GROUPS/TEAMS

When Teams Don't Work, page 600
http://www.bitwise.net/iawww/IAWWW-WP-LEADERSHIP.HTML

LEADING

Building a Personal Mission Statement, page 601
http://www.covey.com/mission/

COMMUNICATION

Exploring the Journal of Computer Mediated Communication, page 601
http://207.201.161.120/jcmc/index.html

HRM/HUMOR

Compensation and Benefits – What are the Options? page 602
http://www.auxillium.com/contents.htm

Dilbert Reflects on the Work Place, page 602
http://www.unitedmedia.com/comics/dilbert

ORGANIZATIONAL CHANGE

Another Perspective on Organizational Change, page 602
http://www.tiac.net/users/praxis/article.html

OPERATIONS MANAGEMENT

Linking to a Variety of Operations Management Web Sites, page 603
http://bradley.bradley.edu/~rf/opman.html

A Look at Agile Manufacturing, page 603
http://web.mit.edu/ctpid/www/agile/atlanta.html

INVENTORY PLANNING

The Inventory Management Newsletter, page 604
http://www.inventorymanagement.com/imnl1997.htm

INFORMATION MANAGEMENT

Data Warehousing and the World Wide Web, page 604
http://www.strategy.com/dwf/v9n6.htm#H

ENTREPRENEURSHIP

10 Great Ideas for Starting a Health, Beauty or Fitness Business, page 605
http://www.entrepreneurmag.com/page.hts?N=1191&Ad=S

Developing an Entrepreneurial Mind Set, page 605
http://www.inc.com/

CAREERS

Careers in Management, page 605
http://jwtworks.com/hrlive/factsfig/index.html

Resume Writing, page 605
http://www.careermag.com/careermag/newsarts/resume.html

FUNDAMENTALS
OF MANAGEMENT

1998 IRWIN/McGRAW-HILL MANAGEMENT TITLES

INTRODUCTION TO BUSINESS

Business: An Integrated Approach
Fred L. Fry, *Bradley University*
Charles R. Stoner, *Bradley University*
Richard E. Hattwick, *Western Illinois University*

PRINCIPLES OF MANAGEMENT

Contemporary Management
Gareth R. Jones, *Texas A&M University*
Jennifer M. George, *Texas A&M University*
Charles W.L. Hill, *University of Washington*

Fundamentals of Management, *10/e*
James H. Donnelly, Jr., *University of Kentucky*
James L. Gibson, *University of Kentucky*
John M. Ivancevich, *University of Houston*

Management, *3/e*
Kathryn M. Bartol, *University of Maryland*
David C. Martin, *American University*

ORGANIZATIONAL BEHAVIOR

Organizational Behavior, *4/e*
Robert Kreitner, *Arizona State University*
Angelo Kinicki, *Arizona State University*

Organizational Behavior, *8/e*
Fred Luthans, *University of Nebraska*

INTERNATIONAL BUSINESS

Global Business Today
Charles W.L. Hill, *University of Washington*

ENTREPRENEURSHIP

Entrepreneurship, *4/e*
Robert D. Hisrich, *Case Western Reserve University*
Michael P. Peters, *Boston College*

HUMAN RESOURCE MANAGEMENT

Human Resource Management, *7/e*
John M. Ivancevich, *University of Houston*

Managing Human Resources, *5/e*
Wayne F. Cascio, *University of Colorado at Denver*

Human Resource Management, An Experiential Approach, *2/e*
H. John Bernardin, *Florida Atlantic University*
Joyce E. A. Russel, *University of Tennessee*

STRATEGIC MANAGEMENT

Strategic Management, *3/e*
Alex Miller, *University of Tennessee*

Strategic Management: Concepts and Cases, *10/e*
Arthur A. Thompson, Jr., *University of Alabama*
A. J. Strickland, III, *University of Alabama*

Crafting and Implementing Strategy: Text and Readings, *10/e*
Arthur A. Thompson, Jr., *University of Alabama*
A. J. Strickland, III, *University of Alabama*

Cases in Strategic Management, *10/e*
Arthur A. Thompson, Jr., *University of Alabama*
A. J. Strickland, III, *University of Alabama*

Readings in Strategic Management, *10/e*
Arthur A. Thompson, Jr., *University of Alabama*
A. J. Strickland, III, *University of Alabama*
Tracy Robertson Kramer, *George Mason University*

Business Strategy Game, *5/e*
Arthur Thompson, Jr., *University of Alabama*
Gregory J. Stappenbeck, *University of Alabama*

BUSINESS ETHICS

Perspectives in Business Ethics
Laura B. Pincus, *DePaul University*

BUSINESS AND SOCIETY

Business and Society: A Managerial Approach, *6/e*
Heidi Vernon, *Northeastern University*

NEGOTIATION

Negotiation, *3/e*
Roy L. Lewicki, *Ohio State University*
John W. Minton, *Appalachian State University*
David M. Saunders, *McGill University*

Negotiation Readings: Exercises and Cases, *3/e*
Roy L. Lewicki, *Ohio State University*
David M. Saunders, *McGill University*
John W. Minton, *Appalachian State University*

LABOR RELATIONS

Labor Relations: Development Structure Process, *7/e*
John A. Fossum, *University of Minnesota*

T E N   T H   E   D   I   T   I   O   N

FUNDAMENTALS OF MANAGEMENT

James H. Donnelly, Jr.
Thomas C. Simons Professor of Business
College of Business and Economics
University of Kentucky

James L. Gibson
Kincaid Professor
College of Business and Economics
University of Kentucky

John M. Ivancevich
Hugh Roy and Lillie Cranz
Cullen Chair and
Professor of Organizational Behavior and Management
University of Houston

Boston, Massachusetts • Burr Ridge, Illinois • Dubuque, Iowa
Madison, Wisconsin • New York, New York • San Francisco, California
St. Louis, Missouri

Irwin/McGraw-Hill

A Division of The McGraw·Hill Companies

This book is printed on acid-free paper.

1 2 3 4 5 6 7 8 9 0   VNH/VNH   9 0 9 8 7   (U.S. Edition)
1 2 3 4 5 6 7 8 9 0   VNH/VNH   9 0 9 8 7   (International Edition)

ISBN 0-256-23237-7

Vice President and Editorial director: *Michael W. Junior*
Publisher: *Craig S. Beytien*
Senior sponsoring editor: *John E. Biernat*
Developmental editor: *Maryellen Krammer*
Marketing manager: *Kenyetta Giles*
Project manager: *Margaret Rathke*
Production supervisor: *Scott Hamilton*
Designer: *Michael Warrell*
Compositor: *Carlisle Communications, Ltd.*
Typeface: *10/12 Times Roman*
Printer: *Von Hoffmann Press, Inc.*

Library of Congress Cataloging-in-Publication Data

Donnelly, James H.
    Fundamentals of management / James H. Donnelly, James L. Gibson,
John M. Ivancevich. — 10th ed.
      p.   cm.
    Includes bibliographical references and index.
    ISBN 0-256-23237-7. — ISBN 0-07-115233-4
    1. Management.   I. Gibson, James L.   II. Ivancevich, John M.
III. Title.
HD31.D594   1998
658—dc21   97-25992

http://www.mhhe.com

To
Gayla Donnelly,
Dianne Gibson,
Dana Louise Ivancevich

We are very much aware that students of management will be studying our book in the 21st century. This reality is both gratifying and challenging. It is gratifying because it tells us our book continues to be a valuable and relevant resource for students and teachers of management. They have found both the structure and the content of the book to be user-friendly. It is challenging because we also know that the world of managers is entering a new and exciting era, one not imaginable only a few years ago. Electronic commerce, interactive television, virtual organizations, e-money, and the information highway are but a few of the features of this new era. Thus to stay abreast of the world of management and to reflect that world in this textbook has been a significant challenge.

We believe we have met this challenge and that the approaches to learning found in this book will prepare students who aspire to manage in these extraordinary times. You will find this edition to be shorter than previous editions. This change increases the potential for exploiting the active learning features of the book. All the changes in this edition reflect our concern for making this book a significant contribution to the education and preparation of tomorrow's managers. We introduce the tenth edition of *Fundamentals of Management* with a deep sense of gratification.

Fundamentals of Management has been identified by management faculty as one of the best management textbooks in the country. It is particularly rewarding for us to hear that our book "has changed the way the introductory management course is taught."

The supplementary resources that accompany our text have been rated among the best available.

Style, organization, and content features that we introduced many editions ago are copied and imitated by competitors, which is the highest form of flattery we can receive.

Recognition serves as an incentive to continue to improve our book. Every revision of *Fundamentals of Management* is a major revision and this edition is no exception. We believe our constant attention to the field and practice of management and our continual updating, revising, and restructuring have been important to the success of the book. The present edition bears little resemblance to the first; however, the rationale remains the same as for previous editions. Management, we believe, will be practiced better by individuals who have had access to high-quality, challenging management textbooks.

To be effective, a textbook must serve two groups well: those who teach the course and those who take the course. We repeat our pledge to faculty and students.

Pledge to Management Faculty.   A textbook of high quality will never compromise the integrity of the field it explores. We pledge to provide a text which in every respect is a quality work of management scholarship that we as academicians can be proud of.

Pledge to Management Students.   A textbook of high quality never loses sight of its ultimate purpose—to help students learn. We pledge to always strive to make our textbook the most contemporary, comprehensive, challenging, readable, and exciting management textbook available today.

The Development of the Tenth Edition

Every revision is guided by extensive market research, interviews with faculty, reviews by commissioned instructors, and classroom experience. The information resulting from these sources enables us to determine which features of the book are effective and which ones should be revised or eliminated.

Based on this research we have made several important changes. An overarching purpose was to increase the active learning components and to decrease the overall length of the book. We eliminated many of the end-of-chapter materials and added video cases. We eliminated one chapter from the previous edition. Thus each chapter now contains one case, most chapters contain a video case, and all chapters contain one experiential exercise, and discussion questions. Internet exercises have also been included (end-of-text appendix) in this edition to draw the student further into the technology highway.

Globalization, quality, competitiveness, diversity, teams and teambuilding, ethics, and entrepreneurship are emphasized throughout the relevant chapters. These topics appear in vignettes, examples, and in the Management Focus features of each chapter.

Our Standards for a High-Quality Textbook

We believe a high-quality management textbook should possess several key characteristics. It should be comprehensive, systematic, scientific, practical—and exciting.

Comprehensive.   This text is comprehensive because it covers the major management topics affecting students, teachers, and practitioners. Research has indicated that our book is being used to cover American Assembly of Collegiate Schools of Business (AACSB) common body of knowledge requirements for both Organizational Behavior/Organization Theory and Production/Operations Management. The materials selected for this book reflect our contacts with teaching colleagues, students, practicing managers, accrediting agencies such as AACSB, and professional societies such as the Academy of Management and the American Management Association.

Systematic.   In studying management, a beginning student can easily be overwhelmed by the vast number of concepts, theories, and topics. The systematic approach of *Fundamentals of Management* helps overcome this tendency. In each chapter's subject matter, readers are able to see where they have been, where they are, and where they will be going.

This book is divided into five parts. And each part is structured around three fundamental managerial tasks common to all organizations: managing work and organizations, managing people, and managing production and operations.

Scientific. *Fundamentals of Management* presents concepts and theories that have been the subject of extensive research. However, our textbook does not attempt to teach social or behavioral science, or operations management. It provides bases for applying many relevant contributions from numerous scientific disciplines to management.

Practical. To become an effective manager, a student must learn to analyze management problems and then solve them by applying relevant management theory. *Fundamentals of Management* stresses a practical approach to learning these vital skills. Subject matter is reinforced with descriptions of how actual managers in real organizations have applied the concepts to solve problems. In addition, case applications, experiential exercises, and Internet exercises bring the chapter material to life in real-world situations.

Exciting. Since the practice of management is exciting, a management textbook should follow suit. We try to convey this excitement to our readers. Every chapter, except for Chapter 1, begins with an account of an organization or individual manager facing a particular management problem or real-life situation that will be discussed in the following pages. In addition, each chapter contains contemporary examples of real-world applications of concepts discussed in the chapter. Important points are illustrated and summarized in each chapter.

An Emphasis on Learning

In addition to the features retained and updated from previous editions, several new features have been strengthened and updated when necessary.

Learning Objectives. Clear, attainable goals are spelled out at the start of each chapter. In each chapter, the student learns to define, describe, discuss, compare, and identify essential issues affecting modern management.

Management in Action. To stimulate reader interest, we continue to use exciting chapter-opening vignettes taken from real-life situations to orient students to concepts and problems discussed in the text.

Management Focus. A series of timely, relevant, real-life examples is drawn from large and small organizations around the world. These examples illustrate problems modern managers confront daily, and they appear at exact points in the discussion where the concept or theory is being discussed.

Cases. A variety of cases is included in the book. Each chapter concludes with a written case to illustrate pertinent issues. In addition a video case also appears at the end of most chapters. These cases feature a variety of types and sizes of organizations and include problems at all levels of management. They are designed to illustrate practical applications of concepts in the chapter.

End of Chapter Features. Every chapter concludes with a concise "Summary of Key Points," a point-by-point summary of key topics. In addition, "Discussion and

Review Questions" are included in every chapter. New questions, which address the major issues explored, have been added to each chapter.

Experiential Exercises.   Experiential exercises are included at the end of each chapter. We included these learning methods in the previous edition, and we received positive reactions to these exercises—so new ones have been added here. They move the material from "seeing" and "hearing" to "doing." The understanding of management concepts is greatly enhanced when students can actively join the learning process. More and more contemporary students seek out courses that include opportunities to learn from experience.

Internet Exercise.   New to this edition is the Internet Appendix (pp. 593–605) which contains 21 Internet exercises, one for each chapter of the book. These exercises further increase the active learning component of the book.

Support for Instructors and Students

We are fortunate to have a complete coordinated and integrated system of support for both teacher and student. As mentioned earlier, the supplementary materials available with *Fundamentals of Management* have been rated the best available. Our goal was to make them even better for the tenth edition.

Support for Instructors

Instructor's Manual/Lecture Resource Manual.   Far more than the traditional instructor's manual, ours is organized to follow each chapter in the text and includes chapter objectives, chapter synopsis, chapter outline with tips and ideas, answers to end-of-chapter cases, answers to discussion and review questions, 12 additional end-of-chapter questions (along with answers) per chapter, suggested transparencies, analyses of experiential exercises, and transparency masters. It is a complete manual in every respect. The Video Guide portion will include teaching hints for use with the videos, a synopsis of the video, a few multiple choice questions for the videos, and a direct tie-in to the chapter.

We believe that even the most experienced and dedicated teacher will find useful hints and insightful ideas in this unique lecture resource guide combined with the IM in this edition. From a pedagogical perspective, we believe this is the real strength of our instructional support system. We encourage those interested in teaching management to examine this element of the system because we believe there is nothing available that approaches its quality and innovativeness. Over 190 sources were used to develop the material.

Color Acetates.   A complete set of high-quality, four-color acetates has been developed specifically for our instructional support system. These transparencies are a separate element in addition to the transparency masters included in the Instructor's Manual/Lecture Resource Manual.

Test Bank.   This examination resource contains a wide variety of materials such as true/false, multiple-choice, short answer, and essay questions. Items are categorized by type of question and include text page references.

McGraw-Hill Higher Education's Computerized Testing Software.   New to this edition, the advanced-feature test generator allows you to add and edit questions; save and reload tests; create up to 99 different versions of each test; attach graphics to questions; import and export ASCII files; and select questions based on type, level of difficulty, or keyword. McGraw-Hill's computerized testing software provides password protection of saved texts and question databases and can run on a network. The versions available are 3.5″ IBM.

PowerPoint Presentation Software. This presentation software provides the means to deliver state-of-the-art technology to enhance any lecture. A complete lecture is provided for each chapter. In addition, the flexibility of the PowerPoint platform allows faculty to edit or import their own lecture material to create a custom presentation.

Support for Students

Videos. Available for the first time with this edition are corresponding chapter videos for 17 of the 21 chapters. A wide variety of company settings gives the videos broad appeal. Video cases have been included, where applicable, at the end of each chapter. Videos and cases can be used to generate in-class discussion and draw students' interest.

Acknowledgments

Scores of people have made important suggestions over the years that have substantially improved the book. In addition, we want to publicly thank and acknowledge the contributions of reviewers of previous editions and of the present edition. Their ideas and suggestions are reflected throughout our book, and they have contributed much to its success.

Reviewers of This and Previous Editions

Nick Blanchard
Eastern Michigan University

Mauritz Blonder
Hofstra University

Arthur H. Boisselle
El Paso Community College

Lyle Brenna
El Paso Community College

Sonya Brett
Macomb County Community College

Donald R. Burke
Villanova University

Douglas D. Cantrell
Eastern Michigan University

Debra R. Comer
Hofstra University

Deborah F. Crown
University of Colorado—Boulder

Helen Deresky
SUNY—Plattsburg

Bernard C. Dill
Bloomsburg State University

Sam Doctors
California State University

Charles Flaherty
University of Minnesota

Frank Flaumenhatt
University of New Haven

David Gray
University of Texas at Arlington

Stan Guzell
Youngstown State University

Lindle Hatton
California State University Sacramento

A. Thomas Hollingsworth
University of South Carolina

Milton Holmen
University of Southern California

Fred C. House
Northern Arizona University

W. Dow Hoyt
San Bernadino Valley College

Carolyn Jacobson
Ohio University

Elias Kalman
*Baruch College of the City University
of New York*

Jack Kappeler
Platte Tech Community College

John E. Kinney, Jr.
Chabot College

Eric A. Larson
Onondaga Community College

Pamela S. Lewis
University of Central Florida

Wendell H. McCulloch
California State University at Long Beach

John Mee
Indiana University

Robert Miller
Upjohn Research Corporation

Jan Muczyk
Cleveland State University

James R. Necessary
Ball State University

Donald D. Nelson
College of DuPage

M. Gene Newport
University of Alabama in Birmingham

James G. Pesek
Clarion State College

Charles K. Phillips
Stephen F. Austin University

Jon Pierce
University of Minnesota

Lawrence Podell
William Patterson College

William Ryan
Indiana University

Mary S. Thibodeaux
University of North Texas

Robert L. Trewatha
*Southwest Missouri State
University*

John J. Vitton
University of North Dakota

Irwin Weinstock
*California State University at
Fresno*

Martin W. Wensman
Cerritos College

Philip Van Auken
Baylor University

Robert K. Robinson
University of Mississippi

John Hall
University of Florida

Anne C. Cowden
*California State University
Sacramento*

Raffaele DeVito
Emporia State University

Douglas M. McCabe
Georgetown University

Thomas Daymont
Temple University

**Reviewers of the
Present Edition**

Elizabeth Cooper
University of Rhode Island

Jack Johnson
Cosumnes River College

M. R. Meredith
University of Southwestern Louisiana

Robert K. Robinson
The University of Mississippi

Ellen Sikes
Campbell University

Charles White
*University of Tennessee at
Chattanooga*

| *Instuctors Manual/Lecture Resource Manual* | Authored by Dr. Amit Shah Frostburg State University |

| *Test Bank and PowerPoint Presentation Software* | Authored by Barbara Gorski University of St. Thomas |

Our thanks to Maryellen Krammer and Maggie Rathke for their efforts on this edition of *Fundamentals of Management.* We hope that working with us was painless, productive, and positive.

We would like to pay a special note of appreciation to the individuals who listen, attempt to read scribbled notes, are magical wizards with word processing, and dig out facts, databases, and statistics that authors sometimes use. Jacque Francos and Ginger Roberts, the quality control gatekeepers, helped us make this edition possible.

We owe the hundreds of thousands of students across the world who have used *Fundamentals of Management* a great intellectual debt because they have helped make our book fulfilling to each of us. And we believe that together we have provided you with another edition of an educationally rigorous but very readable management textbook.

James H. Donnelly, Jr.
James L. Gibson
John M. Ivancevich

CONTENTS

PART IV

MANAGING PRODUCTION AND OPERATIONS
Planning, Organizing, Leading, Controlling

17   Production and Operations Management   476

18   Production and Inventory Planning and Control   500

19   Managing Information for Decision Making 524

20   Entrepreneurship 546

I MANAGEMENT AND THE ENVIRONMENT

1 MANAGERS AND THE EVOLUTION OF MANAGEMENT

Chapter Learning Objectives

After completing Chapter 1, you should be able to:

- **Define** the terms manager and management.
- **Describe** the evolution of management as a field of study and how the three established approaches to management provide the foundations for practicing management.
- **Discuss** why the study of management can be important to almost anyone.
- **Explain** the principles of work management, work simplification, work scheduling, and efficiency.
- **Identify** he tools and techniques used by management scientists.
- **Compare** the human relations and the behavioral sciences approaches.

The way organizations are managed is changing by necessity. Globalization is now an accepted fact of everyday life. The United States, Germany, and Japan—the three dominant world economies—have slower growth than the developing giants, China, India, and Indonesia. To remain or become competitive, managers in the developed countries have to restructure and rethink how people are managed.

In the new global economy that is slowly emerging, human resources, information technology, speedy decision making, strategic alliances, use of the skills of a diverse workforce, and knowledge of how to combine individualism and teamwork can provide competitive edge opportunities for small entrepreneurs, mid-sized companies, or large conglomerate multinational firms. The United States, despite all its critics, has the richest mix of ethnic groups, racial groups, and global experience the world has ever known.[1] Managers who know how to meld this fantastic human resource mix will gain the competitive edge in the new global economy.

As we close the 20th century and enter the new millennium, managers are going to have to use new, as well as proven, methods and tools to manage human resources. Despite an endless list of naysayers, we believe that managers in the United States, Canada, Japan, Germany, and many other nations will be able to adapt to global changes. The history of management suggests that managers are intelligent and can learn new methods. The wake-up call has been sounded, and, as this book will indicate, changes in how management is practiced will be the rule in organizations around the world.[2]

A team of experts was asked to explain what happened to industrial performance in the United States during the past 20 years and to suggest what could be done to improve the situation. This Massachusetts Institute of Technology (MIT) team studied the problem and concluded that American organizations were not producing as well as they should produce, as well as they used to produce, or as well as the organizations in other nations.[3] The team concluded that, "To live well, a nation must produce well." This indictment of American organizations is only partially correct. American organizations certainly need to produce well, but to do this, they must be managed effectively.

The application of effective management principles, programs, and techniques in organizations must become commonplace whether industries produce automobiles, machine tools, semiconductors and computers, or commercial aircraft or are involved in banking, health care, government, or retailing. Although only eight industries were included in the MIT investigation, they constituted about 22 percent of all employment in the United States. Thus, the Made in America report provides important comparative data that contrast the managerial and economic well-being of eight important industries in the United States, Europe, and Japan.[4]

Participative management. Quality assurance. Customer service programs. New technology implementation. Employee stock-purchase programs. Just-in-time production systems. Managing diverse work teams. Making ethical decisions. Leading employees. Reward programs. Entrepreneur programs. Organizational change techniques. All of these management approaches have one thing in common—they must be managed.

The United States is at a crossroads because of the increase in international competitiveness. *Competitiveness* refers to the relative position of a person, unit, firm, or nation in comparison to other individuals, units, firms, and nations.[5] And traditional management approaches that worked yesterday or that have not been modified to fit the current situation are proving inadequate.

Management is the process undertaken by one or more individuals to coordinate the activities of others to achieve results not achievable by one individual acting alone. Peter Drucker believes that the work of management is to make people productive. To regain our competitive edge in the international arena, society must have managerial competence. Drucker states, "Management, its competence, its integrity, and its performance will be decisive both to the United States and to the free world in the decades ahead.[6]

Another view of management is presented in the popular best-seller, *In Search of Excellence,* where Peters and Waterman state:

> There is good news from America. Good management practice today is not resident only in Japan. But, more important, the good news comes from treating people decently and asking them to share, and from producing things that work . . . Even management's job becomes more fun. Instead of brain games in the sterile ivory tower, it's shaping values and reinforcing through coaching and evangelism in the field—with workers and in support of the cherished product.[7]

Drucker's view emphasizes performance, quality, and service. On the other hand, Peters and Waterman emphasize mentorship, a love for managing and working with people; managers are excellent communicators and value shapers, lightning rods to get the job done.

If you learn only two things as you journey through the subject of management and managing, learn that effective managers intend to make their employees productive, and they also have the ability to inspire people.[8] Also, improving the industrial and service performance of any nation will require managers to be in the forefront, applying the best techniques, knowledge, and understanding every single day. How the techniques and knowledge are applied will vary across groups, countries, and situations.

Why Study Management?

Learning about management is important for two reasons. First, our society depends on specialized institutions and organizations to provide the goods and services we desire. These organizations are guided and directed by the decisions of one or more individuals designated as "managers." In capitalistic societies, it is managers who allocate society's resources to various and often competing ends. Managers have the authority and responsibility to build safe or unsafe products, seek war or peace, build or destroy cities, or clean up or pollute the environment. Managers establish the conditions under which we are provided jobs, incomes, lifestyles, products, services, protection, health care, and knowledge. It would be very difficult to find anyone who is neither a manager nor affected by the decisions of a manager.

Second, individuals not trained as managers often find themselves in managerial positions. Many individuals presently being trained to be teachers, accountants, musicians, salespersons, artists, physicians, or lawyers will one day earn their livings as managers. They will manage schools, accounting firms, orchestras, sales organizations, museums, hospitals, and government agencies. The United States is an organizational society, and its approximately 16 million organizations must have managers.

The future success of the United States, Canada, Japan, France, Germany, or any industrialized nation in the global village lies in managing productivity, being able to cope with environmental changes, and properly managing the workforce. These challenges will require well-educated, knowledgeable, and hard-working individuals deciding that a management career is of value to them personally.[9] We believe that the content of this book will clearly indicate that managing is one of the most stimulating and rewarding careers a man or woman can choose.

The Evolution of Management as a Field of Study

Both organizational growth and its increasing influence on our economy and standard of living are relatively recent in history; thus, the study of management is relatively new. Many of the first individuals to study and write about management were practicing managers. They described their own experiences and tried to generalize the principles they believed could be applied in similar situations. Even today, a great deal of what we know about management comes from the autobiographies and memoirs of men and women who are or have been practicing managers.

Now, however, other individuals also are interested in management for scientific reasons. Social and behavioral scientists view the management of organizations as an extremely important social phenomenon worthy of study through scientific inquiry. As scientists, these men and women make no value judgments regarding good or bad management practices. Their objective is to understand and explain the practice of management.

Between the two extremes of management practice and management science are many individuals who have contributed to the study of management. They include engineers, sociologists, psychologists, anthropologists, lawyers, economists, accountants, mathematicians, political scientists, and philosophers.

Such differing perspectives on the same subject cannot be neatly classified. Thus, as a manager, you will have at your disposal many ways of looking at management's tasks. Each may be more useful for some problems than for others. For example, a management theory that emphasizes employee satisfaction may be more helpful in dealing with a problem of high employee turnover than with delays in production. Because there is no single, universally accepted management approach, you should be familiar with the various major theories.

The three well-established approaches to management thought are the **classical approach,** the **behavioral approach,** and the **management science approach.** Although these approaches evolved in historical sequence, later ideas have not always replaced earlier ones. Rather, each new approach has added to the knowledge of the previous ones. At the same time, each approach has continued to develop on its own. And at last, some merging did occur as later theorists attempted to integrate the accumulated knowledge. Two of these attempts to integrate theories—the **systems approach** and the **contingency approach**—are discussed later in this section.

Each of these approaches indicates that managers can make a difference in firms of all sizes. Managers can create opportunities for employees, judge performance accurately, and encourage optimum productivity. When managers accomplish these worthy outputs, people being managed can be very productive. Of course, the study of management also points out errors that managers make by being selfish, insensitive, harsh, and autocratic. As we review the history of managing people, we identify the lessons, principles, and functions that have continuing value for practitioners as we move to the 21st century.

Foundations of Managing Work and Organizations

At the beginning of the 20th century, some managers wanting to improve the practice of management began to put their ideas in writing. These managers were particularly concerned with two issues: (1) increasing the productivity of individuals *performing work* and (2) increasing the productivity of *organizations* within which work is performed. Directing their attention to finding ways to manage work and organizations so that higher levels of output would be produced at lower costs, they created a body of management literature that became known as the classical approach.

The emphasis on rational analysis and the application of scientific rigor to facts and information about productivity led to the use of the term *scientific management* to describe the earliest attempts to manage the work of individuals. The first supporters of scientific management were practicing engineers and managers who believed and then demonstrated that work could be done more efficiently and thus more productively. Believing that the most efficient—the best—way to do a job could be determined through analysis of data, they urged managers to study the actual performance of work and to collect objective data on their observations.

While scientific management ideas were developing, classical organization theory began to evolve. Developers of this theory believed that organizations are the settings within which individuals perform jobs—that the organization is a collection of individual jobs—so the organization should also be designed and managed according to principles and practices that stress efficiency and productivity.

The combination of ideas from scientific management's concern for productive work and classical organization theory's concern for efficient organizations creates an important body of management knowledge, classical management thought. Managers must know and apply this knowledge to survive both domestic and international competition for resources and products. Today's managers and organizations that make headlines for their high performance stress the importance of rational planning, organizing, and controlling the work of individuals and the organization in which the work takes place. But this recognition of the importance of managing did not develop overnight; it took many years to overcome existing management ways.

The Management of Work

To appreciate fully the importance of scientific management as a philosophy and practice, you must understand its major contributions.[10] These contributions were in the areas of work management, work simplification, work scheduling, and efficiency.

As a supervisor at the Philadelphia Midvale Steel Company in the late 1800s, Frederick W. Taylor became interested in ways to improve lathe work. He began gathering facts and applying an objective analysis that was to typify his entire career.[11] He studied the work of individual lathe workers to discover exactly how they performed their jobs; he identified each aspect of each job and measured everything measurable. His goal was to provide the lathe operator with scientifically based, objective standards that would define *a fair day's work.*

Taylor's efforts culminated in four principles for managing work:

1. For each element of a person's work, develop a science that replaces the old rule-of-thumb method.
2. Scientifically select, train, teach, and develop the worker. (In the past, workers chose their own work and trained themselves as best they could.)
3. Cooperate with the workers to ensure that all the work is done in accordance with the science that has been developed.
4. Recognize that there is almost an equal division of work and responsibility between management and workers. Managers take over all work for which they are better fitted than the workers. (In the past, almost all the work and the greater part of the responsibility were thrown on the workers.)[12]

These four principles became the basic guidelines for managing the work of individuals. Taylor was the first individual to study work in a serious manner.[13] His experiments with stopwatch studies and work methods inspired others to undertake similar studies in other industries. One result of the efforts of those who followed was the discovery of ways to simplify work.

Principles of Work Simplification.   Frank and Lillian Gilbreth, a husband and wife team, combined their talents to produce important breakthroughs in work simplification. An untrained but insightful engineer, Frank Gilbreth was an apprentice bricklayer in his first job. His observations of skilled bricklayers' motions convinced him that many of their body movements (bending, reaching, stooping, troweling) could be combined or eliminated. Bricklaying could be simplified, and production could be increased. By combining and eliminating body movements and increasing the number of bricks laid in a given time period, resources (bricklayers' time) are reduced, and output (bricks laid) is increased. The result is an increase in labor productivity.

Principles of Work Scheduling.   A close associate of Taylor was a young graduate engineer, Henry L. Gantt. Like Taylor and the Gilbreths, Gantt was concerned with problems of productivity at the shop-floor level. Gantt's major contribution to scientific management is a chart showing the relationship between work planned and completed on one axis and time elapsed on the other. The *Gantt Chart* is still used in industry as a method for scheduling work.

While Taylor and the Gilbreths focused on the workers, Gantt believed that the way managers did their work could be improved and made more productive. He believed that expertise should be the sole criterion for the exercise of authority and that managers have the moral obligation to make decisions by scientific methods, not by opinion. Thus Gantt broadened the scope of scientific management by including the work of managers as appropriate for analysis.

Principles of Efficiency.   The public became aware of Harrington Emerson in 1910, when he testified as an expert witness before the Interstate Commerce Commission that the railroads could save $1 million per day by using the methods and philosophy of scientific management.

Emerson's ideas are embodied in a set of principles that define the manner in which the efficient use of resources is to be accomplished. His principles encompass the basic elements of the scientific management approach. In summary, they state that a manager should (1) use scientific, objective, and factual analyses; (2) define the aims of the undertaking; (3) relate each part to the whole; (4) provide standardized procedures and methods; and (5) reward individuals for successful execution of the task.

Emerson's contributions go beyond his principles of efficiency. He also recognized the positive lessons to be learned from the military's use of formalized staff and advisory positions. In his capacity as one of the first management consultants, he proposed the creation of an organization whose activities would be defined by clear statements of goals and purposes.

The significant and lasting contribution of scientific management, however, has been the identification of management's responsibilities for managing work. According to the classical approach, management has the following responsibilities:

- *Planning* the work by predetermining the expected quantity and quality of output for each job.
- *Organizing* the work by specifying the appropriate ways and means to perform each task.

- *Leading and influencing* others to engage in work behaviors to achieve the results desired.
- *Controlling* the work by *(a)* selecting and training qualified individuals, *(b)* overseeing the actual job performance, and *(c)* verifying that actual quantity and quality of output meet expectations.

At the work level, the responsibilities of management were defined in functions: planning, organizing, leading, and controlling.

The Management of Organizations

Practicing managers were the first contributors to the literature on classical organization theory. They brought their practical experiences to bear on the problem of coordinating large-scale organizations.

The two lasting contributions of classical organization theory are (1) the principles of management and (2) the principles of organization. Through the application of these principles, supporters of the theory argued, managers can manage *organizations* on the same basis that they manage *work.*

Principles of Management.   Many early writers sought to define the principles of management. Chief among them was a Frenchman named Henri Fayol, manager of a large coal company, who sought to discover principles of management that determine the "soundness and good working order" of the firm.[14] Fayol was not seeking fixed rules of conduct; rather, he sought guidelines to thinking. Deciding on the appropriateness of a principle for a particular situation was, in his view, the art of management. Fayol believed that any number of principles might exist, but he described only those he most frequently applied in his own experience.

Fayol's chief desire was to elevate the status of management practice by supplying a framework for analysis. His framework included a statement of management functions and principles of managing organizations.

Principles of Managing Organizations.   Fayol proposed 14 principles to guide the thinking of managers in managing organizations. These principles are presented in Table 1–1. The principles do not answer questions of how much of each principle should be used; Fayol did not suggest that applying these principles would relieve management from the responsibility for determining what he called "the appropriate balance." Indeed, he emphasized time and again that the moral character of the managers determines the quality of their decisions.

Principles of Organization.   In 1931, James D. Mooney and Alan C. Reiley wrote *Onward Industry,* which was revised in 1947 by Mooney and titled *The Principles of Organization.*[15] This book is a vital part of the literature of classical management thought. It complements Fayol's work and adds a new dimension.

Mooney viewed management as the technique, or art, of directing and inspiring other people. Organization, on the other hand, is the technique of relating specific duties or functions in a coordinated whole. The primary purpose of management, according to Mooney, is to devise an appropriate organization.

Mooney's personal experience led him to believe that natural laws of organizing existed, and it was these natural laws, or principles, that he sought to discover through logic.

TABLE 1–1   Some Principles of Management, circa 1929

1. *Division of labor.* Work should be divided and subdivided into the smallest feasible elements to take advantage of gains from specialization.
2. *Parity of authority and responsibility.* Each jobholder should be delegated sufficient authority to carry out assigned job responsibilities.
3. *Discipline.* Employees should obey whatever clearly stated agreements exist between them and the organization; managers should fairly sanction all instances of breached discipline.
4. *Unity of command.* Employees should receive orders from and be accountable to only one superior.
5. *Unity of direction.* Activities that have the same purpose should be grouped together and operate under the same plan.
6. *Subordination of individual to general interests.* The interests of the organization take precedence over the interests of the individual.
7. *Fair remuneration.* Pay should be based on achievement of assigned job objectives.
8. *Centralization.* Authority should be delegated in proportion to responsibility.
9. *Scalar chain.* An unbroken chain of command should exist through which all directives and communications flow.
10. *Order.* Each job should be defined so that the jobholder clearly understands it and its relationship to other jobs.
11. *Equity.* Established rules and agreements should be enforced fairly.
12. *Stability of personnel.* Employees should be encouraged to establish loyalty to the organization and to make a long-term commitment.
13. *Initiative.* Employees should be encouraged to exercise independent judgment within the bounds of their delegated authority and defined jobs.
14. *Esprit de corps.* Employees should be encouraged to define their interests with those of the organization and thereby achieve unity of effort.

Foundations of Managing People in Organizations

The classical approach to management was built on the notion that if management could properly plan, organize, lead, and control jobs and organizations, productivity would increase. The early approaches also emphasized the technical aspects of work, at the expense of work's personal aspects. Therefore, it is not surprising that theories were developed that challenged some of the early fundamentals. The fundamentals of managing people evolved into two branches with heavy behavioral and humanistic orientations. One branch may be identified as *human relations*; it became popular in the 1940s and early 1950s. The second branch is *behavioral science,* which came into popular use in the early 1950s and today receives much emphasis in the literature on management. Both branches and important characteristics of each are illustrated in Figure 1–1. A report prepared by the American Assembly of Collegiate Schools of Business (AACSB), *Management Education and Development: Drift or Thrust into the 21st Century,* pointed out the need for future managers to learn to use people skills.[16] The report emphasizes that successful managers must be able to communicate, make decisions, lead, create a positive motivational environment, and resolve conflicts. An emphasis on leading needs to be highlighted. The leaders in organizations need to be able to cope with change and understand the firm's history, environment, technology, and employees.[17]

FIGURE 1–1   **Fundamentals of Managing People: Two Approaches**

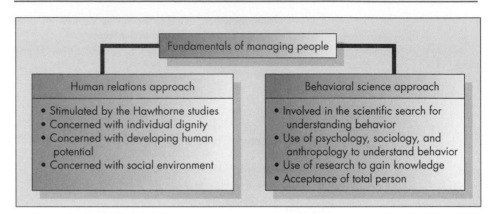

*The Human
Relations Approach*

Human relations writers brought to managers' attention the important role played by individuals in determining the success or failure of an organization. Basically accepting the major premises of the classical approach, the human relations approach showed how these premises should be modified in view of differences in individual behavior and the influence of work groups on the individual—and vice versa. Thus, the formulators of human relations theory concentrated on the *social* environment surrounding the job, while classical writers were concerned mainly with the *physical* environment. For the student of management, the human relations movement has produced a wealth of important ideas, research findings, and values about the role of the individual in an organization.

We do not know if the captains of industry in the 1900s learned any specific lessons from the Hawthorne studies. But before you read about the research, think about Sam Walton, the founder of the Wal-Mart Stores; Fred Smith, who started Federal Express Corporation; David Packard, founder of Hewlett-Packard Company; Mary Ann Keller, Wall Street analyst; and Susan W. Bowen, president of Champion Awards, Inc. Employees of these effective managers say they are trustworthy, interested in creating a pleasant work environment, and willing to listen to what employees have to say. Human dignity, individual self-esteem, and relationships are important considerations when effective managers make decisions. Exploitation, manipulation, and insensitivity toward people are not accepted in organizations with people-oriented management. These leaders stand out as possessing skills, values, ideals, and qualities that others want to possess and be associated with in working within organizations.

*The Hawthorne
Studies*

In 1924, the National Research Council (NRC) of the National Academy of Sciences decided to study how lighting in the workplace influenced individual efficiency. From 1924 to 1927, the NRC studied this relationship at the Cicero, Illinois, Hawthorne Plant of Western Electric. The initial experiments were so inconclusive that everyone was ready to abandon the whole project.[18] Despite the early results, a team of Harvard University industrial psychologists became involved in the Hawthorne studies. This research team originally set out to study the relationship between productivity and physical working conditions.

Research.   The research at Hawthorne can be grouped into four phases. Each successive phase developed as an attempt on the part of the researchers to answer questions raised by the previous phase. The four stages were:

1. Experiments to determine the effects of changes in illumination on productivity.
2. Experiments to determine the effects of changes in hours and other working conditions (e.g., rest periods, refreshments) on productivity (the relay assembly test room experiment).
3. Conducting a plantwide interview program to determine worker attitudes and sentiments.
4. Determination and analysis of social organization at work (the bank wiring observation room experiment).

Experiments in Illumination.   The researchers divided the participating workers into two separate groups. The *experimental* group was exposed to varying intensities of illumination. Another group, called the *control* group, continued to work under constant intensities of illumination. Surprisingly, the researchers found that as they increased the illumination in the experimental group, both groups increased production. When the researchers decreased the intensity, output continued to rise for both groups. Finally, the illumination in the experimental group was reduced to that of moonlight. Then, and only then, was there a significant decline in output. The researchers concluded that illumination in the workplace had little or no effect on the productivity of the two groups. At this point, the research team from Harvard became involved.

Relay Assembly Test Room Experiment.   In the second phase of the study, several persons volunteered to work under controlled conditions isolated from the other workers. Several changes were made in the conditions of the job (for example, workplace temperature and refreshments) with little effect on productivity. In another phase, a group of women employees was placed in an isolated part of the assembly department. The experimental group was given a special group incentive as a wage payment. In this case, output increased for each operator.

Overall, the relay assembly test room experiment was designed to determine the effects of changes in various job conditions on group productivity. The researchers concluded that these factors had little or no effect.

Employee Interviews.   After the first two phases, the researchers concluded that their attempt to relate physical conditions of the job to productivity did not produce any significant results. So they postulated that the *human element* in the work environment apparently had a significantly greater impact on productivity than the technical and physical aspects of the job. The researchers summarized this impact as follows:

> In brief, the increase in the output rate of the women in the relay assembly test room could not be related to any change in their physical conditions of work, whether experimentally induced or not. It could, however, be related to what can only be spoken of as the development of an organized social group and a peculiar and effective relation with its supervisors.[19]

On the basis of their extensive interview program, the researchers proposed that the work group as a whole determined the production output of individual group members by enforcing an informal norm of what a fair day's work should be.

Bank Wiring Observation Room Experiment.   To test the premise formulated at the conclusion of the interview program, the researchers conducted a final experiment. The procedure in this part of the study was similar to that used in the relay assembly test room, except that nine males who assembled terminal banks for telephone exchanges were selected.

This experiment focused on the effect of a group piecework incentive pay plan. The assumption was that the workers would seek their own economic interests by maximizing their productivity and that faster workers would pressure the slower ones to improve their efficiency. However, the researchers found that pressure was actually a form of social behavior. To be accepted in the work group, the worker had to act in accord with group norms and not be a rate buster by overproducing or a chiseler by underproducing. The group defined what constituted a day's work, and as soon as they knew that they could reach this output level, they slacked off. This process was more marked among the faster workers than the slower ones.

The researchers concluded that the work group set the fair rates for each of its members. They found no relationship between productivity and intelligence, dexterity, and other skills. They concluded that the wage incentive plan was less important in determining an individual worker's output than was group acceptance and security.

Review and Critique of the Hawthorne Studies.   The Hawthorne studies have been criticized by some behavioral scientists because of the lack of scientific objectivity used in arriving at conclusions. Some critics feel that there was bias and preconception on the part of the Harvard researchers.

Although they have been criticized, the Hawthorne studies had a significant impact on management practice, teaching, and research. Obviously, the assumptions of early management writers began to be questioned. Subsequent studies of the behavior of workers confirmed criticisms and led to revised assumptions about human nature. Behavioral scientists began attacking the "dehumanizing" aspects of the scientific management approach and bureaucratic forms of organization; a great number of training programs were undertaken to teach managers how to better understand people and groups in the work situation. With this, the pendulum began to swing away from the somewhat depersonalized view of classical management to a more personalized (some would say *over*personalized) view. Consequently, the worker, rather than the job or production standards, became the focus.

The Behavioral Science Approach

The behavioral science approach to management began to appear in the early 1950s, after the Foundation for Research on Human Behavior was established. The goal of this organization was to promote and support behavioral science research in business, government, and other organizations. The behavioral science approach to the study of management can be defined as:

> The study of observable and verifiable human behavior in organizations, using scientific procedures. It is largely inductive and problem centered, focusing on the issue of human behavior and drawing from any relevant literature, especially in psychology, sociology, and anthropology.[20]

Many things about the classical management and human relations approaches bothered advocates of the behavioral science approach. For example, they recognized that managers did indeed plan, organize, lead, and control. But they believed that viewing management solely in this way led mainly to *descriptions* of what managers do rather than to an *analysis* and *understanding* of what they do. Many also believed that, just as the economic man model of the classical writers was an oversimplification, the social man model of the human relations approach was oversimplified. You will see later how the emphasis of the behavioral science approach has shifted more and more to the nature of work itself and the degree to which it can fulfill the human need to use skills and abilities.

When we use the term *behavioral sciences,* we refer to the disciplines of psychology, sociology, and anthropology.

Psychology is the study of human behavior. The many branches of general psychology have provided concepts and theories useful to the study of management. For example, **social psychology** deals with behavior as it relates to other individuals. It studies how groups and individuals influence and modify one another's behavior. **Organizational psychology** deals with behavior and attitudes within an organizational setting. It studies the effect of the organization on the individual and the individual's effect on the organization.

Books such as Robert Levering's *A Great Place to Work* emphasize how widespread psychology's influence on management has become.[21] The list of companies cited and the use of self-motivation, participation, quality of work life, new organizational designs, team building, job enrichment, and other psychologically based techniques fill 312 pages. Does a manager have to be a psychologist in the 1990s to be effective? Definitely and thankfully not. However, the manager would be better able to work with the changing face and nature of the 1990s workforce if she remembered some of the lessons taught in Psychology 101. **Sociology** attempts to isolate, define, and describe human behavior in groups. It strives to develop laws and generalizations about human nature, social interaction, culture, and social organization.

One of sociology's major contributions to management thought has been its focus on emergent groups, which often are treated in management literature as the informal components of organizations. Sociologists also have an interest in formal organizations, which they approach as the study of bureaucracy. They focus on bureaucratic behavior as well as the structural relationships in bureaucratic organizations. Sociologists have provided managers with knowledge regarding leader and follower roles and how patterns of power and authority are applied in organizations. Teams, partnerships, ownership, and cohesiveness are what more and more employees are asking for today.

At Johnsonville Foods in Sheboygan, Wisconsin, the application of sociological principles is very easy to spot. Workers in teams, with no identifiable hierarchy above them, do all the hiring, firing, and evaluation. The result is a cohesive workplace, a family spirit, a pleasant environment. Sociologists have for decades been providing insights and ideas about groups. Some old-line firms still close their eyes and don't look at the success stories. Unless more of such firms familiarize themselves with sociological information, they are not likely to survive the next few years.

Anthropology examines the learned behaviors of people, including all of the social, technical, and family behaviors that are a part of the broad concept known as culture. **Cultural anthropology,** the science devoted to the study of different peoples and cultures of the world, is important to the behavioral sciences because the ways in which individuals behave, the priority of needs they attempt to satisfy, and the means they choose by which to satisfy them are all functions of culture.

The evidence that economists provide to managers is that people, not machines, are the driving force behind economic development. And as increasing numbers of females and foreign-born workers become a major part of the workforce in the last few years of the 1990s, cultural anthropologists inform managers that different people from different backgrounds and cultures will have to be integrated into organizations. To avoid forfeiting economic growth and power to the Japanese, South Koreans, Germans, French, and others, US managers must scientifically study the human resources available for employment, training, and education.[22] Cultural anthropologists have a wealth of knowledge, insight, and recommendations that managers need to use more and more.

While psychology and sociology have had greater impact in shaping management thought, cultural anthropology has made significant contributions regarding the effect of culture on organizations. In the future, as firms expand their activities overseas, anthropology undoubtedly will also provide managers with valuable insights as they attempt to perform the functions of planning, organizing, and controlling in different cultural environments.

Foundations of Managing Production and Operations

The third major contribution to modern management theory and practice is referred to as the **management science approach.** The central theme of management science is *to provide managers with quantitative bases for decisions regarding the operations under their control.* A more complete definition of the field is that it "is the science devoted to describing, understanding, and predicting the behavior of complicated systems of men and machines operating in natural environments."[23] The ideas and concepts of management science are, in fact, extensions of scientific management, which was a major part of the classical approach, just as the behavioral approach is an extension of earlier developments arising out of the Hawthorne studies and human relations. Thus, we can see the thread of continuity that runs through each of the three foundations of contemporary management.

Development of Management Science

The field of management science has formally existed for only approximately 50 years. During this period, individuals associated with the field began to have a noticeable impact on the solution of complex military and business problems through the use of engineering and mathematical skills. Also during this period, a new profession emerged: the management scientist.

The terms *management science* (MS) and *operations research* (OR) are synonymous. In recent years, the field is generally designated MS/OR. The use of different terms for essentially the same set of ideas is a characteristic of emerging bodies of knowledge; management science is no exception. Keep in mind that the aim of management science is *to provide managers with quantitative bases for decisions.*

The activities of management scientists have emphasized the mathematical modeling of systems. Applications of these models by operations research specialists, mostly confined to the production segment of business firms, began after World War II. During the war, operations researchers had successfully solved a number of military problems ranging from those of logistical nature (equipment and troop movements) to developing strategy for submarine warfare. As a result, management science caught on in some of the larger firms in the United States after the war. Such companies as E. I. du Pont de Nemours & Co. and H. J. Heinz Company pioneered the use of early operations research applications. However, not until these bolder firms had tried it with success did civilian operations research make any major headway in the United States.

While it is difficult to place clear boundary lines around the management science process, it is possible to distinguish certain characteristics of its approach. It is generally agreed that most management science tools and techniques possess the following characteristics:

1. *A primary focus on decision making.* The principal end result of the analysis must have direct implications for management action. Decision making is still the central activity for production and operations managers today.

2. *Reliance on economic effectiveness criteria.* A comparison of feasible actions must be based on measurable values that reflect the future well-being of the organization. Examples of such measured variables include costs, revenues, and rates of return on investment.

3. *Reliance on formal mathematical models.* These models, stated in mathematical form, are actually possible solutions to problems. The procedures for manipulating the data must be so explicit that another analyst can derive the same results from the same data. This *replicability* requirement is also a major requirement of the behavioral science approach to management. In fact, replication is the keynote of scientific analysis.

4. *Dependence on computers.* This requirement is necessitated by either the complexity of the mathematical model, the volume of data to be manipulated, or the magnitude of computations needed to implement the model.[24]

Managers were faced with the problems of *planning, organizing, leading, and controlling* their organizations' operations long before the advent of the electronic computer and management science models; they are still performing these functions. Mathematical models can be especially useful as an aid to the manager performing the functions of planning and controlling production and operations, as shown in Figure 1–2. While management scientists were constructing sophisticated quantitative models and theories, managers in organizations were struggling to manage their day-to-day production and operations more efficiently. What has emerged from this partnership of managers and scientists is a distinct area of inquiry, analysis, and application that

FIGURE 1–2   Managing Production and Operations

P/OM stresses the application of management science techniques.

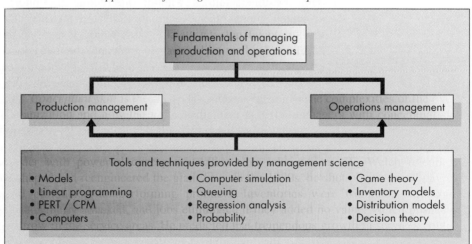

focuses on the management of production and operations in manufacturing and service industries. This area is known as production and operations management (P/OM).[25]

Production and Operations Management

The most widespread application of management science tools and techniques in modern organizations has been in the area of production and operations management.

The term **production** focuses on manufacturing technology and the flow of materials in a manufacturing plant. The production function in a business organization is specifically concerned with the activity of producing goods—that is, the design, implementation, operation, and control of people, materials, equipment, money, and information to achieve specific production objectives. The term **operations** is broader in scope and refers to the goods- or service-producing activity in any organization— public, private, profit, or nonprofit. Thus, a bank and a hospital have operations functions although they have nothing to do with manufacturing technology, production assembly lines, and assembled products. Operations management, therefore, is similar to production management except that it focuses on a wider class of problems and includes organizations whose technologies may be quite different from those of a manufacturing organization. However, there are important similarities between the flow of materials in a manufacturing plant, customers waiting in line at a bank or supermarket, the processing of claims in an insurance company, student registration in a college or university, and the provision of health care in a hospital.

Production and operations management has management science as its foundation. To understand the P/OM approach, it is essential to understand the relationship between the two areas, graphically portrayed in Figure 1–2.

The Role of Mathematical Models.   Mathematical models play a significant role in production and operations management. Before defining mathematical models, however, let us examine two points. First, in a previous section of this chapter, we saw that experimentation is an important part of the scientific approach. However, rarely if ever can a manager perform what would be considered a bona fide scientific experiment to test the feasibility of taking a particular action; the practicalities of the real world preclude this. In other words, a manager cannot usually experiment with inventory to determine which level minimizes carrying costs and ordering costs. However, an accurately constructed mathematical model enables the decision maker to experiment with possible solutions without interrupting the ongoing system. If the model accurately represents the ongoing system, it provides the decision maker with the results of proposed solutions. In other words, it reacts as the real system would react, enabling the decision maker to simulate the behavior of the real system. This experimental role of mathematical models makes them useful to managers.

Second, while there are several different models, the emphasis in P/OM is on mathematical models. Thus, the models examined in this section of the book are quantitative, or mathematical, in nature.

What do we mean by mathematical model? A **mathematical model** *is a simplified representation of the relevant aspects of an actual system or process.* The value of any model depends on how well it represents the system, or process, under consideration. A highly simplified model that accurately describes a system or process still provides a more clearly understood starting point than a vague conception. An accurate model forces the manager to consider systematically the variables in the problem and the relationships among the variables, and forcing the manager to formalize thinking reduces the possibility of overlooking important factors or giving too much weight to minor factors.

You are probably more familiar with models for decision making than you think. The accounting equation A = L + C is a mathematical model. It is a mathematical model showing a simplified relationship between assets, liabilities, and capital. It does not resemble the actual system physically, but it does behave as the real system behaves. It is an abstraction of the financial condition of a particular enterprise at a given moment of time.

Some Useful P/OM Models.

Allocation Models.   Allocation models are useful in a variety of situations in which numerous activities compete for limited resources. These models enable the decision maker to allocate scarce resources to maximize some given objective. In certain departments, the resources may include labor time that the production manager must allocate to several different products to maximize the objective of profit. One of the most widely used allocation models is the linear programming (LP) model. Linear programming expresses the objective in the form of a mathematical function, the value of which is to be maximized (e.g., profits) or minimized (e.g., costs).

Network Models.   Network models are extremely useful in planning and controlling both simple and complex projects. Actually, network models are as old as scientific management. The Gantt chart is one of Henry Gantt's contributions to the managerial task of managing work and organizations. While network models are more sophisticated than the Gantt chart, both are based on the same philosophy. The basic type of network model is PERT (Program Evaluation and Review Technique). PERT is a method of planning and controlling nonrepetitive projects—projects that have not been done before and will not be done again in exactly the same manner (e.g., the first space shuttle).

Inventory Models.   Inventory models provide answers to two questions: how much and when. Just as the business organization is concerned with obtaining goods to be sold at the most favorable price, it must also be concerned with the time at which orders are placed for repeat goods and the quantity of each order. On the one hand, enough inventory must be available at all times to ensure that there are no lost sales or loss of customer goodwill due to stock-outs; on the other hand, frequent orders result in increased costs, such as the storage costs from carrying an excessive inventory. The costs of ordering and carrying an inventory are inversely related: one increases while the other decreases. Inventory models enable the manager to compute the economic order quantity (EOQ) and the optimum reorder point. Because these models can be applied wherever inventories are kept, they have also found wide use in nonbusiness organizations.

Attempts to Integrate the Three Approaches

During the last 30 years, there have been attempts to integrate the three approaches to management—classical, behavioral, and management science. One of these attempts, the *systems approach,* stresses that organizations must be viewed as total systems, with each part linked to every other part. Another, the *contingency approach,* stresses that the correctness of a managerial practice is contingent on how it fits the particular situation in which it is applied. Let us briefly examine each.

FIGURE 1–3   A Systems Perspective of Managing

The systems perspective describes the important and dynamic nature of management.

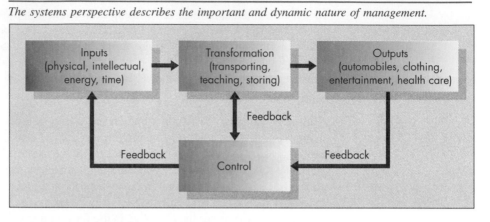

The Systems Approach

The systems approach to management is really a way of thinking about management problems. It views an organization as a group of interrelated parts with a single purpose. Because the action of one part influences the others, managers cannot deal separately with individual parts. In solving problems, managers using the systems approach must view the organization as a dynamic whole and must try to anticipate the intended as well as unintended impacts of their decisions. Such managers do not solve individual problems. Rather, they intervene in a total system of interrelated parts, using the management functions of planning, organizing, and controlling.

Figure 1–3 presents a systems model that illustrates inputs, transformation, outputs, and control. Inputs of labor, raw material, and technology are integrated to obtain finished goods (e.g., computers, automobiles, and furniture) or services (e.g., a well patient discharged from a hospital or a completed banking transaction). The transformation process (e.g., drilling, storing, teaching, diagnosing an illness) involves adding value to the product or service. To ensure that the best quality outputs are obtained, feedback and control are needed. As Figure 1–3 suggests, the action of one element in the model influences other parts of the model. For instance, poor raw materials are likely to result in poor final products.

The age-old confrontation between the production objective of low costs and the marketing objective of a broad product line is another example of the interrelated nature of management problems. Each objective conflicts with the other. For example, to incur the lowest production costs, a firm would produce only one color and one style. To achieve the marketing objective, however, several models and several colors would be required but at higher costs. In this situation, a compromise is necessary for the overall system to achieve its objective. The objectives of the individual parts must be compromised to meet the objective of the entire firm.

Contingency Approach

The systems approach forces managers to recognize that organizations are systems made up of interdependent parts and that a change in one part affects other parts. It seeks to identify the characteristics of jobs, people, and organizations, allowing managers to see the interdependence between the various segments of an organization. The basic idea of the contingency approach is that there is no best way to plan, organize, or control. Rather, managers must find different ways to fit different situations. A method highly effective in one situation may not work in other situations.

The contingency approach seeks to match different situations with different management methods.

Actually, the idea of contingency, or situational, thinking is not new. During the 1920s, an early writer in the classical approach mentioned the "law of the situation." Mary Parker Follett noted that "different situations require different kinds of knowledge, and the man possessing the knowledge demanded by a certain situation tends in the best managed businesses, other things being equal, to become the leader of the moment.[26]

The contingency approach has grown in popularity over the last two decades because research has found that, given certain characteristics of a job and certain characteristics of people doing the job, specific management practices tend to work better than others. For example, rigid plans, clearly defined jobs, autocratic leadership, and tight controls have at times resulted in high productivity and satisfied workers. At other times, the opposite characteristics (general plans, vaguely defined jobs, democratic leadership, and loose controls) have produced the same results.

If, for instance, productivity needs to be increased, the manager should not automatically assume a new work method is needed (a classical solution) or that a new motivational approach needs to be tried (a behavioral solution). Instead, the manager should study the characteristics of the workers, the nature of the job, and his own leadership approach before deciding on a solution.

Managers around the globe use more of a contingency approach to survive. Sole reliance on a classical or a behavioral or a management science approach is not sufficient for organizations. The approaches that worked for Procter & Gamble for 50 years and for the start-up of Apple Computer during its first few years must be modified to fit the changing global environment.[27] Thus, the contingency view has become more relevant and prominent because of the following factors:

1. Increased globalization of enterprise and the need for more government—business alliances to compete internationally.
2. Demands for ethical and socially responsive leadership.
3. Changing demographics and skill requirements of the workforce.
4. The emergence of new organizational structures that emphasize speed in reacting to environmental changes.
5. Changing needs, preferences, and desires of employees for job security, participation, ownership, and personal fulfillment.

As the contingency approach suggests, the student of management preparing for the 21st century must learn multiple ways to compete, innovate, create, motivate, and lead. Both the systems approach and the contingency approach can provide valuable insights and complement the classical, behavioral, and management science approaches.

The Three Tasks of World Class Managers

In introducing the three well-established approaches to management and the systems and contingency approaches, we have established that all modern managers, in any country in this world, essentially face three managerial tasks:

1. Managing work and organizations.
2. Managing people.
3. Managing production and operations.

FIGURE 1–4   The Work of Management

The work of management involves three interrelated tasks: managing work and organizations, managing people, and managing production and operations.

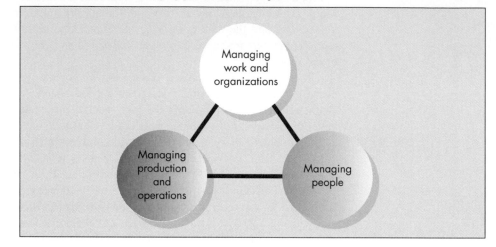

No matter what an organization engages in, its managers face these three tasks. Thus, managing is more than solving behavioral problems; it is more than solving technical problems; it is more than managing individual work; it is more than planning a department's future. The work of management is all of these. Learning to be a manager requires knowledge and skills relevant to each of these three tasks, which provide a point of departure for the study of management. These three fundamental tasks must be learned and practiced in a world that is globalizing, where there is demand and competition for better quality products and services, where the workforce is becoming increasingly culturally diverse, and where the public insists upon ethical and socially responsible decisions. The challenge of managing in the changing world has made management an exciting occupation.

Figure 1–4 illustrates that while each of the three managerial tasks can be discussed separately, they are very much interrelated. The figure also provides us with a framework that we build on throughout this book.

Figure 1–5 summarizes the challenges a modern manager faces and the wide knowledge necessary to plan, organize, lead, and control. Managers must rely primarily on information based on the classical approach to manage work and organizations. To manage people, they need behavioral information. To manage operations, they must have a management science perspective.

Plan for the Book

The purpose of this book is to prepare managers—individuals well versed in all traditions of management—for the future. We must all be contingency-oriented managers who use, when needed, the appropriate classical, behavioral, and management science concepts, tools, and techniques. Managers must be well grounded in the techniques of planning, organizing, leading, and controlling; they must understand the role of human behavior in organizations; and they must be skilled in the various ways to manage operations. Figure 1–6 illustrates the framework followed in the book.

FIGURE 1–5   The Practical Challenges and Required Knowledge of a Modern Manager

This figure illustrates the management tasks, the management functions, and the three approaches to management.

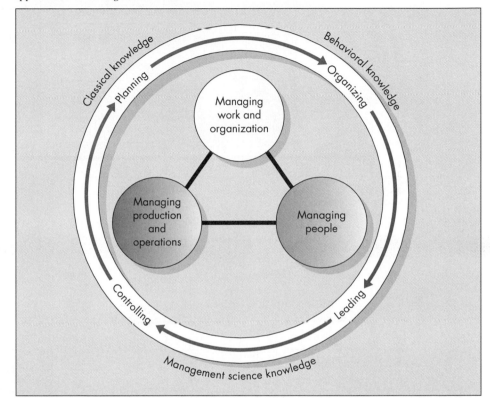

The three main managerial tasks serve as focal points for the three major sections of this textbook:

Part II, "Managing Work and Organizations: Planning, Organizing, Controlling," contains six chapters devoted to various aspects of the three primary management functions: planning, organizing, and controlling.

Part III, "Managing People in Organizations: Leading," concentrates on the behavioral foundations of effective management. This section contains six chapters that discuss such important management topics as motivation, group behavior, leadership, communications and negotiations, and development of the organization and its members.

Part IV, "Managing Production and Operations: Planning, Organizing, Leading, Controlling," focuses on the managerial task. Its three chapters include discussions of production and operations management, decision support systems, and introductory discussions of several tools useful in planning and controlling production and operations.

The book concludes with Part V, "Special Management Topics." Its two chapters discuss the important topics of entrepreneurship and careers in management.

FIGURE 1–6   Plan for the Book

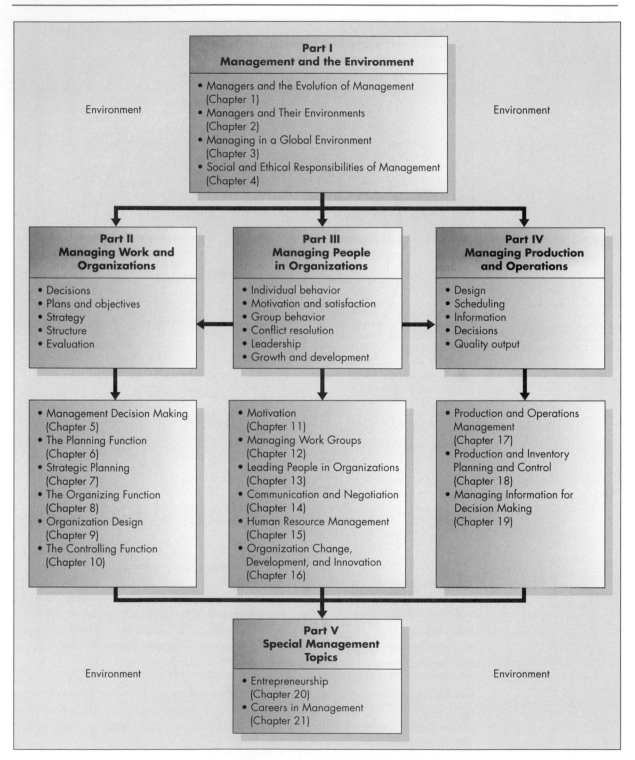

Summary of Key Points

- Management is the process undertaken by one or more individuals to coordinate the activities of others to achieve results not possible by one individual acting alone.
- Three fundamental tasks make up managerial work: managing work and organizations, managing people, and managing production and operations. These three tasks are generally applicable to managers in all organizations.
- Management literature offers a variety of viewpoints and emphases. We have sought to introduce some clarity by identifying three mutually supportive approaches to management: classical, which focuses on the task of managing work and organizations; behavioral, focusing on the task of managing people; and management science, which focuses on the task of managing production and operations.
- The modern era of managing began early in the 20th century when classical theorists, economists, and industrial engineers offered a classical approach to increase the productivity of individuals and organizations.
- The fundamentals of managing people evolved from human relations and behavioral science approaches that stimulated

the most famous management study known as the Hawthorne studies. This four-phase study conducted by Harvard University industrial psychologists has had a significant impact on the practice, teaching, and research of management.
- In the management science approach, managers found numerous quantitative tools and techniques with which to practice their craft. Applications of management science tools and techniques by the government during World War II illustrated that these tools were also applicable and useful in other settings. Today allocation, network, and inventory models and techniques are used in organizations of all sizes around the world.
- Each of the three well-established approaches has value. However, managers have also found that it is important to be system- and contingency-oriented (more flexible, more open minded, more inquisitive) in today's organizations.

Discussion and Review Questions

1. Have you ever managed anything—for example, as part of a job or in a social or civic organization? If so, did you perform the management functions of planning, organizing, leading, and controlling without being aware of it? Discuss your managerial experience and relate it to the functions of management.

2. One writer has stated: "People who don't manage are either too young, too old, or found in institutions for the incompetent." What is this writer trying to say? Do you agree? Why?

3. Are managers really needed in organizations? There are some who believe that managers and their contributions are no longer of much value to organizations or society. What do you believe?

4. Why is it likely that a contingency approach to managing people, information, or change is needed in a rapidly globalizing and interconnected world?

5. What are the advantages of having an ethnically diverse workforce in a globalizing world?

6. Over 70 years have passed since the Hawthorne studies were conducted, and, according to some critics, the "dehumanizing" aspects of various forms of managing still exist. What are some of the "dehumanizing" aspects of management that you are familiar with and can identify? Has the claim of "dehumanization" been exaggerated?

7. How would you determine whether Americans, Japanese, or Germans are better managers? Is it even worthwhile to discuss which country has better managers? Why?

8. Are there significant differences in what is referred to as scientific management and management science? Explain.

9. Talk to a few managers and ask them what is the most rewarding aspect of their job. What is the most frustrating aspect of their job?

10. What were the last three purchases you made? How much competition was there for your money?

Case 1–1
Goya Foods: Competition and Job Creation

Immigrants continue to flock to the United States in large numbers relative to immigration into any other nation in the world. Freedom, opportunities, a high standard of living, and multicultural influences are some of the attractions. There is some backlash occurring due to perceptions that US citizens are losing their jobs to immigrants who are willing to work for lower wages. Of course, another side of this ongoing debate about immigration involves the point that a number of immigrants have been successful in starting businesses and creating jobs. Job creation and business success send the message that the United States can and does benefit from immigration.

The Unanue (U-na-nu-way) family is an example of successful immigration. The family patriarch, Prudencio Unanue, immigrated from Spain to Puerto Rico in 1904 and to New York in 1915. He started what has now become the largest Hispanic-owned company in the United States—Goya Foods. For two decades, Unanue worked odd jobs in the food industry before he started working with a Spanish importer of olives and canned sardines. He lost the job because of poor business and started searching for another way to support his family.

Unanue didn't attend a university to study management, but he clearly understood that he had to plan, organize, lead, and control. He was well aware of the need to practice these functions. He had closely observed how managers in the firms he had worked for handled job assignments, workers, and customers. These lifelong experiences helped shape his view of what it would take to make a company successful.

In addition to being an astute observer of how managers worked, Unanue did his own marketing research. He believed that Spanish and Puerto Rican food was difficult to find and purchase. So, in 1936, he and his wife Carolina started Goya Foods. In 1992, privately owned Goya Foods had revenue of $452 million and over 1,800 employees, making it the largest Hispanic-owned firm in the United States.

For decades, Goya Foods has dominated the Northeast, where it controls 80 percent of the Hispanic-foods market.

It has flooded the market with more than 840 products such as beans, tomato sauce, seasonings, and olive oil. Goya has changed its product line because Hispanics of Mexican and Central American descent enjoy many foods unfamiliar to Hispanics of Caribbean descent, and vice versa. The Mexican food market in supermarkets is also expected to reach $4 billion by 1997. (In 1992, salsa surpassed ketchup as the United States' best-selling condiment.) When Prudencio Unanue began Goya Foods, he had a vision that the Hispanic food business would become a giant, and he was correct.

As immigration from Mexico and Central and South America continues, Goya Foods searches for products to sell to the new immigrants. Goya is now intent on making Goya a national brand name, but competitors are stepping into the market. Campbell's, Knorr, and Heinz all intend to show Goya Foods that competition in the US economy can be stiff. Identifying Hispanic markets, their needs, and their tastes is what Goya Foods has been built on and is what competitors are searching for every day.

The Unanue family learned from Prudencio that there were opportunities to conduct business in the United States. They also learned that business success creates competitors. Once business success is achieved, it is important to continue working hard to stay successful. Prudencio Unanue was so successful that 1,800 people are working hard today to keep Goya Foods in front of the competition.

Questions for Analysis

1. Could Prudencio Unanue have started Goya Foods in a planned communist economy such as North Korea? Why or why not?

2. Why is observing others sometimes an effective way for people to learn how to operate as a manager?

3. What managerial activities was Prudencio Unanue not able to learn by observing managers doing their jobs?

Source: Copyright 1993, *USA Today.* Reprinted with permission.

Video Case
The Evolution of Management

The management profession, as we know it today, is relatively new, even though the issues and problems that confront managers have existed for thousands of years. Management

emerged as a formal discipline at the turn of the century, when rapid industrialization called for better-skilled management of natural resources, capital, and labor. The various management approaches that have been developed can be divided into two major groups: classical approaches and contemporary approaches.

The classical approaches, which extended from the mid-19th century through the early 1950s, emerged as managers tried to cope with the growth of American industry. These approaches were systematic management, scientific management, administrative management, human relations, and bureaucracy.

Systematic management represented the beginning of formal management thought in the United States. It emphasized the way in which manufacturing firms operated because most management problems were focused on manufacturing.

Scientific management was introduced around the turn of the century by Frederick Taylor, an engineer who applied scientific methods to analyze work and determine the "one best way" to complete production tasks. Taylor stressed the importance of hiring and training the proper workers to do those tasks. One of the most famous examples of the application of scientific management is the factory Henry Ford built to produce the Model T. Ford's use of scientific management principles yielded higher productivity and efficiency. For example, by 1914, chassis assembly time had been trimmed from almost 13 hours to 1.5 hours.

Administrative management emerged at about the same time and emphasized the perspective of senior managers within the organization. It viewed management as a profession that could be taught.

The human relations approach to management evolved from the Hawthorne studies conducted from 1924 to 1932 at the Western Electric Company outside Chicago. Various working conditions, particularly lighting, were altered to determine the effects of these changes on productivity. But researchers, led by Harvard professor Elton Mayo, were ultimately unable to determine any relationship between factory lighting and productivity levels. This led the researchers to believe the productivity was affected more by psychological and social factors. This approach highlighted the importance of the human element in the organization. However, critics believed the human relations philosophy of "the happy worker as a productive worker" was too simplistic.

The bureaucracy approach to management was developed by Max Weber, a German sociologist and social historian. He attempted to establish an overall management system by focusing on a structured, formal network of relationships among specialized positions in an organization. Bureaucracy allowed efficient performance of many routine activities.

The contemporary approaches to management, which have been developed since World War II, attempted to overcome the limitations of the classical approaches. The contemporary approaches include quantitative management, organizational behavior, systems theory, and the contingency perspective.

Quantitative management was aided by the development of modern computers. It emphasizes the application of a formal, mathematical model to management decisions and problems.

The organizational behavior approach to management promotes employee effectiveness through the understanding of the complex nature of individual, group, and organizational processes.

The systems theory of management, which originated in the 1950s, was a major effort to overcome the limitations of the earlier approaches by attempting to view the organization as a whole system. Systems theory introduced the concept of equifinality—that there is no "one best way" to reach a goal. And it stresses the notion of synergy—that the whole is greater than the sum of its parts.

The contingency perspective has most recently dominated the study of management. It asserts that situational characteristics, or contingencies, determine the management strategies that will be most effective. This approach argues that no universal principle should *always* be applied. Rather, managers, like those at Trek Bicycle, analyze situations and then, based on their analysis of key contingencies, make decisions regarding the most appropriate ways to manage. Trek, based in rural Wisconsin, has a very open-minded approach to managing, and meeting customer needs.

But the evolution of management doesn't end there. Management thought and practice continues to evolve. Current events and trends are shaping the future of business and of management. Among the major forces now revolutionizing management are: globalization, learning organization, total quality management, and reengineering.

Globalization refers to the rise of multinational enterprises in the ever-expanding global marketplace. Even small firms that don't operate on a global scale must make important strategic decisions based on international considerations. Trek Bicycle recently discovered the importance of the global market. In the mid-1980s, only a small percentage of its revenues came from foreign sales. However, as international sales manager Joyce Keehn said, "When we began to get into other markets like Germany and Japan, their standards were much higher than what we were experiencing here in the States. So, in effect, these countries helped us increase our quality because we wanted to grow our business in these countries. We listened to what the dealers and the market were expecting from us and we implemented those quality changes here." Today, Trek sells its bicycles in 55 countries with international sales accounting for 40 percent of its business.

The learning organization is committed to openness, new ideas, generating new knowledge, and spreading information and knowledge to others. Continuing dialogue and open-mindedness with an eye toward achieving the organization's goals are the foremost concern. Tellabs, a Chicago-area manufacturer of telecommunications products and services, is a learning organization that has emphasized innovation, teams, and mentoring. It seems to be working. Tellabs' stock has increased by more than 1,600 percent over the last five years, outperforming every other publicly traded stock in the nation. Tellabs employee Kris Bean said, "My experience with mentoring has been phenomenal. My life has completely changed by the inputs of other people."

Total quality management, or TQM, refers to an approach to management that produces customer satisfaction by providing high-quality goods and services. Its goal is to solve and then eliminate all quality-related problems. First National Bank of Chicago has an aggressive quality program that includes weekly performance review meetings. In the meetings, managers analyze dozens of charts that are designed to monitor the quality of their performance.

First National's Rich Gilgan said, "You can't manage what you don't understand. And you don't understand what you don't measure. So measurement is critical to understanding where our performance is improving or not improving, where we have problems, and we can go back and identify the root cause of those problems."

Finally, business reengineering is the process of starting all over to rebuild the company and overhaul its ways of doing business. The goal of reengineering is to achieve dramatic improvements in critical performance measures including cost, quality innovation, and speed. Reengineering requires a way of thinking that's quite different from traditional management practices.

From the classical approaches, through the contemporary approaches, and into the forces now revolutionizing management, the history of past efforts, triumphs, and failures has become the guide to future management practice. Since the mid-19th century, change has been the constant in the evolution of management. The marketplace keeps changing, the technology keeps changing, and the workforce keeps changing. Today's manager must learn how to deal with the forces of change affecting management. Only by understanding the implications of change and the challenges it presents will you be prepared to meet it head-on.

Critical Thinking Questions

1. In general, how do contemporary approaches to management differ from classical approaches?

2. What are some modern organizational problems that are a result of classical approaches to managing?

3. The Hawthorne studies are frequently cited as a turning point in management thought. What is the significance of this research?

EXPERIENTIAL EXERCISE
ATTITUDES ABOUT BUSINESS ORGANIZATIONS

Purpose

The purpose of this exercise is to identify attitudes that students have about business and various industries.

The Exercise in Class

1. Individually, each student is to complete the surveys about business and various industries. (See Exhibits 1 and 2.)

2. After individuals complete the surveys, the instructor will form five- to seven-person groups to discuss the individual ratings.

3. Each group will calculate an average group score for each item (adding the individual scores and dividing by the number of individuals in the group to arrive at an average).

4. The average scores will be placed by the group on the board or a flip chart for the class to discuss.

The Learning Message

Differences in student opinions exist. This exercise will display these differences and may also point out why they exist (e.g., backgrounds, pessimism, optimism, values).

Exhibit 1   Survey of Business

In your opinion, have business organizations in general been supportive in each of the following areas? Use the scale below to indicate how supportive you believe business has been, placing the appropriate number in the space after each area of concern.

5—significant support
4—some support
3—undecided
2—little, if any, support
1—no support

Area of concern:

Energy conservation   _____

Improving quality of worker's life   _____

Controlling environmental pollution   _____

Fighting inflation   _____

Helping higher education   _____

Retraining employees with obsolete skills   _____

Developing urban areas   _____

Hiring the disabled   _____

Hiring minorities   _____

Promoting ethical behavior   _____

Technological advancement   _____

Rewarding good performance   _____

Maintaining fair profit margins   _____

A strong government

Exhibit 2   Survey of Industries

Please provide a rating for the industries listed below. In other words, what are your general impressions of these industries? Why do you feel this way? Use values of 1 to 5 according to the scale below. Place the number you choose for the industry in the appropriate blank space.

5—very good
4—generally good
3—unsure
2—generally poor
1—very poor

Industry:

Automobile	_____	Television	_____
Steel	_____	Aerospace	_____
Tobacco	_____	Health care	_____
Food processing	_____	Education	_____
Banking	_____	Fast food	_____
Publishing	_____	Computer	_____
Religion	_____	Paper	_____
Oil	_____	Insurance	_____
Chemicals	_____	Car repair	_____
Electronics	_____	Prescription drugs	_____
Tire and rubber	_____		

Notes

1. John P Fernandez, *The Diversity Advantage* (New York: Lexington Books, 1993).

2. H Thomas Johnson, *Relevance Regained* (New York: Free Press, 1992).

3. Michael L Dertousos, Richard K Lester, and Robert M Solow, *Made in America* (Cambridge, MA: MIT Press, 1989), p. 1.

4. Ibid.

5. Albert T Somners, *The U.S. Economy Demystified* (New York: Lexington Books, 1993), pp. 11–14.

6. Peter F Drucker, *Managing in Turbulent Times* (New York: Harper & Row, 1980), p. 230.

7. Tom Peters and Robert H Waterman, Jr., *In Search of Excellence* (New York: Harper & Row, 1982), p. xxiii.

8. Lynne Joy McFarland, Larry E Senn, and John R Childress, *21st Century Leadership* (New York: Leadership Press, 1993).

9. T George Harris, "The Post Capitalistic Executive: An Interview with Peter F. Drucker," *Harvard Business Review,* May–June 1993, pp. 114–22.

10. Samuel Haber, *Efficiency and Uplift* (Chicago: University of Chicago Press, 1964).

11. Lyndall Urwick, *The Golden Book of Management* (London: Newman Neame, 1956), pp. 72–79.

12. Frederick W Taylor, *Principles of Scientific Management* (New York: Harper & Row, 1911), pp. 36–37.

13. Edwin A Locke, "The Ideas of Frederick W. Taylor," *Academy of Management Review,* January 1982, pp. 14–24.

14. Henri Fayol, *General and Industrial Management,* trans. J A Conbrough (Geneva: International Management Institute, 1929). All subsequent references in this text are to the more widely available translation by Constance Storrs (London: Sir Isaac Pitman & Sons, 1949).

15. James D Mooney, *The Principles of Organization* (New York: Harper & Row, 1947).

16. Lyman W Porter and Lawrence E McKibbon, *Management Education and Development* (New York: McGraw-Hill, 1988).

17. "Treading the Boardrooms," *The Economist,* September 1990, pp. 64–65.

18. See Fritz J Roethlisberger and William H Dickson, *Management and the Worker* (Cambridge, MA: Harvard University Press, 1939). Eugene L Cass and Frederick G Zimmer, *Man and Work in Society* (New York: Van Nostrand Reinhold, 1975).

19. Paul R Lawrence and John A Seiler, *Organizational Behavior and Administration* (Burr Ridge, IL: Richard D. Irwin, 1965), p. 173.

20. Alan C Filley, Robert J House, and Steven Kerr, *Managerial Process and Organizational Behavior* (Glenview, IL: Scott, Foresman, 1976), p. 16.

21. Robert Levering, *A Great Place to Work* (New York: Random House, 1988).

22. Geert Hofstede, "Cultural Constraints in Management Theories," *Academy of Management Executive,* February 1993, pp. 81–94.

23. Gary A Klein, *Decision Making In Action: Models and Methods* (Norwood, NJ: Ablex Methods, 1993), pp. 4–6.

24. Antonio Kovacevic and Nukolas Majluf, "Six Stages of IT Strategic Management," *Sloan Management Review,* Summer 1993, pp. 77–87.

25. Darryl V Landvater, *World Class Production and Operations Management* (Essex Junction, VT: Wight, 1993).

26. The many contributions of Mary Parker Follett are collected in *Dynamic Administration,* ed. Henry C Metcalf and Lyndall Urwick (New York: Harper & Row, 1941), p. 101.

27. Ian Mitroff and Harold A Linstone, *The Unbounded Mind: Breaking the Chains of Traditional Business Thinking* (New York: Oxford University Press, 1993).

2   MANAGERS AND THEIR ENVIRONMENTS

Chapter Learning Objectives

After completing Chapter 2, you should be able to:

- **Define** an organization and its environment in terms of a system.
- **Describe** the internal environment in which a manager must function.
- **Discuss** how a more culturally diverse workforce is becoming a reality in American organizations.
- **Compare** the three basic skills necessary for effective managerial performance.
- **Identify** the various roles managers in organizations must perform.

Managers Are Experiencing Changes in Their Environments

The world and environment of work are changing. The year 2000 will dawn on a Saturday, and a new millennium will be thrust upon managers. There are experts who foresee some changes in organizations and how they will be managed. The average size of US companies will become smaller as fewer people are employed in them. About 133 million Americans will have positions in a new kind of workforce.

The headlines are clear in stating that the largest corporations are engaged in a bruising transition toward a global, information-driven economy. Approximately 11 percent of male, college-educated workers lost their jobs from 1991 through 1993. Of the 8 million new jobs created in the period 1992 through 1995, about 60 percent were managerial and professional positions. Job security, which was a decade ago simply assumed, is now an important issue that blue-collar and white-collar employees give consideration to when considering their futures.

Another change in organizations predicted by some is that the supervisor–subordinate or boss-following type of hierarchy that emphasizes how managers plan, organize, lead, and control will give way to a more horizontal arrangement. Instead of managers using power and au-thority, organizations will need more facilitators, coaches, and mentors. (In place of these "old-fashioned" labels, the term *coordinator* is preferred at Westt, Inc., a custom manufacturing and industrial automation firm in Menlo Park, California.)

Does this mean that *all* firms will be practicing the fundamentals of coordination and not the fundamentals of management? We don't think so. However, more firms will probably experiment with coordinators and not rely solely on managerial hierarchy and power. But whether organizations use coordinators, managers, or technicians, sound planning, organizing, leading, and controlling will have to be practiced. We do not believe that managers will completely disappear in the 21st century. More managers are likely to learn how to make use of coordinators, mentors, and coaches, and more managers are likely to include in their own skill mix an ability to coordinate, mentor, and coach.

Sources: Adapted from Michael J Mandell, "Economic Anxiety," *Business Week*, March 11, 1996, pp. 50–56; W Kiechel III, "How We Will Work in the Year 2000," *Fortune*, May 17, 1993, pp. 38–52; "The Death of Corporate Loyalty," *The Economist*, April 3, 1993, pp. 63–64; and "The Fall of Big Business," *The Economist*, April 17, 1993, p. 13.

Many different forces outside and inside an organization influence managers' performance. The managerial functions of planning, organizing, leading, and controlling must be accomplished under constantly changing conditions. Even if the coordinator, mentor, or coach becomes more widespread in organizations, the managerial functions must be implemented. Managers must deal with both the external environment and the internal environment.

The **external environment** includes all the forces acting on the organization from the outside. Customers, competitors, suppliers, and human resources are some of the obvious forces in an organization's external environment. Other not-so-obvious forces include technological, economic, political, legal, regulatory, cultural, social, and international forces.

The **internal environment** includes the day-to-day forces within the organization in which managers perform their functions. For example, the level in the organization where management is performed has implications for managerial performance: top-level managers do different things from middle-level managers, who, in turn, do different things from first-level managers. Coping with managerial demands in the internal environment requires managers to have different skills and to perform different roles. Skill requirements and role performance are important forces in the internal environment as we see in the discussion that follows.

The External Environment

Individuals often limit their perspective of an organization to the elements and activities that exist within the organization: the employees, managers, equipment, tools, procedures, and other elements that combine to create the organization's product or service. However, this perspective is sorely limited. A complete picture of any organization must include its *external environment,* the large arena that exists outside the organization and comprises many varied forces that have an impact upon the organization's structure, processes, and performance. These forces may be *direct,* exerting an immediate and direct influence on the organization, or they may be *indirect,* influencing the climate in which the organization operates (and becoming direct forces under some conditions).

To some degree, these direct and indirect forces are unpredictable and uncontrollable, and they are usually quite powerful, exerting a significant effect on the organization's performance and well-being. For an organization to succeed, its managers must recognize these external forces, comprehend their interrelationships, and understand their real and potential impacts on the organization. Above all, managers must manage the organization (and, in some cases, the environment) to minimize the environmental forces' negative effects and maximize their positive impacts on the organization.

Direct Forces

The major direct forces of an organization's external environment are the customers that the organization must satisfy, the competitors with whom the organization must effectively compete for customers, the suppliers that provide the organization with essential resources, and human resources—people in the external environment from whom the organization must draw an effectively performing workforce. Figure 2–1 illustrates these direct forces.

FIGURE 2–1   Direct Forces in the Organization's External Environment

---

Direct forces have an immediate impact on the organization.

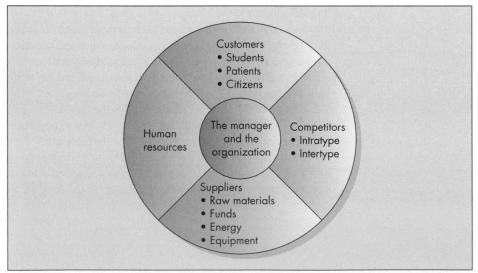

Customers.   Customers purchase an organization's products or services. They may be individuals—for example, a freelance writer who buys an Apple Macintosh personal computer for her writing work. Individual customers differ in many characteristics, such as age, education, income, and lifestyle. Customers may also be organizations. Compaq, for example, powers its personal computers with microprocessors it buys from Intel Corporation. Organizational customers differ in their requirements for service, quality, and delivery times.

Of all the direct forces, customers are perhaps the most vital to organizations. After all, their decision to buy or not buy a firm's output directly determines the company's sales revenues and ultimately its survival. Organizations typically respond to customer forces in the external environment by taking action: They conduct *customer research* that focuses on both present and potential customers. Organizations seek to identify their present customers' degree of satisfaction with their products and services and to discover any changing preferences.

For example, at Lands' End, the mail-order catalog company, telephone operators make meticulous notes of all comments made by customers; these comments are summarized each month in a written report provided to all managers. Even in health care, paying attention to patient needs is becoming a way of providing services. UCLA's satellite clinic in the Fairfax district of Los Angeles specializes in geriatrics for the area's middle-income retirees. The average patient is over 80 with at least five active medical problems. Most of these patients qualify for Medicare.[1]

Many organizations emphasize current-customer research because it is commonly recognized that, done effectively, keeping a current customer incurs about one-fifth the expense of finding a new one.[2] The failure to detect customers' changing preferences is also quite costly. For example, Nike Inc. lost its market leadership in athletic shoes during the mid-1980s partly because it failed to recognize and react to the customers' growing preference for style over performance. However, Nike has since rebounded because it foresaw and reacted to the fickle market's return to preferring performance over style. Nike and Reebok International Ltd. are now battling shoe-to-shoe for market dominance.[3]

Customer research also focuses on potential buyers. Organizations study changes in demographics and other factors to identify groups of possible buyers. Since the late 1980s, for example, more companies have begun to target elderly Americans, given that by the year 2000, over 15 percent of the population will be over 65 years of age.[4]

Beyond these specific examples, US companies nationwide are responding to a major change in customer preferences: a new desire for increased quality in the products and services they buy. Overall, companies are placing greater emphasis on quality, whether it be in speed of service or in the features of a product. This focus on improving quality is discussed further throughout this book.

Competitors.   Competitors are an organization's opponents, the companies against which the organization competes for customers and needed resources (e.g., employees, raw materials, even other organizations) in the external environment. An organization's *intratype competitors* are companies that produce the same or similar products/ services as the organization. General Motors and Ford Motor Company, American and United Air Lines, and Compaq and IBM are intratype competitors that vie for customers. Harvard University and Yale University are also intratype competitors that pursue top-notch students and compete to recruit exceptional faculty.

Intertype competitors are distinctly different and competing organizations. For example, a bank such as Prudential Insurance Co. of America competes against Smith

Barney Shearson for individuals interested in investing money. The Phoenix Suns, Dallas Cowboys, Chicago White Sox, and other professional athletic teams continually compete against universities for talented high school athletes. Hewlett-Packard Company and Microsoft Corporation compete against the US armed forces for talented computer software programmers.

The dynamics of the moves and countermoves made by intertype competitors can occur on many fronts and be fast-paced and difficult to predict. Because of this, competition can be intense, as it is in the soft drink industry, where Coca-Cola Company and PepsiCo compete for market leadership. Each company continually moves and countermoves on a number of fronts—including new product development, distribution, price, and advertising/promotion. In other industries (especially those regulated by the government), the moves and countermoves are less frequent, more stable, and more predictable (e.g., the utilities industry).

To succeed, an organization must make effective moves and countermoves, ones that maintain or advance the company's position in the marketplace and that cannot be easily nullified by competitors' responses. Doing so requires a thorough grasp of the relevant forces in the environment, especially competition. An organization comes to understand its competitors by performing an ongoing *competitor analysis*. It reviews and evaluates information from many sources (the media, suppliers, wholesalers, and associates) to obtain a solid understanding of a competitor's objectives, strategies, and competitive advantages (e.g., a strong distribution network) and weaknesses (e.g., a typically slow response to competitors' moves). A thorough competitor analysis enables an organization to better anticipate a competitor's moves and countermoves.[5]

In this regard, a growing number of companies are establishing competitor intelligence teams typically staffed by two to five employees assigned to obtain specific information about a competitor. Top management uses the information in making critical decisions such as whether to enter new markets.

Overall, organizations strive to establish and protect competitive advantages, particularly strengths that bolster the company's competitive power. In some industries, competitive power has been lost as foreign competition more successfully satisfied customer demands. For example, American firms in the semiconductor industry have lost out to firms in newly industrialized countries (NIC), such as South Korea and Taiwan.

Suppliers.   All organizations require resources—funds, energy, equipment, services, and materials—to produce a product or service that succeeds in the marketplace. Suppliers are organizations that provide these resources. Their outputs are the buyer organization's inputs and can therefore significantly affect the quality, cost, and timeliness of the buyer's product or service. A buyer organization is vulnerable to several potential supplier problems, such as low-quality materials or a supplier's financial crisis or labor strike that prevents the buyer from receiving essential materials. One major problem Reebok faced in 1987 was labor unrest in Korea that prevented the company from filling its retailers' orders.

Because of these potential problems, many organizations reduce their dependence on any one source by spreading their purchases of raw materials and other needed resources across several suppliers. They make sure that the materials they need are standardized and can thus be made by many suppliers. Some companies have gone further, becoming their own suppliers by *backward vertical integration*. These companies manufacture at least some of the raw materials needed to produce the final product or service. This strategy is costly to implement, but it offers the advantages of greater control over materials cost, quality, and delivery. One reason Coors could not compete with Gallo in the wine cooler market was that Gallo has backward vertical integration; it grows its own grapes and makes bottle labels, thus lowering its overall production costs.

However, a growing number of companies in some industries are opting for *single sourcing*—relying on one supplier for particular parts and materials. At Ford Motor Company and General Motors Corporation, over 98 percent of the purchased materials and parts are single sourced. All steering wheels for a particular model, for example, are provided by one supplier. Companies that are single sourcing are willing to risk greater dependence for the higher materials quality they believe the strategy provides. With fewer suppliers, a company can work more easily with a vendor to boost materials quality. With a guaranteed larger volume of purchases, a supplier is more willing to invest in the production equipment that boosts materials quality. Single sourcing also provides greater consistency in materials quality, and with fewer suppliers, a buyer can more easily coordinate production schedules.[6]

Human Resources.   Human resources are the vast resource of people in the external environment from which an organization obtains its employees. People are perhaps an organization's most precious internal resource because they are the organization's lifeblood. They provide the knowledge, skills, and drive that create, maintain, and advance organizations. To be successful, an organization must attract and keep the individuals it needs to achieve its objectives and to thrive.

According to researchers of the US labor force, the following four recent trends concerning human resources pose major challenges for management. They are a more culturally diverse workforce, women in the workforce, the downsizing trend, and an aging population.

A More Culturally Diverse Workforce.   Traditionally, the United States has been considered a melting pot nation. Ethnically and racially diverse workers have eventually become assimilated into American society. Today, however, a diverse workforce means more than ethnic background or skin color.[7] As Figure 2–2 illustrates, diversity refers to an array of other factors as well. People working in organizations are different from one another in *many* ways. The factors presented in Figure 2–2 suggest that managers are faced with attempting to balance the wants, needs, perceptions, and attitudes of an increasingly diverse workforce. The balancing act is difficult since each person has individual characteristics and, further, each group that a person belongs to has unique characteristics. For example, an African-American female worker who is college educated belongs in at least those three groups—African-American, college-educated, and female—and each group has its own values, perceptions, attitudes, and so forth. Managing such diversity will require managers to consider accommodating within reason significant individual and group differences.[8]

The accompanying Management Focus indicates that according to some research studies, different groups place value on different factors. Managing each of these groups will require considering these types of factors.

The increased prominence of minorities in the workforce is becoming an extremely important diversity consideration. The Bureau of Labor Statistics projects 16.5 million African-Americans and over 14 million Hispanics in the workforce by 2000. In the past, the one dominant, visible ethnic majority comprised white males. As we enter the 21st century, many ethnic groups will become dominant.

FIGURE 2–2   Factors Contributing to Diversity

Selected characteristics that result in diversity among individuals.

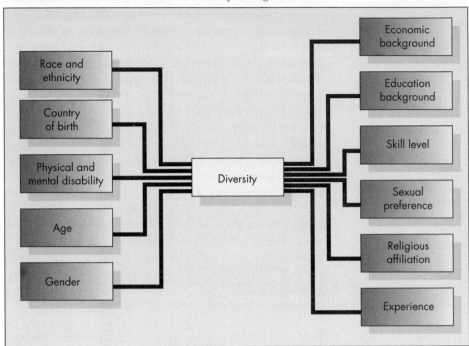

Managers will need to consider a host of factors in attempting to create effective work units and motivational programs. Language and communication, how to motivate people from different cultures and backgrounds, career planning, and the type of training programs to implement are some of the decisions and issues created by the changing mix of the workforce.

Women in the Workforce.   More women are entering the workforce than ever before. Women will be almost 50 percent of the workforce by the year 2000. Today more females are enrolled in college than males. A related shift is also occurring: High-paying, high-status jobs are finally beginning to open up to women.

As more businesses and institutions realize that they have a moral and legal obligation to hire, promote, and develop women, more females will begin to consider management as a viable career option. A decrease in the number of younger workers and appropriately skilled workers should encourage more organizations to find ways to attract, retain, and reward equitably educated and skilled women.

Since women are likely to play a growing role in organizations, it will be important for firms to become more creative in identifying and supporting affordable child care and elder care systems.

The Downsizing Trend.   Some types of jobs are being phased out of existence. Downsizing has become a fact of life, as over the past decade millions of managers, professional employees, and blue-collar workers have lost their jobs. As a result, fear has spread among those who have survived the wave of cutbacks. According to the US

Management Focus

What Diverse Employees Want

Marilyn Loden and Judy B. Rosener are involved in research and training in the area of managing diversity in organizations. Based on their own research and workshops, they have determined that individuals belonging to different groups have various attitudes, needs, and wants. A few of the group wants that Loden and Rosener have identified are the following:

Younger and Older Employees Want:

- More respect for their life experiences.
- To be taken seriously.
- To be challenged by their organizations—not patronized.

Women Want:

- Recognition as equal partners.
- Active support of male colleagues.
- Organizations to proactively address work and family issues.

Men Want:

- The same freedom to grow/feel that women have.
- To be perceived as allies, not as the enemy.
- To bridge the gap between dealing with women at home and at work.

People of Color Want:

- To be valued as unique individuals, as members of ethnically diverse groups, as people of different races, and as equal contributors.
- To establish more open, honest working relationships with people of other races and ethnic groups.

- The active support of white people in fighting racism and colorism.

White People Want:

- To have their ethnicity acknowledged.
- To reduce discomfort, confusion, and dishonesty in dealing with people of color.
- To build relationships with people of color based on common goals, concerns, and mutual respect for differences.

Differently Abled People Want:

- Greater acknowledgment of and focus on abilities, not just on disabilities.
- To be challenged by colleagues and organizations to be the best.
- To be included, not isolated.

Physically Able-Bodied People Want:

- To develop more ease in dealing with differently abled people.
- To appreciate abilities—in addition to understanding disabilities.
- To give honest feedback and appropriate support—without being patronizing or overprotective.

Source: Adapted from M Loden and J B Rosener, *Workforce America* (Burr Ridge, IL: Business One Irwin, 1991), pp. 76–78.

Department of Commerce, between 1987 and 1992 nearly 5 million workers who had held their jobs for at least three years were dismissed.[9]

As downsizing continues, loyalty to the firm is weakening and even disappearing. The absence of firm loyalty has become a concern among managers who have been asked to develop effective teams and high-performing individuals. Instead of building a strong relationship between the firm and employees, a new type of relationship is emerging. Anxiety, low trust, and low job security have created a strong individual orientation toward taking control of one's own destiny.[10] This type of "Darwinian" approach has created a more arm's-length relationship.

An Aging Population.   Today, over 49 percent of the population is under age 35; by 2000, less than 39 percent will be under 35. In sum, there will be fewer younger employees to replace the older employees who retire. At the same time, more older employees are retiring sooner. In 1970, for example, 83 percent of all men from 55 to 64 years of age were employed; in 1991, only 62 percent were employed.[11]

Baby boomers—those born between 1946 and 1964—have consistently been a dominant force. They now number about 76 million and constitute about one-third of the US population. This large segment of the population is now in their 30s and 40s. They are a part of the aging population and one of the reasons the median age of the workforce, which in 1970 was 28 years old, will be about 40 years old in 2000.

These changing demographics present management with two challenges: to find ways to keep older, experienced employees in the workforce and to retrain older workers, such as those who enter an organization to start a second career. To date, retention strategies have included allowing older employees to work fewer hours and redesigning jobs to accommodate them. Challenger, Gray, and Christman, a Chicago outplacement firm, has gathered some interesting data that suggest that the aging worker possesses some valued characteristics. For example, only 3 percent of employees 50 or over change jobs in any year, compared with 10 percent of the entire workforce; and people over 30 tend to use fewer health care benefits than workers with school-aged children.[12]

Indirect Forces

The indirect forces of the external environment can affect managers in at least two ways. First, outside organizations can have a direct influence on an organization or an indirect influence through a direct force. For example, a consumer activist group may lobby for certain causes, such as equal credit opportunities for women. Local media may apply pressure to keep open a plant that management planned to close. Legislation may force managers to alter the way they report certain information concerning hiring practices.

Second, certain indirect forces can influence the climate in which the organization must function. For example, the economy may expand or decline, requiring responses from management. New technological breakthroughs may alter the entire way an organization does business. Imagine, for example, the impact digital watches had on traditional watch manufacturers or the effect of compact disks and cassette tapes on the manufacture of long-playing records. In 10 years, the records' share of the recorded music market declined from over 90 percent to less than 20 percent. The following discussion addresses some of the most important indirect forces in the external environment.

Technological.   Technological forces are developments in technology in the external environment that can have an impact on an organization in two ways. Technological developments can influence an organization's use of knowledge and techniques in producing a product or service and in performing other work (e.g., financial analysis, clerical tasks) of the organization. For example, ultrasound equipment that provides a picture of a patient's heart is an important part of the technology used in diagnosing cardiac diseases, and the advent of laser scanners at cash registers in grocery stores has quickly become a primary element of the technology used in checking a customer's purchases. Second, technological developments also affect the characteristics of an organization's products or services, such as the power of a computer system or the clarity and brightness of a color TV's picture.

Technological forces require that management keep abreast of the latest developments and, where possible, incorporate advancements to maintain the organization's competitiveness. This challenge is made more difficult by the quickening pace of technological change. Consider, for example, the projected technological changes listed in Table 2–1. According to experts, these major advancements will occur within the next 10 years. Moreover, the speed of change is expected to continue to accelerate in the 21st century.

Organizations attempt to keep up with technological change through close contacts with research and development organizations, research scientists, and other individuals involved in technological developments. Companies also update the skills and knowledge of their employees who are responsible for the technology of the organization's work and output. For example, some companies require their engineers to attend technical seminars to keep up-to-date. Many engineering and high-tech firms allow their technical people to take sabbaticals—a several-month paid leave from the company—to upgrade their skills.[13]

Competitor intelligence teams can provide insight into developments in a competitor's work technology. Xerox Corporation, for example, has learned much about the technology its Japanese competitors use in copiers by purchasing their copiers, disassembling them, and studying the machines' parts and structural designs.[14]

Federal Express Corporation developed the computerized technology that has given the company a winning competitive edge in overnight delivery. In an instant, Federal Express can locate any package at every step of its journey from initial pickup to final delivery. Technology also enables Federal Express to come when you call, while chief competitor United Parcel Service (UPS) must maintain a strict pickup schedule.[15] UPS's response: It is implementing the kind of technology that has given Federal Express the competitive advantage.[16]

Economic.   Economic forces are changes in the state of America's economy reflected by such indicators as inflation rates, gross domestic product, unemployment rates, the value of the US dollar, interest rates, and the size of US budget and trade deficits.

Changes in the economy pose both opportunities and problems for managers. In times of continual moderate growth, many organizations enjoy a growing demand for output, and funds are more easily available for plant expansion and other investments. However, when the economy shifts downward (as in a recession), demand plummets, unemployment rises, and profits shrink.

TABLE 2–1   Forecasts for the Year 2000 and Beyond

Music: Individual members of a household and guests will wear electronic pins that communicate with the house's information and entertainment system so each person can listen to a different tune or message—or hear nothing at all.

Movies: In the palm of the hand. A tiny video and audio player that lets you see full-motion video is now (1996) being released.

Schooling: Can begin in the crib. Infotech is producing interactive educational toys to stimulate early development of mental faculties.

Information chips: Information technologies will become small enough to implant into our bodies. Tiny implanted chips will serve as a combination credit card, passport, driver's license, and personal diary.

New professions: As society demands more creative and spiritual fulfillment, new professions will appear such as strategic dreamers to help corporations understand customers' spiritual goals and sensory designers who use colors, scents, and textures to create environments that stimulate particular emotions.

Source: "Recent Forecasts," *The Futurist,* November–December 1996, pp. 27–31.

Organizations must continually monitor changes in the chief economic indicators to minimize threats and capitalize on opportunities. Some organizations utilize projections of future economic conditions in making such decisions as whether to expand plant facilities or enter new markets. However, leading economists often differ in their economic projections, and many organizations are therefore skeptical about economic forecasting.

Political, Legal, and Regulatory.   Numerous laws and a multitude of authorities characterize the political, legal, and regulatory forces in the external environment that have an indirect but strong influence on the organization. For example, legislation by federal and state governments affects the wages and taxes that an organization pays, the rights of employees, and the organization's liabilities for harm done to customers by its products. Federal regulatory agencies influence an organization's hiring and promotion of women and minorities (the Equal Employment Opportunity Commission), its workplace safety (the Occupational Safety and Health Administration), the levels of pollutants its factories can release (Environmental Protection Agency), and the establishment and activities of unions in its workplace (the National Labor Relations Board).[17] More recent laws and judicial decisions have banned the use of polygraphs for employment decisions and restricted an organization's right to fire and its options in testing employees for drug use.

Political, legal, and regulatory forces can act as both constraint and opportunity. For example, while some organizations view antipollution laws as constraints, these laws have stimulated the growth of the pollution control industry. When the government has acted to combat inflation, those actions have constrained builders of single-unit houses, but spurred growth for apartment builders. Though some organizations oppose the government's tariffs on foreign goods imported into the United States, some organizations have clearly benefited. For example, in the early 1980s, motorcycle maker Harley-Davidson approached bankruptcy, battered by the higher-quality and lower-priced Japanese bikes imported by Honda Motor Company, Yamaha Motor Corp., and Kawasaki Motors Corp. At Harley-Davidson's request, the US government in 1983 boosted the import tariffs on the Japanese bikes from 4.4 percent to more than 49 percent, which eliminated the Japanese price advantage and gave Harley-Davidson five years to boost product quality and production efficiency. The company is now highly competitive.[18]

Most observers believe that government involvement in organizations will continue, given that people continue to call on government to protect the consumer, preserve the environment, and push for an end to discrimination in employment, education, and housing. Consequently, many organizations monitor governmental and legislative developments to ensure their own compliance with the law. In some areas, specialists are hired to monitor and ensure compliance—for example, with affirmative action and labor relations regulations in the area of personnel. Some organizations actively attempt to influence the government by making contributions to political candidates and by lobbying state and federal legislators. Although professional political lobbyists often represent the interests of organizational clients, in recent years a growing number of companies have been utilizing their own employees to lead the company's lobbying efforts.[19]

Cultural and Social.   Cultural and social forces are changes in our social and cultural system that can affect an organization's actions and the demand for its products or services. Every nation has a social and cultural system comprising certain beliefs and values. The American culture and social system, for example, promotes the values of individuality, equality, and free enterprise.

Over time, issues emerge and changes occur that can affect organizations. In the 1970s, for example, the ecology movement had a major impact on legislation and numerous industries. Environmental interest groups have lobbied for legislation to further limit industries' emissions of fossil fuels (gas, coal, and oil) that intensify the greenhouse effect—a phenomenon that could produce disastrous changes in the world's climate.[20] America's growing emphasis on good health has led food companies to lower the cholesterol content of their products. And the social shift toward moderation in drinking along with the efforts of Mothers Against Drunk Driving is largely responsible for the continuing decline of sales in the liquor industry over the last nine years.[21]

Organizations should monitor social and cultural forces because these external forces are extremely important to their performance. Interestingly, however, many organizations ignore the potential effects of these indirect forces until they become direct forces.[22] To avoid complacency, managers can adopt principles that commit their organizations to actions defined by society as in accordance with good citizenship. The 1989 ecological disaster following the grounding of the Exxon *Valdez* and the 1991 war with Iraq have heightened our concern for environmental issues, especially in relation to the use of fossil energy. At what price are we willing to risk permanent destruction of human life-support systems in the environment?

This heightened sense of concern for the environment has produced a heated debate among all those who have an interest in the environment, and that includes nearly everyone with an awareness of world events. Considerable sentiment abounds that organizations must take greater safeguards to protect the environment. The Boston-based Coalition for Environmentally Responsible Economies suggests the type of code of principles featured in the accompanying Management Focus.

International.   For most US organizations, the external environment (customers, competitors, human resources, and suppliers) is contained within the boundaries of the United States. However, international forces apply when an organization relies on a foreign supplier for resources or competes with international competitors within the United States. The importance of international forces grows considerably when an organization decides to internationalize and expand its products or services (and sometimes manufacturing operations) into an international market. Venturing abroad, a company confronts an entirely new set of circumstances and environmental forces.[23] Consumer preferences may differ. Pricing and promotional strategies may be very unfamiliar. Governmental policies in the international market may bear little resemblance to those of the US government. And the cultural and social systems in the international market may contrast sharply with America's system of values and beliefs. Once an organization internationalizes, these international elements become direct rather than indirect forces.

Overall, the decision to do business in other countries presents significant challenges to an organization because management must learn to operate in an environment where many of the rules of business are very different from those that succeed in the United States.[24] However, an increasing number of companies *are* entering international markets, for two main reasons. First, a business might pursue internationalization because of weakening opportunities at home. Product demand may have declined, legislative regulation may have become too burdensome, or economic conditions may be weak. Second, the company may be drawn overseas by outstanding

Management Focus

Environmentally Sound Principles of Social Responsibility

Around the world, societies are pursuing two major goals: sustained economic growth and a cleaner environment. A growing list of companies such as AT&T, 3M, UNOCAL, and Xerox believe that these goals do not necessarily have to be in conflict with each other.

A growth- and profit-oriented organization that desires to also make public its commitment to a safe environment can do so by adopting the following principles to govern its conduct:

1. We will minimize and strive to eliminate the release of any pollutant that may cause environmental damage to the air, water, or earth, or its inhabitants.

2. We will make sustainable use of renewable natural resources such as water, soils, and forests.

3. We will minimize the creation of waste, especially hazardous waste, and whenever possible we will recycle materials.

4. We will make every effort to use environmentally safe and sustainable energy sources to meet our needs.

5. We will minimize the environmental, health, and safety risks to our employees and the communities in which we operate by employing safe technologies and operating procedures and by being constantly prepared for emergencies.

6. We will sell products or services that minimize adverse environmental impacts and that are safe as consumers commonly use them.

7. We will be responsible for any harm we cause to the environment by making every effort to restore it fully and to compensate those persons who are adversely affected.

8. We will disclose to our employees and to the public incidents relating to our operations that cause environmental harm or pose health or safety hazards.

9. We will appoint to our board of directors at least one member qualified to represent environmental interests.

10. We will conduct and make public an annual self-evaluation of our progress in implementing these principles and in complying with all applicable laws and regulations throughout our worldwide operations.

What difference would it make if every organization adopted these principles? How would society enforce them?

Sources: Adapted from B Smart, ed., *Beyond Compliance* (New York: World Resources Institute, 1992); and M Zetlin, "The Greening of Corporate America," *Management Review,* June 1990, pp. 12–17.

opportunities to market its products or services in other nations while continuing to do business at home. Such businesses as Kentucky Fried Chicken Corporation, Mc-Donald's Corporation, and The Coca-Cola Company are thriving both internationally and domestically. The accompanying Management Focus depicts Coca-Cola's view of the work and the abundant opportunities that the firm wants to capture.

Whether competition from abroad, opportunities abroad, or dependency on foreign resources is involved, international forces will increase in importance in the next decade. Many experts predict that it is only a matter of time before most US businesses operate in an international environment.

Figure 2–3 illustrates the direct and indirect forces in the external environment, summarizing our discussion of the organization's external environment. It shows the many forces that influence organizational performance. In every case, a major challenge to management is to identify and understand these forces, anticipate and adapt to those beyond its control, and influence those within its control.

Management Focus

Coca-Cola Sees a World of Opportunities

Although The Coca-Cola Company operates today as the world's most global enterprise, not only in terms of geographical diversity but also in terms of country-by-country industry leadership, the fact is that the company is just now seriously entering and developing soft drink markets that account for the majority of the world's population. These new worlds of opportunity are not only heavily populated but also often culturally and climatically ripe for significant soft drink consumption. As a whole, they represent staggering potential for future growth.

But for all its allure, potential is nothing more than just that—potential. The future is far from guaranteed, and talk, particularly about things yet to happen, is cheap. At the same time, a proven track record of success greatly adds to the credibility of potential.

Throughout its history, Coca-Cola has proved its ability to develop new worlds of opportunity. What were once untouched new worlds of opportunity are now huge, thriving businesses with ample growth opportunities of their own. Coca-Cola's flagship business, its operations in the United States, began more than a century ago as the fanciful whim of an Atlanta pharmacist. Today, every man, woman, and child in the United States drinks an average of 296 servings of Coca-Cola's products annually.

Coca-Cola entered Mexico in 1927, and by 1933 the Coca-Cola system was selling more than 1 billion cases of soft drinks annually in that country. Coca-Cola's rate of development has been even faster in West Germany and Japan, where it committed itself to investing heavily in war-ravaged economies following World War II. Today, those mammoth businesses operate as two of Coke's top four unit case volume contributors. And, in a recent example, Coca-Cola has moved with great speed into eastern Germany since unification, raising the annual per capita consumption of its products there to West Germany's consumption level.

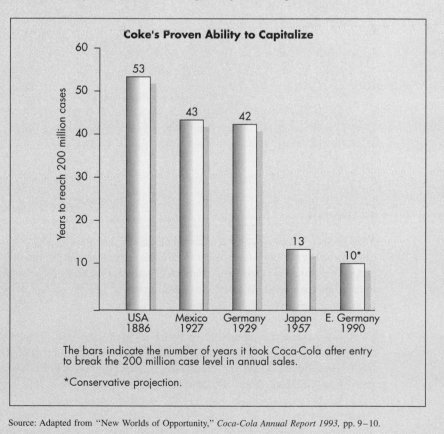

Coke's Proven Ability to Capitalize

The bars indicate the number of years it took Coca-Cola after entry to break the 200 million case level in annual sales.

*Conservative projection.

Source: Adapted from "New Worlds of Opportunity," *Coca-Cola Annual Report 1993,* pp. 9–10.

FIGURE 2–3   **Direct and Indirect Forces of the Organization's External Environment**

An organization's, and therefore a manager's, external environment consists of both direct and indirect forces.

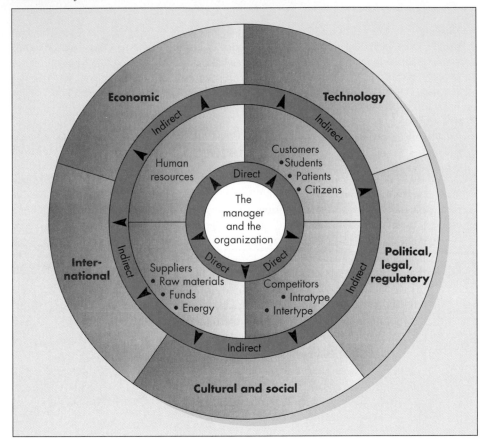

The Internal Environment

This section examines the environment inside the organization in which a manager must function. It identifies the settings where managers work, the day-to-day activities that utilize much of their time, and some generalized skills necessary to cope with the internal environment. We begin by looking at the various *levels* of management, then focus on managerial *skills* and *roles*.

Three Management Levels

Most organizations function on at least three distinct but overlapping levels, each requiring a different managerial focus and emphasis. They include the *operations level*, the *technical level*, and the *strategic level*. Managers at each of these three levels must plan, organize, lead, and control.

Operations Level.   We know from Chapter 1 that every organization, whether it produces a physical product or a service, has an operations function.[25] In any organization the operations level focuses on effectively performing whatever the organization produces or does. A physical product, for instance, requires a flow of materials and supervision of the operations. Colleges must be sure that their students are properly processed, registered, scheduled, and taught and that their records are maintained. Banks must see that checks are processed and financial transactions are recorded accurately and quickly.

The operations function is at the core of every organization. The managerial task here is to develop the best allocation of resources that produces the desired output.

Technical Level.   As an organization increases in size, someone must coordinate the activities at the operations level as well as decide which products or services to produce. These problems are the focus of the technical level. A dissatisfied student complains to the dean of the college. A sales manager mediates disagreements between customers and salespeople. Production schedules and amounts to be produced must be planned for an automobile manufacturer.

At this level, the managerial task is really twofold: (1) managing the operations function and (2) serving as a liaison between those who produce the product or service and those who use the output. In other words, for the operations level to do its work, managers at the technical level must make sure they have the correct materials and see that the output gets sold or used.

Strategic Level.   Every organization operates in a broad social environment. As a part of that environment, an organization is also responsible to it. The strategic level must make sure the technical level operates within the bounds of society. Since the ultimate source of authority in any organization comes from society, the organization must provide goods and services to society in a socially acceptable manner. Thus, the strategic level determines the long-range objectives and direction for the organization—in other words, how the organization interacts with its environment.[26] The organization also may seek to influence its environment through lobbying efforts, advertising efforts, or educational programs aimed at members of society.

Types of Managers and Levels of Management

Understanding the three levels of management can be helpful in determining the primary focus of managers' activities at different levels in an organization. For example, terms widely used in organizations include **top management, middle management,** and **first-level management.** Figure 2–4 indicates that top management corresponds to the strategic level, middle management corresponds to the technical level, and first-level management corresponds to the operations level.

FIGURE 2–4   Managers and the Levels of Management

The primary focus of managers' activities depends on their level in the organization.

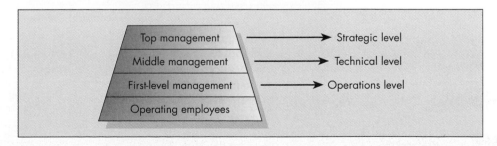

While the terms *top, middle,* and *first-level management* may not always correspond exactly to the three levels, they do provide an understanding of what managers do at each level. The term *manager* covers all three levels.

The actual terms used to identify managers at various organizational levels differ from organization to organization. (Figure 2–5 compares terms typically used in three types of organizations: business, education, and government.) But from the chief executive officer (CEO) to the first-level supervisor, all are managers, although the focus of their activities varies.

Generally speaking, the activities of supervisors, chairpersons, and program managers are similar despite the different terms used to identify them. A chairperson of a department in a college could be expected to spend most of the time dealing with the faculty as individuals. Similarly, CEOs, presidents, and cabinet secretaries spend much of their time being concerned about the work that their organization is doing to meet the expectations of owners, customers, and taxpayers. While we can identify similarities in managerial jobs as a function of their level in the organization, we must recognize that dissimilarities also exist. These dissimilarities arise from the uniqueness of each organization and the environment in which it exists.[27]

Skills of Managers. Certain general skills are needed for effective managerial performance, regardless of the level of the manager in the hierarchy of the organization. However, the mix of skills differs depending on the level of the manager in the organization. These skills and the necessary mixes are illustrated in Figure 2–6.[28] The figure indicates the basic skills—human, technical, and conceptual—needed by all managers.

Managers must accomplish much of their work through other people. For this, *human skill* is essential. A reflection of a manager's leadership abilities, human skill is the ability to work with, communicate with, and understand others.

The importance of human skill is most obvious in those managerial jobs that involve extensive interactions with other employees. A study of more than 1,400 managers at different levels in an organizational hierarchy reconfirms that the essential activities of individuals in first-level supervisory jobs are human skills. First-level

---

FIGURE 2–5   Managers at Different Organizational Levels in Three Types of Organizations

Organizations use various terms to identify managers at different organizational levels.

Level of management / Type of organization	Business organization	Educational institution	Government organization
Top (strategic level)	Chief executive officer	President	Cabinet secretary
Middle (technical level)	Superintendent Manager	Vice president Dean	Commissioner Division director
First (operating level)	Supervisor	Department chairperson	Program manager

---

FIGURE 2–6   Basic Management Skills

Three core skills and their use at the three levels of management.

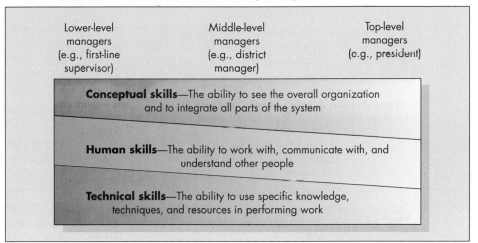

---

managers must provide ongoing feedback to subordinates, resolve interpersonal and performance problems, motivate subordinates to change or improve performance, as well as oversee the other activities involved in managing individual performance. The study also identified several activities that involve teaching and coaching efforts. Clearly these activities require high levels of human skill, the skill to communicate in positive ways the expectations one has for the performance of other individuals.

Technical skill is the ability to use specific knowledge, techniques, and resources in performing work. Accounting supervisors, engineering directors, and nursing supervisors must have the technical skills of the people they manage to perform their management jobs.

Merck & Co., Inc. illustrates the importance of technical skills. Considered by many management experts to be the best-managed company in America, Merck manufactures drugs for medical use. The company's key resource is a top-notch team of scientists. Their technical skills developed a consistent stream of major, productive pharmaceuticals that increased the company's sales by about 20 percent each year during the late 1980s. Merck attracts top talent by paying well and maintaining first-rate lab facilities and a campuslike working environment. Many of its managers possess the same skills—for example, the company's CEO, Roy Vagelos, has a doctorate in medicine.[29]

Conceptual skill is the ability to see the big picture, the complexities of the overall organization and how the various parts fit together. Managers with conceptual skills understand all activities and interests of the organization and how they interrelate.[30]

General Electric's (GE) Chief Executive Officer Jack Welch is an example of a leader with powerful conceptual skills. After taking over GE, Welch relentlessly reshaped and reengineered the giant firm. In the 1980s, he shut plants, pared payrolls, and eliminated nonperforming products. Inventories were trimmed, bureaucratic inefficiencies attacked, and jobs eliminated if they added no value. Welch pushed GE to grow in the service areas. He predicted that tremendous growth in services could be achieved by using GE's core industrial strength to provide the capital and human resources. He was proven correct to push into health care, transportation, power generation, and computer service outsourcing. Services were always overshadowed at GE because of the firm's dependence on production and engineering. Welch forecasted the future and used conceptual skills to help GE grow and cope with an ever-changing world economy.[31]

All three managerial skills are essential for effective performance. Figure 2–6 indicates that the relative importance of the three skills to a specific manager depends on his or her level in the organization. Human skill is critical at the lower levels of management. Because they deal with the day-to-day interpersonal problems in manufacturing and education, a production supervisor and a department chairperson need more human skill than the chief operating officer of a company or a college president.

On the other hand, the importance of conceptual skill increases as one rises in management. The higher one is in the hierarchy, the more involved one becomes in longer-term decisions that can influence many parts of the organization or the entire organization. Thus, conceptual skill is most critical for top managers.

Technical skills are required at each level of management, but they are most crucial to the effectiveness of middle managers. As we noted in our earlier discussion of the technical level of organizations, decisions at this level depend on expertise in the specific functions of the particular organization. The technical level of manufacturing organizations, for example, includes various specialized departments such as production, personnel, engineering, legal, research and development, and marketing. Managers of each of these specialized departments must be able to speak with authority about the technical details of the units they manage. Their ability to do so is vital to their effectiveness as middle managers.

Roles of Managers.   Henry Mintzberg observed and studied the activities of top managers. He followed these managers and recorded each behavior, meeting, and action they engaged in over an extended period of time. Mintzberg concluded that, because their workdays are filled with interruptions, constant changes in plans, and specific demands, managers do not have time to be careful planners, organizational experts, cautious leaders, or strict controllers. He categorized the managers' hectic days in 10 specific, yet related roles. These are illustrated in Figure 2–7. The figure shows that the 10 roles can be separated into three different groupings: interpersonal roles, informational roles, and decisional roles.[32]

Interpersonal Roles.   These roles focus on interpersonal relationships. The three roles of figurehead, leader, and liaison result from formal authority. By assuming them, the manager is able to move into the informational roles that in turn lead directly to the decisional roles.

All managerial jobs require some duties that are symbolic or ceremonial in nature. A college dean hands out diplomas at graduation, a shop supervisor attends the wedding of a subordinate's daughter, the mayor of New York City gives the key to the city to an astronaut. These are examples of the *figurehead role.*

The manager's *leadership role* involves directing and coordinating the activities of subordinates. This may involve staffing (hiring, training, promoting, dismissing) and motivating subordinates. The leadership role also involves controlling—making sure that things are going according to plan.

The *liaison role* gets managers involved in interpersonal relationships outside their area of command. This may involve contacts both within and outside the organization. Within the organization, managers must interact with numerous other

---
FIGURE 2–7   Overlapping Roles of Managers

Although managers perform 10 different roles in three groupings, many of these roles overlap.

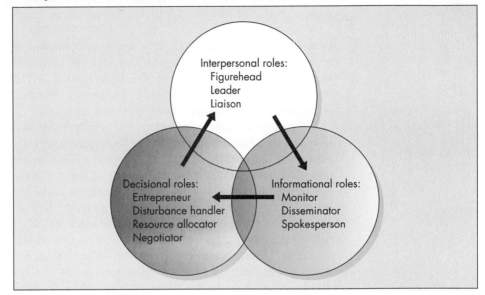

managers and individuals. They must maintain good relations with the managers who send work to the unit as well as those who receive work from the unit. For example, a college dean must interact with individuals all over the campus; a supervisory nurse in an operating room must interact with supervisors of various other groups of nurses; a production supervisor must interact with engineering supervisors and sales managers. Finally, managers often have interactions with important people outside the organization. It is easy to see that the liaison role often can consume much of a manager's time.

Informational Roles.   This set of roles establishes the manager as the central focus for receiving and sending nonroutine information. Through the three interpersonal roles discussed earlier, the manager builds a network of contacts. The interpersonal contacts aid the manager in gathering and receiving information in the monitor role and transmitting that information in the disseminator role and spokesperson role.

The *monitor role* involves examining the environment to gather information about changes, opportunities, and problems that may affect the unit. The formal and informal contacts developed in the liaison role are often useful here. The information may concern competitive moves that could influence the entire organization or knowing whom to call if the usual supplier of an important part cannot fill an order.

The *disseminator role* involves providing important or privileged information to subordinates that they might not ordinarily know about or be able to obtain. In a lunch conversation, the president of a firm hears that a large customer of the firm is on the verge of bankruptcy. On returning to the office, the president contacts the vice president of marketing, who in turn instructs the sales force not to sell anything on credit to the troubled company.

In the *spokesperson role,* the manager represents the department to other people. This representation may be internal, as when a manager makes the case for salary increases for members of the department to top management. The representation also may be external, such as when an executive speaks for the organization on a particular issue of public interest to a local civic organization.

Decisional Roles.   Although developing interpersonal relationships and gathering information are important, these two activities are not ends in themselves. They serve as the basic inputs to the process of decision making. In fact, some people believe that the decisional roles—entrepreneur, disturbance handler, resource allocator, and negotiator—are a manager's most important duties.

The purpose of the *entrepreneur role* is to bring about changes for the better in the unit. The effective first-line supervisor looks continually for new ideas or new methods to improve the unit's performance. The effective college dean constantly plans changes that result in higher-quality education. The effective CEO diligently seeks new ideas.[33]

In the *disturbance handler role,* managers make decisions or take corrective action in response to pressure that is beyond their control. Because there are disturbances, the decisions usually must be made quickly, which means that this role takes priority over other roles. The immediate goal is to bring about stability. When an emergency room supervisor responds quickly to a local disaster, a plant supervisor reacts to a strike, or a first-line manager responds to a breakdown in a key piece of equipment, each is dealing with disturbances in the environment. These responses must be quick and must result in a return to stability.

The *resource allocator role* places a manager in the position of deciding who gets which resources, including money, people, time, and equipment. There are never enough resources to go around; the manager must allocate the scarce resources toward numerous possible ends. Resource allocation, therefore, is one of the most critical of the manager's decisional roles. A first-line supervisor must decide whether an overtime schedule should be established or whether part-time workers should be hired. A college dean must decide, based on available faculty, which courses to offer next semester. The president and the congress of the United States must decide whether to propose a budget allocating more funds to defense and less to social programs, or vice versa.

In the *negotiator role,* managers must bargain with other departments and individuals to obtain advantages for their own units. The negotiations may be over work, performance, objectives, resources, or anything influencing the department. A sales manager may negotiate with the production department over a special order for a large customer; a first-line supervisor may negotiate for new typewriters; a top manager may negotiate with a labor union representative.

Management Level and Management Roles.   A manager's level in the organization influences which managerial roles are emphasized. Obviously, top managers spend much more time in the figurehead role than first-line supervisors do. The liaison roles of top and middle managers involve individuals and groups outside the organization, while the liaison role at the first-line level is outside the unit but inside the organization. Top managers monitor the environment for changes that can influence the entire organization. Middle managers monitor the environment for changes likely to influence the particular function that they manage (for example, marketing). And the first-line supervisor is concerned about what influences his or her department. However, while both the amount of time in the various roles and the activities performed in each role may differ, all managers perform interpersonal, informational, and decisional roles.

Summary of Key Points

* A manager's external environment consists of direct and indirect forces. Direct forces provide an immediate and direct impact on the organization. Indirect forces influence the climate in which the manager functions and often have the potential of becoming direct forces.
* Direct forces include the organization's customers, competitors, suppliers, and human resources. Indirect forces include technology; the economy; political, legal, and regulatory forces; cultural and social forces; and international forces. For an organization to succeed, its management must recognize these forces, understand their real and potential impacts, and manage the organization to minimize their negative and maximize their positive influences on the organization.
* Most organizations function on at least three distinct but overlapping levels. The *operations level* focuses on effective performance, whether the organization produces something or performs a service; the task at this level is to develop the best allocation of resources to produce the desired output. The *technical level* focuses on coordinating the activities at the operations level and serves as a liaison

between those who produce the product or service and those who use the output. The *strategic level* determines the long-range objectives and direction of the organization—that is, how the organization interacts with the environment.
* The terms *top, middle,* and *first-level* managers are closely associated with the strategic, technical, and operations levels, respectively. Together (see Figure 2–5), they are useful in understanding the different activities of managers.
* Three basic skills are required for effective managerial performance: human skill, technical skill, and conceptual skill. However, as Figure 2–6 indicates, a different mix is required, depending on the level of management in the organization.
* Managers at all levels perform a variety of tasks. Specifically, they perform 10 different but closely related roles. The 10 roles can be separated into three different groupings: *interpersonal roles* (figurehead, leader, liaison), *decisional roles* (entrepreneur, disturbance handler, resource allocator, negotiator), and *informational roles* (monitor, disseminator, spokesperson).

Discussion and Review Questions

1. Why should managers be concerned that downsizing has had a negative impact on firm loyalty?
2. What demographic changes suggest that managers must become more effective in working with culturally diverse work groups?
3. If you were trying to identify top managers at the school you attend, which titles would you look for? If you had to identify them based on what they do, what would you look for?
4. Discuss human, technical, and conceptual skills in relation to a college instructor. What, in your opinion, would be a good mix?
5. In your opinion, can human and conceptual skills be taught, or are they inherent?
6. What are the differences between managers' jobs at the top, middle, and first-line levels at the college or university you attend? Use the total university or college as the basis for your analysis, with the

institution's president or chancellor representing top management. As you identify the jobs of these different managers, is it accurate to state that they require different mixes of the three managerial skills? Explain.
7. As the chapter notes, the direct forces in the external environment pose many challenges to organizations. Which challenge, in your view, is the most difficult for managers? Explain.
8. Some observers assert that the importance of each of the various forces in the external environment differs across types of industries. Do you agree? Discuss.
9. If you were being interviewed for a position in a firm and were asked why businesses need to be aware of environmental forces, how would you respond?
10. Some management observers assert that Mintzberg's typology of 10 managerial roles is incomplete. What other roles do managers assume?

CASE 2–1
MANAGERS MAKING DECISIONS

There are many decisions and actions that managers engage in on a daily basis. A series of managerial problems is presented below so that realism is injected into your reading and thinking about managing. There are six short cases for you to make decisions about. How would *you* respond if you were the manager faced with each case situation?

Case Situation 1
Subject: Request for Leave of Absence

Don, a project engineer, has requested a two-month leave of absence beginning in two weeks. He has just won custody of his two sons in an unpleasant divorce settlement. He needs time to make arrangements for child care, and he wants to be absolutely sure that the boys are cared for properly.

Don is the lead person on the SASTEX project, which will involve 35 other engineers and technicians. He is the technical expert who helped the firm land the contract. Without Don, SASTEX may not get off the ground. The Family Medical Leave Act of 1993 doesn't mandate Don's request be granted. However, Don has been a top performer and has pushed hard to get the leave.

Case Situation 2
Subject: Unpaid Debt/Bill of Top Customer

Wilson Beeson has worked closely with Marco Quintana, a Spanish businessman, to create what was up until now a profitable exporting relationship. Beeson is the president of Americana, a machine tool firm that has been providing Quintana's manufacturing plant in Seville, Spain, with machine tools for 15 years.

Until recently, Quintana has been a model customer—very demanding in the quality expected, but prompt with payment. The Spanish economy has dramatically faltered. Inflation has skyrocketed, and unemployment rates are increasing. Quintana has informed Beeson that the $4 million, eight-months-overdue bill simply can't be paid. Although Beeson and Quintana are close friends, the debt has strained their relationship. Beeson's board has instructed him to solve the problem now.

Case Situation 3
Subject: Teamwork

Over the past three years, Mary Higgins has hired an outstanding group of accountants, engineers, scientists, salespeople, and financial analysts. The talent and experience of each individual are impeccable. Despite the individual strengths of those who were hired, Higgins can't get the people to work effectively together. There is gossip, withholding of information, animosity, and hostility displayed within and between groups. The lack of teamwork and cooperation has taken its toll on many people; some customers have stopped doing business with the firm; some employees have quit and gone elsewhere; and Higgins herself has been hospitalized three times this past year for an ulcer. She is at a loss about how to get her key employees to work together as a team. She is thinking about firing the biggest instigators to send a message to the remaining employees.

Case Situation 4
Subject: Company Policy

Trish Cravens is the most productive and dedicated lead technician in Anderson Optical Systems Co. She has worked her way up in the past 10 years and has expressed aspirations to become the division coordinator, a highly rewarded and recognized position. Denise Calkins, the division general manager, just found out that Cravens may be leaving Anderson because her husband, a research scientist who lost his job when his company closed six months ago, has found a job in Colorado.

Anderson has had seven job openings in the past 10 years that fit Cravens's husband's record and experience, but the company has a policy to not employ spouses in the same facility. Calkins has expressed her opinion over the years that this policy has cost Anderson some top talent. She has requested a meeting with the president, who has recently been talking about updating some of Anderson's policies.

Case Situation 5
Subject: Personal Time Management

Typically, Pete Maxville is a bundle of energy, optimistic, and committed to excellence. This has all changed in the last year. Maxville has not been able to return his telephone calls, meet with customers on time, or develop his strategic plan (now six months overdue). He is totally overloaded with requests for his time or presence at meetings. He has been working from 7:00 AM until 9:00 PM for at least nine months, is totally fatigued, and believes that his performance has suffered. He has flown off the handle three times this past week and has had some major arguments at home about trivial matters.

Maxville has attended time management workshops and read everything he can about time management, but nothing seems to improve his attitude, emotions, or behavior. He feels overwhelmed by the job. Budget cutbacks, increased competition, new government regulations and policies, and the retirement of six key managers have all placed new responsibilities and burdens on Maxville. He is searching for a way to get himself back on track.

Case Situation 6
Subject: An Ethical Dilemma

Bob Ogan is the audit manager of Pearl, Lendnini, and Nordstrum, a fast-growing firm in Phoenix. While working on a recent major project, he realized that he was spending 60 to 70 hours more than the company had estimated for the work. He asked another audit manager, Rick Spurgeon, how *he* would handle the excess hours. In a short response, Spurgeon said, "Bury the hours." This is a term used to indicate that excesses above estimates are simply not reported. Coming in with excessive hours was just not acceptable in the firm. True, the firm didn't receive a true picture about the time, but "burying the hours" was the honorable, company-spirited thing to do.

Ogan thinks that although he participated in estimating the time to do the project, it was the senior partner who was the final authority. Ogan feels that he was expected to work longer hours and that "burying" is unethical. He is wondering how he is going to solve this dilemma.

VIDEO CASE
MANAGEMENT CHALLENGE

This video case focuses on the management style of United Airlines, whose headquarters is just outside of Chicago, Illinois. It looks at the company's recent change to becoming employee-owned and what effect that has had on management philosophy as it relates to quality and competitiveness.

On July 12, 1994 United Airlines became the world's largest employee-owned company. In their new role as owners and investors, employees must take advantage of this distinction to position the company for long-term competitiveness in the airline industry. The new owners are working to create a new organizational culture that fosters high commitment to employee involvement, open and honest communication, sharing of ideas, trust, respect for diversity, and teamwork.

One innovation already developed by the new owners is "Customer Problem Resolution teams," a new customer-satisfaction initiative. These teams illustrate the point that, in order to be successful in an intensely competitive global environment, UAL feels it can no longer operate in the traditional ways of having only management involved in the business. Because United is an employee-owned company, now more than ever, it needs the commitment of ideas and the decision making of each "owner" in order to become world class competitors.

UAL's new management style views employee participation, customer focus, and continuous improvement as essential factors to its success and profitability. Management is confronted with the task of becoming more involved in encouraging and empowering employees to solve problems immediately, by themselves. In this regard they have instituted several aggressive new programs emanating from their Culture Change division.

The overarching campaign of this new management approach is their Mission United program. Basically this is a one-day event for all employees for the purpose of gaining an understanding of how they must work together differently in achieving their primary goal: to become the worldwide airline of choice.

Each Mission United event is planned for approximately 150 employees who are mixed from all departments, levels, and job groups within the company. The enrollment process is designed to ensure a maximum mix of employee job groups as well as a cross-function of departments and divisions at each event. At Mission United events, each participant is challenged to:

- Become thoroughly acquainted with United's mission, vision, and values.
- Gain a better understanding of how business decisions are made.
- Heighten awareness of their individual impact on the customer.
- Take a look at the strengths and weaknesses of the company.
- Interact with fellow employees.
- Examine the concept of ownership.
- Share breakthrough successes and learn how employees are working differently.

Through Mission United, employees are oriented to focus on the company's "core values" of teamwork, safety, integrity, respect, community service, customer satisfaction, and profitability. Basically, the company feels that these values are going to help them achieve their goal "to be the worldwide airline of choice," with the top priority of providing a safe airline.

As an outgrowth of this new kind of management approach to employee involvement, United has instituted a new employee participation process to focus on customer service, organizational concerns, and profitability. Taking the best practices from the most successful companies with high commitment to employee involvement, they created the "Best of Best" process. The main thrust of this process involves employees working together in teams to identify and resolve local operational and quality issues that impact the customer. The focus of Best of Best teams is for continuous improvement of services within the boundaries of the team's control. Teams will have a clear understanding of their goals and are empowered at the local level to work on creative new ways of doing business.

The Best of Best program was the first attempt by United to bridge all divisions together to solve problems. It represents the beginning of a long-term cultural transformation to a collaborative, decision-making, learning organization in which employees are encouraged to gain new skills and work differently. Teamwork is valued and rewarded, responsibility and accountability are maximized, personal and professional growth are continuous, and hierarchy is minimized. Self-determination, self-motivation, and self-management are expected, and management is providing the leadership necessary to drive and sustain the empowerment.

Managers have become more visible to the United employees as well. They are making it a point to spend time on the front lines of the business in order to do a better job leading and planning for culture change. In many cases, they are leading by doing and are certainly much more open and available to their employees than they were in the past. The managers have been conducting "road shows" that become interactive question-and-answer sessions to encourage open communication with staff members.

Since becoming an employee-owned company, United Airlines has had to do a lot of internal soul searching to discover a better way of doing things. This major cultural change has served to accelerate the company's strategic shift to becoming more competitive on a global scale. Fortunately, as owners they were forced to focus on new and dynamic ways of doing things. They realized that exceeding the customer's expectations is the only way to compete and achieve their goals. By turning to greater employee involvement and more responsive management, they appear to be headed in the right direction.

Critical Thinking Questions

1. United Airlines managers use an approach called Mission United to orient employees throughout the organization to new initiatives, goals, and competitive position. Discuss in class how managers should conduct these one-day sessions to get maximum employee buy-in and commitment.

2. Best of Best programs are cross-functional teams aimed at creating changes based on identified best practices. Why do you think United organized these teams cross-functionally?

3. Employee ownership has been attempted before in the airline industry at a company called People Express. That company didn't survive, although it was initially successful. What are some steps UAL can take to improve its chances of success?

EXPERIENTIAL EXERCISE
PROFILE OF AN EXTERNAL ENVIRONMENT

Purpose

To enhance students' understanding of the importance, dynamics, and challenges of the external environments in which organizations operate.

The Exercise in Class

The instructor will divide the class into teams, each comprising three to four members. Each team will complete the following steps:

1. Select a company that interests your team and that is well reported in the business literature (several companies discussed in this chapter are excellent in this regard).

Then, for your company, identify two direct forces and two indirect forces in the external environment that are strongly influencing the company's well-being.

2. Go to the library and research the company, focusing on these four forces. For each force, obtain from your research a thorough understanding of the following:

   a. The specific force. (For example, who are the organization's critical competitors and what are their strategies? What social trends and government regulations are influencing the company?)

   b. The current impact of that force on the company.

   c. The company's present strategy for dealing with the force.

3. Prepare a written profile of the company's four external forces that includes the points researched in step 2. Also be sure to include your team's predictions concerning how each force will challenge the company in the future and how the company should respond.

The Learning Message

This exercise should clearly illustrate that the forces in the external environment are very dynamic, at times unpredictable, and that their challenges and impacts vary across different organizations in different industries.

Notes

1. Gloria Lau, "University Extension," *Forbes,* October 21, 1996.
2. Alexander Hiam and C D Scheine, "The Portable MBA in Marketing (New York: John Wiley, 1992), pp. 111–13.
3. Nike, Inc., *1993 Annual Report,* pp. 1–5.
4. Lawrence Mishel and Jared Bernstein, *The State of Working America* (Armonk, NY: Economic Policy Institute, 1993), p. 343.
5. Praveen R Nayyar, "On the Measurement of Competitive Strategy: Evidence from a Large Multiproduct US Firm," *Academy of Management Journal,* December 1993, pp. 1652–69.
6. John H Sheridan, "Betting on a Single Source," *Industry Week,* February 1, 1988, p. 31ff.
7. John P Fernandez, *The Diversity Advantage* (New York: Lexington Books, 1993).
8. Lotte Bailyn, *Breaking the Mold* (New York: Free Press, 1993).
9. Telephone conversation with US Department of Commerce, December 1993.
10. Charles F Hendricks, *The Rightsizing Remedy* (Burr Ridge, IL: IPRO, 1992).
11. *Statistical Abstract of the United States 1992* (Washington, DC: US Department of Commerce, 1993), p. 389.
12. Anne Fisher, "Wanted: Aging Baby-Boomers," *Fortune,* September 30, 1996, p. 204.
13. Douglas T Hall and Victoria A Parker, "The Role of Workplace Flexibility in Managing Diversity," *Organizational Dynamics,* Summer 1993, pp. 5–18.
14. Jon Woronoff, *The Japanese Management Mystique* (Salem, MA: Probus, 1992), pp. 190–95.
15. Tom Peters, *Liberation Management* (New York: Alfred A Knopf, 1992), pp. 428–29.
16. Ibid.
17. Fred S Steingold, *The Employer's Legal Handbook* (Berkeley, CA: Nolo Press, 1996).
18. Joseph F McKenna, "America's Most Admired CEOs," *Industry Week,* December 6, 1993, pp. 22–32.
19. Bruce Smart, *Beyond Compliance* (Washington, DC: World Resources Institute, 1992), pp. 1–6.
20. Stephen Schmidhcing, *Changing Course* (Cambridge, MA: MIT Press, 1992), p. 134.
21. Donna J Wood, *Business and Society* (New York: HarperCollins, 1994), pp. 737–39.
22. Barry G Sheckley, Lois Lamdin, and Morris T Keeton, *Employability in a High Performance Economy* (Chicago: The Council for Adult and Experiential Learning, 1993).
23. Paul W Beamish, "The Characteristics of Joint Ventures in the People's Republic of China," *Journal of International Marketing* 1, no. 2 (1993), pp. 29–48.
24. James E Austin, *Managing in Developing Countries* (New York: Free Press, 1990).
25. Valerie Zeithaml, A Parasuraman, and L Berry, *Delivering Service Quality* (New York: Free Press, 1990); David E Bowen, Richard B Chase, Thomas G Cummings, and Associates, *Service Management Effectiveness* (San Francisco, CA: Jossey-Bass, 1990).
26. George Stalk, Philip Evans, and Lawrence Schuman, "Competing on Capabilities: The New Rules of Corporate Strategy," *Harvard Business Review,* March–April 1992, pp. 57–69.
27. Fred Luthans, "Successful vs. Effective Real Managers," *The Executive,* May 1988, pp. 127–32.
28. Sheckley, Lamdin, and Keeton, *Employability in a High Performance Economy,* pp. 103–18.
29. Carol M Cropper, "Health," *Forbes,* January 3, 1994, p. 158.
30. Philippe Mao, "Capital Goods," *Forbes,* January 3, 1994, pp. 111–13.
31. Tim Smart, "Jack Welch's Encore," *Business Week,* October 26, 1996, pp. 155–160.
32. These managerial roles were first identified and described in Henry Mintzberg, "The Manager's Job: Folklore and Fact," *Harvard Business Review,* July–August 1975, pp. 49–61. Also see Jay W Lorsch, James P Baughman, James Reece, and Henry Mintzberg, *Understanding Management* (New York: Harper & Row, 1978).
33. David B Yaffie, *Strategic Management in Information Technology* (Englewood Cliffs, NJ: Prentice Hall, 1994), pp. 1–9.

3 Managing in a Global Environment

Chapter Learning Objectives

After completing Chapter 3, you should be able to:

- **Define** culture and the ways in which cultures can differ across nations.
- **Describe** the three primary issues that encompass an organization's decision to become a multinational company.
- **Discuss** the assumed benefits of economic alliances such as the European Community and the North American Free Trade Agreement.
- **Compare** the different ways of entering a foreign market.
- **Identify** the major challenges facing expatriate managers in their overseas assignments.

Going Global: A Framework That Can Shape Thinking

Michael Porter, a Harvard business professor, has proposed four environmental elements that are central to remaining competitive in a global economy. Porter suggests that managers and policy makers need to assess and understand these four sets of factors, and they need to be innovative if the firm or nation is to compete. The figure below introduces Porter's four "diamond" factors of competitive advantage.

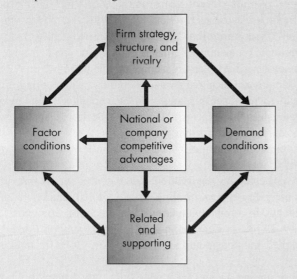

- *Firm strategy, structure, and rivalry*: the conditions in a nation that affect the way organizations interact with one another. Domestic rivalry stimulates innovation (e.g., Compaq versus IBM) and the development of competitive advantage.
- *Demand conditions:* the domestic demand for the products and services of an industry. When customers are demanding, companies must respond with high-quality and innovative products and services.
- *Factor conditions:* the components involved in producing goods and services such as skilled workers, the economic infrastructure, and available raw materials or natural resources.
- *Related and supporting industries:* the availability within the nation or industry of suppliers that compete internationally. Being able to provide resource inputs and essential services to support the production of goods or delivery of services is important.

Porter contends that managers must take action, make decisions, and implement solutions to problems based on the four factors in his diamond. The central role of innovation is highlighted repeatedly in Porter's discussions and presentations. By establishing high-quality standards, working with sophisticated buyers and suppliers, and effectively managing human resources, a firm can remain competitive both domestically and globally. Porter believes managers need to develop and implement strategies to enhance competitive advantage rather than simply increase in size. For example, in reviewing its entrance into China, Mexico, or Nigeria, a firm should consider whether conducting business in these countries adds to its competitive advantage.

As you read this chapter, refer to Porter's approach to competitive advantage and how to achieve it in the global marketplace. Large, medium, and small companies and their managers can learn to appreciate the importance of innovation as markets, joint alliances, and business transactions are evaluated. Learning how to compete in a rapidly changing world is a difficult job that must be done. Porter's competitive advantage diamond is a way to begin that job.

Sources: Michael E Porter, "The Rise of the Urban Entrepreneur," *The State of Small Business,* Nation's Business Report, January 1996, pp. 104–119; G Das, "Local Memoirs of a Global Manager," *Harvard Business Review,* March–April 1993, pp. 38-47; M E Porter, "The Competitive Advantage of Nations," *Harvard Business Review,* March–April 1990, pp. 73-93; M E Porter, *The Competitive Advantage of Nations* (New York: Free Press, 1990).

William Wordsworth complained in a 19th-century poem, "The world is too much with us. Getting and spending, we lay waste our powers." What would he make of the current era of instant communications and global business? These days, the world is too much with almost everyone. Goods, products, services, currencies, and changing cultural values move restlessly around the planet, from country to country, city to village, and group to individual.

What was once considered foreign by many Americans is now considered ours. We have adopted Asian, Mexican, and Italian foods. We wear shoes made in Italy, shirts made in Taiwan, and jeans and slacks made in China. A large number of our automobiles, electronics products, and entertainment items are made in Japan.

Global business is not a one-way street. A growing number of US businesses are venturing overseas, selling and often producing goods and services in foreign countries. Their efforts are contributing to a surge in international trade, which has grown sevenfold since 1970. Today, over one-fourth of the goods and services produced worldwide cross national borders.

Why have a growing number of American businesses become so involved in international business? The reason is simple. Many global markets provide substantial opportunities and higher return on investment for businesses with the ability and determination to succeed in an often unfamiliar environment. Specifically, many companies venture abroad because of declining markets at home and brighter opportunities overseas.[1] For some companies, the US market for their product may be maturing or even in decline, while the market in an overseas country is just taking off. Some businesses venture abroad to use excess manufacturing capacity. Companies such as Caterpillar Tractor established manufacturing facilities worldwide partly to achieve substantial economies of scale that provide them with a significant cost advantage over competitors.[2] Other companies go international to alleviate the risk of operating in only one geographical market.[3]

Whatever the specific motive, businesses internationalize to reap rewards that are not so readily available at home. However, venturing into a global market is an exceptionally challenging strategy. In order to succeed, the type of competitive advantage proposed by Michael Porter is becoming a necessity. Each of Porter's "diamond" factors must be weighed and considered as firms scan the globe for market and business opportunities.

The growing interdependence among nations has created not only a need to learn about and work with other people but also to coordinate the flow of trade. It is trade that sets the tone for business interactions, the creation of joint alliances, and the development of a strategically focused set of international decisions.

International Agreements and Economic Alliances

After World War II, a number of nations decided to create economic alliances to stimulate trade and growth. They believed that cooperation, interaction, and better understanding would lead to a higher standard of living for their citizens.

General Agreement on Tariffs and Trade

An important trade agreement reached in 1947 was the General Agreement on Tariffs and Trade (GATT). Its objective was to establish a set of rules to govern and resolve conflicts in international trade. GATT is headquartered in Geneva, Switzerland, and is supported by the contributions of over 12 nation-members.[4]

GATT has been successful in reducing the tariffs on over 50,000 products, saving about $750 million for more than 120 countries. The eighth round of GATT negotiations, called the Uruguay Round, was started in 1986 and concluded with the creation of a World Trade Organization that for the first time has substantial powers to take action against nations that violate the agreement terms. The Uruguay Round focused on stabilizing worldwide currencies and preventing protection laws that stifle international trade.

Economic Alliances   Often groups of nations form alliances to further the trade agreements and cooperation stimulated by GATT. The major reason for alliances is to open up markets and reduce or remove tariffs or trade restrictions. Table 3–1 lists six major alliances and notes how well each has done in terms of economic integration.

European Community.   The European Community (EC) was established in 1958. Today 12 countries are part of the EC.[5] These countries have formed an alliance that

TABLE 3–1   Economic Communities

These are selected economic partnerships that are working to improve the economic conditions of citizens.

Name and Starting Date	Countries	Level of Integration
European Community (EC), 1958	Belgium Denmark France Germany Greece Ireland Italy Luxembourg Netherlands Portugal Spain United Kingdom	The nations are highly integrated, both economically and politically.
North American Free Trade Agreement (NAFTA), 1994	United States Mexico Canada	Some economic integration
Latin American Integration Association (LAIA), formerly Latin American Free Trade Area (LAFTA), 1960	Argentina Bolivia Brazil Chile Colombia Ecuador Mexico Paraguay Peru Uruguay Venezuela	Some economic integration
Central American Common Market (CACM), 1961	El Salvador Nicaragua Guatemala Costa Rica	Some economic integration
Caribbean Free Trade Association (CARIFTA), 1968	Jamaica Trinidad Tobago Montserrat	Some economic integration
Association of South East Asian Nations (ASEAN), 1967	Singapore Thailand Malaysia Indonesia Philippines Brunei (entered in 1984)	Some economic integration

encourages economic development and growth. The EC agreements include the following:

- Elimination of trade barriers between the 12 member nations in order to allow the free movement of merchandise, people, and capital.
- Creation of uniform technical product standards among the 12 member nations.
- Creation of a uniform set of financial regulations.

The 1992 Maastricht accord encouraged the EC to develop a common central bank and monetary union by the year 2000. The EC is attempting to use a new European currency unit (ECU) in international transactions. The goal of a borderless Europe is making slow progress. Technically, Europe's borders were eliminated in 1992, but the economic integration of 12 member nations will take a number of years. However, the 12-nation EC, with its population of 345 million, is an economic alliance that has a good possibility of becoming a major force in the globalizing world.

The North American Free Trade Agreement.   The North American Free Trade Agreement (NAFTA) created an economic alliance between the United States, Mexico, and Canada on January 1, 1994. NAFTA provides for the phased elimination of tariff and most nontariff barriers on regional trade within 10 years. It also establishes free trade of agricultural products between Mexico and the United States within 15 years.

For Mexico, NAFTA reinforces the extensive market-oriented policy reforms implemented since 1985. For Canada, NAFTA strengthens the ability to trade freely with the United States.[6] For the United States, NAFTA enhances the ability to increase its important export market in Mexico.

Although it is generally viewed favorably by Americans, a heated battle over the value and impact of NAFTA occurred in the United States in 1993. Labor and environmental critics believe that NAFTA will cause the loss of thousands of jobs in the United States because American firms will relocate to Mexico where labor is cheaper. The environmentalists fear that relocation will be attractive because enforcement of environmental laws and regulations is more lax in Mexico than in the United States.

Until NAFTA has been in force for at least five years, it will be difficult to assess its importance and effectiveness. However, it should be noted that free trade agreements will result in *freer* trade, but not *free* trade.[7] The significance of the NAFTA alliance, which created a market larger than that of the EC, is yet to be determined.

The Association of South East Asian Nations.   The Association of South East Asian Nations (ASEAN) was ratified in 1967 by Singapore, Thailand, Malaysia, Indonesia, and the Philippines. Brunei joined in 1984 when it attained its independence. Preferential trading arrangements were established within ASEAN. Members have cooperated on the coordinated development of industry in the region. An ASEAN finance corporation was established to finance joint ventures. In addition, agreements (such as a determination of the value of currencies of different nations) have been reached among the central banks of member countries to reduce exchange-rate frustrations.

ASEAN has resulted in cooperation in education projects, population control, and cultural exchanges. There has also been a sharing of crude oil and oil products. On the

The Pacific Century: An Economic Prediction

The economics of every nation along the Pacific Rim are pulling closer together as this part of the world continues its phenomenal growth. The EC and NAFTA are two great economic alliances that have influenced how business is conducted in both Europe and North America. By the year 2000 there could be a Pacific Rim economic alliance with the potential to dwarf the EC and NAFTA.

During the 1990s, the growth of the Pacific Rim is expected to average about 5 to 6 percent a year, twice the rate that is forecast for North America and 50 percent faster than the most optimistic forecast for Europe. If the Pacific Rim's growth continues at its current rate, by the year 2010 Asia will account for about one-third of the world's production.

In today's Pacific Rim, the atmosphere is almost electric and there is a feeling that anything is possible. For the past 500 years, the focus of power, the center of gravity in the world economy, has been the West. Many predict that based on present trends, the 21st century could be the Pacific Rim Century.

Some Asian experts believe that if a free trade bloc were formed in the Pacific Rim, most countries in the region could become Japan's economic colonies. This is a major fear that Asian business leaders and politicians privately acknowledge having. However, if the EC and NAFTA nations attempt to block business investment or transactions with the Japanese and the rest of Asia, a Pacific Rim economic alliance may become a realistic response.

With the vibrant Pacific Rim business growth, increased trade and cooperation with other parts of the world make a lot of business sense for the Americans and the Japanese. Managers should be learning as much as possible about working and conducting business within the region and various cultures of the Pacific Rim. The world's growth center now exists in East Asia and includes such countries as Japan, Indonesia, China, Singapore, Hong Kong, Malaysia, South Korea, and Taiwan. Fully understanding Asian values and history in the Pacific Rim may become a management learning requirement before long.

Sources: Andrew Tanzer, "The Pacific Century," *Forbes,* July 15, 1996, pp. 108–113; "Time for a Reality Check in Asia," *Business Week,* December 2, 1996, pp. 58–67; R Norton, "Will a Global Slump Hurt the US?" *Fortune,* February 22, 1993, pp. 63-64; "A Target for Protection," *The Economist,* March 27, 1993, pp. 65-66; E Thorton, "Will Japan Rule a New Trade Bloc?" *Fortune,* October 5, 1992, pp. 131-32.

other hand, there have been some problems in ASEAN. The lack of financial resources among member nations has resulted in slower progress in industrial development and conflict in distributing benefits of jointly operated projects.

Japan and China are two of the most economically powerful nations in the Pacific Rim, yet, as of late 1996, neither is part of a specific economic alliance. The potential economic power of a major Pacific Rim alliance that includes Japan and China is significant. These two giants, together with other developing Asian nations, will play a major role in shaping future patterns of international trade. Perhaps history and years of dissension will block any Japan–China economic alliance. As the Management Focus "The Pacific Century" indicates, a new regional economic alliance would certainly be a force for the EC and the NAFTA nations to deal with in global markets.

The Multinational Company

The multinational company (MNC) is an organization doing business in two or more countries. Typically, these firms have sales offices and, in many cases, manufacturing facilities in many countries. They usually define their scope of operation as global. For example, American firms such as Pfizer Inc., Hoover Company, Mobil Oil Corporation, Coca-Cola Company, Xerox Corporation, Dow Chemical Co., Chrysler Corp., and IBM experience the majority of their sales outside the United States.

Multinational companies are large, and they are growing.[8] Today US-based MNCs employ most of the Americans working outside the United States and are responsible for a large proportion of America's imports and exports. In addition, the present growth rate of the world's 200 largest MNCs (most of which are American) is two or three times the growth rate of individual advanced nations. Table 3–2 provides a few examples of various types of MNCs.

The globalization of markets was the most important theme of business strategy in the 1980s.[9] The topic of global management, long ignored by many, is now a subject of great interest to all. To achieve long-term business success, organizations must successfully adapt to a competitive environment based on worldwide competition.

This chapter approaches the topic of global management by focusing on three topics: (1) the aspects of an organization's decision to enter an international market; (2) the primary elements of the international environment and their impact on business; and (3) the application of the key managerial functions in an international context.

The MNC Decision

The decision to become an MNC is truly a major one. Although the choice involves many considerations, the move to become an MNC essentially encompasses three primary decisions.

TABLE 3–2   Examples of Various Types of Multinational Companies

MNCs fall under several different categories.

American-Owned MNCs		
General Motors	Mobil Oil	Bank America
IBM	ITT	Eastman Kodak
General Electric	Ford Motor	Procter & Gamble
F. W. Woolworth	Chevron	Gulf & Western
Sears Roebuck	American Express	
Foreign-Owned MNCs		
Unilever	Honda	Volkswagen
Royal Dutch/Shell	Toyota Motors	Perrier
Nestlé	Sony	Norelco
Datsun (Nissan)		
Nonprofit MNCs		
Roman Catholic Church (Italy)	US Army (United States)	Red Cross (Swiss)
American Firms Owned by Foreign MNCs		
Magnavox	Saks-Fifth Avenue	Capitol Records
Gimbel's Department Store	Bantam Books	Kiwi Shoe Polish
Libby, McNeill & Libby	Baskin-Robbins	Lipton
Stouffer Foods		

International Market to Be Served

Targeting a country (or countries) for international expansion involves considering many aspects of the prospective country's environment. Many international businesses emphasize the market size (both current and potential) in the prospective host country, the country's consumer wealth (per capita income), and the ease of doing business in the market. In assessing this latter criterion, organizations consider such factors as geographical location, language commonality, governmental relations with business, and the availability of employees with the skills that the business will require. Overall, evaluating the prospective host country's cultural, economic, and political environments are important steps in the host country selection. These factors are discussed in more detail later in the chapter.

Products or Services to Be Marketed

What products or services should an organization establish in an international market? In answering this question, many firms opt for the *shot-in-the-dark* method: They simply select one or more of their products (or services) that have done well in their domestic market and introduce them into the chosen international market. Kellogg's Corn Flakes, Coca-Cola, and McDonald's hamburgers were introduced in this manner.[10]

A growing number of companies are utilizing more analytical and deliberate approaches to product or service selection. Some firms utilize a *phased internationalization* approach. They travel to the selected host country and conduct product market research to determine consumer needs in the overall product area in which the company does business. Then the company returns home with the research and designs a product that fits the consumers' needs. The new product (often some variation of the company's product line) is then introduced into the host country. Ferrero's Tic Tac breath mints and IDV's Bailey's Irish Cream liqueur are products specifically developed and marketed based on the research of multiple international markets.[11]

Regardless of the approach taken by an organization, a successful international product or service requires primary attention to the needs, preferences, and idiosyncrasies of the consumers in the selected host country. Many hugely successful American products have failed in international markets because US companies simply ignored international consumer differences.

Other products that failed initially found success once the manufacturer made some seemingly slight though important changes. Consider S. C. Johnson & Son's Lemon Pledge furniture polish. After the product sold poorly in Japan among older consumers, the company conducted marketing research and found that the polish smelled like a latrine disinfectant used throughout Japan during World War II. Johnson & Son reduced the lemon scent in the polish, and sales boomed.

Mattel's Barbie doll was another faltering product in Japan until marketing research determined that few Japanese identified with the Americanized doll. For the Japanese, Barbie was too tall, too long-legged, and her blue eyes were the wrong color. Mattel produced a Japanized Barbie—shorter, with brown eyes and a more Asian figure. Thereafter, 2 million Barbies were sold in two years.

Even name changes can produce positive results. Pillsbury Company changed its "Jolly Green Giant" name in Saudi Arabia once it found that the name translated to "intimidating green ogre"; in China, Coca-Cola instituted a name change after it found that, in Chinese, "Coca-Cola" means "bite the wax tadpole."[12]

Mode of Entry

Once the market and product or service for international expansion have been selected, an organization must decide specifically how it will enter its selected market. The four basic, sequential strategies involved in market entry are illustrated in Figure 3–1. Each strategy increases commitment to the international venture.

FIGURE 3–1   Four Modes of Market Entry

This chart shows ways to enter foreign markets and the degree of control an owner has.

Sourcing.   Sourcing uses labor in countries where labor costs are at the lowest possible level. The maquiladoras use the sourcing approach. US plants perform capital-intensive work, while the Mexican plants perform labor-intensive tasks in assembling the products.

Export.   Exporting involves selling a product in the international market without establishing manufacturing facilities there. Exporting encompasses promotion to stimulate demand for the product, collecting revenues, making credit arrangements for sales, and shipping the product to the market.

Most companies utilize an **agent** to perform some or all of these tasks.[13] The agent may be a sales representative who obtains sales for a commission while the home company handles the shipping and required paperwork. Or an agent may be an export management company that performs all the exporting tasks (e.g., obtaining import licenses, making sales calls, handling shipping documents) for a larger commission fee.[14] However, once a home company becomes accustomed to the exporting business, it may assume most or all of these tasks, often establishing a staff in the host country.

The largest US exporters include such firms as Boeing, General Motors, IBM, Eastman Kodak, and Motorola. Many other large exporters also have investments in foreign nations. For example, Coca-Cola is the world's most recognizable trademark and best-selling soft drink.

Smaller companies venture into exporting for another important reason. Exporting is the least complicated and least risky strategy for entering a foreign market. The strategy involves little or no change in the organization's basic mission, objectives, and strategies, since all production occurs at home. If problems arise in the host country, an exporting organization can easily leave the market. The simplicity of exporting, relative to other strategies for market entry, is more compatible with smaller companies that have less resources.

However, exporting is still a challenging undertaking. When an agent is used to handle the exporting tasks, the organization has little control over the overall exporting situation (such factors as product price, advertising, and distribution). If the company handles many of the exporting tasks, it must contend with language differences, taxes, regulations, customs inspections, differing transportation systems, and time zones.

Foreign Activities.   As the importance of exports increases, the firm may decide that it now can justify its own foreign subsidiary. This decision usually involves establishing production and marketing facilities in the host country. This strategy differs from *direct investment* because it entails some type of association with a local firm or individual. This association usually takes the form of *licensing* or a *joint venture.*

When a firm negotiates a licensing agreement, it is granting to a company in the host country the right to produce the firm's product. A firm may also grant a local company the right to use the firm's intangible assets such as patents or technology. In the 1950s, many US firms transferred technology to Japanese companies via licensing agreements. The licensing firm usually receives a flat payment plus royalties from the sale of the goods produced using the licensed technology.

Licensing can be an effective way to obtain profits from product sales without establishing and managing facilities in the host country. However, a firm loses some control over the asset that is licensed. The company also runs the risk of the outside licensee eventually becoming a competitor.

In the joint venture arrangement, a business joins with local investors to create and operate a business in the host country. Each investor is a partner and shares the ownership of the new venture. Joint ventures are a quite popular strategy for launching a business abroad; over 40 percent of America's largest industrial corporations maintain international joint ventures.[15] They are especially popular with US investors in countries such as China and Japan, where the business and cultural environment is quite different from that of the United States.[16] In recent years, the joint venture has become the cornerstone of McDonald Corporation's global expansion. The company has found the approach ideal for maintaining some 2,000 outlets outside the United States. McDonald's requires that its overseas partners adhere to the company's strict production standards, while providing them the freedom to be creative in marketing, new products, and aspects of the outlet's decor. Such autonomy enables the partner to develop an outlet that caters to local tastes and culture.[17]

The popularity of joint ventures is largely owing to the substantial advantages the strategy can provide. A joint venture is a lower-cost and less-risky approach to establishing production and marketing operations abroad, compared to direct foreign investment. Substantial gains can be reaped when partners with complementary abilities pool their skills and resources in making and selling a product. For example, several US companies such as KFC Corporation have achieved success in the challenging Japanese markets via joint ventures. These companies provide financing and technology while the Japanese partner provides the personnel and knowledge of the Japanese markets and business practices.[18]

However, the failure rates of joint ventures are disturbingly high. Approximately 40 percent of these international arrangements fail; most ventures last only from three to four years.[19] At the core of the arrangement's problems are the difficulties of joint ownership and management. Usually, two partners from different countries and cultures must work together in setting venture objectives and strategy and in operating the new business. Emerging differences in management and cultural styles can create major conflicts between the parties, as can differing objectives for the venture.

Given the inherent difficulties of joint ventures, a company must thoroughly evaluate and carefully select a joint venture partner. Selection should be based on such factors as compatibility of venture objectives, similar value systems, and mutual respect. Partners should reach agreements concerning mechanisms for resolving disputes and the specific roles of each partner in managing the venture.[20]

Direct Investment.   The strongest commitment to becoming a global enterprise is a management decision to begin producing the firm's products abroad with no association with a host country investor. This entry strategy is booming in international business. The amount of U.S. direct investment in Canada (over $65 billion) and the United Kingdom (over $65 million) is the largest.

Businesses build or buy manufacturing facilities abroad for a number of reasons. In some cases, direct investment reduces manufacturing expenses because of lower labor and other costs. This benefit triggered the booming growth of the maquiladoras industry along the Mexican border. Direct investment also enables a business to avoid the tariff and other government-imposed costs associated with exporting. The strategy is an effective means for building major national markets and for maintaining total control over international operations. Also, larger benefits can be gained by establishing a local presence via direct investment. By paying taxes in the host country and providing local employment, a foreign business can build confidence among consumers and receive more equitable treatment from the host government.[21] However, direct investment entails a full commitment to an international venture. When problems arise in the host country (e.g., market decline, economic depression, government instability), leaving the country is often quite difficult and costly.

Environment of the Multinational Manager

Future managers might wonder if multinational enterprises involve unique requirements for effective performance of the managerial functions. Planning, organizing, leading, and controlling are required regardless of the business setting. However, in today's business environment, top managers in global companies are faced with a challenge that may be described as "the managing of a mixed marriage."[22] There are several of these so-called mixed marriages to contend with: the mixed economies involving government either through subsidy or nationalization; the interdependent economies of the industrial nations strongly affected by variances in trade patterns and exchange rates; the conflicting political interests that affect trade and monetary policies; and of course, widely varying social customs and contrasting cultures. All of these elements converge within the international corporation aspiring to conduct business worldwide.

In the opening section of our book, we discussed the importance of environmental factors in managerial performance. Their importance is magnified many times in an international setting. Effective international management requires even more careful consideration and appreciation of potential differences in culture, economics, politics, and technology.

Culture

Culture is a very complex environmental influence, encompassing knowledge, beliefs, values, laws, morals, customs, and other habits and capabilities an individual acquires as a member of society. These elements of culture can all vary a great deal across societies. If an MNC is global, management must adapt its managerial practices to the specific and unique aspects of culture in each host country. An MNC's management must be culturally sensitive in its business practices and learn to bridge the cultural gap that exists between its ways of management and business and those of the host country. In making these adjustments, management must be aware that cultures are *learned,* cultures *vary,* and cultures *influence behavior.*

Cultures Are Learned.   Cultures include all types of learning and behavior, the customs that people have developed for living together, their values, and their beliefs about what is right and wrong. A **culture** is the sum of what humans learn in common with other members of the society to which they belong.

Cultures Vary.   Different societies have different cultures. Various and diverse objectives are prized, and behavior valued in one society may be much less important in another. This cultural diversity affects individual perception and, therefore, individual behavior.

There are substantial differences between Eastern and Western cultures. In Asian countries, a major cultural rule of behavior is to maintain and "save face," essentially to preserve an individual's self-respect, pride, and dignity. This principle governs the ways that Asians communicate and interact with other people. For example, while American culture prizes individuality and frankness, the Asian culture emphasizes conforming to society. Individualism is shunned because, by disagreeing with others' behavior, individualism insults others and causes them to lose face. Frank criticism is avoided because criticizing others causes a loss of face. Asians avoid demonstrations of anger because it is viewed as a humiliating loss of dignity.[23]

In some cultures a payoff or a bribe to bring about a more favorable decision or to seal a deal is an accepted practice. However, in the United States, the manager making the payoff may land in jail. The accompanying Management Focus on ethics outlines the Foreign Corrupt Practices Act and how it prohibits certain behavior. It is necessary for managers to be aware of the act and to practice business in another country with the prohibitions in mind.

Cultures Influence Behavior.   Diversity in human behavior characterizes almost every human activity. Religious ceremonies and beliefs, social values, work habits, food preferences, and recreatinal activities vary endlessly among different cultural environments. At the same time people's deepest needs are probably universally the same, unlike the culturally influenced behavior expressing their needs.

Although human needs may be inherently the same, the cultural environment determines the relative importance of needs and also the means through which needs are satisfied.[24] A study of 116,000 employees in one US MNC with locations across 50 countries found that employees in different countries varied in their perceptions of what were important needs. In contrast to Americans, for instance, employees in the Netherlands and Scandinavian countries valued social needs more highly than self-actualization needs.[25]

Culture influences attitudes of individuals toward work, authority, material possessions, competition, time, profit, risk taking, and decision making. Many employees in Israel, Austria, New Zealand, and Scandinavian countries, for example, prefer consultative over unilateral decision making. In some cultures, time is measured in days and years rather than hours, which can substantially affect work scheduling and control. In some countries, especially Muslim societies, the culture does not emphasize self-determination, in contrast to the strong cultural norm in the United States. People in Muslim societies believe that fate rather than initiative determines the future.[26] Behavior follows accordingly.

Management Focus

Ethics and Doing Business in Other Countries

As business transactions, negotiations, and cooperation among international business people and government officials increase, the issue of corruption or unethical behavior must be addressed. Concern about unethical business behavior was dramatically highlighted upon revelations that the Lockheed aerospace firm had made payoffs to Japanese Premier Kakui Tanaka for his help in securing contracts. In the 1970s, it was determined that firms in industries such as construction, aerospace, electronics, and pharmaceuticals routinely made payments to facilitate contract awards, sales orders, or project clearances by foreign regulating agencies. In response to these findings, the Foreign Corrupt Practices Act (FCPA) was enacted by Congress in 1977 to deal with payments abroad.

FCPA has three major provisions regarding bribes and payoffs. First, it establishes standards for all business transactions. Second, it prohibits the use of gifts, payments, or offers of payments to foreign officials, political parties, or political candidates if the purpose is to influence a better business deal. Third, it establishes sanctions or punishments for violating FCPA. Violations could result in fines of $1 million or imprisonment for up to five years.

Protecting intellectual property rights of US firms in foreign countries is a formidable task. "Pirates" and unethical individuals in other countries produce software, medicines, music, films, books, and hundreds of other products without the approval of their creators (many of whom are Americans). The pirates stalk the open markets of international commerce. The United States is leading the charge against this unethical and illegal piracy because few other countries are willing to voice concerns. Estimated US losses are estimated to be more than $2.5 billion annually for only five industry categories: pharmaceuticals, software, motion pictures, music, and books.

The United States strictly enforces the FCPA. However, some experts believe that American firms are at a disadvantage in competing for business around the world because making payoffs and offering bribes is how business is transacted in many other countries. In Germany, payments for a more favorable deal are considered customary and are accounted for as tax deductible special expenses just as they are in the United Kingdom. In France, there are no restrictions on making "deal" payments to facilitate the development of business. What is considered normal or petty in one country is often labeled unethical or a blatant form of bribery in the United States.

Sources: Jeb Blount, "Hands of Steal," *Latin Trade,* November 1996, pp. 50-58; J G Morone, *Winning in High-Tech Markets* (Boston: Harvard Business School Press, 1993), pp. 237-49; G M Taoka and D R Beeman, *International Business* (New York: HarperCollins, 1991), pp. 295-96.

Economics

The *economic influences* of a host country substantially affect MNC performance. Its income levels, economic growth, inflation rates, and balance of payments can significantly affect an MNC's sales, earnings, and business practices. The MNC must constantly be aware of each host country's economic stability. The rate of inflation and currency stability must be closely monitored.

In economic and overall development, a country is classified either as a *developed country (DC)* or a *less developed country (LDC),* which has a lower level of economic development than a developed country. An LDC usually has a low gross national product, little industry, and underdeveloped educational, distribution, and communication systems. Making up 80 percent of the world's 6.0 billion population, LDCs have an unequal distribution of income that keeps many of their people in deep poverty.

While LDCs include most of the world's population, only about 25 percent of the world's international business activity occurs in these countries.[27] However, the amount of international activity there *is* increasing.

Economic relations between MNCs and LDCs have often been the subject of controversy. People in many LDCs have strong feelings of nationalism. During the last 30 years, in their drive for political independence and freedom from foreign domination, many developing nations have felt the need to consolidate control of their economies by altering the past pattern of relationships with foreign firms. In some LDCs, extensive government regulations have been adopted with the ultimate purpose of limiting the growth of MNCs. More recently, however, there has been a movement away from this trend. The reasons for the shift are changing attitudes and rising direct investment.[28]

Rising Direct Investment.   Improved relations have given rise to a doubling of direct investment, compared to the early 1960s. Apparently, many MNCs believe the possible returns are worth the risk. Also, these direct investments do not reflect the flow of other resources—such as managerial skills, technology, and marketing skills—that may overshadow the monetary contribution.

Despite greater mutual trust and a greater volume of investment, it would be wrong to assume that MNCs and developing countries have achieved total agreement on the questions of exploitation of resources and threats to sovereignty. These issues have divided them for years, and even today, opinions still diverge widely within each group.

In response to a population's concerns about the intentions and impact on a foreign nation's culture, a number of large MNCs have launched efforts to aid in the development of the LDCs where they conduct international business. Ford Motor Company's South American subsidiary, for example, has constructed 128 schools in Mexico over the last 20-plus years. These schools educate about 170,000 children each year. Champion International Corporation subsidizes 13,000 meals each day for its Brazilian employees. Warner-Lambert's Tropicare Inc. provides training in primary health care in the four West African countries where it operates (Cameroon, Ivory Coast, Senegal, and Zaire). These efforts are not totally selfless; the MNCs realize that helping to solve the host country's developmental problems serves both the LDC's and the MNC's interests.[29]

Politics

The political influences in a host country environment can substantially affect all of the managerial functions of an MNC and can frequently determine the ultimate success of an MNC's international operations. Our discussion of the political environment focuses on two topics: the *characteristics* of the host country government that most affect an MNC and the concept of *political risk,* including how MNCs forecast and cope with political uncertainty in their international settings. Concerning the host government, three factors most significantly influence an MNC's operations and performance:

Governmental Attitudes.   Host country governments express their attitudes concerning international imports and investments with actions that can greatly help or hinder an MNC. Governments that encourage investment often provide incentives to persuade foreign companies to establish manufacturing facilities there. Such incentives are often provided by LDCs who want access to the technology, capital, jobs, and educational and managerial skills that an MNC can provide. Singapore, for example, offers low-interest government loans, tax holidays, and accelerated depreciation to foreign investors from certain industries. India provides capital grants to companies that build manufacturing facilities in certain depressed areas of the country. Malaysia waives taxes for as long as 10 years for companies that locate in certain areas.[30]

Although LDC governments are often eager to attract certain foreign investors, they set requirements that seek to obtain as much value as possible from the MNC while not compromising the country's sovereignty. These requirements take a variety of forms. Many LDCs, for example, require a "fadeout," that is, the majority ownership of the MNC's facility in the host country is transferred to a host country investor within a certain number of years. Other LDCs, such as India, set a strict limit on foreign ownership of an MNC facility. India limits foreign ownership of a local facility to 40 percent and must approve the operation's production capacity and entry into new markets. IBM left India after the government refused to agree to IBM's worldwide policy of total ownership of its subsidiaries. Coca-Cola Company left India because it refused to comply with the government's requirement that the company disclose its Coke formula to its Indian partners.[31]

LDCs may require that an MNC hire a specified number of local citizens for employee and management positions to boost the area's employment. Some LDCs require that the MNC sell its technology to local businesses. Many host countries restrict the amount of funds that an MNC can transfer out of the country. To obtain access to markets in developed countries, some LDCs (e.g., Colombia) require that for every good imported by a resident MNC, the MNC must export a Colombian good of equal or higher value.[32]

Efficiency of Government.   Many American business executives become disillusioned with the inefficient bureaucracies they must deal with in many countries. Often, little assistance is provided by foreign governments to American businesspeople. Customs handling procedures are inefficient and burdensome, and market information is nonexistent. Systems of law in each country also can be quite different. For example, the United States has developed its legal system by means of English *common law*: The courts are guided by principles derived from previous cases. In much of Europe and Asia, however, the legal system is one of *civil law*. In such systems, judges are less important, and the bureaucrat (civil servant) is extremely important.

Government Stability.   The stability of the host country's government is perhaps the characteristic that has the greatest impact on an MNC. Highly unstable governments that are subject to volatile change can upend an MNC's operations. The most extreme impact of government instability can occur when an unstable government changes hands. In such cases, the MNC may face *expropriation,* that is, the new leaders in power seize the MNC's facility without compensation. Or under a policy of *nationalization,* the government forces the MNC to sell its facility to local buyers. Since World War II, most takeovers of MNC facilities have occurred in LDCs, particularly in Latin America.

Government instability and the uncertainty of other elements of the political environment introduce a degree of *political risk* into an MNC's operations in the respective host country. Political risk refers to unanticipated changes in the host country's political environment that affect MNC operations. *Macro risk* involves political changes that affect all multinational corporations operating in a host country; *micro risk* encompasses changes that affect certain industries or firms. Saudi Arabia's nationalization of all foreign operations in the country's oil industry in 1974 is one example of micro political change.[33]

In deciding whether to establish operation in a country, few MNCs neglect to consider political risk. Rather, most conduct *political risk analysis,* which involves identifying and assessing the sources of risk and the probabilities that adverse political change will occur in the prospective host country. Several methods of analysis are available. MNCs send representatives to visit the prospective host country and meet with government officials, business executives, and other nationals to obtain their own first-hand assessment of the political environment, or employ panels of individuals who are experts on the country to rate the country on a given number of political risk factors (such as the history of government stability, the role of the military in the host government, and the government's attitude toward foreign investors). There are businesses that produce and publish risk ratings on nations. Business International (BI) rates 70 countries on 55 political risk factors. The ratings are provided by BI specialists who live in the countries they assess.

Rather than hire external experts or rely solely on published risk ratings, a growing number of companies are designing political risk analysis programs that meet the MNC's specific needs. Dow Chemical maintains its own economic, social, and political risk program (ESP). Six to eight line managers trained in political and economic analysis, along with executives from the respective country, provide specific risk analyses of that country. Xerox Corporation maintains its Issues Monitoring System, which regularly identifies the 10 most important political issues for each host country in which Xerox operates. Xerox's managers in the respective country assess the issues, evaluate their potential impact on Xerox, and then offer strategies for dealing with the issues. Using these strategies, "external relations" objectives are then set for each local manager. Part of the manager's yearly bonus is based on the accomplishment of the objectives.[34]

Technology

Technology influences productivity, jobs, interpersonal relationships, and the structure of organizations. And it has obvious impacts on multinational companies. A company's technological superiority in multinational operations is often the major reason for its direct foreign investment and commitment to multinational business. But some nations have an abundance of technological capacity, while others virtually have none. International managers must determine how the levels of technology in foreign countries might affect their operations and sources of raw materials, energy, and transportation.

Management in a Multinational Corporation

Planning Function

The objectives of a multinational company cannot be the same as if it were operating only in the United States. There is too much potential for conflict between corporate objectives and the economic and political objectives of the countries in which the firm operates.[35] In many nations, the role played by government in economic planning heightens the possibility of conflicts with the MNC. For example, Japan's Ministry of International Trade and Industry plans the nation's economy to the point of specifying five-year percentage growth rates in exports of specific products.

In certain situations, a country may have objectives—such as a favorable balance of payments or an improved standard of living for its citizens—that do not coincide with the corporate objectives of the MNC. A common source of conflict is that to achieve a profitable objective, some of the earnings of the foreign subsidiary must be returned to the MNC's headquarters. This outward flow of earnings could have a negative impact on the host country's balance of payments. For this reason and similar ones, some nations place restrictions on multinational companies.

Civil servants who hold influential positions in foreign bureaucracies often dominate the planning functions of many countries. Managers of multinational

TABLE 3–3   **The Planning Environment in Domestic versus Global Settings**

The management function of planning takes on greater complexity in an international environment.

Domestic Setting	Global Setting
Similar culture	Diverse cultures
Limited language differences	Multilingual
One economic system	Multiple economic systems
One political system	Numerous political systems
One legal system	Diverse legal approaches
One monetary system	Multiple monetary systems
Similar markets	Diverse markets

companies must become acquainted with the attitudes and practices of these individuals for an important reason: The civil servants often establish the conditions under which the managers must do their planning.

Table 3–3 presents some factors that can complicate the planning environment for a multinational manager. The greater the number of differing factors, the more complex the planning environment.

Organizing Function

After a company decides to go multinational and its planning function is well along, a structure of jobs and authority for achieving the organizational objectives must be devised.[36] As with planning in international management, organization structures often must be adapted to local conditions. Organizational effectiveness depends greatly on flows of information. And these flows become more difficult to maintain as geographically dispersed decision centers are established. Consequently, an MNC must have an effective worldwide communication system for transmitting information throughout the organization.

Multinational companies usually employ the three basic organizational structures discussed in this textbook:

1. *Product design.* An MNC following the product design structure assigns to a single unit the operational responsibilities for a product or product line. Product design structure is widely used in multinational companies with diverse product lines that are being marketed in geographically dispersed areas. Such multinationals as Unisys Corporation and Clark Equipment Company use this design, illustrated in Figure 3–2.

2. *Geographic design.* With this design, a multinational company groups all functional and operational responsibilities into specific geographical areas. The geographic design is used widely and by such organizations as International Telephone and Telegraph and Pfizer, which do not have highly diversified product lines. The area managers are given decentralized decision-making authority, and they coordinate practically all of the operations within their geographic areas. The geographic design is illustrated in Figure 3–3.

3. *Functional design.* For an MNC using the functional design, managers at the corporate headquarters, who report to the chief executive, are given global

FIGURE 3–2   Product Organization Design

This structure is used when MNCs market diverse product lines in geographically dispersed areas.

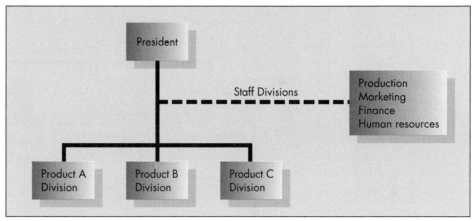

FIGURE 3–3   Geographic Organization Design

Some multinational firms group all functional and operational responsibilities into geographical areas.

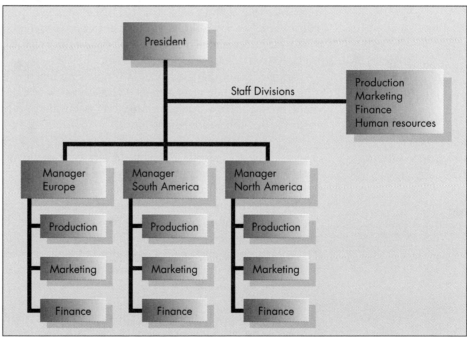

responsibilities for such functions as production, marketing, and financing. Each manager has the authority to plan and control worldwide operations within the function he or she manages. The functional design is useful for an MNC with a very limited product line, because duplication of effort can be avoided. Extractive industries, such as oil and gas, often use this design, illustrated in Figure 3–4.

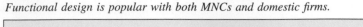

FIGURE 3–4   **Functional Organization Design**

Functional design is popular with both MNCs and domestic firms.

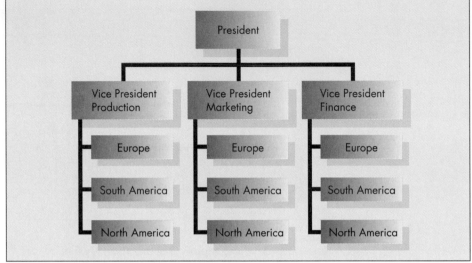

No organization structure is suitable in all cases for either multinationals or companies that operate only at home. A multinational company in a high-technology industry probably would not organize around geographic regions. More likely, it would use a functional design. A company with relatively inexperienced managers probably would not use a product design.[37]

Another factor that influences the organizing function of a multinational company is the degree to which management is home-country oriented, host-country oriented, or world oriented. How management views itself and the organization affects how it organizes the firm in foreign countries.[38]

Leading Function

Leadership is an essential function in any type of organization. Whether a firm is located in Detroit, Maricabo, Moscow, or Osaka, leadership is needed. Leaders are individuals who positively influence the behavior of followers. Exercising influence in solving problems in international markets is a key to successfully operating globally.

In most organizational settings, leadership occurs in two forms: formal and informal. Formal leaders are in appointed or elected positions of formal authority. An MNC organization chart outlines positions of authority. Whether a man or woman in these organizationally sanctioned positions exercises positive influence determines whether he or she is a leader. By definition, a leader can help motivate others to complete tasks.

MNCs also have informal leaders or individuals who become influential because they have special skills, expertise, or charisma that meets the needs of others. The formal and informal leaders of an MNC or any type of organization are the influence centers of authority.

Exactly why one person is recognized as a leader and another is not has puzzled organizational researchers for years. We do not know the exact mix of leadership traits and behaviors that predict success. However, we can and should study how influence works and where it is effective. Of the four management functions, leadership is perhaps the most studied and least understood.

Leadership in either Japan or the United States influences behavior, but how it is practiced or applied differs because of cultural differences. What would be considered a good way to influence somebody in Japan might be considered inappropriate in the United States and vice versa. Research is continually being conducted to illustrate and identify leadership similarities and differences across countries. As more globalization occurs, it will become even more important to determine how leadership works in different countries.

Controlling Function

Effective performance of the controlling function is extremely important in a multinational company. The more global the operation, the more difficult effective management control becomes. The concepts of preliminary control, concurrent control, and feedback control are applicable in controlling multinational companies. However, because of cultural differences, the controlling function may not be used in some countries to the same degree it is used in the United States. For example, such things as performance appraisals and quality controls may have little meaning in certain countries. Nevertheless, the implementation of control in the international environment requires the same three basic conditions needed domestically: standards, information, and action.

In establishing standards for an MNC, consideration must be given both to overall corporate objectives and to local conditions. This often involves bringing local managers into the planning process. As citizens of the country in which they work, the local managers can provide input useful in establishing standards that contribute to organizational objectives without causing intercultural conflicts.

Information must be provided that reports actual performance and permits appraisal of that performance against standards. Problems can occur here that may not appear in domestic organizations. For example, should profitability be measured in local currency or the home currency? The value of different currencies may cause headquarters to arrive at performance measures that differ from those of the local managers. Finally, the long distances between subsidiaries and headquarters can contribute to too much information—or too much irrelevant information—being fed into the MNC's decision support system. Decision support systems must be designed or altered to optimize the amount of information necessary for control.

Managerial action to correct deviations is the final step of the controlling function. The possible actions range from total centralization of decisions—where all operating decisions are made at corporate headquarters—to a situation in which international units are independent and autonomous. In the majority of cases, most actions are taken by international managers with specific guidelines from corporate headquarters. Effective managerial control of a global enterprise is extremely complex but vital to the firm's survival.

In summary, an international operation adds numerous complexities to the planning, organization, leading, and control processes. The most perplexing issues are related to national situation assessments, the evolution of regional infrastructures, the global funding process, technology transfer, leveraging, security, and complex sourcing and production systems.[39]

National situation assessment involves continual monitoring of political risk, governmental regulations, and market trends in both current and target countries. The evolution of regional infrastructures has created the need to increase levels of intelligence, deployment of integrated regional support, and rationalization of sourcing and manufacturing capabilities. The effective use of global funding is becoming increasingly important to fully leverage a firm's financial position in dealing with foreign exchange strategy, capital acquisition and allocation, and financial performance monitoring.

Controlling technology transfer is becoming especially crucial with the proliferation of strategic alliances and increasing overseas deployment of a firm's research facilities. In addition to maintaining a vigorous planning and control system to maximize their technological leverage on a worldwide basis, numerous multinational firms are developing centers of expertise around the world to tap local pockets of technology. Finally, there is an increasing emphasis on rationalizing a firm's global manufacturing infrastructure to balance overall efficiency and flexibility with benefits of local presence. It is clear that multinational companies are faced with a multitude of issues that domestic companies don't have to address.

Managing People in a Multinational Corporation

Effectiveness in managing people can vary from nation to nation because motivational incentives and styles of leadership are influenced by a variety of factors. As with domestic organizations, effective management of a multinational company requires managers who understand the needs, values, and expectations of people in the nations in which the MNC operates. As we noted earlier, attitudes toward work, competition in the marketplace, and perceptions of authority vary greatly across cultures. Thus, leadership styles and motivational techniques that may be effective in the United States, Canada, and Great Britain probably would not work well in Mexico, Africa, Taiwan, or South America. And just as cultures differ greatly, so may the dominant needs of the people in different countries.

Because substantial differences can exist between the leadership styles and ways of doing business in many countries, an important issue in managing the MNC's facility in a host country is whether local or expatriate managers should staff the facility. An *expatriate* is an MNC employee transferred to the facility from the MNC's home base or from a facility in some other country. Approximately 250,000 US citizens work as expatriates in MNC facilities abroad. On the other hand, foreign companies with operations in the United States employ over 4.5 million workers. A few of the largest foreign employers in the United States are presented in Table 3–4.

The staffing decision requires evaluating many factors that both favor and disfavor the use of expatriates abroad. A number of these factors are shown in Table 3–5. For example, the use of expatriates ensures that the MNC facility has the necessary managerial skills to oversee the operations, a key advantage in LDCs where there exists a shortage of managerial skills. However, an expatriate policy is much more costly than hiring local managers; many MNCs estimate that expatriates are three times more expensive than locals. The high costs are due to the double-taxing of an expatriate's compensation and the extra costs such as educational and family-related expenses.[40]

Although many MNCs utilize expatriates, the failure rate of US expatriate managers overseas is significant. Experts estimate that, on average, 30 percent of all expatriate assignments end in failure, often with the manager returning home sooner than expected.[41] Two main reasons account for such disappointing performance: (1) The expatriate often has problems adjusting to the cultural, social, and business environment in the host country, frequently because the MNC has not adequately prepared the manager for the significant cultural differences encountered. (A recent survey of MNCs found that less than 12 percent of the firms provide formal training on

TABLE 3–4   A Sample of the Largest Foreign Employers in the United States

Foreign Parent	Home Office	US Subsidiary	US Employment
Tengelmann	Mulheim, Germany	Great Atlantic & Pacific Tea Co.	74,000
Hanson	London	Hanson Industries	50,000
Nestlé	Vevey, Switzerland	Nestlé Enterprises Alcon Laboratories Carnation	48,027
Honda Motor	Tokyo	American Honda Motor	46,238
ABB–ASEA Brown Boveri	Zurich	ASEA Brown Boveri	40,000
British Petroleum	London	BP America	37,000
Royal Dutch/Shell Group	The Hague	Shell Oil	32,434
Siemens	Munich	Siemens	31,000
Bridgestone	Tokyo	Bridgestone/Firestone	28,000
Sony	Tokyo	Sony Corp. of America	20,000

Source: D J Rachman, M H Mescon, C L Bovée, and J V Thill, *Business Today* (New York: McGraw-Hill, 1993), p. 143.

TABLE 3–5   Should Expatriate or Local Managers Staff a Host Country Facility?

Staffing decisions for foreign facilities involve the consideration of many factors.

In Favor of Expatriates

Expatriates possess technical and managerial skills.

Using expatriates enhances communications between parent and subsidiary.

Presence of expatriates promotes foreign, or MNC, image.

Parent/subsidiary relations are facilitated by presence of expatriates familiar with corporate culture.

Assignment of expatriates is part of their professional development program, and it improves senior management's decision making.

In Favor of Locals

Total compensation paid to locals is usually considerably less than that paid to expatriates.

No host country cultural adaptation is necessary when locals are used.

Using locals is consistent with a promote-from-within policy.

No work permits are needed with locals.

Using locals promotes a local image.

Using expatriates with special employment contracts rather than local nationals may violate local equal employment opportunity regulations.

Source: Adapted from R Grosse and D Kujawa, *International Business: Theory and Managerial Applications* (Burr Ridge, IL: Richard D. Irwin, 1988), p. 480.

the cross-cultural aspects of managing in a foreign country.)[42] (2) Some expatriate managers lack the special characteristics and abilities that an overseas assignment requires, such as communication skills, flexibility, adaptability to change, emotional maturity, and the ability to work with people with different backgrounds, perspectives, and cultures.[43]

Some MNCs carefully screen employees for expatriate assignments. McDonnell Douglas Corporation's selection program involves close questioning about personal habits, religious and political beliefs, medical histories, and family situations. The company looks for anything that may cause problems for the individual or the company once the expatriate is working abroad. McDonnell Douglas also encourages each of its expatriate managers to return home at least once a year (the company pays the round-trip fare) to relieve two potential expatriate problems: homesickness and the "out of sight, out of mind" syndrome. Many expatriates fear that once away from the home office they will be forgotten by the company and that no opportunities will be available for them at the MNC home base when they return.[44]

Summary of Key Points

- Strategic economic alliances in Europe, North America, and the Pacific Rim have resulted in freer trade and more cooperation among the nations included in each region. These economic blocs could change the way global business is transacted.
- The multinational corporation (MNC) presents a critical challenge to future managers—the challenge of managing organizations, people, and operations in an international environment.
- The decision to become an MNC involves determining the international market to be served, the products or services to be produced and marketed, and the strategy for entering the selected market.
- The environment of a multinational manager differs in many respects from the domestic environment. The culture, economics, politics, and technology of the international environment are among the most important differences.
- Cultures may have differing attitudes toward the importance of work, authority, competition, material possessions, time, risk taking, profits, and other factors.
- Economic differences in income levels, growth trends, inflation rates, balance of payments, and the stability of the currency and overall economy can significantly affect MNC performance.
- It is difficult to separate politics and the MNC. The attitudes in host countries toward imports and direct investment, the stability of government, and the efficiency of government vary widely between nations. Each may change rapidly in those nations where governments change rapidly.
- Technology has affected and will continue to affect multinational companies. Often a company's technological superiority in multinational operations is the major reason for

its commitment to multinational business. Technology levels also influence the sources of raw materials, energy, and transportation in a particular area.
- The management function of planning can be more complex in an MNC. The greater the cultural and language differences, the more diverse the economic, political, and legal systems. Also, the more markets and monetary systems it faces, the more complex the planning environment for an MNC.
- MNCs often employ the basic organizational structures of domestic organizations: product design, geographic design, and functional design.
- Effective performance of the controlling function is extremely important in MNCs. Because of cultural differences, the controlling function may not be used in some countries to the same degree that it is used in the United States. Such techniques as performance appraisals and quality control may have little meaning in some cultures. However, the conditions for effective control—standards, information, and corrective action—are still required.
- Managing people will vary across nations because styles of leadership and motivational techniques are influenced by the needs, values, and expectations of the people in the nations in which the MNC operates. Thus, leadership styles and motivation techniques that might be effective in America may not be useful in other parts of the world.
- An important decision for MNCs is whether to utilize expatriate managers for overseas assignments. To date, the effectiveness of US expatriate managers has been limited because of difficulties in adjusting to environmental differences in the host country and their lack of human relations skills required for effectively managing abroad.

Discussion and Review Questions

1. Discuss how culture could affect an employee's willingness to change behaviors.

2. How would a manager use Porter's "diamond" framework and analysis to evaluate the attractiveness of forming a joint venture in Costa Rica?

3. Do you believe that you would be an effective expatriate manager? Explain why or why not.

4. Some managers are calling for the repeal of the Foreign Corrupt Practices Act, charging that the law greatly diminishes their competitiveness abroad. In your view, should the law be repealed? Discuss.

5. Why would an American firm be reluctant to establish a new plant in Saudi Arabia?

6. Why might American managers prefer domestic versus global assignments? What are the advantages and disadvantages of each?

7. Suppose you were the CEO of a computer manufacturing company with plans to establish a production facility in Japan. You want to transfer some of your managers to the Japanese facility. What steps would you take to ensure that your expatriate managers are effective in their new assignments?

8. Could economic alliances such as the EC and NAFTA result in greater trade protectionism against nations not included in the alliance? Explain.

9. Would the social responsibility aspects of managerial actions differ between domestic and international managers? Discuss.

10. Of the economic, cultural, political, and technological factors in the international environment, which factor do you believe has the greatest impact upon MNC performance? Explain.

CASE 3–1
INVEST IN RUSSIA: WHY?

Most Western executives are aware of two very important advantages of investing in Russia: a well-educated, low-cost workforce and a large, completely open market—a market so large it can influence global market shares. Executives of many multinationals also know that even during the Cold War their companies enjoyed good business relations with the Soviet Union. A study carried out in 1988 of 106 American companies that had done a significant amount of business with the USSR found that only 1 percent did not want to increase their operations in the then Soviet Union. The American companies were particularly complimentary of the way their Soviet partners had complied with agreements; only 5 percent said that agreements were sometimes not met, and most of these cases appeared to have been the result of inefficiencies rather than attempts to derive an unfair advantage. Fifty-four percent of American companies rated the Soviet Union in the top half of their foreign customers.

There are good reasons, however, why American companies are not now investing more in Russia. Interestingly, political instability is not often such a reason. While it is an important factor in some of the independent states such as Georgia and Azerbaijan, this is not the case in Russia, particularly now that the Overseas Private Investment Corporation (OPIC) offers political-risk insurance to American corporations investing in Russia.

The reasons why American companies are investing so little are many and complex, but they can be summed up simply: Russians do not understand what they need to do to attract US investors, and Americans need to gain a better understanding of how they can benefit from the opportunities that exist in Russia.

Although the Russian government favors foreign investment, its policies are the primary reason American companies have not invested a great deal more. The sudden imposition of large taxes, such as those on the export of oil, scare off investors for two reasons: (1) these taxes make structuring a satisfactory investment more difficult; and (2) even worse, they make future taxes and regulations uncertain, thus making investment in Russia very risky.

The failure of the Russian government to resolve its judicial problems has also been a major factor. Foreign investors are uncertain about whom they should deal with and how often. When dealing with several levels of government, each citing conflicting laws and decrees pertaining to the project, investors are often frustrated to the point of withdrawing their money.

Another major deterrent to Western investment in Russia is that few Russians understand the value of capital, while foreign companies do not seek "profitable" investments, but rather, investments that maximize the return on capital. Most American companies have a "hurdle rate," which is the minimum return on investment that the company will accept. For many companies, the hurdle rate is about 20 percent after tax for investments made in the United States. The rate increases when an investment is made in a country where the risks are perceived to be higher than in the United States. Hurdle rates are high because investment capital is in high demand. American companies generally have the highest hurdle rates in the world—in part because the low savings rate in the United States limits investment funds and in part because the American economy generates so many investment opportunities.

The difficult living conditions in Russia, particularly outside Moscow and St. Petersburg, have also been a deterrent to investors. One American executive described this problem charitably when he said, "It takes a special kind of person to handle the isolation and the primitive conditions."

Providing quality hotels and restaurants throughout the country is a problem that is being addressed by American entrepreneurs such as Jeff and Belinda Donnely, who have started a real estate agency for Western clients. They renovate and lease apartments.

Despite the fact that conditions in Russia could be better, those American companies that explore opportunities for investment in Russia stand a good chance of finding business that will increase their competitiveness in world markets.

In the present environment, an investment in Russia involves a greater degree of risk than in many other countries, but there is an excellent chance that the environment will change for the better. Many aspects of the present difficulties result from the lack of a market culture after 70 years of Communism, and it is in Russia's self-interest to make the necessary changes. Thus, there is a good case for exploring opportunities and making some investments now in order to be in a position in the long run to move quickly with much larger investments should the timing be appropriate. McDonald's is perhaps the best-known example of a company that has followed this pattern, but there are many others, such as Asea Brown Boveri and Polaroid.

Russia offers excellent opportunities for commercializing new products. New products, even when successful, usually incur heavy losses for several years because of low sales and high marketing costs. The absence of competition in Russia, however, allows a Western company to introduce a new product there without this period of low sales and high marketing costs as the product moves down the experience curve and becomes better and less expensive. In addition, hard currency could be obtained by exporting products to the West for market development.

Questions for Analysis

1. Using Porter's "diamond" analysis, explain why a Western manager would consider entering the Russian market?

2. The case outlines some reasons why American companies in 1997 are not investing heavily in Russia. What are some other business reasons not presented?

3. Why would McDonald's and Polaroid believe that early entry in Russia would provide a competitive advantage at a later time?

Sources: Paul Klebnikov, "Moscow Cowboys," *Forbes,* December 16, 1996, pp. 78–85; J L Hecht, "The Trouble with Russia," *Delovie Lyudi,* March 1993, pp. 52–53; P Lawrence and C Vlachoutsicos, "Joint Ventures in Russia: Put the Locals in Charge," *Harvard Business Review,* January–February 1993, pp. 44–51, 54.

EXPERIENTIAL EXERCISE
LAUNCHING AN INTERNATIONAL BUSINESS

Purpose

This activity is designed to enhance students' understanding of the key elements of the international environment and their impact on expanding a business internationally.

The Exercise in Class

The instructor will divide the class into groups of four students each. Each group should complete the following project:

1. Assume that your group is the top-management team of a manufacturing company. Your team's first task is to select a product that your company manufactures. Once you've selected the product, assume that your company makes the product domestically and wants to expand production overseas. Specifically, your company seeks to produce and sell the product in a Latin American, European, or Asian country.

2. Select a country for your international expansion. Once you've identified the nation, conduct an assessment of the country as an international market for your product:
   a. Conduct library research on the cultural, economic, and political aspects of the country's environment.
   b. Review your research, answering the following questions:
      (1) What is the level of demand for your product in this potential market?
      (2) In what ways do the cultural, economic, and political aspects of the country's environment facilitate the success of your product in the market?
      (3) In what ways do these environmental aspects hinder the success of your product?
      (4) In your team's opinion, what are the primary challenges in establishing manufacturing facilities and launching your product in this market?

3. Prepare a five- to seven-page typed report that provides an overall profile of your selected market, including your responses to these questions. Be prepared to defend your findings in class discussion.

The Learning Message

This exercise effectively illustrates the importance of specific foreign national environments in success or failure of a launch of manufacturing and marketing activities into the international market. Students should quickly realize the complexities in expanding business abroad, which often cause overseas ventures to fail.

Notes

1. Murray Weidenbaum, "The Emerging Transnational Enterprise," *Business and the Contemporary World,* Winter 1993, pp. 160–66.
2. Paul Klebnikov and Caroline Waxler, "The Wild East," *Forbes,* December 16, 1996, pp. 348–350.
3. Louis Kraar, "Daewoo's Daring Drive into Europe," *Fortune,* May 13, 1996, pp. 145–152.
4. Dara Khambata and Riad Ajami, *International Business* (New York: Macmillan, 1992), pp. 154–69.
5. Arvind V. Phatak, *International Business: Concepts and Cases* (Cincinnati: South-Western, 1997), pp. 65–74.
6. Gary C Hufbauer and Jeffrey V Schott, *North American Free Trade* (Washington, DC: Institute for International Economics, 1992).
7. Gary C Hufbauer and Jeffrey V Schott, *NAFTA: An Assessment* (Washington DC: Institute for International Economics, 1993), pp. 120–25.
8. Helen Deresky, *International Management* (New York: HarperCollins, 1994), pp. 20–22.
9. Ibid., pp. 120–141.
10. Patricia Sellers, "How Coke Is Kicking Pepsi's Can," *Fortune,* October 28, 1996, pp. 70–84.
11. Ibid.
12. David A Ricks, *Blunders in International Business* (Cambridge, MA: Blackwell, 1993), p. 34.
13. John D Daniels and Lee H Radebaugh, *International Dimensions of Contemporary Business* (Boston, MA: PWS-Kent, 1993), pp. 35–36.
14. John D Daniels and Lee H Radebaugh, *International Business Environments and Operations* (Reading, MA: Addison-Wesley, 1992), chaps. 14 and 15.
15. Phatak, *International Business,* pp. 261–68.
16. John A Byrne, "Enterprise," *Business Week,* special issue, 1993, pp. 12–18.
17. Peter G Petersen, *Facing Up* (New York: Simon & Schuster,1993).
18. "The Partners," *Business Week,* February 10, 1992, p. 36.
19. Timothy M Collins and Thomas L Doorley, *Teaming Up for the 90s* (Burr Ridge, IL: IPRO, 1991), pp. 100–17.
20. Phatak, *International Business,* pp. 261–68.
21. IMF, *World Economic Outlook,* May 1995, p. 62.
22. For a more detailed discussion, see Klaus E Agthe, "Managing the Mixed Marriage," *Business Horizons,* January–February 1990, pp. 37–43.
23. Louis Kraar, "The Battle for Asia," *Fortune,* November 1, 1993, pp. 126–56.
24. Brent M Longnecker, "Rewarding a Global Workforce: Internationalization of Executive Compensation," *Professional Review,* Summer 1993, pp. 15–18.
25. Geert Hofstede, "National Cultures in Four Dimensions," *International Studies of Management and Organization,* Spring–Summer 1983, p. 68, as cited in Daniels and Radebaugh, *International Dimensions,* p. 99.
26. Thomas Sowell, *Migrations and Cultures: A World View* (New York: Basic Books, 1995).
27. Robert Grosse and Duane Kujawa, *International Business: Theory and Managerial Applications* (Burr Ridge, IL: Richard D. Irwin, 1988), pp. 606–7.
28. Jim Rohiver, *Asia Rising* (New York: Simon & Schuster, 1995).
29. Ibid.
30. Robert Weigand, "International Investments: Weighing the Incentives," *Harvard Business Review,* July–August 1983, pp. 146–52.
31. Dennis J Encarnation and Sushil Vachani, "Foreign Ownership: When Hosts Change the Rules," *Harvard Business Review,* September–October 1985, pp. 152–60.
32. Grosse and Kujawa, *International Business,* pp. 219–27.
33. "Rating Risk in the Hot Countries," *The Wall Street Journal,* September 20, 1991, p. B1.
34. Thomas W Shreeve, "Be Prepared for Political Changes Abroad," *Harvard Business Review,* July–August 1984, pp. 111–18.
35. John A Quelch and James E Austin, "Should Multinationals Invest in Africa?" *Sloan Management Review,* Spring 1993, pp. 107–19.

36. James L Gibson, John M Ivancevich, and James H Donnelly, Jr., *Organizations: Behavior, Structure, and Processes* (Burr Ridge: Irwin, 1997).

37. Matthew J Kiernan, "The New Strategic Architecture: Learning to Compete in the Twenty-First Century," *Academy of Management Executive,* February 1993, pp. 7–21.

38. Donald A Palmer, P Devereaux Jennings, and Xueguang Zhou, "Late Adoption of the Multinational Form by Large US Corporations: Institutional, Political, and Economic Accounts," *Administrative Science Quarterly,* March 1993, pp. 100–31.

39. William D Trotter, "The Global Management of Integrated Planning and Control," *The International Executive,* March–April 1990, pp. 27–28.

40. Joanne S Lublin, "Foreign Accents Proliferate in Top Ranks as US Companies Find Talent Abroad," *The Wall Street Journal,* May 21, 1992, pp. 1B–2B.

41. M Selz, "Hiring the Right Manager Overseas, *The Wall Street Journal,* February 27, 1992, p. 1B.

42. J S Black and H B Gregerson, "The Other Half of the Picture: Antecedents of Spouse Cross-Cultural Adjustments," *Journal of International Business Studies,* Third Quarter 1992, pp. 461–77.

43. "Multinationals," *The Economist,* March 27, 1993, special survey, pp. 1–19.

44. Amanda Bernett, "Path to Top Job Now Twists and Turns," *The Wall Street Journal,* March 15, 1993, pp. B1, B7.

4 SOCIAL AND ETHICAL RESPONSIBILITIES OF MANAGEMENT

Chapter Learning Objectives

After completing Chapter 4, you should be able to:

- **Define** social responsibility in terms that reflect your view of the role of corporations in society.
- **Describe** the manner in which managers' ethics affect their decisions regarding social responsibility.
- **Discuss** the purpose, process, and pitfalls of establishing an effective code of ethics.
- **Compare** arguments for and against a specific corporate action, based on your own ethical standards.
- **Identify** the various actions managers are taking to ensure that their organizations are ethical.

The Growing Green Revolution

In the 1970s, when citizens of the world first demanded a cleanup of the environment, corporations were largely uncooperative. But today, when it comes to green issues, many companies worldwide have turned from rebellious underachievers to active problem solvers. The green revolution is rapidly spreading across the earth, encompassing diverse companies engaged in a wide variety of activities. Indeed, for some companies, engaging in the green revolution has become part of their daily business practices. Three prime examples follow:

Example 1. WMX Technologies, Inc. (previously Waste Management, Inc.) is the world's largest waste-handling company. WMX offers diverse services, including environmental consulting, design, and engineering; landfill construction and management; and waste disposal. A superficial glance at a description of these services might suggest to some people that WMX could be considered among the worst of the environment's enemies. However, this would be totally wrong.

At WMX's giant Settler's Hill landfill in Geneva, Illinois (a Chicago suburb), a park and an 18-hole golf course sit on top of the half of the fill that is now closed. Across the road is the open half of the fill where a steady stream of trucks dump their loads on the open face of the landfill mountain. Yet, there is virtually no odor associated with the dumps, and when the fill is finally closed, there will be 27 holes for golf, several ski slopes, and other recreational facilities. Using methane gas emitted from the site, the landfill also generates enough power to meet WMX's local power needs and to supply electricity to 5,000 homes in Geneva.

Example 2. Devastation of the world's rain forests continues at an alarming rate, but some multinational companies are taking steps to preserve these valued resources. Companies cited for promoting conservation efforts are Merck, Eli Lilly, and Shaman Pharmaceuticals (pharmaceutical giants that are investing millions on new drugs generated from native species); AES Corp. and New England Electric System (power companies that are planting trees in the rain forest to offset carbon dioxide emissions from fossil-fueled power plants in the United States); and Maxus Energy and Chevron (petroleum firms leading multicompany environmental projects in Ecuador and Papua New Guinea).

Example 3. Several Canadian hotels have proved that being earth friendly can save money. The Royal York Hotel in Toronto is saving over $260,000 a year in waste removal costs by compacting and then recycling its garbage. The hotel has also cut an additional $200,000 in annual expenses by fixing leaky steam pipes. L'Hotel, also in Toronto, saved $25,000 in one year when it traded its 40W fluorescent tubes for 30W tubes. Finally, Hotel Vancouver installed a computer system to monitor and control energy use throughout the building and received a $19,000 rebate from the power company in the first month of use. What do these three hotels have in common? All are part of the Canadian Pacific Hotels and Resorts chain, which, since the introduction of its Green Programme in 1990, has been making large cash savings while simultaneously contributing greatly to Canada's environmental policy.

Sources: G Gallarotti, "It Pays to Be Green: The Managerial Incentive Structure and Environmentally Sound Strategies," *Columbia Journal of World Business,* Winter 1995, pp. 38–57; N Chakravarty, "Dean Buntrock's Green Machine," *Forbes,* August 2, 1993, pp. 96–100; F Rice, "Who Scores Best on the Environment," *Fortune,* July 26, 1993, pp. 114–20; and K McDermid, "Canadian Hotels Go Green and Save Cash," *Hospitality,* April 1993, p. 16.

The challenge for most companies is that a new segment of business life, the environment, is being entered on the balance sheet for the first time. Unfortunately, many managers fail to see the benefits of green management. They see it as detrimental to the organization's goals of profitability, market share, and efficiency. Others, however, see the necessity for very practical reasons: (1) they know many countries have strict regulations in force, and (2) they believe that there are many opportunities for managers to profit from environmentally sound strategies.

The terms *social responsibility, business ethics,* and *management ethics* appear frequently in popular and technical literature. Every day, newspapers report incidents involving businesses that some people would call socially irresponsible and unethical.

Yet, other individuals and groups might consider the actions to be quite proper, from both a social and ethical standpoint.

One of the purposes of this chapter is to provide a basis for understanding the meanings and implications of social responsibility and ethics. To accomplish this purpose, we review (1) society's expectations for corporate and managerial behavior and (2) changing business ethics. The social context in which corporate and managerial decisions and actions occur is dynamic and complex. Thus, to understand the meanings of social responsibility and business ethics is to recognize that they change with time and circumstance.[1]

Another purpose of this chapter is to provide guidelines by which managers can determine socially and ethically responsible behavior. Managers must be cognizant of their own responsibilities for instilling acceptable ethical standards throughout their organizations.[2] They must also be cognizant of the necessity to create organizational procedures and policies that encourage disclosure of unethical behavior.[3] The standard of business and managerial behavior for what is minimally responsible and ethical is that which is legal. Legality must be the recognized threshold of all managerial and organizational action.

The Meanings of Social Responsibility

A recent review of the literature identifies no less than nine meanings for social responsibility.[4] These nine meanings can be classified in three general categories: **social obligation, social reaction,** and **social responsiveness.**[5]

Social Responsibility as Social Obligation

According to this view, a corporation engages in socially responsible behavior when it pursues a profit within the constraints of law as imposed by society. Because society supports business by allowing it to exist, business is *obligated* to repay society for that right by making profits. Thus, legal behavior in pursuit of profit is socially responsible behavior, and *any behavior not legal or not in pursuit of profit is socially irresponsible.*

This view is associated with economist Milton Friedman and others who believe that society creates business firms to pursue special and specialized purposes—producing goods and services—and that to engage in other pursuits exaggerates the legitimate place of business in society.[6] As Friedman stated: "There is one and only one social responsibility of business—to use its resources and engage in activities designed to increase its profits so long as it stays within the rules of the game, which is to say, engages in open and free competition without deception or fraud."[7]

Proponents of social responsibility as social obligation offer four primary arguments in support of their view: First, they assert, businesses are accountable to their shareholders, the owners of the corporation. Thus, management's sole responsibility is to serve the shareholders' interests by managing the company to produce profits from which the shareholders benefit.

Second, socially responsible activities such as social improvement programs should be determined by law, by public policy, and by the actions and contributions of private individuals. As representatives of the people, the government (via legislation and allocation of tax revenues) is best equipped to determine the nature of social improvements and to realize those improvements in society. For example, in 1993, the federal government enacted the Family and Medical Leave Act, which provides employees with as many as 12 weeks of leave annually to care for a new baby or an ill family member.[8] Businesses contribute in this regard by agreeing to maintain the employee's group health benefits with employer contributions continuing as if the worker were on the job.

Third, if management allocates profits to social improvement activities, it is abusing its authority. As Friedman notes, these actions amount to taxation without representation. Management is taxing the shareholders by taking their profits and spending them on activities that have no immediate profitable return to the company.[9] And management is doing so without input from shareholders. Because managers are not elected public officials, they are also taking actions that affect society without being accountable to society. Further, this type of nonprofit-seeking activity may be both unwise and unworkable because managers are not trained to make noneconomic decisions.[10]

Fourth, these actions by management may work to the disadvantage of society. In this sense, the financial costs of social activities may, over time, cause the price of the company's goods and services to increase, and customers would pay the bill. Managers will have thus acted in a manner contrary to the interest of the customers and ultimately the shareholders.

Although many people disagree with this meaning, *social responsibility* can refer to behavior directed exclusively (but legally) toward the pursuit of profit. A manager can, with justification, state that he has discharged his obligation to society by creating goods and services in exchange for profit within the limits defined by law.

Social Responsibility as Social Reaction

A second meaning of social responsibility is behavior that is in reaction to "currently prevailing social norms, values, and performance expectations."[11] This pervasive view emphasizes that society has expectations for business and corporate behavior that go beyond the provision of goods and services. At minimum, business must be accountable for the ecological, environmental, and social costs incurred by its actions; at maximum, business must react and contribute to the solving of society's problems (even those that cannot be directly attributed to business).[12]

A somewhat restrictive interpretation of social responsibility as social reaction is that it involves only voluntary actions. This interpretation seeks to separate corporate actions that are *required* by economic or legal imperative and those that are initiated by voluntary, altruistic motives.[13] Thus, this more narrow view would imply that a corporation that pursues only socially obligated behavior is not socially responsible, because such behavior is required, not voluntary.

A leading spokesman for the view that social responsibility goes beyond the law, Keith Davis, states: "A firm is not being socially responsible if it merely complies with the minimum requirements of the law . . . Social responsibility goes one step further. It [social responsibility] is a firm's acceptance of social obligation beyond the requirements of the law."[14] A firm that accepts social obligation in reaction to pressure groups, consumer boycotts, or adverse publicity would not be socially responsible.

Whether the firm's actions are voluntary or involuntary, a broader interpretation of the social reaction view identifies as socially responsible those actions that go beyond the law. Typically, these actions are reactions to the expectations of specific groups— unions, shareholders, social activists, consumerists, and the like.[15] Because the expectations of these groups go beyond legal minimums, firms can decide not to react in such circumstances. Favorable reaction, however, is considered socially responsible behavior in this view.

The essence of this view of social responsibility is that firms are reactive. Demands are made of them by certain groups, and the firms are socially responsible when they react, whether voluntarily or involuntarily, to satisfy these demands. This

Management Focus

The Socially Responsible Body Shop

In today's environment, companies do not exist in a vacuum. It is the corporation's responsibility to consider not only shareholders' desire for profits, but also the needs of its employees, customers, suppliers, the community(ies) where the business resides, and society at large. Is it possible for a company to be active in improving society and still make above-average financial returns? The answer is yes, and a prime example of such a company is The Body Shop.

The Body Shop sells only environmentally safe, natural, nonanimal-tested cosmetics and toiletries. This company's philosophy is to give back to the communities from which it receives its profits. Seven examples follow of how the Body Shop incorporates its philosophy of "trade-not-aid" into its business workings.

1. The Body Shop set up workshops to make foot rollers at six poverty-stricken orphanages in small villages in India. The Body Shop pays first-world prices for these third-world products. As a result, each village now has much higher educational, health, and nutritional standards.

2. The Body Shop found a paper-making plant in Nepal that was destroying the environment through deforestation, causing erosion and landslides. Body Shop employees taught the Nepalese how to make paper from renewable resources like banana skins, and the company now purchases drawer liners, sheet paper, and sachets made from that plant.

3. The Body Shop discovered an abandoned factory in a Glasgow, Scotland, slum where the unemployment rate was higher than the national average. They purchased the building and converted it into a soap factory. The plant now operates at a profit, and 25 percent of the profits generated are being returned to the community for various social projects.

4. The Body Shop sells a hair conditioner that is made from Brazilian nut oil. To acquire the oil, the company first sent anthropologists to live with an Indian tribe in northern Brazil. This was done so that they could learn how to trade with the Indians without disturbing their culture.

5. Each of the 210 Body Shop store windows in Canada is used as a platform for education three times a year to draw attention to selected social and environmental issues.

6. The Body Shop stores sell T-shirts, and for each one that is sold, one dollar is donated to The Body Shop Charitable Foundation.

7. Every Body Shop store sends its staff out to work on community projects of the staff's choosing for an average of four hours per week.

In the mid-90s some critics began saying that Body Shop management was paying too much attention to environmental issues and not enough to business issues. Indeed, often experiencing double-digit sales growth over the previous decade, the company did start to lose some momentum with its mature product line. A new managing director was hired. Since that time The Body Shop has experienced tremendous growth in the Asian market and opened new markets in South Korea and the Philippines. And it is revamping its product line while maintaining its environmental and humanitarian ideals.

Sources: C P Wallace, "Can The Body Shop Shape Up?" *Fortune*, April 15, 1996, pp. 118–20; M Franssen, "Beyond Profits," *Business Quarterly*, Autumn 1993, pp. 15–20; and "Striving to Be Cosmetically Correct," *New York Times*, May 27, 1993, p. B1.

meaning is unsatisfactory for those who believe social responsibility should refer to proactive behavior.

Social Responsibility as Social Responsiveness

According to this view, socially responsible behaviors are anticipatory and preventive rather than reactive and restorative.[16] The term *social responsiveness* has become widely used in recent years to refer to actions that go beyond social obligation and social reaction.[17] The characteristics of socially responsive behavior include taking stands on public issues, accounting willingly for actions to any group, anticipating future needs of society and moving toward satisfying them, and communicating with the government regarding existing and anticipated socially desirable legislation.

A socially responsive corporation actively seeks ways to solve social problems. Progressive managers, according to this view, apply corporate skills and resources to every problem—from rundown housing to youth employment and small business job creation. The Body Shop's active involvement in a wide variety of socially responsible activities, as profiled in the accompanying Management Focus, provides an example of a company deeply committed to taking a proactive approach to social responsibility.

The social responsiveness view is the broadest meaning of social responsibility. It places managers and their organizations in a position of responsibility far removed from the traditional one of being concerned solely with economic means and ends. Advocates of social responsiveness generally assert that this approach to social responsibility is superior to a social obligation or social reaction perspective for three reasons.

First, business's economic activities and goals cannot be neatly separated from the social activities and goals of society. Virtually everything that business does, such as opening or closing a plant or launching a new product line, has distinct social consequences.[18] Therefore, as important participants in American society, businesses have a responsibility to deal proactively with society's major problems and challenges.

Second, contrary to the social obligationist's view that managers are not trained to deal with societal problems, social responsiveness advocates assert that companies "are perhaps the most effective problem-solving organizations in a capitalist society."[19] Their resources and talents can contribute much toward alleviating major social problems.

Third, social responsiveness advocates assert that business's involvement in social problems is not an abuse of authority, as the social obligation view proposes. Shareholders have rarely challenged their business's support of social causes, and companies' efforts are likely to receive substantial approval from consumers, the press, and the public.[20]

A Continuum of Social Responsibility

The three general meanings of social responsibility can be depicted as a continuum. As shown in Figure 4–1, at one extreme is social obligation: business behavior that reflects the firm's economic and legal responsibilities. Occupying the middle position is social reaction: behavior that is demanded by groups having a direct stake in the organization's actions. The furthest extreme, social responsiveness, is anticipatory, proactive, and preventive behavior.

In practice, a corporation can choose to be anywhere along the continuum. To be socially reactive implies the firm's acceptance of social obligation as well. Similarly, to be socially responsive requires both social obligation and social reaction behavior. In a sense, the three meanings refer to different degrees of departure from the usual economic expectations and performance of business firms.

FIGURE 4–1   A Continuum of Social Responsibility

The continuum formed by the three classes of socially responsible behavior ranges from an emphasis on profit making to an emphasis on social and economic concerns.

Type of behavior:	Socially obligated	Socially reactive	Socially responsive
Primary emphasis:	The organization's economic and legal responsibilities	The organization's economic, legal, and social responsibilities	The organization's economic, legal, social, and citizenship responsibilities

One Company's Commitment to Worker Education

In the United States, almost half of all adults possess only limited reading and writing skills. Results of a recent study conducted by the Education Department highlight significant learning handicaps associated with the populace: 40 million adults can perform only simple routine tasks involving brief and uncomplicated texts and documents, and another 50 million adults have only a slightly higher literacy level, able to calculate the total cost of a purchase or determine the difference in price between two items. Responding to this deficiency, the Better English Campaign, a national drive to improve literacy in the workplace, kicked off in 1996.

A primary concern of US employers is that they will find the numbers of skilled workers that will be necessary to compete in a global economy. Workforce requirements and needs are changing so rapidly that employers fear skills considered sufficient today will not be adequate in the years to come. Rather than sit by idly and depend solely on the efforts of the secondary school systems, some companies, recognizing the crucial importance of literacy and other learning skills, have taken it upon themselves to provide advanced education to their workforce.

One such company is Milford Fabricating Company, in Detroit, Michigan. Milford is a specialty-item, prototype supplier to automakers. Milford's technicians take designs from the automakers and produce tools and parts that are then used in the production of automobiles. Because of the technical work of the company, Milford's employees must possess a high degree of literacy and be highly trained in specialized processes. To ensure continuing quality, Milford designed an employee educational program that includes a balance of on-the-job training and advanced education.

The Milford apprentice program recruits students from mainly Detroit-area high schools and trade centers. The apprentice program takes five years to complete, and all employees are required to go through it. Employees can participate in manufacturing (i.e., tool-and-die making) or maintenance (i.e., machine repair) apprenticeships. What sets the Milford program apart from other apprenticeship programs is the requirement that workers must also complete 24 courses (including classes in math, drafting, and programming) at an area community college. Applicants who qualify for recruitment are interviewed and informed of the commitment they must make to be considered for placement in the Milford program.

The cost to Milford of this program for an average of 70 apprentices is high. Milford's annual training and education bill exceeds $300,000 because the company covers all training expenses, including tuition, books, and work time lost to training. Once their apprenticeship is completed, Milford then offers employees an incentive to further their education: pay increases are given as courses are completed. Opportunities for advancement in the company also directly relate to the number of courses the employee has taken after completion of the apprentice program. In fact, all of Milford's top management people have come from inside the corporation.

Sources: "Campaign Spells Out Concern for Adult Literacy," *People Management,* April 18, 1996, pp. 6–7; P C Nwakeze and L H Seller, "Adult Literacy Programs: What Students Say," *Adult Learning,* September–October 1993, pp. 17–24; T Henry, "90 Million Can Barely Read, Write," *USA Today,* September 9, 1993, p. 1A; and "A Burgeoning Movement," *American Machinist,* August 1993, p. 42.

Specific Socially Responsible Activities

So far, the discussion has revolved around *abstract* concepts of social responsibility. However, an organization translates its particular abstract concept of social responsibility into concrete expressions via specific, deliberate activities.

Socially responsive activities can be classified in different ways. One such classification provides eight categories of socially responsible actions. A business can take socially responsible actions in its *marketing practices,* for example, by being truthful and complete in its product advertising. The business can also do the same in its *product line* by manufacturing safe, reliable, and high-quality products. For example, Procter & Gamble has developed refill cartons for its laundry detergents;

Scott Paper has developed recycled facial tissues; and Church and Dwight Co. has brought to market a 98 percent phosphate-free dishwashing detergent.[21] Socially responsible activities in *employee education and training* can include effectively preparing employees to perform jobs well and providing them with the means to advance their careers. The accompanying Management Focus provides an example of a company's taking such actions. Concerning *environmental control,* a business may be socially responsible by implementing production technology that reduces the amount of pollutants produced by manufacturing processes.

Actions in *employee relations, benefits, and satisfaction with work* can include providing benefits that accommodate important but unfulfilled employee needs such as providing an on-site day care facility for parent employees. In the area of *employment and advancement of minorities or women,* businesses may choose to be socially responsible by focusing efforts on hiring minorities and encouraging their professional development. Efforts to provide a clean, safe, and comfortable working environment are socially responsible activities in the realm of *employee safety and health.* Finally, some businesses, especially large corporations, focus socially responsible efforts in the area of *corporate philanthropy,* by making donations to universities, arts and cultural foundations, the underprivileged, community development projects, and other groups and causes in society.

Another way to classify socially responsible actions is to identify the *beneficiaries* of each action. As the preceding discussion indicates, the organization's customers benefit in some instances; in others, the employees benefit. Beyond employees and customers are definable interest groups, such as racial and ethnic groups, women's groups, and governmental agencies. In a sense, these groups are other organizations that transact business with the corporation. The focus of these transactions is not exchange of economic goods and services but exchange of concessions based on relative power. In addition to customers, employees, and interest groups, there are ill-defined beneficiaries such as future generations, society at large, and the common good. Activities such as assistance to the arts are directed to these beneficiaries. For simplicity, two general classes of beneficiaries can be identified: *internal* and *external.*

Internal Beneficiaries

Three groups of internal beneficiaries are apparent: *customers, employees,* and *shareholders* (owners). Each of these groups has an immediate and often conflicting stake in the organization. Corporate activities in response to each group can be classified as obligatory, reactive, or responsive.

Responsibilities to Customers.   The issue of social responsibility toward customers is relatively fixed at one extreme (as in instances where specific legal directives define product safety) and quite fluid at the other (as in instances where there are general expectations regarding price–quality relationships). Many firms choose to meet their responsibilities to customers by responding promptly to complaints, by providing complete and accurate product information, by implementing advertising programs that are completely truthful regarding product performance, and by taking an active role in developing products responding to customers' social concerns. For example, Carrier Corporation recently addressed consumers' growing environmental concerns by introducing refrigerators that have no or low ozone-depletion potential, improve indoor air quality, maintain noise levels to a minimum, use materials more efficiently, and are smaller in size.[22] And in the home furnishings industry, emphasis has also been placed on targeting the environmentally friendly product niche with the introduction of all-natural fabrics as a substitute for synthetic furniture coverings.[23]

Responsibilities to Employees.   Management's responsibilities to employees can be minimally discharged by meeting the legal requirements that relate to employee–employer relationships. Such laws address issues associated with the physical conditions of work (particularly the safety and health issues), wage and hour provisions, unions and unionization, and the like. The thrust of these laws is to encourage management to create safe and productive workplaces within which employees' basic civil rights are not compromised. In addition to these responsibilities, the modern corporate practice of providing fringe benefits—retirement funds, health and hospitalization insurance, and accident insurance—has extended the range of socially obligated activity. In some instances, these practices are in response to concerted employee pressure, typically through union activity.

A company may assume other socially responsible activities, such as providing comprehensive employee training, career development, and counseling, and establishing employee assistance programs (EAPs) to help employees with drug and alcohol problems. In 1991, three-fourths of all Fortune 500 companies and approximately 12,000 smaller firms had EAPs.[24]

More companies are realizing that employees are experiencing greater difficulties in meeting the responsibilities of job and family. The growing incidence of two-career couples with children and the longer life span of the elderly mean that more employees need assistance in caring for their children and aging parents.

Companies are responding in several ways. One of the tools used by firms is flextime.[25] The concept of flextime refers to a variety of flexible arrangements including unconventional hours, job sharing, leaves of absence, and working at home. From a company's perspective, allowing employees to work fewer and more pliable hours is a powerful way to attract and retain top-caliber people.

A growing number of businesses provide some form of assistance for elder and child care. In 1987, IBM launched the first nationwide elder care referral service for its employees after learning that over 30 percent of its workforce cares for elderly relatives. Over 4,000 of IBM's employees and 33,000 retirees called for help during the service's first month of activity.[26] Lancaster Laboratories and Stride Rite Shoes are innovative in that they both provide on-site, intergenerational care centers.[27] These centers provide day care for both the elderly and children in one location, taking advantage of the natural attraction between youngsters and elders.

These efforts are socially reactive in nature if they are responses to pressures from employees or external parties. The efforts are socially responsive if the organization proactively initiates these activities in the absence of any substantial pressure. Note, however, that like many socially responsible actions, activities undertaken in the interest of employees also benefit the organization. For example, several companies that have proactively established day care centers report substantial improvement in attendance and productivity among participating employees.[28]

Some employee benefits result in a trade-off between the employer and employee. In many companies, executives are asked to work longer hours. A recent poll of CEOs reveals that 62 percent of the respondents believe that company executives are working longer hours today than 10 years ago.[29] Expectations are that middle managers and high-level executives should work between 50 to 59 hours per week. Corporate restructuring, employee cutbacks, and heightened global competition are all factors contributing to this trend. The danger is that increases in the amount of work demanded by corporations of their managers can lead to higher levels of stress and employee burnout. Indeed, in Japan when a worker dies from exhaustion, they call it *karoshi* or "death from overwork." American corporations must become increasingly cognizant of the demands placed on their employees.

Responsibility to Shareholders.   Management has a responsibility to disclose fully and accurately to shareholders its use of corporate resources and the results of those uses. The law guarantees shareholders the right to financial information and establishes minimums of public disclosure. The fundamental right of a shareholder is not to be guaranteed a profit but to be guaranteed information on which a prudent investment decision can be based. The ultimate action that a shareholder can take is to sell the stock and cease to have an ownership interest.[30]

Many individuals would argue that management's first responsibility is to the shareholder. In fact, those persons would contend that any managerial action that goes beyond socially obligated behavior to the benefit of any group other than shareholders is a violation of management's (and therefore social) responsibility. At the same time, there is evidence that firms that aggressively pursue socially responsive behavior are more profitable than those that do not. The evidence to support this position is controversial because there is little agreement on how social responsibility can be measured and how it should be related to performance measures such as profit and stock prices, the interests of shareholders. Two published reviews suggest that if there is a relationship between socially responsible behavior and corporate performance, it is one that must be taken on faith.[31]

The internal beneficiaries of corporate actions are the focus of much of management's socially obligated behavior. In their relations with customers, employees, and shareholders, managers are most likely to be judged socially responsible. The relationships between the corporation and its internal beneficiaries are so circumscribed by law, regulation, and custom that the corporation is bound to act out of legal obligation. To do so involves no particular accomplishment for the corporation. Failure to act legally or in the perceived best interests of shareholders, whether intentional or not, can lead to all sorts of legal problems and social condemnation of the corporation and its management. Today, more and more individual shareholders and investor groups are challenging management's actions either through legal suits, shareholder resolutions, or outright battles for control of the company's board of directors.[32] Increasingly, managers and shareholders are having to forge new relationships in which shareholders are more patient in exchange for being given more say.[33]

Corporations have greater opportunities to be socially reactive and responsive in matters involving external beneficiaries.

External Beneficiaries

The external beneficiaries of corporate behavior are *specific* and *general*. Both types benefit from the organization's action, even though they may have no direct or apparent stake in it.

Specific External Beneficiaries.   Modern societies consist of diverse interest groups working to further the well-being of their members. These groups represent rather well-defined populations of individuals seeking to redress historical grievances: minorities and ethnic groups, women, the disabled, and the aged. Such groups pursue their interests by bringing political and popular opinion to bear on corporate actions. Some are able to have laws implemented that force corporations to support their efforts. For example, equal employment opportunity and affirmative action legislation creates corporate obligations to recruit, hire, and train women and members of minority and ethnic groups. The fundamental contention of these groups is that they have been discriminated against in the past and that corporations have played a big role in that discrimination. Thus, a larger burden of responsibility must be borne by corporations to erase the vestiges of historical discrimination and to create a new environment of equal access to employment opportunities and economic advancement.

Corporate actions involving specific external beneficiaries can be obligatory, reactive, or responsive. Obligatory actions are in response to antidiscrimination laws and regulations. The corporation can be judged both socially and legally irresponsible if it violates these laws. But beyond minimal compliance, a corporation has considerable latitude in the rigor with which it pursues affirmative action programs. How rapidly it fills its managerial ranks with minorities and women is largely a matter of discretion, so long as good faith can be demonstrated. A corporation can be deemed socially reactive if it goes beyond the letter of the law in implementing affirmative action. Socially responsive behavior not only seeks solutions to the immediate problems but also attempts to go to the very heart of the causes. Such behavior could include doing business with minority-owned businesses, creating programs to train the chronically unemployed, and initiating career development programs for women. When such efforts are not prompted by law or pressure, they are clearly socially responsive.

The most important characteristic of these actions—whether they be obligatory, reactive, or responsive—is that the economic, social, and political well-being of a specific group of individuals is enhanced through the corporation's efforts.

General External Beneficiaries.   Programs involving general external beneficiaries often are considered socially responsible because they elicit corporate efforts to solve or prevent general social problems. Companies have launched efforts to solve or prevent environmental or ecological problems such as water, air, and noise pollution and waste and radiation disposal. Actions by several companies provide examples of activities in this area.[34] Japan's Hitachi Corporation pioneered the technology for removing nitrogen oxides from power plant exhausts and also supplies sulfur-removal and heat-recovery systems to customers worldwide. Saab-Scania NA, the Swedish auto company, is redesigning its car air conditioners to reduce the destruction of the ozone layer. Hewlett-Packard Company produces equipment that analyzes waste samples to identify the toxic chemicals present. On a worldwide basis, companies are taking a more proactive approach to managing and monitoring their environmental operations. A more in-depth look at what several American companies are doing in this area was profiled in the Management in Action section, "The Growing Green Revolution," at the beginning of this chapter.

Other organizations have acted to upgrade education, the arts, and community health through gifts and donations of executive time. For example, New York Life Insurance Company is one of a growing number of companies donating funds for AIDS research and public education programs. New York Life donated over $1 million to fund an AIDS public information advertising campaign in New York and sponsored a fund-raising benefit that raised $2 million for AIDS research.[35]

Some organizations have launched efforts to improve the quality of governmental management by granting leaves of absence for executives who take government positions. Other organizations have contributed to philanthropic causes such as the United Way to help upgrade the quality of community life. Companies have also made contributions to overall community development. One notable example is the Minnesota 5 Percent Club, a group of 45 companies. Each member donates at least 5 percent of its taxable profits to the development of the twin cities, Minneapolis–St. Paul.[36]

Corporations have considerable freedom in this area of social responsibility. They can choose which specific problems to become involved with—or they can choose not to become involved at all. But business leaders recognize the growing importance of issues such as the condition of the environment. For example: "In recent industrial history, few public policy issues have had the social, political, and economic impact that this one [health, safety, and the environment] is having on many companies."[37]

Changing Expectations for Corporate Performance

No thoughtful person can question the responsibility of a corporation to act within the law. Society expects no less of an individual citizen. Even so, people disagree over other corporate responsibilities—those described in the previous section as socially reactive and socially responsive behavior. Does a corporation have any responsibility to support the arts, rebuild inner-city housing, or make charitable contributions? Some people argue that corporations have been legally required to bear a disproportionate share of the cost of correcting historical discrimination in employment and damage to the environment. Yet the prevailing mood is that large organizations, particularly corporations, are not only *capable* of contributing to social progress beyond that of producing safe and reliable goods and services but are *responsible* for doing so. This attitude did not appear suddenly. It is simply a contemporary expression of the dynamic and evolutionary relationship between society and its institutions.

The Historical Evolution of Expectations

One scholar has observed that the relationship between organizations and society has changed in the aftermath of three business crises.[38]

The Crisis of 1870.   The industrialization of America and the incorporation of its business occurred during the pre– and post–Civil War eras; the great impetus for the development of corporate power was the mobilization required by the Civil War. During the 1860s, the captains of industry—John D Rockefeller, J Pierpont Morgan, Jay Gould, and Andrew Carnegie—were creating the great railroad, steel, coal, sugar, tobacco, and oil corporations. In comparison to smaller, more traditional proprietorships and partnerships, these corporations had tremendous power—for good and for evil. The abuse of this power, in the form of kickbacks, discriminatory pricing, lockouts, and the manipulation of commodity prices, led to a public outcry for legal action. Consequently, Congress enacted various laws related to rate regulation, fair-trade practices, and labor. The landmark legislation was the Sherman Act of 1890.

The Crisis of 1930.   The passage of the Sherman Act did not reverse the trend toward larger and larger business organizations because the underlying forces were irreversible. Business organizations tended then, as today, to equate growth with profitability—the bigger, the better. Three merger movements occurred in 1870, 1890, and 1920.[39] The effect of these mergers was to create even larger legal corporate entities that enabled the country to mobilize and fight a world war. By 1914, the production of goods and services in the United States was *more than a third of the world's total industrial output.*[40]

The Roaring Twenties were aptly named. More and more people were sharing the fruits of America's industrial development. Thus, the circle of beneficiaries of corporate action widened beyond a small group of owners. Many Americans owned shares of stock. Ever more Americans worked for big business. And ever more Americans were daily affected by the actions of corporations.

The Great Depression brought an abrupt halt to the euphoric attitude that unchecked business could bring prosperity to all. In fact, the blame for the Great Depression was placed squarely on business. In a sense, the country felt that business had betrayed the country's faith. As a result, the power of government to regulate and monitor business practice increased sharply through the efforts of President Franklin D Roosevelt and supporters of his New Deal reforms. Government action cemented a relationship between corporations and society that placed responsibility on business for fair treatment of customers, employees, stockholders, suppliers, and other groups in society that have a *direct stake* in the corporation's actions. Much of contemporary corporate legal responsibility (obligatory responsibility) can be traced to the crisis of 1930. The era following the 1930 crisis also marked the beginning of society's expectations for socially reactive behavior. After World War II—a watershed historical event—business regained the country's confidence as a provider of industrial goods. Employment soared, savings accounts swelled, and corporations converted to production of consumer goods. The country put behind it the experience, if not the memory, of the Depression. Thus, society turned again to the corporation as a singular source of the good life, but the definition of the good life was beginning to change.

The Crisis of 1970.   The closer one gets to contemporary history, the more unreliable hindsight becomes. Whether this crisis began in 1970 or 1960, the fact remains that society now expects more of its corporations than it did in 1930 and much more than in 1870.[41] But how much more? And specifically for what? The answers to these questions are now being hammered out in political debates, shaped by public relations efforts, and argued in public forums.

The background of the 1970 crisis was an uninterrupted 20-year period during which two economies came into being. One economy, the *public economy,* is run by the government. It regularly intervenes in business practice, redistributes income through taxation and entitlement programs, and regulates labeling, packaging, advertising, and many other business factors. According to some estimates, the public economy makes up one-fourth of the national social system.[42] The second economy, the *private economy,* makes up the remaining three-fourths. Of this portion, the 500 largest firms account for two-thirds of all manufacturing. These two economies confront and accommodate each other. Each has power over the other, and each represents different yet compatible interests.

But in the 1960s and 1970s, the business/government-as-usual relationship was challenged. New ideas—such as consumerism, feminism, environmentalism, and ecology—grew out of the social unrest fed by the unpopular Vietnam War and the Watergate scandal. As a result, new demands were made on business that went far beyond social obligations as defined by law.

The Contemporary Expectation for Corporate Social Responsiveness

Events of the 1980s and 1990s have reinforced the attitude that corporations must react to problems created by their own actions. More important, the 1970 crisis initiated the idea that corporations should be proactive, that they should be responsive to a wide range of social problems because they have the expertise and power to do so. The current debate on the social responsibility of business is not concerned with obligatory behavior: business must be law abiding. The debate is seldom stated in terms of reactive behavior: business should be responsible for its actions. Rather, the debate has to do with socially responsive behavior.

Managerial Ethics

The word **ethics,** as commonly understood, refers to principles of behavior that distinguish between good, bad, right, and wrong.[43] The purpose of ethics, or a code of ethics, is to enable individuals to make choices among alternative behaviors. The importance of ethics increases in proportion to the *consequences* of the outcome of a behavior. As an individual's actions become more consequential for others, the ethics of that individual become more important.

The role and state of ethics in American businesses have become a growing concern among managers and the public. Several factors have contributed to this concern. First, scandals involving unethical activities by several major corporations (e.g., NYNEX, General Electric, Shearson Lehman, and General Dynamics Corporation) have been widely publicized.[44] Over the past 15 years, over two-thirds of the Fortune 500 companies have been involved in some form of illegal behavior.[45]

Studies also indicate that many managers feel pressured by their employers to commit ethically questionable acts. In one study of 1,500 top, middle, and first-level managers, more than 40 percent of the respondents reported they had compromised their personal principles to meet an organizational demand.[46] Other recent surveys have found that many managers—on average about 75 percent of those polled—feel pressured to compromise their ethical values to meet corporate objectives.[47] These developments have led many individuals and managers to believe that the level of ethics in business has declined over the last decade.[48]

A second factor causing business ethics to become a topic of concern has been the realization that ethical misconduct by management can be extremely costly for the company and for society as a whole. Shearson Lehman and General Electric, for example, each paid several million dollars in criminal penalties and fines for their managers' misconduct. Beech-Nut Nutrition Corporation has yet to recover from the damage done to its reputation caused by its selling tainted apple juice. Unethical behavior on the part of several key executives of Drexel Burnham Lambert not only forced the company into bankruptcy proceedings but also cast a pall over the entire junk bond market.[49]

Third, both managers and the public are realizing that the dynamics of ethics in management decision making are often a complex and challenging phenomenon; determining what is and isn't ethical is often difficult to do. In some situations, the task is easy. We know, for example, that accepting bribes from a supplier is clearly unethical, as is falsifying records or dishonest advertising in promoting a product. However, the ethics of a business situation are often more complex. Every day, managers face ethical questions that have no easy answers. What, for example, is a "fair" profit? What is a "just" price for a product? How "honest" should a company be with the press?

Because the ethics of a business situation are often complex, managers sometimes differ in their views of which actions are ethical. In most business situations, ethical decision making does not involve a choice between what's right and what's wrong; rather, it involves "conflicts of right versus right."[50] Currently, several ethical issues are being debated in the business environment. For example, managers are grappling with the ethics of employee surveillance (monitoring their computer work and telephones to measure employee productivity) and of testing employees for drug use and AIDS.[51] One upcoming ethical controversy in the US business community is the projected future use of genetic testing by employers.

Because the ethics of managerial decision making are often complex and managers often disagree on what constitutes an ethical decision, two subjects are particularly relevant: (1) the basis that the individual manager can use for determining which alternative to choose in a decision-making situation, and (2) what organizations can do to ensure that managers follow ethical standards in their decision making. We discuss these topics in the following section.

Ethical Standards

Managers must reconcile competing values in making decisions. They make decisions that have consequences for themselves, the organization that employs them, and the society in which they and the organization exist. For example, managers can be called on to make decisions that can be good for them but bad for the organization and society. In general, managers' decisions affect people's lives and well-being, determine "fair" resource allocation, and implement and interpret organizational rules and policies.[52]

Philosophers, logicians, and theologians have studied ethical issues. Their ideas provide guidelines, but only guidelines, for making value-laden decisions. Figure 4–2 depicts a simplified model of ethical behavior with three different bases for developing ethical guidelines.[53]

Maximum personal benefits (egoism), depicted on the vertical axis, can be the sole basis for decision making. A completely selfish individual would always do what is personally beneficial. An extreme view of this ethical approach is that individuals should always seek that which is pleasurable; and conversely, one should avoid pain. Managers driven by egoism would evaluate alternative actions in terms of personal benefit—salary, prestige, power, or whatever they consider valuable. If the action also proves beneficial to the organization and society, all well and good. But these other benefits are incidental and not the primary intent of the manager.

Maximum social benefits (altruism), depicted on the horizontal axis, can also be the sole consideration in decision making. An altruistic individual selects courses of action that provide maximum social benefit. A manager who follows this ethical guideline would measure right and wrong as the greatest happiness to the greatest number. As a practical matter, decisions based on only altruistic concerns are particularly difficult to make. For example, altruism provides no means for judging the relative benefits to individuals, unless one is willing to assume that each has the same interest in and receives the same benefit from a decision.

Obligation to a formal principle is shown between the extremes of egoism and altruism. Egoism contends that an act is good if the individual benefits from it. Altruism contends that an act is good if society benefits from it. The criteria for both are consequences. In contrast to them, the ethic of adhering to a formal principle is based on the idea that *the rightness or wrongness of an act depends on principle, not consequences.*

Those who adhere to principle in judging their actions could, for example, follow the Golden Rule: "Do unto others what you would have others do unto you." Or they

---

Figure 4–2   **An Ethical Framework**

Ethical behavior involves choosing what is good for the individual—egoism—and what is good for society—altruism—with possible formal principles.

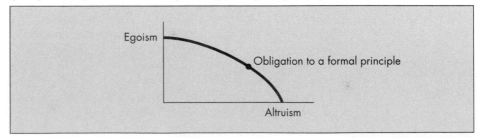

might decide that each action should be judged by the **categorical imperative**: "Act as if the maxim of your action were to become a general law binding on everyone."

This idea that actions can be judged by one particular principle is unacceptable to many individuals. Some prefer a *pluralistic* approach that would contain several principles arranged in a hierarchy of importance. For example, one writer proposes that managers can be guided in decision making by adhering to the following principles: (1) Place the interests of society before the interests of the organization. (2) Place the interests of the organization before managers' private interests. (3) Reveal the truth in all instances of organizational and personal involvement.[54] These three principles provide guidelines but not answers. The manager must determine the relative benefits to society, company, and self. The determination of benefits and beneficiaries is seldom simple, but the advantage of a pluralistic approach to ethical decision making is that the decision maker who intends *to do right* has the basis for evaluating decisions.

The Organization's Role in Ethical Behavior

The approaches to developing guidelines for ethical behavior have so far focused on the individual manager. Indeed, a critical first step in evaluating the ethics of an organization is to understand the level of ethics development among its employees.[55] However, many observers assert that the organization should play a major role in ensuring that its managers act ethically in managing the firm. The organization's participation is understandable, given that the organization is ultimately responsible for the consequences of the decisions that its managers make.

Although a company is ultimately responsible, surprisingly few organizations have traditionally provided managers with specific guidelines concerning ethics in decision making. However, given the increasing concern about ethics in organizations, a growing number of companies are attempting to provide guidance for their managers.[56]

At the core of many companies' efforts is the development of a corporate *code of ethics* (often called a *code of conduct*). Typically established by top management, a code usually consists of a written statement of a company's values, beliefs, and norms of ethical behavior.[57] Johnson & Johnson's (J&J) credo, one example of a corporate code of ethics, is shown in Figure 4–3. Like many codes, J&J's credo specifies its values and beliefs concerning its relationships and responsibilities toward its different constituents (i.e., customers, employees, community, and shareholders). The credo also states Johnson & Johnson's objectives concerning each constituency and norms of behavior such as "supporting good works and charities" and "encouraging civic improvements."

Ideally, a code of ethics should provide employees with direction in dealing with ethical dilemmas, clarify the organization's position regarding areas of ethical uncertainty, and achieve and maintain overall ongoing conduct that the organization views as ethical and proper.[58] For example, a code of conduct might contain policies addressing the following specific areas:

- Confidentiality
- Conflicts of interest
- Accepting gifts
- Sexual harassment
- Supporting equal employment rights
- Environmental issues

FIGURE 4–3   Johnson & Johnson's Code of Ethics

A code of ethics that illustrates straight-forward language.

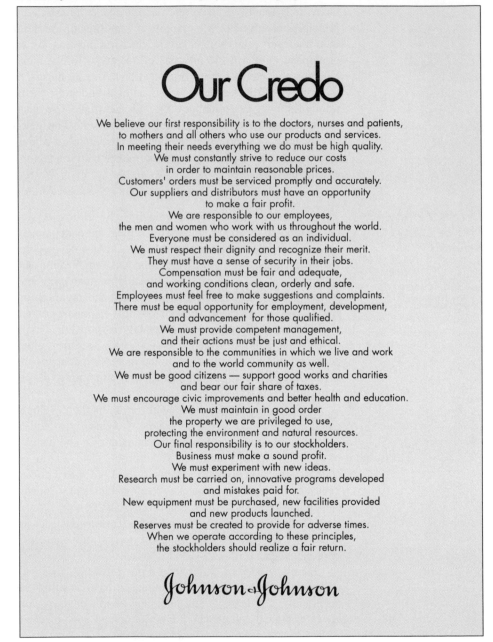

Our Credo

We believe our first responsibility is to the doctors, nurses and patients,
to mothers and all others who use our products and services.
In meeting their needs everything we do must be high quality.
We must constantly strive to reduce our costs
in order to maintain reasonable prices.
Customers' orders must be serviced promptly and accurately.
Our suppliers and distributors must have an opportunity
to make a fair profit.
We are responsible to our employees,
the men and women who work with us throughout the world.
Everyone must be considered as an individual.
We must respect their dignity and recognize their merit.
They must have a sense of security in their jobs.
Compensation must be fair and adequate,
and working conditions clean, orderly and safe.
Employees must feel free to make suggestions and complaints.
There must be equal opportunity for employment, development,
and advancement for those qualified.
We must provide competent management,
and their actions must be just and ethical.
We are responsible to the communities in which we live and work
and to the world community as well.
We must be good citizens — support good works and charities
and bear our fair share of taxes.
We must encourage civic improvements and better health and education.
We must maintain in good order
the property we are privileged to use,
protecting the environment and natural resources.
Our final responsibility is to our stockholders.
Business must make a sound profit.
We must experiment with new ideas.
Research must be carried on, innovative programs developed
and mistakes paid for.
New equipment must be purchased, new facilities provided
and new products launched.
Reserves must be created to provide for adverse times.
When we operate according to these principles,
the stockholders should realize a fair return.

Johnson & Johnson

Used with permission of Johnson & Johnson Co.

- Product and workplace safety
- Employee health screening
- Stakeholder interests[59]

Yet, all too often, even with policies in place, codes of conduct do not achieve their purposes. Indeed, many are surprisingly ineffective. Results of a recent study found that organizations with ethics codes were more often found in violation of federal regulations than were organizations with no established codes.[60]

Codes can be ineffective for several reasons. Many ethics codes tend to be legalistic, focusing more on explaining the strict legalities and illegalities of doing business than on tackling the more difficult and complex question of ethics and values.[61] Many codes also tend to focus on conflicts of interest and infractions that employees commit against the company that affect profits, rather than on infractions committed by the company that affect the community and other constituencies.[62]

Further, codes of ethics must be framed in the context of world citizenry so employees have the ability to adapt to local customs while still complying with the values that define the corporate charter.[63] Business ethics have not yet been globalized, and the norms of ethical behavior continue to vary widely in different nations. For example, expensive gift giving is considered an acceptable way of doing business in Japan. However, in the United States, such actions can be construed as an unethical form of bribery. Therefore, company policies must be established that simultaneously acknowledge foreign customs while providing acceptable codes of conduct for US managers to follow.

US companies are not alone in being accused of unethical organizational behavior. In South Korea, the diversified industrial giants or *chaebol* have been accused of manipulating land prices and thus depriving Korean citizens of affordable housing.[64] Actions have been taken by the Korean government to force companies such as Hyundai Electronics, Lucky-Goldstar Group, Samsung Electronics, and Daewoo International to sell millions of meters of land back to the public.

Many codes fail because they simply are not proactively implemented or enforced. According to recent studies, fewer than 20 percent of companies with codes have ethics committees to oversee and enforce the codes; less than 10 percent of the companies have officials to help employees deal with ethical issues; and fewer than 1 percent of the companies have published procedures to deal with code violations. As a result, the codes lie dormant and ultimately serve little more than a public relations purpose.[65]

However, organizations have achieved effective, "living" codes of ethics, typically by following a multistep implementation strategy. They first translate values and beliefs into specific ethical standards of behavior. Some standards may exist in the code itself; often even more specific standards for particular situations are developed. For example, a specific behavioral standard for Johnson & Johnson's credo objective of high product quality may be immediately reporting to management any evidence that a product does not meet the company's quality standards.[66] At Northrop, anonymous reporting procedures have been established so employees can come forward when they see instances of wrongdoing without fear of retribution—fear of being labeled as the messenger of bad news.[67]

Besides translating the code into behavior standards, companies with effective ethics codes have determined the actions to be taken when code violations occur, communicated the penalties to employees, and implemented the penalties to ensure code compliance. Xerox Corporation, for example, has dismissed employees both for violations that are serious (taking bribes) and for those that are relatively insignificant (petty cheating on expense accounts). Chemical Bank has likewise fired employees for violating the code, even when such violations were not unlawful. In both cases, actions were taken to communicate the company's commitment to the code and the importance of maintaining ethical behavior.[68]

Many organizations also periodically conduct ethics seminars to keep employees sensitive to the place of ethics in the company and to help them develop skills in handling ethical dilemmas. At Chemical Bank, the company's corporate social policy department provides an ethics course based on ethics cases written by the department and founded on interviews with a cross-section of Chemical Bank managers. The cases represent the most common and perplexing ethics problems encountered on the job, and the training focuses on providing managers with analytical tools and approaches to think through the problems and find solutions.[69]

Many companies with effective ethics programs emphasize the importance of setting realistic performance objectives for subordinates.[70] Setting unreasonable goals has the effect of encouraging unethical behavior to achieve those objectives (e.g., cutting corners, making ethical compromises), especially when the performance goals are tightly linked to rewards.

Establishing the position of an ethics advocate is another often recommended action.[71] The ethics advocate is normally a top-level executive who, in a sense, serves as the organization's full-time ethical conscience. The advocate evaluates the organization's actions from an ethical perspective and vigorously and openly questions the ethical implications of proposed plans of action. At some companies, the ethics advocate also serves as an ombudsperson, someone to whom employees can, with guaranteed anonymity, report ethics violations they have witnessed or express ethical concerns. In many cases, the advocate/ombudsperson is an outsider (such as a retired executive), which ensures independence from management and builds credibility with employees.[72]

Other companies have gone even further in their efforts to be good corporate citizens, hiring lawyers and consultants to act as watchdogs over their activities. For example, California Steel Industries, Inc., a $600 million steelmaker, retained a lawyer to advise them on how to avoid getting sued before they engaged in cleanup activities at a mill site.[73]

Ethics and Social Responsiveness

The relationship between a manager's ethical standards and social responsiveness should be apparent. Ethics serve as a basis for assessing the rightness of potential actions. In a sense, ethical standards are filters that screen actions according to relative rightness. The ideas that have been developed in our discussion of social responsibility, expectations for corporate behavior, and ethics can be integrated as shown in Figure 4–4. Here the corporation is seen as a *means* for achieving the *ends* of various claimants. Social responsibility involves deciding *what* means and *whose* ends are right and good. Ultimately, it is the task of corporate managers to decide the relative rightness of each demand; and ethical standards are the basis for their decisions.

FIGURE 4–4   The Corporation's Social Responsibility and Managerial Ethics

In the final analysis, managerial ethics determine a corporation's socially responsive actions.

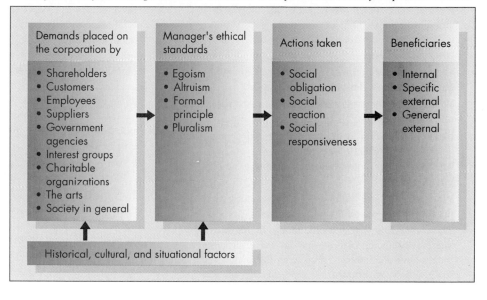

Summary of Key Points

- The term *social responsibility* is popularly used to prescribe and proscribe corporate activity, yet the meaning of social responsibility has many variations. Therefore, it is imperative to define the term when discussing the issue. The various meanings can be sorted into three categories: social obligation, social reaction, and social responsiveness.
- Social obligation means that business is socially responsible when it meets its primary obligation: to pursue a profit for owners within the law. Conversely, a business is socially irresponsible when it pursues activities not related to improving the economic well-being of owners.
- Social reaction means that business is socially responsible when it reacts to prevailing social norms, values, and expectations. The business must sense, understand, and react to what society articulates as representing its expectations. These expectations change with time and place, but in modern times, society has expected business to go beyond its socially obligated behavior of profit seeking as prescribed by law.
- Social responsiveness includes obligatory and reactive behavior but also requires that corporations be proactive and take action to prevent social problems. This meaning places considerable emphasis on the corporation's obligations above and beyond what is legal and expected.
- The activities through which corporations meet their social responsibilities range from producing safe, reliable, quality products to supporting the arts; from providing safe and healthful working conditions to assisting minority enterprises. Each of these activities benefits some group, often

to the disadvantage of some other group. Managers must make choices among various interests both inside and outside the corporation.
- The beneficiaries of corporate action are either internal or external. Internal beneficiaries include customers, owners, and employees. External beneficiaries include groups representing minorities, women, the disabled, and the aged.
- The contemporary demands placed on corporations are the result of an evolutionary process. In earlier times, when corporations were relatively insignificant, society expected them to meet their social obligations. As corporations became larger and more pervasive, society's expectations shifted toward social reaction and responsive corporate behavior.
- Managers are the referees of competing demands on corporate resources. Their ethical standards—criteria for rightness and goodness—filter these demands and determine which will be satisfied. Ethical standards are influenced by the principles of maximum personal benefits (egoism), maximum social benefits (altruism), and obligation to a formal principle.
- Managers and the public are increasingly concerned about ethics in US business because many believe that ethics have declined in the last decade, the costs of unethical conduct by management are often high, and the dynamics of ethics in management are complex and challenging.
- Some organizations are responding to these concerns by developing ethics codes, establishing training seminars in ethics for employees, and creating the position of ethics advocate/ombudsperson.

Discussion and Review Questions

1. Describe the steps an organization could take to become more socially responsible. In your discussion, include some examples of how these steps would apply to both internal and external beneficiaries.

2. How can an organization, through its guidelines and actions, influence an individual manager to make ethical decisions? Provide some examples.

3. Which of the three meanings of social responsibility reflects your opinion? Explain.

4. Identify a situation in which an organization might be socially responsible to one group of internal beneficiaries but not socially responsible to another group.

5. What are the basic arguments for and against each of the three meanings of social responsibility?

6. The corporation is responsible to a wide range of interest groups, on both an internal and external basis. Should any one interest group (e.g., employees, shareholders, government, or the general public) be given more priority? Why?

7. Can you think of a situation you have been in where your attitudes and views toward ethical behavior and/or social responsibility conflicted with those of your peers? Explain.

8. One manager's comment: "Since most foreign competitors do not follow or even *have* strict codes of ethics, it is unfair to expect American companies to adhere to rigid standards. Rather, when operating overseas, American companies should have the right to discard domestic standards of ethical conduct." Do you agree? Explain.

9. In your opinion, what is the greatest challenge in developing an ethical environment within a business?

10. Much has been written of responsibilities in achieving ethical standards of behavior in a company's relations with internal and external beneficiaries. However, little has been mentioned of these beneficiaries' responsibilities to the corporation. Do you believe they have any? Why or why not?

CASE 4–1
BUILDING ETHICS AT GENERAL DYNAMICS

For years, General Dynamics Corporation enjoyed a productive relationship with the federal government as the nation's largest defense contractor. However, through much of the 1970s and 1980s General Dynamics came under heavy fire for allegedly overcharging the government. At one point, according to a federal investigative agency, the Pentagon froze all payments to the company to retrieve almost $250 million in overcharge billings. Criminal charges were filed against General Dynamics by the Justice Department.

Most observers asserted that something was clearly wrong at General Dynamics. Indeed, the situation culminated in an agreement with the Navy to either implement an ethics program or lose the Navy's business. Faced with this prospect, top management at General Dynamics set about building a sense of ethical conduct at the company via development of such a program. The official objectives of the ethics program were to support individual employees in their daily business conduct, to enhance the administrative performance of the company in basic relationships, and to help build trust between the company and its customers, suppliers, employees, shareholders, and the communities in which the company functioned. Specifically, the ethics program included the following:

A Written Code of Conduct

The core of the company's efforts was a 20-page publication that provided guidelines for ethical conduct in business situations and decision making. This blue book described employees' responsibilities for maintaining the company's stipulated ethical standards and stated the penalties for violation of the standards. The book also specified individuals with whom employees could discuss problems or questions concerning the application of the company's code. The code also contained an invaluable squeal clause that protected employees who identified individuals violating the ethical standards.

About 103,000 employees of General Dynamics received blue books during sessions with their supervisors. In the sessions, the standards were discussed along with how to apply them in different on-the-job situations. Employees were asked to sign an acknowledgment card stipulating that they understood the code of conduct and that the code was company policy. Most workers signed the cards although they were not required to. However, reading the blue book and signing the acknowledgment card became a prerequisite of employment for new applicants.

Ethics Training

General Dynamics conducted ethics awareness seminars for all employees. The workshop's format included a film concerning the company's values, exercises about ways to resolve ethical dilemmas encountered on the job, and information and discussion about the company's overall ethics program. Seminars for upper-level managers included participation in case studies of ethics.

Ethics Program Directors

Throughout the corporation, about 40 employees were named to serve as ethics program directors. Their responsibility was to answer employees' questions about the company's code and to counsel employees on how to handle particular ethics dilemmas. Each director was to report directly to the respective subsidiary president.

Ethics Hot Line

General Dynamics established 30 hot lines throughout the company and a toll-free number for calling company headquarters. Ethics program directors operated the hot lines. The purpose of the hot lines was to provide a mechanism for requesting information or counsel in handling ethical dilemmas and for reporting incidents of potential misconduct. In one year of the hot lines' operations, over 3,600 calls were received. As a result, General Dynamics imposed more than 100 sanctions for misconduct. The sanctions ranged from warnings to dismissal and referral for criminal prosecution.

Program Structure

General Dynamics's overall ethics program was coordinated by a full-time corporate ethics director. This person worked with the company's ethics steering committee, composed of the heads of the company's major functional departments. The committee provided overall program direction and was responsible for policy development. A committee of outside directors was also formed, holding responsibility for reviewing and approving ethics policy for General Dynamics.

Has the ethics program worked? In many respects, yes. Results of numerous studies conducted among General Dynamics employees indicate overall satisfaction with the program's effectiveness. As evidence, respondents cite high usage of the various channels for complaints and inquiries, high levels of employee trust in the program, fair and timely investigations and appropriate corrective actions, and positive attitudes among new employees toward customers and positive public relations.

During the course of the years following implementation of the program, General Dynamics has not been involved in the series of sweeping scandals involving government contractors. Further, representatives of the Navy and other government agencies give high marks to the ethics program as an example of a "model program" for other contractors to follow.

However, a closer look reveals the fact that some questionable activities are still occurring within the company and that some discontent exists among employees. The ethics program was originally sold to employees using two arguments: Being ethical is good business, and being ethical will enhance the quality of work life. As a result, employees came to expect increased concern for their welfare by managers, increased humanistic treatment by their supervisors, and increased participation in work-related decisions. By all accounts, a significant number of employees still feel these expectations have not been realized.

There have also been numerous complaints regarding supervisor use of subtle forms of retaliation (i.e., assigning undesirable tasks or creating inflexible working conditions) against employees who were known to use the ethics hot line. Further, while General Dynamics has succeeded in placating government officials, it has drawn the ire of other internal beneficiaries. In 1993, charges were filed against top officials by stockholders alleging that the company had misled investors in order to buy back its stock at artificially low prices. Thus, in some respects, the program has failed to live up to its billing.

Questions for Analysis

1. Do you feel General Dynamics took a reactive or proactive approach to developing an ethics program? Does the choice of approach influence a program's outcomes? Why or why not?

2. Evaluate the effect that implementation of the ethics program had on the various internal beneficiary groups. Were employee expectations regarding improvements in the quality of work life realistic? Discuss.

3. Based on your reading of this case, what recommendations would you provide to companies that do not currently have ethics programs in place? What further actions would you recommend that General Dynamics take?

Sources: Anonymous, "The Problem with Bribery," *Harvard Business Review*, September–October 1996, p. 58; R. A. Barker, "An Evaluation of the Ethics Program at General Dynamics," *Journal of Business Ethics* 12 (1993), pp. 165–77; "General Dynamics, Its Chairman Named in Holder's Lawsuit," *The Wall Street Journal*, March 8, 1993, p. B4.

Video Case

The High Bid Dilemma

This video case provides students with the opportunity to view the possibility of conflict of interest when dealing with an outside vendor.

A purchasing agent (PA) and his assistant are reviewing bids from seven companies to determine which company should receive a contract for bronze-facing a clutch. The PA's assistant proposes that the bid should be awarded to Metaltech, the low bidder, which is located some 300 miles away. His boss, the PA agent, leans toward Spin Cast Systems, a nearby company, which has submitted a much higher bid. Both companies submitting bids have the ability to provide a quality product complete with delivery and support capabilities.

The PA attempts to persuade his assistant that the contract award should be awarded to Spin Cast Systems despite its higher bid that will create a budgetary problem. He informs his assistant that he has used Spin Cast's services previously.

Moreover, Greg Sommers, the president of Spin Cast, is his personal friend, his fraternity brother, and his sailing companion. The PA tells his assistant, "You take care of your suppliers and they'll take care of you." In fact, to show his assistant that Sommers is a "nice guy," the PA will ask Sommers to invite the assistant to a house party.

Critical Thinking Questions

1. Does the issue of a "conflict of interest" surface in this exercise? If so, how? If not, why not?
2. Will the purchasing assistant compromise his own ethics if he allows his boss to award the bid to Spin Cast Systems even though such an award will create a budget overrun and does not follow company regulations?
3. Does the purchasing agent's assistant have any possible options if his boss decides to award the bid to Spin Cast?

Experiential Exercise
Ethical Dilemmas

Purpose

This activity is designed to illustrate the complexity of ethical decision making and how people can differ in their views of what is and is not ethical behavior.

The Exercise in Class

The following four situations are often encountered in the workplace and raise ethical issues. Read each scenario and place yourself in the position of the respective decision maker. What would you do?

The Roundabout Raise.   When Joe asks for a raise, his boss praises his work but says the company's rigid budget won't allow any further merit raises for the time being. Instead, the boss suggests that the company "won't look too closely at your expense accounts for a while." Should Joe take this as authorization to pad his expense account on the grounds that he is simply getting the same money he deserves through a different route, or should he not take this roundabout raise?

Your decision:

The Faked Degree.   Bill has done a sound job for more than a year. The boss learns that Bill got the job by claiming to have a college degree, although he actually never graduated. Should his boss dismiss him for submitting a fraudulent résumé or overlook the false claim because Bill has otherwise proved to be a conscientious and honorable worker, and making an issue of the lack of a degree might ruin Bill's career?

Your decision:

Sneaking Phone Calls.   Helen discovers that a fellow employee regularly makes about $100 a month worth of personal long-distance telephone calls from an office telephone. Should Helen report the employee to the company or disregard the calls on the grounds that many people make personal calls at the office?

Your decision:

Cover-Up Temptation.   Bill discovers that the chemical plant he manages is creating slightly more water pollution in a nearby lake than is legally permitted. Revealing the problem will bring considerable unfavorable publicity to the plant, hurt the lakeside town's resort business, and create a scare in the community. Solving the problem will cost the company more than $100,000. It is unlikely that outsiders will discover the problem. The violation poses no danger whatever to people. At most, it will endanger a small number of fish. Should Bill reveal the problem despite the cost to his company or consider the problem as little more than a technicality and disregard it?

Your decision:

1. Write your decision for each scenario on a sheet of paper.
2. After everyone has completed step 1, your instructor will discuss the class responses to each situation. The instructor will also provide you with the general responses of about 1,500 adults and 400 middle

managers who completed the exercise as a part of a *Wall Street Journal*/Gallup Poll on ethics in America.

3. Compare your responses to those of the general public and the executives. What factors account for any differences between your responses and their decisions?

The Learning Message

This exercise demonstrates the complexities of ethical considerations in decision making and the sources of the complexities: individuals' differing perspectives concerning what is ethical, their differing interpretations and assessments of situations, and their differing goals, needs, and values.

Source: The scenarios are reprinted by permission of *The Wall Street Journal*, 1983 Dow Jones & Company, Inc. All Rights Reserved Worldwide.

Notes

1. Ronald L Crawford and Harold A Gram, "Social Responsibility as Interorganizational Transaction," *Academy of Management Review,* October 1978, p. 880.
2. George Strother, "The Moral Codes of Executives: A Watergate-Inspired Look at Barnard's Theory of Executive Responsibility," *Academy of Management Review,* April 1976, pp. 13–22. L Peach; "Managing Corporate Citizenship," *Personnel Management,* July 1985, pp. 32–35.
3. L D Alexander and W F Matthews, "The Ten Commandments of Corporate Social Responsibility," *Business and Society Review,* Summer 1984, pp. 62–66; Robert Boulanger and Donald Wayland, "Ethical Management: A Growing Corporate Responsibility," *CA Magazine,* March 1985, pp. 54–59.
4. Archie B Carroll, "A Three-Dimensional Conceptual Model of Corporate Performance," *Academy of Management Review,* October 1979, pp. 497–505.
5. Suggested by S Prakash Sethi, "A Conceptual Framework for Environmental Analysis of Social Issues and Evaluation of Business Response Patterns," *Academy of Management Review,* January 1979, pp. 63–74.
6. Milton Friedman, *Capitalism and Freedom* (Chicago: University of Chicago Press, 1962).
7. Milton Friedman, "The Social Responsibility of Business Is to Increase Its Profits," *New York Times Magazine,* September 1970, pp. 33, 122–26.
8. Richard B McKenzie, "The Mandated Benefit Mirage," *Business Horizons,* May–June 1993, pp. 30–39.
9. Friedman, "The Social Responsibility of Business," pp. 33, 122–26.
10. Henry Mintzberg, "The Case for Corporate Social Responsibility," *Journal of Business Strategy,* Fall 1983, pp. 5.
11. Sethi, "A Conceptual Framework," p. 66.
12. Mintzberg, "Case for Corporate Social Responsibility"; Sethi, "A Conceptual Framework."
13. H Manne and H C Wallich, *The Modern Corporation and Social Responsibility* (Washington, DC: American Enterprise Institute for Public Policy Research, 1972), as noted in Carroll, "A Three-Dimensional Conceptual Model," p. 498.
14. Keith Davis, "The Case for and against Business Assumption of Social Responsibilities," *Academy of Management Journal,* June 1973, p. 313.
15. Crawford and Gram, "Social Responsibility," p. 880.
16. Sethi, "A Conceptual Framework," p. 66.
17. Peter Arlow and Martin J Gannon, "Social Responsiveness, Corporate Structure, and Economic Performance," *Academy of Management Review,* April 1982, p. 235.
18. Mintzberg, "Case for Corporate Social Responsibility," p. 12.
19. H Gordon Fitch, "Achieving Corporate Social Responsibility," *Academy of Management Review,* January 1976, p. 45.
20. Leonard Silk, "The New (Improved) Creed of Social Responsibility," *Business Month,* November 1988, p. 110.
21. Jennifer Lawrence, "Green Products Sprouting Again: More Focused Efforts Avoid Controversy," *Advertising Age,* May 10, 1993, p. 12.

22. "Carrier Emphasizes Environmentalism in Products Introduced at the Show," *Air Conditioning, Heating, & Refrigeration News,* February 15, 1993, pp. 64–66.

23. Donna Boyle Schwartz, "Natural Evolution: Retailers and Manufacturers Spotlight 'Environmentally Friendly' Growth Opportunities," *HFD—The Weekly Home Furnishings Newspaper,* May 24, 1993, pp. 29–30.

24. Stuart Fedeman, "Today's EAP's Make the Grade," *Personnel,* February 1991, p. 3.

25. The discussion of flextime is based on D Keith Denton, "Using Flextime to Create a Competitive Workplace," *IM,* January–February 1993, pp. 29–31.

26. Janice Castro, "Home Is Where the Heart Is," *Time,* October 3, 1988, p. 48.

27. Linda Thornburg, "Day Care for Kids and Elders Is a Natural," *HR Magazine,* January 1993, pp. 48–50.

28. Fern Schumer Chapman, "Executive Guilt: Who's Taking Care of the Children?" *Fortune,* February 16, 1987, pp. 30–37.

29. Sally Solo, "Stop Whining and Get Back to Work," *Fortune,* March 12, 1990, pp. 49–50.

30. Howard R Bloch and Thomas J Lareau, "Should We Invest in 'Socially Irresponsible' Firms?" *Journal of Portfolio Management,* Summer 1985, pp. 27–31.

31. Kenneth E Aupperle, Archie B Carroll, and John D Hatfield, "An Empirical Examination of the Relationship between Corporate Social Responsibility and Profitability," *Academy of Management Journal,* June 1985, pp. 446–63; Arieh A Ullman, "Data in Search of Theory: A Critical Examination of the Relationships among Social Performance, Social Disclosure, and Economic Performance of US Firms," *Academy of Management Review,* July 1985, pp. 540–57.

32. Neasa MacErlean, "D&O: Do You Need It?" *Accountancy,* March 1993, pp. 40–41.

33. Judith H Dobrzynski, "Shareholders Unfurl Their Banner: 'Don't Tread on Us,' " *Business Week,* June 11, 1990, pp. 66–67.

34. The following discussion is based on information contained in the special section, "Agenda for the 21st Century: Managing Earth's Resources," *Business Week,* June 18, 1990, pp. 16, 40.

35. Milton R Moskowitz, "Company Performance Roundup," *Business and Society Review,* 1987, p. 69.

36. James O'Toole, *Vanguard Management: Redesigning the Corporate Future* (Garden City, NY: Doubleday, 1985), p. 359.

37. Francis W Steckmest, *Corporate Performance: The Key to Public Trust* (New York: McGraw-Hill, 1982), p. 109.

38. Stahrl W Edmunds, "Unifying Concepts in Social Responsibility," *Academy of Management Review,* January 1977, pp. 38–42.

39. Ibid., p. 40.

40. Frederick D Sturdivant, *Business and Society: A Managerial Approach,* 3d ed. (Burr Ridge, IL: Richard D. Irwin, 1985), p. 102.

41. Thomas J Zenisek, "Corporate Social Responsibility: A Conceptualization Based on Organizational Literature," *Academy of Management Review,* July 1979, pp. 359–68, suggests that 1960 marks the beginning of contemporary dialogue regarding the role of corporations in society.

42. Edmunds, "Unifying Concepts," p. 40.

43. Verne E Henderson, "The Ethical Side of Enterprise," *Sloan Management Review,* Summer 1982, p. 38.

44. For example, see Larue T Hosmer, *The Ethics of Management* (Burr Ridge, IL: Richard D. Irwin, 1987), pp. 151–52; Larue T Hosmer, "The Institutionalization of Unethical Behavior," *Journal of Business Ethics,* 1987, pp. 439–47; William J Ferguson, "Building a Solid Ethical Foundation in Business," *Executive Speeches,* June–July 1993, pp. 31–34.

45. This finding is the conclusion of Professor Amitai Etzioni, as reported by Saul Gellerman in "Why 'Good' Managers Make Bad Ethical Choices," *Harvard Business Review,* July–August 1986, p. 85.

46. Barry Z Posner and Warren H Schmidt, "Ethics in American Companies: A Managerial Perspective," *Journal of Business Ethics,* 1987, pp. 383–91.

47. Beth Brody, "Ethics 101: Can the Good Guys Win?" *U.S. News & World Report,* April 13, 1987, p. 54.

48. Roger Ricklefs, "Executives and General Public Say Ethical Behavior Is Declining in U.S.," *The Wall Street Journal,* November 1, 1983, pp. 23ff; Roger Ricklefs, "Public Gives Executives Low Marks for Honesty and Ethical Standards," *The Wall Street Journal,* November 2, 1983, pp. 29ff; Stanley J Modic, "Are They Ethical?" *Industry Week,* February 1, 1988, p. 20.

49. Brett Duval Fromson, "Did Drexel Get What It Deserved?" *Fortune,* March 12, 1990, pp. 81–88.

50. Andrew Stank, "What's the Matter with Business Ethics?" *Harvard Business Review,* May–June 1993, pp. 38–48.

51. John Hoerr, "Privacy," *Business Week,* March 28, 1988, pp. 61ff.

52. Gerald L Blakely and Cindy L Martinec, "Executive Development: Corporate Response to Business Ethics," *Journal of Education for Business,* November–December 1992, pp. 110–13.

53. The discussion that follows is based on Grover Starling, *The Changing Environment of Business* (Boston: Kent, 1980), pp. 252–58.

54. Robert W Austin, "Code of Conduct for Executives," *Harvard Business Review,* September–October 1961, p. 53, as cited in Sturdivant, *Business and Society,* p. 147.

55. Ralph E Welton and James R Davis, "Understanding Ethics and Employee Behavior," *Internal Auditing,* Winter 1993, pp. 63–69.

56. John A Byrne, "Businesses Are Signing Up for Ethics 101," *Business Week,* February 15, 1988, pp. 56–57.

57. Earl A Molander, "A Paradigm for Design, Promulgation, and Enforcement of Ethical Codes," *Journal of Business Ethics,* 1987, pp. 619–31.

58. Fred Luthans, Richard M Hodgetts, and Kenneth R Thompson, *Social Issues in Business* (New York: Macmillan, 1984), pp. 97–105.

59. Jerry G Kreuze and Dwight M Owsen, "What Can Be Done about Deteriorating Ethics," *The Small Business Controller,* Winter 1993, pp. 43–45.

60. Rick Wartzman, "Nature or Nurture? Study Blames Ethical Lapses on Corporate Goals," *The Wall Street Journal,* October 9, 1987, p. 21.

61. Ibid. See also, Donald Robin, Michael Giallourakis, Fred R David, and Thomas E Moritz, "A Different Look at Codes of Ethics," *Business Horizons,* January–February 1989, pp. 66–73.

62. William C Frederick, "The Culprit Is Culture (An Ethics Roundtable)," *Management Review,* August 1988, pp. 48–50.

63. The discussion on global ethics comes from David Fagino, "Ethics in a Changing World," *Management Review,* March 1993, p. 2; and David Vogel, "The Globalization of Business Ethics: Why America Remains Distinctive," *California Management Review,* Fall 1992, pp. 30–49.

64. Laxmi Nakarmi, "Roh Cracks His Whip at the Chaebol," *Business Week,* May 28, 1990, p. 40.

65. Thomas J Murray, "Ethics Programs: Just a Pretty Face?" *Business Month,* September 1987, pp. 30ff.

66. Luthans et al., *Social Issues in Business,* p. 104.

67. Kent Kresea, "Ethics: Right Values, Right Choices," *Executive Speeches,* June–July 1993, pp. 17–20.

68. Byrne, "Businesses Are Signing Up," p. 57.

69. Rita Kay Meyer, "Chemical's Executive Training Emphasizes Ethics," *American Banker,* June 17, 1988, p. 16.

70. Archie B Carroll, *Business and Society: Managing Corporate Social Performance* (Boston: Little, Brown, 1981), pp. 78–79.

71. Ibid., p. 85.

72. Murray, "Ethics Programs," p. 30. Also see, Michael Brody, "Listen to Your Whistleblower: Smart Managers Find Out about Nasty Problems before the Story Shows Up on the 11 O'clock News," *Fortune,* November 24, 1986, pp. 77–78.

73. Joseph Weber, "Rebel with a Cause—Actually, Several," *Business Week,* June 18, 1990, p. 157.

II MANAGING WORK AND ORGANIZATIONS:

Planning, Organizing, Controlling

5 MANAGEMENT DECISION MAKING

Chapter Learning Objectives

After completing Chapter 5, you should be able to:

- **Define** programmed and nonprogrammed decisions.
- **Describe** how the types of decisions managers make are related to their levels in organizations.
- **Discuss** the process of decision making.
- **Compare** individual and group decision making.
- **Identify** the major sources for locating problems that require management decisions.

Decisions—Decisions—Decisions!

Anyone familiar with Apple Computer knows that their continuing saga is always full of surprises. The latest installment in the saga includes a series of decisions that, if successful, could return the company to its place of prominence as the industry innovator. The popular Mac and its various versions carried the company throughout the 1980s and into 1990. And in 1991, nifty design techniques put Apple's PowerBook computer way ahead of the crowd when it was introduced. In fact, the Power-Book became the first notebook computer to top $1 billion in sales. However, the success has been short-lived as rivals' products now compete effectively against the PowerBook.

Apple can no longer count on the sale of higher-priced Macs and the PowerBook to sustain the company's future growth. Indeed, events in 1992 and 1993 confirm this claim: Market share has dropped; the stock price has plunged; and Apple CEO John Scully has resigned. To many customers and investors, Apple has relied too much on past successes.

Recent discussions among Apple executives have been primarily concerned with finding means to turn the company's fortunes around. What must the company do to reverse the slide? Among the decisions made over the last few years by Apple executives were the following:

1. The company would delay until 1997 the introduction of Apple's long-awaited new Copland operating system for its Macintosh computer.

2. The company would cut prices and begin offering rebates on Macs in an attempt to increase market share and profits.

3. A new line of Macintosh computers, targeted for graphical applications and complex networking, would be introduced.

4. Advertising and marketing expenditures would be significantly increased in order to increase global recognition of the Apple name, and promote Apple as a total systems integrator.

5. A heretofore unheard of deal was reached with Wal-Mart stores to distribute Apple products. As part of the agreement, 1,400 Wal-Mart stores would begin selling Macintosh computers.

6. The Apple Newton, a personal digital assistant, would be unveiled to the market. Key features of the Newton include its ability to offer intelligent assistance, serve also as a paging device, present information in a visually attractive display, and transmit E-mail or send documents to printers, fax machines, or personal computers.

7. An agreement was reached with IBM and Motorola to jointly develop and market a new microprocessor chip, the PowerPC Chip.

8. Apple would participate in a joint venture with IBM to develop software that would make it easier for programmers to combine video, sound, data, and graphics in multimedia CDs.

Nearly every stock analyst believes that the effects of these decisions must be positive in the coming years if Apple is to have a chance of regaining the luster it once possessed. In fact, if Apple does not recover, it may become just another minor player in the communications market rather than the leader it once was. Clearly, these seven decisions and many others supporting them are crucial.

Sources: M Hayes, "Copland Release Delayed," *Informationweek,* April 29, 1996, p. 15; P Burrows, "Do a Few Things Incredibly Well," *Business Week,* May 20, 1996, p. 36; J Jaben, "Apple Fills Up Its Marketing Cart," *Business Marketing,* September 1993, pp. 12–14. A Deutschman, "Odd Man Out," *Fortune,* July 26, 1993, pp. 42–56; M McGuire, "Apple Counting on Newton, Multimedia PC for Relief," *PC Week,* July 19, 1993, pp. 1–2; and R M Breyer, "Wal-Mart Signs Agreement with Apple, Dell Computers," *Discount Store News,* June 7, 1993, p. 34.

In an organization, managers at all levels make decisions. The ultimate influence of these decisions may extend to something as vital as the survival of the organization itself or to something as seemingly minor as the starting salary of a new college trainee. All decisions, however, have some influence—large or small—on performance. Thus, managers must develop decision-making skills. As the Management in Action that opened this chapter illustrates so well, the future of an important American company, Apple Computer, depends on the quality of the decisions that its management made in response to market and competitive conditions.

The quality of managers' decisions is the yardstick of their effectiveness and of their value to the organization. Like it or not, managers are evaluated and rewarded on the basis of the importance, number, and results of their decisions. Indeed, results of a recent study, conducted to determine what attributes contribute to being an effective European manager, indicated that decision-making ability is the most desirable skill a manager can possess.[1]

Types of Managerial Decisions

Although managers in business organizations, government offices, hospitals, and schools may be separated by background, lifestyle, and distance, they must all make decisions. The manager as decision maker is a problem solver, charged with either selecting from available alternatives or inventing an alternative different in meaningful ways from any that now exist.[2] In this section, we discuss various types of decisions.[3]

Programmed and Nonprogrammed Decisions

When a particular problem occurs often, managers develop a routine procedure for solving it. Thus, **programmed decisions** have repetitive and routine solutions. The managers of most organizations face great numbers of programmed decisions in their daily operations. Such decisions should be made without expending unnecessary time and effort on them.

When a problem contains elements that management has not previously confronted or if a problem is complex or extremely important, it requires a different and, perhaps, unique solution. **Nonprogrammed decisions** are solutions for novel and unstructured problems. The management of Apple Computer made important and difficult nonprogrammed decisions in their effort to turn around the company's fortunes. The two classifications are broad, but the distinction is important.[4] Table 5–1 presents examples of programmed and nonprogrammed decisions in different organizations.

What is important, however, is that the need for nonprogrammed decisions be properly identified. On the basis of this type of decision making, billions of dollars in resources are allocated in our nation every year. Government organizations make decisions that influence the lives of every citizen; business organizations make decisions to manufacture new products; hospitals and schools make decisions that influence patients and students years later.

TABLE 5–1   Types of Managerial Decisions
Programmed and nonprogrammed decisions result from different types of problems and use different types of procedures.

Decision	Problem	Procedures	Examples
Programmed	Repetitive, routine	Rules Standard operating procedures Policies	Business: Processing payroll vouchers College: Processing admission applications Hospital: Preparing a patient for surgery Government: Using a state-owned motor vehicle
Nonprogrammed	Complex, novel	Creative problem solving	Business: Introducing a new product College: Constructing new classroom facilities Hospital: Reacting to a regional disease epidemic Government: Solving a spiraling inflation problem

Unfortunately, very little is known about nonprogrammed human decision making.[5] Such decisions have always been the outcome of inner problem-solving processes, judgment, intuition, and creativity.[6] Although some managers are uncomfortable with basing decisions on intuition, modern management techniques have not made the same advances in improving managerial performance in nonprogrammed decision making as they have in programmed decision making.[7]

Coping with nonprogrammable decisions is always a formidable task, especially in small firms. The small-business manager just may not have the managerial and financial resources to deal with difficult situations when they arise. Such managers must consider the possibility of hiring someone else to make the decision.

Types of Decisions and Level of Management

Problems that come up frequently and have a great deal of uncertainty surrounding them are often of a strategic nature and should be the concern of top management. Problems that occur frequently and have fairly certain outcomes should be the concern of lower levels of management.[8]

Middle managers in most organizations concentrate mostly on programmed decisions. As Figure 5–1 indicates, the nature of the problem, how frequently it arises, and the degree of certainty surrounding it should dictate the appropriate level of management for making the decision.

The Process of Decision Making

There are numerous approaches to decision making. Which approach is best depends on the nature of the problem, the time available, the costs of individual strategies, and the mental skills of the decision maker.

Decisions are means rather than ends. They are processes by which a manager seeks to achieve some desired state. They are the manager's (and hence the

---

FIGURE 5–1   Types of Problems, Types of Decisions, and Management Level in the Organization

Programmed decisions are made at lower levels of management; nonprogrammed decisions are made at higher levels of management.

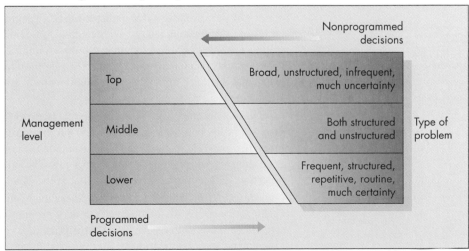

organization's) responses to problems. Every decision is the outcome of a dynamic process influenced by many forces including the organizational environment and the manager's knowledge, ability, and motivation.[9] Thus, decision making is the process of thought and deliberation that results in a decision. However, the process should not be viewed as the all-important strategic objective. The decision itself is of primary, strategic importance. There is tremendous temptation, especially on the part of large organizations, to start focusing more on how decisions are made rather than on what is decided. This type of activity can lead to decision paralysis, an inability on the part of managers to make decisions on a timely basis. Indeed, the difficulties that IBM, Sears, and General Motors have recently experienced can be directly attributed to company cultures that emphasized the process over the results of decision making.[10]

The Management Focus on AT&T provides an example of how one formerly bureaucratic organization took steps to avoid such paralysis through creating an environment that stimulates and rewards active decision making.

Decision making is not a fixed procedure, but it is a sequential process.[11] In most decision situations, managers go through a number of stages that help them think through the problem and develop alternative strategies. The stages need not be rigidly applied; their value lies in their ability to force the decision maker to structure the problem in a meaningful way. Figure 5–2 enables us to identify each stage in the normal progression that leads to a decision. You may find it helpful to develop your own list of stages for the decision-making process.

The process represented in Figure 5–2 applies more to nonprogrammed than to programmed decisions. Problems that occur infrequently with a great deal of uncertainty surrounding the outcome require the manager to utilize the entire process.[12] In contrast, problems that occur frequently are often handled by policies or rules, so it is not necessary to develop and evaluate alternatives each time these problems arise.[13]

Problem Identification

Identifying problems is not as easy as it may seem. If the problem is incorrectly identified or defined, any decisions made are directed toward solving the wrong problem.[14]

Warning Signals.   To locate problems, managers rely on several different indicators:

1. *Deviation from past performance.* A sudden change in some established pattern of performance often indicates that a problem has developed. When employee turnover increases, sales decline, student enrollments decline, selling expenses increase, or more defective units are produced, a problem usually exists. If, for example, the error rate among tellers has always been below the standard until this year, this departure from the historical pattern could signal a problem.

2. *Deviation from the plan.* When results do not meet planned objectives, a problem is likely—for example, a new product fails to meet its market share objective, profit levels are lower than planned, the production department is exceeding its budget, or the teller error rate exceeds the performance objective. These occurrences signal that some plan is off course.

3. *Outside criticism.* The actions of outsiders may indicate problems. Customers may be dissatisfied with a new product or with their delivery schedules; a labor union may present a grievance; investment firms may not recommend the organization as a good investment opportunity; alumni may withdraw their support from an athletic program.

A New Style of Decision Making at AT&T

Jerre Stead never closes his office door. Leaving the door open is both a symbol and an invitation—to customers, employees (Stead refers to them as associates), ideas, and information. He tells his associates to call him "coach" because that is how he sees himself. Stead aggressively focuses on making timely decisions that benefit both customers and financial results. In fact, Stead has been quoted as saying, "If you're in a meeting, any meeting, for 15 minutes, and we're not talking about customers or competitors, raise your hand and ask why. If it goes for half an hour, leave! Leave the meeting!"

Stead provides just one example of the new breed of decision makers at AT&T who have succeeded in moving profits upward while simultaneously quadrupling stock prices. Robert Allen, AT&T CEO, originally installed Stead as president of AT&T's Global Business Communications Systems (a division that had been bleeding billions of dollars) in September of 1991. Within months, the division was turning a profit. Allen was so impressed with Stead's performance that in March 1993, Stead was promoted to head of NCR.

AT&T is no longer the slow, lethargic, and bureaucratic giant it once was. CEO Allen has modernized management in ways employees of the old Ma Bell would scarcely recognize. AT&T is thriving because new managers, with their unique decision-making styles, have turned around business after business. AT&T practices a hands-off management strategy that promotes teamwork and openness with the customer as the focus. Servicing customers is what AT&T is excellent at doing in both the domestic and the international markets.

CEO Allen defines AT&T goals simply: to bring people together and give them easy access to each other and the information they want and need to make effective decisions—anytime, anywhere. Since becoming CEO, Allen has done the following:

- Installed a new corporate structure that encourages cooperation among otherwise independent businesses, including the formation of cross-unit teams that search for new opportunities.
- Spent large amounts of time promoting a set of company values he calls "our common bond."
- Shaken up the organization and ended a tradition of insularity by recruiting executives from outside AT&T.
- Reduced the size of the workforce by 40,000.
- Built new ties with AT&T's unions, even while making it clear that the company can no longer promise lifetime employment.
- Invested in other companies with critical technologies or attractive positions in their prospective markets (e.g., NCR, McCaw Cellular).

Through efforts such as these, Allen has succeeded in eliminating hundreds of policies and guidelines established in the old, heavily regulated environment. In their place, all AT&T business units have been given only two mandates to utilize in guiding decision processes: Grow and be profitable in your own right, but make sure you contribute to the success of the core telecommunications network.

Sources: J Nocera, "Living with Layoffs," *Fortune*, April 1, 1996, pp. 69–71; H Gold, "Brave New AT&T," *Barrons*, March 11, 1996, pp. 33–39; B Ziegler, "AT&T's Bold Bet," *Business Week*, August 30, 1993, pp. 26–30; and D Kirkpatrick, "Could AT&T Rule the World?" *Fortune*, May 17, 1993, pp. 55–66.

Sources of Difficulties in Problem Identification.   It is easy to recognize that some problems exist when a gap occurs between desired results and actual results. However, identifying the exact problem is often made more difficult by one or more factors:

Perceptual Problems.   Our individual perceptions may protect or defend us from unpleasant realities. Thus, negative information may be selectively perceived to distort its true meaning. It may also be totally ignored. Recent research has revealed that managers who initiate projects and are held responsible for success or failure will tend to continue the projects even if they are unprofitable. In this case, the manager is ignoring the best interests of the organization in making the decision to continue.[15]

FIGURE 5–2   The Process of Decision Making

In the decision-making process, taking certain specific steps contributes to high-quality decisions.

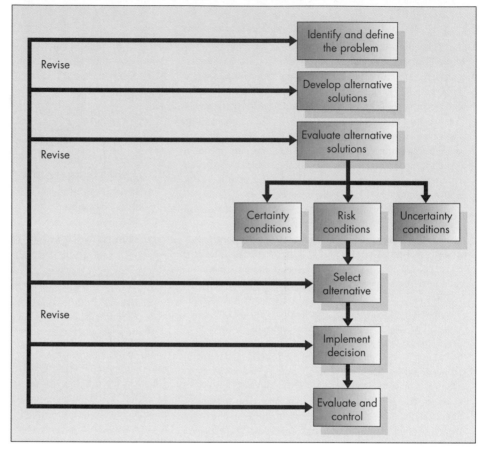

Defining Problems by Solutions.   This is really a form of jumping to conclusions. For example, a sales manager may say, "The decrease in profits is due to our poor product quality." The sales manager's definition of the problem suggests a particular solution: the improvement of product quality in the production department. Certainly, other definitions—and solutions—may be possible. Perhaps the salesforce has been inadequately selected or trained. Perhaps competitors have a less expensive product.

Identifying Symptoms as Problems.   "Our problem is a 32 percent decline in orders." While it is certainly true that orders have declined, the decline is actually only a symptom of the real problem. Not until the manager identifies the real problem can the cause of the decline in orders be found.[16]

Types of Problems.   Problems are usually of three types: opportunity, crisis, or routine. Crisis and routine problems present themselves and must be attended to by the managers.[17] Opportunities, in contrast, must usually be found; they wait to be discovered. Often they go unnoticed and are eventually lost by an inattentive manager. Because, by their very nature, most crises and routine problems demand immediate attention, a manager may spend a great deal of time handling minor crises and solving routine problems and may not have time to pursue important new opportunities. Many well-managed organizations try to draw attention away from crises and routine problems and toward longer-range issues through planning activities.

Developing Alternatives

Once the problem is defined, feasible alternatives (actually, potential solutions) to the problem should be developed, and the potential consequences of each alternative should be considered. This search process investigates the relevant internal and external environments of the organization to provide information that can be developed into possible alternatives.[18] Obviously, this search for solutions is conducted within certain time and cost constraints because only so much effort can be devoted to developing alternatives.[19]

However, sufficient effort should be made to develop a wide range of alternatives. Contrary to what one may think, there is a positive linkage between the number of alternatives considered and the speed with which decisions can be reached.[20] Not generating enough detailed and varied alternatives can actually wind up costing both time and resources, the very commodities organizations seek to conserve.

Evaluating Alternatives

Once alternatives have been developed, they must be evaluated and compared. In every decision situation, the objective in making a decision is to select the alternative that produces the most favorable outcomes and avoids the least favorable outcomes. For example, in many business decisions, the most favorable outcome would be the one that maximizes shareholder wealth.[21] Other possible decision criteria could be minimizing costs, improving customer satisfaction, winning the Baldrige Quality Award, or meeting mandatory deadlines.[22] This again points out the importance of objectives and goals, since in selecting an alternative, the decision maker should be guided by these previously established goals and objectives. The alternative–outcome relationship is based on three possible conditions:

1. *Certainty.* The decision maker has complete knowledge of the outcomes of each alternative.
2. *Risk.* The decision maker has some probabilistic estimate of the outcomes of each alternative.
3. *Uncertainty.* The decision maker has absolutely no knowledge of the probability of the outcome of each alternative.

Decision making under conditions of risk is probably the most common situation.[23] Statisticians and operations researchers have made important contributions to decision making in evaluating alternatives under these conditions. Their methods have proved especially useful in the analysis and ranking of alternatives.

We illustrate the process of evaluating alternatives in the context of planning by describing a typical decision that publishers of specialty books must make: how many units to produce.

Conditions of Certainty.   If the publisher knows with certainty how many books will be demanded at each possible and feasible price, the number of books to produce is obvious. (Some business decisions do occur with certainty; for example, we all know with certainty that we must pay our taxes by April 15.)

Perfect knowledge of demand is rare, particularly for a publisher of commemorative books. Often a book commemorates a special event such as the nation's bicentennial celebration. Because the book is unique, the publisher may have only sketchy information about its potential sales. When the publisher has some, but not complete, knowledge, the condition of risk may prevail.

Conditions of Risk.   Conditions of risk occur when the planner/decision maker has enough information to allow the use of probability in evaluating the alternatives. We are all aware of probability as a basis for making decisions; every time we play bridge, poker, or backgammon we are making decisions under conditions of risk, which is to say, we could know the probability associated with the decision we make.

We can estimate probability in one of two ways: *Objective* probability reflects historical evidence. For example, the probability of obtaining either heads or tails on the fair toss of a coin is .50 (50 percent); the coin is equally likely to come up either heads or tails, and we can verify this distribution of outcomes by tossing the coin a thousand times and seeing that each side does come up about the same number of times.

In many instances, planners do not have historical evidence but may have sufficient information to enable them to arrive at a *subjective* probability. Some managers seem to do better than others when estimating probabilities, perhaps owing to their experience, intelligence, or intuition. When the planner has access to probability information, the criterion for decision making is to maximize the **expected value** of the decision. For example, the publisher would use probability estimates of each level of feasible demand for the specialty book and from this information calculate the expected value for the alternative.

What if the decision maker has absolutely no basis for making probability estimates? When the decision involves absolutely no information, it is a nonprogrammed decision in the purest sense of the term. Next we discuss how a planner can decide among alternatives when no information exists, creating a condition of complete uncertainty.

Conditions of Uncertainty.   When no information exists relevant to the outcomes of possible alternatives, the personality characteristics of the decision maker become more important for determining which decision is made. Although it is possible to enumerate countless characteristics that could affect which alternative a decision maker would choose, the following four suffice for describing what most of us would do:

The Optimistic Decision Maker.   Some decision makers think optimistically about the events that influence decisions. Such individuals always choose the alternative that maximizes the maximum outcomes. That is to say, they always act as though no matter what they do everything will come out to their benefit; consequently, why not go for broke? They cannot, so they believe, go broke. Many entrepreneurs utilize this type of decision-making strategy, possessing a strong belief that what they do will always work. Some large companies, including 3M and General Electric, have also succeeded in implementing this type of entrepreneurial thinking within their organizations.[24] In our publishing example, the publisher would print the maximum number of books, with the expectation that they would all be sold.

The Pessimistic Decision Maker.   Other decision makers believe the worst possible outcome will occur no matter what they do. Under these circumstances, they estimate the worst outcomes associated with each alternative and select the best of these worst outcomes. Thus, a pessimistic publisher would produce the minimum number of books.

The Regret Minimizing Decision Maker.   Regret minimizers want to minimize the amount of dissonance they experience after the fact. They try to make decisions that have outcomes not too far removed from the best outcome possible under the circumstances. The regret minimizing publisher would publish a number of books somewhere between what the optimist and the pessimist would publish.

The Insufficient Reasoner Decision Maker.   The last group of decision makers would simplify the decision by making the assumption that all possible outcomes of the decision have an equal chance of occurring. The assumption follows the reasoning that if no information exists to support the relative advantage of one alternative, one might as well assume that all alternatives have an equal chance. This criterion would cause the publisher to assign equal probabilities to each feasible production run and then decide on the basis of maximum expected value.

Thus, the evaluation of alternatives comes down to evaluating outcomes through the use of information. When sufficiently valid information exists, the chances that planners would choose an alternative reflecting relevant facts are greater. When insufficiently valid information exists, the chances that planners would choose an alternative reflecting personal and personality factors are greater. The next section introduces additional complications in the choice of alternatives.

Choosing an Alternative

The purpose of selecting an alternative is to achieve a predetermined objective by solving a problem. This point is an important one. It means that a decision is not an end in itself but only a means to an end. While the decision maker chooses an alternative expected to result in the achievement of the objective, the selection of that alternative should not be an isolated act. If it is, the factors that led to and lead from the decision are likely to be excluded. Specifically, the steps following the decision should include implementation, control, and evaluation. The critical point is that decision making is more than an act of choosing; it is a dynamic process.

Unfortunately for most managers, situations rarely exist in which one alternative achieves the desired objective without having some positive or negative impact on another objective. Situations often exist in which two objectives cannot be optimized simultaneously. If one objective is optimized, the other is suboptimized. In a business organization, for example, if production is optimized, employee morale may be suboptimized, or vice versa. Or a hospital superintendent optimizes a short-run objective such as maintenance costs at the expense of a long-run objective such as high-quality patient care. Thus, the multiplicity of organizational objectives complicates the real world of the decision maker.

A situation could also exist in which an organizational objective would be attained at the expense of a societal objective. The reality of such situations is clearly seen in the rise of ecology groups, environmentalists, and the consumer movement. As we discussed in Chapter 4, these groups question the priorities (organizational as against societal) of certain organizational decision makers. In any case, whether an organizational objective conflicts with another organizational objective or with a societal objective, the values of the decision maker strongly influence the alternative chosen. The influence of individual values on the decision-making process should be clear.

Thus, in managerial decision making, optimal solutions are often impossible. This is because the decision maker cannot possibly know all of the available alternatives, the consequences of each alternative, and the probability of occurrence of these consequences.[25] Thus, rather than being an optimizer, the decision maker is a satisfier, selecting the alternative that meets an acceptable (satisfactory) standard.

Implementing the Decision

Any decision is little more than an abstraction if it is not implemented. In other words, a decision must be effectively implemented to achieve the objective for which it was made. It is entirely possible for a good decision to be hurt by poor implementation. In this sense, implementation may be more important than the actual choice of the alternative.[26]

Because implementing decisions involves people in most situations, the test of the soundness of a decision is the behavior of the people affected by the decision. While a decision may be technically sound, it can easily be undermined by dissatisfied subordinates or by partners who view things differently.

Control and Evaluation

Effective management involves periodic measurements of results. If deviations exist when actual results are compared with planned results (the objective), changes must be made. Here again, we see the importance of setting measurable objectives. If such objectives do not exist, there is no way to judge performance. If actual results do not match planned results, changes must be made in the solution chosen, in its implementation, or in the original objective if it is deemed unattainable. If the original objective must be revised, the entire decision-making process is reactivated. Once a decision is implemented, a manager cannot assume the outcome will meet the original objective. Some system of control and evaluation is necessary to make sure the actual results are consistent with the results planned when the decision was made.

Individual Decision Making

Several individual differences influence the decision-making process.[27] Some of these differences influence only certain aspects of the process, while others influence the entire process. However, each may have an impact and, therefore, must be understood to fully appreciate decision making as a process in organizations. Four individual differences—values, personality, propensity for risk, and potential for dissonance—are discussed in this section. Each of these individual differences has a significant impact on the decision-making process.

Values

In the context of decision making, values are the guidelines that a person uses when confronted with a situation in which a choice must be made. Values are acquired early in life and are a basic—yet often taken-for-granted—part of an individual's thoughts. The influence of values on the decision-making process is profound:

> In establishing objectives, it is necessary to make value judgments regarding the selection of opportunities and the assignment of priorities.
>
> In developing alternatives, it is necessary to make value judgments about the various possibilities.
>
> In choosing an alternative, the values of the decision maker influence which alternative is chosen.
>
> In implementing a decision, value judgments are necessary in choosing the means for implementation.
>
> In the evaluation and control phase, value judgments cannot be avoided when corrective action is taken.[28]

It is clear that values pervade the decision-making process. They are reflected in the decision maker's behavior before making the decision, in making the decision, and in putting the decision into effect.[29]

Personality

Decision makers are influenced by many psychological forces, both conscious and subconscious. One of the most important of these forces is personality. As we observed in our discussion of decision making under conditions of uncertainty, decision makers' personalities are strongly reflected in the choices they make. Studies have examined the effect of selected variables on the process of decision making.[30] These studies have generally focused on the following sets of variables:

1. Personality variables include the attitudes, beliefs, and needs of the individual.
2. Situational variables pertain to the external, observable situations in which individuals find themselves.
3. Interactional variables pertain to the momentary state of the individual as a result of the interaction of a specific situation with characteristics of the individual's personality.

The most important conclusions concerning the influence of personality on the decision-making process are as follows:

1. It is unlikely that one person can be equally proficient in all aspects of the decision-making process. The results suggest that some people do better in one part of the process, while others do better in another part.
2. Such characteristics as intelligence are associated with different phases of the decision-making process.
3. The relation of personality to the decision-making process may vary for different groups on the basis of such factors as sex and social status.

Thus, we can see how the personality traits of the decision maker combine with situational and interactional variables to influence the decision-making process.

Propensity for Risk

Decision makers vary greatly in their propensity for taking risks: the optimistic decision maker takes risks by assuming that the outcome will always be favorable. Female managers have been found to possess a strong propensity for taking risks.[31] Toward this end, many female managers are leaving the security associated with working for large organizations and, instead, are starting their own businesses. (In fact, female-owned businesses are currently being founded at a five-times-greater rate than male-owned businesses.) The accompanying Management Focus, "Making Tough Decisions," provides some examples of how women who have chosen to stay with corporations have become valued additions to the decision-making process.

A decision maker who has a low aversion to risk establishes different objectives, evaluates alternatives differently, and selects different alternatives than another decision maker in the same situation who has a high aversion to risk. The latter attempts to make choices for which the risk or uncertainty is low or for which the certainty of the outcome is high. Many people are bolder and advocate greater risk-taking in groups than as individuals. Apparently, such people are more willing to accept shared risk as members of a group.

Potential for Dissonance

Traditionally, researchers have focused much of their attention on the forces and influences on the decision maker before a decision is made, and on the decision itself. Only recently, however, has attention been given to what happens after a decision has been made. Specifically, behavioral scientists have focused their attention on postdecision anxiety, or cognitive dissonance.

Management Focus

Making Tough Decisions

The past two decades have seen a rise in the number of women entering the workforce. Coinciding with this overall growth trend, there has also been an increase in the number of women joining the managerial ranks at corporations throughout the United States. Overall, 42 percent of managers today are women. However, this increase has not come easily. In fact, a recent study of 461 female executives in Fortune 1000 companies found that 52 percent believed that male stereotyping was the biggest barrier to women's progress up the corporate ladder. In their quest to reach the top, women have had to work hard to prove they were capable of joining their male counterparts. The following are two examples of women who are taking an active role in the decision-making process at large companies:

Tommye Jo Daves only wanted to earn enough money to purchase a washing machine when she began working at Levi Strauss & Company more than 35 years ago. But today, as plant manager of Levi's Murphy, North Carolina, plant, she is one of the few female plant managers in her company and industry. Daves began her climb up the corporate ladder by persuading Levi's to help blue-collar workers get the training and education they needed to become better equipped and eligible for promotions.

Donna Ecton, Vencor Inc.'s first female director, joined the board in early 1993. Because of her skills and knowledge gained as CEO of candy maker Van Houton Inc., Donna was immediately able to help the Louisville, Kentucky, hospital operator navigate through a series of complex acquisition decisions, which would map the future strategy of the company. In an extremely short period, Ecton gained recognition as one of Vencor's most valuable advisors.

Today, more women than in the past are reaching senior-management levels. As this happens, businesses are tapping record numbers of women for board positions. The proportion of corporate boards appointing women recently surged to an all-time high of 60 percent. And with a growing number of women entering the nation's executive suites, corporate America's decisions are being reshaped.

Women's board power becomes even more formidable when several women hold director's seats at a particular corporation. That is already happening at Sears, Roebuck & Company. Women hold three of its nine board member seats and control two committees. Thanks largely to the joint efforts of these women, Sears has been able to make some tough decisions, such as divesting its nonretail subsidiaries and more actively courting working-women shoppers. Edward Brennan, Sears CEO, firmly believes female directors understand consumers better and, in the future, anticipates having even more women join the Sears board.

Finally, it is interesting to note that a recent study found that female managers not only are more effective than male managers at the "softer" management skills of communication, feedback, and empowerment but also are more decisive and effective in planning and facilitating change.

Sources: E Davis, "Women at The Top," *HR Focus,* May 1996, p. 18; H Collingwood, "Women as Managers: Not Just Different—Better," *Working Women,* November 1995, p. 14; "Clearing a New Path to the Top," *Working Woman,* January 1993, pp. 24–26; and J Lopez, "Once Male Enclaves, Corporate Boards Now Comb Executive Suites for Women," *The Wall Street Journal,* January 22, 1993, p. B1.

Such anxiety is related to a lack of consistency or harmony among an individual's various cognitions (attitudes, beliefs, and so on) after a decision has been made.[32] As a result, the decision maker has doubts and second thoughts about the choice that was made. In addition, the intensity of the anxiety is likely to be greater when any of the following conditions exist:

1. The decision is psychologically or financially important.
2. There are a number of forgone alternatives.
3. The forgone alternatives have many favorable features.

When dissonance occurs, people can reduce it by admitting that a mistake has been made. Unfortunately, many individuals are reluctant to admit that they have made wrong decisions. These individuals are more likely to use one or more of the following methods to reduce their dissonance:

1. Seek information that supports their decisions.
2. Selectively perceive (distort) information in a way that supports their decisions.
3. Adopt a less favorable view of the forgone alternatives.
4. Minimize the importance of the negative aspects of the decisions and exaggerate the importance of the positive aspects.

While each of us may resort to some of this behavior in our personal decision making, it is easy to see how a great deal of it could be extremely harmful to organizational effectiveness. The potential for dissonance is influenced heavily by one's personality, specifically one's self-confidence and persuasibility. In fact, all of the behavioral influences are closely interrelated and are isolated here only for purposes of discussion.[33]

Group Decision Making

The first part of this chapter focused on individuals making decisions. In most organizations, however, a great deal of decision making is achieved through committees, teams, task forces, and other groups. Managers frequently face situations in which they must seek and combine judgments in group meetings. This is especially true for nonprogrammed problems, which are novel, with much uncertainty regarding the outcome. In most organizations, it is unusual to find decisions on such problems being made by one individual on a regular basis. The increased complexity of many of these problems requires specialized knowledge in numerous fields, usually not possessed by one person. This requirement, coupled with the reality that the decisions made must eventually be accepted and implemented by many units throughout the organization, has increased the use of the collective approach to the decision-making process. The result for many managers has been an endless amount of time spent in meetings of committees and other groups. Many managers spend as much as 80 percent of their working time in committee meetings.

Individual versus Group Decision Making

There has been considerable debate over the relative effectiveness of individual versus group decision making. In some cases, groups can take more time to reach a decision than individuals, but bringing together individual specialists and experts has its benefits because the mutually reinforcing impact of their interaction results in better decisions.[34] In other cases, a group can actually make quicker decisions. At General Motors, the major decision-making process has become faster with the establishment of the North American Operations Strategy Board.[35] The board replaces a previously cumbersome decision process whereby proposals had to be approved by three separate levels of management. Now, for example, pricing decisions that used to take three weeks to make are being made in one.

A great deal of research has shown that consensus decisions with five or more participants are superior to individual decision making, majority vote, and leader decisions.[36] Unfortunately, open discussion has been found to be negatively influenced by such behavioral factors as the pressure to conform, the influence of a dominant personality type in the group, status incongruity (which causes lower-status participants to be inhibited by higher-status participants and go along even though they believe that their own ideas are superior), and the attempt of certain participants to influence others because these participants are perceived to be experts in the problem area.[37]

Certain decisions appear to be better made by groups, while others appear better suited to individual decision making. Nonprogrammed decisions appear to be better suited to group decision making. Such decisions usually call for pooled talent in arriving at a solution; the decisions are so important that they are usually made by top managers and to a somewhat lesser extent by middle managers.

In the decision-making process itself, the following points concerning group processes for nonprogrammed decisions can be made:

1. In *establishing objectives,* groups are probably superior to individuals because of the greater amount of knowledge available to groups.

2. In *identifying alternatives,* the individual efforts of group members are necessary to ensure a broad search in the various functional areas of the organization.

3. In *evaluating alternatives,* the collective judgment of the group, with its wider range of viewpoints, seems superior to that of the individual decision maker.

4. In *choosing an alternative,* group interaction and the achievement of consensus usually result in the acceptance of more risk than would be accepted by an individual decision maker. In any event, the group decision is more likely to be accepted as a result of the participation of those affected by its consequences.

5. *Implementation* of a decision, whether made by a group or not, is usually accomplished by individual managers. Thus, since a group cannot be held responsible, the responsibility for implementation necessarily rests with the individual manager.

Figure 5–3 summarizes the research on group decision making. It presents the relationship between the probable quality of a decision and the method utilized to reach the decision. It indicates that as we move from individual to consensus, the quality of the decision improves. Note also that each successive method involves a higher level of mutual influence by group members. Thus, for a complex problem requiring pooled knowledge, the quality of the decision is likely to be higher as the group moves toward achieving consensus.

Creativity in Group Decision Making

If groups are better suited to making nonprogrammed decisions than individuals, companies must create an atmosphere fostering group creativity. In this respect, group decision making may be similar to brainstorming in that discussion must be free flowing and spontaneous. All group members must participate, and the evaluation of individual ideas must be suspended in the beginning to encourage participation. However, a decision must be reached, and this is where group decision making differs from brainstorming. Table 5–2 presents guidelines for developing the permissive atmosphere necessary for creative decision making.[38]

Techniques for Stimulating Creativity

Even though in many instances group decision making is preferable to individual decision making, we have all heard the statement, "A camel is a racehorse designed by a committee." Thus, while the necessity and the benefits of group decision making are

FIGURE 5–3   **Probable Relationship between Quality of Group Decision and Method Utilized**

The quality of decision making is related to the degree to which managers can attain consensus within the group.

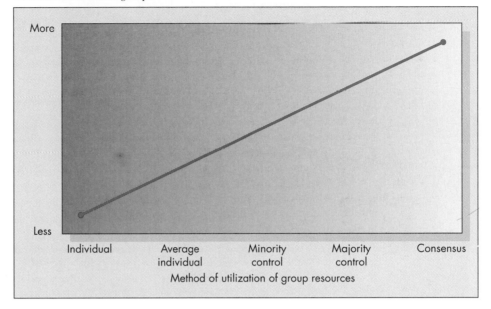

recognized, numerous problems are also associated with it, some of which have already been noted. Practicing managers need specific techniques enabling them to increase the benefits from group decision making while reducing the problems associated with it.

We examine three techniques that, when properly utilized, are extremely useful in increasing the creative capability of a group in generating ideas, understanding problems, and reaching better decisions. Increasing the creative capability of a group is especially necessary when individuals from diverse sectors of the organization must pool their judgments to create a satisfactory course of action for the organization. The three techniques are brainstorming, the Delphi technique, and the Nominal Group Technique.

Brainstorming.   In many situations, groups are expected to produce creative or imaginative solutions to organizational problems. In such instances, *brainstorming* has often enhanced the creative output of the group. The technique of brainstorming includes a strict series of rules. The purpose of the rules is to promote the generation of ideas while at the same time avoiding the inhibitions of members that are usually caused by face-to-face groups. The basic rules are:

No idea is too ridiculous. Group members are encouraged to state any extreme or outlandish idea.

Each idea presented belongs to the group, not to the person stating it. In this way, group members utilize and build on the ideas of others.

No idea can be criticized. The purpose of the session is to generate, not evaluate, ideas.

TABLE 5–2   Creative Group Decision Making

Groups develop particular characteristics that enable them to undertake creative decision making.

Group Structure

The group is composed of heterogeneous, generally competent personnel who bring to bear on the problem diverse frames of reference, representing channels to each relevant body of knowledge (including contact with outside resource personnel who offer expertise not encompassed by the organization), with a leader who facilitates the creative process.

Group Roles

Each individual explores with the entire group all ideas (no matter how intuitively and roughly formed) that bear on the problem.

Group Processes

The problem-solving process is characterized by the following:

1. Spontaneous communication between members (not focused on the leader).
2. Full participation from each member.
3. Separation of idea generation from idea evaluation.
4. Separation of problem definition from generation of solution strategies.
5. Shifting of roles, so interaction that mediates problem solving (particularly search activities and clarification by means of constant questioning directed both to individual members and to the whole group) is not the sole responsibility of the leader.
6. Suspension of judgment and avoidance of early concern with solutions, so that the emphasis is on analysis and exploration, rather than on early commitment to solutions.

Group Style

The social-emotional tone of the group is characterized by the following:

1. A relaxed, nonstressful environment.
2. Ego-supportive interaction, where open give-and-take between members is at the same time courteous.
3. Behavior that is motivated by interest in the problem, rather than concern with short-run payoff.
4. Absence of penalties attached to any espoused idea or position.

Group Norms

1. Are supportive of originality and unusual ideas and allow for eccentricity.
2. Seek behavior that separates source from content in evaluating information and ideas.
3. Stress a nonauthoritarian view, with a realistic view of life and independence of judgment.
4. Support humor and undisciplined exploration of viewpoints.
5. Seek openness in communication, where mature, self-confident individuals offer spontaneous ideas to the group for mutual exploration without threat to the individuals for "exposing" themselves.
6. Deliberately avoid giving credence to short-run results or short-run decisiveness.
7. Seek consensus but accept majority rule when consensus is unobtainable.

   Brainstorming is widely used in advertising and some other fields, where it is apparently effective. In other situations, it has been less successful. Brainstorming groups normally produce fewer ideas than do the equivalent number of individuals working by themselves, and there is no evaluation or ranking of the ideas generated.[39] Thus, the group never really concludes the problem-solving process.

The Delphi Technique.   This technique involves the solicitation and comparison of anonymous judgments on the topic of interest through a set of sequential questionnaires that are interspersed with summarized information and feedback of opinions from earlier responses.

The *Delphi process* retains the advantage of having several judges while removing the biasing effects that might occur during face-to-face interaction. The basic approach has been to collect anonymous judgments by mail questionnaire. For example, the members independently generate their ideas to answer the first questionnaire and return it. The staff members summarize the responses as the group consensus and feed this summary back along with a second questionnaire for reassessment. Studying this feedback, the respondents independently evaluate their earlier responses. The underlying belief is that the consensus estimate results in a better decision after several rounds of anonymous group judgment. While it is possible to continue the procedure for several rounds, essentially no significant change occurs after the second round of estimation.

An interesting application of the Delphi process was undertaken by the American Marketing Association in order to determine the principle international issues most likely to have a significant impact on marketing in the year 2000.[40] Twenty-nine experts on international marketing participated in the study. The major issues identified by the experts included the environment, globalization, regional trading blocks, the internationalization of service industries, and higher foreign direct investment.

The Nominal Group Technique (NGT).   NGT has gained increasing recognition in health, social service, education, industry, and government organizations. The term *Nominal Group Technique* was adopted by earlier researchers to refer to processes that bring people together but do not allow them to communicate verbally. Thus, the collection of people is a group nominally, or in name only. In its present form, NGT actually combines both verbal and nonverbal stages.

Basically, NGT is a structured group meeting that proceeds as follows: A group of 7 to 10 individuals sit around a table but do not speak to one another. Rather, each person writes ideas on a pad of paper. After five minutes, a structured sharing of ideas takes place. Each person around the table presents one idea. A person designated as recorder writes the ideas on a flip chart in full view of the entire group. This continues until all the participants indicate that they have no further ideas to share. There is still no discussion.

The output of this phase is usually a list of between 18 and 25 ideas. The next phase involves structured discussion in which each idea receives attention before a vote is taken. This is achieved by asking for clarification or stating the degree of support for each idea listed on the flip chart. The next stage involves independent voting, in which each participant privately selects priorities by ranking or voting. The group decision is the mathematically pooled outcome of the individual votes.

Both the Delphi technique and NGT have proven to be more productive than brainstorming.[41] Each has had an excellent success record. The basic differences between the Delphi technique and NGT follow:

- Delphi participants are typically anonymous to one another, while NGT participants become acquainted.
- NGT participants meet face-to-face around a table, while Delphi participants are physically distant and never meet face-to-face.

· In the Delphi process, all communication between participants is by way of written questionnaires and feedback from the monitoring staff. In NGT, communication is direct between participants.

Practical considerations, of course, often influence which technique is used. For example, such factors as the number of working hours available, costs, and the physical proximity of participants influence which technique is selected.

Our discussion has not been designed to make anyone an expert in the Delphi process or NGT. Our purpose throughout this section has been to indicate the frequency and importance of group decision making in every organization. The three techniques discussed are practical devices whose purpose is to improve the effectiveness of group decisions.

Decision making is a common responsibility shared by all executives, regardless of functional area or management level. Every day, managers are required to make decisions that shape the future of their organizations as well as their own futures. Some of these decisions may have a strong impact on the organization's success, while others are important but less crucial. However, all of the decisions have some effect (positive or negative, large or small) on the organization.

Summary of Key Points

· Planning and decision making are two managerial activities that cannot be separated. Every stage of planning involves decision making.

· The quality of management decisions determines to a large extent the effectiveness of plans.

· Managers are evaluated and rewarded on the basis of the importance, number, and results of their decisions. To a large degree, decision making is the most valuable skill a manager can possess.

· Decisions may be classified as programmed or nonprogrammed, depending on the problem. Each type requires different kinds of procedures and applies to very different types of situations.

· Decision making is a many-phased process. The actual choice is only one phase.

· Decisions should be thought of as means rather than ends. They are a manager's responses to problems and the results of a process of thought and deliberation. Toward this end, managers must realize that the process of decision making should not overshadow the importance of the decision itself.

· Different managers may select different alternatives in the same situation. This is because of differences in values and in attitudes toward risk.

· Managers spend a great deal of time in group decision making. This is especially true for nonprogrammed decisions. Much evidence exists that, in certain situations, group decisions are superior to individual decisions. However, there are exceptions, and group decision making itself can create problems.

· A great deal of nonprogrammed decision making occurs in group situations. Much evidence exists to support the claim that in most instances group decisions are superior to individual decisions. Three relatively new techniques (brainstorming, the Delphi technique, and the Nominal Group Technique) have the purpose of improving the effectiveness of group decisions. The management of collective decision making must be a vital concern for future managers.

Discussion and Review Questions

1. What is a decision?
2. We make decisions daily. Describe in detail two programmed decisions you make each day. Why do you consider them to be programmed? Were they ever nonprogrammed? If so, discuss why.

3. Describe a nonprogrammed decision that you recently made. Describe the circumstances surrounding the decision and state why you believe it was nonprogrammed. Did this belief influence your decision-making approach? In what ways?

4. Describe the organizational factors that could possibly lead to decision paralysis, the inability to make decisions in a timely fashion. How could an organization avoid such situations?

5. Select and describe a business situation where the Delphi Technique or Nominal Group Technique could be utilized effectively as part of the decision-making process.

6. Describe a business situation in which there is a strong, positive relationship existing between the number of alternatives generated and the quality of the decision itself.

7. Describe a group decision-making situation in which you were involved. Did any problems develop?

Describe them in detail. Was the decision reached by the group different from the one you would have made as an individual? Do you think that the group decision was better? Why?

8. Why are the management function of planning and the process of decision making so closely related?

9. Think of a corporate executive who you believe is a good decision maker. What traits make this executive effective?

10. Describe a situation you have encountered in which a decision made by an individual could have been better made by a group. Why do you feel this way?

Case 5–1

One Manager's Tough Decision

At 4 PM Monday, December 6, Kimberly Brouchous, district sales manager for Sigma Industries, sat at her desk contemplating how she should go about making a decision that was forced upon her during the course of the previous week. The decision she had to make would greatly affect both the future prospects for her district and the lives of the 10 individuals Sigma employed as salespeople within her district.

Three days before, top management had decided, as a result of worsening financial conditions, that each district had to cut its sales personnel expenses by a minimum of 10 percent. The options given to district sales managers were to reduce the number of salespeople employed within their districts, increase the amount of sales individuals would need in order to reach quota and begin receiving their commissions, or take an action that combined the first two alternatives. The home office wanted a decision on which action(s) would be taken by no later than December 15. At the present time, the Sigma salespeople in Kimberly's district were averaging $40,000 in earnings, 50 percent of which was salary and 50 percent commissions. All salespeople had been with the company for at least four years. In order to meet top management's demands, Kimberly would have to choose between three alternatives. First, she could lay off two salespeople, which would result in salary savings of $40,000. The remaining eight salespeople could expect to see their commissions increase by an average of $5,000. This would result from their taking over the accounts previously handled by the laid-off individuals.

Second, she could raise the quota needed for salespeople to begin collecting commissions. This would result in an average decrease of $4,000 in each salesperson's earnings. Finally, she could decide to eliminate one salesperson, while

simultaneously raising the quota. The effect of this action would be to keep each remaining salesperson's average earnings at the $40,000 level.

Two factors added to the complexity of Kimberly's decision. On December 1, Joe Sancho, one of the district's top salespeople, had stopped by Kimberly's office. Joe had been with Sigma for 19 years. During his visit, Joe informed Kimberly that he was going to retire in June. At that time, he would be eligible for full retirement benefits, having been with the company for 20 years. Should Joe leave the company prior to June 1, he would be ineligible for fully paid medical insurance and would lose monthly retirement payments equaling $100 per month.

Prior to the company's decision to cut back personnel expenses, Kimberly had planned to hire and train a new salesperson to replace Joe. This salesperson would have accompanied Joe on customer visits during his remaining months and, upon Joe's retirement, taken over his accounts. Now, this option was no longer viable.

Second, Kimberly's work was interrupted by an urgent phone call from Tom Eliason, who was employed in Sigma's personnel department. Tom had attended college with Kimberly. During that time, they had developed a friendship that still continued. The purpose of Tom's call was to inform Kimberly that Brian Kinder, the newest salesperson in her district, had just submitted a receipt for an antidepressant medication. Further, Brian had requested a two-month unpaid medical leave of absence beginning January 1. Several times during the course of the call, Tom told Kimberly that the information he was giving her had to be kept secret as Sigma's personnel guidelines clearly forbade disclosure of employee medical information outside the personnel department. Under normal company procedures, Kimberly would not be informed of the company's decision on approval of the leave of absence until at least December 20. Kimberly hung up the phone in a state of shock, as she had spent the entire morning with Brian, going over his January sales call plan.

Questions for Analysis

1. Is the decision that Kimberly has to make a programmed or nonprogrammed one? Explain.

2. How do Kimberly's personal values and sense of ethical responsibility have an impact upon her decision?

3. Should Kimberly involve her salespeople in the decision-making process? Why or why not?

Video Case
Decision Making

In a global economy, sound business decisions require consideration of a number of important factors that may potentially affect a company's ability to meet its goals. The quality of managerial decisions can determine a company's success or failure. A recent study concluded that managers spend approximately 50 percent of their time dealing with the consequences of bad decision making.

It's important to understand decision making as it occurs in the business world. In this video case of two successful businesses—the Second City Theater in Chicago, Illinois, and Heavenly Ski Resort in Lake Tahoe, Nevada—we explore the following decision making topics:

1. Managers make different decisions under different business conditions.
2. When managers take steps to explore and evaluate alternatives, it leads to more effective decisions.
3. All managers need to be aware of the many factors that can affect the decision-making process.

Broadly defined, decision making is a process of choosing among alternative courses of action. In the business world, this process takes place under varying conditions of certainty and risk. Decision making is more likely to be effective when approached in a series of steps that explore and evaluate alternatives.

1. Identify the problem.
2. Generate alternative solutions.
3. Evaluate the alternatives.
4. Select the best alternative.
5. Implement the decision.
6. Evaluate the decision.

In order to evaluate a decision, managers must gather information that can shed light on its effectiveness. Although most managers would prefer to follow all of these decision making steps, time and circumstances don't always allow it. This decision making process can also be influenced by other important factors such as intuition, emotion and stress, confidence, and risk propensity.

Although Second City and Heavenly Lake Tahoe are very different businesses, they are both examples of companies that have made successful decisions under conditions of risk and uncertainty. Second City has grown from its roots as a small "mom and pop" theater, to a large, internationally known corporate enterprise. Rather than in investing all its resources into its immensely popular old-town Chicago improv theater, Second City has decided to translate its expertise into other ventures, such as television, corporate training, and other theaters in Toronto, suburban Chicago, and Detroit.

Joe Keefe, producer of Second City communications, said, "So much of what we do is in having people approach the decision-making process from a group point of view, and allowing for input. It's difficult many times to find the time to listen to everyone but I literally try to book out time weekly to meet with people. I meet with the directors after every project. I know what the heck happened: What do they think? How do they feel? What does the client feel? By the time you have all that information, the decision is usually self-evident. It's a matter of making certain that you get accurate information immediately, that your client response issues are done immediately, and then your intuition will tell you what's the right thing to do. Ninety-nine percent of my decisions are self-evident once you have the right information."

Heavenly Lake Tahoe accommodates nearly 750,000 skiers per year, and competes as one of eight large Tahoe-area resorts. Like the Second City Theater, managers at Heavenly must make decisions affecting the growth of the company in less than ideal conditions. Malcolm Tibbets, vice president of mountain operations said, "Quick decisions happen every hour of the day. Looking at the level of business coming into the base areas and making a quick decision to open an additional lift that was not otherwise scheduled or vice versa shutting down a lift in order to save some cost because the level of business is not going to warrant the operation of that lift. Whether to start the snow plows at midnight or wait until 3:00 in the morning. These kinds of decisions are continuous. You have to have people in positions that are unafraid to make those decisions without calling six people and wasting time collecting all the data. That's just part of the way this business works."

Although following the six decision-making steps may lead to a sounder decision-making process, theory doesn't always play out in practice. Management may follow some steps, but perhaps not all of them, depending on the factors affecting the decision-making process. "Most of the managers are encouraged to make a decision right away and don't hold on to the problem. It's such a fast pace that I want them to just go on to the next thing and not hold the problem back. I've empowered them to pretty much make their own decisions. They were hired to do a job so I let them do the job. If there's something wrong we can discuss that later, but business must go on," said Steve Jacobson, director of food and beverage at Heavenly.

Sometimes it's easier to follow the steps of the decision-making model. Kelly Leonard, associate producer at Second City, said, "Our northwest theater in Rolling Meadows we had seriously considered moving to Oakbrook. These people wanted us to move in, they were going to pay to have us move in and we had the luxury of a great deal of time to decide if we should leave or not. We decided not to primarily because the risk wasn't worth it at that point. We really had a chance to make our lists of pros and cons which is exactly what we did and we finally decided to say no."

Making people laugh takes a lot of hard work and courage, as well as creativity and insight. Decisions about artistic design don't always fit the mold of the decision-making model. Certain factors, such as intuition, emotion and stress, or confidence and risk propensity can affect the decision-making process. Leonard said, "We did a show which was a parody of Our Town and it was at times brilliant and at times not. It got great reviews, it was very intricate in its knowledge of Our Town. However, it demanded a certain understanding of the play and of the Second City form to

really get all the jokes. What we found is that though critics loved it and many of us loved it here, the audience didn't understand it. We tried an advertising campaign to support it, though to that time we had not advertised much, and it didn't work and people wouldn't come. So we had to switch over the show."

Not all factors affecting the decision-making process are negative. Some, such as intuition, can assist an experienced manager in making decisions under pressure.

Both the Second City Theater and Heavenly Lake Tahoe face the challenge of providing entertainment to consumers. In their day-to-day operations, both companies experience the need to make decisions in varying conditions of certainty, uncertainty, and risk. Both companies follow the steps of the decision-making model when feasible: Identifying a problem, generating alternatives, evaluating the alternatives, selecting the best alternative, implementing the decision, and evaluating the decision. Factors such as intuition, emotion and stress, and confidence or risk propensity can also have an impact on the decision-making process. Awareness of the nature of decision making, its important steps, and influential factors may help managers minimize the time they spend responding to the consequences of poor decision making. This can enable managers to spend more time maximizing opportunities for growth.

Critical Thinking Questions

1. Decision making is described in the video as a series of steps. Do you agree with the six steps as outlined in the video? What additional procedures might be added to the process?

2. There are situations where decision making requires input from many people, and times when decisions have to be made by an individual. Describe a situation that would require wide input, and one where an individual should make a decision without outside input. How do these situations differ?

3. Managerial decision making is affected by something called "risk propensity." What does this term mean? How can managers improve their risk propensity?

EXPERIENTIAL EXERCISE
LOST-AT-SEA DECISION MAKING

Purpose

The purpose of this exercise is to offer you the opportunity to compare individual and group decision making.

The Exercise in Class

You are adrift on a private yacht in the South Pacific. As a consequence of a fire of unknown origin, much of the yacht and its contents have been destroyed. The yacht is now slowly sinking. Your location is unclear because of the destruction of critical navigational equipment and because you and the crew were distracted trying to bring the fire under control. Your best estimate is that you are approximately 1,000 miles south-southwest of the nearest land.

Exhibit 1 contains a list of 15 items that are intact and undamaged after the fire. In addition to these articles, you have a serviceable rubber life raft with oars, large enough to carry yourself, the crew, and all the items listed here. The total contents of all survivors' pockets are a package of cigarettes, several books of matches, and five $1 bills.

1. Working independently and without discussing the problem or the merits of any of the items, your task is to rank the 15 items in the order of their importance to your survival. Under column 1, place the number 1 by the most important item, the number 2 by the second most important, and so on through number 15, the least important. When you are through, *do not discuss* the problem or your rankings of items with anyone.

2. Your instructor will establish teams of four to six students. The task for your team is to rank the 15 items, according to the group's consensus, in the order of importance to your survival. Do not vote or average team members' rankings; try to reach agreement on each item. Base your decision on knowledge, logic, or the experiences of group members. Try to avoid basing the decision on personal preference. Enter the group's ranking in column 2. This process should take between 20 and 30 minutes, or as the instructor suggests.

3. When everyone is through, your instructor will read the correct ranking, provided by officers of the US Merchant Marine. Enter the correct rankings in column 3.

4. Compute the accuracy of your individual ranking. For each item, use the absolute value (ignore plus and minus signs) of the difference between column 1 and column 3. Add up these absolute values to get your *individual accuracy index*. Enter it on the worksheet.

5. Perform the same operation as in step 4, but use columns 2 and 3 for your group ranking. Adding up the absolute values yields your *group accuracy index*. Enter it on the worksheet.

6. Compute the *average* of your group's individual accuracy indexes. Do this by adding up each member's individual accuracy index and dividing the result by the number of group members. Enter it.

7. Identify the *lowest* individual accuracy index in your group. This is the most correct ranking in your group. Enter it on the worksheet.

Exhibit 1

	Worksheet		
Items	(1) Individual Ranking	(2) Group Ranking	(3) Ranking Key
Sextant	_____	_____	_____
Shaving mirror	_____	_____	_____
Five-gallon can of water	_____	_____	_____
Mosquito netting	_____	_____	_____
One case of US Army MRE rations	_____	_____	_____
Maps of the Pacific Ocean	_____	_____	_____
Seat cushion (flotation device approved by the Coast Guard)	_____	_____	_____
Two-gallon can of oil-gas mixture	_____	_____	_____
Small transistor radio	_____	_____	_____
Shark repellent	_____	_____	_____
Twenty square feet of opaque plastic	_____	_____	_____
One quart of 160-proof Puerto Rican rum	_____	_____	_____
Fifteen feet of nylon rope	_____	_____	_____
Two boxes of chocolate bars	_____	_____	_____
Fishing kit	_____	_____	_____

Individual accuracy index	_____
Group accuracy index	_____
Average of group's individual accuracy indexes	_____
Lowest individual accuracy index (correct ranking)	_____

The Learning Message

This exercise is designed to let you experience group decision making. Think about how discussion, reflection, and the exchange of opinions influenced your final decision.

Notes

1. Duncan Boldy, Sagar Jain, and Kristine Northey, "What Makes an Effective European Manager?" *Management International Review* 33 (1993), pp. 157–69.

2. Allen R Solem, "Some Applications of Problem-Solving versus Decision Making to Management," *Journal of Business and Psychology,* Spring 1992, pp. 401–22.

3. Bernard M Bass, *Organizational Decision Making* (Burr Ridge, IL: Richard D. Irwin, 1983).

4. Herbert Simon, *The New Science of Management Decision* (New York: Harper & Row, 1960), pp. 5–6.

5. Neil M Agnew and John L Brown, "Executive Judgment: The Intuition/Rational Ration," *Personnel,* December 1985, pp. 48–54.

6. Paul C Nutt, "Types of Organizational Decision Processes," *Administrative Science Quarterly,* September 1984, pp. 414–50.

7. Weston Agor, "The Logic of Intuition: How Top Executives Make Important Decisions," *Organizational Dynamics,* Winter 1986, pp. 5–18.

8. Anna Gandori, "A Prescriptive Contingency View of Organizational Decision Making," *Administrative Science Quarterly,* June 1984, pp. 192–209.

9. Robert Libby and Joan Luft, "Determinants of Judgment Performance in Accounting Settings: Ability, Knowledge, Motivation, and Environment," *Accounting Organizations and Society* 18 (1993), pp. 425–50.

10. For a discussion of this topic, see Carol J Loomis, "Dinosaurs?" *Fortune,* May 3, 1993, pp. 36–42.

11. James E Hopper and Kenneth J Euske, "Facilitating the Identification and Evaluation of Decision Objectives," *Cost and Management,* July–August 1985, pp. 36–40.

12. Jane M Booker and Maurice C Bryson, "Decision Analysis in Project Management: An Overview," *IEEE Transactions on Engineering Management,* February 1985, pp. 3–9.

13. J W Boudreau, "Decision Theory Contributions to HRM Research and Practice," *Industrial Relations,* Spring 1984, pp. 198–217.

14. David A Cowan, "Developing a Process Model of Problem Recognition," *Academy of Management Review,* October 1986, pp. 763–77.

15. Paul D Harrison and Adrian Harrell, "Impact of Adverse Selection on Managers' Project Evaluation Decisions," *Academy of Management Journal* 36 (1993), pp. 635–43.

16. George P Huber, *Managerial Decision Making* (Glenview, IL: Scott, Foresman, 1980).

17. Dean Tjosvold, "Effects of Crisis Orientation on Managers' Approaches to Controversy in Decision Making," *Academy of Management Journal,* March 1984, pp. 130–38.

18. David B Jamison, "The Importance of Boundary Spanning Roles in Strategic Decision Making," *Journal of Management Studies,* April 1984, pp. 131–52.

19. Paul Shrivastava, "Knowledge Systems for Strategic Decision Making," *Journal of Applied Behavioral Science,* Winter 1985, pp. 95–108.

20. William Q Judge and Alex Miller, "Antecedents and Outcomes of Decision Speed in Different Environmental Contexts," *Academy of Management Journal* 34 (1991) pp. 449–63.

21. Bill Parks, "Rate of Return—The Poison Apple," *Business Horizons,* May–June 1993, pp. 55–57.

22. Don Swann, "Decisions, Decisions: First, Get the Facts," *Management Review,* April 1993, pp. 58–61.

23. J E Hodder and H E Riggs, "Pitfalls in Evaluating Risky Projects," *Harvard Business Review,* January–February 1985, pp. 128–35.

24. Donald F Kuratko, Jeffrey S Hornsby, Douglas W Naffziger, and Ray V Montagno, "Implement Entrepreneurial Thinking in Established Organizations," *SAM Advanced Management Journal,* Winter 1993, pp. 28–39.

25. Paul Shrivastava and I I Mitroff, "Enhancing Organizational Research Utilization: The Role of Decision Makers' Assumptions," *Academy of Management Review,* January 1984, pp. 18–26.

26. Paul C Nutt, "Tactics of Implementation," *Academy of Management Journal,* June 1986, pp. 232–61.

27. Paul C Nutt, "Strategic Decisions Made by Top Executives and Middle Managers with Data and Process Dominant Types," *Journal of Management Studies,* March 1990, pp. 173–94.

28. E Frank Harrison, *The Managerial Decision Making Process* (Boston: Houghton Mifflin, 1975), p. 42.

29. Linda K Trevino, "Ethical Decision Making in Organizations: A Person–Situation Interaction Model," *Academy of Management Review,* July 1986, pp. 601–17.

30. Patricia A Renwick and Henry Tosi, "The Effects of Sex, Marital Status, and Educational Background on Selected Decisions," *Academy of Management Journal,* March 1978, pp. 93–103.

31. For a discussion of this topic, see Marcia A Brodsky, "Successful Female Corporate Managers and Entrepreneurs," *Group & Organization Management,* September 1993, pp. 366–78.

32. Leon Festinger, *A Theory of Cognitive Dissonance* (New York: Harper & Row, 1957).

33. J Richard Harrison and James G March, "Decision Making and Postdecision Surprises," *Administrative Science Quarterly,* March 1984, pp. 26–42.

34. John P Wanous and Margaret A Yountz, "Solution Diversity and Quality of Group Decisions," *Academy of Management Journal,* March 1986, pp. 149–58.

35. Phil Frame, "Strategy Board Turbocharges GM Decision-Making Process," *Automotive News,* March 15, 1993, pp. 3–4.

36. David M Schweiger, William R Sandburg, and James W Ragan, "Group Approaches for Improving Strategic Decision Making," *Academy of Management Journal,* March 1986, pp. 51–71.

37. The classic experiment which suggested these factors is Solomon Asch, "Studies of Independence and Conformity," *Psychological Monographs,* 1956, pp. 68–70.

38. Andre L Delbecq, Andrew H Van de Ven, and David H Gustafson, *Group Techniques for Program Planning* (Glenview, IL: Scott, Foresman, 1975).

39. R Brent Gallupe, Lana M Bastianutti, and William H Cooper, "Unblocking Brainstorms," *Journal of Applied Psychology,* February 1991, pp. 137–42.

40. "Study Spots Global Marketing Trends (Global Marketing 2000: Future Trends and Their Implications, a Delphi Study)," *Marketing News,* October 14, 1991, p. 9.

41. Brian Mullen, Craig Johnson, and Eduardo Salas, "Productivity Loss in Brainstorming Groups: A Meta-Analytic Integration," *Basic and Applied Social Psychology,* March 1991, pp. 3–23.

C   H   A   P   T   E   R

6   THE PLANNING FUNCTION

Chapter Learning Objectives

After completing Chapter 6, you should be able to:

- **Define** the planning function in terms of managerial responsibilities and decisions.
- **Describe** the planning function's four principal elements.
- **Discuss** why the planning function must begin with the determination of objectives.
- **Compare** arguments for and against the alternative means for implementing a plan.
- **Identify** the most useful forecasting technique for a particular set of circumstances.

A Plan to Get Back in the Game

So far, the 1990s have proved to be turbulent times for the manufacturers and marketers of many leading consumer products. Consumers seem to have fallen out of love with higher-priced, branded products; instead, they are focusing on value—a combination of both quality and price. Legions of private-label competitors (who at times seem intent on giving away their products for free) have sprung up out of nowhere to serve this ever-growing, price-conscious market segment. As a result, many once-leading companies have resorted to quick fixes, such as increasing their promotional spending, desperately holding onto the fading hope that if market share is retained, profits will somehow magically reappear.

At Procter & Gamble (P&G), however, executives have a feeling that the marketplace changes are indeed permanent. P&G's CEO, Edwin Artzt, strongly believes that resorting to short-term fixes is the equivalent of walking into a bottomless pit; once you get in, there's no way out. Instead, P&G managers have emphasized planning as their primary weapon to combat these market threats and regain lost profits. As a result, the night-lights have burned brightly at the headquarters of the Cincinnati giant with managers focusing on what P&G aims to accomplish and how.

In a series of moves that have shocked retailers and are being closely watched by other rivals, P&G has drastically revamped many of the company's time-honored selling techniques. What follows is a description of several of the actions P&G has taken to date toward achieving the company's long-term objective of regaining market supremacy and associated profit levels.

1. *The simplification and consolidation of product lines.* P&G has trimmed back on many of the size, color, and flavor variations offered in the past.

2. *A drastic reduction in the use of coupons and consumer promotions.* Rather than inundate consumers with coupons targeted solely at increasing short-term sales of its products, P&G decided to permanently lower the retail price of many brands and to provide free samples for new products only. By 1996 the company decided it liked the results and decided to expand its low price strategy to other products as well as to expand its decision to eliminate coupons.

3. *A massive cut in discounts offered to retailers.* In lieu of providing retailers with trade discounts (i.e., discounts, fees, and allowances), P&G decided to lower the wholesale prices charged to channel members. The intent of this action has been to stop the wild swings in price that formerly took place at the retail level.

4. *A reduction in workforce size.* As a result of taking the above actions, demand for products is less erratic, and the number of production changes needed to prepare lot runs of differing size and brand variations has been reduced. As a result of realizing production efficiencies and cutting back on unnecessary activities, P&G has been able to trim back its workforce.

Sources: C Murphy, "P&G Escalates Pricing Conflict," *Marketing*, April 1996, p. 3; J Quinn, "Will P&G Test Mean Curtains to Coupons?" *Incentive*, April 1996, p. 7; G Stern, "P&G Gains Little from Diaper Price Cuts," *The Wall Street Journal*, October 28, 1993, p. B6; Z Schiller, "Procter & Gamble Hits Back," *Business Week*, July 19, 1993, pp. 20–22; and J Riddle, "Procter & Gamble Sets Sweeping Employee Cuts to Stay Competitive," *Brandweek*, July 19, 1993, pp. 1, 6.

Managers have a primary responsibility for planning. In fact, some managers see planning as the primary management function and think that organizing and controlling are secondary. Whatever its relative importance to other management functions, planning is essential if organizations are to achieve effective levels of performance.[1] Companies can no longer afford to forgo change if they want to sustain competitive advantage in global markets.[2] The ability or inability of a firm to successfully implement and adapt to such change is linked directly to its planning system. The Management in Action that opened this chapter provides an example of the important role planning plays in an organization's ability to keep abreast of changing marketplace conditions.

The Focus of Planning

Planning focuses on the future: what is to be accomplished and how. In essence, the planning function includes those managerial activities that determine *objectives for the future and the appropriate means for achieving those objectives*. The outcome of the planning function is a plan, a written document that specifies the courses of action the firm will take.

The Elements of Planning

The planning function requires managers to make decisions about four fundamental elements of plans: objectives, actions, resources, and implementation.

Objectives specify future conditions that a manager hopes to achieve. For example, the statement, "The firm's objective is to achieve a 12 percent rate of return on investment by the end of fiscal year 1996," refers to a condition (12 percent rate of return) that the manager hopes to achieve at a specific time in the future (by the end of fiscal year 1996).

Actions are the means, or specific activities, planned to achieve the objectives. A course of action intended to result in a 12 percent return might be to engage in a product development effort aimed at introducing five new products in the two-year period—1995 and 1996. Establishing objectives and choosing courses of action also

---

Management Focus

A Woman with a Plan

More people are employed by woman-owned businesses than by all of the Fortune 500 companies. The number of these businesses has increased at a rate greater than 20 percent annually, now totalling more than 6.5 million. Without question, women business owners are carving out a growing marketplace niche. Lillian Vernon, the specialty catalog marketer, provides a good example of the increasingly important role that woman-owned businesses are playing in the growth of the US economy.

The company began in 1951 when Vernon, as a young housewife, placed a $495 ad in *Seventeen* magazine, offering free personalization of a purse or belt. From there, the business took off. In 1987, the Lillian Vernon Corporation went public, using the proceeds to fund the company's continued growth. To keep up with the ever-increasing volume of orders shipped, the company opened a national distribution center in Virginia Beach, Virginia, in 1988. As the 90s come to an end, the organization has seen sales advance every year in addition to revenues, operating profits, and net worth.

Vernon's secret? Offer customers high-quality merchandise, such as household, gardening, decorative, and children's products, at exceptionally good values. The cost of an average item in one of Lillian Vernon's 19 catalogs is $17, and the average customer order is only $39. Yet, in the last year alone, Lillian Vernon shipped more than 4.3 million orders. Today, the Lillian Vernon Corporation stands as one of the largest mail-order companies in the United States.

Entrepreneurs who are successful in starting and growing a business share two common traits. First, in the deepest sense, they are willing to take risks (for Vernon, the risk was the $495 cost of the first ad) to achieve what they believe in. And second, they effectively plan, taking actions toward achieving their objectives. Vernon's plan was seemingly simple: offer useful, low-priced, high-quality items for sale by mail. The payoff? A thriving business that is poised to take even further advantage of the current trend toward in-home catalog shopping.

Sources: R Brammer, "Mail-order Bride," *Barrons*, March 4, 1996, p. 20; M Oneal, "Just What Is an Entrepreneur?" *Business Week*, Enterprise Special Issue, Fall 1993, pp. 104–12; E J Bamford, "Woman, America's Top Women Business Owners," *Working Woman*, May 1993, pp. 49–64.

require *forecasting* the future. A manager cannot plan without giving consideration to future events and factors that could affect what will be possible to accomplish.

Resources are constraints on the course of action. For example: "The total cost to be incurred in the development of five new products must not exceed $10 million." A plan should specify the kinds and amounts of resources required, as well as the potential sources and allocations of those resources. Specifying resource constraints also involves *budgeting*—identifying the sources and levels of resources that can be committed to the courses of action.

Finally, a plan must include ways and means to implement the intended actions. *Implementation* involves the assignment and direction of personnel to carry out the plan.

Although the four elements of the planning function are discussed separately, they are in fact related. Objectives must be set according to what is possible, given the forecasts of the future and the budgeting of resources. Moreover, availability of resources can be affected by the very actions management is planning. In the preceding example, if a 12 percent return is not achieved, $10 million may not be available because shareholders, bondholders, or other sources of capital will not invest the funds. Then, other action may not be feasible.

In some organizations, planning is the combined effort of managers and other personnel. In other organizations, planning is done by the top management group. In still others, as seen in the Management Focus on Lillian Vernon, the initial planning is performed by one individual. Depending on the size and type of organization, the number of individuals holding responsibility for planning will vary. Normally, the larger the organization, the greater the number of individuals involved in the planning process.

Planning activities can range from complex, formal procedures to simple and informal ones. Although the form of planning activities varies from organization to organization, the substance is the same. Plans and planning always involve objectives, actions, resources, and implementation directed toward improving an organization's performance in the future. Figure 6–1 outlines the planning function.

FIGURE 6–1   The Planning Function

The planning function is a set of related steps by which management determines what is to be done and how it will be done.

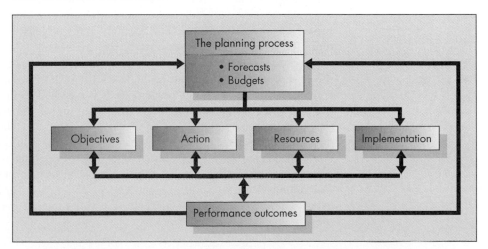

The Importance of Planning

Planning can occur at all levels in an organization. A production manager who identifies standard output and directs subordinates in using standard procedures is engaged in planning. Sales managers who define sales quotas and assign salespeople to particular territories are engaged in planning. In both instances, these managers determine objectives (standard output, sales quotas), actions (standard procedures, assignment to territories), and resources (production workers, salespeople).

In other companies, planning is being pushed down to lower levels of the organization.[3] Many American companies are discovering that workers can manage themselves. These so-called superteams arrange their own schedules, set profit targets, have a say in hiring and firing decisions, order material and equipment, and in some cases, devise strategy. General Mills, Federal Express Corporation, 3M Company, Aetna Life & Casualty Company, and Chaparral Steel are examples of companies that have instituted this process. Superteams aren't appropriate in all situations. They make sense only if a job entails a high level of dependency among workers in a complex environment. The aim of a superteam is to take advantage of cross-functionalism, drawing people with different jobs or functions together. A major goal of the team is to free managers from time-consuming supervisory tasks, thus allowing the manager additional time to engage in long-term planning and coordination activities. In the future, as the average company becomes smaller and employs fewer managers, the trend toward increased worker involvement in the planning process should continue to grow.[4]

The fact that most managers plan in some form is ample evidence of planning's importance in management. We can identify the following four specific benefits.[5]

Coordinating Efforts

Management exists because the work of individuals and groups in organizations must be coordinated, and planning is one important technique for achieving coordinated effort. An effective plan specifies objectives both for the total organization and for each part of the organization. By working toward planned objectives, the behavior of each part contributes to and is compatible with goals for the entire organization.

Preparing for Change

An effective plan of action allows room for change. The longer the time between completion of a plan and accomplishment of an objective, the greater the necessity to include contingency plans. Yet, if management has considered the potential effect of the change, it can be better prepared to deal with it. History provides some vivid examples of what can result from failure to prepare for change. The collapse of many banks, savings and loans, and airlines in the last few years was caused in large part by those industries' managements' lack of preparedness.

Indeed, as one executive states, "Forewarned is forearmed."[6] The combining of the European Community into a single market is an example of the critical need for contingency plans. Although past emphasis was placed on the years 1992 and 1993 as the time when all regulatory barriers would be removed, it is clear now that this event may not happen until the end of the decade if at all. The European Community countries represent a $4.5 trillion market with 320 million people. Currently, US companies draw only 9 percent of their sales from this region.[7] The most astute companies, while realizing that many changes must take place before the European Community is a truly single market, are already engaged in market planning for this event. These companies have developed a wide range of contingency plans to better prepare for all possible outcomes.

Developing Performance Standards

Plans define expected behaviors, and in management terms, expected behaviors are performance standards. For example, the success of a plan by a bank to improve service quality is highly dependent on the expected behavior of the individuals carrying out the task. If bank employees are unable to provide customers with quick decisions, a minimum of waiting, personalized caring service, and front-line responsiveness and empathy, then the plan to improve service quality will most definitely fail.[8]

As plans are implemented throughout an organization, the objectives and course of action assigned to each individual and group are the bases for standards, which can be used to assess actual performance. In some instances, the objectives provide the standards: A manager's performance can be assessed in terms of how close her unit comes to accomplishing its objective. In other instances, the courses of action are the standards: A production worker can be held accountable for doing a job in the prescribed manner. Through planning, management derives a rational, objective basis for developing performance standards. Without planning, performance standards are likely to be nonrational and subjective.

Developing Managers

Good planning involves the art of making difficult things simple.[9] Toward this end, the act of planning requires high levels of intellectual activity. Those who plan must be able to deal with complex, abstract ideas and information. Planners must think systematically about the present and the future. Through planning, the *future* state of the organization can be improved if its managers take an *active* role in moving the organization toward that future. Planning, then, implies that managers should be *proactive* and *make* things happen rather than *reactive* and *let* things happen. Through the act of planning, managers not only develop their ability to think futuristically but, to the extent that their plans are effective, their motivation to plan is also reinforced. The *act* of planning sharpens managers' ability to think as they consider abstract ideas and possibilities for the future.[10] Thus, both the result and the act of planning benefit the organization and its managers.[11]

The accompanying Management Focus provides an example of how one person's ability to focus on the abstract led to the creation of a successful business.

Setting Objectives and Priorities

The planning function begins with the determination of future objectives, and these objectives must satisfy the expectations of many and often conflicting groups in the organization's environment. Whether the organization is a business, university, or government agency, the environment supplies the resources that sustain it. In exchange for these resources, the organization must supply the environment with goods and services at an acceptable price and quality. The increasing interdependence between organizations and their environments has caused corporate managers to turn more and more to formal planning techniques.[12] Moreover, the evidence is clear that organizations that use formal approaches to planning are more profitable than those that do not.[13]

Management initiates planning to determine the *priority* and *timing* of objectives. In addition, management must also resolve *conflict* between objectives and provide *measurement* of objectives so that results can be evaluated.[14]

Management Focus

Starbucks—The Power of Vision

In the age of fiber optics and biotechnology, an old-time commodity like coffee is not an obvious business opportunity, especially at $2 per cup. After all, coffee sales have declined steadily since the 1960s, primarily due to health concerns about caffeine. Yet, only seven years after purchasing Starbucks from its founders, owner Howard Schultz has transformed the gourmet coffee company into one of the fastest-growing businesses in North America.

Starbucks's history originally dates back to 1971, when three entrepreneurs started selling whole-bean coffee in Seattle's Pike Place Market. They named their store Starbucks, after the first mate in *Moby Dick*. In 1982, Schultz was asked to join the company as manager of retail sales and marketing. While on a buying trip in Italy, Schultz was struck by a vision. He saw the special relationship Italian culture has with coffee and determined that this same type of relationship was also possible in America, and that Starbucks could capitalize on it because of the premium quality of Starbucks coffee. However, the owners did not agree with Schultz's vision. Consequently, Schultz left the company and wrote a business plan for this new venture.

In 1986, Schultz opened his first coffee bar, with the financial aid of Starbucks's owners. The coffee bar was named *Il Giornale,* after an Italian newspaper, and Schultz served Starbucks coffee. It was an immediate success, and Schultz opened two more coffee bars—another one in Seattle and one in Vancouver. The following year, Schultz bought out Starbucks for $4 million.

From the beginning, Schultz built his business around a plan of cautious growth. Immediately following the purchase of Starbucks, his first move (after a careful audit of his new company) was to write a new business plan. He laid out his vision and has adhered to it faithfully ever since. Schultz's philosophy is as follows: If you build a solid infrastructure, hire an all-star management team, and serve the finest product, the customers will come. And indeed they have; in 1996 Starbucks celebrated its 25th anniversary with nearly 1,000 stores nationwide.

Coffee giants Procter & Gamble, Nestlé, and Kraft General Foods concede that the growing popularity of fancier brews, such as the ones Starbucks serves, is hurting their sales. The "big three" have always focused more on building brand names than on creating better coffees. The growing demand for special coffees represents a big change in consumer behavior, a change these coffee giants did not identify. As a result, they have lost sales to upstarts like Starbucks. As we close out the decade, Starbucks and similar cafes hold almost 25 percent of the market.

Sources: M Matzer, "Starbucks Restyles for 25th Bash," *Brandweek,* September 1996, pp. 1,6; A J Slywotzky and K Mundt, "Hold The Sugar," *Across the Board,* September 1996, pp. 39–43; K Veveny, "For Coffee's Big Three, a Gourmet-Brew Boom Proves Embarrassing Bust," *The Wall Street Journal,* November 4, 1993, pp. B1 & B9; E P M Reilly, "Coffeehouse Craze Scalds Some Owners," *The Wall Street Journal,* November 3, 1993, p. B1.

Priority of Objectives

The phrase *priority of objectives* implies that at a given time, accomplishing one objective is more important than accomplishing others. For example, to a firm having difficulty meeting payrolls and due dates on accounts, the objective of maintaining a minimum cash balance may be more important than achieving minimum profitability. Priority of objectives also reflects the relative importance of certain objectives regardless of time. For example, survival of the organization is a necessary condition for the realization of all other objectives.

Managers always face alternative objectives that must be evaluated and ranked, and they must establish priorities if they want to allocate resources in a rational way. Managers are particularly concerned with the ranking of seemingly interdependent objectives. For example, many African-American-owned businesses dedicate themselves to boosting economic opportunities at the community level while simultaneously pursuing profits.[15] Because determining objectives and priorities is a judgmental decision, it is a difficult process. Indeed, a reality of modern business is that necessary trade-offs may, in the short run, result in seemingly inconsistent priorities and standards.[16]

Several Japanese firms, including Toyota Motor Corporation, Toshiba, Inc., Pioneer Electronics, and Sony Corporation, have recently experienced problems in their attempts to balance objectives.[17] As both foreign and domestic competitors rushed new products to market, increased pressure was placed on these companies to cut production costs and speed up new product development. New parts and materials were integrated into products without proper testing. As a result, quality problems surfaced that potentially threaten these companies' previously earned reputations for producing quality goods.

Perhaps, the greatest fault of these Japanese companies was that they lost sight of what should have been their overriding priority: the creation of customer satisfaction. As more and more American companies have come to realize, customer satisfaction is highly related to issues of quality. In fact, customer satisfaction can be considered the backbone of all Total Quality Management programs.[18]

Time Frame of Objectives

Time dimensions imply that an organization's activities are guided by different objectives, depending on the duration of the action being planned. Managers usually identify short-run, intermediate, and long-run objectives. Short-run objectives can be accomplished in less than a year; intermediate objectives require one to five years; and long-run objectives extend beyond five years. The relationship between priority and timing is quite close, since long-run objectives are those that must be accomplished to ensure the long-term survival of the organization.

The time dimension is reflected in the practice many organizations have of developing specific plans for different periods of time. The long-run objective of a business firm could be a desired rate of return on capital, with intermediate and short-run plans stated in objectives that must be accomplished to realize the ultimate goal. Management is then in a position to know the effectiveness of each year's activities in achieving not only short-run but also long-run objectives.

In some instances, short-run objectives and long-run objectives may appear to conflict. Many observers of contemporary business management argue that the emphasis on short-run goals, such as achieving market share, detracts from efforts to make commitments to such long-term objectives as improving worker productivity or profits. For example, Chrysler used to focus on market share as the key indicator of short-term success.[19] This narrow focus led to decisions that ended up alienating customers, shaving margins, planning capacity for unachievable sales volumes, and causing many other ill-fated actions. Today, Chrysler's sole, short-term objective is to work toward continuous quality improvement, a goal that company executives believe is linked directly to long-term profitability.

In recent years, the increasing pace of environmental change has prompted many organizations to adopt *strategic planning,* which focuses on the definition of long-term objectives and strategies to achieve those objectives. This is in contrast with *functional,* or *operational, planning,* which is done in the individual units within the organization and focuses on more intermediate objectives and problems. Because of its growing importance, strategic planning is the focus of Chapter 7.

Conflicts among Objectives

At any time, shareholders (owners), employees (including unions), customers, suppliers, creditors, and government agencies are all concerned with the operation of the firm. The process of setting objectives must not overlook these interest groups, and plans must incorporate and integrate their interests.[20] The form and weight to be given to any particular interest group illustrates precisely the nature of management's dilemma. Yet management's responsibility is to make these judgments. Some of the most common planning trade-offs faced by managers in business organizations are as follows:

1. Short-term profits versus long-term growth.
2. Profit margin versus competitive position.
3. Direct sales effort versus development effort.
4. Greater penetration of present markets versus developing new markets.
5. Achieving long-term growth through related businesses versus achieving it through unrelated businesses.
6. Profit objectives versus nonprofit objectives (that is, social responsibilities).
7. Growth versus stability.
8. Low-risk environment versus high-risk environment.

Management must consider the expectations of the diverse groups on whom the firm's ultimate success depends. For example, present and potential customers hold ultimate power over the firm. If they are not happy with the price and quality of the firm's product, they withdraw their support (stop buying), and the firm fails because of lack of funds. Suppliers can disrupt the flow of materials to express disagreement with the firm's activities. Government agencies have the power to enforce the firm's compliance with regulations. The existence of these interest groups and their power to affect the objectives of the firm must be recognized by managers. A business firm exists only as long as it satisfies the larger society.[21]

Studies of objectives that business managers have set for their organizations confirm the difficulty of balancing the concerns of interest groups. These studies also suggest that the more successful firms consistently emphasize profit-seeking activities that maximize the stockholders' wealth. This is not to say that successful firms seek *only* profit-oriented objectives but rather that such objectives are dominant.

Evidently, such firms are managed by persons who value pragmatic, dynamic, and achievement-oriented behavior.[22] At the same time, these persons recognize that businesses have an increasing responsibility to do what is best for society.[23] The interrelationship of the manager's values, society's needs, and organizational objectives has been aptly summarized: "*What to make, what to charge, and how to market the wares* are questions that embrace moral as well as economic questions. The answers are conditioned by the personal value system of the decision maker and the institutional values which affect the relationships of the individual to the community."[24]

Measurement of Objectives

Objectives must be understandable and acceptable to those who will help to achieve them. In fact, many people believe that specific, measurable objectives increase the performance of both employees and organizations and that difficult objectives, if accepted by employees, result in better performance than do easier objectives. In practice, effective managerial performance requires establishing objectives in every area that contributes to overall organizational performance. Management expert Peter Drucker has stated that objectives should be established in at least eight areas of organizational performance:

1. Market standing
2. Innovations
3. Productivity
4. Physical and financial resources

5. Profitability
6. Manager performance and responsibility
7. Worker performance and attitude
8. Social responsibility[25]

This classification in no way implies relative importance. Depending on the specific organization, the importance of any one objective may vary. For example, American companies tend to emphasize profitability objectives (e.g., ROI—return on investment—and capital gains to shareholders) as being most important, while Japanese companies accord highest priority to market-standing objectives such as market share and product introduction rates.[26]

Drucker has observed that "the real difficulty lies indeed not in determining what objectives we need, but in deciding how to set them."[27] This involves determining what should be measured in each area and how it should be measured. Immediately, one can recognize the difficulty of measuring performance in certain areas. For example, how can a manager measure employee attitudes and social responsibility? The more abstract the objective, the more difficult it is to measure performance.[28]

Nevertheless, effective planning requires measurement of objectives. As a result, effective measurement must become an integral part of the management process.[29] A variety of measurements exist to quantify objectives in the eight areas that Drucker suggests.

Profitability Objectives.   Profitability objectives include the ratios of profits to sales, profits to total assets, and profits to capital (net worth). The tendency in recent years has been to emphasize the ratio of profits to sales as an important measure of profitability. Both quantities in this ratio are taken from the income statement, which management generally regards as a better test of performance than the balance sheet.

However, other managers believe that the true test of profitability must combine the income statement and the balance sheet. These managers would use either the profit-to-total-asset ratio or the profit-to-net-worth ratio. Which of these two measures is preferred depends on whether the *source* of capital is an important consideration. The profit-to-total-asset ratio measures management's use of all resources, regardless of origin (that is, creditors or owners). The profit-to-net-worth ratio measures how management used the owner's contribution.

The measures are not mutually exclusive. All three ratios are profitability objectives because each measures and therefore evaluates different yet important aspects of profitability.

The purposes of profit are to measure efficiency, recover one cost element of being in business (return on invested capital), and provide funds for future expansion and innovation. The minimum profitability is that which ensures the continuous stream of capital into the organization, given the inherent risks of the industry in which the organization operates.

Marketing Objectives.   Marketing objectives measure performance relating to products, markets, distribution, and customer service objectives. They focus on the prospects for long-run profitability. Thus, well-managed organizations measure performance in such areas as market share, sales volume, number of outlets carrying the product, number of new products developed, and levels of customer satisfaction. Taken together, these measures can be viewed as a total quality indicator, for quality must permeate the organization's entire marketing function, extending to how the firm identifies and meets customer expectations, develops and delivers new products, and runs and staffs its operations.[30]

Productivity Objectives.   Productivity is measured with ratios of output to input. Other factors being equal, the higher the ratio, the more efficient is the use of inputs.

Drucker has long proposed that the *ratios of value added to sales and to profit* are the superior measures of productivity.[31] He believes that a business's objective should be to increase these ratios and that departments in the firm should be evaluated on the basis of these increases. The argument for value added is that it measures the increase in value of the purchased materials owing to the combined efforts of the firm, since value added is equal to the difference between the purchase price and the market value of materials and supplies. In this way, the efficiency of the firm's efforts is measured directly. This measure of productivity could also be used for comparisons among the individual departments in the firm.

Physical and Financial Objectives.   Physical and financial objectives reflect the firm's capacity to acquire resources sufficient to achieve its objectives. Measurement of physical and financial objectives is comparatively easy since numerous accounting measures can be used. Liquidity measures, such as the current ratio, working capital turnover, acid-test ratio, debt-to-equity ratio, and accounts receivable and inventory turnover, can be used in establishing objectives and evaluating performance in financial planning.

Other Objectives.   Objectives for profitability, market standing, productivity, and physical and financial resources are amenable to measurement. Objectives for innovation, employee attitudes, manager behavior, and social responsibility are, however, not so easily identifiable or measurable in concrete terms. This is important because, without measurement, any subsequent evaluation is inconclusive. For example, a company that desires to encourage and achieve diversity in the workplace may use measures such as the number of minority employees hired and/or promoted, diversity training sessions developed and run, internal advocacy groups established, and flexible work policies enacted to gauge its progress in this area.[32] Some other selected measures of performance are summarized in Table 6–1.

RJR-Nabisco, Inc., recognizes multiple objectives may be desirable.[33] As part of its compensation plan, RJR-Nabisco offers managers the opportunity to earn bonuses. The amount of the bonus awarded depends on the manager's performance in meeting several objectives. For example, at Nabisco Brands, bonuses are tied to targets for cash flow, net income, market share, and discretionary programs such as specific product launches.

An Example of Objectives in Planning

Stating objectives clearly is a critical element of planning.[34] Our discussion of objective setting is summarized in Table 6–2, which is based on one organization's actual experience in establishing objectives. This organization established seven objectives that management ranked in the order of priority shown in the table.

Clear objectives can be converted into specific targets and actions. Note that management also stated each objective in Table 6–2 in more specific secondary objectives, which can become objectives for individual departments. For example, the secondary objective associated with objective 1 can serve as a financial management objective; those associated with objective 2 can be marketing objectives; and those associated with objective 3 can be the goals of the personnel department.

TABLE 6–1   Selected Measures of Objectives

Management must decide which measures to use to indicate whether objectives are being achieved.

Objective	Possible Measures
Profitability	1. Ratio of profit to sales 2. Ratio of profit to total assets 3. Ratio of profit to capital
Marketing	1. Market share 2. Sales volume 3. Rate of new product development 4. Number of outlets
Productivity	1. Ratio of output to labor costs 2. Ratio of output to capital costs 3. Ratio of value added to sales 4. Ratio of value added to profit
Physical and financial	1. Current ratio 2. Working capital turnover 3. Ratio of debt to equity 4. Accounts receivable turnover 5. Inventory turnover

---

TABLE 6–2   The Development of Objectives

Management can subdivide some objectives and develop fairly specific indicators of achievement.

Objective	Possible Secondary Objectives	Possible Indicators
1. Achieve a 15 percent return on investment.	a. Earn maximum return on idle funds.	Interest income.
2. Maintain a 40 percent share of the market.	a. Retain 75 percent of old customers. b. Obtain 25 percent of first-time customers.	Percent replacement purchases. Percent initial purchases.
3. Develop middle managers for executive positions.	a. Develop a merit review system by year-end. b. Select 10 managers to attend industry-sponsored executive school.	Report submitted on November 1. Number selected by January 1.
4. Help to ensure that clean air is maintained in all geographical areas in which the firm has plant locations.	a. Reduce air pollution by 15 percent.	By April 1, pollutants to be 125 pounds/hour measured at stack by electrostatic.
5. Provide working conditions that constantly exceed industrywide safety levels.	a. Automate loading process in plant B. b. Reduce in-plant injuries by 10 percent by year-end.	Installation to be 50 percent complete by January 1. Ratio of labor days lost to total labor days.
6. Manufacture all products as efficiently as possible.	a. Increase productivity by 5 percent through installation of new punching machine.	Installed by August 1. Ratio of output to total labor hours.
7. Maintain and improve employee satisfaction to levels consistent with those in our own and similar industries.	a. Improve employee satisfaction levels in all functional areas by 15 percent by year-end.	Ratio of quits to total employees. Attitude survey questionnaires administered to all employees.

Courses of Action

Actions, the second element of the planning function, are the catalysts that can determine success or failure in meeting objectives. Planned courses of action are called *strategies* and *tactics,* usually differentiated by the scope and magnitude of the action. Whatever the name, a planned action is directed toward changing a future condition—that is, achieving an objective. For example, if an objective is to increase productivity from five units of output per labor hour to six units per labor hour, a course of action has to be identified and implemented.

In some instances, managers simply do not know what action to take. When President John F Kennedy stated as a national objective the placing of an American on the moon by 1970, no one knew exactly what action was necessary to accomplish that objective. In other instances, numerous alternative courses of action may be possible. For example, productivity increases can be achieved through a variety of means, including improved technology, employee training, management training, reward systems, and improved working conditions. In such cases, managers must select the least costly but most effective alternative. Often, several possible courses of action exist for top managers who are planning for the total organization. As the plan becomes more localized to a simple unit in the organization, the number of alternatives tends to become fewer yet more familiar.

The important point is that courses of action and objectives are causally related; the objective is caused to occur by the courses of action. The intellectual effort required in planning involves knowing not only *what* alternatives will accomplish an objective but also *which* one is most efficient. Planning is a management process, deductive in nature and designed to produce orderly results.[35] In some instances, managers can test the effects of a course of action by forecasting. Forecasting is *the process of using past and current information to predict future events.*

A typical objective in business planning is to maintain or increase sales volume. Sales volume is a primary source of liquid resources (e.g., cash, accounts receivable, and notes receivable), which managers can use to finance the firm's activities. Courses of action that affect sales include price changes, marketing and sales activities, and new product development. Factors beyond the control of management also affect sales. Such external factors include the price of competing and substitute products, competitors' marketing/sales activities, and general economic conditions (expansion, recession, inflation). Although managers cannot control many of the factors that determine sales volume, forecasting remains a valuable managerial tool.[36]

Forecasting Sales Volume

Managers currently use four methods to forecast future events. Although we present them in the context of forecasting sales volume, the methods are generally applicable to forecasting other events.

1. *Hunches.* Estimates of future sales can be based on past sales data, comments by salespeople and customers, and instinctive reaction to the general state of affairs. This approach is relatively cheap and usually effective in firms whose market is stable or at least changing at a predictable rate.

2. *Market survey.* Estimates of future sales can be based on the opinions customers express to the organization's salespeople. More sophisticated statistical sampling techniques yield more refined information; the forecaster can specify both the range of projected sales and the degree of confidence in the estimates.

3. *Time-series analysis*. Estimates of future sales can be based on the relationship between sales and time. The movement of sales over time is affected by at least three factors: seasonal, cyclical, and trend. This means that a firm's sales can vary in response to seasonal factors, to cycles common to business activity generally, and to trends of long duration. The management of a brewery knows that peak sales occur during the summer months. But it also is aware of the cyclical nature of beer consumption, as beer drinkers shift to liquor when their incomes increase and shift back when their incomes decline. For long-term planning, the manager also must know something about the trend in beer consumption. Consumer preferences change with time and with the introduction of new products.

4. *Econometric models*. These allow a forecaster to evaluate the impact of a number of variables on sales. Even though these techniques are the most sophisticated of the methods, they offer no hope for the elimination of all uncertainty; management judgment is still needed. The econometric approach begins with the identification of those variables that affect the sales of the firm's products. Among the obvious variables are price, competing products, and complementary products. Variables such as the age of existing stocks of the goods, availability of credit, and consumer tastes are less obvious. Measurements of these variables are obtained for previous years and matched with sales of the product for those same years.

No perfect method exists for forecasting future sales. Hunches, market surveys, time-series analysis, and econometric models provide estimates that may or may not be reasonable, and they can be no better than the information that goes into them. As technological breakthroughs in information processing occur, we can expect sales forecasts to become more accurate and consequently to be better guides for planning. At present, however, forecasting requires a great deal of managerial judgment.

Resources

The third phase of the planning function is budgeting resources for each important plan. The sales forecast presumes that a firm has a product to sell, so managers must first utilize resources to acquire or produce that product. And just as managers use forecasts to approximate income from sales, they must also forecast the future availability of major resources, including people, raw materials, energy, and money.[37] Indeed, results of such forecasts may influence management to attempt to leverage its resources.[38] This can be done in many different ways including concentrating resources on few versus many strategic goals; accumulating resources more efficiently (i.e., through strategic research alliances); complementing one kind of resource with another (i.e., blending technologies); conserving resources whenever possible (i.e., recycling innovations across product lines); and recovering resources from the marketplace in as short a time as possible (i.e., reducing time to market).

Techniques for forecasting resources are the same as those employed to forecast sales: hunches, market surveys, time-series analysis, and econometric models. The only difference is that the manager is seeking to know the quantities and prices of goods that can be purchased rather than those to be sold.

The sales forecast, whether for 1 or for 10 years, predicts the firm's level of activity. At the same time, the prediction is conditioned by the availability of resources, by economic and social events beyond the control of management, and by the predetermined objectives. Given an adequate supply of resources, the manager's next task is the allocation of resources necessary to implement a plan. The principal technique management uses in this phase of the planning function is the *budget*.

A very close relationship exists between budgeting as a planning technique and budgeting as a control technique.[39] However, this section is concerned only with the preparation of budgets as a part of planning, prior to operations. After the organization has been engaged in activities for a time, actual results are compared with the budgeted (planned) results and may lead to corrective action. This, as we see later, is the management function of controlling.[40]

The complexity of the budget phase is shown in Figure 6–2. The sales forecast plays a key role, as is evident in the placement of the sales budget; all other budgets are related to it either directly or indirectly. The production budget, for example, must specify the materials, labor, and other manufacturing expenses required to support the projected sales level. Similarly, the marketing expense budget details the costs associated with the level of sales activity projected for each product in each sales region. Administrative expenses also must be related to the predicted sales volume.

FIGURE 6–2   The Budgeting Process

The budgeting process consists of actions and decisions that affect the entire organization.

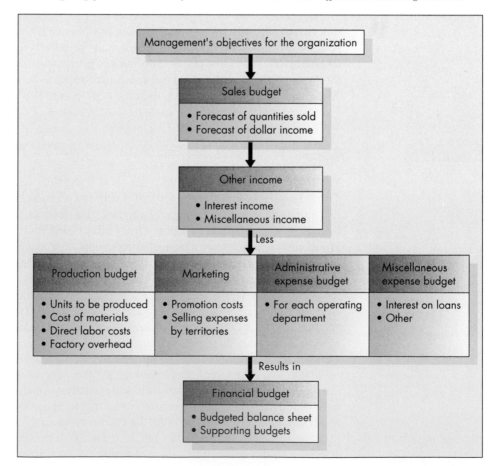

The projected sales and expenses are combined in the financial budgets, which consist of pro forma financial statements, inventory budgets, and the capital additions budget.

Forecast data are based on assumptions about the future. If these assumptions prove wrong, the budgets are inadequate. So the usefulness of financial budgets depends mainly on the degree to which they are flexible to changes in conditions. Two principal means exist to provide flexibility: variable budgeting and moving budgeting.

Variable budgeting provides for the possibility that actual output deviates from planned output. It recognizes that variable costs are related to output, while fixed costs are unrelated to output. Thus, if actual output is 20 percent less than planned output, it does not follow that actual profit will be 20 percent less than that planned. Rather, the actual profit varies, depending on the complex relationship between costs and output. Table 6-3 shows a variable budget that allows for output variations. It demonstrates the behavior of costs and profits as output varies.

To be complete, variable budgeting requires adjustments in all supporting budgets. The production, marketing, and administrative budgets must likewise allow for the impact of output variation.

Moving budgeting is the preparation of a budget for a fixed period (say, one year), with periodic updating at fixed intervals (such as one month). For example, a budget is prepared in December for the next 12 months, January through December. At the end of January, the budget is revised and projected for the next 12 months, February through January. In this manner, the most recent information is included in the budgeting process. Premises and assumptions are constantly being revised as management learns from experience.

Moving budgets have the advantage of systematic reexamination; they have the disadvantage of being costly to maintain. Although budgets are important instruments for implementing the objectives of the firm, they must be viewed in perspective as one item on a long list of demands for a manager's time.

Recently, many experts have begun to question the value of budgets.[41] The major criticism is that by strictly adhering to a decision-making process based solely on numbers and dollars, companies tend to overlook critical variables such as quality and customer service. In addition, these critics claim that budgets encourage thoughtless moves—cutting prices too sharply or wooing weak customers—and discourage thoughtful ones such as investing for growth. To overcome several of the flaws associated with the budget process, companies including 3M Company, Emerson Electric Company, and Digital Equipment Corporation have developed guidelines for developing budgets. These guidelines include the necessity to plan first, budget later;

TABLE 6-3   Hypothetical Variable Budget

A variable budget recognizes that planned profit and total costs do not vary proportionately with sales.

Output (units)	1,000	1,200	1,400	1,600
Sales (at $5.00 per unit)	$5,000	$6,000	$7,000	$8,000
Variable costs (at $3.00 per unit)	3,000	3,600	4,200	4,800
Fixed costs	1,000	1,000	1,000	1,000
Total costs	4,000	4,600	5,200	5,800
Planned profit	$1,000	$1,400	$1,800	$2,200

budget for managers, not accountants; measure output, not input; and design budgets to protect against turf wars.

Implementation of Plans

All the planning in the world does not help an organization realize objectives if plans cannot be implemented. (Implementation of plans involves resources and actions, as shown in Figure 6–1.) In some instances, the manager can personally take all the necessary steps to apply resources in planned actions to achieve objectives. But in most cases, the manager must implement plans through other people, motivating them to accept and carry out the plan. *Authority, persuasion,* and *policy* are the manager's means of implementing plans.

Authority

Authority is a legitimate form of power in the sense that it accompanies the position, not the person. That is, the nature of authority in organizations is the right to make decisions and to expect compliance with these decisions. Thus, a manager can reasonably expect subordinates to carry out a plan so long as it does not require illegal, immoral, or unethical behavior. Authority is often sufficient to implement relatively simple plans that involve no significant change in the status quo. But a complex and comprehensive plan can seldom be implemented through authority alone.

Indeed, a by-product of the highly centralized management structure that many firms adopted during the 1980s was a lessening of the formal span of control that any one manager possessed.[42] Toward this end, formal authority was diminished. In its place, persuasion came to represent an increasingly important tool that managers utilize in effectively implementing plans.

Persuasion

Persuasion is a process of selling a plan to those who must implement it— communicating relevant information so individuals understand all implications. In this sense, persuasion requires convincing others to base acceptance of the plan on its merits rather than on the authority of the manager.

A key variable influencing the effectiveness of persuasive efforts is the degree to which employees are loyal to their organization.[43] The longer employees stay with a company, the more familiar they become with the business, and the better able they are to evaluate the relative pros and cons of any one plan.

Policy

When plans are intended to be long-term or permanent fixtures in an organization, management develops policies to implement them. **Policies** usually are written statements that reflect the basic objectives of the plan and provide guidelines for selecting actions to achieve those objectives. Once plans have been accepted by employers who must carry them out, policies become important management tools for implementing them. Effective policies have these characteristics:

1. *Flexibility.* A policy must strike a reasonable balance between stability and flexibility. Conditions change, and policies must change accordingly. On the other hand, some degree of stability must prevail if order and a sense of direction are to be maintained. No rigid guidelines exist to specify the exact degree of flexibility; only managerial judgment can determine the appropriate balance.

2. *Comprehensiveness.* If plans are to be followed, a policy must be comprehensive enough to cover any contingency. The scope of the policy depends on the scope of action controlled by the policy itself. If the policy is directed toward very narrow ranges of activity—for example, hiring policies—it need not be as comprehensive as a policy concerned with, say, public relations.

3. *Coordination.* A policy must provide for coordination of the various subunits whose actions are interrelated. Without coordinated direction provided by policies, each subunit is tempted to pursue its own objectives. The ultimate test of any subunit's activity should be its relationship to the policy statement.

4. *Ethics.* A policy must conform to society's prevailing codes of ethical behavior. The increasingly complex and interdependent nature of contemporary society has resulted in a great number of problems involving ethical dilemmas. And as we saw in the previous chapter, the manager is ultimately responsible for the resolution of issues that involve ethical principles.

5. *Clarity.* A policy must be written clearly and logically. It must specify the intended aim of the action it governs, define the appropriate methods and action, and delineate the limits of freedom of action permitted to those who are to be guided by it.

The ultimate test of the effectiveness of a policy is whether or not the intended objective is attained. Policies must be subjected to reexamination on a continual basis. If a policy does not lead to the objective, it should be revised.

Key Planning Issues

We have seen that planning, a fundamental activity of managers, can cover any time span from the short to the long run. We also have surveyed some of the most important forecasting and budgeting techniques. These do not cover the entire range of problems and issues associated with planning.[44] Our discussion has, however, underscored the fact that planning is the essence of management; all other managerial functions stem from planning.

In fact, one additional point needs to be made prior to leaving the topic of planning. A positive relationship has been found to exist between the extent of planning activities and the performance of small, as well as large, businesses.[45] Specifically, the benefits derived (by small businesses and their owners) from engaging in formal planning activities include the ability to develop a more complete knowledge of the environment, choose from and implement a wider range of strategy options, develop new products, engage in cooperative agreements with other firms, and secure equity investments. Thus planning by no means should be thought of as an activity that only large organizations pursue.

How does a manager begin the planning process? Many professionals agree that much of the task consists of asking the appropriate questions. Table 6–4 suggests the basic ones. Other, more specific questions might well be asked, but the fundamental questions are appropriate regardless of the type and size of the organization.

TABLE 6–4 Key Managerial Planning Issues

Asking the right questions for each element of the plan is critical.

Planning Element	Key Managerial Decisions
Objectives	1. Which objectives will be sought? 2. What is the relative importance of each objective? 3. What are the relationships among the objectives? 4. When should each objective be achieved? 5. How can each objective be measured? 6. Which person or organizational unit should be accountable for achieving the objective?
Actions	1. Which important actions bear on the successful achievement of objectives? 2. What information exists regarding each action? 3. What is the appropriate technique for forecasting the future state of each important action? 4. Which person or organizational unit should be accountable for the action?
Resources	1. Which resources should be included in the plan? 2. What are the interrelationships among the various resources? 3. Which budgeting technique should be used? 4. Which person or organizational unit should be accountable for the preparation of the budget?
Implementation	1. Can the plan be implemented through authority or persuasion? 2. What policy statements are necessary to implement the overall plan? 3. To what extent are the policy statements comprehensive, flexible, coordinative, ethical, and clearly written? 4. Who or what organizational units would be affected by the policy statements?

Summary of Key Points

- Companies can no longer afford to forgo change if they want to compete in global markets. The planning function includes those managerial activities that result in predetermined courses of action. Planning necessarily focuses on the future, and management's responsibility is to prepare the organization for the future.

- Planning requires managers to make decisions about objectives, actions, resources, and implementation. These four factors are essential to effective planning.

- Good planning involves the art of making difficult things simple. Through planning, management coordinates efforts, prepares for change, develops performance standards, and manages development.

- Objectives are statements of future conditions that, if realized, are deemed satisfactory or optimal by the planner. Managers always face alternative objectives that must be evaluated and ranked. All sets of objectives have three characteristics: priority, timing, and measurement. Because determining objectives is a judgmental decision, it is a difficult process. Necessary trade-offs may, in the short run, result in seemingly inconsistent priorities.

- To be useful in planning, objectives should be stated in measurable terms and should relate to significant organizational performance determinants. In particular, objectives should be set for profitability, marketing, productivity, physical and financial resources, innovation, manager behavior, employee attitudes, and social responsibility. Depending on the specific organization, the importance of any one objective may vary.

- Courses of action to achieve objectives must be specified. The terms *strategies* and *tactics* refer to planned courses of action. An important part of specifying courses of action is forecasting future demand for the organization's output and future availability of resources.

- Resource requirements of a plan must be forecast and specified by budgets. Management can select the type of budget that best suits the planning needs of the organization.

- The fourth part of planning is implementation, a phase in which it is recognized that plans usually are carried out by other people.

- The three approaches to implementation use authority, persuasion, and policy. Approaches can be used individually or in combination.

- Implementation by policy has the advantage of continuously reinforcing the plan for those who must implement it. Effective policies produce the planned course of action.

- Planning should not be thought of as an activity that only large businesses pursue. A positive relationship exists between the extent of planning activities and the performance of small businesses.

Discussion and Review Questions

1. Discuss the problems an organization would face if it failed to plan. Specifically, address the impact that failing to plan would have on employees, the organization's ability to compete effectively, and the organization's chances for long-run survival.

2. A manager is overhead saying, "Plan? I never have time to plan. I live from day to day just trying to survive." Comment.

3. Is it accurate to say that since it involves value judgments, planning is the implementation of the manager's value system? Why?

4. Describe the possible similarities and differences in the objectives set by nonprofit organizations and those set by for-profit organizations.

5. Describe a situation in which an organization you belonged to had to choose among several conflicting objectives. What was the basis for assigning a higher priority to one of the objectives over the others?

6. How would the planning process differ between a small business and a large business? Should the one place a stronger emphasis on planning than the other? Why or why not?

7. Why is it important when forecasting future events to utilize both qualitative (e.g., hunches, gut feelings, experiences) and quantitative (e.g., time series) methods? Are there occasions when one method is clearly superior to the other? Explain.

8. Several companies are experimenting with programs that shift most of the responsibility for planning to the lower levels of the organizations. Discuss possible advantages and disadvantages to be realized from such programs.

9. Describe through use of an example how a lack of available resources could cause a change in an organization's ability to reach its planned objectives. In what stage of the planning process would this lack of resources be most likely to be noticed?

10. Discuss how a bank manager could utilize authority and persuasion in motivating his staff to implement a plan to improve customer service.

CASE 6–1
PLANNING FOR CHANGE LEADS TO A CHANGE IN PLANS

In the current business environment, companies must be dynamic, unafraid of bucking conventional wisdom, and capable of change. The trend of large corporations in the 1980s was toward a centralized decision-making structure, and Hewlett-Packard Company was no exception. Although the company had been set up originally in a decentralized manner, it followed the lead of general business and, by the end of the 80s, came to possess a highly bureaucratic organizational setup. Consequently, Hewlett-Packard (HP) faced many of the same problems in the early 90s as its closest rivals, IBM and DEC.

The problems these three companies faced were brought about by decades of heavy growth in the computer industry, followed by a sharp downturn in demand, the result being highly competitive yet simultaneously sluggish market conditions. Fortunately, Hewlett-Packard possessed a weapon in its arsenal that rivals lacked, two founders, David Packard and William Hewlett, who could return to the company and provide much needed direction to the planning function at HP. The two founders, both approaching 80 years of age and long retired from the company, returned in the nick of time. In 1990, Hewlett-Packard stock was trading as low as $25 a share. Today, Hewlett-Packard stock has regained its market luster and trades well above $70. Interestingly, the three competing electronics companies, Hewlett-Packard, IBM, and DEC, had grown at least tenfold over the previous quarter century preceding 1990, and all were profitable, prosperous, complacent, and paternalistic, each possessing no-layoff policies during this period. However, while all have since undergone dramatic change, only Hewlett-Packard has emerged as healthy as ever, its two rivals continuing to stumble. What makes Hewlett-Packard and the leadership of its two founders so different?

First, unlike the leaders of their rivals, Hewlett and Packard, upon their return, had the power to effect change. Between them, they owned one quarter of HP's stock, and, more important, as engineers they commanded the respect, even reverence, of the employees. Second, realizing that the company had become too centralized, Hewlett and Packard immediately began moving people and power away from headquarters. The result was divisional independence, which has led to increased innovation and shortened decision times.

Third, HP was quicker than its rivals in recognizing that as markets change, HP must also change. Toward this end, HP borrowed its marketing strategy metaphor from the language of war: "Don't attack a well-entrenched competitor. Early on, stake out your own hill and fortify."

Hewlett-Packard uses this metaphor to guide all its actions. Sometimes it beats its competitors to market; Hewlett-Packard was the first to enter the palmtop computer market. Sometimes it invests heavily in an alternative technology; Hewlett-Packard never built a mainframe computer but bet millions on Unix-based minicomputers (now marketed as mainframe alternatives). And, sometimes it simply buys market share; Hewlett-Packard acquired Apollo Computer to boost its workstation business.

Fourth, with the benefit of management's vision, Hewlett-Packard has strategically mustered its resources to benefit from three prominent computing trends: reduced instruction set computing (RISC), which enables computers to operate faster; open systems (as opposed to proprietary systems), which stress compatibility with other manufacturers' offerings; and desktop networks of personal computers. Finally,

Hewlett-Packard's emphasis on customer service and product support has become an important strategy in and of itself.

Businesses, both large and small, can benefit from the wisdom of Hewlett-Packard. In order to plan for change, a company must effect a change in plans.

Questions for Analysis

1. Discuss how past successes could contribute to the inability of managers to successfully plan for the future.

2. Describe how William Hewlett's and David Packard's authority and persuasiveness influenced the planning process at Hewlett-Packard.

3. How was the use of the marketing strategy metaphor able to effectively guide the development of specific objectives and deployment of resources at Hewlett-Packard?

4. What is meant by the final statement in the case, "In order to plan for change, a company must effect a change in plans"?

Sources: J Yarbrough, "Putting It All Together," *Sales and Marketing Management,* September 1996, pp. 68–77; R D Hoff, "Hewlett-Packard Digs Deep for a Digital Future," *Business Week,* October 18, 1993, pp. 72–75; T Clark, "Marketing Key to HP's Battle Plan," *Business Marketing,* July 1993, pp. 15–16; T Clark, "CEO Platt Not Afraid to Strike Back," *Business Marketing,* July 1993, p. 16.

VIDEO CASE
PLANNING AND STRATEGIC MANAGEMENT AT FORD MOTOR COMPANY

Ford Motor Company, like the other two major automobile manufacturers in the United States, experienced difficult times during the early 1980s. Ford and the others had seen their market share severely eroded by better quality cars from international competitors. Ford was able to weather the competitive storm, and has seen its fortunes rebound, through effective strategic planning.

Donald Peterson was Ford's CEO during the company's recovery period. To create an atmosphere of trust between employees, and between employees and management, Peterson and his fellow managers at Ford emphasized the use of employee teams to solve corporate problems. This emphasis, Peterson explained, was based on the assumption that employees want to contribute, and they want to do the right thing.

As the environment within Ford began to change, the leadership initiated a process to establish a strategic vision for the company. This process culminated in a written statement proclaiming the company's mission, values, and guiding principles (MVGP). The statement provided strategic focus for all of the company's employees. The mission

statement is a definition of the purpose of the company. The key values are people, process, and profits, and the guiding principles are the code of conduct for Ford's people as they conduct the company's business worldwide.

Reflecting on how he was able to steer Ford through the thicket of intense competition, employee skepticism, and consumer dissatisfaction, and create the MVGP statement, Peterson said, "As we were working through the extraordinarily difficult early 1980s, when we were losing so much money, we had many gatherings of groups of our employees, talking about our problems and talking about what we had to do to solve them. And it became very clear that there was a pattern in these conversations of a request from people in the company to understand clearly what it is we stand for—what is the basic core culture of this company. We set about the process of letting the people think about that very question. And then, they in turn selected a group of themselves to continue the process in a series of meetings with top Ford executives to work out what we call our mission, values, and guiding principles."

In a video presentation to all Ford employees in 1985, Peterson introduced the MVGP statement. He explained that he wanted the statement to be a "basic platform" upon which the board and all of Ford's employees would stand together. Peterson told the video audience that he hoped all employees would understand and embrace what the statement means, what is behind it, and what it would take to live the values and guiding principles in day-to-day work.

As a result of the broad acceptance of the MVGP statement, Ford has made employee involvement and team work a way of life inside the company. People at all levels of the organization have learned new skills to help them contribute to the continuous improvement of quality. The team Taurus project, for example, is legendary for its efficiency in the design, development, manufacture, and marketing of the Ford Taurus. The new employee spirit was articulated by Chip and Scratch Coordinator Leon Garner, who said, "I look at each car as if I'm buying it."

The MVGP statement also led to a renewed emphasis on quality throughout the company. Terry Holcomb, Statistical Process Control Coordinator in the trim department at Ford's Atlanta assembly plant, noted, "There's always room for improvement. The day that there's not room for improvement I guess I'll quit." Holcomb's plant won Ford's internal Q1 (the "Q" stands for "quality") award in 1991. One improvement that Holcomb's plant made during 1990 was the placement of a monoroof control relay. The relay had been located behind the glove box and interfered with the smooth functioning of the glove box door. Using a "management by facts" approach, his team determined the best way to fix the problem. Their improvement lowered the plant's TGW (things gone wrong) rate from 18 in the second quarter of 1990, to just 2 in the first quarter of 1991.

Bob Anderson, the Atlanta Plant Manager, said, "When management and the workforce settle on a common goal, and that goal being productivity and quality, you end up with the same results. But you've got to have that common goal and

everyone willing to get behind that common goal." Harold Poling, Chairman of the Board and Chief Executive Officer, summarized the impact of the MVGP statement on Ford's operations: "I think that if our employees recommit themselves to the basics of the business, which were the things that helped us achieve our success in the 80s, quality, product, cost, and employee relations and relations with our dealers and suppliers, then we'll be successful in the years ahead. It's a team effort and that's what we had in the decade of the 80s. And I'm confident that with that same teamwork we'll be successful in the decade of the 90s."

Critical Thinking Questions

1. Ford is a complex organization with a highly diverse workforce and worldwide operations. Do you think it is possible that the statement of mission, vision, and guiding principles can be applied in all of the company's transactions? What are the limits of such a statement?

2. According to the video, Ford put together its MVGP statement through lengthy discussions with employees. Why do you think it was desirable for Ford executives to include employees in the drafting of the statement? Do you think this is the most *efficient* way to complete this project? Explain.

3. One of the reasons the automobile industry in America lost its competitive standing to foreign competition was that the internal organizational structure of each of the Big Three auto manufacturers had become stagnant. One lesson that has been learned by many companies in a variety of industries is that stagnation leads to competitive decline. Do you think a statement such as Ford's MVGP will help the company continue to change? Explain.

EXPERIENTIAL EXERCISE
USING THE ELEMENTS OF PLANNING IN YOUR OWN LIFE

Purpose

The purpose of this exercise is to apply the elements of planning to your own life.

The Exercise in Class

Every person in the class should apply the four major elements of planning to a personal situation and answer the following questions:

1. What one important *objective* would you like to achieve in the next six months? It may be a personal objective pertaining to weight loss, exercise, caloric intake, diet, grade point average, major purchase, or personal relationship. Or it may be a professional objective such as a promotion, pay raise, or income level. Make sure you adhere to such criteria as time frame and measurement, discussed in the chapter.

2. What specific *actions* (strategies and tactics) do you intend to undertake to achieve your objective?

3. What *resources* will be required for you to achieve your objective? Remember to also include nonmonetary resources such as time, effort, and other people.

4. How do you intend to *implement* the actions you have decided to take to achieve your objectives?

The instructor will randomly select members of the class to present their plans. Other members of the class should make sure the presenters have adhered to the basic elements of planning discussed in the chapter.

The Learning Message

The purpose of the elements of planning is to provide a blueprint for management action. This exercise should illustrate the benefits of formal planning (for individuals as well as for organizations).

Notes

1. Arthur C Beck and Ellis D Hillman, *Positive Management Practices: Bringing Out the Best in Organizations and People* (San Francisco: Jossey-Bass, 1986).

2. Rocco W Belmonte and Richard J Murray, "Getting Ready for Strategic Change," *Information Systems Management,* Summer 1993, pp. 23–29.

3. Brian Dumaine, "Who Needs a Boss?" *Fortune,* May 7, 1990, pp. 52–60.

4. For a discussion of trends that will affect the planning process in the future, see Walter Kiechel III, "How We Will Work in the Year 2000," *Fortune,* May 17, 1993, pp. 38–52.

5. Arthur A Thompson, Jr., and A J Strickland III, *Strategic Management: Concepts and Cases,* 4th ed. (Burr Ridge, IL: Richard D. Irwin, 1987), chaps. 1 and 2.

6. "Marketing for EC 1992: Keep Your Powder Dry," *Marketing Briefing by the Conference Board,* February–March 1990, pp. 1–3.

7. Rene Riley-Adams, "Hands across the Sea," *International Management,* July–August 1993, pp. 22–25.

8. Oren Harari, "Think Strategy when You Think Quality," *Management Review,* March 1993, pp. 58–60.

9. For a discussion of this topic, see Norman L Mulgrew, "Why Can't Stupid Keep It Simple," *IM,* September–October 1992, pp. 31–32.

10. Dale P McConkey, "Planning for Uncertainty," *Business Horizons,* January–February 1987, pp. 40–45.

11. Bernard Taylor, "Corporate Planning for the 1990s: The New Frontiers," *Long Range Planning,* December 1986, pp. 13–18.

12. Milton Moskowitz, "Lessons from the Best Companies to Work For," *California Management Review,* Winter 1985, pp. 42–47.

13. Ibid. Also see, V Ramanujan and N Vankatramen, "Planning and Performance: A New Look at an Old Problem," *Business Horizons,* May–June 1987, pp. 19–25.

14. Max D Richards, *Setting Strategy Goals and Objectives,* 2d ed. (St. Paul, MN: West, 1986).

15. Earl G Graves, "Agents of Change," *Black Enterprise,* June 1993, pp. 15–16.

16. Leonard R Sayles, "Doing Things Right: A New Imperative for Middle Managers," *Organizational Dynamics,* Spring 1993, pp. 5–13.

17. Robert Neff, "Now Japan Is Getting Jumpy about Quality," *Business Week,* March 5, 1990, pp. 40–41.

18. For a discussion on the relationship between customer satisfaction and TQM programs, see Noriaki Kano, "A Perspective on Quality Activities in American Firms," *California Management Review,* Spring 1993, pp. 12–31.

19. Jerry Flint, "Volume Be Damned," *Forbes,* April 12, 1993, pp. 52–53.

20. John E Prescott, "Environments as Moderators of the Relationship between Strategy and Performance," *Academy of Management Journal,* June 1986, pp. 329–46.

21. D Quinn Mills, "Planning with People in Mind," *Harvard Business Review,* July–August 1985, pp. 97–105.

22. C Don Burnett, Dennis P Yeskey, and David Richardson, "New Roles for Corporate Planners in the 1980s," *Journal of Business Strategy,* Spring 1984, pp. 64–68.

23. For relevant discussions of these and related management problems, see M J Gimpl and S R Daken, "Management and Magic," *California Management Review,* Fall 1984, pp. 125–36; and R T Pascale, "The Paradox of Corporate Culture: Reconciling Ourselves to Socialization," *California Management Review,* Winter 1985, pp. 26–41.

24. Clarence C Walton, *Ethos and the Executive* (Englewood Cliffs, NJ: Prentice Hall, 1969), p. 192.

25. Peter Drucker, *The Practice of Management* (New York: Harper & Row, 1954); reemphasized in Peter Drucker, *Management: Tasks, Responsibilities, Practices* (New York: Harper & Row, 1974). For recent work by this renowned management writer, see

Managing in Turbulent Times (New York: Harper & Row, 1980); and *Innovation and Entrepreneurship* (New York: Harper & Row, 1985).

26. For a discussion on differences between the objectives of American and Japanese firms, see John C Beck and Terry Hansen, "Lessons from Japan: American and Japanese Strategies and Goals in the 1990s," *The International Executive,* September–October 1993, pp. 445–60.

27. Drucker, *The Practice of Management,* p. 64.

28. George S Odiorne, "Measuring the Unmeasurable: Setting Standards for Management Performance," *Business Horizons,* July–August 1987, pp. 69–75.

29. For a discussion of how one company utilizes measures as an integral part of the planning process, see Robert S Kaplan and David P Norton, "Putting the Balanced Scorecard to Work," *Harvard Business Review,* September–October 1993, pp. 134–47.

30. For an example of how this concept applies to the banking industry, see Diogo Teixeira and Joseph Zisken, "Achieving Quality with Customer in Mind," *The Bankers Magazine,* January–February 1993, pp. 29–35.

31. Drucker, *The Practice of Management,* pp. 71–73.

32. For a discussion on this topic, see Patricia Galagan, "Diversity," *Training & Development,* April 1993, pp. 39–43.

33. Judith H Dobrzynski, "How Long Can Nabisco Keep Doing More with Less?" *Business Week,* April 23, 1990, pp. 90–95.

34. See Edwin A Locke and Gary P Latham, *Goal Setting: A Motivational Technique That Works!* (Englewood Cliffs, NJ: Prentice Hall, 1984), for a related discussion and additional examples.

35. John P Kotter, "What Leaders Really Do," *Harvard Business Review,* May–June 1990, pp. 103–11.

36. S Makridakis, S Wheelwright, and V McGee, *Forecasting Methods and Applications* (New York: John Wiley & Sons, 1982).

37. Arthur A Thompson, Jr., "Strategies for Increasing Cost Businesses," *Academy of Management Proceedings,* August 1982, pp. 17–21.

38. For an in-depth discussion of this topic, see Gary Hamel and C K Prahalad, "Strategy as Stretch and Leverage," *Harvard Business Review,* March–April 1993, pp. 75–84.

39. Neil Churchill, "Budgeting Choice: Planning vs. Control," *Harvard Business Review,* July–August 1984, pp. 150–64.

40. Robert N Anthony, John Deardon, and Norman Bedford, *Management Control Systems,* 5th ed. (Burr Ridge, IL: Richard D. Irwin, 1984), pp. 12–13.

41. Thomas A Stewart, "Why Budgets Are Bad for Business," *Fortune,* June 4, 1990, pp. 179–90.

42. A Richard Krachenberg, John W Henke, Jr., and Thomas F Lyons, "The Isolation of Upper Management," *Business Horizons,* July–August 1993, pp. 41–47.

43. Frederick F Reichheld, "Loyalty-Based Management," *Harvard Business Review,* March–April 1993, pp. 64–73.

44. Peter Mills, *Managing Service Industries* (Cambridge, MA: Ballinger, 1986), discusses the problems of managing organizations whose product is human performance and not a tangible product.

45. For a discussion of this topic, see Marjorie A Lyles, Inga S Baird, J Burdeanne Orris, and Donald F Kuratko, "Formalized Planning in Small Business: Increasing Strategic Choices," *Journal of Small Business Management,* April 1993, pp. 38–49.

7 STRATEGIC PLANNING

Chapter Learning Objectives

After completing Chapter 7, you should be able to:

- **Define** strategic planning in terms of the direction it gives to the entire organization.
- **Describe** how the mission and strategies of an organization should mesh.
- **Discuss** why strategic planning has grown in importance in recent years.
- **Compare** organizational objectives and operational objectives.
- **Identify** appropriate strategies for each business type identified in a portfolio matrix.

Strategic Planning Works

Strategic management fundamentally entails two activities: deciding the actions an organization must take to get from where it is now to where it needs and wants to be in the future and making sure all actions taken to get to this point are performed smoothly and successfully. The following are examples of various activities that three CEOs, possessing strategic visions, pursued in guiding their organizations' passage to business success.

Beyond Cheesecake. CEO John H Bryan initiated a new strategic direction for Sara Lee, the baked-goods giant, to follow when the economy began softening a few years ago. Recognizing that the mature American food industry held little future appeal, he took the company's strength—selling branded products—into new areas. Sara Lee, through a series of acquisitions, began focusing on marketing a wide range of brands (including L'eggs hosiery, Hanes underwear, and Coach leather products), in addition to its traditional Sara Lee line of products. Today, about 40 percent of Sara Lee's revenues come from outside the United States while almost 60 percent of sales are generated by nonfood brands.

Thinking Big. Many analysts feared that Blockbuster's megagrowth would be zapped by expanding cable channels and more pay-per-view movie offerings. But CEO H Wayne Huizenga had no intention of watching the company, which he had built from a base of 18 stores in 1987 to more than 3,000 currently, go into decline. Instead, Blockbuster began positioning itself as an entertainment powerhouse, recently announcing deals to own and operate major league baseball and hockey teams, acquire Sound Warehouse, codevelop music stores with Virgin Retail, take an ownership stake in Spelling Entertainment, and coproduce a monthly preview tape with CBS. Recently, Sears and Blockbuster announced that they are joining forces. Blockbuster will manage music departments at three Sears stores in Florida on a trial basis.

More than Kid's Play. When Geraldine Laybourne first took over as president, Nickelodeon was a tiny, unprofitable network. Airing boring educational shows and toymakers' pet programs, kids shunned the network. Laybourne decided radical surgery was necessary. She took action to develop original, quality shows and allow paid advertising in order to cover the program development costs. She then made use of the time that youngsters are in bed by enticing their parents to watch oldies but goodies like *Get Smart*. More recently, Nickelodeon has added news programs targeted at children and has begun airing shows in Britain. As the result mainly of Laybourne's vision, Nickelodeon has been transformed from a backwater network that was struggling to survive to a dominant force in cable television.

Source: Reprinted from the January 1996 issue of *Money* by special permission; copyright 1996, Time, Inc.

The preceding chapter examined the four phases of planning and introduced important planning terminology. However, before a production manager, marketing manager, or human resources manager can develop plans for his or her individual department, a larger plan—a blueprint—for the entire organization must be developed. Otherwise, on what would the individual departments' plans be based?

The planning activities conducted throughout the organization require the larger framework that we consider in this chapter. A large business organization, such as General Electric or Philip Morris, usually has several business divisions and several product lines within each division. At the corporate level, planning is primarily concerned with selecting the businesses the company should be in, balancing earnings and cash flow, and achieving synergy between business units.[1] The Management in Action described how three innovative CEOs performed this type of planning.

At the business unit level, planning has the objective of achieving competitive advantage and, thereby, superior performance over competitors. At the functional level within the business unit (marketing, finance, production, etc.), planning is concerned with developing the actions necessary to implement the business level plan.

In other words, planning and subsequent strategy development have different meanings at the various levels of the organization. Objectives and strategies established at the top level provide the planning context for each of the individual divisions and functions. As a result, division and functional managers can develop their plans only within the constraints developed at the higher levels.[2]

The Growth of Strategic Planning

Some of the most successful business organizations are here today because many years ago they offered the right product at the right time to a rapidly growing market. The same can also be said for nonprofit and governmental organizations. Many of the critical decisions of the past were made without the benefit of strategic planning or thinking. Whether these decisions were based on wisdom or were just luck is not important; they worked for these organizations. However, a sadder fate befell countless other organizations. Over three-fourths of the 100 largest US corporations of 70 years ago have fallen from that category.[3] These corporations at one time dominated their markets, controlled vast resources, and had the best-trained workers. In the end, they all made the same critical mistake. Their management failed to recognize that business strategies must reflect changing business environments. Instead, they attempted to carry on business as usual.

Present-day managers are increasingly recognizing that wisdom and innovation alone are no longer sufficient to guide the destinies of organizations, both large and small. Over the course of the past decade, markets have become increasingly global, technology has evolved at an accelerated pace, novel forms of distributing products and services have proliferated, and firms have continually invented new organizational forms—all while customer needs and preferences have continually shifted in sometimes unpredictable ways.[4] Fifteen years ago, few would have predicted that Sears, the world's largest retailer for over half a century, would be struggling for survival while three relative newcomers, Wal-Mart, Kmart, and Target would become market leaders.[5] Likewise, few would have thought that IBM and General Motors would be engaged in fierce competition for market supremacy with Microsoft and Toyota.

Organizations today not only need to function in a competitive and hostile environment but must also be able to cooperate with other companies, perhaps even with those that in other respects may be competitors.[6] For these and countless other reasons, managers have turned to strategic planning as a means to ensure competitive viability.[7] Strategic planning is a process that involves the review of market conditions; customer needs; competitive strengths and weaknesses; sociopolitical, legal, and economic conditions; technological developments; and the availability of resources that lead to the specific opportunities or threats facing the organization.[8] In practice, *the development of strategic plans involves taking information from the environment and deciding on an organizational mission, objectives, strategies, and portfolio plan.* The **strategic planning process** is depicted in Figure 7–1. To develop a sense of unity of purpose across the organization and to keep participants moving in the same direction, senior managers must, through the strategic planning process, provide a strong, compelling vision.[9] This vision must then be tied to objectives and goals at all levels of management. At Matsushita Electric Industrial Company, for example, department managers provide three plans every six months: a five-year plan that incorporates technological and environmental changes, a two-year plan that translates strategies into new products, and a six-month operating plan, developed by department managers, that addresses monthly projections for production, sales, profits, inventories, quality control, and personnel requirements.

Strategic planning plays a key role in achieving a balance between the short and the long term.[10] Managing principally for current cash flows, market share, and earnings tends to mortgage the firm's future. An intense focus on the near term can produce an aversion to risk that dooms a business to stagnation. However, an overemphasis on the long run is just as inappropriate. Companies that overextend themselves betting on the future may penalize short-term profitability and other operating results to such an extent that the company is vulnerable to takeover and other threatening actions.

The Strategic Planning Process

The output of the strategic planning process is a strategic plan. Figure 7–1 shows the four components of such plans: mission, objectives, strategies, and portfolio plan. Let's examine each one.[11]

Organizational Mission

The organization's environment supplies the resources that sustain the organization, whether it is a business, a college or university, or a government agency. In exchange for these resources, the organization must supply the environment with goods and services at an acceptable price and quality. In other words, every organization exists to accomplish something in the larger environment, and that purpose or mission usually is clear at the start. As time passes, however, the organization expands, the environment changes, and managerial personnel change. And one or more things are likely to occur. First, the original purpose may become irrelevant as the organization expands into new products, new markets, and even new industries. Second, the original mission may remain relevant, but some managers begin to lose interest in it. Finally, changes in the environment may make the original mission inappropriate. The result of any or all of these three conditions is a drifting organization, without a clear mission or purpose to guide critical decisions.[12] When this occurs, management must renew the search for purpose or restate the original purpose.

FIGURE 7–1   The Strategic Planning Process

Strategic planning emphasizes the impact of the environment on the organization.

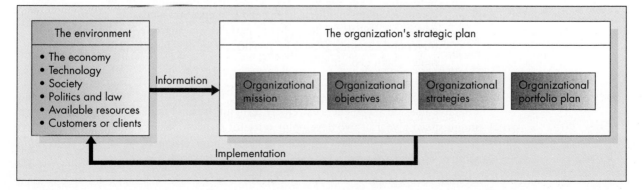

The mission statement should be a definition of what the organization is striving to become in the long run.[13] This vision refers to a company's far-reaching sense of purpose and the ways in which it intends to pursue that objective.[14] In essence, the mission statement defines the direction in which the organization is heading and the unique aims that will succeed in differentiating it from similar organizations.

The basic questions that must be answered are "What is our business?" and "What should it be?"[15] The need is not for a stated purpose (e.g., "to produce the highest-quality products at the lowest possible price") that would enable shareholders and managers to feel good or that would promote public relations. Rather, the need is for a stated **mission** that provides direction and significance to all members of the organization, regardless of their level. Further, all employees should be made aware of the mission statement and how it fits in with their jobs.[16] The Management Focus on General Electric describes how one CEO's vision provided direction and guidance to an organization that, at the time, was ill prepared for the future.

Developing a Statement: Key Elements.   In developing a mission statement, management must take into account three key elements: the organization's history, its distinctive competencies, and its environment.[17]

1. *History.* Every organization, large or small, profit or nonprofit, has a history of objectives, accomplishments, mistakes, and policies. A study of the organization's history will reveal the critical characteristics and events of the past that must be considered in developing future strategy.[18] For example, it would not make sense for McDonald's to become a chain of gourmet restaurants or for Yale University to become a community college, even if such moves were opportunities for growth in the future.

2. *Distinctive competencies.* While an organization may be able to do many things, it should seek to do what it can do best. Distinctive competencies are the things that an organization does well—so well, in fact, that they offer an advantage over similar organizations. Procter & Gamble probably could enter the oil business, but such a decision certainly would not take advantage of its major distinctive competence: knowledge of the market for low-priced, repetitively purchased consumer products. No matter how appealing an opportunity may be, the organization must have the competencies to capitalize on it. An opportunity without the competence to exploit it is not really an opportunity for the organization[19] It is an illusion.

3. *Environment.* The organization's environment dictates the opportunities, constraints, and threats that must be identified before a mission statement is developed.[20] For example, technological developments in the communications field (e.g., long-range picture transmission, closed-circuit television, and the picture phone) may have a negative impact on business travel and certainly should be considered in the mission statement of a large motel chain and an airline.

Characteristics of a Mission Statement.   Needless to say, writing a useful and effective mission statement is extremely difficult. It is not unlikely that an organization might spend a year or two developing a useful mission. When completed, an effective mission statement focuses on *markets rather than products;* it is also *achievable, motivating,* and *specific.*[21]

Management Focus

Strategic Planning at General Electric

In the early 80s, General Electric's chief executive officer, Jack Welch, embarked on a crusade to reshape GE. Welch went at his task with such zest that *Newsweek* began calling him "Neutron Jack," in recognition of his facility for detonating employees while leaving the business structures they once occupied untouched.

At the time Welch began his crusade, GE could have been considered operationally dysfunctional. For example, the company was overburdened by management that spent too much time pursuing wasteful paper exercises. In fact, the annual strategic plan review required anywhere from six to eight months of preparation and monthly sector reviews effectively took a week out of the work calendar for 20 managers.

Welch took an axe to GE's organizational chart by eliminating one-third of the company's employees and the substratum of executive vice presidents that sat between Welch himself and GE's individual business heads. Perhaps Welch's greatest accomplishment, and one that is hard to quantify, was to persuade the remaining GE employees to accept and internalize a vision of shared values that embraced all the management buzzwords now in vogue: empowerment, boundarylessness, intuitiveness, and so on. One observer comments that GE is a contradictory combination of teamwork and competition, but it works.

More than a decade later, Welch is still CEO at GE and is not planning on retiring until at least the year 2000. His tenure at GE has proved the most wrenching in the corporation's history and yet simultaneously appears to be the most strategically satisfying. Clearly, GE's earnings growth can be directly attributed to Welch's ability to increase productivity. Welch is currently pursuing a strategy that is attempting to shift the company's focus from the industrialized world to Asia and Latin America. By the end of the decade, Welch hopes that these markets will provide more than $20 billion in revenues, double their current level, and contribute more than 25 percent of GE's total sales.

GE has also established the goal of becoming a Six Sigma quality company by 2000. The Six Sigma is a level of quality rarely achieved. It involves a change in approach from fixing products so that they are perfect to fixing processes so that they produce perfect or defect-free products and services all the time.

Sources: D Bollier, "Building Corporate Loyalty while Rebuilding the Community," *Management Review,* October 1996, pp. 17–22; J F Welch, Jr., "Quality 2000," *Executive Excellence,* September 1996, pp. 4–5; T Smart, "GE's Brave New World," *Business Week,* November 8, 1993, pp. 64–70; and M K Ozanian, "The Prize," *FW,* September 14, 1993, pp. 24–26.

---

1. *Market rather than product focus:* The customers or clients of an organization are critical in determining its mission. Traditionally, many organizations defined their businesses by what they made ("our business is glass") and, in many cases, named the organization after the product or products (e.g., National Cash Register, Harbor View Savings and Loan Association). Often such organizations have found that when products and technologies become obsolete, their missions are no longer relevant and their names may no longer describe what they do. Thus, a more enduring way of defining the mission is needed.

   In recent years, a key feature of mission statements has been an *external* rather than *internal* focus. In other words, the mission statement should focus on the broad class of needs that the organization is seeking to satisfy (external focus), not on the physical product or service that the organization is offering at present (internal focus). This has been clearly stated by Peter Drucker:

   > A business is not defined by the company's name, statutes, or articles of incorporation. It is defined by the want the customer satisfies when he buys a product or service. To satisfy the customer is the mission and purpose of every

business. The question "What is our business?" can, therefore, be answered only by looking at the business from the outside, from the point of view of customer and market.[22]

While Drucker was referring to business organizations, the same necessity exists for both nonprofit and government organizations.[23] They need to state their missions in terms of serving a particular group of clients or customers and/or meeting a particular class of need.

2. *Achievable:* While the mission statement should stretch the organization toward more effective performance, it should at the same time be realistic and achievable. In other words, it should open a vision of new opportunities but should not lead the organization into unrealistic ventures far beyond its competencies. Examples would be a pen manufacturer stating it is in the communications business or an antique car restorer viewing its mission as transportation.

3. *Motivational:* One of the side (but very important) benefits of a well-defined mission is the guidance it provides employees and managers working either in geographically dispersed units or on independent tasks. A well-defined mission provides a shared sense of purpose *outside* the various activities taking place within the organization. Therefore, end results (sales, patients cared for, reduction in violent crimes) are the product of careful pursuit and accomplishment of the mission and are not the mission itself.

4. *Specific:* As mentioned earlier, public relations should not be the primary purpose of a statement of mission. This statement must be specific and provide direction and guidelines for management's choices between alternative courses of action. In other words, "to produce the highest-quality products at the lowest possible cost" sounds very good, but it does not provide direction for management.

Table 7–1 presents actual mission statements of various types of organizations. While some have been abbreviated, each clearly illustrates its purpose as defined by management. Review each one with respect to the four criteria just discussed.[24]

The questions related to the mission statement need to be asked and answered at the inception of an organization and whenever it is experiencing serious problems. However, a successful organization should also ask them from time to time.[25] The reason for this should be clear: Because of the ever changing environment, sooner or later even the most successful definition of purpose becomes obsolete. Thus, the process of periodically addressing the issue forces management to anticipate the impact of environmental changes on the organization's mission, objectives, markets, and products.

Finally, the mission statements of many organizations also include major policies the organizations plan to follow in the pursuit of their missions. For example, some organizations are using mission statements as a means of encouraging ethical behavior by employees.[26] Such policies establish the ground rules for the organization in its relationships with government, customers or clients, suppliers, distributors, and creditors. An example of such a document is shown in Table 7–2.

*Organizational
Objectives*

In the previous chapter, we saw that a critical phase of planning is the determination of future outcomes. These desired future outcomes are objectives. Organizational objectives are the end points of an organization's mission and are what it seeks through

TABLE 7–1   Actual Mission Statements

A mission statement reflects the role the organization plays in its environment.

Organization	Mission
1. Office equipment manufacturer	We are in the business of problem solving. Our business is to help solve administrative, scientific, and human problems.
2. Credit union	To produce a selected range of quality services to organizations and individuals to fulfill their continuing financial needs.
3. Large conglomerate	Translating new technologies into commercially salable products.
4. Consumer products paper company	The development and marketing of inedible products for food stores.
5. State department of health	Administering all provisions of law relating to public health laws and regulations of the state board of health, supervising and assisting county and regional boards and departments of health, and doing all other things reasonably necessary to protect and improve the health of the people.
6. Appliance manufacturer	A willingness to invest in any area of suitable profit and growth potential in which the organization has or can acquire the capabilities.

TABLE 7–2   A Mission Statement That Includes Organizational Policies

Mission and policy statements express an organization's highest standards.

It is the basic purpose of this organization, in all of its decisions and actions, to attain and maintain the following:

1. A continuous, high level of profits, which places it in the top bracket of industry in its rate of return on invested capital.
2. Steady growth in profits and sales volume, and investment at rates exceeding those of the national economy as a whole.
3. Equitable distribution of the fruits of continuously increasing productivity of management, capital, and labor among shareholders, employees, and the public.
4. Design, production, and marketing, on a worldwide basis, of products and services that are useful and beneficial to its customers, to society, and to mankind.
5. Continuous responsiveness to the needs of its customers and of the public, creating a current product line that is "first in performance" and a steady flow of product improvements, new products, and new services that increase customer satisfaction.
6. A vital, dynamic product line, by continuous addition of new products and businesses and prompt termination of old products and businesses when their economic worth, as measured by their profit performance, becomes substandard.
7. The highest ethical standards in the conduct of all its affairs.
8. An environment in which all employees are enabled, encouraged, and stimulated to perform continuously at their highest potential of output and creativity and to attain the highest possible level of job satisfaction.

the ongoing, long-run operations of the organization. The organizational mission is stated as a general set of specific and achievable organizational objectives.

As with the statement of mission, organizational objectives are more than good intentions. In fact, if formulated properly, they:

1. Can be converted into specific actions.
2. Provide direction: serve as a starting point for more specific and detailed objectives at lower levels in the organization. Each manager then knows how her objectives relate to those at higher levels.
3. Establish long-run priorities for the organization.
4. Facilitate management control, because they serve as standards for evaluating overall organizational performance.

Organizational objectives are necessary in any and all areas that may influence the performance and long-run survival of the organization. These were identified in the previous chapter as market standing, innovations, productivity, physical and financial resources, profitability, manager performance and responsibility, worker performance and attitude, and social responsibility.

The preceding objectives are by no means exhaustive; an organization may very well have additional ones. For example, some organizations are specifying their primary objective as the attainment of a specific level of quality, either in the making of a product or the providing of a service. These organizations believe that objectives should reflect an organization's commitment to the customer rather than to its own finances.[27] The important point is that management must translate the organizational mission into specific objectives that support the realization of the mission. Table 7–3 presents some examples of organizational objectives. Note that they are broad statements that serve as guides and that they are of a continuing nature. They specify

---

TABLE 7–3   Sample Organizational Objectives: Manufacturing Firm

Specific objectives are needed for all areas of an organization to work toward realizing the mission.

Area of Performance	Possible Objective
1. Market standing	To make our brands number one in their field in market share.
2. Innovations	To be a leader in introducing new products by spending no less than 7 percent of sales for research and development.
3. Productivity	To manufacture all products efficiently, as measured by the productivity of the workforce.
4. Physical and financial resources	To protect and maintain all resources—equipment, buildings, inventory, and funds.
5. Profitability	To achieve an annual rate of return on investment of at least 15 percent.
6. Manager performance and responsibility	To identify critical areas of management depth and succession.
7 Worker performance and attitude	To maintain levels of employee satisfaction consistent with our own similar industries.
8. Social responsibility	To respond appropriately whenever possible to societal expectations and environmental needs.

the end points of an organization's mission and the results that it seeks in the long run, both externally and internally. Most important, however, the objectives in Table 7–3 are all capable of being converted into specific targets and actions for *operational plans* at lower levels in the organization.

Organizational Strategies

When an organization has formulated its mission and developed its objectives, it knows where it wants to go. The next management task is to develop a grand design to get there.[28] This grand design comprises the organizational strategies. The role of strategy in corporate planning is to identify the general approaches that the organization utilizes to achieve its organizational objectives.[29] Strategy involves the choice of major directions the organization takes in pursuing its objectives.[30] It involves thinking through how the company is to be positioned to either create uniqueness in current markets or conquer new markets.[31]

Thus, organizations achieve objectives in two ways: by better managing what the organization is presently doing and by finding new things to do. In choosing either or both of these paths, management must decide whether to concentrate on present customers, to seek new ones, or both. Figure 7–2 presents the available strategic choices. Known as a product–market matrix, it shows the strategic alternatives available to an organization for achieving its objectives. It indicates that an organization can grow in a variety of ways by concentrating on present or new products and on present or new customers.

Market Penetration Strategies.   These strategies focus on improving the position of the organization's present products with its present customers. For example:

- A snack products company concentrates on getting its present customers to purchase more of its products.
- A charity seeks ways to increase contributions from present supporters.
- A bank concentrates on getting present credit card customers to use their cards more frequently.

Such a strategy may involve devising a marketing plan to encourage customers to purchase more of a product. Tactics used to carry out the strategy could include price reductions, advertising stressing the many benefits of the product, packaging the product in different-sized packages, or making the product available at more locations. Likewise, a production plan may be developed to produce more efficiently what is being produced at present. Implementation of such a plan could include increased

FIGURE 7–2   Product–Market Matrix

An organization's basic strategy involves decisions about products and markets and about the directions in which it chooses to grow.

Products / Market	Present Products	New Products
Present Customers	Market penetration	Product development
New Customers	Market development	Diversification

production runs, the substitution of preassembled components for individual product parts, or the automation of a process previously performed manually. In other words, market penetration strategies concentrate on improving the efficiency of various functional areas in the organization.

Market Development Strategies.   Following this strategy, an organization would seek to find new customers for its present products. For example:

- A manufacturer of industrial products may decide to develop products for entrance into consumer markets.
- A governmental social service agency may seek out individuals and families who have never utilized the agency's services.
- A manufacturer of automobiles decides to sell automobiles in Eastern Europe because of the transition to a free market system.
- An athletic clothing and footwear company decides to develop a line of fitness clothing for children.

Market development strategies may involve much more than simply getting the product to the new market. Before considering sales techniques such as packaging and promotion, companies often find they must first establish a foothold. Scott Paper Company serves as a good example of a company that successfully adapted to the European market. Europeans have traditionally consumed far fewer paper napkins and tissues than their American counterparts. Despite this, Scott Paper has made over $1 billion in revenue from sales in the European Community by following a strategy of quality improvement.

Product Development Strategies.   In choosing either of the remaining two strategies, the organization, in effect, seeks new things to do. With this particular strategy, the new products developed would be directed to present customers. For example:

- A candy manufacturer may decide to offer a fat-free candy.
- A social service agency may offer additional services to present clients.
- A college or university may develop programs for nontraditional students.
- A soft drink manufacturer may develop a clear cola.

Diversification.   An organization diversifies when it seeks new products for customers it is not serving at present. For example:[32]

- A discount store purchases a savings and loan association.
- A cigarette manufacturer diversifies into real estate development.
- A college or university establishes a corporation to find commercial uses for the results of faculty research efforts.
- A cosmetics manufacturer acquires a baby care products company.

On what basis does an organization choose one (or all) of its strategies? Of extreme importance are the directions set by the mission statement. Management should select those strategies consistent with its mission and capitalize on the organization's distinctive competencies that lead to a sustainable competitive advantage.[33] A sustainable competitive advantage can be based on either the assets or skills of the organization. Technical superiority, low-cost production, customer service/ product support, location, financial resources, continuing product innovation, and

Management Focus

Strategic Mistakes at Borden

At the beginning of this decade, executives at Borden Inc. implemented two restructuring strategies aimed at turning around the ailing food giant. At the time of the second one, Borden had just suffered a severe income drop caused by lower sales and the continuing reorganization costs. Despite management's noble efforts, one year later the company still reported dismal operating results.

Where did the company go wrong? Blame for these increasingly poor results can be directly attributed to company management, which developed and pursued a flawed strategy of national branding. The strategy led to mistakes in marketing, pricing, and management. Examples of some of the mistakes that Borden committed follow.

Mistake 1.   When raw milk prices fell, Borden refused to lower its prices to compete on a local market basis. This inaction allowed regional competitors to underprice Borden and reap what should have been Borden's share of the profits. As a result, milk sales dropped more than 7 percent, and the division, which used to make $80 to $100 million per quarter, began operating at a loss.

Mistake 2.   Borden ignored strong regional pasta brands such as Prince in the Northeast and Anthony's in the West, instead giving all of its advertising support to Creamette, the leading national brand. As a result, regional brand sales stagnated, and, in addition, Creamette sales failed to take off. Pasta division sales dropped 8 percent in the first nine months of the campaign.

Mistake 3.   Borden's Snacks company tried to roll out a national brand of chips even though test marketing results were not encouraging. As a result, Borden's total market share in the potato chip market fell by 16 percent, hit especially hard by Frito-Lay's aggressive price promotions and Anheuser-Busch's deep pockets for its Eagle brand.

All is not lost at Borden, however. Realizing the folly of their past decisions, management has continued to take aggressive action through another restructuring in an attempt to rectify the situation and put the company's operations back on course. First, through internal job promotions and external hirings, Borden has assembled a new management team. Second, Borden has begun committing millions of dollars to support its regional brands, hoping to regain lost sales.

Finally, the company has recently introduced The Big Cheese, a two-flavor line of individually wrapped sliced cheese and launched a national campaign for its $3 billion dry pasta and sauce business. They also brought Elsie the cow back from retirement hoping that Elsie will help turn around sales of lagging brands.

Whether these and other soon-to-be-taken actions succeed is anybody's guess. But for the executives at Borden, hope rests on fulfilling the corporate credo, attributed to founder Gail Borden: "I tried and failed; I tried again and again and succeeded."

Sources: S Hume, "Sive/Y+R Takes Borden's Big Cheese Line From Concept to Customer," *Adweek,* March 18, 1996, p. 3; B Spethmann, "Borden Tries Category Management in Pasta," *Brandweek,* January 1, 1996, p.3; E Lesley, "Why Things Are So Sour at Borden," *Business Week,* November 22, 1993, pp. 78–85; and B Spethmann, "Borden Shakeup Designed to Milk Dairy Products Division," *Brandweek,* September 13, 1993, p. 14.

overall marketing skills are all examples of distinctive competencies that can lead to a sustainable competitive advantage.

The Management Focus on Borden provides an example of an organization that, by failing to take advantage of its distinctive competencies, has experienced poor operating results.

Organizational Portfolio Plan

The final phase of the strategic planning process is the formulation of the organizational portfolio plan. In reality, most organizations at a particular time are portfolios of businesses. For example, an appliance manufacturer may have several product lines (e.g., televisions, washers and dryers, refrigerators, stereos), as well as two divisions (consumer appliances and industrial appliances). A college or university has numerous schools (e.g., education, business, law, architecture) and several programs within each school. The YMCA has hotels, camps, spas, and schools. Some widely diversified organizations such as Philip Morris Companies are in numerous unrelated businesses, such as cigarettes, land development, paper products, and breweries.

Managing such groups of businesses is made a little easier if resources and cash are plentiful and each group is experiencing growth and profits. Unfortunately, providing larger and larger budgets each year to all businesses is sometimes no longer feasible. Many may not be experiencing growth, and profits or resources (financial and nonfinancial) may be growing more and more scarce. In such a situation, choices must be made. Management must decide which businesses to build, maintain, or eliminate or which new businesses to add. Some method is needed to help management make the choices. Perhaps the best-known method to accomplish this is the business portfolio matrix developed by the Boston Consulting Group.[34]

The Business Portfolio Matrix. The first step in this approach is to identify each division, product line, and so forth, that can be considered a business. When identified, these are **strategic business units** (SBUs). Each SBU:

- Has a distinct mission.
- Has its own competitors.
- Is a single business or a collection of related businesses.
- Can be planned for, somewhat independent of the other businesses of the total organization.

Thus, depending on the organization, an SBU could be a single product, product line, division, college department of accounting, or state mental health agency. Once the managers have identified and classified all of the SBUs, they need some method of determining how resources should be allocated among the various SBUs. This is the important contribution of the Boston Consulting Group's (BCG) approach.

Using this approach, the organization would classify all of its SBUs in the business portfolio matrix. (An example is shown in Figure 7–3.) The matrix's basic purpose is to assist management in deciding how much resource support should be budgeted to each SBU.

The business portfolio matrix illustrates two business indicators of great strategic importance. The vertical indicator, *market growth rate,* refers to the annual rate of growth of the market in which the product, division, or department is located. For

---

FIGURE 7–3   Business Portfolio Matrix

Each SBU can be classified according to projected market growth rate and estimated market share.

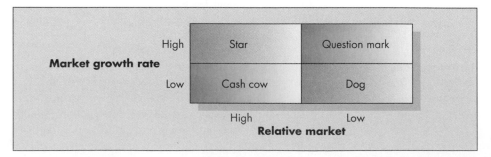

example, the number of individuals of college age is declining, and the impact on enrollments has been felt. However, enrollments in some fields of study have been increasing. Thus, certain departments in a college would have different market growth rates.

The horizontal indicator, *relative market share,* illustrates an SBU's market share relative to that of the most successful competition. This indicator ranges from high to low relative share of the market. As illustrated, four classifications of SBUs can be identified:

1. *Stars* are SBUs with a high share of a high-growth market. Because high-growth markets attract competition, such SBUs are usually cash users because they are growing and because the firm needs to protect their market share position.

2. *Cash cows* are often market leaders, but the market they are in is not growing rapidly. Because these SBUs have a high share of a low-growth market, they are cash generators for the firm.

3. *Question marks* are SBUs with a low share of a high-growth market. They have a good deal of potential but require great resources if the firm is to successfully build market share.

4. *Dogs* are SBUs that have a low share of a low-growth market. If the SBU has a very loyal group of customers, it may be a source of profits and cash, but dogs are not usually large sources of cash.

Strategic Choices.   Thus, depending on whether the SBUs are products, product lines, entire divisions, or departments, an organization may have one star, three cash cows, two question marks, and two dogs. After classifying each SBU according to the business portfolio matrix, management must decide which type of strategy to follow for each. In general, the strategy should focus on the decision of whether the organization wants to gain shares, hold shares, lose shares, or sell off shares.[35] Descriptions follow of the four general types of strategy options that organizations employ.

1. *Build.* If an organization has an SBU that it believes has the potential to be a star (probably a question mark at present), this would be an appropriate objective. Thus, the organization may even decide to give up short-term profits to provide the necessary financial resources to achieve this objective.

2. *Hold.* If an SBU is a very successful cash cow, a key objective would certainly be to hold or preserve the market share so that the organization can take advantage of the very positive cash flow.

3. *Harvest.* This objective is appropriate for all SBUs except those classified as stars. The basic objective is to increase the short-term cash return without too much concern for the long-run impact. It is especially worthwhile when more cash is needed for a cash cow whose long-run prospects are not good because of a low market-growth rate.

4. *Divest.* Getting rid of SBUs with low shares of low-growth markets is often appropriate. Question marks and dogs are particularly suited for this objective.

SBUs change position in the business portfolio matrix. As time passes, question marks may become stars, stars may become cash cows, and cash cows may become dogs.[36] In fact, one SBU can move through each category as the market growth rate declines. How quickly these changes occur is influenced by the technology and competitiveness of the industry. This underscores the importance and usefulness of viewing an organization in terms of SBUs, and the necessity of constantly seeking new ventures as well as managing existing ones.[37]

There have been several major criticisms of the BCG business portfolio matrix, on account of its focus on market share and market growth as the primary indicators of preference. First, the BCG matrix assumes market growth is uncontrollable.[38] As a result, managers can become too preoccupied with setting market share objectives instead of trying to grow the market. Second, assumptions regarding market share as a critical factor affecting firm performance may not hold true, especially in international markets.[39] Third, the BCG matrix assumes that the major source of SBU financing comes from internal means. Fourth, the BCG matrix does not take into account any interdependencies that may exist between SBUs, such as shared distribution channels.[40] Fifth, and perhaps most important, the thrust of the BCG matrix is based on the underlying assumption that corporate strategy starts with an analysis of competitive position. By its very nature, a strategy developed entirely on competitive analysis will always be a reactive one.[41] While the above criticisms are certainly valid ones, managers (especially of large firms) across all industries continue to find the BCG matrix useful in assessing the strategic position of SBUs.[42]

Strategic Planning: Using the Process

Strategic planning provides direction for an organization's mission, objectives, and strategies, facilitating the development of plans for each of the organization's functional areas.[43] A completed strategic plan guides each area in the direction the organization wishes to go and allows each area to develop objectives, strategies, and programs consistent with those goals.[44] The relationship between strategic planning and operational planning is an important concern of managers.

For example, Digital Equipment Corporation has established Digital Competence Centers (DCCs) in key commercial areas throughout Europe.[45] The DCCs ensure the development and implementation of industry strategies that are globally consistent within Digital yet take into account European customers' specific needs. This is accomplished by close contact between the DCCs and organizational headquarters in the United States, thus providing an organizational basis for information exchange.

Relating the Strategic Plan and Operational Plans

Most managers in an organization do not directly develop the organization's strategic plan.[46] Those who are interested in the benefits and results of planning are frequently not responsible for implementation of the plan. It is an incongruent activity, relying on inputs from some and interpretation by others. However, managers may be involved in this process in two important ways. First, they usually influence the strategic planning process by providing information and suggestions relating to their particular areas of responsibility. For example, at the Elyria Foundry, managers in each of the five departments identify 5 to 10 potential performance goals, which are then condensed into the company's annual list of objectives.[47] Second, they must be completely aware of what the process of strategic planning involves as well as the results, because everything their respective departments do, the objectives they establish for the areas of responsibility, should all be derived from the strategic plan. To a large degree, corporate success depends on this sharing of information, for employee knowledge can be viewed as a critical ingredient contributing to the plan's success.

In well-managed organizations, therefore, a direct relationship exists between strategic planning and the planning done by managers at all levels.[48] The focus of the planning and the time perspectives will, of course, differ. Figure 7–4 illustrates the relationship between the strategic plan and operational plans. It indicates very clearly that all plans should be derived from the strategic plan while at the same time contributing to the achievement of the strategic plan.

Relating Organizational Objectives and Strategies to Operational Objectives and Strategies

If done properly, planning results in a clearly defined blueprint for management action *at all levels* in the organization.[49] Figure 7–5 illustrates the *hierarchy of objectives and strategies,* using only one objective and two strategies from the strategic plan. In the figure, all objectives are related to other objectives at higher and lower levels in the organization. We have illustrated only four possible operational objectives. Obviously, many others could be developed, but our purpose is to clearly explain how objectives and strategies from the strategic plan for the entire organization (above the dotted line) relate to objectives and strategies that are part of operational plans for individual departments (below the dotted line). As we move from the top of the organization toward lower levels (in terms of who does the planning), we increase the detail and specificity of the objectives, and we decrease the time span. Although the scope, time span, and issues confronted by operational plans differ, they are all derived from those in the strategic plan.[50]

At this point it may be worthwhile for the reader to review Chapters 6 and 7 as a unit. Together they present a comprehensive perspective on the management function

FIGURE 7–4   Relationship between the Organization's Strategic Plan and Operational Plans

While the strategic plan provides direction for individual departments' plans, these operational plans are simultaneously contributing to the success of the strategic plan.

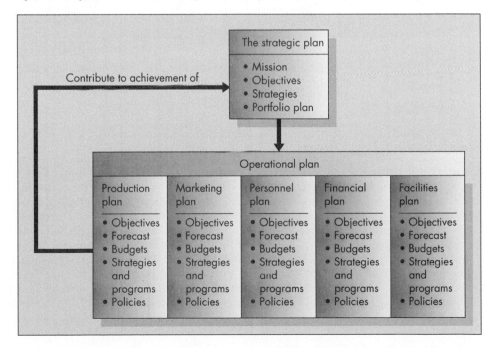

FIGURE 7–5   **The Hierarchy of Objectives and Strategies in the Organization**

If planning is effective, the objectives of individual departments will contribute to the achievement of overall objectives.

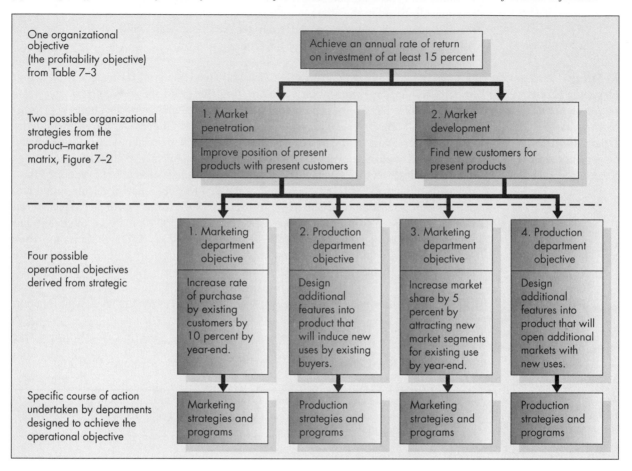

of planning. All other management functions reflect the decision managers make during the planning function.

Summary of Key Points

- Strategic planning involves the total organization in that it specifies the organization's relation to its environment in terms of mission, objectives, strategies, and portfolio plan. The importance of strategic planning has increased as organizations seek more rational responses to environmental change and uncertainty.

- The organization's mission specifies the organization's basic purpose, its reason for being. The mission statement should be a definition of what the organization is striving to become in the long run and should take into account the organization's history, distinctive competencies, and environment.

- To be useful, the mission statement should focus on markets rather than products and should be achievable, motivational, and specific.

- Organizational objectives are derived from the mission. They are guideposts for assessing the degree of movement toward achieving the mission. They are the bases for establishing operational objectives for the subunits and departments of the organization.

- Organizational strategies are the broad approaches the organization takes to achieving its objectives. Strategy development involves thinking through how the company is to be positioned to either create uniqueness in current markets or conquer new markets. Business firms can follow four basic growth strategies: market penetration, market development, product development, and diversification. The strategies selected by the organization must not only contribute to the achievement of objectives but also be compatible with the mission.

• Organizational portfolios present the relative strength of each strategic business unit and the relative growth rate of the industry in which the business competes. The portfolio analysis suggests corporate strategies based on the positioning of strategic business units in the portfolio matrix. Although many criticisms have been leveled at portfolio matrixes, they continue to be widely utilized.

• The corporate objectives and strategies contained in the strategic plan are converted into operational objectives and strategies. Through strategic planning, organizations can achieve unity and continuity of action.

Discussion and Review Questions

1. Discuss the statement, "Why should companies bother to engage in long-term planning? They have enough problems coping with planning for the short run."

2. Explain why you agree or disagree with the following statements:
   a. Planning is the easiest when environmental change is minimal.
   b. Planning is most valuable when environmental change is great.

3. Describe how a company, through placing too much emphasis on achieving long-term objectives, could jeopardize its short-term profitability and other operating results. Use an existing company as an example in formulating your response.

4. Discuss the potential problems an organization could encounter if its mission statement failed to provide a long-run vision of what the company is striving to become.

5. Choose a company and describe its distinctive competencies. Do you believe that these competencies are capable of leading the company to a sustainable competitive advantage? Why or why not?

6. This chapter states that an effective mission statement focuses on markets rather than products and is achievable, motivating, and specific. Select three of the actual mission statements presented in Table 7–1 and evaluate them based on these criteria.

7. What is the relationship between organizational mission, organizational objectives, and organizational strategies?

8. Discuss how a company that manufactures and markets children's toys could pursue growth through utilization of the strategies presented in Figure 7–2.

9. Do you believe each of the criticisms of the BCG Business Portfolio Matrix is valid? Why or why not?

10. Explain, through use of some examples, how managers and employees at lower levels of an organization influence the development and implementation of the strategic plan.

Case 7–1
Encouraging Diversity as Part of the Strategic Planning Process

At the Chemical Group of the Monsanto Corporation (Monsanto), managing diversity is treated as a long-term process one of whose goals is helping employees become more efficient and effective in their interpersonal relationships on the job. Toward this end, management has created a strategic action plan called the Process for Diversity Management. The intent of the plan is to establish, recognize, and reward new behaviors in people management; indeed, this road map represents a radical change in the corporate culture.

Monsanto's diversity efforts encompass a three-part strategy aimed at raising employee awareness of diversity-related issues; establishing accountability as a measure of perfor-mance; and changing the processes that support the ways in which people are managed. The strategy is based on a model that presumes the following: As diversity in the workplace increases, perceived homogeneity decreases. Left untouched, the result is the building of barriers that inhibit effective interpersonal relationships and thereby reduce worker productivity. For this reason, Monsanto management views diversity as a strategic business issue, wanting to allow the differences, talents, and capabilities of all their employees to interact in a manner that is synergistic, effective, and free of friction.

The Monsanto approach to diversity specifically seeks to raise the awareness and change the behavior patterns of white males. This reflects a strong management belief that, while diversity-related issues affect all, the environment in which change needs to be induced is largely controlled by white males. Further, the potentially biggest obstacle to progress—the attitudes and behaviors of this group—also presents the largest opportunity for positive change.

In the past, as was the case with many large organizations, Monsanto's corporate culture was predominately based upon the values and beliefs of white males. Monsanto had its eyes opened to the problems associated with this phenomenon by scrutinizing the retention rates among employees who might be considered to be outside the old mainstream culture. Through undertaking such an examination, the company found that members of minorities and women were leaving at a rate almost twice as high as that of white males. Further, in the case of minority women, the incidence of departure escalated to three to four times the normal rate. These patterns were deemed unacceptable and a waste of talent.

The company took several steps to address the problems that were causing women and minority members to leave. The first step involved the creation of Consulting Pairs. Each pair consists of two employees who receive 13 days of special training in addressing and solving problems related to diversity issues.

The second step involved the institutionalization of formal discussions to take place between managers and their individual subordinates. These discussions, called "join-ups," are facilitated by a Consulting Pair. During the two-hour join-up sessions, the Consulting Pair assists the manager and the new employee in undertaking discussions related to topics such as job responsibilities, organizational norms, expectations, and the mission of the work group. In this session, both the manager and the employee present their "hot buttons" or personal pet peeves to each other. For example, the manager might say, "Expect me to get mad if you miss a staff meeting," or the employee might admit, "I hate it when a boss looks over my shoulder." Since 1989, nearly 1,000 employees have taken part in the join-up program. To lend credence to the program's objectives, Robert G Potter, president of the Chemical Group, has participated as a facilitator at numerous sessions.

Another integral part of Monsanto's diversity strategy involves changing processes that support how people are managed. Monsanto has implemented programs to target barriers preventing its employees (both managers and subordinates) from understanding diversity. The eight process barriers defined by Monsanto are as follows:

1. Denial of issues.
2. Lack of awareness of problems.
3. Restrictions on bringing bad news up the organizational ladder.
4. A lack of trust about how others will perceive and respond to diversity issues.
5. The need to be in control of one's job.

6. A compulsion to fix "them" rather than "us."
7. Issues outside one's reality.
8. Past, well-intended, diversity actions.

Positive new behaviors are reinforced by a climate in which line managers assume responsibility for valuing differences, in which candid feedback is given to all employees for competency-based development plans, and in which managers, who achieve financial and business results and who value and develop their people, are recognized and rewarded.

The company's cause is also supported by actions taken by corporate headquarters. Monsanto, as a corporation, has taken a strong stance in supporting universities that are predominately attended by minority students. For example, the company recently renewed a partnership program with Howard University, awarding a four-year, $860,000 grant for the university's chemistry, chemical engineering, and business programs. The partnership program requires Monsanto to supply technical expertise as well as grants for Howard's laboratory renovation, undergraduate scholarships, research fellowships, and graduate stipends. In return, Monsanto is able to recruit highly qualified minority graduates who enhance the company's efforts and success in promoting diversity.

In essence, Monsanto's mission incorporates the *work environment* as an integral aspect of achieving business objectives. Improving work relationships by eliminating barriers is now seen as strategically vital to the company's mission.

Like Monsanto, many other companies, both large and small, are beginning to provide diversity training for their workforces. The focus of the training is generally on creating a workplace conducive to retaining and promoting a diverse workforce. Some large corporations even link executive pay increases partly to the achievement of diversity goals. And some small companies have used diversity training to smooth tensions in the workplace before a crisis erupts.

Questions for Analysis:

1. Why did Monsanto address diversity-related issues as part of its strategic planning process?
2. Assume that you were hired to solve the problems related to employee turnover at Monsanto. What would you have done differently or in addition to the actions taken?
3. Choose three of the eight barriers presented in the case. Explain why these barriers do, in fact, prevent employees from understanding diversity.
4. In general, how can actions taken toward achieving diversity assist organizations in becoming more competitive?

Sources: S. P. Talbot, "Building a Global Workforce Starts with Recruiting," *Personal Journal,* March 1996, pp. 9–11; P. A Galagan, "Trading Places at Monsanto," *Training & Development,* April 1993, pp. 44–49; "Diversity Training Extends Beyond U.S.," *The Wall Street Journal,* March 13, 1993, p. B1.

Video Case
A Conversation with Ben and Jerry

Ben & Jerry's Homemade Ice Cream, Inc., is unique because of the way Ben Cohen and Jerry Greenfield decided to organize and manage their company. Annual sales have increased to more than $120 million dollars since Ben & Jerry's was founded in the late 1970s. Commenting on his firm's remarkable record and his partner's contributions to that success, Jerry said, "What Ben brings is a real sense of experimenting, trying new things, no sense of failure whatsoever. Ben has often said that he would rather fail at something new than succeed at something that has already been done. I think another major thing that Ben brings is that he's never satisfied. So, no matter what we do he's always looking to improve it. I'm very good at routine things. I don't mind doing the same thing over and over again, which is good when you're trying to make ice cream. We didn't really regard ourselves as going into business or setting up a business or anything like that. We looked at ourselves as ice cream makers, having this little homemade parlor and doing it for two or three years and then doing something else. So we weren't looking at what form of legal structure we needed to put together for a business as it would grow and evolve over the years."

Ben corroborated Jerry's story about the pair's initial nonchalance about corporate legal form stating: "I think we talked to some lawyer and he said we should form a corporation and so we did. The lawyer talked about sub S versus not sub S for a while and then we said, which do you think we should do? and he said not sub S and so we said OK."

Starting the company on a shoestring wasn't frightening to the young partners because they didn't have really high expectations. As Jerry put it, "We had $12,000. Sure it was our life savings and everything, but we didn't look at this as some huge thing that we were getting into. When we were getting into business it was a lark, something fun to do, to work together, to be our own bosses. The question of legal liability and putting together a corporation and stock and things like that wasn't on our minds."

A Ben and Jerry's stockholder meeting is something to behold. Their meetings aren't the stuffy, formal, technical number sessions of Wall Street. A Ben & Jerry's annual meeting is more like a county fair. One shareholder said, "It was like nothing I had ever seen before. It was part of a festival weekend that Ben & Jerry's was hosting. It was under a tent. The chairman of the board and many of the executives were in Bermuda shorts and T-shirts." You won't find may of the people complaining about that irreverence, however. Last year the value of Ben & Jerry's stock increased 150 percent and the company reported record earnings of $3.7 million.

Jerry points out that, despite the fun of the shareholder meetings, the company has always felt the same pressures as any other entrepreneurial firm, especially the pressure for more money. He said, "We always needed more money. It's funny how everybody keeps telling you you'll need more money and you don't think it's true but as you grow in your business you need more money." Ben supported Jerry's remarks stating, "We went public because we had a need to raise capital in order to expand. We went public just in the state of Vermont. It was the first ever just intrastate Vermont public stock offering. And the idea was that if we could make the members of the community as owners of the business as the business prospered the community would automatically prosper."

Ben & Jerry's has always been run with an exceedingly open management style. Ben pointed out that "all the accountants, lawyers and financial advisors were telling us we were crazy when we wanted to become a public held company and have to open our books to everybody. We said that's the only kind of business we want to run, where we can open our books to everybody and be proud of it. You know, they said you really ought to take venture capital because if you need more money the venture capitalists will give you more money, and we realized that if we took venture capital that that would be a few rich people that would loan us a whole lot of money in order to get richer and what we wanted to do was we wanted to give the opportunity to the people of limited wealth to achieve some money. So we had a very low minimum buy—for $126.00 you could become an owner of Ben & Jerry's. At the end of the IPO, 1 out of every 100 Vermont families had bought stock in the company."

Ben & Jerry's is famous for its ice cream, but it's also famous for its overall business philosophy that encourages giving back to the community. The two founders spoke eloquently about their founding and guiding philosophy. "Ben and I are not really capable of looking at an accounting report and making a whole lot of sense out of it," said Jerry. "We can see if we're making money or not, if some expenses are out of line, or sales are out of line, but I'd say beyond that we don't have a very sophisticated take on financial matters here. That's not to say that financial information here doesn't get used, it just doesn't get used by us." Ben added, "Right, that's definitely true. The financial information gets used a lot and I encourage it. You know when our business was first starting out the financial advisors, the business pundits, the advisors and accountants were saying our concern for the community and our use of our company resources to improve the quality of life in the community was going to be our downfall. Now we're realizing that it's really those things that have driven our success. And what we have discovered is that there's a spiritual aspect to business just as there is to the life of individuals. As you support the community the community supports you back. It's really not so crazy."

Critical Thinking Questions

1. Ben and Jerry began with low expectations for the company, and thus had little concern for the corporate legal form they adopted. What consequences can arise from choosing the wrong legal form when starting a business?

2. Ben and Jerry both commented that they have little sophistication for understanding the financial condition of their firm. What do you think are some of the absolutely essential financial considerations that any entrepreneur or business person must understand?

3. Ben & Jerry's has made its mark because it has a good product, but also because it has been a good corporate citizen. How do these two factors work in the company's favor?

EXPERIENTIAL EXERCISE
THE IMPORTANCE OF THE PLANNING FUNCTION

Purpose

The purpose of this exercise, which requires some out-of-class homework, is to emphasize the importance of planning in organizations in various industries.

The Exercise in Class

The organizations for the exercise:

General Motors Corporation
Standard Brands Paint Company
Walt Disney Company
General Mills, Inc.
Levi Strauss & Co.
Sears, Roebuck & Co.
Revlon, Inc.
Bell Atlantic
Tennaco, Inc.
Genentech, Inc.
Topps Co.
WordPerfect Corp.

1. Every person in the class should be assigned the same organization from the above list and answer these questions:

   a. What events in this organization's environment should be considered in developing a strategic plan for the successful achievement of objectives?

   b. How likely are important events to occur? That is, what is the probability of an event (e.g., energy shortage, shortage of qualified job candidates, increase or decrease in demand, increase or decrease in competition)?

   c. How can managerial planning improve the organization's chances of surviving and/or benefitting from the occurrence of positive and/or negative events cited in your answer to question *b*?

2. After each student completes the first part of the exercise, the instructor will form groups of four to six students. Each group will be assigned a different organization from the preceding list.

3. Your group should answer questions 1*a,* 1*b,* and 1*c* and report your answers to the class.

The Learning Message

This exercise will show that some organizations need planning more than others because of the events they must deal with in the environment.

Notes

1. For a discussion of this topic, see Ray Suutari, "The Case for Strategic Thinking," *CMA Magazine,* June 1993, pp. 17–21.

2. John H Grant and William R King, *The Logic of Strategic Planning* (Boston: Little, Brown, 1982), chap. 1.

3. Joe Dodson, "Strategic Repositioning through the Customer Connection," *Journal of Business Strategy,* May–June 1991, pp. 4–7.

4. G S Day, K E Jocz, and H P Root, "Domains of Ignorance: What We Most Need to Know," *Marketing Management,* Winter 1992, pp. 9–14.

5. H H Beam, "Strategic Discontinuities: When Being Good May Not Be Enough," *Business Horizons*, July–August 1990, pp. 10–14.
6. Peter Lorange and Johann Roos, "Why Some Strategic Alliances Succeed and Others Fail," *Journal of Business Strategy*, January–February 1991, pp. 25–30.
7. Jane E Dutton and Susan E Jackson, "Categorizing Strategic Issues: Links to Organizational Action," *Academy of Management Review*, January 1987, pp. 76–90; Jane E Dutton and Edward Ottensmeyer, "Strategic Issue Management Systems: Forms, Functions, Contexts," *Academy of Management Review*, April 1987, pp. 355–65.
8. See Henry Mintzberg, "The Strategy Concept I: Five Ps for Strategy," *California Management Review*, Fall 1987, pp. 11–24; Henry Mintzberg, "The Strategy Concept II: Another Look at Why Organizations Need Strategies," *California Management Review*, Fall 1987, pp. 25–32.
9. Alexander Hiam, "Strategic Planning Unbound," *Journal of Business Strategy*, March–April 1993, pp. 46–52.
10. See F Paul Carlson, "The Long and Short of Strategic Planning," *The Journal of Business Strategy*, May–June 1990, pp. 15–19, for a discussion of this subject.
11. David K Hurst, "Why Strategic Management Is Bankrupt," *Organizational Dynamics*, Autumn 1986, pp. 4–27, critiques the conventional strategic management model.
12. Jerome H Want, "Corporate Mission: The Intangible Contribution to Performance," *Management Review*, August 1986, pp. 46–50.
13. James Whelan and James D Sisson, "How to Realize the Promise of Strategic Planning," *Journal of Business Strategy*, January–February 1993, pp. 31–36.
14. Chris Lee, "The Vision Thing," *Training*, February 1993, pp. 25–33.
15. Peter Drucker, *Management: Tasks, Responsibilities, Practices* (New York: Harper & Row, 1974), chap. 7.
16. David Calfee, "Get Your Mission Statement Working!" *Management Review*, January 1993, pp. 54–57.
17. Philip Kotler, *Marketing Management: Analysis, Planning, and Control*, 6th ed. (Englewood Cliffs, NJ: Prentice Hall, 1986), chap. 2.
18. William French, "Aiming for Success," *Journal of Housing*, January–February 1993, pp. 37–39.
19. For a study of the relationship between distinctive corporate competencies and firm performance in 185 industrial firms, see M A Hitt and R D Ireland, "Corporate Distinctive Competence, Strategy and Performance," *Strategic Management Journal*, July–September 1985, pp. 273–93.
20. C Smart and I Vertinsky, "Strategy and the Environment: A Study of Corporate Responses to Crises," *Strategic Management Journal*, April–June 1984, pp. 199–214. This study of the largest US and Canadian companies examines the relationship between a firm's external environment and its supply of strategic responses to cope with crises. For a different view of the environment, see L Smircich and C Stubbart, "Strategic Management in an Enacted World," *Academy of Management Review*, October 1985, pp. 724–36.
21. Drucker, *Management*, pp. 77–89; Kotler, *Marketing Management*, chap. 2.
22. Drucker, *Management*, p. 79.
23. See Paul C Nutt, "A Strategic Network for Nonprofit Organizations," *Strategic Management Journal*, January–March 1984, pp. 57–76; Peter Smith Ring and James L Perry, "Strategic Management in Public and Private Organizations: Implications of Distinctive Contexts and Constraints," *Academy of Management Review*, April 1985, pp. 276–86.
24. Practical ideas for developing a mission statement can be found in Mark Frohman and Perry Pascarella, "How to Write a Purpose Statement," *Industry Week*, March 23, 1987, pp. 31–34; also see, John A Pearce II and Fred David, "Corporate Mission Statements: The Bottom Line," *Academy of Management Executive*, May 1987, pp. 109–15.
25. Drucker, *Management*, p. 87.
26. For a discussion of this topic, see Alan Farnham, "State Your Values, Hold the Hot Air," *Fortune*, April 19, 1993, pp. 17–20.
27. Martha H Peak, "More than Syntax," *Management Review*, January 1993, p. 1.
28. Ellen Earl Chaffee, "The Models of Strategy," *Academy of Management Review*, January 1985, pp. 89–98.
29. Michael Goold and Andrew Campbell, "Many Best Ways to Make Strategy," *Harvard Business Review*, November–December 1987, pp. 67–73.
30. Ari Ginsberg, "Operationalizing Organizational Strategy: Toward an Integrated Framework," *Academy of Management Review*, July 1984, pp. 548–57.
31. Thomas L Brown, "Bringing Strategy to Life," *Industry Week*, April 5, 1993, p. 19.
32. See Jeffrey L Kerr, "Diversification Strategies and Managerial Rewards: An Empirical Study," *Academy of Management Journal*, March 1985, pp. 155–79, for a study of the relationship between diversification and the design of managerial reward systems in 20 large industrial firms. Also see Paulette Dubofsky and P Varadarajan, "Diversification and Measures of Performance: Additional Empirical Evidence," *Academy of Management Journal*, September 1987, pp. 597–606.
33. David A Aaker, "Managing Assets and Skills: The Key to a Sustainable Competitive Advantage," *California Management Review*, Winter 1989, pp. 91–106.

34. There are other portfolio models; each has its supporters and detractors. The one presented here, while among the most popular, is also not without critics. The important point is the concept of viewing an organization as a portfolio of businesses or activities, each competing for resources. The interested reader should consult Richard G Hammermesh and Roderick E White, "Manage beyond Portfolio Analysis," *Harvard Business Review*, January–February 1984, pp. 103–9; J A Seeger, "Revising the Images of BCG's Growth/Share Matrix," *Strategic Management Journal*, January–March 1984, pp. 93–97.

35. William Rothschild, "Avoid the Mismatch between Strategy and Strategic Leaders," *Journal of Business Strategy*, January–February 1993, pp. 37–42.

36. Gareth R Jones and John E Butler, "Costs, Revenue, and Business-Level Strategy," *Academy of Management Review*, April 1988, pp. 202–13.

37. For a related discussion that focuses on small businesses, see Gerald d'Amboise and Marie Muldowney, "Management Theory for Small Business: Attempts and Requirements," *Academy of Management Review*, April 1988, pp. 226–40.

38. P Rajan Varadarajan, Terry Clark, and William M Pride, "Controlling the Uncontrollable—Managing Your Market Environment," *Sloan Management Review*, Winter 1992, pp. 39–47.

39. Reed E Nelson, "Is There Strategy in Brazil?" *Business Horizons*, July–August 1992, pp. 15–23.

40. Peter S Davis and Patrick L Schill, "Addressing the Contingent Effects of Business Unit Strategic Orientation on the Relationship between Organizational Context and Business Unit Performance," *Journal of Business Research* 27 (1993), pp. 183–200.

41. Michel Roberts, "Times Change, but Do Business Strategists?" *Journal of Business Strategy*, March–April 1993, pp. 12–15.

42. Donald L McCabe and V K Narayanan, "The Life Cycle of the PIMS and BCG Models," *Industrial Marketing Management*, November 1991, pp. 347–52.

43. James J Chrisman, Charles W Hofer, and William R Boulton, "Toward a System for Classifying Business Strategies," *Academy of Management Review*, July 1988, pp. 413–28.

44. For interesting support of this view, see Ed Bukszar and Terry Connolly, "Hindsight Bias and Strategic Choice: Some Problems in Learning from Experience," *Academy of Management Journal,* September 1988, pp. 628–41.

45. For a more complete discussion, see Lee W Sargeant, "Strategic Planning in a Subsidiary," *Long Range Planning* 23, no. 2 (1990), pp. 43–54.

46. David M Reid, "Where Planning Fails in Practice," *Long Range Planning* 23, no. 2 (1990), pp. 85–93.

47. Leslie Brokaw, "One-Page Company Game Plan," *Inc.*, June 1993, pp. 111–13.

48. G David Wallace, "America's Leanest and Meanest," *Business Week*, October 5, 1987, pp. 78–84.

49. Frederick W Gluck, "A Fresh Look at Strategic Management," *Journal of Business Strategy*, Fall 1985, pp. 4–19.

50. While developing strategy is important, implementing it is also critically important. For excellent works devoted entirely to implementation, see Paul J Stonich, *Implementing Strategy: Making Strategy Happen* (Cambridge, MA: Ballinger, 1982), and Jay Galbraith and Robert K Kazanjian, *Strategy Implementation: Structure, Systems and Process*, 2d ed. (St. Paul, MN: West, 1986).

8 THE ORGANIZING FUNCTION

Chapter Learning Objectives

After completing Chapter 8, you should be able to:

- **Define** the organizing function in terms of required management decisions.
- **Describe** the effects of the span of control on the manager and the organization.
- **Discuss** the relationships between the planning and organizing functions.
- **Compare** two organizations, using the dimensions of structure as the bases for the comparison.
- **Identify** the ways to describe differences among jobs.

Innovations in Organization Structures in Global and Small Organizations

Organizations around the world have been experimenting with different ways to organize the way they do business. These organizations are some of the most influential and publicized in the world, and their actions will surely influence other organizations to attempt similar innovations. This Management in Action summarizes only some of these experiments.

Motorola learned in the mid-1980s that its products were not competitive on the global market and that the primary cause for this poor quality was the way the company had traditionally designed jobs. The event that instigated Motorola's search for quality was its winning of an antidumping suit against Japanese manufacturers of cellular phones.

But that suit did not solve Motorola's underlying problem of poor quality. The company's product was simply not up to standards of competition, and product quality improvement became the most important management problem to be solved. Management responded by shifting responsibility for quality control from inspectors at the end of the assembly line to individual production workers.

Then, to encourage individual workers to be familiar with and capable of doing all the jobs on the line so as to recognize potential and actual sources of quality failures, Motorola revised its compensation plan to reward individuals who learned a variety of jobs. The company then revised its selection and training approaches to reflect the new job requirements.

The First National Bank of Chicago reported increases in profitability, productivity, customer satisfaction, and staff morale as a consequence of its approach to job design in the unit that issues letters of credit. The unit employs 110 people who traditionally had performed fragmented tasks on what they referred to as their paperwork assembly line.

Over a period of six months the employees of the unit recently participated with management in designing their jobs around whole jobs that required greater skill and talent. The newly designed jobs were different in content, requirements, and context. The additional content meant that employees had to undergo further training to be capable of undertaking these expanded responsibilities, but the result has been an increase in pay because of their increased productivity.

Rohm & Haas Bayport, a relatively small manufacturer, was founded in 1981 to produce specialty chemicals. The plant is located in LaPorte, Texas, and its 67 employees play active roles in management because their jobs are designed with that activity in mind. The company's philosophy is to provide autonomy and responsibility in each individual's job and, consequently, to enable employees to feel a sense of "ownership" of key decisions and actions. Every person in the organization is trained to be and to act like a manager. The 46 process engineers and technicians and 15 engineers and chemists report to one of the two manufacturing unit managers, who in turn report to the executive team.

Lechmere Inc., a 27-store retail chain owned by Dayton Hudson, opened an outlet in Sarasota, Florida, in 1987. It faced an unusual circumstance of being unable to employ its typical workforce of part-timers such as teenagers and homemakers. The unemployment rate in the area was less than 4 percent, and entry-level people were in short supply. Retailers such as Lechmere rely on part-time employees because they are able to use them at the times and hours of peak activity. But in the absence of these types of employees, Lechmere needed to adopt a different approach by designing jobs that included a considerable range of activities. They hired full-time employees but then rewarded them for learning about and taking on many different job responsibilities.

Volvo Corporation, under the leadership of Pehr Gyllenhammar, has, since 1971, been experimenting with innovative ways to manufacture automobiles. Gyllenhammar took a keen interest in the experiments of Ingvar Barrby, head of the upholstery department, in job rotation (termed *job alternation* at Volvo). The reduction in turnover from 35 percent to 15 percent encouraged the new managing director to adopt other aspects of job redesign. For example, group management and work modules are used at the Torslanda car assembly plant. Employees, in groups, follow the same auto body for seven or eight workstations along the line for a total period of 20 minutes.

Sources: N Dixon, "New Routes to Evaluation," *Training and Development,* May 1996 pp. 82–85; R Galvin, "Knowledge Makes A Difference at Motorola," *Strategy and Leadership,* March–April 1996, pp. 42–43; J Noe, "Regaining Customer Appreciation," *America's Community Banker,* April 1996, pp. 16–20; C Ponicki, "Improving the Efficiency of Small-Business Lending at First National Bank of Chicago," *Commercial Lending Review,* Spring 1996, pp. 51–60; L Thornburg, "Winners Touch Many Lives," *HRMagazine,* September 1995, pp. 47–55; S Caudron, "Diversity Ignites Effective Work Teams," *Personnel Journal,* September 1994, pp. 54–63; J Ettlie, "European Manufacturing: The Big Comeback?" *Production,* August 1995, p. 18; and C Berggren, P Adler, and R Cole, "NUMMI vs. Uddevalla; Rejoinder," *Sloan Management Review,* Winter 1994, pp. 37–49.

Business historians will have every reason to describe the 1980s and 1990s as the era of "reorganization." Headline after headline in *The Wall Street Journal, Business Week, Forbes, Fortune,* and countless other periodicals and newspapers report how America's great corporations have reorganized to be more effective competitors in their markets. The headlines invite us to read and learn how IBM and US Shoe have decentralized, how General Motors has reduced the number of managers and increased the number of people reporting to each manager, how Procter & Gamble has increased the number of managers by superimposing another level of management on the existing management, and how Kodak has redefined the bases for grouping jobs. Evidently, the way jobs are organized has important implications for attaining organizational performance.[1]

The purpose of the organizing function is to achieve coordinated effort through the design of a structure of task and authority relationships: The two key concepts are design and structure. Design, in this context, implies that managers make a conscious effort to predetermine the way employees will do their jobs; structure refers to relatively stable relationships and aspects of the organization. Some management experts think of organizational structure as "the anatomy of the organization, providing a foundation within which the organization functions."[2]

Thus the structure of an organization, similar to the anatomy of a living organism, acts as a framework within which the dynamic activity and processes of people doing work take place. The idea of structure as a framework "focuses on the differentiation of positions, formulation of rules and procedures, and prescriptions of authority."[3] In this context, the purpose of structure is to regulate or at least reduce the uncertainty regarding the behavior of individual employees.

The organizing function involves breaking down the overall task into individual jobs with specific duties and assigning authority to carry out those duties and aggregating the individual jobs into departments of specific bases and sizes. Thus, we can describe the organizing function in terms of dividing tasks into jobs, delegating authority, determining the appropriate bases for departments, and deciding the appropriate size of each department.

The decisions managers make regarding division of tasks, delegation of authority, bases of departments, and size of departments can cause organizations to be different in very important ways. As we shall see, tasks can be more or less specialized, authority can be centralized or decentralized, departments can contain jobs that are more or less alike, and the number of jobs (people) assigned to a department can be relatively few or many. The challenge of management when engaged in the organizing function is to design the most appropriate organization structure by making the appropriate decisions about jobs, authority, and departments.

This chapter and Chapter 9 should be considered as one unit of learning, separated for reasons of convenience and brevity. This chapter has two major purposes: to develop an understanding of the ways in which organization structures differ along certain dimensions and to demonstrate the ways that managers can make organization structures different by their decisions related to jobs and departments. Chapter 9 continues the discussion by reviewing the factors that managers should take into account when they design or redesign organization structures. We begin the discussion of this chapter by introducing three dimensions of organization structure, which differentiate one structure from another.

Dimensions of Structure

Researchers and practitioners of management have attempted to develop their understanding of relationships between organization structure and performance, attitudes, satisfaction, and other variables thought to be important. The development of understanding has been hampered not only by the difficulty of the relationships themselves, but also by the difficulty of defining and measuring the concept of organization structure.

Although universal agreement on a common set of dimensions that measure differences in structure is neither possible nor desirable, some suggestions can be made. We can conveniently use three dimensions to describe and analyze differences in organization structures. They are formalization, centralization, and complexity.[4]

Formalization

The dimension of formalization refers to the extent to which expectations regarding the means and ends of work are specified, written, and enforced. An organization structure that is described as highly formalized would be one in which rules and procedures are available to prescribe what each individual should be doing.[5] Such organizations would have written standard operating procedures, specified directives, and explicit policy. We should recognize that the idea of formalization as referring to written rules and procedures may not be totally satisfactory. For example, some organizations, such as research laboratories and colleges, often have unwritten rules of conduct that every employee knows about and obeys. The importance of examining this dimension is to point out that some organizations, but not others, can predetermine in considerable detail what their employees should do in particular situations.

Centralization

Centralization refers to the location of decision-making authority in the hierarchy of the organization. More specifically, the concept refers to the delegation of authority among the jobs in the organization. Typically, we think of centralization in terms of making decisions and exacting obedience (i.e., upper-level managers in the organization make all the significant decisions, and managers at all levels can command their subordinates to undertake legitimate work-related activities).

The idea of centralization can be difficult to grasp in a particular organization for several reasons. For example, people at the same level in an organization can have different decision-making authority: one department chair of a university can make all hiring decisions, yet peers in the same university cannot make this decision without approval of their dean. Moreover, all decisions are not of equal importance in organizations. For example, a typical management practice is to delegate authority to make routine operating decisions (i.e., decentralization), but to retain authority to make strategic decisions (i.e., centralization). Finally, individuals may not perceive that they really have authority even though their job descriptions include it. Thus objectively they have authority, but subjectively they do not.[6]

Complexity

Complexity is the direct outgrowth of dividing work and creating departments. Specifically, this dimension refers to the number of distinctly different job titles, or occupational groupings, and the number of distinctly different units, or departments. The fundamental idea is that organizations with a great many different kinds and types of jobs and units create more complicated managerial and organizational problems than those with fewer jobs and departments.

Complexity, then, relates to differences among jobs and units. It is not surprising therefore that differentiation is often used synonymously with complexity. Moreover it has become standard practice to use the term *horizontal differentiation* to refer to the number of different jobs at the same level; *vertical differentiation* refers to the number of levels in the organization.[7] Thus an organization that has eight managerial levels from the chief executive to the line employee would be more complex than one that has only five levels. Similarly, an organization that has 100 different job titles would be more complex than one that has only 25 job titles.

These three dimensions vary independently. Organizations can be more or less formal, centralized, and complex. The important point, however, is not that organizations are different along these three dimensions, but that these differences can make a difference in the organization's performance. Managers can affect the extent to which their organizations are formal, centralized, and complex through their decisions regarding division of labor, delegation of authority, departmental bases, and departmental size. Thus we have introduced the important concepts of this chapter and the next, which are summarized in Table 8–1. We think that these three concepts can be very important aids in developing an understanding of this crucial managerial responsibility. Let us now move to the discussion of division of labor as a key decision in the organizing function.

Division of Labor

Division of labor concerns the extent to which jobs are specialized. Managers divide the total task of the organization into specific jobs having specified activities. The activities define what the person performing the job is to do and to get done. For example the activities of the job "accounting clerk" can be defined in terms of the methods and procedures required to process a certain quantity of transactions during a period of time. Other accounting clerks could use the same methods and procedures to process different types of transactions. One could be processing accounts receivable; the others process accounts payable. Thus jobs can be specialized both by method and by application of the method.

Management's most important organizing responsibility is to design jobs that enable people to perform the right tasks at the right time. In fact, the ability to divide

TABLE 8–1   Distinctions among Organizing Function, Organizational Structure, and Organization Dimensions

The organizing function, organizational structures, and organization dimensions are different, but related, concepts.

Organizing Function	*Organizational Structure*	*Organization Dimensions*
Refers to decisions managers make about:	Refers to results of managers' decisions as reflected by:	Refers to distinguishing organizational characteristics:
Specialization of jobs Delegation of authority Departmental bases Size of departments	Job designs that specify job requirements, activities, outcomes, and authority Organizational departments that contain specific types and numbers of jobs	Complexity Formalization Centralization

overall tasks into smaller and specialized tasks is the chief advantage of organized effort.[8]

All organizations consist of specialized jobs—people doing different tasks. A major managerial decision is to determine the extent to which jobs will be specialized. Historically, we have seen that managers will tend to divide jobs into rather narrow specialties because of the advantages of division of labor.[9] Two such advantages are as follows:

1. If a job consists of few tasks, you can quickly train replacements for personnel who are terminated, transferred, or otherwise absent. The minimum training effort results in a lower training cost.
2. When a job entails only a limited number of tasks, the employee can become highly proficient in performing those tasks. This proficiency can result in a better quality of output.

The gains derived from narrow divisions of labor can be calculated in purely economic terms: As the job is divided into ever smaller elements, additional output is obtained. As long as the relative increase in output exceeds the relative increase in costs of performing the smaller job elements, increases from specialization result. However, at some point, the costs of specialization (labor and capital) begin to outweigh the increased efficiency of specialization (output), and the cost per unit of output begins to rise as shown in Figure 8–1.

Specialization of Labor at the Job Level

Specialization, or division, of labor at the job level is measured in relative terms. One job can be more or less specialized than another. In making comparisons of degrees of specialization, it is useful to identify five aspects that differentiate jobs:

1. *Work pace.* The more control the individual has over how fast she must work, the less specialized the job.
2. *Job repetitiveness.* The greater the number of tasks to perform, the less specialized the job.

Figure 8–1   The Economics of Specialization

There are limits to the gains realized from specialization of labor.

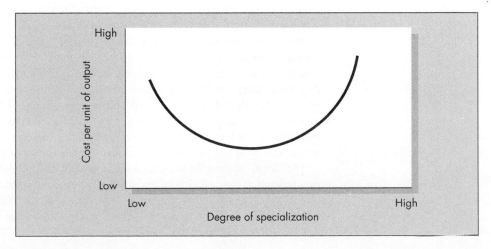

3. *Skill requirements.* The more skilled the jobholder must be, the less specialized the job.

4. *Methods specification.* The more latitude the jobholder has in using methods and tools, the less specialized the job.

5. *Required attention.* The more mental attention a job requires, the less specialized it is.

If you now reexamine the job specialization continuum, you can identify the specific characteristics of jobs that are relatively high or low in specialization.

Specialization	
High	*Low*
1. No control over pace.	1. Control over pace.
2. Repetitive.	2. Varied.
3. Low skill requirements.	3. High skill requirements.
4. Specified methods.	4. Unspecified methods.
5. No required attention.	5. Required attention.

The principle of specialization of labor has been the traditional guideline for managers when determining the content of individual jobs.[10] In recent years, management's attention has been directed to alternative ways of designing jobs that focus on teams doing work rather than on individuals doing work. The automobile industry in particular has emphasized the importance of designing jobs that are performed in the context of teams rather than by individuals.[11]

The Team Approach to Job Design

An innovation in job design has challenged traditional views. This approach reflects increasing respect for the power of teams and teamwork to get work done. For example, the traditional way to make cars reflects the ideas of Scientific Management, first popularized by Frederick W Taylor some 90 years ago. According to Taylor the jobs of making cars should be reduced to small, repetitive, and specialized tasks requiring little individual initiative and decision making. Over time these specialized jobs have been incorporated in bargaining agreements, and they have become very rigid and inflexible. Rigid job classifications and the accompanying work rules hamper the ability of the auto industry to utilize modern technology and to be competitive with foreign automakers.

The team approach to car making is more flexible and would enable the automakers to respond quickly to market changes. The basic elements are teams consisting of from 5 to 20 individuals who already work next to one another. But rather than doing only one job, team members learn several jobs. Work can then be organized as needed with different individuals doing different jobs as they are required. As the number of different jobs is reduced, the number of different job classifications and work rules are reduced. The reduction in work rules provides management with the flexibility to achieve higher levels of productivity and quality.

The team approach to job design results in individual jobs that take on characteristics at the left side of the specialization continuum. They enable employees to exercise relatively more discretion over pace and methods. They also reduce the amount of supervision needed and require considerably more skill. The team approach to job design has captured the attention of managers around the globe, and many have implemented this approach in their organizations. However, the team approach has not proved to be a cure-all for organizing issues, as Procter & Gamble discovered.

Procter & Gamble changed the degree of specialization of the company's sales representatives by having them concentrate on selling a specific line of products rather than a broad range of products.[12] Prior to the change, P&G had used a team approach in its sales organizations. Instead of having different sales representatives for each P&G division calling on a single customer, sales reps, as members of multi-function teams representing a broad spectrum of products, had been calling on customers. For example, sales representatives as well as specialists in finance, information, and logistics would work as team members to enable big customers, such as Wal-Mart Stores, to control inventory costs. The team approach had also enabled P&G to cut costs and to develop new products. But some costs were associated with these benefits.

For example, sales representatives who have an interest in developing strong ties with customers lose their competitive instinct. Some team members devoted too much energy to building relationships within the team and with the customers and too little attention to building volume and profit. For these reasons, P&G reversed the team approach in favor of sales representatives who would represent narrow sectors such as soap and food products.

One organizational effect of P&G's decision has been the creation of separate sales groups within each of the sectors. In terms of specialization of labor, the sales representatives now have more specialized jobs—they sell fewer different products—and the organization will now have more specialized units—the sales units in each of the sectors. P&G has become a more complex organization as a result of the increase in horizontal differentiation (more specialized jobs) and vertical differentiation (additional organizational units).

Organizations that utilize highly specialized jobs are relatively formal, complex, and centralized compared to those that use less specialized jobs, such as team-based jobs. Highly specialized jobs are usually rather narrow in scope, with predictable outcomes, thus lending themselves to standardized, written procedures. Such organizations are complex because of the many different specialties requiring much more managerial attention and, in unionized organizations, many more unions to deal with. Typically such organizations are centralized because of the same reasons: Relatively specialized jobs having little individual impact on the organization contain little in the way of authority to make significant decisions.

Delegation of Authority

Managers decide how much authority should be delegated to each job and each job-holder. As we have noted, authority refers to the right of individuals to make decisions without approval by higher management and to exact obedience from others. Delegation of authority refers specifically to making decisions, not to doing work. A sales manager can be delegated the right to hire salespeople (a decision) and the right to assign them to specific territories (obedience). Another sales manager may not have the right to hire but may have the right to assign territories. Thus the degree of delegated authority can be relatively high or relatively low with respect to both aspects of authority. And any particular job involves a range of alternative configurations of authority delegation.[13] Managers must balance the relative gains and losses of alternatives.

Why Delegate
Authority?

Relatively high delegation of authority encourages the development of professional managers. No doubt Philip G Barach, CEO of US Shoe Corporation, has this point in mind when he describes his management style as organized anarchy because he tends to leave his managers alone without any direction from his office (until things go wrong!).[14] Organizations that decentralize (delegate) authority enable managers to make significant decisions, gain skills, and advance in the company. By virtue of their right to make decisions on a broad range of issues, managers develop expertise that enables them to cope with problems of higher management. Managers with broad decision-making power often make difficult decisions. Consequently, they are trained for promotion into positions of even greater authority and responsibility. Upper management can readily compare managers on the basis of actual decision-making performance. The advancement of managers on the bases of demonstrated performance can eliminate favoritism and personality conflicts in the promotion process.

Second, high delegation of authority can lead to a competitive climate within the organization. The managers are motivated to contribute in this competitive atmosphere since they are compared with their peers on various performance measures. A competitive environment in which managers compete on how well they achieve sales, cost reduction, and employee development targets can be a positive factor in overall organizational performance.

Competitive environments can also produce destructive behavior if the success of one manager occurs at the expense of another. But regardless of whether it is positive or destructive, significant competition exists only when individuals have authority to do those things that enable them to win.

Finally, managers who have relatively high authority are able to exercise more autonomy and thus satisfy their desires to participate in problem solving. This autonomy can lead to managerial creativity and ingenuity, attributes that contribute to the organization's ability to respond to change. Many organizations, large and small, choose to follow the policy of decentralization of authority.

Hewlett-Packard (HP), for example, began in 1991 to rethink decisions the company had made in the 1980s.[15] Those 1980s decisions had the effect of centralizing operations at the expense of autonomy of product managers. The impetus for the decision to centralize was the increasing cost of duplication at the local level. For example each HP unit once manufactured its own circuit boards for its own products, even though the circuit boards were interchangeable. This arrangement enabled local managers to have control and flexibility over volume and quality. But the cost of duplication became intolerable as competition forced down the prices of HP products. Circuit-board production was thus consolidated in a few manufacturing sites and under the direction of a single manager.

The downside of the decision was the creation of committees and procedures and, consequently, a seemingly impenetrable maze of paperwork. In October 1990, the company reversed its earlier decision to centralize, announcing a major reorganization. John Young, HP's CEO, decided to go the way of many competitors, including IBM, by reducing the number of managerial levels in the organization structure and decentralizing decisions to managers of more-or-less independent operating units. Each unit now has its own salesforce concentrating on selling the unit's product. No doubt the reorganization will be worked out over a long time and with mixed results, but the HP way of the future seems assuredly to rest on decentralization rather than centralization.

Thus HP has attempted to exploit the benefits of decentralization of authority, but these benefits are not without costs. Organizations that are unable or unwilling to bear these costs will find reasons to centralize authority.

Why Should Authority Not Be Delegated?

Numerous reasons can be cited to justify centralized authority. First, managers must be trained to make the decisions that go with delegated authority. Formal training programs can be quite expensive, and the expense can more than offset the benefits.

Second, many managers are accustomed to making decisions, and they resist delegating authority to their subordinates. Consequently, they may perform less effectively because they believe that delegation of authority involves losing control.

Third, administrative costs are incurred because new or altered accounting and performance systems must be developed to provide top management with information about the effects of their subordinates' decisions. When lower levels of management have authority, top management must have some means of reviewing the use of that authority. Consequently, they typically create reporting systems that inform them of the outcomes of the decisions made at lower levels in the organization.

The fourth and perhaps most pragmatic reason to centralize recognizes that decentralization means duplication of functions. Each autonomous unit must be truly self-supporting to be independent. But that involves the potentially high cost of duplication, and some organizations find that the cost of decentralization outweighs the benefits.[16]

Nevertheless, organizations must choose the appropriate balance between centralization and decentralization. Organizations all around the globe have had to confront the centralization–decentralization issue. Nowhere has this choice caused more difficulty than in the countries formerly part of the Soviet Union, but other managers in other countries have had a good deal of difficulty with the decision as well.

Delegation of Authority in International Settings

Russian factory managers have begun to learn about Western ways of managing. The critical decision of degree of centralization within a specific factory has been particularly difficult for Russian factory managers to deal with because of their previous experience. In the past, the central planning agency, Gosplan, held these managers accountable for meeting specific, but negotiable, effectiveness criteria. As a result the factory managers emphasized short-term outcomes such as efficiency and production. This short-term orientation, combined with the hostility of middle- and lower-level bureaucrats toward decentralization has created real barriers to pushing decision making down to the factory level.[17]

A report from England indicates that the cost of duplication within divisionalized organizations has led to increased centralization of activities common to all divisions. The study focused on firms in the insurance business that had diversified into several lines of insurance and had established divisionalized structures to manage these different businesses. Although many observers thought that these insurance firms managed quite well with decentralized structures, the study points to the contrary: These firms had to take into account the cost of duplicative functions and thus decided to centralize them.[18]

An American firm had a similar experience with decentralization. Norwest Financial Information Services has evaluated the effects of information technology on its operations and decided that the advantages of decentralization do not offset its disadvantages. In particular, the company centralized certain operations that rely on either getting or sending information to the field. By making the information accessible to field offices through computerized technology, the company can seemingly have the advantages of both centralization and decentralization.[19]

*Empowerment:
Specialization and
Delegation*

Contemporary organizations have in recent years undertaken efforts to empower their employees. In fact, employee empowerment has become a cornerstone in those organizations attempting to implement total quality management. Now that we have reviewed some of the basic concepts of specialization of labor and delegation of authority, we can see that employee empowerment involves designing jobs that are relatively unspecialized, having considerable delegated authority to make decisions about job-related issues. The relationship between empowerment, specialization of labor, and delegation of authority is shown in Figure 8–2.

Despite its widespread publicity, employee empowerment cannot succeed in all organizations. As experts have pointed out, employee empowerment will have the best chance of succeeding when the organization institutes a cross-training program to provide employees with skills to exercise additional responsibility and authority, encourages and rewards innovative behavior, provides access to all pertinent information, and supports employee decision making even in risky situations. Only through the development of a sense of ownership, these experts state, can an organization achieve the high levels of quality that customers and clients have come to expect.[20] The accompanying Management Focus describes some examples of employee empowerment in small firms.

Like most managerial issues, whether authority should be delegated in high or low degrees cannot be resolved simply. As usual, in managerial decision making, whether to centralize or decentralize authority can only be guided by general questions. However, in terms of the dimensions of organization structure, delegation of authority bears a direct relationship to centralization: The more authority is delegated to lower levels in the organization, the less centralized is the organization. Conversely, the less authority is delegated, the more centralized the organization.

FIGURE 8–2   The Relationship between Empowerment, Specialization, and Delegation

Empowering people influences how jobs are designed and the amount of delegated authority.

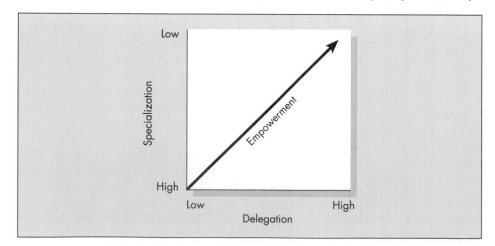

Employee Empowerment in Small Companies

Empowering employees by enabling them to do important work and to make important decisions might be the hidden secret of success in business today, and not just for large organizations. For example, LifeUSA, a relatively new Minneapolis-based insurance company, believes in empowering its people by making them more than just employees. All 275 people on LifeUSA's payroll are also owners who receive approximately 10 percent of their compensation in stock options. LifeUSA founder and CEO Robert W MacDonald claims LifeUSA, with fewer people, will write more new business than 98 percent of the competition because its employees have an ownership stake in the company.

MacDonald created a company unlike those of the past. LifeUSA and other newer companies empower people at all levels to make decisions. To make good decisions, employees need training as well as access to appropriate information. These new companies ensure that everyone has access to the information necessary to make good decisions. The balance sheet is no longer just the province of the accounting department and top management in this new generation of companies; it is available to everyone.

Another company, Wabash National—an Indiana-based truck manufacturer—has offered free classes for employees in finance, quality techniques, and manufacturing processes. Over 90 percent of Wabash's employees have taken the classes on their own time. LifeUSA and Wabash National have been successful partly because of the steps each has taken to empower employees.

Sources: S Armstrong, "Despite the Perils, Agents Create Carriers," *Best's Review,* March 1994, pp. 56–58; L Croghan, "Wabash National: It's a Truck, It's a Train, It's . . . RoadRailer?" *Financial World,* February 21, 1995, p. 14; J Case, "A Company of Businesspeople," *Inc.,* April 1993, pp. 79–93; and J Thomas, "Equipped for Success," *Distribution,* June 1993, pp. 46–50.

The two organizing decisions that most effect individual jobs are division of labor (specialization) and delegation of authority (centralization). The remaining two decisions, departmental bases and size of departments, relate more specifically to the way jobs are grouped in the organization.

Departmental Bases

The rationale for grouping jobs rests on the necessity for coordinating them. The specialized jobs are separate, interrelated parts of the total task, the accomplishment of which requires the accomplishment of each of the jobs. But the jobs must be performed in the specific manner and sequence intended by management when they were defined. As the number of specialized jobs in an organization increases, there comes a point when they can no longer be effectively coordinated by a single manager. Thus to create manageable numbers of jobs, they are combined into smaller groups, and a new job is defined—that of manager of the group.

The crucial managerial consideration when creating departments is the determination of the basis for grouping jobs. Of particular importance is the determination for the bases for departments that report to the top management position. In fact numerous bases are used throughout the organization, but the basis used at the highest level determines critical dimensions of the organization.

Five of the more widely used departmentalization bases[21] are described in the following sections. The first two bases, functional and process, refer to internal activities of the organization; the other three bases—product, customer, and geographic—are external to the organization.

Functional Departmentalization

Managers can combine jobs according to the functions of the organization. Every organization must undertake certain activities in order to do its work. These necessary activities are the organization's functions. The necessary functions of a manufacturing firm include production, marketing, finance, accounting, and personnel. These activities are necessary to create, produce, and sell a product. The necessary functions of a commercial bank include taking deposits, making loans, and investing the bank's funds. The functions of a hospital include surgery, psychiatry, housekeeping, pharmacy, nursing, and personnel.[22] Each of these functions can be a specific department, and jobs can be combined according to them. The functional basis is often found in relatively small organizations providing a narrow range of products and services. It is also widely used as the basis in divisions of large multiproduct organizations.

Manufacturing organizations are typically structured on a functional basis as depicted in Figure 8–3. The functions are marketing, production, finance, personnel, and research and development. The functional basis has wide application in service as well as in manufacturing organizations. The specific configuration of functions that appear as separate departments varies from organization to organization.

The principal advantage of the functional basis is its efficiency. That is, it seems logical to have a department that consists of experts in a particular field such as production or accounting. By having departments of specialists, management creates highly efficient units. An accountant is generally more efficient when working with other accountants and other individuals who have similar backgrounds and interests. They can share expertise to get the work done. General Motors attracted considerable attention when it combined its traditional product divisions into two functional departments—production and sales, and now, under the direction of a new Chief Operations Officer (COO), GM has accelerated its consolidation of its auto divisions

---

FIGURE 8–3   Departmentalization Based on Internal Operations

Internal operations-oriented departments can be based on functions of the organization or technical processes.

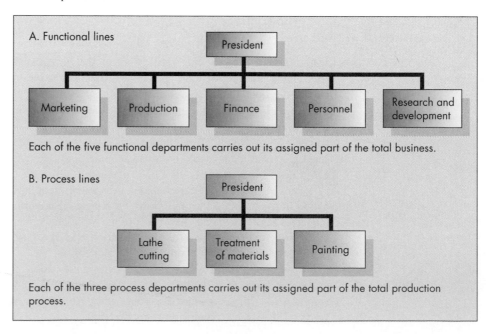

into one functionally organized entity.[23] The driving force behind GM's reorganization was to reduce the cost of developing and marketing automobiles by realizing the efficiencies of a function-based organization structure.

A major disadvantage of this departmental basis is that because specialists are working with and encouraging one another in their area of expertise and interest, the organizational goals may be sacrificed in favor of departmental goals. Accountants may see only their problems and not those of production or marketing or the total organization. In other words, the culture of, and identification with, the department are often stronger than identification with the organization as a whole and *its* culture.

Process Departmentalization

Organizations that use processes as the bases for departments at the highest level are typically small firms, such as manufacturers of limited product lines. Processes in this context refer to the technical operations that are required to manufacture the product and that are undertaken by specialists trained to do the particular operation. Figure 8–3B depicts the organization chart of a manufacturing firm that uses three different processes to produce the product: lathe cutting, treatment of materials, and painting. Employees would be assigned to one of the three departments depending upon whether they were skilled in the operation undertaken in that particular department. Thus lathe operators would report to the lathe cutting department, materials treaters would report to their department, and painters would, of course, be assigned to the painting department.

The advantages and disadvantages of process-based departments parallel those of function-based departments. These two bases, function and process, emphasize the internal operations of the organization. As such, they encourage skillful and efficient performance of necessary work-related activity. Other bases emphasize the organization's products, customers, and location. These external bases are discussed next.

Product Departmentalization

Managers of many large diversified companies group jobs on the basis of product. All the jobs associated with producing and selling a product or product line will be placed under the direction of one manager. Product becomes the preferred basis as a firm grows by increasing the number of products it markets. As a firm grows it is difficult to coordinate the various functional departments and it becomes advantageous to establish product units. This form of organization allows personnel to develop total expertise in researching, manufacturing, and distributing a product line. Concentration of the authority, responsibility, and accountability in a specific product department allows top management to coordinate actions. Figure 8–4 depicts an organization with five different product departments reporting to top management.

The organization structure that uses products as the basis for departments has been a key development in modern capitalism. The term "divisional organization" refers to this form of organization structure, and most of the major and large firms of developed countries use it to some degree. The product-based divisions are often free-standing units that can design, produce, and market their own products, even in competition with other divisions of the same firm.[24]

General Motors pioneered the divisional structure when it evolved into the five separate auto divisions: Chevrolet, Pontiac, Oldsmobile, Buick, and Cadillac. As we noted in our discussion of the functional form above, General Motors has begun a process of moving away from the purely product-based, divisional form.

Product-based organizations foster initiative and autonomy by providing division managers with the resources necessary to carry out their profit plans. But such organizations face the difficult issue of deciding how much redundancy is necessary.

FIGURE 8–4   **Output-Oriented Departmentalization**

Output-oriented departments can be based on products, customers, or geography.

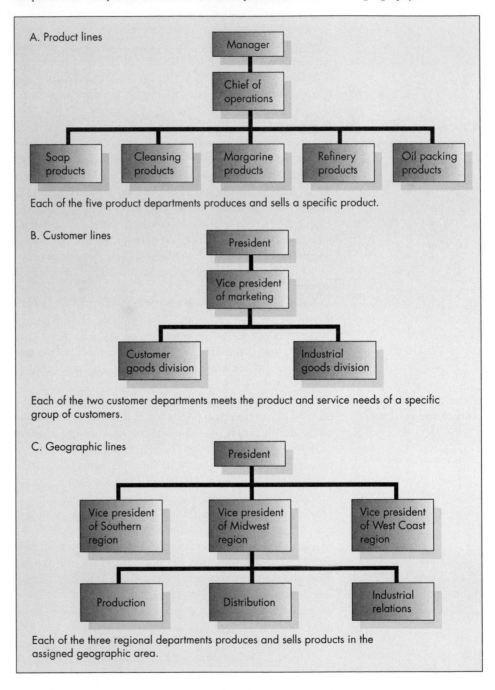

A. Product lines

Manager

Chief of operations

Soap products | Cleansing products | Margarine products | Refinery products | Oil packing products

Each of the five product departments produces and sells a specific product.

B. Customer lines

President

Vice president of marketing

Customer goods division | Industrial goods division

Each of the two customer departments meets the product and service needs of a specific group of customers.

C. Geographic lines

President

Vice president of Southern region | Vice president of Midwest region | Vice president of West Coast region

Production | Distribution | Industrial relations

Each of the three regional departments produces and sells products in the assigned geographic area.

Divisional structures contain some degree of redundancy, because each division wants its own research, engineering, marketing, production, and all other functions necessary to do business. Thus technical and professional personnel are found throughout the organization at the division levels.

Customer Departmentalization

Customers and clients can be a basis for grouping jobs.[25] Examples of customer-oriented departments are the organization structures of educational institutions. Some educational institutions have regular (day and night) courses and extension divisions. In some instances, a professor will be affiliated solely with the regular division or extension division. In fact, the title of some faculty positions often specifically mentions the extension division.

Another form of customer departmentalization is the loan department in a commercial bank. Loan officers are often associated with industrial, commercial, or agricultural loans. The customer will be served by one of these three loan officers. Figure 8–4 depicts the organization chart for a firm that has identified customers as the basis for organizing its market department. Evidently the selling strategies for consumer goods are different from those required to sell to industrial customers.

The importance of customer satisfaction has stimulated firms to search for creative ways to serve customers and clients better. Since the Bell System broke up, competition for customers has forced AT&T to organize into customer-based units that identify with the needs of specific customers. Prior to the breakup, the firm was organized around functions. The move toward customer-based departments at Bell Labs was accompanied by efforts to implement total quality management, a customer-focused management practice that is reinforced in the customer-based structure.[26]

Some department stores are departmentalized to some degree on a customer basis. They have groupings such as university shops, men's clothing, and boys' clothing. They have bargain floors that carry a lower quality of university, men's, and boys' clothing. Organizations with customer-based departments are better able to satisfy customer-identified needs than organizations that base departments on noncustomer factors.[27]

Generally, organizations relying on function-based departments are somewhat more formal, complex, and centralized than those that rely on territorial, product, or customer departments. Function-based departments rely heavily on specialization of labor and centralized authority to coordinate the work of employees. Consequently, they create relatively more job titles and layers of organizations, all tied together by formal rules and procedures and centralized authority. By contrast, organizations that are based around territory, products, and customers must provide employees with latitude to act and make decisions that respond to the needs of the local situation. These organizations will design relatively despecialized jobs, delegate more authority for decision making, and reduce reliance on rules and procedures.

Geographical Departmentalization

Another basis for departmentalizing is to establish groups according to geographical area. The logic is that all activities in a given region should be assigned to a manager. This individual would be in charge of all operations in that particular geographical area. Territorial departments are advantageous in organizations with widespread geographical dispersion because physical separation of activities makes centralized coordination difficult. For example, it is extremely difficult for someone in New York to manage salespeople in Kansas City. It makes sense to assign the managerial job to someone in Kansas City. Figure 8–4 shows a manufacturing organization that has used geography as the basis for departments reporting to top management and function as the basis for departments reporting to regional management.

Large multiunit retail stores are often organized along territorial lines. Specific retail outlets in a geographic area will comprise units, often termed divisions, that report to a regional manager who in turn may report to a corporate manager. For example, the manager of the Lexington, Kentucky, retail store of a national chain reports to the president, Midwest Division. The Midwest Division reports to the headquarters unit.

Geographical departmentalization provides a training ground for managerial personnel. The company is able to place managers in territories and then assess their progress in that geographical region. The experience managers acquire in a territory away from headquarters provides valuable insights into how products and services are accepted in the field.

Multiple
Departmental Bases

Large corporations use different bases at different levels. For example, corporations such as General Motors and General Electric use product as the basis for departmentalizing at the highest level. Each product department, usually termed a division, will have all the resources to act as an independent business unit. The departmental basis at the next level down is typically function. Note in Figure 8–5 that the vice president of product B has three functional departments: marketing, production, and personnel. The next level is departmentalized by geography (West Coast and East Coast reporting to marketing), process (manufacturing and finishing reporting to production), and clientele (managerial-related and nonmanagerial-related reporting to personnel). Thus, at each level different bases can exist among and within departments.

Combined Bases for
Departmentalization:
The Matrix
Organization

The matrix organization structure attempts to maximize the strengths and minimize the weaknesses of both the functional and product bases. In practical terms, the matrix design combines functional and product departmental bases.[28] Companies such as American Cyanamid, Avco, Carborundum, Caterpillar Tractor, Hughes Aircraft, ITT,

---

FIGURE 8–5   Organizational Design Using Mixed Departmentalization

At different levels in the large organization, different bases are used for departmentalization.

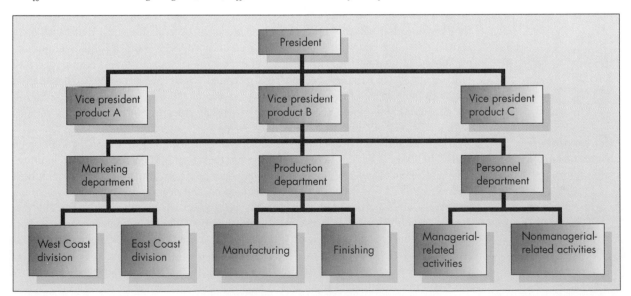

Monsanto Chemical, National Cash Register, Prudential Insurance, TWR, and Texas Instruments are only a few of the users of matrix organization. Public sector users include public health and social service agencies.[29] Although the exact meaning of matrix organization is not well established, the most typical meaning sees it as a balanced compromise between functional and product organization, between departmentalization by function and by product.[30]

Matrix organizations achieve the desired balance by superimposing, or overlaying, a horizontal structure of authority, influence, and communication on the vertical structure. In the arrangement shown in Figure 8–6, personnel assigned in each cell belong not only to the functional department, but also to a particular product or project. For example, manufacturing, marketing, engineering, and finance specialists are assigned to work on one or more projects or products A, B, C, D, and E. As a consequence, personnel report to two managers, one in their functional department, and one in the project or product unit. The existence of a dual authority system is a distinguishing characteristic of matrix organization.

Matrix structures are found in organizations that require responses to rapid change in two or more environments, such as technology and markets; that face uncertainties that generate high information-processing requirements; and that must deal with financial and human resources constraints.[31] Managers confronting these circumstances must obtain certain advantages that are most likely to be realized with matrix organization.[32]

Matrix organization facilitates the utilization of highly specialized staff and equipment. Each project, or product unit, can share the specialized resource with other units, rather than duplicating it to provide independent coverage for each. This concept of sharing resources is particularly advantageous when projects require less than the full-time efforts of the specialist. For example, a project may require only half a computer scientist's time. Rather than having several underutilized computer scientists assigned to each project, the organization can keep fewer of them fully utilized by shifting them from project to project.

Such flexibility results in quicker response to competitive conditions, technological breakthroughs, and other environmental changes. Also, these interactions encour-

---

FIGURE 8–6   Matrix Organizations

An organizing approach is based on forming temporary teams from the ranks of the functional units until the project is completed.

Projects, products	Functions			
	Manufacturing	Marketing	Engineering	Finance
Project or product A				
Project or product B				
Project or product C				
Project or product D				
Project or product E				

age cross-fertilization of ideas, such as when a computer scientist must discuss the pros and cons of electronic data processing with a financial accounting expert. Each specialist must be able to listen, understand, and respond to the views of the other. At the same time, specialists maintain ongoing contact with members of their own discipline because they are also members of a functional department.

An important United Kingdom car manufacturer, The Rover Group, has been developing innovative management practices that incorporate matrix organization, teamwork, and total quality management.[33] Among its most successful achievements has been the development of the K series engine, Rover's first volume car engine in 30 years. The K series engine developmental effort began in 1986, and to spur the process along, Rover used a matrix organization approach. This management approach combines the time and talents of individuals from all functional departments throughout the organization. The company selected members for the K series project team on the basis of their ability and willingness to adapt to constant change. The 18 members of the team were trained to work with other people from different functions and with different educational and technical expertise. Although the team members were a part of the K series project, they continued to report to the managers of their functional departments.

As the cross-functional matrix approach proved successful, management created project groups to deal with quality problems and to launch the Land Rover Discovery four-wheel-drive vehicle. Each project group contains functional experts with demonstrated technical and interpersonal skills. Rover has found that the project groups integrate from the beginning all the concerns of the functional groups that must eventually bring the car to the market—from product design to production to marketing to sales. In traditional automobile manufacturing plants, the functional departments work in isolation—and only after they have received information and specifications from the preceding department in the developmental process.

A fully developed matrix organization has product management departments along with the usual functional departments. Figure 8–7 depicts an organization that has a product manager reporting to top management and subproduct managers for each product line. In some instances, the subproduct managers are selected from specific functional departments and would continue to report directly to their functional managers. In other instances, the product managers are permanently assigned to the product management department. There is considerable diversity in the application of matrix organization, yet the essential feature is the creation of overlapping authority and, thus, the existence of dual authority.

Departmentalization in Multinational Corporations

Corporations that cross national boundaries must decide how to include the foreign activity in the organization. How should the international activities be coordinated? In fact, the foreign activities are but extensions of the domestic businesses, and how they are coordinated to achieve strategic outcomes involves issues not much different from those of local activities.[34] The outstanding success of Japanese corporations in international markets has initiated great interest in the ways firms can and should organize if they are to compete successfully with the Japanese. At the heart of the discussion is which departmental basis is appropriate under which circumstances.[35]

The most prevalent departmental basis is territory. The arrangement has the national and regional managers reporting to a headquarters in the same national or regional area. Territorial-based organizations for multinational corporations (MNCs) have the same characteristics as those for domestic organizations. Each national or regional office has all the resources necessary to produce and market the product or

---

Figure 8–7   Fully Evolved Matrix Organization

This is a more permanent dual-reporting relationship, because functional and project (product) units are often permanent. Thus, managers may report to both functional and product managers regularly.

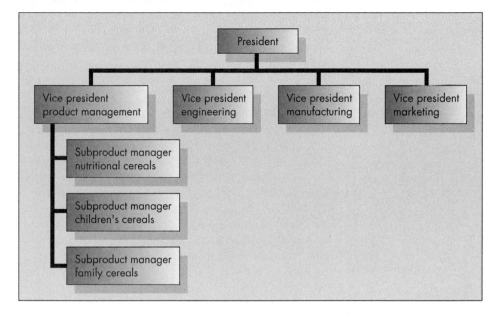

service. This organizational form is suitable for organizations such as ITT and Charles Pfizer Corporation, which have limited product lines.

MNCs having a diversified product line will find certain advantages in the product-based organization structure. This structure assigns worldwide responsibility for a product or product line to a single corporate office and all foreign and domestic units associated with that product report to the corporate product office. Kodak Company uses the product-based structure to assign responsibility for worldwide research and development, manufacturing, marketing, and distribution of its products. The basic product unit, termed a line of business (LOB), makes its own decisions and succeeds or fails accordingly. Kodak believes this structure enables managers to respond more quickly to market conditions.[36]

MNCs with very restrictive product lines, such as firms in the extractive industry, will use the function approach. According to this structure, a corporate office for each business function, such as production, marketing, and finance, has authority over those functions wherever they take place throughout the world. Thus the production personnel in Europe, South America, and, say, North America will report to corporate officials in charge of production.[37]

Although MNCs share certain common managerial and organizational problems, how they deal with them will reflect their own national culture as well as the host country's culture. Japanese firms, for example, typically concentrate on a relatively narrow set of business activities, unlike their typical Western counterparts, which enter several lines of business.[38] One of the effects of this difference is that Japanese employees perform relatively fewer specialized jobs with relatively more homogeneous skills and experiences on account of the fewer business specialties to be performed.

The typical Japanese manufacturing job has less range than the typical Western manufacturing job. The authority associated with each job is relatively less in Japanese firms, although the Japanese practice of participative management enables individual workers to have a say in matters that immediately affect their own jobs. Middle managers in Japanese firms are expected to initiate opportunities for workers to be involved, and they are evaluated on this criterion as well as on economic and performance criteria.

The departments in Japanese firms are more often based on function and process than on product, customer, or location. The preference for the internal-oriented bases reflects again the preference of Japanese firms to do business in fewer industries such that more complex divisional firms are not as likely to develop. There are, of course, many diversified organizations in Japan, but these firms typically follow holding company patterns of organization. The Japanese have developed the practice of creating close ties with supplier organizations and thus have avoided the necessity of vertical integration as is the case with many Western business organizations.

The differences between organization structures in Japan and those in the West can be accounted for by differences in business practices. These business practices are no doubt due to national and cultural developments in the ways business is conducted in a country, not in the ways organizations are structured.

Departmentalization is a key decision in organization design. Generally organizations that rely on function and process as departmental bases are relatively more complex, specialized, and formalized than those that rely on product, customer, and geography. Thus the choice of departmental bases can have important implications for organizational structure. An equally important decision is the determination of each manager's span of control.

Span of Control

The determination of appropriate bases for departmentalization establishes the kinds of jobs that will be grouped together. But that determination does not establish the number of jobs to be included in a specific group. That determination is the issue of span of control. Generally, the issue comes down to the decision of how many people a manager can oversee; that is, will the organization be more effective if the span of control is relatively wide or narrow? The question is basically concerned with determining the volume of interpersonal relationships that the department's manager is able to handle. Moreover, the span of control must be defined to include not only formally assigned subordinates, but also those who have access to the manager; a manager is always responsible for *immediate* subordinates, but he or she may also be the chairperson of several committees and task groups, thereby broadening span of control.

The number of potential interpersonal relationships between a manager and subordinates increases geometrically as the number of subordinates increases arithmetically. This relationship holds because managers potentially contend with three types of interpersonal relationships: direct single, direct group, and cross. Direct-single relationships occur between the manager and each subordinate individually—that is, in a "one-on-one" setting. Direct group relations occur between the manager and each possible arrangement of subordinates. Finally, cross relationships occur when subordinates interact with one another.

The critical consideration in determining the manager's span of control is not the number of potential relationships. Rather, it is the frequency and intensity of the actual relationships that is important. Not all relationships will occur, and those that do will vary in importance. In fact, only the actual required relationships have importance for determining the optimum span of control, and thus the size of an organizational unit.

Actual Relationships   If we shift our attention from potential to actual relationships as the bases for determining optimum span of control, at least three factors appear to be important: required contact, degree of specialization, and ability to communicate.

Required Contact.   In research and development, medical, and production work there is a need for frequent contact and a high degree of coordination between a superior and subordinates. The use of conferences and other forms of consultation often aid in the attainment of communication goals within a constrained time period. For example, the research and development team leader may have to consult frequently with team members so that a project is completed within a time period that will allow the organization to place a product on the market. Thus, instead of relying upon memos and reports, it is in the best interest of the organization to have as many in-depth contacts with the team as possible. A large span of control would preclude contacting subordinates so frequently, and this could have detrimental effects on completing the project. In general, the greater the inherent ambiguity that exists in an individual's job, the greater the need for supervision to avoid conflict and stress.[39]

Degree of Specialization.   The degree of specialized employees is a critical consideration in establishing the span of control at all levels of management. It is generally accepted that a manager at the lower organizational level can oversee more subordinates, because work at the lower level is more specialized and less complicated than at higher levels of management. Management can combine highly specialized and similar jobs into relatively large departments, because the employees may not need close supervision.

Ability to Communicate.   Instructions, guidelines, and policies must be communicated verbally to subordinates in most work situations. The need to discuss job-related factors influences the span of control. The individual who can clearly and concisely communicate with subordinates is able to manage more people than one who cannot do so.

Span of Control and Downsizing   The widespread practice of downsizing and "flattening" organizations of all kinds and types has direct implications for the span of control decision. As Figure 8–8 clearly demonstrates, one effect of increasing the span of control is to reduce the number of managerial levels and the number of managers. Downsizing reduces the number of total employees, but relatively more managers—usually middle managers—than nonmanagers.[40] The result is an increase in the number of nonmanagers per manager, and consequently, the average span of control of each manager increases. Whether the factors of required contact, degree of specialization, and ability to communicate have any bearing on the resultant spans of control can be debated. In fact, many of the middle managers whose spans of control have been widened may believe that top management made the downsizing decision without regard to these factors.

Nearly every firm in the global economy either has downsized or has considered the implications of doing so. Some of the giants in the basic industries, such as IBM, GM, Ford, HP, and Chrysler, as well as many of the 21 winners to date of the prestigious Baldrige Award, have already reduced the number of middle managers and

FIGURE 8–8   **Relationship of Span of Control to Organizational Structure**

The shape of the organization changes as the average span of control changes.

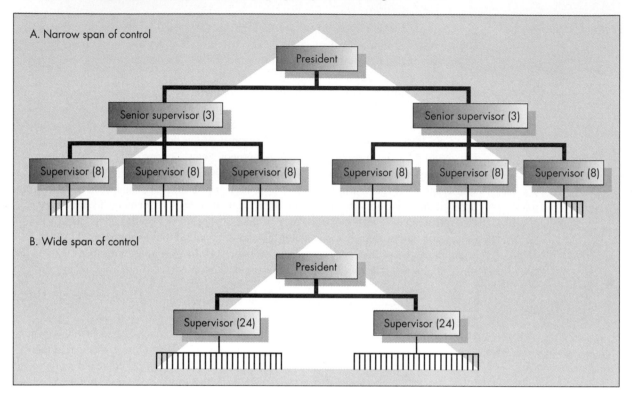

A. Narrow span of control

B. Wide span of control

increased the spans of control of all managers. The accompanying Management Focus describes some of the implications of downsizing.

The rationale for this decision relies on the idea that more highly trained individuals throughout the organization, empowered with authority and competence, can manage themselves. The idea is not new; the widespread application of the idea is new. Many firms, large and small, have reported their experiences with wider spans of control; some have been positive, others negative. The positive experiences stress the renewed commitment of employees who have the benefits of empowerment; the negative experiences stress the additional pressures placed on managers to be responsible for the work performance of more employees.

One observer points out that for flattening to reach its full potential, managers and employees must exercise initiative to "add value" to the directives they receive.[41] The idea of adding value implies that individuals take the directive and evaluate its full potential for adding to the organization's well-being and effectiveness.

Other observers of flattening in the US banking industry state that whether the practice works out depends upon the willingness and ability of employees at the local level to provide quality service and high performance, even peak performance, of their assigned duties.[42] But perhaps the most important factor bearing on the success of the practice is the manager's ability to comprehend the new relationship between managers and nonmanagers: No longer can managers set themselves apart from those

The Implications of Downsizing

Procter & Gamble (P&G), the consumer products giant once known for its innovative brand-management organizational structure, joined the ranks of other American corporate giants like IBM, Sears, and General Motors (GM) by creating a new, leaner structure, which the company hopes is also more efficient and effective. As is the case with IBM, Sears, and GM, leaner will mean fewer employees working for P&G. P&G will close 20 percent of its plants worldwide and reduce employees by 13,000 by 1996 through voluntary separations and early retirement. P&G executives hope its new structure will better position it to meet increased international and low-price competition.

The current downsizing binge, as illustrated by P&G, has implications not often considered during the decision to downsize. For example, many US firms offering early retirements receive an excessively enthusiastic response and lose some of their best talent. Moreover, downsizing also has a demoralizing effect on those who stay, as was the case with Duracell, Inc. It found that after two reorganizations in three years, the remaining employees required as much attention as those who left the company.

Another example is the downsizing of the US military during the first part of the 1990s, resulting in a loss of 1 million uniformed and civilian defense jobs. While the contraction of the military pushed much needed technical talent into other industries, many middle managers and blue-collar workers found it difficult to match their former wages.

Other implications of downsizing include increased reliance on information technology, the use of outside consultants rather than expensive senior executives, and increased use of temporary agencies. For example, employment by temporary agencies increased by 240,000 in 1992.

Finally, the massive layoffs of the late 1980s and early 1990s resulted in over 3.5 million lost jobs. Yet, a recent survey of over 500 companies that downsized during the same period found that only 43.5 percent had improved profit margins. While corporate restructuring by downsizing may produce quick savings, no substantial evidence exists to illustrate that reductions in employees will improve long-term profits.

Sources: P Glasser, "Surviving the (Big) Blues," *CIO*, April 15, 1996, p. 14; "Procter & Gamble Hits Back," *Business Week*, July 19, 1993, pp. 20–22; M De Vries, "The Human Side of Downsizing," *European Management Journal*, April 1996, pp. 111–20; G Stern, "P&G Will Cut 13,000 Jobs, Shut 30 Plants," *The Wall Street Journal*, July 16, 1993, p. A3; and M Barrier, "Base Closings: The Last Roundup," *Nation's Business*, April 1996, pp. 62–63.

they manage; they must develop helping and coaching relationships with their subordinates.

Thus, we see the profound effects of managers' organizing decisions on the organization structure. In Chapter 9, we will review the more important ideas, which give some guidelines to managers who must decide how formal, centralized, and complex the organization they design should be.

Summary of Key Points

- The structure of an organization consists of relatively fixed and stable relationships among jobs and groups of jobs. The primary purpose of organization structure is to influence the behavior of individuals and groups so as to achieve effective performance.

- Organizational structures differ as a consequence of management decisions. In order to measure these differences, it is necessary to identify measurable attributes, or dimen-

sions, of structure. Three often-used dimensions are complexity, centralization, and formalization.

- Complexity refers to the extent to which the jobs in the organization are relatively specialized; centralization refers to the extent to which authority is retained in the jobs of top management; and formalization refers to the extent to which policies, rules, and procedures exist in written form.

- Four key managerial decisions determine organization structures. These decisions are dividing work, delegating authority, departmentalizing jobs into groups, and determining spans of control.
- The four key decisions are interrelated and interdependent, although each has certain specific problems that can be considered apart from the others.
- Dividing the overall task into smaller, related tasks or jobs depends initially on the technical and economic advantages of specialization of labor.
- Delegating authority enables an individual to make decisions and to exact obedience without approval by higher management. Similar to other organizing issues, delegated authority is a relative, not absolute, concept. All individuals, whether managers or nonmanagers, in an organization have some authority. The question is whether they have enough to do their jobs.
- The grouping of jobs into departments requires the selection of common bases such as function, process, product, customer, and geography. Each basis has advantages and disadvantages that must be evaluated in terms of overall effectiveness.
- The matrix form of organization provides some opportunities to realize the advantages of function and product as bases for departments in combination. The principal disadvantage is the creation of dual reporting channels for members of product departments and groups.
- The optimal span of control is no one specific number of subordinates. Although the number of potential relationships increases geometrically as the number of subordinates increases arithmetically, the important consideration is the frequency and intensity of the actual relationships.
- The current practice of downsizing has important implications for the spans of control of managers in organizations that downsize. As a consequence of the reduced number of managers relative to nonmanagers, the average spans of control will necessarily increase.

Discussion and Review Questions

1. What managerial and organizational purposes does the structure of an organization accomplish? What would be the evidence that would establish whether these purposes have been achieved?

2. What would be the characteristics of firms that would have relatively complex, specialized, and formal organizational structures? What would be the characteristics of firms that would have relatively simple, generalized, and informal organizational structures?

3. Explain the relationships between the four organizing decisions (division of labor, delegation of authority, departmental bases, and span of control) and the dimensions of organizational structure.

4. Identify the bases for the departments in the college you attend or in the firm where you work. What alternative bases can you think of that might make a difference in the way the college or firm performs its work?

5. How does the culture of a country influence the way the organizations in that country specialize jobs? For example does the Japanese culture encourage different levels of specialization than the American culture does?

6. Explain the differences between potential and actual relationships among subordinates and managers and why actual, not potential, relationships are important for assessing the appropriate span of control.

7. Obtain information about the spans of control among chairpeople of departments in the college you attend. Chances are, no two chairpeople have the same span of control. What accounts for these differences?

8. Using the same chairpeople as in question 7, determine the degree of decentralization of authority for each by documenting the decisions that all chairpeople can make without checking first with the dean. Then determine whether and why some chairpeople have more authority compared with their peers.

9. Explain the relationships among downsizing, the four organizing decisions, and the dimensions of organizational structure.

10. What is meant by employee cmpowerment, and what is the relationship between empowerment, division of labor, and delegation of authority?

CASE 8–1
ORGANIZATION STRUCTURE OF SAXE REALTY COMPANY

Saxe Realty Company, Inc., located in the San Francisco Bay area, was founded in 1938 by Jules and Marion Saxe. For most of its history, the company was a single-office agency run by its founders. Over time, the company grew in size and sales revenue, which increased from $1 million in 1973 to over $10 million in 1979. Rather than a single office, the company had six branches in the San Francisco and Marin County areas.

The firm grew for many reasons. An important reason was the founders' ability to do certain things very well. They knew how to select locations, time moves, and design offices. They recruited and hired people with above-average ability and trained them to be effective salespeople. The rewards of growth were enjoyed by the Saxe family and employees of their firm.

But with growth came problems stemming from the mismatch between the firm's organization structure, management practices, and the requirements of a large firm compared to a small one. In the early days, Saxe Realty could handle its business matters in simple and informal ways. After all, it was a family corporation, and family members ran it as a family, not as a business.

Some of the problems that surfaced with growth included the absence of clearly defined roles and areas of responsibility. People were in jobs because of family relationships rather than skills. Important decisions were made by relatively few people, who often did not have knowledge of all available information. The firm, moreover, had no strategic plan. It responded and reacted to opportunities rather than being proactive. In a sense, the firm's success had simply outgrown its organization.

Saxe consequently had to make many changes in its operations and organization structure, the overriding goal being to move Saxe away from an entrepreneurial-style firm toward a professionally managed one. The change itself involved a process of preparation and implementation.

The organization structure that Saxe adopted relies on geography as the basis for departmentalization. There is a central office, and the branch offices report to it. Geographic departmentalization encourages decentralization, one of the outcomes sought by Saxe's top management. Branch managers are responsible for the day-to-day activities of their offices. The central office maintains overall direction through planning and controlling processes. For example, all branch offices participate in the annual planning process, during which objectives for each branch are developed. These objectives are then the targets and the responsibility of branch managers.

Saxe's top management developed formal descriptions for all key positions, defining the responsibilities of each job with special attention to avoiding overlap and duplication of effort. The company's experience during its entrepreneurial stage was that things were often left undone because everyone assumed that someone else was doing them. In other instances, several people would assume responsibility for a task when it required the attention of only one person. A key consideration in the new organization structure was to define explicitly and formally the work expected from each individual job.

The new structure provides for reporting channels from each branch associate to the chief executive officer. The chain of command is the channel for progress reports on planned objectives, financial and sales reports, and other informational needs. In comparison with the previous organization, the chain of command is much more explicit and formal. Individuals are encouraged to go through channels.

The entire change at Saxe has been both extensive and time consuming. Nearly every aspect of the firm's operations has been affected, and the changes took two years or more to fully implement.

Questions for Analysis

1. Draw an organization chart that depicts the structure being implemented at Saxe.
2. Which alternative structures could Saxe have implemented, and what would be the advantages of each in comparison to the one Saxe did implement?
3. What are the relationships between the planning function and the organization function as depicted in the Saxe case?

VIDEO CASE
THE RESPONSIVE ORGANIZATION

In the past, a corporation was structured much like the military, with a formal chain of command and division of labor. Over time, many companies came to realize that the bureaucratic structure of the traditional corporation can often cause breakdowns in communication and lower efficiency.

Manufacturers of products in relatively unchanging environments often take a mechanistic approach to production. In such environments, employees strictly adhere to their job descriptions. However, companies that depend on their ability to continuously introduce new innovations usually take a more organic approach, giving employees more room to make decisions and communicate outside the chain of command. Some companies may choose to radically modify or reengineer their structure.

Big Apple Bagels and St. Louis Bread Company are two rapidly growing businesses that share a similar market. However, each organization is structured quite differently. Whatever the structure, for an organization to be successful, it must be responsive to its customers. This operating principle runs a lot deeper than just making sure the right kind of cheese gets put in a turkey sandwich.

Many companies are finding that changing the way in which they are organized improves their responsiveness. For example, they may choose to simplify their structure and reduce the layers of management, thus reducing the layers in the chain of command. Another option is to widen the spans of control. The traditional organization has a tall structure and a narrow span of control. This means managers have few subordinates who report directly to them. A company with a flat organizational structure has a wide span of control with fewer reporting levels.

Many companies are empowering their employees and allowing them to make decisions on their own rather than insisting that they report to various levels of management. When Paul Stolzer opened the first Big Apple Bagel store in 1985, he had no idea that in the short span of seven years his small store would grow into a franchise that boasts 75 stores with more opening all the time. Stolzer said, "The stores have changed quite extensively over the years. We are actually a fourth or fifth generation store right now. Initially the stores were set up as strictly bagel bakeries with the predominant product being bagels and cream cheese. We've progressed to a more aggressive stature, adding a few more dimensions to our operation in that we have dine-in facilities, a more extensive sandwich menu, and a very, very strong coffee program. We're still progressing. That's one thing that never ends."

One thing that hasn't changed is Big Apple Bagels' open-door policy. From top management to line workers, communication channels are wide open. Jim Lentz, director of training for the company said, "At Big Apple Bagels we have an open-door policy between the franchisee and the franchisor, and between the ultimate consumer and the franchisor, in that we encourage people to come up with suggestions, new products, new ideas. We're never further than a phone call or a stop away. We're continually in the franchisees' stores to make sure that their operation meets our specifications."

In 1987, Ken Rosenthal opened his first St. Louis Bread Company store in Kirkwood, Missouri, with used baking equipment. Today, St. Louis Bread company operates over 50 stores in the St. Louis area, with stores opening in other midwestern markets as well. The growth happened quickly, forcing the company to change its organizational structure. Originally, it was a small store with 17 employees. When it became a large chain, employing over 1,000 people, a more traditional organizational structure was needed.

When a company is growing, it may need to use some of the concepts of reengineering. Reengineering entails the radical redesign of business processes to achieve major gains in cost, service, or time. For example, by mid-1992, St. Louis Bread was growing at a frantic pace. The partners decided it was time to slow down and take a breath. They began to realize that the opportunistic approach wouldn't work anymore.

They had reached a point where the controls and information systems they had in place were inadequate for a larger operation. New equipment was purchased to automate processes on the line. Thirty thousand dollar point-of-purchase cash registers were installed to track everything from sales per hour to sales per stockkeeping unit to sales by stores.

Doron Berger said, "The organization at St. Louis Bread Company is probably not atypical of many organizations. While we have a hierarchical structure in terms of someone is ultimately accountable for the results of the business. We do fight vigorously to maintain a flat organization. In other words, there aren't a lot of layers between the president CEO and the people who are on the front lines. I think we have succeeded because of the effort we have put into that."

In November of 1983, Au Bon Pain, the dominant bakery/cafe chain in the country, acquired St. Louis Bread Company. Au Bon Pain's stores were all in urban areas. St. Louis Bread would enable them to tap into the suburban market. David Hutkin said, "Our organizational structure has not changed dramatically. It really hasn't changed since the acquisition. We've continued to run the company very independent of the parent company, and we're still building stores and expanding the concept. As far as the organization, basically we're still doing the same things as we were doing before."

A company like Big Apple Bagels is considered to be a boundaryless organization. In such an organization, the corporate structure is more horizontal than vertical. Boundaryless businesses are typically organized around core customer-oriented processes, such as communication, customer contact, and managing quality. In order to enjoy the benefits a horizontal organization offers, four boundaries must be overcome:

- Authority
- Task
- Political
- Identity

Even a relatively boundaryless company has an authority boundary. Some people lead, others follow. To overcome problems that may arise, managers must learn how to lead and still remain open to criticism. Their "subordinates" need to be trained and encouraged not only to follow but also to challenge their superiors if there is an issue worth considering. As one Big Apple executive said, "I think there are some natural boundaries that occur between a franchisor and a franchisee, or an employee and an employer. What we try to do at Big Apple Bagels is to eliminate those boundaries by keeping the phone line open at all times as well as the fact that a lot of us have been franchisees as well as now being a franchisor so we know what it's like to sit on both sides of the table and to be able to talk to the franchisee from the standpoint of we were there at one time as well and we have that empathy for their position."

The task boundary arises out of the "it's not my job" mentality. A task boundary can be overcome by clearly defining who does what when employees from different departments divide up work.

The political boundary derives from the differences in political agendas that often separate employees and can cause conflict. This is closely related to the identity boundary. The identity boundary emerges due to an employee tendency to identify with those individuals or groups with whom they have shared experiences, or with whom they share fundamental values.

To overcome the identity boundary, employees and management need to be trained to gain an understanding of the business as a whole and avoid the "us versus them" mentality. A good way to do this is by forming cross-functional teams, in which tasks are shared and cross-training simply happens as a result of employee interaction.

The new boundaryless organization relies on self-managed work teams. It reduces internal boundaries that separate functions and create hierarchical levels. A horizontal corporation is structured around core, customer-oriented processes.

Lines of communication are very open, allowing line-level employees to communicate their questions and concerns directly to those at the management and executive level. Not all organizations are structured the same way. There are factors to consider such as organizational size, culture, and production volume. These factors may indicate that under some circumstances, a tall organizational structure may be more appropriate than a flat structure. Companies in the future may change or alter the way they operate but customer satisfaction, quality, and efficiency will always be the primary goals.

Critical Thinking Questions

1. If companies today are working so hard to break down boundaries, why is it that there are boundaries in the first place?

2. What are some new technologies that will help managers keep lines of communication open to employees? To customers?

3. The video mentions that St. Louis Bread Company had to use a more traditional organizational structure when it grew rapidly. Why do you think that was necessary? What do you think the company gains by adopting such a structure? What does it lose?

4. What new communication tools do you think lie on the horizon? To finish your class presentation, describe what new communication tools you think will be available in the workplace in 20 years. Be creative. Remember that 20 years ago not many people would have been able to envision the communication tools that we now take for granted.

EXPERIENTIAL EXERCISE
DESIGNING THE NEW ORGANIZATION

Purpose

The purpose of this exercise is to provide students with first-hand experience in organizing a new business venture.

The Exercise in Class

Scenario.   A few years ago, George Ballas got so frustrated trying to keep his lawn neatly trimmed around the roots of oak trees that he developed what is now called the Weed Eater. The original Weed Eater was made from a popcorn can that had holes in it and was threaded with nylon fishing line. Weed Eater sales in 1972 totaled $568,000, but by 1978, sales were in excess of $100 million. There are now 20 or so similar devices on the market.

Two brothers from Pittsburgh, George and Jim Gammons, are starting a new venture called Lawn Trimmers, Inc. They are attempting to sell trimmers that do not wear out for over 2,000 trimming applications. The Weed Eater and similar products often have breaks in the nylon lines that require the user to turn off the trimmer and readjust the line. The Gammons brothers have developed a new cutting fabric that is not physically harmful and cuts for over 2,000 applications.

To sell the Lawn Trimmers, the Gammons brothers will have to market their product through retail establishments. They will make the products in their shop in Pittsburgh and ship them to the retail establishments. The profits will come entirely from the sales of the Lawn Trimmers to retail establishments. The price of the product is already set, and it appears that there will be sufficient market demand to sell at least 6,000 Lawn Trimmers annually.

Activity.   The instructor will set up teams of five to eight students to serve as experts who will provide the Gammons brothers with the best structure for their new venture. Each group should do the following:

1. Establish a structure that would be feasible for the Gammons at this stage in their venture.
2. Select a spokesperson to make a short presentation of the group's organizational structure for the Gammons.

The class should compare the various structures and discuss why there are similarities and differences in what is presented.

The Learning Message

This exercise will show deciding on an organizational structure necessitates making assumptions about the market, competition, labor resources, scheduling, and profit margins, to name just a few factors.

Notes

1. Henry Mintzberg, "The Effective Organization: Forces and Forms," *Sloan Management Review,* Winter 1991, pp. 54–67.
2. George P Huber and Reuben R McDaniel, "The Decision-Making Paradigm of Organizational Design," *Management Science,* May 1986, p. 573.
3. Dan R Dalton, William D Todor, Michael J Spendolini, Gordon J Fielding, and Lyman W Porter, "Organization Structure and Performance: A Critical Review," *Academy of Management Review,* January 1980, pp. 49–64.
4. Richard S Blackburn, "Dimensions of Structure: A Review and Reappraisal," *Academy of Management Review,* January 1982, pp. 59–66.
5. James P Walsh and Robert D Dewar, "Formalization and the Organizational Life-Cycle," *Journal of Management Studies,* May 1987, pp. 215–32.
6. Jeffrey D Ford, "Institutional versus Questionnaire Measures of Organizational Structure," *Academy of Management Journal,* September 1979, pp. 601–10.
7. Richard L Daft and Patricia J Bradshaw, "The Process of Horizontal Differentiation: Two Models," *Administrative Science Quarterly,* September 1980, pp. 441–56.
8. Phoebe M Carillo and Richard E Kopelman, "Organization Structure and Productivity," *Group and Organization Studies,* March 1991, pp. 44–59.

9. Richard E Kopelman, "Job Redesign and Productivity: A Review of the Literature," *National Productivity Review,* Summer 1985, p. 239.
10. Donald J Campbell, "Task Complexity: A Review and Analysis," *Academy of Management Review,* January 1988, pp. 40–52.
11. "Detroit vs. the UAW. At Odds over Teamwork," *Business Week,* August 24, 1987, pp. 54–55.
12. Zachary Schiller, "Ed Arnst's Elbow Grease Has P&G Shining," *Business Week,* October 10, 1994, pp. 84–86.
13. Jeffrey A Alexander, "Adaptive Change in Corporate Control Practices," *Academy of Management Journal,* March 1991, pp. 162–93.
14. "Why US Shoe is Looking down at the Heel," *Business Week,* July 4, 1988, p. 60.
15. "Hewlett-Packard Rethinks Itself," *Business Week,* April 1, 1991, pp. 76–79; Nancy Stevens, "The Challenge of Change," *Business Week,* April 1996, pp. 84–86.
16. Jay Greene and Judith Nemes, "To Centralize or Not to Centralize: Centralization Paying Off at Not-for-Profits, For-Profits Cut Back at Corporate," *Modern Healthcare,* October 8, 1990, pp. 30–36.
17. Michael Kublin, "The Soviet Factory Director: A Window on Eastern Bloc Manufacturing," *Industrial Management,* March–April 1990, pp. 21–26.

18. Hillary Ingham, "Organizational Structure and Internal Control in the UK Insurance Industry," *Service Industries Journal,* October 1991, pp. 425–38.

19. Barbara E Van Gorder, "Moving back to Centralization," *Credit,* May–June 1990, pp. 12–15.

20. John H Dobbs, "The Empowerment Environment," *Training and Development,* February 1993, pp. 55–57; Joseph D O'Brian, "Empowering Your Front-Line Employees to Handle Problems," *Supervisory Management,* January 1993, p. 10.

21. Mariann Jelinek, "Organization Structure: The Basic Conformations," in *Organization by Design,* ed. Mariann Jelinek, Joseph A Litterer, and Raymond E Miles (Plano, TX: Business Publications, 1981), pp. 293–302.

22. Peggy Leatt and Rodney Schneck, "Criteria for Grouping Nursing Subunits in Hospitals," *Academy of Management Journal,* March 1984, pp. 150–64.

23. James R Treece and John Templeman, "Jack Smith Is Already on a Tear at GM," *Business Week,* May 11, 1992, p. 37.

24. Joseph T Mahoney, "The Adoption of the Multidivisional Form of Organization: A Contingency Approach," *Journal of Management,* January 1992, pp. 49–72.

25. Frank Cornish, "Building a Customer-Oriented Organization," *Long-Range Planning,* June 1988, pp. 105–7.

26. Michael Maccoby, "Transforming R&D Services at Bell Labs," *Research-Technology Management,* January–February 1992, pp. 46–49.

27. Jay R Galbraith and Robert K Kazanjian, "Organizing to Implement Strategies of Diversity and Globalization: The Role of Matrix Organizations," *Human Resource Management,* Spring 1986, pp. 37–54.

28. Kenneth Knight, "Matrix Organization: A Review," *Journal of Management Studies,* May 1976, p. 111.

29. Ibid., p. 114.

30. Paul R Lawrence, Harvey F Kolodny, and Stanley M Davis, "The Human Side of the Matrix," *Organizational Dynamics,* September 1977, p. 47; George J Chambers, "The Individual in a Matrix Organization," *Project Management Journal,* December 1989, pp. 37–42, 50.

31. The following discussion is based upon Knight, "Matrix Organization."

32. Christopher A Bartlett and Sumantra Ghosal, "Organizing for Worldwide Effectiveness: The Transactional Solution," *California Management Review,* Fall 1988, pp. 54–74; James K McCollum and J Daniel Sherman, "The Effects of Matrix Organization Size and Number of Project Assignments on Performance," *IEEE Transactions on Engineering Management,* February 1991, pp. 75–78.

33. Frank Muller, "A New Engine of Change in Industrial Relations," *Personnel Management (UK),* July 1991, pp. 30–33.

34. Mohammed M Habib and Bart Victor, "Strategy, Structure, and Performance of US Manufacturing and Service MNCs: A Comparative Analysis," *Strategic Management Journal,* November 1991, pp. 589–606.

35. David J Lemak and Jeffrey A Bracker, "A Strategic Contingency Model of Multinational Corporate Structure," *Strategic Management Journal,* September–October 1988, pp. 521–26.

36. Wilber J Prezzano, "Kodak Sharpens Its Focus on Quality," *Management Review,* May 1989, pp. 39–41.

37. Christopher A Bartlett, "How Multinational Organizations Evolve," *Journal of Business Strategy,* Winter 1982, pp. 20–32.

38. Richard D Whitley, "Eastern Asian Enterprise Structures and the Comparative Analysis of Forms of Business Organization," *Organization Studies* 11, no. 1 (1990), pp. 47–74.

39. Lawrence B Chonko, "The Relationship of Span of Control to Sales Representatives, Experienced Role Conflict and Role Ambiguity," *Academy of Management Journal,* June 1982, pp. 452–56.

40. Robin Bellis-Jones and Max Hand, "Improving Managerial Spans of Control," *Management Accounting (UK),* October 1989, pp. 20–21; John S McClenahen, "Managing More People in the '90s," *Industry Week,* March 20, 1989, pp. 30–38.

41. Emmett J McTeague, "Adding Value," *Executive Excellence,* January 1990, pp. 11–12; A Bird, "Organizational Flattening within the US Banking Industry," *Bankers Magazine,* July–August 1991, pp. 67–70.

42. Suzanne Weixel, "Flat Management Requires Juggling," *Computerworld,* August 20, 1990, pp. 70–71.

9 ORGANIZATION DESIGN

Chapter Learning Objectives

After completing Chapter 9, you should be able to:

- **Define** organization design in terms of the universalistic and contingency viewpoints.
- **Describe** the implications of technology, environmental uncertainty, and strategy for the design of organization structure.
- **Discuss** the fundamental differences between classical and neoclassical organization design.
- **Compare** the alternative arguments that conclude there exists no one best organization design.
- **Identify** criticisms of the universalistic viewpoint by those who support the contingency viewpoint.

The Virtual Corporation

The successful organization of tomorrow will have little in common with the successful organization of yesterday if a group of business futurists are correct. According to Jan Hopeland, a Digital Equipment Corporation executive, tomorrow's organization will focus on its core competencies and, rather than becoming a large, capital-intensive, vertically integrated company, it will outsource the rest to outsiders.

Hopeland coined the phrase virtual corporation, which is a temporary network of independent companies linked to share skills, costs, knowledge, and access to one another's markets. This new and evolving model is flexible, modular, and able to react quickly to the most fleeting opportunities. The advantage of forming virtual corporations and outsourcing noncore activities is reduced investments in the development of new products, thus lowering unit costs and freeing up capital to invest in what the company does best. For example, Nike and Reebok contract virtually all their production to Asian countries, allowing them to concentrate on what they do best—designing and marketing high-tech, high-fashion footwear. Nike's and Reebok's sparse investment in fixed assets has translated into a greater than 16 percent return on assets, fifth and sixth respectively on the Fortune Service 500.

Dell Computer does not own any plants, and it leases two small factories to assemble computers from outsourced parts. Yet not only is it able to sell personal computers to customers at a lower price than IBM or Compaq; it also customizes products for its customers.

Corning, Inc., is one of the most successful organizations at putting together alliances. Its management believes technology is changing so rapidly that no one can go it alone. Corning has 19 partnerships, which account for 13 percent of its profits. Strategic alliances have allowed Corning to develop and sell new products faster, wield more power in the marketplace, and avoid making large investments in capital.

One of America's biggest export success stories has operated this way for a long time. Since the old Hollywood studio system collapsed, virtual corporations make most of the movies—alliances of independent talents who come together for a specific movie project and then go their separate ways when the project is complete.

Apple Computer, Inc., CEO John Scully predicts that in 10 or 20 years there will be an explosion of entrepreneurial industries that will form tens of thousands of virtual corporations.

However, creating virtual corporations will require a new managerial mind-set. Managers will have to become adept at negotiating win–win deals with outsiders, sharing information, and trusting one another.

Sources: S Hill, "The 'Virtual' Corporation," *Manufacturing Systems,* March 1996, pp. 32–40; H Chesbrough and D Teece, "When Is Virtual Virtuous? Organizing for Innovation," *Harvard Business Review,* January–February 1996, pp. 65-71; J Byrne, "The Virtual Corporation," *Business Week,* February 8, 1993, pp. 98–102; and S Tully, "The Modular Corporation," *Fortune,* February 8, 1993, pp. 106–15.

Managers who set out to design the structures of new organizations or to redesign the structures of existing ones must choose among alternatives for which clear-cut criteria for wise choices do not exist. The organization design decision is, therefore, inherently difficult. Contemporary management theory provides some general guidelines that managers can use when designing organizations.[1] These guidelines contain assumptions that managers must recognize when they decide upon a particular design. The Management in Action points out some of the assumptions of contemporary firms when they have undertaken to reduce the size and complexity of their organizations.

This chapter reviews the present state of knowledge regarding the design of organizations. Our purpose is to provide tentative bases for making choices among organization design alternatives.

Contemporary organization design theory can be divided into two categories of opinion. One category is based upon the premise that there is one best way to design an organization, regardless of the situation. The body of opinion that supports this premise is termed the *universalistic approach.* The second category of opinion states that the best way to organize depends upon the situation. This category is termed the *contingency approach.* Within each of these two categories lie differences of opinion as to what precisely is the "one best way" and as to what factors in the situation must be taken into account. Table 9–1 summarizes the differences between these two approaches to organizational design.

Universalistic Approach

In reality, there is no single universalistic design. Instead, researchers and practitioners have proposed two designs. And rather than being complementary, the two designs are quite different. They are the classical design and the neoclassical design.

*Classical
Organization Design*

The characteristics of the classical organization design include the following:

- High complexity
- High formalization
- High centralization

The arguments that support the classical design have been very influential in the development of modern management theory.

The writers of the scientific management and classical schools of management made forceful arguments for the superiority of classical organization design in comparison to any alternative design. According to their reasoning, the classical design is a natural extension of labor specialization to the organizational level.

Organization structures with high levels of complexity, formalization, and centralization reflect the assumption that the design of jobs determines the design of organizations. Figure 9–1 diagrams this assumption and its consequence.

The use of classical designs was widespread during the late 1800s when industrialization of Western civilization was at its height. A primary social, and therefore managerial, concern was efficient use of resources and maximum production. Out of this time period emerged two different, yet compatible, sets of ideas. One set has come to be associated with bureaucracy as an "ideal type" of organization. The other set belongs to the classical school.

*Bureaucratic
Organization Design*

Bureaucracy refers to the form of organization first described in public-administration literature as government by bureaus (i.e., unelected civil servants). It is usually associated with the negative consequences of large organizations, such as "red tape,"

TABLE 9–1   Universalistic and Contingency Approaches to Organizational Design

The universalistic and contingency approaches are quite different ways of thinking about organizational structures.

Universalistic Approach	*Contingency Approach*
Management selects either classical or neoclassical design theory as the one best way in **all** situations depending on the relative importance of task versus human considerations.	Management selects either classical or neoclassical design theory as the one best way in **particular** situations depending on the relative importance of technological, environmental, and strategic issues.

FIGURE 9–1   Classical Design Assumptions

Classical design theory assumes that job design is the principal determinant of organization design.

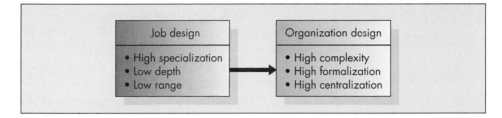

unexplained delays, and general frustration. However, its more important definition is an organizational design that its early proponents believed to be "superior to any other form in precision, in stability, in the stringency of its discipline and its reliability. It thus makes possible a high degree of calculability of results for the heads of the organization and for those acting in relation to it."[2]

The characteristics of a bureaucracy are as follows:

- It has a clear division of labor with each job well defined, clearly understood, and quite routine.
- Each manager has a clearly defined relationship with other managers and subordinates; the relationships follow a formal hierarchy.
- Each employee relies on specific rules, policies, and procedures to guide behaviors.
- Favoritism is minimized through the impersonal application of rules, policies, discipline, and rewards.
- Rigid and equitable selection criteria are used to hire candidates for vacant jobs.

An organization structure that ranks high on each of these five characteristics is an "ideal type." That is, such an organization would be ideally suited to achieving efficient results. An organization that scores low on any one or all of them would be less than "ideal," and therefore less efficient than it could be.

As Max Weber observed, the bureaucratic design compares with other designs "as does the machine with nonmechanical modes of production."[3] Weber based this conclusion on extensive analyses of the Prussian civil service and military organizations. He believed that the advantages of bureaucracy were applicable in any context, whether government, military, or business. The bureaucratic organization approach provides a workable set of guidelines. A manager who is persuaded by the arguments of the approach would design and redesign structures by comparing the proposed (or actual in the case of redesign) design with the "ideal type." The objective would be to design the actual structure so that it is congruent with the characteristics of the "ideal type."

Classical School Organization Design

The classical school's approach to organization design refers to ideas that were expressed in the early 1900s. These ideas propose that certain principles of organization should guide managers who are attempting to design organization structures.[4] Managers who follow these principles would thus design a certain type of organization structure (i.e., a classical design).

The important principles of organization are as follows:

- *Division of labor.* Work should be divided and subdivided to the highest possible degree consistent with economic efficiency.
- *Unity of direction.* Jobs should be grouped according to function or process (i.e., jobs should be grouped in departments).
- *Centralization of authority.* Accountability for the use of authority is retained at the executive, or top-management, level.
- *Authority and responsibility.* A jobholder must have authority commensurate with job responsibility.
- *Unity of command.* Each jobholder should report to one and only one superior.

The application of these principles results in organizations in which jobs are highly specialized, departments are based upon function and process, spans of control are narrow, and authority is centralized. Such organizations tend to be relatively "tall," with several layers of management through which communications and instructions must pass. Taken together, bureaucratic and classical design theories describe the essential features of *classical organization design.*

It is evident that the five classical principles are comparable to the five bureaucratic characteristics. Each set of guidelines stresses specialization of labor and centralized authority; each attempts to design a structure of jobs that minimizes the impact of those who hold the jobs.

Proponents of classical organization design stress the importance of predictable and reliable human behavior. The effects of high complexity, formalization, and centralization include not only more predictable human behavior, but also high levels of efficiency and production.

One example of a firm that has used classical principles to design its organization structure is United Parcel Service (UPS). UPS competes directly with the United States Postal Service in the delivery of small packages.[5] Even though the Postal Service is subsidized and pays no taxes, UPS has been able to compete successfully by stressing efficiency of operations. It apparently achieves great efficiency through a combination of automation and organization design.

Specialization and formalization are highly visible characteristics of UPS's structure. UPS makes use of clearly defined jobs and an explicit chain of command. The tasks are arranged in a hierarchy of authority consisting of eight managerial levels. The high degree of specialization enables management to use many forms of written reports such as daily worksheets, which record each employee's work quotas and performance. Company policies and practices are in written form and routinely consulted in hiring and promotion decisions. Apparently UPS has found the classical principles of organization well suited to its purposes.

Despite the success of classical design principles in some organizations, its critics note certain costs associated with using the principles. These critics argue that an alternative design, the neoclassical design, is a superior design.

Neoclassical Organization Design

In a historical sense, *neoclassical organization design* is a reaction to classical design. The characteristics of neoclassical design include the following:

- Low complexity
- Low formalization
- Low centralization

These characteristics describe organization structures in which jobs are relatively despecialized, departments contain a heterogeneous mix of jobs, spans of control are wide, and authority is decentralized. Thus, the neoclassical design can be viewed as the opposite of the classical design.

The arguments supporting neoclassical design are based on two assumptions. One assumption is that the uniqueness of individuals cannot be ignored. The second assumption is that the demands of situations cannot be ignored. Figure 9–2 outlines the neoclassical approach to organization design.

The Uniqueness of Individuals.   The impact and importance of individuals were first noted in the famous Hawthorne studies, a series of experiments carried out at the Western Electric plant in Hawthorne, Illinois.[6] These studies were the bases for the contention that high specialization of labor and centralized authority underestimate the complexity of employees. Rather than being passive and inert beings, mindlessly performing assigned tasks, the employees are unique, multifaceted people who seek more than monetary rewards from work. The researchers at the Hawthorne plant found that workers were members of friendship groups that defined the level of output considered fair and equitable. These groups seemed to exert far greater influence on employees than their managers, even though the groups had no authority to back up their influence.

Classical Design's Inherent Flaws.   Other studies supported the findings of the Hawthorne studies that classical organization design contains inherent flaws. For example, a very early study analyzed the relationship between rules and job behavior.[7] The study results indicated that extensive use of rules, as is characteristic of organizations that are highly complex, formal, and centralized, encourages individuals to follow rules as though they are ends rather than means. Such behavior maintains the status quo because rules cannot cover all circumstances.

A later study supported the idea that rules define minimum levels of expectations and that extensive use of rules discourages innovative behavior.[8] The classical design

---

FIGURE 9–2   Neoclassical Design Assumptions

Neoclassical design theory assumes that individual differences and situational characteristics are the principal determinants of organization design.

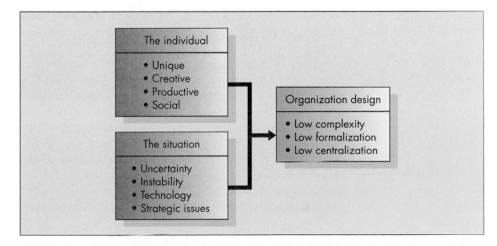

appears to reward the wrong behavior because it fails to take into account all the consequences of human behavior in the workplace.

Chris Argyris, a significant proponent of neoclassical ideas, believes that classical design suppresses the development and growth of employees.[9] According to him, the domination of subordinates through the use of formal rules and centralized authority causes subordinates to become passive, dependent, and uncreative. Such conditions are not congruent with the human need for autonomy, self-expression, accomplishment, and advancement. Consequently, the organization forfeits a considerable portion of its human resources through the use of classical design.

The Demands of Situations.   The assumption that the situation makes a difference is based upon considerable research. As noted earlier, classical designs gained in popularity during the early periods of industrialization and economic development—the late 1800s and early 1900s. That period of relatively stable and predictable change eventually gave way to instability and uncertainty. Advanced technology in communications, transportation, manufacturing processes, and medicine has created the necessity for organizations to be adaptable and flexible so that new ways of doing work can be quickly utilized.

A leading advocate of neoclassical design is Rensis Likert.[10] After considerable study, Likert proposed that, in contemporary society, neoclassical organizations utilize human and technical resources more fully than classical design.

Neoclassical design emphasizes the importance of decentralized authority and nondirective, participative managerial behavior. Relatively wide spans of control and heterogeneous departments facilitate the interaction of multiple and diverse points of view. Consequently, as circumstance and technology change, the organization is able to respond because of the diverse perspectives that can be brought to bear on any issue or problem that it confronts.

The most ardent proponents of neoclassical design believe that even if the organization exists in a relatively stable environment, the neoclassical way is the best way. Their contention reflects the assumption that individuals have fuller and more satisfying work lives in neoclassical organizations. Thus, the most ardent advocates of neoclassical organization design believe that it is universally applicable. They believe that it is the best way to organize in modern society. Neoclassical design is therefore seen as the superior alternative in comparison with classical design.

An alternative point of view, termed "the contingency approach," is that either classical or neoclassical can be the best way to organize depending upon the nature of such underlying factors as the organization's strategy, environment, and technology. Table 9–2 summarizes the distinctions between classical and neoclassical organizational design theory.

Many different types of organizations have used the ideas of neoclassical theory to design their structures. One such user is Aid Association for Lutherans (AAL), a fraternal society that operates a huge insurance business.[11] It has transformed its organization from a classical to a neoclassical structure in an effort to take advantage of the benefits of the self-directed team concept. Prior to reorganization, AAL was organized according to the traditional functions of the insurance industry, and employees were highly trained to deal with processing, underwriting, valuations, and premium-service functions. The specialization resulted in considerable efficiency when dealing with customers requiring the attention of one of the functions. But when multiple functions were involved, the organization became bogged down.

TABLE 9–2   Comparison of Classical and Neoclassical Designs

Classical and neoclassical designs differ in the ways certain important processes occur in organizations.

Processes	Classical Design	Neoclassical Design
Leadership	Includes no perceived confidence and trust. Subordinates do not feel free to discuss job problems with their superiors, who in turn do not solicit their ideas and opinions.	Includes perceived confidence and trust between superiors and subordinates in all matters. Subordinates feel free to discuss job problems with their superiors, who in turn solicit their ideas and opinions.
Motivation	Taps only physical, security and economic motives, through the use of fear and sanctions. Unfavorable attitudes toward the organization prevail among employees.	Taps a full range of motives through participatory methods. Attitudes are favorable toward the organization and its goals.
Communication	Information flows downward and tends to be distorted, inaccurate, and viewed with suspicion by subordinates.	Information flows freely throughout the organization—upward, downward, and laterally. The information is accurate and undistorted.
Interaction	Closed and restricted. Subordinates have little effect on departmental goals, methods, and activities.	Open and extensive. Both superiors and subordinates are able to affect departmental goals, methods, and activities.
Decision	Relatively centralized. Occurs only at the top of the organization.	Relatively decentralized. Occurs at all levels through group process.
Goal setting	Located at the top of the organization, discouraging group participation	Encourages group participation in setting high realistic objectives.
Control	Centralized. Emphasizes fixing of blame for mistakes.	Dispersed throughout the organization. Emphasizes self-control and problem solving.
Performance goals	Low and passively sought by managers, who make no commitment to developing the human resources of the organization.	High and actively sought by superiors, who recognize the necessity for full commitment to developing, through training, the human resources of the organization.

Source: Adapted from R Likert, *The Human Organization* (New York: McGraw-Hill, 1967), pp. 197–211.

AAL's management explored the potential benefits of establishing teams of employees that could handle all the details of any customer transaction, whether it related to health, life, or casualty insurance. The teams consist of individuals who once were responsible for functions; now they are responsible for customers, and they take initiative that once required management prodding. As a result of the teams' assumption of responsibility for their own management, three levels of management have been eliminated from the organization. The organization is now simpler and more decentralized than before its transformation.

Saturn's Neoclassical Structure

In a breakaway from the typical, classical, bureaucratic structure of General Motors, its subsidiary Saturn was established to resemble many of the features of a neoclassical structure. Saturn is organized as a collection of small, self-directed units made up of employees who are empowered with the authority to manage everything from inventory control and hiring to budget planning. Furthermore, Saturn employees are empowered to carry out their ideas and plans without the direct approval of top management.

The added responsibility at Saturn seems to have had the additional benefit of reducing employee absenteeism. Saturn absenteeism averages only 2.5 percent versus 10 to 14 percent at other General Motors plants.

One other benefit of the neoclassical structure is that Saturn employees show a higher-than-average level of commitment to their company. To create teams that are more effective and efficient, Saturn employees spend at least 5 percent of their time in comprehensive training programs.

Sources: F Barrett, "Creating Appreciative Learning Cultures," *Organizational Dynamics,* Autumn 1995, pp. 36-49; G LaBarr, "Safety at Saturn," *Occupational Hazards,* March 1994, pp. 41-44; D Holzman, "Where Workers Run the Show," *Working Woman,* August 1993, pp. 38–41; D Woodruff, "Saturn: Labor's Love Lost?" *Business Week,* February 8, 1993, pp. 122–24; and K Doyle, "Can Saturn Save GM?" *Incentive,* December 1992, pp. 30–37.

Other organizations have implemented organization design principles following neoclassical ideas. One notable example is highlighted in the Management Focus.

Contingency Approach

The contingency approach to organization design is based on the idea that different organization designs facilitate different purposes. Classical organizations are relatively more efficient and productive but relatively less adaptive and flexible than neoclassical organizations. A particular organization, whether a business firm, government agency, hospital, university, or a particular unit *within* an organization, should be structured depending upon whether it must be relatively efficient and productive or adaptive and flexible. The critical issue then becomes determining the circumstances that create the necessity to be relatively efficient and productive or adaptive and flexible.

The researchers and practitioners who have contributed to the ideas of contingency design have suggested a number of circumstances, or variables, that influence the design decision. Among these variables are age of the organization, size of the organization, form of ownership, technology, environmental uncertainty, strategic choice, member (employee) needs, and current fashion.[12] Older organizations tend to be more complex, formalized, and centralized than newer establishments. Also, researchers have noted the tendency of large organizations to be designed more along classical than neoclassical prescriptions. No attempt will be made here to discuss all the evidence related to each of these variables. Rather, the three that have the most apparent implications for management will be analyzed. They are technology, environment, and strategic choice.

Technology and Organization Design

The concept of technology can be narrowly defined as "the manufacturing, as distinct from administrative or distributive, processes employed by manufacturing firms to convert inputs into outputs."[13] Alternatively, it can be broadly defined as "the types and patterns of activity, equipment and material, and knowledge or experience used to perform tasks."[14] Regardless of how one defines the concept, whether narrowly or broadly, it is obvious that performing any kind of work—whether it be making cars, shoes, or computers or serving clients, patients, customers, or students—involves technology. The technology can be machines or it can be knowledge.

Technology as a Contingency.   The role of technology as a contingency variable is shown in Figure 9–3. There we see that technology affects the design of jobs, which in turn affects the design of organizations. The organization design, then, is contingent upon the degree of technology that management incorporates in the design of individual jobs.

Joan Woodward's studies stimulated the interest in the relationship between technology and structure.[15] In one study, Woodward classified technologies as unit, mass, or process production. Unit production referred to production to meet a customer's specific order. Here the product is developed after an order is received. The manufacture of custom-made shirts is an example of unit production technology. Mass production refers to the production of large quantities, such as on an assembly line. Zenith Corporation uses mass production technology to make television picture tubes. Process production refers to producing materials or goods on the basis of weight or volume. Processing 3 million barrels of oil or producing vats of paint at Sherwin-Williams are examples of production in this category.

Woodward found that a strong relationship existed between performance and both organizational design and technology. The highest-performing organizations with unit and process technologies used neoclassical design. However, the highest-performing organizations with mass production technologies used a classical design. These findings are summarized in Figures 9–4 and 9–5. The effects of unit and process manufacturing technology are jobs with low specialization and high depth and range. These jobs are best organized in a structure with relatively low complexity, formalization, and centralization. The rationale is that employees must have considerable latitude, discretion, and freedom of choice in the use of such technologies. Mass production, on the other hand, requires no such latitude on the part of employees, and accordingly, a classical design fits the situation.

FIGURE 9–3   Technology and Organization Design

Technology affects organization design through its impact on job design.

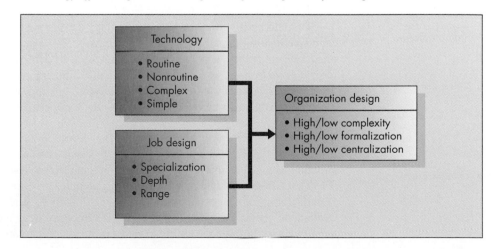

FIGURE 9–4   Unit and Process Production Technology and Organization Design

Complex technologies such as unit and process manufacturing methods require complex jobs that must be managed through neoclassical organization designs.

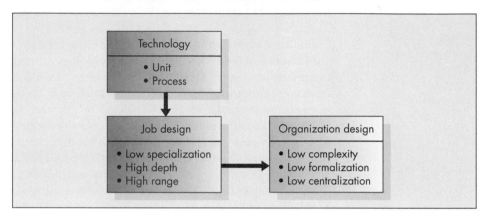

FIGURE 9–5   Mass Production Technology and Organization Design

Simple technologies such as mass production manufacturing methods require relatively simple jobs that can be managed through classical organization designs.

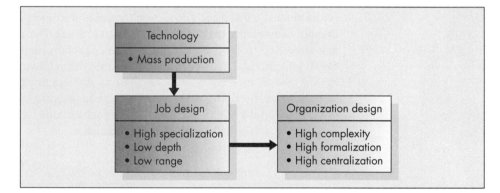

The successful firms in each technology category seem to employ the design characteristics suggested by the three principles. The idea that an organization design must be compatible with the technology it uses to achieve optimal performance is termed *organization "fit."* That is to say, an effective organization fits its technological requirements. A recent review of all the literature bearing on the relationship between technology and structure supports Woodward's earlier results.[16]

Flexible Manufacturing Technology.   The development of modern manufacturing methods has made the understanding of the relationships between technology and structure even more important. One development, flexible manufacturing technology (FMT), enables management to use the computer to integrate marketing, design, manufacturing, inventory control, materials handling, and quality control into a continuous operation.[17] The effect of this technology is to increase the flexibility of manufacturing through the ability to transfer information, material, and other resources throughout the organization; to design products quickly in consultation with customers, manufacturing personnel, and marketing personnel; and to set up machines to manufacture only the needed quantity of parts and components, thus reducing the need for inventory.

Flexible manufacturing technology makes it possible to combine the positive attributes of job order, mass production, and process technology in ways that were not previously contemplated.[18] The major effect of FMT on organization structure is to challenge the case for classical designs in mass production firms. FMT in mass production settings creates managerial problems similar to those in job order and process manufacturing settings. The principal managerial problem is managing interdependent activities that must respond to rapidly changing conditions. But with FMT, the possibilities are unlimited, including the ability to be more responsive to changing customer needs and preferences.[19]

One of the most notable experiences with FMT has been that of Ford Motor Company.[20] Most analysts consider Ford Motor Company to be the strongest of the American auto manufacturers, but the company has had to make major changes in how it manages its employees as well as how it builds its cars to retain this respect. Even with this hard-earned respect, however, the company had reason to be concerned as it moved into the 1990s. When 1991 came to a close, Ford's worldwide sales were off 15 percent, and the outlook continued to be gloomy as the global economy sputtered. Nevertheless, Ford persisted in its efforts to change the way it manages its employees.

One of the biggest changes has been in the way employees perform their jobs. Jobs at Ford are now less specialized; nonmanagerial personnel now perform tasks once reserved for managers, such as scheduling production and assuring quality. They work in teams under the general supervision of managers who have been trained in the development of teamwork.

Ford can now combine the advantages of job order, assembly line, and process manufacturing without suffering the disadvantages of either of the technologies. Manufacturing facilities can change, add, and customize autos for specific customers within time frames unheard of only a few years ago. The utilization of FMT has necessitated the development of neoclassical organization design features throughout Ford Motor Company.

The paradox of FMT and other revolutionary developments in manufacturing is that it enables different parts of the company to become more independent of one another even as they become more dependent.[21] The concept of integration is a key element in discussions of the relationship between environmental uncertainty and organization design.

Environment and Organization Design

Every organization must operate within an environment. There are competitors, suppliers, customers, creditors, and the government, each making demands on the organization. Each of these external forces can have an effect on the organization's design.

Environmental Types.   The environment can be a stable one—that is, one in which change is unpredictable. In a stable environment, customer tastes remain relatively unchanged. New technology is rare, and the need for innovative research to stay ahead of competition is minimal. There has been little change in the environments affecting the manufacturers of accordions, zippers, and book covers.

Another type of environment is referred to as changing. There are changes in the competition's strategy and in market demands, advertising, personnel practices, and technology. The changes are rather frequent and somewhat expected. Automobile manufacturers operate in a changing environment.

A turbulent environment exists when changes are unexpected and unpredictable. New competitive strategies, new laws, and new technology can create a turbulent condition. Electronic firms such as IBM, Hewlett-Packard, and Honeywell face unexpected environmental forces.

Mechanistic and Organic Structures.   Matching an organizational design to the environment would require accurate managerial assessment of the environmental forces. Are they stable, changing, or turbulent? A group interested in organizational design studied 20 English and Scottish firms. Through analysis of interview responses it concluded that two types of organizational systems exist, which the group labeled *mechanistic* and *organic*.[22] Mechanistic structures had the same characteristics as classical designs; organic structures had the characteristics of neoclassical designs.

After completing its study, the group concluded that classical designs were optimal in stable environments. However, the neoclassical was most suited to turbulent environments. The relationship between environmental characteristics and organization design is summarized in Figure 9–6. Stable, placid environments do not cause unexpected events that employees must deal with. Consequently, their jobs can be designed to include minimal depth and range and maximal specialization. Changing, turbulent environments, on the other hand, create unexpected events and circumstances that cannot be anticipated. Jobs must be designed so as to give the employees considerable range and depth. The compatible organization design for such jobs is one with low complexity, formalism, and centralization—neoclassical design.

Designing Organizational Subunits.   An American research group proposed that organizations should be designed with an emphasis on the different subunits, or departments of the organization.[23] Those departments that face highly uncertain and turbulent environments should follow neoclassical design prescriptions—they should be relatively despecialized, informal, and decentralized. On the other hand, a department that faces certain and predictable environments should follow classical design ideas and be specialized, formalized, and centralized. The contingency viewpoint is reflected in the researchers' conclusion that "the internal functioning of

FIGURE 9–6   Environmental Characteristics and Organization Design

Characteristics of the organization's environment can affect its design.

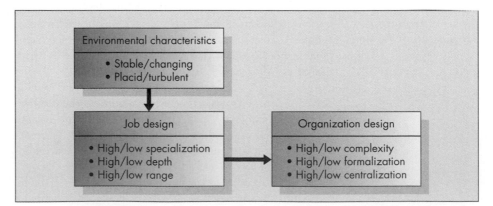

organizations must be consistent with the organization task, technology, or external environment, and the needs of its members if the organization is to be effective."[24]

Environmental characteristics, such as uncertainty, change, turbulence, and volatility, affect the design of organizational subunits by defining the characteristics of the jobs. This effect at the overall organizational level is shown in Figure 9–6. The effect holds true at the subunit, or departmental, level as well. The managerial implications of this effect relate to the possibility of having a diverse range of organizational designs among departments within the same organization.

For example, a manufacturing firm typically must deal with three critical subenvironments. One subenvironment consists of the market for its products. This subenvironment is the source of pressure to compete for customers through pricing, promotion, product development, and other marketing activities. The dominant characteristic of the market subenvironment can range from being highly uncertain to highly certain. The degree of certainty would be influenced by the reliability of available information on customer preferences and competitors' actions, and the rate of change in those preferences and actions.

A relatively certain market subenvironment is one for which reliable information exists regarding stable customer preferences and competitors' actions. An uncertain market subenvironment would be the opposite: unreliable information and changing preferences and actions. Firms in plastics and computer manufacturing face relatively uncertain market subenvironments. Public utilities and container manufacturers face relatively certain market environments.

The environmentally contingent model specifies that the organization design of departments "fit" the demands of the department's subenvironment. Accordingly, the organization design of the marketing departments that face *uncertain* environments would take on characteristics of the neoclassical approach. Those that face *certain* environments would organize according to the classical approach. Thus, there is no best way to organize a marketing department.

Most manufacturing firms face two other important subenvironments in addition to the market subenvironment. The technical-economic subenvironment refers to the external sources of information and resources that are required in the production of the firm's product. This subenvironment can be certain or uncertain depending upon knowledge and rates of change in the technology of production, sources, types, and supplies of human, physical, and natural resources. Production departments must be organized to reflect the state of this subenvironment.

The third subenvironment is the scientific knowledge and know-how that firms relate to through their research and development departments. Research and development units are typically closer to neoclassical structures than any other department because of the relatively higher degree of uncertainty in the scientific subenvironment compared to market and technical-economic subenvironments. After all, the fundamental characteristic of research is the revelation of the unknown. But in some industries the scientific subenvironment can be relatively stable and certain in comparison with those of other industries. For example, the container industry scientific subenvironment is far more certain than the personal computer industry.

The process of designing the organization structure on a department-by-department basis can result in considerable diversity of designs within the same organization. The environmental perspective emphasizes the fitting of departments to subenvironments and then designing methods to coordinate the departments toward organizational objectives. The methods can range from strict applications of rules and procedures to the use of cross-departmental groups and individuals.

Management Focus

Examples of How Global Firms Cope with Uncertainty

Many manufacturing organizations delegate sole responsibility for product and process innovation to research and development units. Other firms recognize the need for involving people with multiple skills and specialties in order to remain innovative. Sony Corporation, which develops an average of four new products a day, looks for people who are *"neyaka,"* which translated means optimistic, open minded, and wide ranging in interest. At Sony, technicians move around among product groups and try technologies they have not previously worked with. To reduce redundant projects and foster the sharing of technology within the company, an umbrella organization, Sony Corporate Research, oversees the efforts of 23 business groups and hundreds of product teams.

Honda Motor Company developed its City model by forming a project team consisting of research and development (R&D), sales and marketing, and production personnel. Members of the project team interacted intensively at every step of the innovation process and, through mutual efforts, coordinated all functional aspects of developing a new automobile.

Matsushita Electric Industrial Company developed its Home Bakery product by involving research personnel as well as sales and manufacturing experts. One result of this collaboration was a design change early in the development process resulting in the discovery of a totally new way to make homemade bread.

Epson America, Inc., involves individuals from all levels of its hierarchy in new product development. It goes even further by creating multiple groups to deal with the same opportunities. The resulting competition inevitably creates some conflict, but out of the conflict emerge innovative products and ways to produce the products.

Sources: E Updike and D Woodruff, "Honda's Civic Lesson," *Business Week,* September 18, 1995, pp. 71–76; B R Schlender, "How Sony Keeps the Magic Going," *Fortune,* February 24, 1992, pp. 76–84; Wim G Biemans, "Organizational Networks: Toward a Cross-Fertilization between Practice and Theory," *Journal of Business Research,* January 1996, pp. 29-39; and I Nonaka, "Redundant, Overlapping Organization: A Japanese Approach to Managing the Innovation Process," *California Management Review,* Spring 1990, pp. 27–38.

An organization that consists of departments predominantly designed along classical lines could achieve interdepartmental coordination through rules, procedures, and policy. But an organization made up of departments designed according to neoclassical guidelines could achieve coordinated effort only through cross-departmental teams and individuals.

Organizations devise numerous ways to cope with the need to innovate and be responsive to uncertain environments. The accompanying Management Focus describes what some have done.

Creating External Networks of Cooperative Relationships. One of the fastest-developing practices in business throughout the world involves firms in cooperative relationships with their suppliers, distributors, and even competitors. These networks of relationships enable organizations to achieve both efficiency and flexibility—to exploit the advantages of the mechanistic and the organic organization designs. These "network organizations" have become so pervasive that some experts refer to them as the models for twenty-first century organizations.[25] The effect of the cooperative relationships enables the principal organization to rely upon the smaller, closer-to-the-market partner to sense the impending changes in the environment and to respond at the local level, thus relieving the parent organization of that necessity.

The exact form of the network organization varies.[26] Some organizations develop relationships only with key suppliers. Other organizations will develop relationships with marketers and distributors. In the extreme case, the parent organization functions much like a broker and deals independently with product designers, producers, suppliers, and markets. The critical managerial and organizational decisions involve which of the functions to buy, which of the functions to produce, and how to manage the relationships with their partners. Managers in these network organizations have less environmental uncertainty to deal with because they have, in a sense, subcontracted that responsibility to their counterparts in the network. Such organization structures are, in a sense, boundaryless organizations.[27]

The exact form of the network organization can take different shapes. Some forms follow the Japanese practice of establishing alliances. These alliances take the form of cooperative agreements, consortia, and equity ownership agreements to establish networks of businesses.

In Japan this form of doing business is termed *keiretsu,* and it involves a very large financial institution, a very large industrial conglomerate, and smaller firms in a network of relationships that enable the large firm to produce the product and the smaller firms to supply components, do research and design, and perhaps distribute and market. The participating bank provides the financial requirements to support the network of cooperative relationships. This form of interorganizational network has enabled Japanese industry to grow without experiencing supply bottlenecks and damaging competition from domestic firms.

American firms are now learning to play this game, and as the twenty-first century looms, the network organization emerges as a dominant form of organization structure for firms desiring to compete in the global marketplace.[28] The examples of cooperative arrangements run the gamut of American industry. General Motors, Chrysler, and Ford have entered into an agreement to develop battery technology for electric cars. IBM and DEC own equity shares of key suppliers of component parts. IBM will often pay suppliers prior to receiving shipment of the supplies as a way to assist them with their cash flow. Deere & Company enables its employees to work with their counterparts at supplier firms, such as McLaughlin Body Company, to solve problems that stand in the way of quality parts and timely delivery. Ford Motor Company belongs to eight different consortia doing research on a range of issues from environmental impact to engineering techniques.

The matter of how these relationships should be organized and managed has just begun to be examined. Although the Japanese experience provides some guidelines, much is left to be learned and put into practice. The development of these cooperative relationships represents yet another reaction from organizations that must maintain flexibility to deal with the dynamic changes of the global economy.

Strategy and Organization Design

As noted in our discussion of the planning function (see Chapter 6), strategy involves the selection of missions and objectives and appropriate courses of action to achieve these objectives. Logically several courses of action could be identified for any given objective, and for each alternative strategy, an alternative organization design exists. Thus, the specific organization design should follow from a specified strategy.

Generic Strategies.   One influential writer in the field of corporate strategy states that corporations can adopt one of three general (generic) strategies.[29] The three strategies are cost leadership, differentiation, and focus.

Cost leadership implies that the firm will outstrip its competition by being the low-cost producer. It will build efficient-scale facilities, pursue cost control policies, avoid marginal customers, and generally be cost conscious in all areas of the business. In other words, the firm will emphasize efficiency and productivity. With lower costs, the firm can afford lower prices, and with lower prices, it can generate larger sales volumes. Two firms that have achieved notable success by striving for cost leadership are Briggs and Stratton, and Lincoln Electric.

The organization design that facilitates overall cost leadership must be one that encourages efficiency and productivity. The classical design, with its emphasis on complexity, formalization, and centralization, fits this strategy.

Differentiation means the firm is creating products that are perceived to be unique. The perception of uniqueness (differentiation) can be based upon a variety of factors such as brand image, product features, customer service, and a dealer network. To be effective, differentiation requires creativity, basic research skill, strong marketing, and a reputation for quality. Firms such as Mercedes, Jenn-Air, Coleman, and Caterpillar have successfully pursued differentiation. Differentiation strategy does not imply that cost control is ignored—only that it is not the primary strategic consideration.

The emphasis on differentiation requires flexible response to changing customer preferences and perceptions. The organization design that facilitates the strategy would tend toward neoclassical characteristics. Neoclassical designs, with their emphasis on low specialization, low formality, and decentralized authority, encourage the freedom of action required for the differentiation strategy to be successful.

Focus, the third generic strategy, means achieving either cost leadership or differentiation or both in a particular segment of the market. Rather than competing throughout the market, the firm focuses on one segment. For example, Porter Paint attempts to serve the needs of the professional painter rather than the do-it-yourself market segment. Thus, the focus strategy implies a trade-off between market share and profitability.

The compatible organization design for a focus strategy includes a mix of classical and neoclassical characteristics because the firm can attempt both cost leadership and differentiation aimed at its segment. The point here is not to depict the relative benefits of any of the three generic strategies. Nor are we concerned with whether these are, in fact, the three generic strategies. Rather the point is to demonstrate the relationship between strategy and structure. Although Porter's ideas regarding this relationship have been widely received, they rest on ideas previously developed.

Growth Strategies.   The contemporary impetus for the idea that structure should reflect strategy is the work of Chandler.[30] After a study of the history of 70 of America's largest firms, Chandler concluded that organization structures follow the growth strategies of firms. He also found that growth strategies tended to follow a certain pattern. In their initial stage, firms are typically plants, sales offices, or warehouses in a single industry, in a single location, and performing a single function such as manufacturing, sales, or warehousing. But they grow if successful, and their growth follows fairly standard paths.

The first stage of growth is through *volume expansion,* in which firms manufacture, sell, or distribute more of their product or service to existing customers. The next stage of growth is *geographic expansion,* through which the firm continues to do what it has been doing but in a larger geographic area by means of field units. The third growth stage is *vertical integration,* in which firms either buy or create other functions. For example, manufacturers integrate either backward, by acquiring or creating sources of supply, or forward, by acquiring or creating sales and distribution functions. The final growth stage, *product diversification,* involves the firm in new industries either through mergers, acquisitions, or creation (product development).

As a firm moves through each stage, it must change its organization structure. Initially, classical design is appropriate because volume expansion of a single product or service in a single industry stresses low unit cost (efficiency) and maximum resource utilization (production), with relatively low concern for response to change and uncertainty. But as the firm moves through the steps of geographic expansion and, ultimately, product diversification, it becomes increasingly concerned about adaptability and flexibility because it faces diverse and complex environments. Thus, the organization structures of highly diversified firms are characterized by product-based divisions and departments, decentralized authority, and relatively wide spans of control. The strategic choice of contingency approach is diagrammed in Figure 9–7.

Companies that have diversified into related and unrelated products rely on divisional forms of organization. Rumelt's study of Fortune 500 firms found an inexorable movement toward product-based divisional forms of organization.[31] But there is some question as to whether such divisional structures always follow neoclassical design principles.[32] Organizations such as Philip Morris, which consists of divisions producing and marketing products as diverse as beer, cigarettes, and soft drinks, are more complex than General Motors, whose divisions produce and market different makes of trucks and automobiles.

We also have some evidence that the relationship between growth strategy and organizational structure holds for organizations in various countries. For example, Hamilton and Shergill report a strong relationship between strategy and structure for New Zealand firms.[33] The idea that organization design should change to reflect the organization's strategic choice implies growth-oriented strategy. It also implies that managers will know the need for changing the structure.[34] This orientation toward change and knowing is termed a *process approach* to organization design. A process approach places its emphasis on how and why an organization moves from one design to another. Implicit in this approach is the assumption that managers know that they should alter the organization design as they change the firm's strategy from volume expansion to product diversification.

FIGURE 9–7   Strategic Choices and Organization Design

The growth strategy that managers choose requires an organization design appropriate to carry out that stratgey.

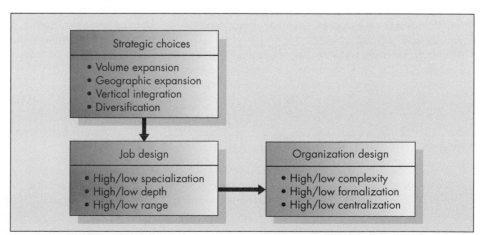

But the same could be said for other approaches to organization design. Both the technology and uncertainty approaches assume that managers know what design to use in a particular situation. The simpler, one-best-way approaches also recognize the importance of competent managers. The proponents of contingency approaches often present their ideas without giving explicit attention to the role of the organization's management, particularly the cognitive and psychological traits of managers.

Summary of Key Points

- The decision to design or redesign an organization involves choosing from among a number of alternatives. These alternative designs can be classified as either universalistic or contingency based.
- Universalistic designs are based upon the assumption that there is one "best way" to organize regardless of the situation. The best way can be either a classical design (defined by complexity, formalism, and centralization) or neoclassical design (defined by simplicity, informalism, and decentralization).
- The classical design, with its high degree of specialization (complexity), written rules and policies (formalism), and low degree of delegation (centralization), places emphasis on obtaining maximum production and efficiency.
- The neoclassical design, with its low degree of specialization (simplicity), unwritten but implicit rules and policies (informalism), and high degree of delegation (decentralization), places emphasis on obtaining maximum flexibility and adaptability, and employee satisfaction.
- The alternative to the universalistic approach is the contingency approach. Contingency designs are based on the assumption that the best way to organize depends upon the situation or setting. The best design can tend toward either the classical or the neoclassical one.
- The contingency approach is the more widely accepted in contemporary management theory and practice. However, there is little consensus among its proponents as to what specific factor or set of factors determines which organization design is preferable.
- One factor that many believe to be important is technology. According to this view, firms that use either job order or process technology will be more effective and productive if

their designs tend toward neoclassical characteristics. Firms that use mass-production technology will benefit from classical characteristics. The development of flexible manufacturing technology (FMT) suggests a renewed interest in neoclassical design principles even among traditional users of classical design.
- A second factor often linked to organization design is environmental uncertainty. This body of opinion notes that organizations facing uncertain environments require flexibility and adaptability to survive and should therefore use neoclassical designs. In contrast, firms facing certain environments must seek high levels of production and efficiency; thus the classical design is appropriate.
- The environmental contingency approach encourages managers to design the total organization in terms of departmental structures. According to this perspective, the organization's environment actually consists of subenvironments, and the organization must design departments to deal with the demands and conditions inherent to those subenvironments.
- The virtual, or network, organization form has emerged in recent years as firms attempt to cope with increasing environmental uncertainty and the need to innovate. Alliances enable organizations to combine the distinctive competencies of several participating organizations in a loosely controlled federation.
- The strategy the organization undertakes implies a particular organization structure. Least cost can best be undertaken through the application of classical principles, while differentiation can best be undertaken with neoclassical principles.

Discussion and Review Questions

1. Contrast the main arguments of universalistic and contingency approaches to organization design. Which of the two approaches is easier to implement in practice? Explain.

2. Contrast the main features of the classical and neoclassical organization designs.

3. Compare what you believe to be the popular meaning of the term "bureaucracy" with the meaning in management literature. Why do the terms *bureaucracy* and *bureaucratic* have negative connotations?

4. Explain why an organization with classical design characteristics is likely to be more efficient and

productive but less flexible and adaptable than an organization with neoclassical design characteristics.

5. Compare two organizations that you know about, either through employment or membership, in terms of classical and neoclassical design characteristics. What explains the differences you find in the two organizations?

6. What are the bases for the opinion that technology is an important contingency variable? Do you believe that technology is the primary factor to be considered when management designs a structure? Explain.

7. What are the relevant subenvironments of business firms? Of hospitals? Of universities? What subunits, or departments, exist in typical business firms, hospitals, and universities to deal with those subenvironments?

8. What are the bases for the opinion that environmental uncertainty is an important contingency variable? Do you believe that environmental uncertainty is the primary factor to be considered when management designs a structure? Explain.

9. What are the bases for the opinion that strategy is an important contingency variable? Do you believe that strategy is the primary factor to be considered when management designs a structure? Explain.

10. Develop an explanation of the important contingency variables that would integrate the technology, environmental, and strategy points of view.

CASE 9–1
GENERAL MOTORS: ITS CHANGING ORGANIZATION DESIGN

The trials and tribulations of General Motors (GM) during the 1980s and 1990s mirror those of organizations in the United States and around the world. GM's position of market leader in automobile production and sales began to falter in the early 1980s along with market leaders in other industries. Competitive forces throughout the world were forcing US firms to rethink their strategies and their organization designs. As more and more competitors from Asia and Europe challenged GM's market supremacy and as technological developments in manufacturing and information processing challenged GM's production advantages, GM's management responded by implementing changes in its organization design that continue into the second half of the 90s.

The first signs of problems began to appear in 1981 when the company reported its first loss since 1921. This report coincided with the appointment of Roger Smith as CEO, the sixth GM CEO since Alfred P Sloan, Jr., who served from 1937 to 1956. Sloan created the modern version of GM through the development of the divisional organizational structure, which consisted of five independent divisions—Chevrolet, Pontiac, Oldsmobile, Buick, and Cadillac—and the competing product strategy. The competing product strategy encouraged each division to compete for customers by delegating complete authority to each division to design, produce, market, and sell its own particular line of cars. The only limitation placed on the division was the overall corporate strategy of encouraging car buyers to think of "trading up" as each year's new models hit the showfloors. Thus, the Chevrolet Division produced the starter cars, relatively inexpensive and within the price range of the first-time car buyer. But with increases in income the car buyer would be encouraged through promotion and selling efforts to consider the more expensive Pontiac and Oldsmobile vehicles, and ultimately the Buick and Cadillac.

This traditional divisional design was in place throughout the post–World War II period when General Motors grew into the largest manufacturing organization in the world. But something happened along the way. The divisional structure as it evolved over time began to be identified as an impediment to progress and market response. One of the outgrowths of the structure was the development of a massive corporate support staff, which when created was supposed to provide expert advice and consultation to the divisions. But over time these staff members began to take over the decision making of the line units, and the decision making began to grind to a halt in endless discussions in endless committee meetings at corporate headquarters. As these corporate staff units increased their influence through the provision of valued information, they sought and received formal authority over many of the day-to-day decisions.

Thus, when Roger Smith took the reins in 1981, he began the process that continues even to this day: redesigning GM's organizational structure with the specific purpose of pushing decision making down into the operating divisions and reducing the number of staff at corporate headquarters. In 1984, he announced his first move: the creation of two autonomous groups, BOC and CPC. BOC consisted of what had been the Buick, Oldsmobile, and Cadillac divisions, and CPC consisted of what had been Chevrolet, Pontiac, and GM of Canada. Smith delegated complete authority to each of the groups to organize in whatever way the managers thought was necessary to get GM back on track—to regain its competitive, growing, and profitable status.

BOC decided to organize around four completely autonomous product groups—strategic business units (SBUs). Each product group would operate as Sloan had envisioned his divisional structure would operate, exercising complete authority to design, produce, and sell cars. By contrast, CPC organized around functional lines with centralized authority, but with a matrix overlay to facilitate communication across functional lines.

When 1993 rolled around, GM had replaced Robert Stempel, who had replaced Roger Smith, with Jack Smith. Stempel had been in office barely two years, yet the board of directors was unhappy with his deliberate management style. He simply was moving too slowly in carrying out the turnaround that Roger Smith had begun. The new CEO responded to the news that GM's market share had dropped to its lowest point in 23 years, 29 percent, by creating a single operating division, North American Operations (NAO); paring corporate staff from 13,500 to 2,500; reducing the number of car models from 62 to 54; combining 27 different purchasing departments into one; and eliminating nearly 16,500 hourly jobs by offering early retirement. These seemingly harsh measures were necessary according to Jack Smith to assure GM's very survival as an automaker.

The organizational design that GM now counts on to enable it to survive and compete identifies the five traditional divisions—Chevrolet, Pontiac, Oldsmobile, Buick, and Cadillac—as marketing units. But all production, product design, and purchasing will be done in one separate unit. The story of GM's reorganization efforts remains unfinished. In fact, what progress the company makes will depend upon Jack Smith's success at eliminating the remaining vestiges of bureaucracy that persist even in the midst of massive efforts to make the company more responsive to market conditions and technological developments. Centralization or decentralization? Which is the appropriate response: centralize some functions, such as purchasing and production, and decentralize other functions such as marketing?

Despite all the efforts of its CEOs from Roger Smith to Jack Smith, GM continues its long slide down the profitability curve. The efforts to reverse this slide through organization redesign and other measures seem to have yielded little gain. If General Motors cannot cope with the rigors of global competition, can the country?

Questions for Analysis

1. Identify the environmental forces that have driven General Motors to change its organizational design.

2. Have the changes in structure been in the appropriate direction? Have they been misguided? Explain your answer and your reasoning.

3. Discuss the possibility that redesigning the organizational structure is actually an irrelevant response to what ails General Motors.

Sources: F Washington, "A Different Kind of Car Guy," *Ward's Auto World,* March 1996, p. 125; B Moskal, "General Motors," *Industry Week,* October 16, 1995, pp. 33–34; and K Kerwin, "Can Jack Smith Fix GM?" *Business Week,* November 1, 1993, pp. 65–67.

EXPERIENTIAL EXERCISE
ORGANIZATIONAL DESIGN IN THE CAMPUS SETTING

Purpose

This exercise enables students to use certain theories of organization design to describe the organizational design of units that make up their college or university.

The Exercise in Class

The instructor will divide the class into groups of 8 to 10 students. Each group will:

1. Select a particular organizational unit on campus. The unit can be an academic department, division, or college, or it can be an administrative, maintenance, or athletic unit. Your group should select the unit for which it can obtain the greatest amount of information.

2. Select one of the contingency theories of organization design discussed in the text (technology, environmental uncertainty, and strategic choice).

3. Use the theory to describe and analyze the unit's organizational design. Emphasize the points of difference between what the theory predicts and what actually exists. Also suggest reasons for the differences.

4. Present the group's analysis to the class, examining the extent to which the organizational structure contributes to or detracts from the unit's effectiveness.

The Learning Message

This exercise is very effective at reinforcing students' understanding of the purposes, strengths, and limitations of theory in the context of management.

Notes

1. William A Pasmore, *Designing Effective Organizations* (New York: John Wiley, 1988).

2. Max Weber, *The Theory of Social and Economic Organization,* trans. A M Henderson and Talcott Parsons (New York: Oxford University Press, 1947), p. 334.

3. Max Weber, *Max Weber: Essays in Sociology,* trans. H H Gerth and C W Mills (New York: Oxford University Press, 1946), p. 214; John I Foster, "Bureaucratic Rigidity Revisited," *Social Science Quarterly,* June 1990, pp. 223–38, is a recent review of the evidence regarding the effectiveness of bureaucratic structure to control all the job-relevant behavior of employees.

4. See Henri Fayol, *General and Industrial Management,* trans. C Storrs (London: Pitman, 1949), pp. 19–42, for the original statement of classical principles.

5. Peter Capelli and A Crocker-Hefter, "Distinctive Human Resources Are Firm's Core Competencies," *Organizational Dynamics,* Winter 1996, pp. 7–22; Kent C Nelson, "Quality in a Service Organization," *Executive Speeches,* August–September 1995, pp. 11-14.

6. Fritz J Roethlisberger and W H Dickson, *Management and the Worker* (Cambridge, MA: Harvard University Press, 1939).

7. Robert K Merton, "Bureaucratic Structure and Personality," *Social Forces,* 1940, pp. 560–68.

8. Alvin W Gouldner, *Patterns of Industrial Bureaucracy* (New York: Free Press, 1954).

9. Chris Argyris, *Personality and Organization* (New York: Harper & Row, 1975); Guy Benveniste, *Professionalizing the Organization: Reducing Bureaucracy to Enhance Effectiveness* (San Francisco: Jossey-Bass, 1987).

10. Rensis Likert, *New Patterns of Management* (New York: McGraw-Hill, 1961); Rensis Likert, *The Human Organization* (New York: McGraw-Hill, 1967).

11. Robert Janson and Richard L Gunderson, "The Team Approach to Companywide Change," *National Productivity Review,* Winter 1990–91, pp. 34–44; Marc Hequet, "Paying for Knowledge in 'Paper Factories,' " *Training,* September 1990, pp. 69–77; John Hoerr, "Work Teams Can Rev Up Paper-Pushers, Too," *Business Week,* November 28, 1988, pp. 64, 68, 72.

12. W Alan Randolph and Gregory G Dess, "The Congruence Perspective of Organization Design: A Conceptual Model and Multivariate Research Approach," *Academy of Management Review,* January 1984, pp. 114–27; Robert Drazin and Andrew H Van de Ven, "Alternative Forms of Fit in Contingency Theory," *Administrative Science Quarterly,* December 1985, pp. 514–39.

13. Charles Perrow, "A Framework for the Comparative Analysis Organizations," *American Sociological Review,* April 1967, p. 195; see Michael Withey, Richard L Daft, and William H Cooper, "Measures of Perrow's Work-Unit Technology: An Empirical Assessment and a New Scale," *Academy of Management Journal,* March 1983, pp. 45–63.

14. Denise M Rousseau, "Assessment of Technology in Organizations: Closed versus Open Systems Approaches," *Academy of Management Review,* October 1979, p. 531.

15. Joan Woodward, *Industrial Organization: Theory and Practice* (London: Oxford University Press, 1965). A recent study based on Woodward's research is reported in Frank M Hull and Paul D Collins, "High-Technology Batch Production: Woodward's Missing Type," *Academy of Management Journal,* December 1987, pp. 786–97.

16. C Chet Miller, William H Glick, Yau-De Wang, and George P Huber, "Understanding Technology-Structure Relationships: Theory Development and Meta-Analytical Theory Testing," *Academy of Management Journal,* June 1991, pp. 370–99.

17. Charles Snow, Raymond E Miles, and Henry J Coleman, "Managing 21st Century Network Organizations," *Organizational Dynamics,* Winter 1992, pp. 5–19.

18. Mary J Maffei and Jack Meredith, "Infrastructure and Flexible Manufacturing Technology," *Journal of Operations Management,* December 1995, pp. 273–98; Raghavan Parthasarthy and S Prakash Sethi, "The Impact of Flexible Automation on Business Strategy and Organizational Structure," *Academy of Management Review,* January 1992, pp. 86–111.

19. William R C Blundell, "Prescription for the '90s: The Boundary-Less Company," *Business Quarterly (Canada),* Autumn 1990, pp. 71–73.

20. Ian Spaulding, "Ford Motor Company: School to Work Transition Is Job One," *Training and Development,* November 1994, p. 34; Frank Petrock, "Ford's Teamwork Training Gets Employees Involved," *Human Resources Professional,* Spring 1991, pp. 30–32.

21. Patricia L Nemetz and Louis W Fry, "Flexible Manufacturing Organizations: Implications for Strategy Formulation and Organization Design," *Academy of Management Review,* October 1988, pp. 627–38.

22. Tom Burns and G M Stalker, *The Management of Innovation* (London: Tavistock, 1961).

23. Paul R Lawrence and Jay W Lorsch, *Organization and Environment* (Burr Ridge, IL: Richard D. Irwin, 1967).

24. Ian C MacMillan and Patricia E Jones, "Designing Organizations to Compete," *Journal of Business*

Strategy, Spring 1984, pp. 11–26; Balaji S Chakravarthy and Peter Lorange, "Managing Strategic Adaptation: Options in Administrative System Design," *Interfaces,* January–February, 1984, pp. 34–46.

25. Raymond E Miles and Charles C Snow, "The New Network Firm: A Spherical Structure Built on a Human Investment Philosophy," *Organizational Dynamics,* Spring 1995, pp. 4–18.

26. Ravi S Achrol, "Evolution of the Marketing Organization: New Forms for Turbulent Environments," *Journal of Marketing,* October 1991, pp. 77–93.

27. Blundell, "Prescription for the '90s," pp. 71–73.

28. "Learning from Japan," *Business Week,* January 27, 1992, pp. 52–55, 58, 59; Frank Hull and Eugene Slowinski, "Partnering with Technology Entrepreneurs," *Research-Technology Management,* November–December 1990, pp. 16–20; Colin Coulson-Thomas, "The Responsive Organization," *Journal of General Management (UK),* Summer 1990, pp. 21–31.

29. Michael E Porter, *Competitive Strategy* (New York: Free Press, 1980), pp. 34–46.

30. Alfred D Chandler, *Strategy and Structure* (Cambridge, MA: MIT Press, 1962); Robert E Hoskisson, "Multidivisional Structure and Performance: The Contingency of Diversification Strategy," *Academy of Management Journal,* December 1987, pp. 625–44, reports a recent study of the relationship between strategy and structure.

31. R P Rumelt, *Strategy, Structure, and Economic Performance* (Cambridge, MA: Division of Research, Graduate School of Business Administration, Harvard University, 1974).

32. Peter H Grinyer and Masoud Yasai-Ardekani, "Dimensions of Organizational Structure: A Critical Replication," *Academy of Management Journal,* September 1980, pp. 405–21.

33. R T Hamilton and G S Shergill, "The Relationship between Strategy-Structure Fit and Financial Performance in New Zealand: Evidence of Generality and Validity with Enhanced Controls," *Journal of Management Studies,* January 1992, pp. 95–113.

34. Tom Peters, "Restoring American Competitiveness: Looking for New Models of Organizations," *Academy of Management Executive,* May 1988, pp. 103–9.

10　THE CONTROLLING FUNCTION

Chapter Learning Objectives

After completing Chapter 10, you should be able to:

- **Define** the controlling function in terms of the three features of effective control.
- **Describe** representative standards, information, and corrective action for general methods.
- **Discuss** the difference between preliminary, concurrent, and feedback control methods.
- **Compare** the control techniques designed to maintain quality of inputs with those designed to maintain quality of outputs.
- **Identify** the different standards used to assess potential profitability of capital investments.

Reengineering at Barr & Stroud

Reengineering represents the ultimate in control practices. Today, the trend toward reengineering is so in vogue that the label is being used to describe diverse actions ranging from mundane requests for new chairs to across-the-board organizational layoffs. However, true reengineering entails the radical redesign of business processes to achieve major gains in cost, service, or time. The goal of business process redesign (BPR) is to change the fundamental way the work of the organization is done in order to achieve dramatic improvements in speed, cost, and quality.

Reengineering, unlike automation, does not simply speed up an existing business function. Instead, it completely recasts or reengineers the core system or process. Computers and other information technology play an integral role in BPR by empowering management to exercise greater, unobtrusive control in all facets of business activity. Reengineering efforts are not limited to domestic companies; they have gained a large following in the international business arena. Barr & Stroud is a Canadian company that has recently utilized reengineering processes to its advantage.

For defense contractor Barr & Stroud, the decline of the Soviet Union was bad news. With the perception in the West of a lessening of the threat from the former Soviet Union, demand for military periscopes, the main product manufactured by the company, faltered. Rather than idly sit back and watch the demise of the company, executives at Barr & Stroud began radical change to regain profitability.

The end results for Barr & Stroud of undertaking BPR include a flattened organizational structure through removal of five levels of management reporting; a single employee negotiating body instead of the previous seven; equal sickness and holiday entitlements for all employees; elimination of special perks formerly accorded to management; and the formation of highly efficient work teams, which are organized by business and product. To achieve these gains, both management and employees had to buy into the critical notion that BPR doesn't just incrementally improve, it dramatically *changes,* former ways of doing business.

In addition to merely cutting costs through use of BPR, Barr & Stroud has also employed information technology to better monitor, and thus regain control of, its manufacturing operations. The outcome has been almost 100 percent on-time delivery of products, leading to higher customer satisfaction and increased revenues and profits. For Barr & Stroud, the use of BPR has certainly led to a peacetime dividend.

Sources: I King, "The Road to Continuous Improvement: BPR and Project Management," *IIE Solutions,* October 1996, pp. 22–27; T Stewart, "Reengineering: The Hot New Managing Tool," *Fortune,* August 23, 1993, pp. 40–48; R S Barton, "Business Process Reengineering," *Business Quarterly,* Spring 1993, pp. 101–3.

The third management function, the **controlling function,** includes *all activities the manager undertakes in attempting to ensure that actual results conform to planned results.*[1] In this chapter, the controlling function is presented in three primary topics. First, we describe the conditions that determine the effectiveness of the controlling function. Managerial control is effective when *standards* can be established for the variables that are to be controlled, when *information* is available to measure the established standards, and when managers can take *corrective action* whenever the variable deviates from its desired state, or standard. The Management in Action section provided a description of the corrective actions taken by a Canadian defense contractor in response to deviations from past results.

Second, we provide a basis for classifying and understanding managerial control procedures. Using this classification scheme, we discuss the third topic: managerial control procedures. Managers utilize a number of control procedures, and these *practical* applications are emphasized in this chapter.

Managers in all disciplines are expected to make sound decisions based either on their personal knowledge or on information provided by others. In the past, a key problem facing decision makers was how and where to obtain information. With today's "information explosion," a major problem facing managers lies in determining which of the vast amounts of information available are appropriate and accurate for use in decision making.[2] Toward this end, standards must be established.

Standards are derived from, and have many characteristics of, objectives. Standards are targets. To be effective, they must be stated clearly and related logically to objectives of the unit. Standards are the criteria against which future, current, or past actions are compared, and thus they provide the basis for identifying the type of information needed to make valid comparisons. Standards are measured in a variety of ways, in physical, monetary, quantitative, and qualitative terms. The various forms that standards can take are made clear in our subsequent discussions of control methods.

Managers must provide information that reports actual performance and permits comparison of the performance against standards. Such information is most easily acquired for activities that produce specific and concrete results; for example, production and sales activities have results that are easily identifiable and for which information is readily obtainable. The performance of legal departments, research and development (R&D) departments, and human resource departments, however, is quite difficult to control because the outcomes of such activities are hard to measure.

Managerial actions to correct deviations depend on the discovery of the need for action and the ability to implement the desired action.[3] People responsible for taking corrective steps must know that they are indeed responsible and that they have the assigned authority to take action. Unless managers' job and position descriptions include specific statements clearly delineating these two requirements, the control function falls short of its objective.

In many organizations, responsibility and authority for corrective action are often ambiguous.[4] Numerous organizations consist of so many interdependent units that corrective action must often be taken by individuals who lack the delegated authority but who must nonetheless influence others to accept solutions.

In summary, the control function involves the implementation of methods that provide answers to three basic questions: What are the planned and expected results? By what means can the actual results be compared to planned results? What corrective action is appropriate from which authorized person? All of the planning in the world will be of little value if management fails to establish some type of control system. Planning and controlling are closely related management functions as we will see in this chapter.

Three Types of Control

Figure 10–1 describes three types of managerial control based on the focus of the control.[5] They are preliminary control, concurrent control, and feedback control.

Preliminary control focuses on preventing deviations in the quality and quantity of resources used in the organization. Human resources must meet the job requirements as defined by the organization: Employees must have the physical and intellectual capabilities to perform assigned tasks.[6] Further, these employees must be made aware of the importance of control procedures and therefore view the control function as a critical corporate undertaking.[7] The materials must meet acceptable levels of quality and must be available at the proper time and place. In addition, capital must be on hand to ensure an adequate supply of plant and equipment. Finally, financial resources must be available in the right amounts and at the right times.

FIGURE 10–1   The Controlling Function

Control methods focus on specific elements of the system, either inputs, processes, or outputs.

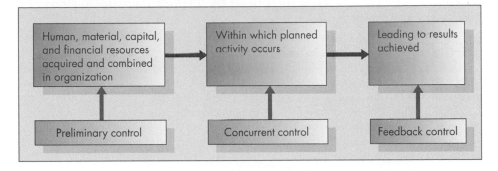

Methods that enable management to implement preliminary control are described later in this chapter.

Concurrent control monitors ongoing operations to ensure that objectives are pursued. The standards guiding ongoing activity are derived from job descriptions and from policies resulting from the planning function. Concurrent control is implemented primarily by the supervisory activities of managers. Through personal, on-the-spot observation, they determine whether the work of others is proceeding in the manner defined by policies and procedures.[8] Delegation of authority provides managers with the power to use financial and nonfinancial incentives to effect concurrent control.

The accompanying Management Focus provides an interesting example of how one company uncovered and was able to correct problems associated with implementation of a new operating procedure.

Feedback control methods focus on end results. Corrective action is directed at improving either the resource acquisition process or the actual operations. This type of control derives its name from the fact that *historical* results guide *future* actions. An illustration of feedback control (see Figure 10–2) is a thermostat, which automatically regulates the temperature of a room. Since the thermostat maintains the preset temperature by constantly monitoring the actual temperature, future results (temperature) are directly and continually determined by historical results (again, temperature). The feedback methods employed in business include budgets, standard costs, financial statements, quality control, and performance evaluation.

In the three types of control, examine the *focus* of corrective action. As shown in Figure 10–3, preliminary control methods are based on information that measures some attribute or characteristic of resources; the focus of corrective action is in turn directed at the resources. That is, the variable measured is the variable acted upon. Similarly, concurrent control methods are based on information related to some activity, and that activity is then acted upon. However, the focus of corrective action associated with feedback control is not that which is measured (results). Rather, resources and activity are acted upon.[9]

This distinction between preliminary, concurrent, and feedback control permits classification of some of the more widely used control techniques, as shown in Table 10–1. As we present the 10 techniques in the remainder of this chapter, our emphasis is on the standards, information, and corrective action appropriate for each technique.[10]

Management Focus

Intangibles Do Affect Business Profits

By and large, executives judge the health and worth of their organization by the value of its financial standing. But there is something going on in successful companies that the most astute and penetrating financial analysts cannot ascertain. Beneath or beyond the frenzy of measuring and quantifying everything from sales revenues to value added throughout the manufacturing process, there are managers who care deeply about the work they do, their employees, and the organization they represent. To ignore this basic human value—caring—is one of the most devastating mistakes that an organization can make.

DuPont Canada recently rediscovered the important relationship between the employee value safety and company operating results when a self-management "thrust" aimed toward increasing profits at one manufacturing facility was implemented. Before the new thrust, DuPont had had an outstanding safety record. However, while productivity, quality, and profits all rose once the new program began, accident reports increased too as employee priorities shifted and stress increased. Deeply concerned about their employees' welfare, top management decided to reemphasize, as the main company priority, three principles that had guided DuPont safety for many decades. These principles were (1) safety has overriding priority; (2) safety is a line responsibility; and (3) any employee deviations from safety rules and practices will not be tolerated.

To put these renewed principles into action, DuPont conducted a series of workshops starting with one led by the company president that was aimed at senior management. This first workshop was immediately followed by others conducted throughout the entire organization. Gradually, the basic commitment to safety that had been entrenched in DuPont Canada employees again prevailed, and while still pursuing the self-management thrust, employees went back to considering safety as one of the most integral aspects of their work. By the mid-90s, the company had gone over two years and almost 20 million worker-hours without a lost workday injury to any of its 4,000-plus employees. And surprisingly, DuPont's return on equity stayed at a level of 10 percent, which put it among the top 15 companies in Canada.

Some estimate that 96 percent of all workplace injuries result from the action of people. Clearly, organizations must develop safety systems that identify these unsafe actions and focus on changing unsafe behaviors. DuPont Canada now conducts regular safety audits that emphasize the behavior of people. All employees participate.

Sources: R Thorburn, "Safety Audits: Focusing on People, Not Things," *PEM: Plant Engineering and Maintenance,* September 1996, p. 86; T E Benson, "Intangibles, The Real Bottom Line," *Industry Week,* August 16, 1993, pp. 19–22; and J M Stewart, "The Multi-Ball Juggler," *Business Quarterly,* Summer 1993, pp. 33–39.

Preliminary Control

Preliminary control procedures include all managerial efforts to increase the probability that actual results compare favorably with planned results. From this perspective, policies are important means for implementing preliminary control, since policies are guidelines for future action. Yet, it is vital to distinguish between *setting* policies and *implementing* them.[11] Setting policy is included in the planning function, whereas implementing policy is a part of the control function.[12] For example, development of a corporate code of conduct is a planning activity. The monitoring and enforcement of the code, on the other hand, can be considered a control activity.[13] Similarly, job descriptions are aspects of the control function, because they predetermine the activity of the jobholder.[14] At the same time, however, it is necessary to distinguish between *defining* and *staffing* the task structure. Defining jobs is part of the organizing function; staffing them is part of the controlling function.

An ominous threat to American business comes from the Japanese *keiretsu,*[15] or business society. The keiretsu serving large manufacturers are composed of several

FIGURE 10–2   Simple Feedback Control System

Feedback control systems are self-correcting.

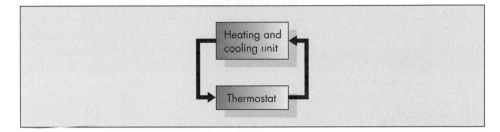

FIGURE 10–3   The Three Types of Control as Distinguished by Focus of Corrective Action

The focus of corrective action may not always be the variable that is measured.

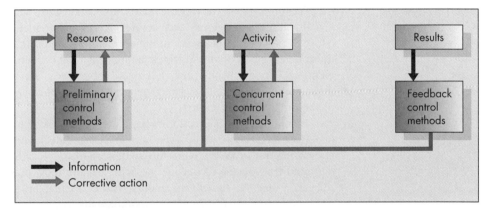

TABLE 10–1   Control Types and Techniques

Managers may use any of the many control techniques available to take corrective action.

Types of Control	Control Techniques
Preliminary	Selection and placement
	Staffing
	Materials inspection
	Capital budgeting
	Financial budgeting
Concurrent	Direction
Feedback	Financial statement analysis
	Standard cost analysis
	Quality control procedures
	Employee performance evaluation

layers of subcontractors. The Mitsubishi group, one of Japan's best-known keiretsu, consists of 28 companies bound together by cross-ownership and other financial ties, interlocking directorates, long-term business relationships, and social and historical links. These keiretsu serve by giving some Japanese companies the ultimate means of preliminary control, a 100 percent probability that suppliers and other associated vendors conform to the manufacturer's plans and objectives.

In addition, use of a keiretsu effectively dictates that US nationals will never be integrated into mainstream management positions in Japanese companies, an aspect that has ominous implications for future trade relations between the United States and Japan.[16]

Human Resources: Selection and Staffing

To succeed, managers must first surround themselves with good people and then give them the tools, training, and encouragement they need to work to their full potential.[17] The organizing function defines the job requirements and predetermines the skill requirements of the jobholders. These requirements vary in degree of specificity, depending on the nature of the task. At the shop level, the skill requirements can be specified in physical attributes and manual dexterity. On the other hand, the job requirements of management and staff personnel are more difficult to define in concrete measurements.[18]

Preliminary control is achieved through procedures that include the selection and placement of managerial and nonmanagerial personnel.[19] We should distinguish between procedures designed to obtain qualified subordinate managers (staffing) and those designed to obtain qualified nonmanagers and operatives (selection and placement). Although basic procedures and objectives are essentially the same, the distinction is important because managerial competence is a fundamental determinant of the organization's success.

Today, employee selection ranks among the most important tasks that managers undertake, for more than ever, employees at all levels of the organization are responsible for making a wide variety of decisions.[20] Candidates for positions must be recruited from inside or outside the firm, and the most promising applicants must be selected from the list of contenders, based on matching an applicant's skills and personal characteristics to the job requirements.

Materials

The raw material that is converted into a finished product must conform to standards of quality.[21] At the same time, a sufficient inventory must be maintained to ensure a continuous flow to meet customer demands. The techniques of inventory control are discussed in a later chapter; at this point, we are concerned only with the quality of incoming materials.

In recent years, numerous methods that use statistical sampling to control the quality of materials have been devised. Samples are inspected rather than the entire lot. These methods take less inspection time, but there is the risk of accepting defective material if the sample does not happen to contain any defective.

A complete discussion of statistical sampling is beyond the scope of this book, but the essence of the procedure can be explained easily. Suppose, for example, that management sets a standard 3 percent level of defective items as a maximum that it will accept from the supplier. The material is inspected by selecting a random sample and calculating the percentage of defective items in that sample. The decision that must then be made, based on the sample, is whether to accept or reject the entire order or to take another sample. Errors can be made in sampling, so that a lot is accepted when it contains more than 3 percent defectives or is rejected when it contains less than 3 percent defectives. The control system constructed is based on balancing the relative costs of these two types of errors.[22]

The preliminary control of materials illustrates a control system that is quite routine. The standard is easily measured, and information (the sample) is readily available. The question of whether to accept or reject materials recurs frequently, and decisions must be made on a fairly regular basis. The decision to accept or reject (or take another sample) is based on straightforward instructions; given the sample results, the decision is automatic. The inspector's instructions may read: "If sample defectives are equal to or less than 3 percent, accept the lot; if sample defectives are equal to or more than 5 percent, reject the lot; if sample defectives are between 3 and 5 percent, take another sample." When a second sample is required, the inspector's actions are determined by another set of instructions.

Capital

The acquisition of capital reflects the need to replace existing equipment or to expand the firm's productive capacity. Capital acquisitions are controlled by establishing criteria of potential profitability that must be met before the proposal is authorized. Such acquisitions ordinarily are included in the *capital budget,* an intermediate and long-run planning document that details the alternative sources and uses of funds. Managerial decisions that involve the commitment of present funds in exchange for future funds are termed *investment decisions.* The methods that serve to screen investment proposals are based on economic analysis.

In this section, we discuss a number of widely used methods. Each involves formulating a standard that must be met to accept the prospective capital acquisition.

The Payback Method.   The simplest method is the payback method. This method calculates the number of years needed for the proposed capital acquisition to repay its original cost out of future cash earnings. For example, a manager is considering a machine that would reduce labor costs by $4,000 per year for each of the four years of its estimated life. The cost of the machine is $8,000, and the tax rate is 50 percent. The additional after-tax cash inflow from which the machine's cost must be paid is calculated as follows:

Additional cash inflow before taxes		
(Labor cost savings)		$4,000
Less: Additional taxes		
Additional income	$4,000	
Depreciation ($8,000 ÷ 4)	2,000	
Additional taxable income	$2,000	
Tax rate	.5	
Additional tax payment		1,000
Additional cash inflow after taxes		$3,000

The payback period can be calculated as follows:

$$\frac{\$8,000}{\$3,000} = 2.67 \text{ years}$$

The proposed machine would repay its original cost in two and two-thirds years; if the standard requires a payback of three years or less, the machine would be an appropriate investment.

The payback method suffers many limitations as a standard for evaluating capital resources. It does not produce a measurement of profitability. More important, it does not take into account the time value of money; that is, it does not recognize that a dollar today is worth more than a dollar at a future date. Other methods include these important considerations.

Despite its flaws, the payback method is still the most widely used method of financial analysis for capital investment decisions.[23] A recent survey found that the payback method is extensively used by corporations in the United States, Japan, and Korea. Seventy-one percent of US corporations, 75 percent of Korean corporations, and 86 percent of Japanese corporations use this approach as an important criterion in long-term investment decisions. The primary reason given for using the payback method is that in situations where the technology changes rapidly and new products become obsolete quickly, corporations should look for investment opportunities that pay back within a short period of time. In this situation, the use of the payback method (along with some other methods) is justified.

Rate of Return on Investment.   One alternative measure of profitability, consistent with methods ordinarily employed in accounting, is the simple rate of return. Using the preceding example, the calculation would be as follows:

Additional gross income		$4,000
Less: Depreciation ($8,000 ÷ 4)	$2,000	
Taxes	1,000	
Total additional expenses		3,000
Additional net income after taxes		$1,000

The rate of return is the ratio of additional net income to the original cost:

$$\frac{\$1,000}{\$8,000} = 12.5\%$$

The calculated rate of return would then be compared to some standard of minimum acceptability, and the decision to accept or reject would depend on that comparison. The measurement of the simple rate of return has the advantage of being easily understood. It has the disadvantage, however, of not including the time value of money. The discounted rate of return method overcomes this deficiency.

Discounted Rate of Return.   The discounted rate of return is a measurement of profitability that takes into account the time value of money. Similar to the payback method, only cash inflows and outflows are considered. The method is widely used because, like the payback method, it can be applied to virtually any capital investment project.[24] In addition, the discounted rate of return considers all the cash inflows an investment will generate, not just those up to the payback point. Based on the preceding example:

$$\$8,000 = \frac{\$3,000}{(1 + r)} + \frac{\$3,000}{(1 + r)^2} + \frac{\$3,000}{(1 + r)^3} + \frac{\$3,000}{(1 + r)^4}$$

$$r = 18\%$$

The discounted rate of return *(r)* is 18 percent, which is interpreted to mean that an $8,000 investment repaying $3,000 in cash at the end of each of four years yields a return of 18 percent.

The rationale of the method can be understood by thinking of $3,000 inflows as cash payments received by the firm. In exchange for each of these four payments of $3,000, the firm must pay $8,000. The rate of return, 18 percent, is the factor equating cash inflows and present cash outflow.[25]

Financial Resources   Adequate financial resources must be available to ensure payment of obligations arising from current operations. Materials must be purchased, wages paid, and interest charges and due dates met. The principal means of controlling the availability and cost of financial resources is budgeting—particularly the budgeting of cash and working capital.

Budgeting should be viewed as an activity undertaken by all managers, not just accountants.[26] Budgets represent plans for future time periods, revealing how management will deal with an uncertain future. More specifically, cash and working capital budgets anticipate the ebb and flow of business activity when materials are purchased, finished goods are produced and inventoried, goods are sold, and cash is received.[27] This operating cycle results in a problem of timing the availability of cash to meet obligations. The simple relationship between cash and inventory is shown in Figure 10–4. When inventories of finished goods increase, the supply of cash decreases as materials, labor, and other expenses are incurred and paid. As inventory is depleted through sales, cash increases. Preliminary control of cash requires that cash be available during the period of inventory buildup and be used wisely during periods of abundance. This requires the careful consideration of alternative sources of short-term financing during inventory buildup and alternative short-run investment opportunities during periods of inventory depletion.

To aid in the process, managers use certain financial ratios. For example, the control standard may be stated in the current ratio (the ratio of current assets to current liabilities), and a minimum and a maximum are set. The minimum ratio could be set at 2:1 and the maximum at 3:1, which would recognize the cost of both too little and too much investment in liquid assets. The control would be in terms of corrective action taken when the actual current ratio deviates from the standard. Other financial ratios contributing to control of financial resources include the acid-test ratio,

---

FIGURE 10–4   Simple Relationship between Cash and Inventory

Understanding cash flows and how they relate to inventory is a critical management skill.

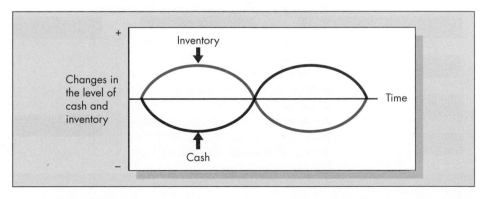

inventory turnover, and average collection period. These ratios are discussed in greater detail in the section on feedback control methods.

Concurrent Control

Concurrent control consists primarily of actions of supervisors who direct the work of their subordinates. **Direction** refers to the acts of managers when they instruct subordinates in proper methods and procedures and oversee subordinates' work to ensure that it is done properly.

Direction follows the formal chain of command, since the responsibility of each superior is to interpret for subordinates the orders received from higher levels. The relative importance of direction depends almost entirely on the nature of the tasks performed by subordinates. The supervisor of an assembly line that produces a component part requiring relatively simple manual operations may seldom engage in direction. On the other hand, the manager of a new product research unit must devote considerable time to direction. Research work is inherently more complex and varied than manual work. So it requires more interpretation and instruction.

Directing is the primary function of the first-line supervisor, but at some time every manager in an organization engages in directing employees. The direction given is guided by the stated goals and policies of the organization as determined in the planning function. As a manager moves up the hierarchy, the importance of directing diminishes as other functions become relatively more important. For example, the chief executive officer devotes considerably more time to the planning and organizing functions.

The scope and content of the direction phase vary according to the nature of the work being supervised, as noted earlier.[28] Also, a number of other factors determine differences in the form of direction. For example, since direction is basically the process of personal communications, the amount and clarity of information are important factors. Subordinates must receive sufficient information to carry out the task and must understand the information that they receive. On the other hand, too much information and too much detail can be damaging. The manager's mode and tone of expression also greatly influence the effectiveness of direction.

The tests of effective direction are related to the characteristics of effective communication. To be effective, a directive must be reasonable, understandable, appropriately worded, and consistent with the overall goals of the organization. Whether these criteria are met is not the manager's decision to make. Rather, it is the subordinate who decides. Many managers have assumed that their directives were straightforward and to the point, only to discover that their subordinates failed to understand or to accept them as legitimate.

The process of direction includes not only the manner in which directives are communicated but also the mannerisms of the person who directs. Whether the supervisor is autocratic or democratic, permissive or directive, considerate or inconsiderate influences the effectiveness of direction as a concurrent control technique.[29] A later chapter delves deeply into leadership behavior and how it influences the performance of individuals and groups.

Direction involves day-to-day oversight of the subordinates' work. As deviations from standards are identified, managers take immediate corrective action through demonstration and coaching their subordinates to perform assigned tasks appropriately.

Management Focus

Control in the Age of Information

Comdisco Disaster Recovery Services, headquartered in Rosemont, Illinois, provides businesses with the ultimate form of control for their information systems. The company offers backup, hot-site facilities for data storage and help in disaster contingency planning to businesses of all kinds, both large and small. Following the occurrence of a disaster at an organization's facility(ies), backup copies of major application programs and other data files can be recovered within 2 to 24 hours from the so-called hot sites.

Regulations exist that require backup plans and storage facilities for data centers operating in the United States. The primary value of Comdisco's services is their providing storage for information contained in personal computer networks primarily used by the marketing and sales functions of an organization, for which type of data there are no laws mandating backup storage facilities.

The aftermath of the 1993 World Trade Center bombing in New York City proved to organizations that greatly rely on information systems the need for having in place a comprehensive disaster-recovery plan. Following the bombing, some companies headquartered in the World Trade Center, including Fiduciary Trust Company International and Fuji Bank Ltd, were able almost immediately to move personnel to Comdisco's office space in North Bergen, New Jersey, and reestablish operations. Since computer professionals backed up data nightly onto tape, these companies' employees needed only to grab the day's trading tickets and data tapes before fleeing the bomb site.

Many other companies were not as fortunate, as millions of TV viewers witnessed. Employees of these companies were shown desperately struggling to lift and move bulky computer equipment as they were being forced to evacuate the scene. In many instances, weeks and even months of valuable data were permanently lost.

More recent disasters such as hurricanes, fires, floods, and "new" disasters such as computer viruses have also underscored the need for control of an organization's information resources. The continuity of business for a company can depend on how quickly they can recover from a disaster. Many companies are now realizing the importance of information control in the age of information.

Sources: T Hoffman, "Disaster Recovery Put to The Test," *Computerworld,* September 16, 1996, p. 12; R Tetzeli, "How to Prepare for a Bombing," *Fortune,* April 5, 1993, pp. 14–16; J Holusha, "The Painful Lessons of Disruption: Exiles from the Trade Center Learn the Drawbacks of the Computer Era," *New York Times,* March 17, 1993, p. C1.

Feedback Control

The distinguishing feature of feedback control methods is a focus on *historical* outcomes as the bases of correcting *future* actions. For example, the financial statements of a firm are used to evaluate the acceptability of historical results and to determine the desirability of making changes in future resource acquisitions or operational activities. In addition, feedback control can be utilized as the basis for making a variety of other decisions, including those related to prices charged for products or services, the dropping of programs or products, reductions or additions to employment, and other means of improving operating results.[30]

This section outlines four feedback control methods widely used in business: financial statement analysis, standard cost analysis, quality control, and employee performance evaluation. Our discussion of these four examples demonstrates the general features of feedback control techniques.

Financial Statement Analysis

A firm's accounting system is a principal source of information from which managers can evaluate historical results. In order to be effective, the system must supply information in a form usable to managers.[31] For example, a manufacturing company may be in the process of implementing a plan to double the growth of a product line over a five-year period. During the course of this process, corporate decision makers would need access to financial information that reported, among other things, sales and profits related to the specific product line. The accompanying Management Focus provides an interesting example of the significance that management places on always having access to up-to-date information.

Managers holding responsibility for overseeing business operations periodically receive a set of financial statements that usually includes a balance sheet, an income statement, and a sources-and-uses-of-funds statement. These statements summarize and classify the effects of transactions in assets, liabilities, equity, revenues, and expenses—the principal components of the firm's financial structure.[32]

A detailed analysis of the financial statements' information enables management to determine the adequacy of the firm's earning power and its ability to meet current and long-term obligations. Managers must have measures of and standards for profitability, liquidity, and solvency. Whether a manager prefers the rate of return on sales, on owner's equity, on total assets, or a combination of all three, it is important to establish a meaningful norm—one that is appropriate to the particular firm, given its industry and stage of growth. An inadequate rate of return negatively affects the firm's ability to attract funds for expansion, particularly if a downward trend over time is evident.

The measures of liquidity reflect the firm's ability to meet current obligations as they become due.[33] The widest known and most often used measure is the current ratio: the ratio of current assets to current liabilities. The standard of acceptability depends on the particular firm's operating characteristics. Bases for comparison are available from trade associations that publish industry averages. A tougher test of liquidity is the acid-test ratio, which relates only cash and near-cash items (current assets, excluding inventories and prepaid expenses) to current liabilities.

The relationship between current assets and current liabilities is an important one. Equally important is the composition of current assets. Two measures that indicate composition and rely on information found in both the balance sheet and income statement are the accounts receivable turnover and the inventory turnover. The accounts receivable turnover is the ratio of credit sales to average accounts receivable. The higher the turnover, the more rapid is the conversion of accounts receivable to cash. A low turnover would indicate a time lag in the collection of receivables, which in turn could strain the firm's ability to meet its own obligations. The appropriate corrective action might be a tightening of credit standards or a more vigorous effort to collect outstanding accounts. The inventory turnover also facilitates the analysis of appropriate balances in current assets. It is calculated as the ratio of cost of goods sold to average inventory. A high ratio could indicate a dangerously low inventory balance in relation to sales, with the possibility of missed sales or a production slowdown. Conversely, a low ratio might indicate an overinvestment in inventory to the exclusion of other, more profitable assets. Whatever the case, the appropriate ratio must be established by the manager, based on the firm's experience within its industry and market.

Another financial measure is solvency, the ability of the firm to meet its long-term obligations—its fixed commitments. The solvency measure reflects the claims of creditors and owners on the assets of the firm. An appropriate balance must be maintained—a balance that protects the interests of the owners yet does not ignore the advantages of long-term debt as a source of funds. A commonly used measure of solvency is the ratio of net income before interest and taxes to interest expense. This indicates the margin of safety; ordinarily, a high ratio is preferred. However, a very high ratio combined with a low debt-to-equity ratio could indicate that management has not taken advantage of debt as a source of funds. The appropriate balance between debt and equity depends on many factors. But as a general rule, the proportion of debt should vary directly with the stability of the firm's earnings.

The ratios discussed earlier are only suggestive of the great number and variety of methods used to evaluate the financial results of the firm. (Accounting as a tool of analysis in management has a long history.)[34] The point here is that financial statement analysis as a part of the management process is clearly a feedback control method.

Standard Cost Analysis

In low-growth business environments, which many organizations are facing, cost reduction is one of few options available to improve performance.[35] Standard cost systems, a major contribution of the scientific management era, provide a means for managers to monitor costs with an aim toward ultimate reduction. A standard cost system provides information that enables management to compare actual costs with predetermined (standard) costs. Management can then take appropriate corrective action or assign to others the authority to take action. The first use of standard costing was to control manufacturing costs. In recent years, standard costing has also been applied to selling, general, and administrative expenses.[36] Here we discuss standard manufacturing costs.

The three elements of manufacturing costs are direct labor, direct materials, and overhead. For each of these, an estimate must be made of cost per unit of output. For example, the direct labor cost per unit of output consists of the standard usage of labor and the standard price of labor. The standard usage derives from time studies that fix the expected output per labor hour; the standard price of labor is fixed by the salary schedule appropriate for the kind of work necessary to produce the output. A similar determination is made for direct materials. Thus, the standard labor and standard materials costs might be as follows:

Standard labor usage per unit	2 hours
Standard wage rate per hour	$ 5.00
Standard labor cost (2 × $5.00)	$10.00
Standard material usage per unit	6 pounds
Standard material price per pound	$ .30
Standard material cost (6 × $.30)	$ 1.80

The accounting system enables the manager to compare incurred costs and standard costs. If during the period covered by the report, for example, 200 units of output were produced, the standard labor cost is $2,000 (200 × $10.00), and the standard material is $360 (200 × $1.80). If the actual payroll cost for that same time period was $2,400 and the actual material cost was $400, there was an *unfavorable labor variance* of $400 and an *unfavorable material variance* of $40. Management must determine the reasons for the variances and decide what corrective action is appropriate.

Assuming that the standards are correct, the manager must analyze the variance and fix the responsibility for restoring the balance between standard and actual costs. It is obvious that if actual labor costs exceed standard labor costs, the reason for the difference is found in labor usage and labor wage rates. Either actual labor usage exceeded standard labor usage or actual wage rates exceeded standard wage rates, or some combination of both. Suppose that, in this example, the accountant reports the actual payroll consisted of 450 actual hours at an average wage rate of $3.33. The questions management must resolve are now narrowed to two: What happened during the period to cause output per labor hour to go down (to produce 200 units of output should require 400 labor hours)? And why was the average wage rate more than the standard wage rate? The answers to these questions are found in the resources and activity stages of the cycle (see Figure 10–3).

Similar analyses are made to discover the causes for the unfavorable material variance. The first step is discovering the relationship between actual and standard usage and between actual and standard price. As with the labor, the manager may find actual material usage exceeded that specified by standard and/or the actual price exceeded the standard price. Once the cause is isolated, the analysis must proceed to fix responsibility for corrective action. The analysis of manufacturing-overhead variance is considerably more complicated than that for labor and material.[37] However, it is still necessary to isolate the causes through comparisons with standards and budgets.

Today, cost accounting practices are undergoing significant changes to keep pace with the rapidly evolving manufacturing environment.[38] A new system of cost accounting based on activity has been advocated by many academicians and practitioners. The underlying principle of activity-based accounting is that activities consume resources and products consume activities. The labor costs of supporting departments can be traced to activities by assessing the portion of each person's time spent on each activity, which can then allow for restatement of departmental cost in activities and their associated costs. Activity costs are then traced to the product based on the amount of activity volume each product consumes. Thus, activity-based costing provides a more accurate means of analyzing costs and distributing overhead. Increasingly, more and more companies, including IBM, Cummins Engine, Unipart, and British Aerospace, have begun implementing forms of activity-based costing.[39]

Quality Control Analysis

The quality of a product measures how closely it conforms to customer expectations.[40] Quality control uses information regarding attributes and characteristics of output to ascertain whether the manufacturing process is in control (i.e., producing acceptable output). To make this determination, the manager must specify the crucial product characteristic. It may be weight, length, consistency, or defects. A major development in the last 10 years or so has been the emergence of concern for product quality, perhaps mostly because of the influx of Japanese imports with a reputation for quality.[41] American business managers have responded by instituting quality-improvement programs.

Management must often be concerned with consistent quantity as well as quality.[42] For example, a peanut butter manufacturer must maintain a minimum quantity of 12 ounces of peanut butter in each container. The company could weigh each container when it is filled—that is, 100 percent of the output could be inspected. An alternative is to inspect samples of output to make inferences about the process, based on the sample information. This latter approach is termed *statistical quality control.* This method makes use of statistical sampling theory, and since the amount of time devoted to inspection is reduced, the cost of inspection is also reduced. Moreover, the acceptable standard of 12 ounces is achieved.

During the past two decades, management thinking about the relationship between quality and productivity has drastically changed.[43] Historically, quality has been viewed largely as a controlling activity that takes place somewhere near the end of the production process, an after-the-fact measurement of production success. As such, efforts to ensure quality increase the costs associated with making available the good

FIGURE 10–5   How Improved Quality Increases Productivity (The Deming Chain Reaction)

Improvements in quality can also result in improvements in productivity.

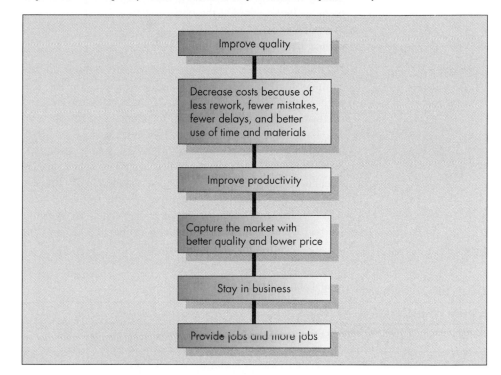

or service. For that reason, quality and productivity have been viewed as conflicting; one is increased at the expense of the other. This assumption has clearly hindered quality improvement in many companies.

Over the years, more and more managers have come to realize that quality is not something that is measured at or near the end of the production process but rather is an essential ingredient of the product or service being produced. As such, quality is an overall approach to doing business and becomes the concern of all members of the organization. When quality comes to be viewed this way, the following conditions prevail:

- The number of defects decreases, which causes output to increase.
- Making it right the first time reduces many of the rejects and much of the rework.
- Making employees responsible for quality eliminates the need for inspection.

These conditions also apply to service quality, whether the service is performed for the customer or for some other department in the same organization. The ultimate result is that quality is viewed as reducing rather than increasing costs.

Today, almost all companies, large and small, try to ensure that their products and services meet the highest quality standards.[44] They have incorporated the concept of quality into their overall strategy through Total Quality Management (TQM) programs, which establish a clear process to understand customer values and perceptions of quality.[45] Customer satisfaction measurements are linked with internal measures of quality to ascertain areas where improvements can be made.

Many of the practices being implemented are based on the work of Dr. W. Edwards Deming, who is credited with helping to make Japan's products world class. Management in some Japanese companies observed 45 years ago that improvement of quality naturally and inevitably leads to improvements in productivity. Once management in Japan adopted the chain reaction illustrated in Figure 10–5, quality became everyone's aim.[46]

Employee Performance Evaluation

No doubt, the most important and difficult feedback control technique is performance evaluation. It is so important because people are the most crucial resource in any organization. As is so often said, "People make the difference."[47] A basic goal of any performance appraisal system is to maintain or improve work performance.[48]

Evaluating people is difficult for several reasons. First, standards for performance are seldom objective and straightforward; many managerial and nonmanagerial jobs do not produce outputs that can be counted, weighed, and evaluated in objective terms. Second, because incentives and rewards are usually based on attainment of standards, managers face discontent when they assign mediocre or low evaluations to employees.[49] Third, the same performance or evaluation system is unlikely to be effective across the spectrum of nations in which a company operates.[50] Because of the

---

TABLE 10–2   Summary of the Controlling Function

Effective control techniques must have standards, information, and corrective action.

Technique	Standards	Information	Corrective Action
1. Job description	Job specifications—skills, experience, education bearing on job success.	Test scores, credentials, background data.	Hire/no hire; remedial training.
2. Selection	Job specifications—skills, experience, education bearing on job success.	Test scores, credentials, background data.	Place/no place; remedial training.
3. Materials inspection	Percent of number defective within tolerance limits.	Sampling of inputs.	Accept, reject, or retest.
4. Capital budgeting	Simple rate of return; payback period; discounted rate of return.	Projected cost, revenue, and engineering data.	Accept, reject.
5. Financial budgeting	Requirements arising out of the forecasting step of planning.	Projected cost, revenue, and engineering data.	Accept, reject; revise.
6. Direction	Required job behavior in end results.	Plans and job specifications.	Change plans and/or job specifications; train, fire people.
7. Financial statement analysis	Relevant data found in trade, banking, and rule-of-thumb sources.	Balance sheet, income statement.	Revise inputs; revise direction.
8. Standard cost analysis	Standard times/usage from engineering studies.	Cost accounting system.	Revise inputs; revise direction.
9. Quality control	Percent or number defective consistent with marketing strategy.	Sampling procedures.	Revise inputs; revise direction.
10. Employee performance evaluation	Job-related performance criteria.	Managerial observations; self-reports.	Retrain, replace personnel; change assigned jobs.

importance of employee performance evaluation, Chapter 15 presents an in-depth discussion of the topic.

Our discussion of the controlling function is conveniently summarized in Table 10–2. The techniques are compared in terms of the standards, information, and corrective action relevant for each one. The table also brings into focus the relationship between the planning function as a source of standards and the organizing function as a source of information. The overriding managerial responsibility is to integrate the three functions into a coherent management process that enables the organization to achieve the levels of performance expected by the individuals and groups that sustain it.

Summary of Key Points

- The controlling function includes activities of managers to ensure that actual results conform to planned results. The controlling function logically follows the planning and organizing functions.
- The three necessary requirements for effective control are predetermined standards, information, and corrective action.
- Three types of control can be identified that are based on the focus of corrective action. Preliminary control focuses on inputs; concurrent control focuses on ongoing operations; feedback control focuses on inputs and ongoing operations.
- The controlling function is highly developed in management practice. A great number of methods and systems allow managers to attain high levels of performance in the controlling function.
- Preliminary control methods require standards of acceptable quality and quantity of inputs, such as material, financial, capital, and human resources.

- Information permitting managers to determine whether resources meet standards allows for corrective action.
- Concurrent control methods require standards of acceptable behavior, activity, and execution of ongoing operations. The primary source of information for concurrent control is supervisors' observations; the corrective action is directed toward improving the quality and quantity of resources and improving the operations.
- Feedback control methods require standards of acceptable quality and quantity of outputs. The information must reflect the desired characteristics of the output. But unlike preliminary and concurrent control, the focus of corrective action is not that for which the standard is set (output). Rather, managers take corrective action to improve inputs and operations.

Discussion and Review Questions

1. Using an example, explain why the planning and control functions cannot exist without one another. Should one function be given priority status over the other? Why or why not?
2. Standards are derived from objectives. How might the setting of inappropriate objectives lead to the setting of inappropriate standards? Illustrate, using an example.
3. Describe how managers at a bank could utilize preliminary control procedures. Would their efforts differ significantly from those of managers at a manufacturing company? Why or why not?
4. A lack of organizational control can lead to disastrous results. When could too strict adherence to organizational control mechanisms lead to disastrous results?
5. Describe how the owner of a small bakery could utilize cost and quality control procedures to improve the operating performance of her business.

6. A number of standards have been discussed as measures of investment profitability. These measures include the payback period, the rate of return, and the discounted rate of return. Illustrate cases in which each of these profitability measures may be considered superior to the others.
7. How might an organization utilize control procedures to help ensure that employees adhere to high ethical standards?
8. Under which circumstances would the use of feedback control procedures be inappropriate?
9. Why might managers have to make trade-offs between adherence to various types of control mechanisms (e.g., between cost and quality controls)?
10. If employee performance evaluations have to be based on subjective criteria, should they be utilized at all? What is the reasoning behind your answer?

CASE 10–1
BENCHMARKING PRACTICES AT XEROX

Benchmarking deserves credit for inspiring some legendary corporate turnarounds; Ford's resurgence with the Taurus and Sable models and Motorola's dramatic improvements in quality and cycle times are just two examples. Benchmarking has become a mainstream tool, used by many organizations to remain competitive in the global marketplace. To be effective, benchmarking not only needs solid support from top management, but must also become an integral part of the entire organization, cascading down to every employee.

In today's business environment, benchmarking projects are numerous and cottage industries have sprung up to support them; in the last year alone, over half a dozen books on benchmarking have hit the stands and the number of benchmarking consultants has grown considerably.

The formal definition of benchmarking is the continuous process of measuring products, services, and business practices against those of the toughest competitors or companies renowned as leaders. Xerox pioneered benchmarking in the late 70s when it suddenly found that the Japanese had more than a 40 percent cost advantage in copiers and that Xerox's own market share in copiers had severely declined. Xerox CEO David Kearns initially launched the successful "Leadership through Quality" program to boost product quality and reduce manufacturing costs. Since then, Xerox senior management has required all organizations within Xerox to pursue benchmarking.

There are four major types of benchmarking activities pursued at Xerox: internal, functional, generic, and competitive. The theory behind *internal* benchmarking maintains that, because large organizations have multiples of the same units set up to perform similar activities, information can easily be shared among similar units to the company's advantage. At Xerox, the company utilizes internal benchmarking as a device to transfer opinions, ideas, and information (regarding best internal practices) among its divisions. In keeping with this idea, for example, the US customer operations division chose its sister affiliate in Canada as the benchmark for improving its customer service process.

Functional benchmarking is the story of Xerox's learning relationship with L L Bean. In the early 1980s, the members of Xerox's benchmarking review team asked, "Who's the best external benchmark for customer order processing?" Surprisingly, the answer was not other high-tech companies such as IBM, Cannon, or Minolta. Rather, it was L L Bean, which picked its orders manually as did Xerox. The big difference was that Bean was three times faster. Thus, Bean became Xerox's functional benchmark in the area of order processing. In essence, functional benchmarking focuses on determining and subsequently implementing best practices, regardless of the industry they are found in.

Generic benchmarking has become one of Xerox's most important focal points. Xerox identified numerous basic business processes, such as order taking, in which they sought improvement. One individual was assigned to oversee improvements in each of 10 areas encompassing the 67 identified processes. These process owners became responsible for documenting specific means of improving processes, overseeing implementation of organizational benchmarking activities regarding the individual processes, and resolving cross-functional disputes arising from resource allocation.

Finally, *competitive* benchmarking entails uncovering competitor practices that can then be implemented and improved upon within an organization. For example, prior to benchmarking, Xerox had four places where it stored and handled material. After reviewing top-competitor practices, Xerox changed its materials management structure to be more in line with that of its competitors. As a result, materials-handling operations have been significantly streamlined without any accompanying loss of service quality.

In total, has benchmarking paid off for Xerox? Well, consider this. Since embarking on its benchmarking quest, Xerox has been able to cut manufacturing costs in half, reduce inventories by two-thirds, increase overall organizational productivity significantly, and achieve almost 100 percent parts acceptance from customers. As a result, Xerox has been able to reclaim the market leadership position that had once been threatened.

Questions for Analysis

1. Can benchmarking be used successfully by all businesses, both large and small? Why or why not?

2. A critical component of functional benchmarking is identification of companies that employ best practices. How would an organization go about finding such companies?

3. What incentives exist for an organization like L L Bean to share the secret of its "best practice" with Xerox?

4. Provide examples of how one or several actual companies (besides those mentioned in the case) could employ each of the four types of benchmarking activities to improve operating results.

Sources: J M Vezmar, "Competitive Intelligence at Xerox," *Competitive Intelligence Review,* Fall 1996, pp. 15–19; R C Camp, "A Bible for Benchmarking by Xerox," *Financial Executive,* July–August, 1993, pp. 23–27; L S Pryor and S J Katz, "How Benchmarking Goes Wrong (and How to Do It Right)," *Planning Review,* January–February 1993, pp. 6–14.

VIDEO CASE
ORGANIZATIONAL CONTROL

Managerial control is the process of measuring progress toward planned performance and, if necessary, taking corrective action. Typically, managerial control includes the use of financial controls, quality controls, and human resource controls. To ensure that planned activities occur in each of these critical areas, managers must set performance standards, measure performance, compare performance with the standard, and take corrective action if it's needed. Emphasizing the need for *measurable* goals, First National Bank of Chicago Senior Vice President Richard J. Gilgan said, "You can't manage what you don't understand, and you don't understand what you don't measure. So measurement is critical to understanding where our performance is improving or not improving, where we have problems, and we can then go back and identify the root causes of those problems."

All managers are involved in controlling one or more of the three critical areas identified in the videotape, financial, quality, and human resources. Techniques and examples are discussed for each.

Financial Controls

Financial controls are implemented by a company so that it can measure and control activities that yield quantitative data such as sales (in dollars), inventory (in units), and productivity per worker. Budgeting is the most common type of financial control. Every company develops budgets that compare past, present, and anticipated future performance. Budgets allow managers to plan for and track the success of their business. Some of the work processes that are controlled through budgeting include sales and income forecasts; production budgets for input, output, and capacity of machinery; and cash budgets that measure anticipated receipts and expenses so a company can determine its working capital needs.

As an example of financial control through the use of budgets, consider the potato chip sales of Nalley Fine Foods. Sales of potato chips generate revenue for the company. All of the materials that go into producing the chips are expenses or costs. Besides the cost of materials, there are other costs that must be accounted for, such as direct labor costs, machinery costs, and additional overhead such as management and administrative expenses, marketing costs, and distribution expenses. A simple budget for potato chip sales for Nalley Fine Foods might look something like the following:

	Sales
−	Expenses
	Profit

A more detailed budget would provide a line item for each expense, and would probably include a line item by customer for sales. With such detail, Nalley managers could determine ways to reduce costs or improve sales. Even with the extra detail, however, in essence the budget is summarized by the simple equation above.

Other types of financial controls that businesses typically use are the balance sheet, profit and loss statement, and financial ratios. These measures give managers a clear picture of how their business is performing from a financial perspective.

Quality Controls

The emphasis of the quality control function is to eliminate manufacturing defects, improve customer service, and to institute procedures that emphasize doing things right the first time. Effective quality controls can often lead to cost reductions and higher rates of customer satisfaction. Motorola, for example, has made quality control a centerpiece of its overall operations. Their famous "Six-Sigma" quality program strives to attain a defect rate of no more than 3.4 per million. To attain this remarkably low defect rate, Motorola has made use of statistical quality control techniques a part of every employee's job. Former Motorola CEO Robert Galvin, the man who brought the quality approach to the company said, "Quality saves money, and makes products appealing and attractive. Anything that's wrong is costing you money. If you get the process exactly right, it's going to be cheaper and it's going to be better."

Quality management is a process that continually improves performance at every level of the organization. Management takes responsibility for the quality of what's produced, and develops cooperative systems with employees to create solutions to organizational problems. The complete changeover to a quality management approach may take time, but the benefits can be worth it. A successful quality management approach creates a work environment where all workers can achieve high performance and participate in all levels of decision making.

Human Resource Controls

The human resources of an organization are a vital key to its success. To effectively manage the use of human resources, management needs a control system that includes two basic components: valid and acceptable performance standards, and adequate information communicated between employees and management. Setting appropriate standards incorporates all important aspects of performance, and strikes a balance between too few controls and too many. Employee participation in decisions that directly affect their jobs is one way of ensuring reasonable, acceptable standards. Feedback from employees is necessary to accomplish this. The workforce also gains important information about accepted performance through feedback from management.

Listening to the staff enables empathy, trust, and esteem to grow within an organization. One way a manager can demonstrate how to use listening skills is to get out on the floor and actively participate in the work that is being done. This has been called "management by walking around" or MBWA. As one hospital administrator put it, "If you want to improve service in an organization, you have to make the frontline people feel as if they're valued. And if they're well treated, they'll pass it on."

By establishing valid and acceptable standards, and by providing adequate information and feedback to employees, a companywide commitment is fostered. The primary goal of the managerial controlling function is to measure actual performance, and to implement corrective action, so that performance meets expected plans. This goal is achieved through the four steps of the control process:

- Setting standards.
- Measuring performance.
- Comparing performance with standards.
- Taking corrective action.

The understanding of managerial control gives management insight into questions like "What can be done to increase sales revenue?" or "What can be done to increase this organization's efficiency?" The answers to these questions are the starting points for feedback or corrective action processes in organizational control.

Critical Thinking Questions

1. The videotape identified the three primary types of organizational control as financial, quality, and human resources. Describe instances in which controlling one of these areas may influence organizational performance in another. How should managers deal with this interaction?

2. Managerial control requires establishing clear performance standards. Why do you think it's necessary to have measurable standards? Can you think of some types of organizational performance that will be difficult to measure?

3. Quality control is becoming an increasingly important element of the overall performance of organizations. Even business schools are concerned about the quality of services they provide. Think of some quality control measures that a business school could use to determine its performance. Do you think your business school is performing at an optimal level on these measures? How could it improve?

EXPERIENTIAL EXERCISE
PAPER PLANE CORPORATION

Purpose

The purpose of this exercise is to work on a task that requires planning, organizing, and controlling.

The Exercise in Class

Unlimited groups of six participants each are used in this exercise. These groups may be directed simultaneously in the same room. Approximately a full class period is needed to complete the exercise. Each person should have assembly instructions and a summary sheet plus ample stacks of paper (8 by 11 inches). The physical setting should be a room large enough so individual groups of six can work without interference from other groups. A work area should be provided for each group.

The participants are doing an exercise in production methodology. Each group must work independently of the other groups. The objective is to make paper airplanes in the most profitable manner possible.

Scenario.   Your group is the complete workforce for Paper Plane Corporation. Established in 1943, Paper Plane has led the market in paper plane production. Currently under new management, the company is contracting to make aircraft for the US Air Force. You must establish a plan and organization to produce these aircraft. You must make your contract with the Air Force under the following conditions:

The Air Force will pay $20,000 per airplane.

The aircraft must pass a strict inspection.

A penalty of $25,000 per airplane will be imposed for failure to meet the production requirements.

Labor and other overhead will be computed at $300,000. Cost of materials will be $3,000 per bid plane. If you bid for 10 but make only 8, you must pay the cost of materials for those you failed to make or that did not pass inspection.

Summary Sheet

Round 1:

Bid: _____ aircraft @ $20,000.00 per aircraft

= _____

Results: _____ aircraft @ $20,000.00 per

aircraft = _____

Less: $300,000.00 overhead

_____ × $3,000 cost of raw materials

_____ × $25,000 penalty

Profit: _____

Round 2:

Bid: _____ aircraft @ $20,000.00 per aircraft

= _____

Results: _____ aircraft @ $20,000.00 per

aircraft = _____

Less: $300,000.00 overhead

_____ × $3,000 cost of raw materials

_____ × $25,000 penalty

Profit: _____

Round 3:

Bid: _____ aircraft @ $20,000.00 per aircraft

= _____

Results: _____ aircraft @ $20,000.00 per

aircraft − _____

Less: $300,000.00 overhead

_____ × $3,000 cost of raw materials

_____ × $25,000 penalty

Profit: _____

Activity.   Use the summary sheet to record the activities of the groups in each round of the exercise. Rounds are timed events utilizing competition among the groups:

1. Your group should choose a manager and an inspector, and the remaining participants will be employees.

2. The facilitator will give the signal to start each 10-minute round, during which your group should act out the above scenario.

3. After the first round, your group should report its production and profits to the entire class, explaining the manner in which you planned, organized, and controlled for the production of the paper airplanes.

4. This same procedure is followed for as many rounds as there is time.

The Learning Message

This exercise is an application of the planning, organizing, and controlling management functions. It illustrates how these functions, if applied, can improve the end result or performance.

Instructions for Aircraft Assembly

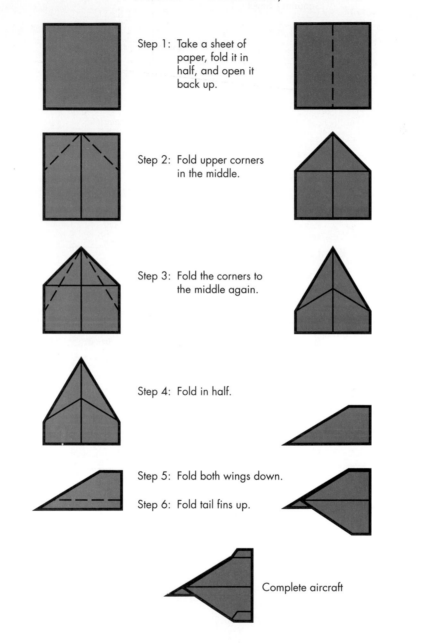

Step 1: Take a sheet of paper, fold it in half, and open it back up.

Step 2: Fold upper corners in the middle.

Step 3: Fold the corners to the middle again.

Step 4: Fold in half.

Step 5: Fold both wings down.

Step 6: Fold tail fins up.

Complete aircraft

Notes

1. For other definitions of management control, see Kenneth A Merchant, *Control in Business Organizations* (Marshfield, MA: Pitman, 1985); Robert J Mockler, *The Management Control Process* (Englewood Cliffs, NJ: Prentice Hall, 1972).

2. George Kress, "Turning Information into Knowledge," *IM,* March–April 1993, pp. 30–32.

3. Richard L Daft and Norman B Macintosh, "The Nature and Use of Formal Control Systems for Management Control and Strategy Implementation," *Journal of Management,* Spring 1984, pp. 43–66.

4. Michel Lebas and Jane Weigenstein, "Management Control: The Role of Rules, Markets, and Culture," *Journal of Management Studies,* May 1986, pp. 259–72.

5. In this section, we identify feedback control as a separate type. Feedback is also viewed as part of the broader concept of control insofar as it refers to the information reported to the manager. Also see Peter Lorange, M F S Morton, and S Goshal, *Strategic Control* (St. Paul, MN: West, 1985).

6. Preliminary control of human resources is one element of personnel management. See John M Ivancevich and William Glueck, *Foundations of Personnel,* 5th ed. (Burr Ridge, IL: Richard D. Irwin, 1992).

7. For a discussion of how organizations educate employees regarding the importance of control procedures, see Allena Leonard and William Bradshaw, "Assessing Management Control," *CMA Magazine,* April 1993, pp. 25–30.

8. Lawrence L Steinmetz and H Ralph Todd, Jr., *First-Line Management,* 3d ed. (Burr Ridge, IL: Richard D. Irwin, 1986).

9. Stephen G Green and M Ann Welsh, "Cybernetics and Dependence: Reframing the Control Concept," *Academy of Management Review,* April 1988, pp. 287–301.

10. See Kiyoshi Suzaki, *The New Manufacturing Challenge: Techniques for Continuous Improvement* (New York: Free Press, 1987). The theme of this work is that control is an ongoing and continuing process.

11. Peter Lorange and Declan Murphy, "Considerations in Implementing Strategic Control," *Journal of Business Strategy,* Spring 1984, pp. 27–35.

12. George Schreyogg and Horst Steinman, "Strategic Control: A New Perspective," *Academy of Management Review,* January 1987, pp. 91–103.

13. Mahendra Gujarathi and K Raghunandan, "Management Reporting on Internal Control: An Update," *Internal Auditing,* Summer 1993, pp. 13–23.

14. See Luis R Gomez-Mejia, Henry Tosi, and Timothy Hinkin, "Managerial Control, Performance, and Executive Compensation," *Academy of Management Journal,* March 1987, pp. 51–170.

15. For a detailed explanation of keiretsu and their impending threat to American companies, see Charles H Ferguson, "Computers and the Coming of the U.S. Keiretsu," *Harvard Business Review,* July–August 1990, pp. 55–70; William J Holstein, et al., "Mighty Mitsubishi Is on the Move," *Business Week,* September 24, 1990, pp. 98–107.

16. Simon Beechler, "International Management Control in Multinational Corporations," *ASEAN Economics Bulletin,* November 1992, pp. 149–68.

17. David Fagiano, "Old Wine in New Bottles," *Management Review,* September 1993, p. 4.

18. For a related discussion, see Richard E Walton, "From Control to Commitment in the Workplace," *Harvard Business Review,* March–April 1985, pp. 76–84.

19. Ivancevich and Glueck, *Foundations of Personnel,* chap. 2.

20. "The Future of Middle Managers," *Management Review,* September 1993, pp. 51–53.

21. At this point, note that quality is important in services as well as products. Later in the chapter, we discuss service quality.

22. See Joel G Siegel and Matthew S Rubin, "Corporate Planning and Control through Variance Analysis," *Managerial Planning,* September–October 1984, pp. 33–36, for a related discussion.

23. Il-Woon Kim and Ja Song, "U.S., Korea, and Japan: Accounting Practices in Three Countries," *Management Accounting,* August 1990, pp. 26–30.

24. For a discussion on the merits of calculating cash flows, see Julie Gable, "Net Present Value: A Financial Tool for Complicated Times," *Records Management Quarterly,* January 1992, pp. 3–5, 18.

25. The time value of money is explicitly considered in the method in the following way. If we remember that 18 percent is the rate of return and that there are four distinct and separate future receipts of $3,000, we can see that $8,000 is the *present value* of the future proceeds.

   $2,542 = Present value of $3,000 to be received = $3,000 in 1 year, or $2,542 × 1.18

   $2,155 = Present value of $3,000 to be received = $3,000 in 2 years, or $2,155 × $(1.18)^2$

   $1,826 = Present value of $3,000 to be received = $3,000 in 3 years, or $1,826 × $(1.18)^3$

   1,547 = Present value of $3,000 to be received = $3,000 in 4 years, or $1,547 × $(1.18)^4$

   $8,070 = Total present value; error due to rounding

26. For a discussion of the importance of involving all managers in the budgeting process, see Robert G Finney, "Budgeting: From Pain to Power," *Management Review,* September 1993, pp. 27–31.

27. Frank Collins, Paul Munter, and Don W Finn, "The Budgeting Games People Play," *Accounting Review,* January 1987, pp. 29–49.

28. For an excellent discussion of problems in managing professional employees, see Joseph A Raelin, "The Basis for the Professional's Resistance to Managerial Control," *Human Resource Management,* Summer 1985, pp. 147–75.

29. Barry Waldon, "The Human Side of Control," *Supervisory Management,* June 1985, pp. 34–39.

30. Ronell B Raaum and Edwin Soniat, "Measurement Based Performance Audits: A Tool for Downsizing Government," *Government Accountants Journal,* Summer 1993, pp. 61–71.

31. For a discussion of this topic, see Lucy R Ricciardi, "Is Your Data Integrated—And under Your Control?" *Financial Executive,* July–August 1993, pp. 30–32.

32. Burton A Kolb and Richard DeMong, *Principles of Financial Management,* 2d ed. (Burr Ridge, IL: Richard D. Irwin, 1988); Diane Harrington and Brent D Wilson, *Corporate Financial Analysis,* 2d ed. (Burr Ridge, IL: Richard D. Irwin, 1986).

33. Avi Rushinek and Sara F Rushinek, "Using Financial Ratios to Predict Insolvency," *Journal of Business Research,* February 1987, pp. 74–77.

34. A C Littleton, *Accounting Evolution to 1900* (New York: Russell & Russell, 1966).

35. Rodgers L Harper, "Practical Approaches to Making Cost Reduction Work," *The Bankers Magazine,* May–June 1993, pp. 16–21.

36. Ralph H Garrison, *Managerial Accounting: Concepts for Planning, Control, Decision Making,* 5th ed. (Burr Ridge, IL: Richard D. Irwin, 1988).

37. The reader can consult any text in cost accounting and management accounting for discussions of standard cost analysis. We also recommend Robert S Kaplan, "One Cost System Isn't Enough," *Harvard Business Review,* January–February 1988, pp. 63–70.

38. For a full explanation of activity-based accounting systems, see Henry J Johansson, "Preparing for Accounting System Changes," *Management Accounting,* July 1990, pp. 37–41.

39. Neasea MacErlean, "A New Dawn for Western Management?" *Accountancy,* June 1993, pp. 40–41.

40. For a discussion of costs related to quality, see Wayne J Morse, "A Handle on Quality Costs," *CMA Magazine,* February 1993, pp. 21–24.

41. Several excellent works are available on quality control and approaches to quality improvement. Especially noteworthy are W Edwards Deming, *Quality, Productivity, and Competitive Position* (Cambridge, MA: MIT Press, 1982); A V Feigenbaum, *Total Quality Control* (New York: McGraw-Hill, 1983); Richard J Schonberger, *World Class Manufacturing: The Lessons of Simplicity Applied* (New York: Free Press, 1986), pp. 123–43.

42. David A Garvin, "Competing on the Eight Dimensions of Quality," *Harvard Business Review,* November–December 1987, pp. 101–9.

43. Everette E Adam, Jr., James C Hershauer, and William A Ruch, *Productivity and Quality* (Englewood Cliffs, NJ: Prentice Hall, 1981).

44. For a discussion of quality efforts being undertaken by small businesses, see Michael Price and E Eva Chen, "TQM in a Small, High-Technology Company," *California Management Review,* Spring 1993, pp. 96–117.

45. Kaye Hamilton-Smith and Ted Morris, "What Management Accountants Should Know about Market-Driven Quality," *CMA Magazine,* May 1993, pp. 23–25.

46. Summarized from W Edwards Deming, *Out of the Crises* (Cambridge, MA: MIT Center for Advanced Engineering Study, 1986). For some interesting examples of quality improvement efforts by US businesses, see Otis Port, "The Push for Quality," *Business Week,* June 8, 1987, pp. 130ff.

47. This important but often overlooked point is forcefully made in Tom Peters, *Thriving on Chaos* (New York: Alfred A. Knopf, 1987).

48. See David A Waldman and Ron S Kenett, "Improve Performance by Appraisal," *HR Magazine,* July 1990, pp. 66–69, for a detailed discussion of the use of performance appraisals.

49. For a discussion of this topic, see Alfie Kohn, "Why Incentive Plans Cannot Work," *Harvard Business Review,* September–October 1993, pp. 54–62; Kevin J Murphy, "Performance Measurement and Appraisal: Merck Tries to Motivate Managers to Do It Right," *Employment Relations Today,* Spring 1993, pp. 47–62.

50. Graeme L Harrison, "Reliance on Accounting Performance Measures in Superior Evaluative Style—The Influence of National Culture and Personality," *Accounting Organizations and Society* 18 (1993), pp. 319–39.

III MANAGING PEOPLE IN ORGANIZATIONS

Leading

11   MOTIVATION

Chapter Learning Objectives

After completing Chapter 11, you should be able to:

- **Define** the meaning of motivation.
- **Describe** the difference between content, process, and reinforcement theories of motivation.
- **Discuss** why most behavior is thought to be goal directed.
- **Compare** the distinguishing characteristics of the reinforcement and expectancy theories of motivation.
- **Identify** the five core motivational dimensions used in job enrichment.

Work Ethics, Fairy Tales, and Motivation

Is motivation a part of a society's moral and social fabric? In 1904, Max Weber proposed that Protestant values as articulated by the followers of John Calvin helped motivate people to work hard. The presence of the Protestant work ethic of working hard is still claimed to be an important indication of a society's ability to achieve.

In *The Achieving Society,* social psychologist David McClelland stated that achievement is built into a society that has a Protestant work ethic. Our society projects values that are embedded in our children's stories. The key to economic growth is proposed to be a deeply felt *need* to achieve. America's Protestant work ethic has been influenced by the melting pot and cultural differences among Germans, Irish, Mexicans, Haitians, Iranians, Swedes, Pakistanis, Indians, Nigerians, Vietnamese, and many others who have brought with them their own work ethics, fairy tales, and needs.

As trade barriers come down in Mexico, Latin America, Africa, and Eastern Europe, the notion of worker motivation has become a serious concern. Do the Russians, Argentines, Nigerians, and Hungarians have the values and orientation to produce a motivated workforce that can compete with workers of other nations, such as Japan, Germany, and the United States?

For example, a McClelland-type analysis of the East European societal makeup might suggest that a work ethic just doesn't exist. When the society is not motivated, how can Vladimir, Miroslav, and Yani be motivated in these societies?

The fairy tales that Russian children read have no work ethic themes. For example, one hero is the crafty peasant Yemeh whose central ambition is to lie atop a warm oven and get what he wants by magic. Yemeh doesn't work hard to achieve. He just slumbers and waits for magic to happen.

Some of the newer fairy tales in the former Soviet Union, however, do emphasize hard work. One example is the tale of the tiger who gets his stripes back. The tiger lost his stripes because he was afraid of everything. One stormy night, the tiger's mother became ill. The tiger braved bad weather, cold, and danger, and rowed across a lake to find a doctor. The mother was saved, and the tiger recovered his stripes.

Like Americans, most individuals are influenced by the folklore, fairy tales, work orientation, and also the diversity of their society. Economic growth, productivity, and improved standards of living can possibly be affected by stories of magic, laziness, dishonesty, and hocus-pocus. The work ethic of a society plays a role in the motivation profiles, patterns, and orientations of individual workers.

Although this chapter illustrates individual examples, the societal fabric discussed by Weber and McClelland plays a role in our levels of motivation. Which fairy tales did *you* read, hear about, and memorize? Those stories, as well as your whole cultural background, probably help explain your motivational makeup.

Sources: Adapted from Robert Hayles and Armida Mendez Russell, *The Diversity Directive* (New York: McGraw Hill, 1997); Maurice Meisner, *The Deng Xiaoping Era* (New York: Hill and Wang, 1997); Joan Warner, "Where on Earth You Can Turn," *Business Week,* December 30, 1996, pp. 100–2; M Kueter, "The Smorgasbord of Life," *Business Ethics,* October 1993, p. 46; and Y Ambartsumov, "The Urgency of Reform," *Business in the U.S.S.R.,* October 1990, p. 13.

Motivation is concerned with the "why" of human behavior. Why do people do things? Why does Harry have frequent run-ins with the boss? Why does Dianne work so much harder than Jim? Answering such questions is greatly aided by an understanding of human motivation. In this chapter, motivation is the main focal point because it is important to management for three reasons: First, employees on the job must be motivated to perform at an acceptable level; second, managers themselves must be motivated to do a good job; third, employees (managerial and nonmanagerial) must be motivated to join the organization.

What Is Motivation?

Motivation has been defined as "all those inner-striving conditions described as wishes, desires, drives, etc. . . . It is an inner state that activates or moves."[1] From a manager's perspective, a person who is motivated:

FIGURE 11–1   **The Process of Motivation**

Motivation starts with an unsatisfied need and drives behavior toward satisfaction.

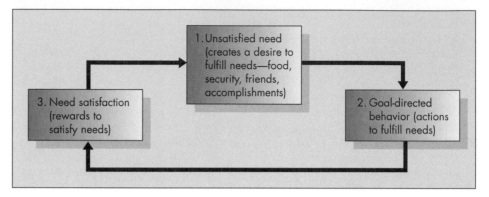

- Works hard.
- Sustains a pace of hard work.
- Has self-directed behavior toward important goals.

Thus, motivation involves effort, persistence, and goals.[2] It involves a person's desire to perform. The actual performance is what managers can evaluate to determine indirectly the person's desire.

When a person's performance is determined to be unsatisfactory, low motivation is often considered the problem. Certainly, in many cases, that is true. However, performance problems are not automatically caused by low levels of motivation. Other factors, such as shortage of resources or lack of skills, may be the cause of poor performance. It is important not to immediately conclude that performance difficulties are motivation problems. As the accompanying Management Focus describes, some individuals simply "hit" what is called the "motivation wall." That is, they are simply burned out and can't get themselves started or energized.

The Motivation Process

An **unsatisfied need** is the starting point in the process of motivation. A deficiency of something within the individual, it is the first link in the chain of events leading to behavior. The unsatisfied need causes tension (physical or psychological) within the individual, leading the individual to engage in some kind of behavior to satisfy the need and thereby reduce the tension. Note in Figure 11–1 that this activity is directed toward a goal. Achieving the goal satisfies the need, and the process of motivation is complete. For example, an achievement-oriented person is driven by the desire to succeed and is motivated by a desire for a promotion and/or accomplishment to satisfy the need.

Each year *Fortune* publishes a list of fascinating, exceptional business leaders who join its "Wall of Business Fame."[3] The descriptive stories for each honored member indicate that goal directedness is a common characteristic of each person. A few of the goal-oriented leaders presented in *Fortune* follow:

- *Lee Iacocca,* past chairperson of Chrysler Corporation and retired president of Ford Motor Co., was totally goal oriented as a top executive. His goal was to run a car company that put pride into the label "Made in America." Iacocca enjoyed his accomplishments, such as turning Chrysler around, putting the convertible back on the road, and presiding over the Mustang.

- *Katharine Graham* became publisher of the *Washington Post* following the death of her husband. Although she lacked business expertise, she was intelligent and determined to succeed. She surrounded herself with talented managers. Her goal was to operate a successful newspaper, and she accomplished it through hard work.

- *Samuel Curtis Johnson,* president of S. C. Johnson & Son, believed that environmentalism and sound management would be good for business. He was right. In the mid-1970s, scientific reports warned that chemicals in aerosol sprays might harm the earth's ozone layer. Johnson studied the reports and made up his mind to change his products. His company was one of the largest sellers of aerosol cans—Raid bug spray and Glade air freshener. Johnson set a goal of being environmentally safe long before it became accepted practice in corporate America.

- *Jack Welch,* CEO General Electric, is an enthusiastic supporter of "stretch goals"—goals that are very challenging and difficult to accomplish. Welch believes that stretch goals were used by Toshiba to produce its new VCR. Welch states that Toshiba had a stretch goal to produce the new VCR with half the parts, in half the time, and at half the cost.[4]

Is everyone goal directed? A lot of people are asking this question. The obvious answer is no. There is, however, enough evidence to suggest that most people are goal directed.

Companies such as AT&T, Apple Computer, McDonald's Corporation, and Merck & Co. have paid $1,000 and up to send employees to a course that emphasizes goals.[5] The goals-oriented course occurs at Pecos River Learning Center near Santa Fe, New Mexico. The originator of the mostly physical approach to goal setting was the Outward Bound program. At the center, employees are expected to work in teams and complete a number of physically demanding tasks such as climbing a mountain, scaling a 25-foot-high telephone pole with wooden rungs, and riding a cable that stretches above the Pecos River. These tasks demand strategy, teamwork, some physical exertion, and taking risks.

The Pecos River Learning Center experience points out that goal-directed behavior can be channeled, it can be inspirational, and it can result in need satisfaction. Climbing a wall or riding a cable zip line across the river is not so different from attempting to manage 10 employees, taking a new job, or preparing a report with very little time available. Goals are what we all point toward every day in our personal lives, at work, and in our communities.

Understanding Motivation: The Use of Theories

Many theories of motivation exist that managers can use to improve their understanding of why people behave as they do. None provides a universally accepted explanation of human behavior. People are far too complex. Our purpose in presenting the most popular theories is not to identify the one best approach. Rather, it is to introduce ideas that managers can use to develop their own motivational approaches.

Management Focus

Hitting the Motivation Wall

Many people have achieved great fame and fortune before turning 40. Mozart died five years before reaching 40. Alexander the Great conquered Asia Minor and died at age 34. Steve Jobs cofounded Apple Computer in his late 20s, and Tom Monaghan founded Domino's, which is now one of the largest home-delivery pizza chains, when he was 23 years old. When comedian Jack Benny was in his 60s and 70s, he used to get laughs by claiming to be 39 instead of what he really was, say 74. Why did Benny pick 39?

Some consider 39 to be the last gasp of youth. In business, the goal to be president or the ambition to invent a world-renowned product may run smack into reality at 40. A 40-year-old often has a long history of work experience, including a few scars from failures.

Many 39-year-olds and even younger men and women have accomplished a lot. They may have been promoted every three or four years, and their compensation packages may be in six figures. They may also have realized that the corporate program or the management hierarchy is becoming narrow and that their opportunities are decreasing. The first 15 years in the workforce are often years of advancement, recognition, autonomy, and high expectations. Motivational inspiration is all around. However, reality, burnout, fatigue, long hours, and travel are also common. By 40, motivational inspiration may be harder to find. A few examples will highlight how self-motivation becomes a very serious concern for many people around 40 years old.

Tim hit the wall at about 38 years old. He was a senior product manager at Borden's Consumer Products Division in Columbus, Ohio. He had always wanted to be president of a company. At 38 he realized that, at Borden, this wouldn't happen. His goals were being stalled. He left Borden and joined a manufacturing firm in Dayton. Today, at 44, as vice president for sales, marketing, and engineering applications for Freund Precision, he is happier and more realistic. He wants to be financially independent at 55, but he is not going to drive himself to exhaustion.

Juanita was a fast tracker when the birth of her son made her rethink her goals. The Princeton graduate had been only 34 when she stepped up to the top rung of the management ladder as president of telemarketing for Time-Life Libraries. At 36 she started to assess her life, the dizzying schedules and the frequent travel. She concluded that a person *can* have it all—but not all at the same time. By all, she meant success, power, money, recognition, time, energy, and influence. Juanita is now enjoying motherhood. When she wants to go back to managing, she will go back to work. She is confident, satisfied, and very aware of the costs and benefits of being a mother, wife, and management superstar.

About 4 million Americans turn 40 each year. Forty is the age at which reality, pyramid narrowing, and self-assessment become crucial. However, success can be measured in many ways. How a person copes depends on many things. Self-confidence, talent, resourcefulness, goals, and adaptability all count. People who love their work, have strong work ethics, and know themselves well will not be stymied by the "40" wall. The over-40 successes are the ones who, like Jack Benny, have a passion to accomplish, achieve, and be creative well into old age without feeling a day over 39.

The two most discussed groups of theories are content theories and process theories. **Content theories** are concerned with identifying what it is within an individual or the work environment that energizes and sustains behavior.[6] That is, what specific things motivate people?

On the other hand, **process theories** try to explain and describe the process of how behavior is energized, directed, sustained, and finally stopped. Process theories first attempt to define the major variables necessary for explaining choice (e.g., Should I work hard?), effort (e.g., How hard do I need to work?), and persistence (e.g., How long do I have to keep this pace?).

First, we discuss two content theories—Maslow's need hierarchy and Herzberg's two-factor theory—and second, two process theories—expectancy and reinforcement. After each theory, we show how it can be applied by managers.

Content Theories of Motivation

Maslow's Hierarchy of Needs

Maslow's need hierarchy theory has enjoyed widespread acceptance since it was introduced. His theory of motivation stresses two fundamental premises:

1. We are wanting animals whose needs depend on what we already have. Only needs not yet satisfied can influence behavior. In other words, a satisfied need is not a motivation.

2. Our needs are arranged in a hierarchy of importance. Once one need is satisfied, another emerges and demands satisfaction.

Maslow hypothesized five levels of needs: physiological, safety, social, esteem, and self-actualization.[7] He placed them in a framework referred to as the **hierarchy of needs** because of the different levels of importance. This framework is presented in Figure 11–2.

Maslow states that, if all of a person's needs are unsatisfied at a particular time, satisfaction of the most predominant needs is most pressing. Those that come first

---

FIGURE 11–2   Maslow's Hierarchy of Needs Theory

According to Maslow, people have and attempt to satisfy five basic needs.

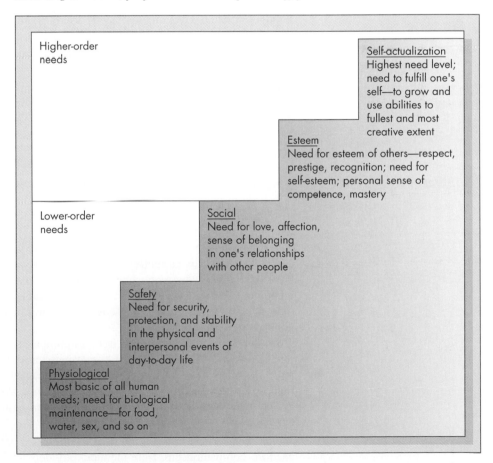

must be satisfied before a higher-level need comes into play. Let us briefly examine each need level:

1. *Physiological needs.* This category consists of the human body's primary needs, such as food, water, and sex. Physiological needs dominate when they are unsatisfied, and no other needs serve as a basis for motivation. As Maslow states, "A person who is lacking food, safety, love, and esteem probably would hunger for food more strongly than for anything else."[8]

   Once upon a time in 1981, IBM employees were assured of satisfying their physiological needs. The firm was growing at a rapid rate, layoffs were unheard of and being a member of the "By Blue" (IBM team) was an ego booster.[9] In fact, an IBM orientation booklet contained the following paragraph:

   > In nearly 40 years, no person employed on a regular basis by IBM has lost as much as one hour because of a layoff. When recessions come or there is a major product shift, some companies handle the work-force imbalances that result by letting people go. IBM hasn't done that, hope never to have to . . . . It's hardly a surprise that one of the main reasons people like to work for IBM is the company's all-out-effort to maintain full employment.

   In Maslow's terms IBM employees were assured that their lower and higher needs would be satisfied. A lot has changed since 1981. IBM has gone from 405,000 to about 225,000 employees and has scrapped a sacred no-layoffs policy. Physiological needs do not dominate IBM employees' thoughts, but because of uncertainties and significant changes brought about by competitors, it is no longer a foregone conclusion that lower- and higher-order needs will be routinely satisfied.

2. *Safety needs.* When physiological needs are adequately met, the next higher level of needs assumes importance. Safety needs include protection from physical harm, ill health, economic disaster, and the unexpected. From a managerial standpoint, safety needs show up in an employee's attempts to ensure job safety and fringe benefits.

   The media for the past few years (1990–96) have placed a spotlight on downsizing or the reducing in the number of employees in order to make an organization more cost efficient and competitive. From 1978 to 1996 the workforces, managers and nonmanagers, of the largest 100 American firms have been reduced by over 3 million employees.[10] This size reduction has had a ripple affect across all firms and economic insecurity is a concern. Although, the US is currently experiencing steady economic growth and there is relatively low employment by international standards, there is still a feeling of job insecurity. People who used to think their jobs were safe and their standard of living would rise each year no longer take either for granted or as guaranteed.[11]

   Job security is still a pressing issue as companies such as Sears, IBM, Shell, Xerox, Siemens, Daimler-Benz, American Airlines, and thousands more lay off millions of managers and nonmanagers.[12] The need for job security is strong in all societies. Layoffs certainly do not reduce this need, but the rash of layoffs (downsizing) continues to reduce the numbers of employees.[13]

3. *Social needs.* These needs are related to the social nature of people and their need for companionship. Here the hierarchy departs from the physical or

quasi-physical needs of the two previous levels. Nonsatisfaction of this level of need may affect the mental health of the individual.

4. *Esteem needs.* The need for both awareness of importance to others (self-esteem) and actual esteem from others is included. Esteem from others must also be felt as warranted and deserved. Satisfaction of these needs leads to a feeling of self-confidence and prestige.

   At most firms, receptionists aren't given the authority to spend $1,000 on equipment. Zytec Corporation in Eden Prairie, Minnesota, a manufacturer of electronics supplies, empowers receptionists and any other employee to spend up to $1,000 anytime, no questions asked, to help improve customer service.[14] Building pride and self-esteem is what Zytec management is attempting to accomplish. The employees in the plant have taken the responsibility very seriously, and expressions of self-confidence and feeling good about helping solve a problem are made every day.

5. *Self-actualization needs.* Maslow defines these needs as the "desire to become more and more what one is, to become everything one is capable of becoming."[15] This means that the individual will realize fully the potentialities of talents and capabilities. Obviously, as the role of an individual varies, so will the external aspects of self-actualization. In other words, whether the person is a college professor, corporate manager, parent, or athlete, the need is to be effective in that particular role. Maslow assumes that satisfaction of the self-actualization needs is possible only after the satisfaction of all other needs. Moreover, he proposes that the satisfaction of the self-actualization needs tends to increase the strength of other needs. Thus, when people are able to achieve self-actualization, they tend to be motivated by increased opportunities to satisfy that need.[16]

   Harry Quadracci is an example of a self-actualized person. He is the founder and president of Quid/Graphics in Peewaukee, Wisconsin. He loves to work himself and to allow other people to grow on the job. He encourages everyone to be an active risk-taker. Quadracci considers himself growing to realize his potential every day of his life. The $600 million printing company he leads is also growing every day.[17]

Applying Maslow's Theory in Management.   The need hierarchy theory is widely accepted and referred to by practicing managers. Although it does not provide a complete understanding of human motivation or the means to motivate people, it does provide an excellent starting point for students of management. The hierarchy is easy to comprehend, has a great deal of commonsense appeal, and points out some of the factors that motivate people in business and other types of organizations. Through wages or salary, individuals are able to satisfy their and their families' physiological needs. Organizations also help to satisfy most security or safety needs through both salary and fringe benefit programs. Finally, they aid in satisfying social needs by allowing interaction and association with others on the job. Some work-related examples that managers can influence under each of the five need categories are presented in Table 11–1.

Criticisms of Maslow's Theory.   Maslow's theory is often presented as being universally accepted as accurate. However, people in various firms, positions, or countries differ. Individual differences certainly exist. An accountant in Budapest, Hungary, working for the Hungarian Credit Bank may be concerned about a

TABLE 11–1   Areas of Management Influence in the Five Need Hierarchy Categories

Managers can help employees satisfy needs.

Need Category	Management Influence Areas
Self-actualization	Challenges in job Advancement opportunities Chances for creativity Motivation toward high achievement
Esteem	Public recognition of good performance Significant job activities Respectful job title Responsibility
Social	Social interaction opportunities Group stability Encouragement toward cooperation
Safety	Safe working conditions Job security Fringe benefits
Physiological	Fair salary Comfortable working conditions Heat, lighting, space, air-conditioning

comfortable work area, a salary to help support her family, and receiving some time off during the summer months. However, an accountant at Chase Manhattan Bank in New York City may have extensive self-actualization needs and not be overly concerned with physiological and security needs.

Another criticism of the need hierarchy is that needs overlap and can fit in more than one, or even all, of the categories. An equitable salary, for example, may satisfy needs in all five categories; the salary received by a person has an impact on many different needs.

Critics also state that Maslow's need hierarchy is static. Needs change over time, in various situations, and when people make comparisons between their satisfaction and the satisfaction of others. A 22-year-old recent college graduate perceives, experiences, and copes with needs differently from a 62-year-old preparing for retirement and leisure activities.

Herzberg's Two-Factor Theory

Another content explanation of motivation was advanced by Frederick Herzberg in 1959. He based his theory on a study of need satisfactions and on the reported motivational effects of these satisfactions on 200 engineers and accountants. The theory is referred to as the two-factor theory of motivation.[18]

In the study of engineers and accountants, Herzberg and his associates asked the subjects to think of times both when they felt especially good and when they felt especially bad about their jobs. Each employee was then asked to describe the conditions that led to these particular feelings. The employees named different kinds of conditions as causes of each of the feelings. For example, if recognition led to a good feeling about the job, the lack of recognition was seldom indicated as a cause of bad feelings. Based on the study, Herzberg reached two conclusions:

1. Some conditions of a job operate primarily to dissatisfy employees when they (the conditions) are not present. However, the presence of these conditions does not build strong motivation. Herzberg called these **maintenance factors,** since they are necessary to maintain a reasonable level of satisfaction. He also noted that many of these have often been perceived by managers as factors that can motivate subordinates but that they are, in fact, more potent as dissatisfiers when they are absent. He named 10 maintenance factors:

   Company policy and administration.
   Technical supervision.
   Interpersonal relations with supervisor.
   Interpersonal relations with peers.
   Interpersonal relations with subordinates.
   Salary.
   Job security.
   Personal life.
   Work conditions.
   Status.

2. Some job conditions build high levels of motivation and job satisfaction. However, if these conditions are not present, they do not prove highly dissatisfying. Herzberg described six of these **motivational factors,** or satisfiers:

   Achievement.
   Recognition.
   Advancement.
   The work itself.
   The possibility of personal growth.
   Responsibility.

In summary, the maintenance factors cause much dissatisfaction when they are not present but do not provide strong motivation when they are present. On the other hand, the factors in the second group lead to strong motivation and satisfaction when they are present but do not cause much dissatisfaction when they are absent. Herzberg's study of engineers and accountants suggested to him that the opposite of satisfaction is not dissatisfaction but simply "no satisfaction." Figure 11–3 compares his view of job satisfaction to a traditional view.

Note that Herzberg's motivational factors are job centered; that is, they relate directly to the job itself, the individual's performance, the job's responsibilities, and the growth and recognition obtained from it. Maintenance factors are peripheral to the job itself and more related to the external environment of work. Another important finding of the study is that when employees are highly motivated, they have a high tolerance for dissatisfaction arising from the maintenance factors. However, the reverse is not true.

The distinction between motivational and maintenance factors is similar to what psychologists have described as *intrinsic* and *extrinsic* motivators. Intrinsic motivators are part of the job and occur when the employee performs the work. The opportunity to perform a job with intrinsic motivational potential is motivating because the work itself is rewarding. Extrinsic motivators are external rewards that have meaning or value after performing the work or away from the workplace. They provide little, if any, satisfaction when the work is being performed. Pay, of course, is a good example

FIGURE 11-3   Contrasting Theories of Satisfaction and Dissatisfaction

Herzberg's view of satisfaction and dissatisfaction departed from the traditional view.

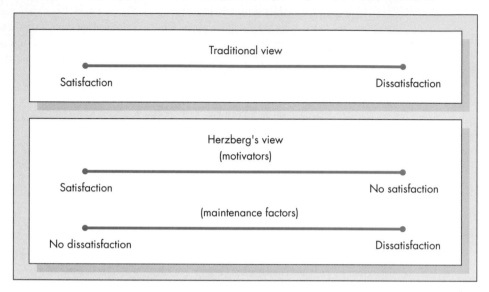

of what Herzberg classifies as a maintenance factor and what some psychologists call an extrinsic motivator.

Applying Herzberg's Theory in Management.   Herzberg certainly has extended Maslow's ideas and made them more applicable to the work situation. He has drawn attention to the critical importance, in work motivation, of job-centered factors previously given little attention by behavioral scientists. This insight has resulted in an increased interest in **job enrichment,** an effort to restructure jobs to increase worker satisfaction.

Herzberg's response to motivation problems is an important one. Traditionally, managers would respond to motivation problems with more money, increased fringe benefits, and improved working conditions. Often, the result of such actions was still no more effort to work harder. Herzberg's theory offers an explanation for this phenomenon. If managers focus only on maintenance factors, motivation will not occur. The motivators must be built into the job to improve motivation. A survey of 200 human resource executives by Goodrich & Sherwood indicates Herzberg's view, which was first stated in 1959, still has validity today. The factors that the executives listed as extremely important for employee motivation were responsibility and autonomy, respect and recognition from superiors, a sense of well-being on the job, and the opportunity to have one's ideas adopted. These are motivational factors.[19]

The importance of recognition in motivating people is spelled out by the style of Mary Kay Ash. She is one of the most effective motivators in the world. The accompanying Management Focus indicates how Ash works at motivating others.

Criticisms of Herzberg's Theory.   One limitation of Herzberg's original study and conclusions is that the subjects consisted of engineers and accountants. Individuals in such positions had the motivation to seek advanced education and expected to be rewarded. The same may not hold true for the nonprofessional worker. In fact, some

Mary Kay Ash: A Motivator Who Understands Women

Some claim that the best motivator of a large workforce is Mary Kay Ash of Mary Kay Cosmetics. She is the chairperson emeritus of a company that had sales of $198,000 in 1963 and sales over $613 million in 1993. Ash has built a salesforce of 300,000, of whom more than 6,500 are driving complimentary Cadillacs and other expensive cars. She has helped create 74 "millionaires"—women who have earned commissions of $1 million or more.

Ash built her empire by practicing a sound motivation principle: The way to motivate people is through recognition. She advocates giving her beauty consultants (saleswomen) recognition. Every consultant buys products from Ash's Dallas headquarters at the same price; the company treats everyone equally. Résumés count for nothing. If an applicant states that she was formerly a brain surgeon, Ash is unimpressed. All that counts is the woman's work ethic and willingness to represent the company's cosmetics positively.

There's no cap on how much a woman can earn. As her sales increase and she recruits more consultants, she advances to sales director and eventually to national sales director. More than 36,000 consultants attended the 1993 summer sales convention and seminar in Dallas. Color-coded suits, sashes, badges, crowns, and emblems showed how far each woman had come in the company.

Recognition from Ash is what the consultants seem to thrive on the most. She personally crowns four queens of the seminar—women who have excelled in sales or recruiting. Ash also tells her own story of making it up the ladder. She was a saleswoman with Stanley Home Products; she started at the bottom and is now a multimillion-aire. She was passed over for a promotion at Stanley and thus decided to quit and start her own company. She wanted to create a business that would treat women well and help build their self-esteem.

Ash's system of motivation includes extrinsic rewards such as bonuses and intrinsic rewards such as feeling good about doing the job well. Concern about recognizing and rewarding good performance seems to improve the self-esteem of the thousands of beauty consultants at Mary Kay Cosmetics. Ash appears to understand how motivation works and the role it plays in directing the behavior of the beauty consultants. Ash's reward-by-recognition motivation approach works well with women and should also work well with men. Husbands who attend the conference and seminar report that they tell their employers that praise is a key to motivation that needs to be used more. Money at Mary Kay Cosmetics is only one of the motivators. Applause, prizes, emblems, praise, and recognition also seem to be powerful motivators.

Sources: Adapted from A Farnham, "Mary Kay's Lessons in Leadership," *Fortune,* September 20, 1993, pp. 68-77.

testing of Herzberg's model on blue-collar workers showed that certain factors considered maintenance factors by Herzberg (pay and job security) are considered by blue-collar workers to be motivational factors.[20]

Some critics believe that Herzberg's inference concerning differences between dissatisfiers and motivators cannot be completely accepted and that the differences between stated sources of satisfaction and dissatisfaction in Herzberg's study may be the result of defensive processes within those responding. Detractors point out that people are apt to attribute the causes of satisfaction to their own achievements but likely to attribute their dissatisfaction more to obstacles presented by company policies or superiors than to their own deficiencies.[21]

Other critics believe that the two-factor theory is an oversimplification of the true relationship between motivation and dissatisfaction as well as between the sources of job satisfaction and dissatisfaction.[22] Reviews of several studies show that one factor can cause job satisfaction for one person and job dissatisfaction for another.

Herzberg assumes that there is a strong relationship between satisfaction and productivity. But his research examined only satisfaction, not productivity. Other researchers have questioned the conclusion that satisfaction and productivity are highly and positively related.[23]

Since his original work, Herzberg has cited numerous replications of the original study that support his position.[24] These subsequent studies were conducted on professional women, hospital maintenance personnel, agricultural administrators, nurses, food handlers, manufacturing supervisors, engineers, scientists, military officers, managers ready for retirement, teachers, technicians, and assemblers. And some were conducted in other cultural settings: Finland, Hungary, Russia, and Yugoslavia. However, some researchers have used the same research methods employed by Herzberg and obtained results different from what his theory would predict,[25] and several using *different* methods have also obtained contradictory results.[26]

Comparing Herzberg's and Maslow's Models

There is much similarity between Herzberg's and Maslow's models. A close examination of Herzberg's ideas indicates that what he is actually saying is that some employees may have achieved a level of social and economic progress such that the higher-level needs of Maslow (esteem and self-actualization) are the primary motivators. However, they still must satisfy the lower-level needs for the maintenance of their current state. Thus, money might still be a motivator for nonmanagement workers (particularly those at a low wage level) and for some managerial employees. In addition, Herzberg's model adds to Maslow's model because it breaks down the five need levels into two job-oriented categories: maintenance and motivational. Figure 11–4 compares the structure of the two. Table 11–2 compares areas in which they differ.

Process Theories of Motivation

In contrast to the two content theories—Maslow's need hierarchy and Herzberg's two-factor model—equity theory and expectancy theory are process theories. They

---

Figure 11–4   Maslow's and Herzberg's Theories: Similarities

Maslow and Herzberg proposed similar ideas with different labels.

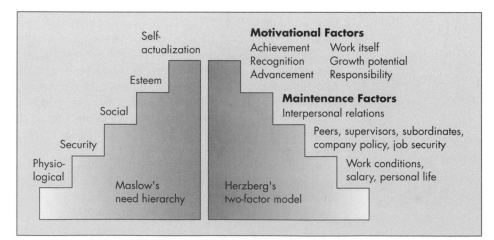

Source: Also see K Davis, *Human Behavior at Work* (New York: McGraw-Hill, 1977), p. 53.

TABLE 11–2   Maslow's and Herzberg's Theories: Differences

Maslow and Herzberg have basic differences in five points of comparison.

Topic	Maslow's Need Hierarchy	Herzberg's Two-Factor Theory
1. Relevance	To people in society in all types of jobs and in retirement.	Mostly to white-collar and professional employees.
2. Impact of needs on behavior	All needs can motivate behavior.	Only some intrinsic needs serve as motivators.
3. Role of financial rewards	Can motivate.	Is not a key motivator.
4. Perspective	Applies to all people and their lives.	Is work centered.
5. Type of theory	Descriptive (what is).	Prescriptive (what should be).

concentrate on how motivation occurs—that is, how behavior is initiated, directed, sustained, and stopped.

Equity Theory

Equity theory is a motivation approach popularized by the work of University of North Carolina professor J Stacy Adams.[27] The theory proposes that perceived inequity is a motivational force. When a person believes that she has been inequitably treated in comparison with others, she will attempt to eliminate the inequity. People are believed to evaluate equity by a ratio of inputs to outputs. Inputs to a job include experience, effort, and ability. Outcomes from a job include pay, recognition, promotions, and benefits.

Figure 11–5 shows how equity comparisons occur. Inequities occur whenever people feel that the outcomes received are unfair in comparison to what other persons appear to be receiving.

Research suggests that being under-rewarded—an inequitable situation—is far more frequent than being over-rewarded.[28] Believing that you are inequitably rewarded often results in attempts to change the situation or the referent other person. Specific methods to reduce inequity could include the following:

- Quitting the job.
- Changing the inputs that are put into the job, such as working less or being absent more frequently.
- Changing the outcomes by asking for and receiving an increase in pay or requesting and receiving additional benefits.
- Changing how the job outcomes already received are perceived. A person may reconsider his rewards to be more substantial than when the original comparison was made.

Applying Equity Theory in Management.   Managers are made aware of comparisons that employees make. Changing pay, work schedules, benefits, or any reward for an employee is likely to be compared with what is being received by other employees. It is important for managers to understand the importance of perceptions. Feelings of equity and inequity are based on perceptions. It is how the recipients of rewards match them up with what others receive that needs to be evaluated. Unless a reward system is carefully administered, it could result in perceived inequity problems. One point for

FIGURE 11–5   **Equity Comparisons**

Comparisons are made by examining or perceiving inputs and outcomes.

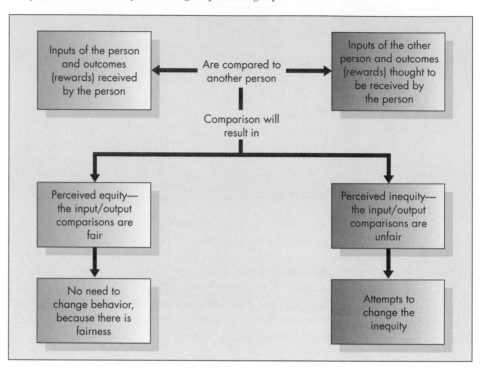

managers to consider is how to carefully communicate the *intended value* of rewards as well as the *reasons* for providing those rewards to individuals.

Criticisms of Equity Theory.   Equity theory fails to provide specific methods for restoring equity.[29] This omission leaves the how-to-correct activities up to managers or to those who must usually guess what should be done. There is also the issue of the comparison or referent person. Who is the person and what can managers possibly do if it is a friend, a family member, or an imaginary figure? There is also the fact that most research on equity theory has been focused on pay. What about other rewards? Are the comparisons similarly made? These are serious questions, since pay is just one of a list of valued rewards.

Vroom's Expectancy Theory   The expectancy theory of motivation as initially presented in 1964 by psychologist Victor Vroom views motivation as a process governing choices.[30] Vroom suggests that individuals are motivated at work to make choices among different behaviors—for example, intensities of work effort. A person may choose to work at a moderate rate or an accelerated rate. The choice is made by the individual. If a person believes that her work effort will be adequately rewarded, there will be motivated effort; a choice will be made to work so that a preferred reward is received. The logic of expectancy motivation is that *individuals exert work effort to achieve performance that results in preferred rewards.*

Three primary variables in the expectancy theory of motivation are choice, expectancy, and preference.[31] *Choice* designates the individual's freedom to select from a number of alternative behaviors. For example, a person's work may be fast or slow, hard or moderate; the employee may stay home or come to work. In some cases, working fast may lead to more pay if compensation is based on the number of units produced. *Expectancy* is the belief that a particular behavior will or will not be successful. It is a subjective probability. Expectancy would be zero if a person believed that it was impossible to produce, say, 50 units a day; it would equal one if a person felt certain of being able to produce 22 units a day. *Preferences,* also referred to by Vroom as *valences,* are the values a person attaches to various outcomes (rewards or punishment).

Another issue covered in the **expectancy motivation model** is *instrumentality—* the probability that a person assigns to the performance–outcome link. It is the probability that a particular performance level will lead to a specific outcome.

Figure 11–6 gives a general explanation and a work-oriented example of the expectancy theory. The work-oriented example is presented to show how the theory can be applied. To predict whether a person will select path A or B, you need to examine the interrelationships of the variables in the model. The motivation to work is expressed as:

$$M = E \times I \times P$$

FIGURE 11–6   How the Expectancy Theory of Motivation Works

This example of expectancy theory shows how the theory works in a job situation.

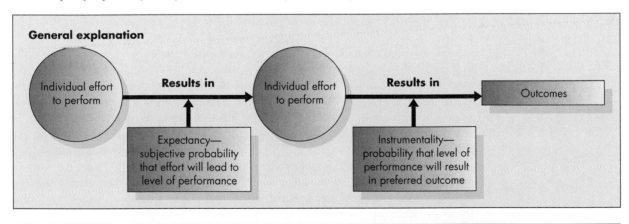

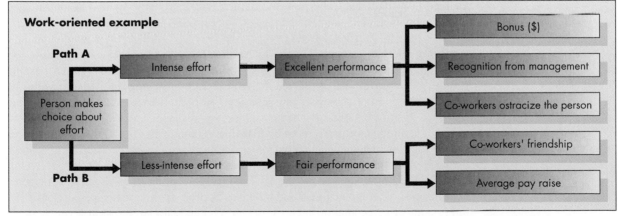

That is, motivation to work (*M*) results from expectancy (*E*) times instrumentality (*I*) times preference (*P*). Because this is a multiplicative interrelationship, think about the consequences if *E, I,* or *P* approaches zero in value.[32]

Suppose that the work example in Figure 11–6 applies to Nan Brewer and her manager Nick. Nick is not sure whether a pay bonus will motivate Nan to perform better. Using the expectancy theory, Nick would predict that Nan's motivation to work hard would be low if:

1. Expectancy is low: Nan feels that she really can't achieve the bonus level of performance.
2. Instrumentality is low: Nan is uncertain about whether excellent performance will result in the bonus money.
3. Preference is low: Nan doesn't value receiving the bonus.
4. Any combination of 1, 2, and/or 3.

The expectancy theory of motivation requires a manager such as Nick to know three things when applying the theory: first, what the person's beliefs are about working hard and achieving a particular level of performance (expectancy); second, whether the person believes that various outcomes (positive or negative) will result from the achievement of the particular level of performance (instrumentality); and third, how much value a person assigns to outcomes (preferences).

In one study, 1,000 employees were asked to rank-order 10 work-related factors.[33] If Nick reviewed this type of research, he would understand how the sex, age, income level, job type, and organizational level influence expectancy and preferences. Not everyone prefers a promotion or job security. Table 11–3 summarizes the results of the study.

In the old days money, bonuses, and economic rewards were assumed to be the key to excellent or improved performance. However, the change in the makeup of the workforce with millions of women attempting to balance career and family, immigrants thankful to have a job, and others who want more leisure, flextime, and personal improvement benefits has complicated the picture. Money is still a powerful tool in any motivational approach that appeals to the majority of individuals whose concern about salary may always be that it isn't enough.[34] Nonmonetary rewards range from Autodesk, a software development firm, allowing its employees to pick their days of work, to Illinois Trade Association, which pays for chiropractic care, herbal therapy, and other forms of alternative medical care. Illinois Trade's employees requested these forms of health care and management provides them. Other firms such as Hewlett-Packard in Santa Rosa, California, and Barnett Banks in Jacksonville, Florida, sponsor public schools at their work sites to satisfy employees' preferences.

Applying the Expectancy Theory in Management.   Managers can influence expectancies by selecting (hiring) individuals with particular skills and abilities, training people to improve their skills and abilities, and providing individuals with the leadership support to achieve a particular level of performance. The manager also can influence instrumentalities by being supportive, realistic, and offering advice. The manager can influence preferences by listening to employee needs, guiding employees to help them accomplish desired outcomes, and providing proper resources to achieve the desired performance.

Managers must understand the vital role of perception in motivation. A person's expectancies, instrumentalities, and valences depend on his or her perceptions. The importance of perceptual differences among workers with similar skill levels is made

TABLE 11–3   What Workers Want (Ranked by Subgroup)

Many factors influence employees' individual job-related expectations and preferences.

	Work Factors									
Subgroup	Interesting Work	Full Appreciation of Work Done	Feeling of Being In on Things	Job Security	Good Wages	Promotion and Growth in Organization	Good Working Conditions	Personal Loyalty to Employees	Tactful Discipline	Sympathetic Help with Personal Problems
Sex										
Men	2	1	3	5	4	6	7	8	9	10
Women	2	1	3	4	5	6	7	8	9	10
Age										
Under 30	4	5	6	2	1	3	7	9	8	10
30–41	2	3	4	1	5	6	7	9	10	8
42–40	3	2	1	4	5	8	7	6	9	10
Over 50	1	2	3	7	8	9	4	5	10	6
Income level										
Under $12,000	5	4	6	2	1	3	8	7	10	9
$12,001–18,000	2	3	1	4	5	6	7	8	9	10
$18,001–25,000	1	3	2	4	6	5	7	8	9	10
Over $25,000	1	2	4	3	8	7	6	5	10	9
Job type										
Blue collar										
Unskilled	2	1	5	4	3	6	9	8	7	10
Skilled	1	6	2	3	4	5	7	9	10	8
White collar										
Unskilled	1	3	5	7	6	4	2	9	10	8
Skilled	2	1	4	5	6	3	7	8	9	10
Organization level: nonsupervisory										
Lower	3	4	5	2	1	6	7	8	9	10
Middle	1	2	3	4	6	5	7	8	9	10
Higher	1	2	3	6	8	5	4	7	10	9

Ranked from 1 (highest) to 10 (lowest).

Source: Adapted from K A Kovach, "What Motivates Employees? Workers and Supervisors Give Different Answers," *Business Horizons*. September–October 1987, p. 61.

obvious by the expectancy theory. Different levels of motivation among people with similar skills could be explained by perceptual differences.

Criticisms of Expectancy Theory.   Many critics believe the expectancy theory is more complex than either Maslow's or Herzberg's theory.[35] There also are problems of measuring and studying the main variables in the model. How should preferences be determined? How should expectancy be determined? However, despite the lack of tested validity, the expectancy model still adds insight into the role that perception plays in choices, expectancy, and preferences.[36]

We might ask each reader: Do you make choices? Do you have expectancies? Do you have reward preferences?

Reinforcement Theory

The content and process theories explain behavior in terms of decisions made by a person. On the other hand, reinforcement theory is based on the idea that behavior results from consequences. **Reinforcement theory** considers the use of positive or negative reinforcers to motivate or create an environment of motivation. This theory of motivation, based largely on the work of B F Skinner, is not concerned with needs or why people make choices. Instead, this theory focuses on the environment and its consequences for the person. That is, behavior is considered to be environmentally caused. For example, suppose John Lofton, a hard-working employee, is given a $100 bonus for doing a good job. In the future, John continues to work hard, expecting another bonus payment. Why does John continue to work hard? When John first worked hard, his behavior was reinforced by a $100 bonus. This reinforcement is an environmental consequence of good performance.

The explanation of why John continued to work hard, according to reinforcement theory, centers on Thorndike's law of effect, which states that *behavior that results in a pleasing outcome is likely to be repeated; behavior that results in an unpleasant outcome is not likely to be repeated.*[37] We learn as children that doing your homework results in better grades and that touching a hot stove causes an injury. These kinds of learning experiences support the validity of Thorndike's law.

Operant conditioning is a powerful tool used for changing employee behavior. The term *operant conditioning* in management literature applies to controlling work behavior by manipulating the consequences. It is based on the research work of psychologist B F Skinner and is built on two principles: Thorndike's law of effect and the idea that properly scheduled rewards influence individual behaviors.[38] *Behavior modification* is the contemporary term that describes techniques for applying the principles of operant conditioning to control individual behavior.

Applying Reinforcement Theory in Management.   Suppose you are a manager and your employee Mary Banner is often late with required budget reports. You could use four types of reinforcement: First, you could focus on reinforcing the desired behavior (which, in this example, is preparing budget reports on time) by using positive or negative reinforcement. **Positive reinforcement** would include rewards such as praise, recognition, or a pay bonus. **Negative reinforcement** also focuses on reinforcing the desired behavior. However, instead of providing a positive reward, the "reward" is that the employee avoids some negative consequence. Thus, Mary would complete the report on time to avoid the negative consequence of being reprimanded by her manager.

Alternatively, the manager might focus on reducing the tardiness of submitting the budget report by use of two other reinforcements: extinction or punishment. Through the use of **extinction** (withholding positive reinforcement), Mary might unlearn her bad habit of submitting late reports. Another method that reduces the frequency of undesired behavior is **punishment**. In this case, punishment could involve the public reprimand of Mary by the manager for submitting a late report.

Positive and negative reinforcement address the issue of having employees learn desired behaviors. On the other hand, unlearning undesired behaviors involves the use of extinction or punishment. Figure 11–7 summarizes the Mary Banner example.

In applying positive reinforcement to motivate desired behaviors, managers can use different schedules. A **continuous reinforcement** schedule involves administering

FIGURE 11–7   **Reinforcement Options Available to Managers: Illustration**

A manager can use four types of reinforcement to affect employees' behavior.

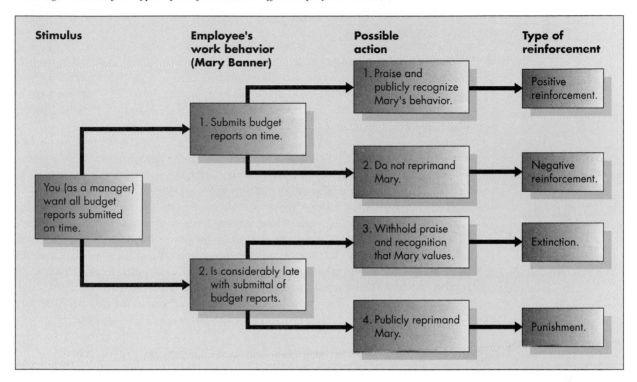

a reward each time a desired behavior occurs. For example, every time a budget report is submitted on time, Mary would be rewarded. An **intermittent reinforcement** schedule involves rewarding desired behavior only periodically. According to research results:

- Continuous reinforcement schedules usually result in the fastest learning.
- Intermittent reinforcement schedules result in slower learning but stronger retention of what is learned.[39]

Criticisms of Reinforcement Theory.   Some critics state that the idea of rewarding or reinforcing performance is bribery and that it is used to manipulate one person to fit a manager's concept of the ideal employee.[40] This raises ethical concerns about controlling the behavior of others. Should anyone be allowed to control and manipulate the behavior of another person? The difficulty rests on what constitutes control and manipulation. What is control to one person is positive guidance to another person.

Others argue that motivating employees through behavior modification relies solely on extrinsic rewards such as pay. What about intrinsic rewards, such as feeling the challenge of doing a good job?[41] Other issues of concern include: Which reinforcers should be used? For whom? How long will a reinforcer be successful? Can reinforcers be effectively used with employees who are independent, creative, and self-motivated?

It is helpful to keep these criticisms in mind when considering the managerial use of reinforcement theory. They help illustrate some of the problems associated with this approach. Also, a word of caution: Reinforcement theory (like any of the other motivation theories) is not a solution to every motivation problem.

An Integrating Model of Motivation

The motivation theories presented here contain the theme that motivation is goal directed. Although the theories use different terms and appear to be quite different, they are not in conflict with one another. Basically, each looks at some segment of overall motivation or looks at the same aspect of motivation from a slightly different perspective.

Porter–Lawler Model

Psychologists Lyman Porter and Edward Lawler offer a model that integrates ideas, variables, and relationships presented in other explanations of motivation such as the need hierarchy, two-factor theory, expectancy theory, and reinforcement theory.

The Porter–Lawler model is presented in Figure 11–8. It points out the relationship of performance, satisfaction, and rewards and introduces the importance of having individuals performing jobs for which they have the proper skills, abilities, and traits. There also is the issue of performance measurement. Performance must be measured accurately and systematically so that rewards can be distributed equitably. If they are not distributed fairly, expending the necessary effort to do the job seems senseless to employees. If no meaningful difference in rewards is made between high

---

FIGURE 11–8   An Integrative Motivational Model (Bringing Together Content and Process Theories)

Effective management must combine theories of motivation.

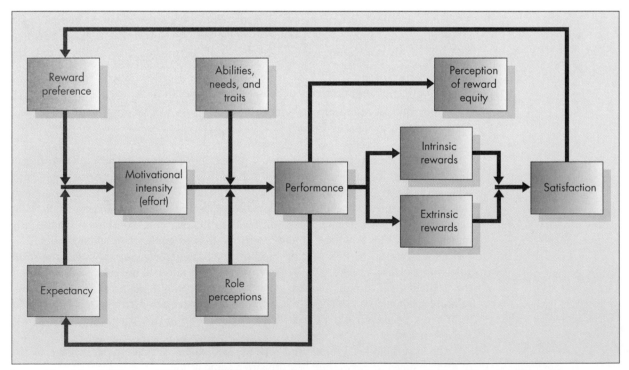

Source: Adapted from L W Porter and E E Lawler III, *Managerial Attitudes and Performance* (Burr Ridge, IL: Richard D. Irwin, 1968), p. 165.

and low performers, high performers lose motivational intensity and probably cut back on their performance.

The integrative model uses motivational concepts discussed so far. For example, expectancy theory predicts that an employee will exert intense effort (motivation) if she perceives strong relationships between effort and performance, performance and rewards, and rewards and satisfaction. For effort to lead to performance, the individual must have a clear understanding of her expected role, abilities, needs, and other characteristics. The performance–reward relationship is strong if the person perceives that intrinsic and extrinsic rewards are equitable. If there is perceived equity (fairness), satisfaction results. Rewards that are reinforcing and satisfying can lead to future encouragement of goal-directed behavior.

Using the Model

The Porter–Lawler model and the individual theories discussed in this chapter point out that motivation is a complex process. Managers should consider the types of variables shown in the integrative model. Certainly, it indicates that motivation holds some important keys for understanding performance and satisfaction. A periodic review of the motivation process can be beneficial if managers ask themselves:

- What are the needs of this subordinate?
- Can I play a role in helping this subordinate satisfy these needs?
- Are the rewards that I control and administer contingent on performance? Are they sufficient to induce the type of effort needed to do the job?
- Does the employee have the skill, traits, behaviors, and experience necessary to perform the job?
- Am I accurately measuring performance? If not, why not?
- For how long will the employees continue to be motivated? What must I do to sustain motivation?

Steven Kerr, Chief Learning Officer in charge of General Electric's Cotonville, New York, Leadership Center, offers a set of simple rules that managers can apply when using a Porter–Lawler-type model.[42] Kerr pushes the overarching notion that a key to effectively using compensation to motivate is to directly and specifically link it to performance. A sample of Kerr's straightforward rules are as follows:

1. Don't tie pay to power. GE has cut the number of salary grades from 29 to 6. This gives employees more opportunities to get a raise without a promotion.
2. Make compensation understandable. Too many firms present their pay packages in convoluted terms.
3. Spread the news. If bonuses are handed out tell everyone.
4. Forget about the calendar. A reward delayed is almost as bad as a reward denied. Too many employees are reviewed and not rewarded for months afterward. GE rewards people on the spot with its "Quick Thanks" program. A well done job can mean a $25 gift certificate. Over the last year GE gave out 10,000 such awards.
5. Make rewards reversible. If a judgment is incorrect or conditions change, reducing base pay may be in order.

Kerr's rules when combined with the type of questions initiated by the Porter–Lawler model listed above are a good starting point for dealing with motivation situations.

Motivation, Cultural Diversity, and Cross-Cultural Issues

In the past, white males made up the dominant majority in the workplace. Today, across the United States, there are many cultural groups represented. Asians with ties to Japan, China, and Thailand; Hispanics from Mexico, El Salvador, Cuba and Spain; and an array of Russian immigrants, Middle Eastern immigrants, and many other culturally diverse individuals make up the workforce. Do the motivation theories presented work the same way for *all* of these culturally diverse individuals? The answer to this question is important for managers who wish to create an optimal motivational climate for their workers, whether it be in a domestic firm or a foreign-based, American-owned firm.

The changing nature of the complexion, gender, and ethnicity of the workforce has illustrated the variety of needs, work ethics, values, and behavior norms that are culturally rooted. Assessing needs, preferred rewards, work patterns, and sensitivity to workplace practices has become an important part of managerial practices. One recommended way to effectively manage employees with different cultural backgrounds, experiences, and histories is to study the fundamentals of various cultures.[43] Of course, as the makeup of the work team consists of people from around the world, it becomes too difficult to adapt to each culture.

The minority share of the workforce will continue to grow from about 17 percent in the early 1990s to over 25 percent in the early part of the twenty-first century.[44] California is leading the way in becoming a culturally diverse state. It is expected that by the year 2005 more than 50 percent of the population of California will be people of color, who will be speaking over 80 languages. Managers will have to learn how to adapt to this multilingual, ethnically diverse workforce.

Diversity means that organizations recruit, select, retain, and motivate individuals from different cultural backgrounds. The diverse workforce can result from many types of differences. Figure 11–9 presents primary and secondary diversity dimensions.

Digital Equipment Corporation (DEC) illustrates how Figure 11–9 is much more than a graphical representation of diversity. A DEC plant in Boston has 350 employees who were born in 44 different countries and who speak 19 languages.[45] Bulletin-board material and various memos are presented in English, Spanish, Chinese, Portuguese, Vietnamese, and Haitian Creole. This type of multicultural workforce means that various motivational assumptions about news, perceived equity, expectancy, and job satisfiers need to be carefully examined.

A New Management Approach

All of the demographic changes require rethinking about, as well as some experimentation in, motivation, leadership, and many other management practices. Cox and Blake provide a framework for considering how managers will have to proceed.[46] The management of a culturally diverse workforce will be very challenging. It will require considering the types of issues that Cox and Blake point out. Determining how to best motivate a culturally diverse workforce will become a top priority because of the importance of human resources in organizations. In order to optimize the performance of the emerging culturally diverse workforce, organizations and managers will have to learn more about the motivational needs, goals, and reward preferences of employees. Ignoring cultural diversity and differences in people is likely to be costly in terms of performance and overall effectiveness.

Cross-Cultural Motivation

Studying Americans, Maslow concluded that five needs explained much of their behavior. Herzberg, in his studies of American engineers and accountants, reached a

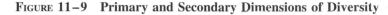

FIGURE 11–9   Primary and Secondary Dimensions of Diversity

These are some primary and secondary differences in people that result in diversity.

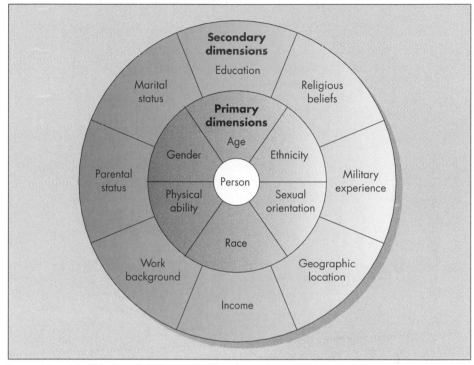

Source: Adapted for M Loden and J B Rosener, *Workforce America!* (Burr Ridge, IL: Business One Irwin, 1991), p. 20. Use with permission.

conclusion that he called the two-factor theory of motivation. Hofstede's research cautions managers to reexamine the predominantly American-based motivation theories.[47] *His* four dimensions are **power distance** (the level of acceptance in a society of the unequal distribution of power in organizations); **uncertainty avoidance** (the extent to which people in a society feel threatened by ambiguous situations); **individualism** (the tendency of people to look after themselves and their immediate family and neglect the needs of society); and **masculinity** (the degree of achievement preference, assertiveness, and materialism that exists in a society). Hofstede studied over 60,000 people in more than 50 countries. A helpful summary of Hofstede's cultural dimensions is presented in Table 11–4.

In fact, Hofstede's work that displays differences on the value dimensions also illustrated some significant similarities across cultures and types of occupational groups in the 50 countries that Hofstede studied. For example, professionals around the world ranked self-actualization as their top need; clerks from around the world ranked social needs as important; and unskilled workers selected the lower order, Maslow-type needs as most important.

There appear to be differences across cultures, as well as significant similarities. Managers must search for ways to motivate workers in the culture and setting in which they practice management. Because many cultures in the world emphasize *group* relationships[48] and most of the content, process, and reinforcement theories of motivation focus on *individual* needs, goals, and consequences, the overall picture

TABLE 11–4   Hofstede's Dimensions Around the World

This table shows Hofstede's analysis of individuals from different cultures.

	Hofstede's Dimensions				
Region/ Country	*Individualism– Collectivism*	*Power Distance*	*Uncertainty Avoidance*	*Masculinity– Femininity*	*Other Dimensions*
North America (USA)	Individualism	Low	Medium	Masculine	
Japan	Collectivism	High and low	High	Masculine and feminine	*Amae* (mutual dependence); authority is respected but superior must be a warm leader
Europe Anglo	Individualism	Low/medium	Low/medium	Masculine	
Germanic West Slavic West Urgic	Medium individualism	Low	Medium/high	Medium/high masculine	
Near Eastern Balkanic	Collectivism	High	High	Medium masculine	
Nordic	Medium/high individualism	Low	Low/medium	Feminine	
Latin Europe	Medium/high individualism	High	High	Medium masculine	
East Slavic	Collectivism	Low	Medium	Masculine	
China	Collectivism	Low	Low	Masculine and feminine	Emphasis on tradition, Marxism, Leninism, and Mao Zedong thought
Africa	Collectivism	High	High	Feminine	Colonial traditions; tribal customs
Latin America	Collectivism	High	High	Masculine	Extroverted; prefer orderly customs and procedures

Source: R Nath and K K Sadhu, "Comparative Analysis, Conclusions, and Future Directions," in *Comparative Management—A Regional View,* ed. Raghu Nath (Cambridge, MA: Ballinger, 1988), p. 273.

provided by cross-cultural motivation research suggests that universal acceptance of these theories is questionable.

Management Strategies for Increasing Motivation

Behavioral scientists have called attention to a number of programs that motivate workers to improve performance. Two programs that have been beneficial to some managers are job enrichment and relating pay to job performance.

Job Enrichment

The idea of quality of work life has received much attention from practicing managers, government officials, and union leaders.[49] It appears that many workers become increasingly dissatisfied and frustrated by routine, mechanically paced tasks. They react negatively with output restrictions, poor-quality work, absenteeism, high turnover, and pressure for higher wages, expanded fringe benefits, and greater participation in decisions that directly affect their jobs.

Earlier, we discussed the Herzberg two-factor theory. The practical contribution of Herzberg's theory is a motivational technique known as **job enrichment,** supported by many managers as a solution to the problem of the quality of life at work.[50] As Herzberg describes it, job enrichment

> seeks to improve both task efficiency and human satisfaction by means of building into people's jobs, quite specifically, greater scope for personal achievement and recognition, more challenging and responsible work, and more opportunity for individual advancement and growth. It is concerned only incidentally with matters such as pay and working conditions, organizational structure, communications and training, important and necessary though these may be in their own right.[51]

Herzberg emphasizes the importance of differentiating between job enrichment and **job enlargement.** He views job enrichment as providing the employee with an opportunity to grow psychologically and mature in a job, while job enlargement merely makes a job larger by increasing the number of tasks. Job enrichment, when applied, attempts to make a job motivational.[52] Research has indicated that jobs higher in job enrichment factors result in higher satisfaction and lower boredom and absenteeism than found with other job design techniques. However, research also indicates that enriched jobs require more training time and result in slightly higher anxiety and stress.[53]

Basically, what this means is that job enrichment occurs by increasing a job's range and depth.[54] **Job range** refers to the number of activities performed on the job, while **job depth** refers to the autonomy, responsibility, and discretion or control over the job. Job enrichment means that the range and depth of a job are increased. On the other hand, job enlargement means that a job's range, but not necessarily its depth, is increased.

The Core Dimensions of Jobs.   Building on Herzberg's work, Richard Hackman and others have identified five core dimensions that, if present, provide enrichment for jobs.[55] Hackman, after conducting research on many different occupations, concludes that these core dimensions are often not found in many managerial and blue-collar jobs. He also noted large individual differences in how employees react to core dimensions. Not all employees want or can benefit from enriched jobs.

1. *Variety.* The first core dimension is variety in the job. Variety allows employees to perform different operations, using several procedures and perhaps different equipment. Jobs that are high in variety are often viewed as challenging because they use all of an employee's skills.
2. *Task identity.* The second core dimension, task identity, allows employees to perform a complete piece of work. Overspecialized jobs tend to create routine job duties that result in a worker performing one part of the entire job. There is a sense of loss or of nonaccomplishment in doing only a part of a job. Thus, broadening the task to provide the worker with a feeling of doing a whole job increases task identity.
3. *Task significance.* The amount of impact that the work being performed has on other people is task significance. This impact may be within the organization or outside in the community. The feeling of doing something worthwhile is important to many people. For example, an employer may be told by a respected supervisor that she has done an outstanding job that has contributed to the overall success of the department. The task has significance because it is recognized as being important in this realm.

4. *Autonomy.* The fourth core dimension, autonomy, refers to the idea that employees have some control over their job duties and work area. This seems to be an important dimension in stimulating a sense of responsibility. The popular practice of management by objectives is one way of establishing more autonomy, because it provides employees with an opportunity to set work goals and personal goals.

5. *Feedback.* Feedback, the fifth core dimension, refers to information that workers receive on how well they are performing. People in general have a need to know how they are doing. They need this feedback frequently so that necessary improvements can be made.

An Organizational Application of Job Enrichment.   An attempt to enrich jobs was built into a General Foods Corporation plant. The new plant management established work teams of 7 to 14 employees. Teams were given large amounts of autonomy and frequent feedback. There also was a high degree of variety built into each job. Most routine work was mechanized. The five core dimensions appear to have been provided, to a large extent. Preliminary results indicated that the plant compared favorably with more traditionally operated plants; productivity was greater, and absenteeism and turnover were less. Now, after 22 years of improvements, the plant remains ahead of others in the field. Several hundred other organizations have followed the General Foods lead, and the term today to describe them is *high involvement firms.* Some of these high involvement firms such as Procter & Gamble and the General Motors Saturn plant in Spring Hill, Tennessee, claim that they have over 30 percent quality and productivity gains since applying job enrichment strategies.[56]

Relating Pay to Job Performance

The money that employees receive for working is actually a package made up of pay and various fringe benefits, such as health insurance, vacation pay, life insurance, and sick leave. Each of the content and process theories of motivation suggests that money can have some influence on effort and persistence.

In Maslow's need hierarchy, pay has the potential to satisfy each of the five needs. However, according to Herzberg's two-factor model, pay is a maintenance factor that should not contribute significantly to workers' motivation. Expectancy theory would indicate that since pay can satisfy a variety of needs, it has an attraction; pay would be a good motivator if workers perceive that good performance is instrumental to obtaining it. In equity theory, pay is a major outcome that one person compares with another person. The input–outcome ratios are especially reviewed in terms of pay. Perceptions of pay inequity may cause employees to take action to restore equity. Reinforcement theory would view pay as an environmental consequence that could be used to stimulate positive work behaviors.

A number of research studies suggest to managers that a pay plan, in order to motivate, must create a belief that good performance leads to high levels of pay, minimize the negative consequences of good performance, and create conditions so that desired rewards other than pay are seen to be related to good performance.[57] Research findings suggest that many organizations, although they try, do not do a very good job of relating pay to performance in either managerial or nonmanagerial jobs.[58]

Figure 11–10 illustrates some of the potentially negative consequences of being dissatisfied with pay. Managers must understand that pay is very important to some people and is a highly valued reward. It can serve to satisfy needs and to increase the motivation intensity of the employee. If a worker's desire for more pay is not satisfied, the consequences could be reduced performance, filing of grievances, interest in going

FIGURE 11–10   Consequences of Pay Dissatisfaction

Pay is very important to some employees and being dissatisfied with pay has negative consequences.

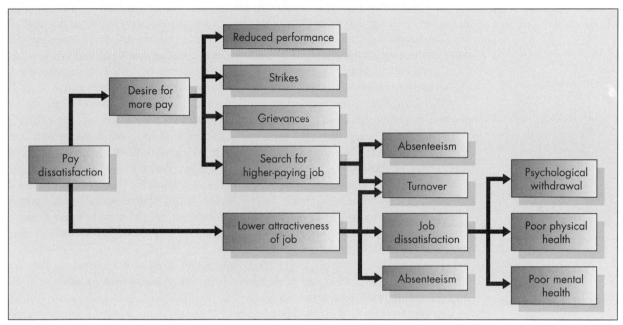

Source: From E E Lawler, *Pay and Organizational Effectiveness: A Psychological View* (New York: McGraw-Hill, 1971). Used with permission of McGraw-Hill Book Company.

on strike, or even seeking a job elsewhere. To head off pay dissatisfaction problems, a number of organizations have used some innovative plans.

Money as a Motivator.   Nucor Corporation has a management team that, unlike Herzberg, believes that money is the best motivator. Most Nucor employees are unskilled and semiskilled when they are hired. Furthermore, Nucor employees seem to place a high value on job security, which management attempts to provide.

Nucor, headquartered in Charlotte, North Carolina, currently operates five steel joist fabrication plants. The entire corporation has five organizational levels from the president to the operating employee. There are no assistant managers, group managers, or directors. All of Nucor's facilities are in rural areas. These organizational features and plant locations are rather unusual in the steel joist fabrication industry.[59]

The company currently has four incentive compensation programs. The focal point of these programs is groups, not individuals. The incentive systems are for production employees; department heads; secretaries, accounting clerks, accountants, and engineers; and senior officers. The groups range in size from 25 to 30. Approximately 5,500 Nucor employees are under the main program, called the production incentive system.[60]

To a certain extent, Nucor views each of the 25 to 30 groups of production employees as being in business for itself. What workers earn is largely dependent on their performance. There are no bonuses paid when equipment is not operating. The rules for absenteeism at Nucor are simple. There are four grace days per year. Additional days off are approved for military service or jury duty. Anyone not there for other days loses the week's bonus. Additionally, being more than a half-hour late means losing the bonus for the day.

The production incentive program is only one part of the Nucor system. At the department-head level, the company has an incentive compensation program based on the contribution of the particular department to the company as a whole.

The third incentive plan applies to employees who are neither in a production function nor at the department-manager level: accountants, secretaries, clerks, and so on. The bonus they receive is based on either the division's return on assets or the corporation's return on assets. Every month, each division receives a report showing, on a year-to-year basis, its return on assets. This chart is posted in the employee cafeteria or break area, together with the chart showing the bonus payout.

The fourth Nucor program is for senior officers. They receive no profit sharing, no pension or retirement plans, or other similar perks. More than half of each officer's compensation is based directly on company earnings. If the firm is doing well, the executives do well. Their base salaries are set at 70 percent of what an individual in a comparable position with another company would receive.

Nucor does not have a retirement plan that is actuarially based; rather, it has a profit-sharing plan with a deferred trust. Under the plan, 10 percent of the firm's pretax earnings is put into profit sharing annually. Of this amount, 20 percent is set aside to be paid to employees in March of the following year as cash profit sharing. The remainder is put into a trust.

Vesting in the profit-sharing trust is much like that of a retirement plan. An employee is 20 percent vested after a year in profit sharing, with an additional 10 percent vesting each year thereafter.

Another example of an incentive at Nucor is the service awards program. Instead of handing out pen and pencil sets, money clips, or gift certificates for seniority, Nucor issues company stock. After five years of service, employees receive five shares of Nucor stock. Another five years of service and they receive another five shares, and so on.

Lincoln Electric's Shift In Pay Plan.   The superstar firm for relating pay to job performance has been Cleveland-based Lincoln Electric Co. For years the size of worker bonuses at Lincoln was the talk of all industry. To learn how Lincoln did it thousands of managers would visit each year to look, first-hand, at the pay-for-performance bonus system.[61] However, because of global competition and some management mistakes Lincoln has had to overhaul its bonus system, which in some years paid employees up to 100 percent of their wages in annual performance-linked bonuses.

Lincoln employees under the new bonus arrangements are still considered self-managing entrepreneurs who are minimally supervised. Each employee is accountable for the quality of his or her work and is rated twice a year on quality, output, dependability, cooperation, and ideas. The average Lincoln factory employee earns $16.54 an hour versus $14.25 average manufacturing wage in the Cleveland area. The 1995 average bonus was 56 percent of wages, which is the lowest in years.

Lincoln guarantees work to employees with three years experience. No one has been laid off since 1948, and turnover is less than 4 percent. The slimmer bonuses, however, reflect a change in thinking and led to employee protests outside headquarters. To study the change Lincoln has set up a committee to come up with a new bonus formula. Even though Lincoln has slimmed its bonuses, it still is likely to remain a pay-for-performance benchmark firm for others.

Employee Stock Ownership Plans (ESOPs)

In over 10,000 organizations, about 10 million employees at all levels own stock in the company in which they work. The total market value of employee ownership is about $150 billion with 40 percent in employee stock ownership plans (ESOPs) and the remainder in profit sharing, Sec. 401(k), savings, and stock purchase plans.[62] There is some evidence that employee ownership may increase motivation, commitment, and loyalty. Changes in the federal tax laws in the 1980s and 1990 have made employee stock ownership plans a method for profit sharing and funding pension funds. Firms such as Kroger's (33 percent employee ownership stake), Morgan Stanley (57 percent employee ownership stake), and Rockwell International (41 percent employee owner-ship stake) have implemented ESOPs. It is suggested that although motivation can be improved by use of ESOPs, the increased use of employee ownership has resulted primarily from tax benefits, restructuring, and fending off raiders interested in taking over a company. ESOPs give employees the right to vote their ownership shares, which can serve as a defense against an unfriendly takeover.

There are some potential negative consequences associated with ESOPs. When employees buy out companies to save their jobs or because of poor financial conditions, there is a risk that the investment will be lost. Financial pressures or risks can prove to be negative in terms of motivation. There is also the question of participation. Does owning stock in a company mean that employees will have more say in major decisions? Critics point out that the key participants in major decision making in employee-owned forms are trustees of the ESOP. There is actually no increase in employee participation in decision making because the trustees, often managers (executives), are the key figures.

Flexible Working Hours

As indicated earlier, managers are faced with an increasingly diverse workforce that includes single parents with young children, employees with elder care responsibili-ties, and employees attending school to improve their English language skills. The concept of flexible working hours or flextime has motivational appeal to many employees. **Flextime** is a term used to describe a work schedule that gives employees a choice in when they will be present at work. A sample flexible working schedule is presented in Figure 11–11. In the sample, employees are able to select one of three options presented. In all cases employees must be present at the 9:00 AM–12:00 noon and 2:00 PM–4:00 PM core times. The three options allow employees greater autonomy in scheduling work and personal time. Individuals can complete personal errands, sleep late, or leave earlier than other workers by selecting the best option for them. Flextime schedules recognize that individuals have different needs and preferences concerning when they will work.

Research on flextime suggests that it can be motivational in that absenteeism and tardiness are reduced, as well as job satisfaction improved.[63] Despite the difficulty of coordinating schedules, flextime provides managers with a method to recognize the diverse needs of employees in terms of managing their time. The ability to accommo-date employees' nonwork needs is a positive approach to motivation that should continue to appeal to managers and employees.[64]

Sam Rivera, an assistant foreman at Fel-Pro, Inc., a Skokie, Illinois, autoparts maker with 1,100 employees, is a manager who understands the flextime needs of his employees and makes a real effort to accommodate people. He is viewed as being fair, flexible, and understanding toward the group he supervises. His 50 workers include 29 Hispanics, 11 Caucasians, 9 African-Americans, and 1 Asian Pacific Islander. There are 4 women and 46 men.[65]

At one point, Sam gave one of his workers three days of emergency leave so he could work with Fel-Pro's psychologist to extricate his son from a street gang. A host of examples like this help explain why Sam's unit produces about 120 percent above the norm. "As long as the job gets done," is Sam's motto, which, apparently, his 50 workers have also adopted.

FIGURE 11–11   A Three-Option Flextime Work Schedule

This flextime schedule covers the 7 AM to 6 PM workday.

Flextime	Core Time*	Flextime	Core Time*	Flextime

| 7 AM | 9 AM | 12 noon | 2 PM | 4 PM | 6 PM |

Sample Schedules

    Option I   7:00–4:00

    Option II   8:00–5:00

    Option III   9:00–6:00

*All employees must be present and work each core period.

Implementation

Flextime is intended to ensure that work is accomplished efficiently and at a high-quality level and, at the same time, to permit employees and their supervisors to establish work schedules, within limits, that recognize individual and family needs.

- Flextime schedules may be approved for employees with permanent positions of employment.
- Employees must work 40 hours per week.
- Offices must be open from 8:00 AM to 5:00 PM.
- A minimum of one half-hour is required for each person as a lunch period.
- Individual work schedules are approved in advance by the department head for a minimum of one month. Work schedules must conform to the needs of the department. Managers responsible for a work unit may require a change in work schedules to meet the needs of the unit.

Summary of Key Points

- Motivation is an inner state that helps describe the wishes, desires, drives, and needs of individuals.
- Two important content theories of motivation are Maslow's need hierarchy theory and Herzberg's two-factor theory. Maslow arranges five needs in a hierarchy based on different levels of importance. Herzberg presents two sets of job conditions: maintenance and motivational. The maintenance factors are external to the job and cause dissatisfaction when they are not present. The motivational factors are job centered and tend to motivate individuals.
- Equity theory proposes that perceived inequity is a motivational force. When a person believes that he has been inequitably treated in comparison with the treatment of others, he will be motivated to correct the inequity.
- The expectancy theory of motivation is a process theory that suggests that individuals are motivated to make choices among different behaviors or intensities of work effort. An individual exerts effort to achieve performance that results in receiving preferred rewards.

- The reinforcement theory of motivation relies on the use of reinforcers (positive, negative, extinction, and punishment) to motivate. It is concerned with the environment and its consequences for the person.
- Job enrichment seeks to improve both task efficiency and human satisfaction by building into jobs greater range for personal achievement and recognition, more challenging and responsible work, and more opportunity for individual advancement and growth.
- A pay plan motivates when it creates a belief that good performance leads to high levels of pay, minimizes the negative consequences of good performance, and creates conditions so that desired rewards other than pay are related to good performance.
- Employee stock ownership plans (ESOPs) involve employees' owning a portion of the company.
- Flextime is a term used to describe a work schedule that allows employees some choice in when they will be present at work.

Discussion and Review Questions

1. How is reinforcement theory used by the instructor in the course you are now taking?

2. The Protestant work ethic is used to describe societal values. Is it still applicable to the increasingly culturally diverse workforce?

3. The manager of a team of engineers in a manufacturing plant was overheard to say, "I believe that money is the best of all possible motivators. You can say what you please about all that other nonsense, but when it comes right down to it, if you give a guy a raise, you'll motivate him. That's all there is to it." In light of what we have discussed in this chapter, advise this manager.

4. Whom do you make school, job, or friendship comparisons with on a regular basis? Have you ever perceived inequity when making comparisons? If so, how do you handle the inequity?

5. Flextime has gained popularity in recent years. Is this type of work schedule motivational? Why?

6. What events have occurred in the United States in the past few years that suggest that job security is now more uncertain?

7. This chapter emphasized that managers must be familiar with the fundamental needs of people to motivate employees successfully. Select two individuals you know well. Do they differ with respect to the strength of various needs? Discuss these differences and indicate how they could affect behavior. If you were attempting to motivate those persons, would you use different approaches for each? Why?

8. Can a student's "job" be enriched? Assume that you are to consult with your professor about applying the two-factor motivation model in your class. You are to answer these questions: Can you apply this approach to the classroom? Why? If you can, differentiate between maintenance and motivational factors and develop a list of motivational factors your professor can use to enrich the student's job.

9. Assume that you have just read Vroom's thoughts on how the *goals* of individuals influence their *effort* and how the behavior the individual selects depends on an assessment of the probability that the behavior will successfully lead to the goal. What is your goal in this management course? Is it influencing your effort? Do you suppose another person in your class might have a different goal? Is that person's effort (behavior) different from yours? If your professor was aware of this, could it be of any value?

10. Evaluate the pay system used at Nucor Corporation. What do you like about the system?

Case 11–1
Executive Pay: Worth It or a Disgrace?

"The Americans are crazy!" roars Rolf Dahlems, manager of German consultants Ward Howell Unternehmensberater. "No executive is so good that he can justify these sums."

Every time a major publication like *Forbes* or *Fortune* publishes lists of US executive compensation, pundits and media naïfs around the globe take their cheap shots about how much more selfless and compassionate chief executives are in other parts of the world. Last year Japan's influential *Yomiuri* newspaper ran a cartoon depicting a Detroit-made car heading downhill, weighed down with overpaid US auto executives. The Japanese car was portrayed racing smartly uphill, transporting Japan's lighter, modestly paid auto executives. Taking the bait, *Business Week* declared, "Disparities in American and Japanese pay are stunning."

Not so fast, folks. The disparities aren't what they seem. Outside the United States there is not much public disclosure of executive compensation, and what disclosure there is sheds only a murky light on the subject. So reviews of tax filings, corporate footnotes, and several scores of interviews with local business people, headhunters, and compensation consultants are needed. *Forbes*'s researchers conducted a thorough analysis of cash compensation—salary plus bonus—of the highest-paid chief executives of publicly traded companies in the United States; for Japan and Germany, *Forbes* used a sampling of highly paid chiefs. At this level, there's no question: US bosses earn more. According to the calculations, the 20 best-paid US executives earned on average $4.8 million in cash salary and bonus in 1992, versus an estimated $1.8 million in Germany and an estimated $530,000 in Japan.

However, *Forbes* discovered, these are not apple versus apple comparisons but asparagus versus bananas. "Each country has a different system," concedes 64-year-old Fumio Sato, the mild-mannered president of Japan's Toshiba Corp. "I don't think the salary gap [between US and Japanese bosses] is so strange."

In the United States, executives tend to take their salary right up front—where it is exposed to income and social security taxes. But in France, for example, marginal tax rates and social security deductions can equal 65 percent of a senior executive's cash compensation. No surprise, then, that in countries with high tax rates, companies throw in lots of nontaxable compensation.

How? One way is by paying the same executive several salaries, one for the home country, for example, and others from subsidiaries outside the home country. Alone among major industrial countries, the United States taxes all of an American citizen's income, no matter where earned. Other countries tax income earned within their borders. Thus while a German chief executive may receive one publicly reported paycheck, another ends up—perfectly legally—in a foreign bank account. Odile Ledesert, consultant at Towers Perrin in Paris, says circumspectly, "We wouldn't learn about bonuses paid in Switzerland or the Bahamas." Horst Brocker, of headhunters Egon Zehnder International GmbH in Munich, makes an educated guess: "There is strong indication that maybe 20 percent of the salary [of a German chief executive with foreign duties] is paid abroad."

Suppose a German boss earns a 20 percent split-salary bonus on a $1.5 million base. Assuming that a $300,000 bonus would probably escape most taxation, it's worth $640,000 in pretax dollars, given Germany's high income tax rates.

"With [marginal] personal income tax rates at 53 percent in Germany, there is little incentive for increases in cash," says Thierry Hamon, partner at Wyatt Co. in Dusseldorf.

There are other hidden payments to European executives. German chief executives are usually given some kind of housing allowance and are often provided with household help. The value to the executive of a typical housing allowance and maid may be up to $130,000 in pretax money terms, if structured properly.

A 1991 court case in Stuttgart revealed that a German chief executive was allowed to charge against the company $300,000 in plane fares to his summer home in Majorca. He was also allowed to charge his employer for some of the villa's renovation, ostensibly for "security" reasons.

German chief executives enjoy a special bonus—a network of external board directorships. We are talking about serious money. It is not uncommon for executives like Hilmar Kopper of the Deutsche Bank or Wolfgang Roller of the Dresdner Bank to supplement an official cash salary and bonus in the region of $1.5 million with another $350,000 or so in directorship fees.

Take the value of a housing allowance, a number of vacation tickets and other company-paid expenses, plus a complement of directorships. Add these to the $1.8 million base earned by the well-paid German boss. It all adds up to the aftertax equivalent of around $2.7 million—half again as much as was reported.

Japan? As in Germany, there are some discreet—and valuable—forms of untaxed compensation in Japan, where the top tax rate rises to about 65 percent after income exceeds just $180,000. Entertaining clients is a big perk in Japan; in a survey, American Express found that Japanese firms spent three times more on entertainment than did US firms. Top Japanese executives are entertained by geisha in private tatami rooms overlooking bamboo gardens at Kanetanaka, an elite Tokyo establishment. Cost: around $700 a person. Yes, US executives have big expense accounts, but they are not as big as in Japan.

Japanese chief executives may also be enriched by "gift" giving, an act that is ingrained in Japanese culture. Corporate golf club memberships are popular Japanese perks. Toshiba's Sato has two company-paid golf memberships. According to the editor of a Japanese golf magazine, a member at a high-class golf club can shell out $1,600 to $1,800 to entertain three guests with a round of golf plus food and drink.

Every country has its favorite perks. French bosses often get first-rate chefs; British executives may get cars with drivers for private use. So prevalent is the car perk—even with middle managers—that over 60 percent of all new cars in Britain are bought by businesses. "It can happen a chief executive has a Jaguar with driver and a BMW for himself, all paid by the company," says Andrew Christie, a director at Noble Lowndes & Partners Ltd.

In Hong Kong, top executives at the largest firms nominally earn between $400,000 and $700,000 in cash. But add to that a generous housing allowance, several club memberships, children's education, maids, car and driver, and subsidized loans. With all the add-ons, the executive's pretax compensation package could easily be worth $1 million. And note this: In Hong Kong the top tax rate is just 15 percent. On a $700,000 salary, a Hong Kong executive takes home almost $600,000. An American counterpart would need $1 million to do as well after taxes.

Now here's a surprise: Towers Perrin ranked global executive pay based on the pay package's net purchasing power. Its conclusion: Mexican and Brazilian chief executives were the best paid in the world, earning a third more than US executives. The firm says currency changes can change the picture, but still it provides an idea of how hard these packages are to compare.

Also, the claim made by a number of politicians in the 1996 US Presidential campaign that "greedy corporations are squeezing down employee wages while pumping up profits" is not substantiated by the facts. Over a number of decades, workers have received about the same share of the corporate pie, over 60 percent of revenue. In the 1990s the payout to workers is a little higher at 65 percent of revenue in wages and fringe benefits than it was in the 1950s to 1980s.

Questions for Analysis

1. Do you think that any executive is worth the kind of pay and perks provided to American chief executives presented in the case?

2. The federal government has made some statements that it might intervene to control or cap what executives are paid for performance. Do you think that the government should play a role? Why?

3. Do you believe that chief executives make comparisons of their pay with other chief executives' pay like the comparisons to referent persons we discussed in connection with equity theory? Why?

Sources: Adapted from R Morais and Joe Spiers, "The Myth of Corporate Greed," *Fortune,* April 15, 1996, pp. 67–68; "Executive Pay: Random Numbers," *The Economist,* June 3, 1995, pp. 62 and 65; "The Global Boss' Pay: Where (and How) the Money Is," *Forbes,* June 7, 1993, pp. 90–98; A Bennett, "Managers' Incomes Aren't Worlds Apart," *The Wall Street Journal,* October 12, 1992, pp. B1 and B5; "Executive Pay: The Party Ain't Over Yet," *Business Week,* April 26, 1993.

Video Case
Employee Motivation at Tellabs, Inc.

It's important to understand the reasons why effective managers must be concerned with employee motivation. After identifying some of the factors contributing to motivation, this video looks at how Tellabs, Inc., has successfully applied motivation theory.

Tellabs is based in the Chicago area, but is internationally known for its telecommunications products and services. However, recently the company gained fame when its stock increased 1,683 percent over a five-year period, making Tellabs the best performing stock at that time on the New York Stock Exchange, the American Stock Exchange, and Nasdaq. Tellabs was founded in 1975 by a group of engineers brainstorming at a kitchen table, and grew from 20 employees with annual sales of $312,000 to 2,600 employees with annual sales of $494 million in 1994. Tellabs currently designs, manufactures, markets, and services voice and data transport and network access systems.

One of the principal reasons for Tellabs' remarkable success has been its ability to motivate its workforce. In simple terms, employee motivation refers to an employee's willingness to perform in his or her job. Effective managers must be concerned with motivating employees toward common goals that will improve the success of the company. At Tellabs, a motivated workforce has enhanced the quality of its products and services.

Tellabs' manager of quality, Joe Taylor, explains what's behind the company's motivated workers: "In the past 10 years we've found that to improve our quality we had to invest in our employees through training programs. Specifically, they have the tools and the resources now to make a difference within our processes in the factory and provide us with process improvements."

A motivated workforce contributes to increased quality in goods and services, greater efficiency in work processes, and improved customer service. Grace Pastiak said, "When I look at the improvements that Tellabs has made since implementing just-in-time and Total Quality Commitment, by far the biggest gain has been exciting employees to do their best and giving them the opportunity to implement their own ideas."

At its core, motivation results from an individual's desire to satisfy personal needs or goals. Every person has a set of needs or goals that influences his or her behavior. Abraham Maslow postulated that needs can be placed in a hierarchy and that as each need level in the hierarchy is satisfied, the person will concentrate on meeting needs at the next level.

Frederick Herzberg conducted a study in the 1960s that concluded that factors pertaining to the work itself, such as achievement, recognition, and responsibility, tended to actually motivate employees. Other factors, such as supervision, pay, and company policies, might increase job satisfaction, but not necessarily employee motivation.

A third approach to motivation, developed by Douglas McGregor, involves two opposing theories about the nature of human behavior. Theory X holds that some employees are lazy or unwilling to work unless motivated by negative factors such as threats and constant supervision. Theory Y holds that employees want to work and do a good job and are motivated best by incentives, responsibility, and ownership of their work.

Maslow's hierarchy, Herzberg's factors, and McGregor's theories suggest that it's in a company's best interest to offer employees adequate rewards and to appeal to their pride of workmanship. At Tellabs, many employees say that the entrepreneurial atmosphere nurtured by managers makes them feel good about themselves. So Tellabs clearly takes a Theory Y approach.

Effective managers help create a work environment that encourages, supports, and sustains improvement in work performance. At Tellabs, managers have implemented job rotation systems and a cadre of high performance teams to help enrich jobs and create an innovative working environment.

Some companies may use a combination of motivation theories. In 1992, Tellabs presented its corporate goals, known as Strategic Initiatives, to its employees. The corporate mission statement emphasized the company's goals quality, customer satisfaction, profits, growth, its people, and its corporate integrity.

Tellabs' total compensation plan includes an Employee Stock Option Plan and retirement investments, such as 401(k). Also employees receive an annual bonus based on the company's productivity.

At Tellabs, employee motivation and performance are enhanced by an atmosphere in which employees are openly told they are valued and trusted. Managers encourage calculated risk taking and innovation. They empower workers through cross-functional teams so that they are able to identify problems and develop effective solutions.

Tellabs' Career Development System trains internal candidates for key management positions, while its competitive compensation plan shares the wealth, contributes to employee satisfaction, and encourages peak performance.

Critical Thinking Questions

1. McGregor's Theory X and Theory Y have totally different views of the typical worker. Which of the two theories do you think managers should adopt? Explain. Describe how adopting Theory X would affect a manager's behavior toward employees. Do the same for Theory Y.

2. What are some of the potential pitfalls of using employee empowerment as a motivational device in the workplace?

3. Herzberg's theory says workplace factors lead to employee motivation. What are some workplace factors not mentioned in the video that could affect employee motivation?

EXPERIENTIAL EXERCISE
YOUR JOB PREFERENCES COMPARED WITH OTHERS'

Purpose

This exercise is designed to identify what makes a job attractive or unattractive to you. Preferences of employees, if known, could be used as information by managers to develop and restructure jobs that are more attractive, rewarding, and generally more fulfilling. This type of information permits a manager to create a positive motivational atmosphere for subordinates.

The Exercise in Class

1. Think about your present job or the type of job you would like. Decide which of the following job factors is most important to you. Place a 1 in front of it. Then decide which is the second most important to you and place a 2 in front of it. Keep ranking the items in order of importance until the least important job factor is ranked 14. Individuals differ in the order in which these job factors are ranked. What is your present preference?

_____ Advancement (opportunity for promotion).
_____ Pay (income received for working).
_____ Fringe benefits (vacation period, insurance, recreation facilities).
_____ Schedule (hours worked, starting time).
_____ Location (geographic area: Midwest, South, West, East, Northeast, Southwest).
_____ Supervisor (a fair, influential boss).
_____ Feedback (receiving prompt, meaningful, and accurate feedback on job performance).
_____ Security (steady work, assurance of a future).
_____ Challenge (interesting and stimulating work).
_____ Working conditions (comfortable and clean work area).
_____ Co-workers (colleagues who are friendly, interesting).
_____ The organization (working for a company you are proud of).
_____ Responsibility (having responsibility to complete important job).
_____ Training and development opportunities (the ability to receive training and development in the organization or through external sources).

2. Now rank the job factors as you think other members of your class would rank them. Look around and think how the average person in your class would rank the job factors.

_____ Advancement.
_____ Pay.

_____ Fringe benefits.

_____ Schedule.

_____ Location.

_____ Supervisor.

_____ Feedback.

_____ Security.

_____ Challenge.

_____ Working conditions.

_____ Co-workers.

_____ The organization.

_____ Responsibility.

_____ Training and development opportunities.

3. The instructor will form four- to six-person groups to discuss the *individual* and *other* rankings. Each group

should calculate averages for both rankings. What does this show? The members of your group should discuss these average scores.

4. The average individual and average other rankings should be placed on the board or flip chart and discussed by the entire class.

The Learning Message

Individuals consider different factors important. Can a manager realistically respond to a wide range of different preferences among subordinates?

Notes

1. Bernard Berelson and Gary A Steiner, *Human Behavior: An Inventory of Scientific Findings* (New York: Harcourt Brace Jovanovich, 1964), p. 239.

2. Frederick F Reichheld, "Loyalty-Based Management," *Harvard Business Review,* March–April 1993, pp. 64–73.

3. Peter Nulty, "The National Business Hall of Fame," *Fortune,* April 5, 1993, pp. 108–16.

4. Marshall Loeb, "Jack Welch Lets Fly on Budgets, Bonuses, and Buddy Boards," *Fortune,* May 29, 1995, pp. 145–47.

5. Betsy Wiesendanger, "Take Me to the River," *Sales and Marketing Management,* October 1990, pp. 62–67.

6. John P Campbell, Marvin D Dunnette, Edward E Lawler III, and Karl E Weick, Jr., *Managerial Behavior, Performance and Effectiveness* (New York: McGraw-Hill, 1970), p. 341.

7. Less described and hence not as well known are the cognitive and aesthetic needs hypothesized by Maslow. Examples of cognitive needs are the need to know or understand and the manipulation of the environment as the result of curiosity. The aesthetic needs are satisfied by moving from ugliness toward beauty. Maslow did not include them in the formal hierarchy framework. See, Abraham H Maslow, *Motivation and Personality* (New York: Harper & Row, 1954), pp. 93–98.

8. Ibid., p. 82.

9. Joseph Nocera, "Living with Layoffs," *Fortune,* April 1, 1996, pp. 69–71.

10. "Economic Anxiety," *Business Week,* March 11, 1996, pp. 49–56.

11. "Reflections on the Downsizing Debate," *HR Focus,* July 1996, pp. 9–11.

12. "The Death of Corporate Loyalty," *The Economist,* April 3, 1993, p. 63.

13. Julia Lawlor, "More Layoffs: Hurt Morale, and Curb Economy," *USA Today,* September 20, 1993, p. B1.

14. Steve Perstein, "Blank Checks," *Business Ethics,* January–February 1993, p. 14.

15. Maslow, *Motivation and Personality,* p. 81.

16. Ibid.

17. "Harry V Quadracci," *Business Ethics,* May 1993, pp. 19–21.

18. See Frederick Herzberg, B Mausner, and G Snyderman, *The Motivation to Work* (New York: John Wiley & Sons, 1959).

19. "Money Isn't Everything," *Personnel,* September 1990, p. 6.

20. Michael R Malinovsky and John R Barry, "Determinants of Work Attitudes," *Journal of Applied Psychology,* December 1965, pp. 446–51. For a discussion of other alternative interpretations of the two-factor theory and the research support for the various interpretations, see N King, "Clarification and Evaluation of the Two-Factor Theory of Job Satisfaction," *Psychological Bulletin,* July 1970, pp. 18–31; D A Ondrack, "Defense Mechanisms and the Herzberg Theory: An Alternate Test," *Personnel Psychology,* March 1974, pp. 79–89.

21. See the classic Victor H Vroom, *Work and Motivation* (New York: John Wiley & Sons, 1964), pp. 128–29.

22. For one of the earliest criticisms, see R J House and L A Wigdor, "Herzberg's Dual-Factor Theory of Job Satisfaction and Motivation: A Review of the Evidence and a Criticism," *Personnel Psychology,* Winter 1967, pp. 369–89.

23. R J Caston and R Braito, "A Specification Issue in Job Satisfaction Research," *Sociological Perspectives,* April 1985, pp. 175–77.

24. Frederick Herzberg, *Work and the Nature of Man* (Cleveland: World, 1966). This is a classic work by Herzberg.

25. An early study is Donald P Schwab, H Wiliam De Vitt, and Larry L Cummings, "A Test for the Adequacy of the Two-Factor Theory as a Predictor of Self-Report Performance Effects," *Personnel Psychology,* Summer 1971, pp. 293–303.

26. Marvin D Dunnette, John P Campbell, and Milton D Hakel, "Factors Contributing to Job Satisfaction and Job Dissatisfaction in Six Occupational Groups," *Organizational Behavior and Human Performance,* May 1967, pp. 143–74.

27. J Stacy Adams, "Inequity in Social Exchanges," in L Berkowitz, ed., *Advances in Experiential Social Psychology* (New York: Academic Press, 1965), pp. 267–300.

28. T P Summers and Angelo S DeNisi, "In Search of Adams' Other: Reexamination of Referents Used in the Evaluation of Pay," *Human Relations,* June 1990, pp. 497–511; Robert P Vecchio, "An Individual Differences Interpretation of Conflicting Predictions Generated by Equity Theory and Expectancy Theory," *Journal of Applied Psychology,* August 1981, pp. 470–84.

29. J Greenberg, "Equity and Workplace Status: A Field Experiment," *Journal of Applied Psychology,* November 1988, pp. 606–13.

30. Vroom, *Work and Motivation,* p. 129.

31. Ibid.

32. Because the preference variable is also called valence, the expression may be $M = E \times I \times V$.

33. K A Kovach, "What Motivates Employees? Workers and Supervisors Give Different Answers," *Business Horizons,* September–October 1987, pp. 58–65.

34. Kerry A Dolan, "When Money Isn't Enough," *Forbes,* November 18, 1996, pp. 164–70.

35. See Victor H Vroom, "Organizational Choice: A Study of Pre- and Post-Decision Processes," *Organizational Behavior and Human Performance,* August 1966, pp. 212–25; J R Galbraith and L L Cummings, "An Empirical Investigation of the Motivational Determinants of Task Performance: Interactive Effects between Instrumentality-Valence and Motivation-Ability," *Organizational Behavior and Human Performance,* August 1967, pp. 237–57. For a critical review of field research or expectancy, see D P Schwab, "Expectancy Theory Predictions of Employee Performance: A Review of the Theory and Evidence," *Psychological Bulletin,* July 1972, pp. 1–9.

36. Terence Mitchell, "Expectancy-Value Models in Organizational Psychology," in N Feather, ed., *Expectancy, Incentive, and Action* (Hillsdale, NJ: Erlbaum & Associates, 1980).

37. E L Thorndike, *Animal Intelligence* (New York: McGraw-Hill, 1911), p. 244.

38. B F Skinner, *Science and Human Behavior* (New York: Macmillan, 1953); B F Skinner, *Contingencies of Reinforcement* (New York: Appleton-Century-Crofts, 1969).

39. H Davis and H M Hurwitz, eds., *Operant-Pavlovian Interactions* (Hillsdale, NJ: Erlbaum & Associates, 1977).

40. Laurence D Smith, "On Production and Control: B F Skinner and the Technological Ideal of Science," *American Psychologist,* February 1992, pp. 216–23.

41. John B Miner, *Role Motivation Theories* (New York: Routhedge, 1993).

42. Steven Kerr, "Risking Business: The New Pay Game," *Fortune,* July 22, 1996, pp. 94–96.

43. John P Fernandez, *The Diversity Advantage* (New York: Lexington Books, 1993), pp. 16–32.

44. David Jamison and Julie O'Mara, *Managing Workforce 2000* (San Francisco: Jossey-Bass, 1991), pp. 5–12.

45. Joel Dreyfuss, "Get Ready for the New Workforce," *Fortune,* April 29, 1990, pp. 165–81.

46. Taylor H Cox and Stacy Blake, "Managing Cultural Diversity: Implications for Organizational Competitiveness," *Academy of Management Executive,* August 1991, pp. 45–46.

47. "A conversation with Geert Hofstede," *Organizational Dynamics,* 1993, pp. 53–61; Geert Hofstede, *Cultures and Organizations: Software of the Mind* (New York: McGraw-Hill, 1991).

48. Helen Deresky, *International Management* (New York: Harper Collins, 1994), pp. 323–51.

49. A report on a major project is found in Barry A Macy, "A Progress Report on the Bolivar Quality of Life Project," *Personnel Journal,* August 1979, pp. 527–30, 558–59.

50. Frederick Herzberg, "One More Time: How Do You Motivate Employees?" *Harvard Business Review,* January–February 1968, p. 53.

51. William J Paul, Jr., Keith B Robertson, and Frederick Herzberg, "Job Enrichment Pays Off," *Harvard Business Review,* March–April 1969, p. 61.

52. Michael A Campion and Paul W Thayer, "How Do You Design a Job?" *Personnel Journal,* January 1989, pp. 43–46.

53. Michael A Campion, "Interdisciplinary Approaches to Job Design," *Journal of Applied Psychology,* August 1988, pp. 467–81.

54. James L Gibson, John M Ivancevich, and James H Donnelly, Jr., *Organizations: Behavior, Structure, Processes,* 9th ed. (Burr Ridge, IL: Richard D. Irwin, 1997), pp. 364–66.

55. J Richard Hackman, Greg Oldham, Robert Janson, and Kenneth Purdy, "A New Strategy for Job Enrichment,"

California Management Review, Summer 1975, pp. 57–71.

56. Tom Christensen, "A High Involvement Redesign," *Quality Progress,* May 1993, p. 108.

57. An interesting discussion of pay and performance can be found in Thomas P Flannery, David A Hofrichter, and Paul E Platten, *People, Performance and Pay* (New York: Free Press, 1996).

58. Shawn Tully, "Your Paycheck Gets Exciting," *Fortune,* November 1, 1993, pp. 83–96.

59. Tom Peters, *Thriving on Chaos* (New York: Alfred A. Knopf, 1987), pp. 335–36.

60. Dana Milbank, "Low Steel Prices May Hold Down Nucor's Earnings," *The Wall Street Journal,* May 1, 1992, pp. B7–8; Michael Schroeder and Walecia

Konrad, "Nucor: Rolling Right into Steel's Big Time," *Business Week,* November 19, 1990, pp. 76–81.

61. Zachary Schiller, "A Model Incentive Plan Gets Caught in a Vise," *Business Week,* January 22, 1996, pp. 89 and 92.

62. "Employee Ownership," *Employee Benefit Plan Review,* July 1992, p. 14.

63. J L Pierce, J W Newstrom, R B Dunham, J A E Barber, *Alternative Work Schedules* (Neutham Heights, MA: Allyn and Bacon, 1989).

64. S Shellenberger, "Managers Navigate Uncharted Waters Trying to Resolve Work-Family Conflicts," *The Wall Street Journal,* December 7, 1992, pp. B1 and B7.

65. "Sam Rivera: An Easygoing Boss and a Master Motivator," *Business Week,* June 28, 1993, p. 84.

12 MANAGING WORK GROUPS

Chapter Learning Objectives

After completing Chapter 12, you should be able to:

- **Define** such terms as groupthink, group development acculturation, and group conflict.
- **Describe** the important characteristics of groups in organizations.
- **Discuss** how cohesiveness can influence a group's overall performance.
- **Compare** the causes of and solutions to intragroup and intergroup conflict.
- **Identify** the key reasons why informal groups appear in organizations.

Individualism and Teamwork: It Works at Bell Labs

Before the breakup of AT&T, Bell Labs was considered a national treasure. It was supported by a kind of hidden tax included in telephone bills from the monopoly company. Bell Labs' work was meant to benefit the nation. From the labs in New Jersey emerged the transistor, the laser, the solar cell, the first transistorized digital computer, the cellular radio, and a galaxy of other world-class technologies that resulted in whole new industries.

Now, the labs work only on projects likely to bear fruit for AT&T owners—and they work fairly quickly. Bell Labs has narrowed its focus and now concentrates on areas of research and development with close connections to AT&T businesses. The change in orientation and company culture has not dulled the eminence of Bell Labs, but how work is done has been altered. Star individual scientists are still held in high esteem, but group work among a number of scientists is now also a part of Bell Labs. The company now believes that it is not enough to pay attention to the star scientist performers; star and middle performers have to work together.

The Bell Lab engineers usually work in groups because the scale of work is beyond the scope of any one person's capabilities. For example, it can take from 5 to 150 engineers to complete a software application in anywhere from six months to two years. No single engineer, despite her stardom, can understand every aspect of a project or specific job.

Bell Labs has instituted an "expert model" for its engineers that attempts to integrate nine work strategies that will result in outstanding performance. The integration approach highlights individual and group characteristics.

The nine work strategies are as follows:

1. *Self-management:* Regulating your own performance level.
2. *Networking:* Having access to co-workers with expertise and sharing your expertise with others.
3. *Taking initiative:* Accepting responsibility above and beyond your job.
4. *Teamwork:* Accomplishing shared goals with co-workers.
5. *Leadership:* Building consensus with others on common goals.
6. *Fellowship:* Helping the leader accomplish organizational goals.
7. *Perspective:* Viewing your job in a layer context and considering other viewpoints of the work team, customer, and manager.
8. *Show-and-tell:* Presenting your ideas in written and oral form.
9. *Organizational savvy:* Working toward cooperation, resolution of conflict, and accomplishment of tasks.

Instead of focusing only on the individual or only on groups, Bell Labs has blended the strengths of individualism and teamwork. Productivity improvement, improved teamwork, and supporting Bell Lab efforts to employ more women and minorities in key positions have all resulted from using the nine strategies.

Sources: Adapted from Harold J Leavitt and Jean Lysman-Blumen, "Hot Groups," *Harvard Business Review,* July–August 1995, pp. 109–17; R Kelley and J Caplan, "How Bell Labs Creates Star Performers," *Harvard Business Review,* July–August 1993, pp. 128–39; D Kirkpatrick, "Could AT&T Rule the World?" *Fortune,* May 17, 1993, pp. 55–56.

Few managers question the existence of work groups or what some are now referring to as teams. For our purpose the terms *groups* and *teams* will be used interchangeably. A team is a formal group made up of interdependent individuals.[1] All teams are groups, but only formal groups can be teams. This is a detail that many leave out of discussions of groups and teams. For years, behavioral scientists have paid special attention to the processes occurring within groups and affecting individuals and organizations. Therefore, any examination of the fundamentals of managing people must provide a framework for understanding the nature of work groups. This chapter provides a classification of the different types of work groups, the reasons for formation and development of work groups, the characteristics of groups, and the consequences of group membership.

A work group or team is a collection of employees (managerial or nonmanagerial) who share certain norms and who strive to satisfy their needs through the attainment of the group goal(s). Students often ask why work groups or teams should be studied in a management text. Many different answers can be provided:

- The formation of work groups is inevitable. Managers create some work groups to perform work and tasks. Others form to satisfy employees' social needs. Therefore, it is in management's interest to understand what happens within work groups because they are found throughout the organization.
- Work groups or teams strongly influence the overall behavior and performance of members. Companies such as Apple Computer, Ford, General Foods, Levi Strauss, and Xerox have realized that self-managed teams (groups) are achieving superior performance. To understand the forces of influence exerted by the group requires a systematic analysis.
- Group membership can have both positive and negative consequences for the organization. If managers are to avoid the negative consequences, it is in their best interest to learn about work groups.

The common thread found in most answers is that groups do exist and affect the attitudes and behaviors of employees. Managing a group is a skill managers must learn and practice. Whether one manages a committee, scout troop, project team, or sports team, there are some principles to consider.

Kurt Lewin, a recognized scholar, perhaps explained it best in a classic speech on why groups need to be understood:

> Although the scientific investigations of group work are but a few years old, I don't hesitate to predict that group work—that is, the handling of human beings not as isolated individuals, but in the social setting of groups—will soon be one of the most important theoretical and practical fields. . . It is easier to affect the personality of 10 people if they can be melted into a group than to affect the personality of any 1 individual separately.[2]

Lewin's explanation made over four decades ago is still very accurate.

Classification of Work Groups

Every organization has technical requirements that arise from its objectives. The accomplishment of these objectives requires certain tasks to be performed, and employees are assigned to groups to perform these tasks. In addition, other groups form that are not the result of deliberate design. Accordingly, we can identify two broad classes of groups in organizations: formal and informal.

Most employees belong to a group based on their position in the organization. These **formal groups or teams** are the departments, units, and so forth that management forms to do the work of the organization. The demands and processes of the organization lead to the formation of these groups.

On the other hand, whenever employees associate on a fairly continuous basis, they tend to form groups whose activities may be different from those required by the organization. These **informal groups** are natural associations of people in the work situation in response to social needs. In other words, they do not arise as a result of deliberate design but rather evolve naturally. While this distinction is convenient for our discussion on specific types of groups in organizations later in the chapter, both formal and informal groups exhibit the same general characteristics.

The Hawthorne studies (see Chapter 1) illustrated the powerful influence that work groups can exert over their members. This influence can be economic, social, psychological, or even physical. Table 12–1 compares some of the main characteristics of formal and informal groups.

Formation of Work Groups

Chapter 11 stated that individuals have a number of needs, most of which are satisfied when interacting with others. Groups form because they sustain and satisfy these needs. There is no single reason why individuals join groups.

Physical Reasons

In organizations, a typical procedure is to place together workers in similar occupations. For example, in the construction of a home, bricklayers perform their jobs in close proximity to one another. The same situation exists in offices where secretaries are located elbow to elbow. People in close proximity to one another tend to interact and communicate with one another. If workers are not able to do this on a fairly regular basis, group formation is less likely.[3]

Economic Reasons

In some situations, work groups form because individuals believe they can derive more economic benefits from their jobs if they form into groups. For example, individuals working at different stations on an assembly line may be paid on a group incentive basis. Whatever the particular group produces determines the wages for each member. Because of the interest of the workers in their wages, they interact and communicate with one another. By working as a group instead of as individuals, they may perceive and actually obtain higher economic benefits.

Japan's Auto Alley has pointed out how American employees and Japanese managers have formed alliances and teams for economic reasons.[4] The economic motive has resulted in Mazdas being made in Michigan, Hondas in Ohio, Toyotas in Kentucky, and Nissans in Tennessee. The Japanese managers have trained and motivated American workers to work as teams to turn out cars of quality comparable to the made-in-Japan original.

Sociopsychological Reasons

Workers in organizations also are motivated to form work groups to satisfy safety, social, esteem, and self-actualization needs.

Safety.   Work groups can protect members from outside pressures, including serving as a buffer from management's demands for better quality and quantity of production,

---

TABLE 12–1   **Formal and Informal Groups: A Comparison**

Formal and informal groups differ in a number of important dimensions.

Dimension	Formal Group (Team)	Informal Group
1. Major objectives	Profit, efficiency, service.	Member satisfaction, member security.
2. Origin	Planned by organization.	Spontaneous.
3. Influence on members	Position authority, monetary rewards.	Personality, expertise.
4. Communication	Flows from top down, uses formal channels.	Grapevine, person-to-person, using all channels.
5. Leader	Appointed by organization.	Emerges from group.
6. Interpersonal relations	Established by job and workflow pattern.	Developed spontaneously.
7. Control	Reliance on threat, use of monetary rewards.	Strong social sanctions.

insistence that they punch the clock on time, and recommendations for change in their work area layouts. By being a member of a group, individual employees can become involved in group activities and openly discuss these management demands with fellow workers who usually support their viewpoint. Without the group to lean on when various management demands are made, employees often assume that they stand alone against management and the entire organization. This aloneness leads to a degree of insecurity.

Another form of safety need occurs in instances when a new employee is asked to perform a difficult job task over an extended period of time. Not wanting to contact the supervisor continually for help in correctly performing the job, the employee depends largely on the group for help, gaining a form of needed security. Whether the supervisor believes that continual requests for help by a new employee are signs of inability to perform the job is not the main issue. The important point is how new workers perceive their situation and job security.

Social.   Employees often join work groups because of their need for affiliation. The basis of affiliation ranges from wanting to interact with and enjoy other employees to more complex desires for group support of self-image. A management atmosphere that does not permit interaction and communication suppresses the desire of employees to feel a sense of belonging.

Esteem.   Some employees are attracted to a work group because they think they gain prestige by belonging. In an organization, a particular group may be viewed by employees as being a top-notch work group. Consequently, membership among the elite bestows on the members prestige that is not enjoyed by nonmembers. This prestige is conferred on members by other employees (nonmembers), often leading to more gratification of the esteem need. And by sharing in the activities of a high-prestige work group, the individual identifies more closely with the group.

Self-Actualization.   The desire of individuals to utilize their skills with maximum efficiency and to grow and develop psychologically on the job may be called the self-actualization need. Employees often believe that rigid job requirements and rules do not enable them to satisfy this need sufficiently. One reaction is to join a work group, which is viewed as a vehicle for communicating among friends about the use of a job-related skill. The particular jargon and the skill employed are appreciated by the knowledgeable group members; this can lead to a feeling of accomplishment. This and other similar feelings related to a sense that one is creative and skillful can lead to further growth and satisfaction of the self-actualization need.

Specific Types of Groups in an Organization

Both managers and nonmanagers belong to a number of different groups within the organization. Memberships in multiple groups often overlap.[5] In some instances, individuals are members of a group because of position in the organization. However, through group contacts, they begin to affiliate with some of its members on an informal basis.

To illustrate the point that individuals rarely belong to just one group, look at the case of Joe DiNardo, an electrical engineer who works for American Bridge and Iron in Chicago. DiNardo is friendly with each worker on his project team (a formal group): a senior mechanical engineer, an industrial designer, a safety specialist, and three technicians. He also regularly discusses project problems with two electrical engineers and the design specialists who work at the Barrington, Illinois, project site. DiNardo always eats lunch with office accountant Mickey Wright, drafting supervisor Don Spellman, and production analyst Mike Jackson. And every Wednesday he bowls with Wright, as well as ironworker Mel Perkowski and district manager Mitch Kelso. Each of the groups to which DiNardo belongs has a different membership. Some of the groups are formal and some are informal.

Another, more specific way to classify groups is to refer to them as command, task, interest, and friendship groups.[6] Command and task groups are formal groups because they are defined by the organization structure; interest and friendship groups are not defined by the organization structure and thus are informal groups.

Command Groups/Teams

The command group is represented in the organization chart as the subordinates who report directly to a given supervisor. The relationship between the department manager and the three supervisors in a machine shop is spelled out in the organization chart. As the span of control of the department manager increases, the command group increases in number.

Task Groups/Teams

Employees who work together to complete a project or job are considered a task group. Assume that three office clerks are required for securing a file of an automobile accident claim; checking the accuracy of the claim by contacting persons involved; and typing the claim, securing the required signatures of those involved, and refiling the claim.

These activities create a situation in which three clerks must communicate and coordinate with one another if the file is to be handled properly. Their activities and interactions facilitate the formation of the task group. Joe DiNardo's project team, mentioned previously, can be referred to as a task group.

Cross-functional task teams are more widely used as organizations attempt to improve coordination and integration.[7] Cross-functional task teams take many forms, but they are most often created to make decisions and are usually temporary until a project or task is completed. Each member has an identity with another more permanent command group. Cross-functional task teams are expected to be creative, reduce cycle time, and disseminate organizational learning. Examples of cross-functional task teams include project teams, quality teams, planning teams, product development teams, and process improvement teams. For example, the product development team would combine diverse sources of expertise in order to develop innovative new products.[8]

Interest Groups

Another type of group formation occurs when workers organize to present a united front on a particular issue. This group is an interest group, since the members have joined together to achieve some common objective, such as an equitable pension plan. Its members may or may not be members of the same command or task group.

When the desired objective has been achieved or is thought to be within reach, the interest group might disband. Thus, it typically exists for a shorter time than other groups.

Friendship Groups

Because of some common characteristic, such as age, ethnic background, political sentiment, interest in sports, or desire to drink coffee in the lounge at 10:30 AM, employees may form a friendship group. Such groups often extend their interaction and communication to off-the-job activities. For example, they get to know one another in the workplace and then bowl together or take their families on picnics. Mickey Wright and Joe DiNardo eat lunch together and bowl together, thus forming a friendship group.

The membership patterns of interest and friendship groups are not tightly controlled by the organization. However, managerial actions, such as laying out a work area, allowing workers to take coffee breaks at a specific time, and demanding a certain level of productivity, can influence the interaction and communication patterns of employees, causing certain individuals to affiliate with one another so that interest and friendship groups emerge.

Committees: Special Kinds of Groups

Many unkind things have been said about committees: "A camel is a horse designed by a committee"; "A committee is a body that keeps minutes and wastes hours"; and "A committee is a group that works hard at making common sense seem difficult."[9] Despite this, the use of committees in organizations is very common for such purposes as resolving conflict, recommending action, generating ideas, and making decisions.[10]

Behavioral scientists recommend that a committee be kept relatively small, since size affects the quality of a group's decision and the ability of its members to communicate.[11] As size increases, a growing number of members seem to feel threatened and less willing to participate actively; this can increase stress and conflict.

Committee Chairperson.   In most committees, a chairperson is expected to provide direction. Successful committees often have chairpeople who understand group processes and keep the committee moving toward its objectives without becoming constrained by endless debates, conflict, and personality clashes.

A committee chairperson must walk a fine line; a passive one may lose the members' respect. On the other hand, an overly dominating one does not usually acquire the group's acceptance. Without group respect, the chairperson is a leader without a group.

A few managerial guidelines that can aid committee chairpersons are:

- Listen carefully and with an open mind.
- Allow each member to voice opinions and do not place your opinions above others.
- Get everyone involved in the committee's activities.
- Display an active interest in the purpose of the committee and the ideas of the membership.
- Help the committee focus on the task at hand and the progress being made.[12]

Committee Members.   The image of a committee is a group cooperating to reach an objective. But what is found in some committees is negative competition and a general lack of cooperation. Behavioral studies indicate that in cooperative groups, as distinguished from competitive groups, one finds stronger motivation to accomplish the task, more effective communication, more ideas generated, more membership satisfaction, and more group productivity.

Unfortunately, committees are often made up of competitive individuals, lack a strong chairperson, and have strict time limitations imposed. For example, a committee in a small plastics manufacturing firm discussed replacing an injured secretary.[13] The committee consisted of a division manager, six department heads, and three section heads. The committee spent 50 minutes debating whether a new permanent person or a temporary replacement should be hired. The discussion took most of the committee's time, and the new fluorescent lighting system was never discussed. The lighting decision involved several departments and a $28,000 investment. The secretarial decision involved a single department. In this case, the committee had reversed the priority order of the topics to be discussed.

To overcome committee paralysis and the tendency not to complete important priority discussions, Norman Sigband offers six concise and important suggestions for keeping a committee focused and helping it to be productive.[14]

1. Hold meetings only when they really need to be conducted.
2. Establish an overall purpose and series of objectives to be covered.
3. Invite only those individuals who are needed and can make a contribution.
4. Distribute an agenda and necessary handouts before the meeting.
5. Make all room and layout arrangements ahead of time (e.g., location, desks, chairs, slide equipment, overheads).
6. Be punctual in beginning and ending the meeting.

These six sound suggestions can be invaluable in the work and output of committees. They do not guarantee success, but they can improve the probability that something productive will result from a committee.

Quality Circles: An Action-Oriented Group Approach

The term *quality circles* originated in Japan in 1962. The history of quality circles, however, goes back to the 1940s. The evolution of quality circles can be broken into three phases: studying statistical quality control, adapting the techniques, and forming quality circles.[15]

The concept of statistical quality control was introduced in Japan by individuals such as W Edwards Deming, the American engineer who played a major role in Japan's resurrection as an economic power. *Statistical quality control* is the use of tools and techniques in a disciplined way to solve problems in order to improve performance. Deming and others showed the Japanese how to use statistical techniques to improve the quality of products. The Japanese thought so highly of Deming's contributions to their society that they founded the much-coveted Deming Prize.

The Japanese had to determine how to best teach statistical quality control to managers and workers. They established seminars, symposiums, and radio broadcasts.[16] They worked very hard at adopting the techniques so that they could be taught.

A magazine, *Genba to QE,* was introduced in 1962 and discussed quality circles. Thus, quality circles as a new term was introduced into management literature. NTT Corporation became registered as the first quality circle firm in Japan in 1962 soon after *Genba to QE* introduced the concept. Today, there are hundreds of thousands of quality circles around the world. These quality circles meet on a regular basis to study quality control and productivity improvement techniques and to identify and solve work-related problems. Some specific features of quality circles are as follows:

· Small groups ranging in size from 4 to 15 members. Eight- or 9-member groups seem to be the most popular size.
· Members working in the same area.
· A work area supervisor usually, though not always, leading the circle.
· Voluntary participation.
· Meetings once every week on company time for a half-hour to an hour with pay.

- Training in the techniques of problem solving (e.g., brainstorming, cause-and-effect analysis, flowcharts).
- Choice of the problems and projects that members work on.
- Circles exist as long as the members wish to meet.[17]

Quality circles typically follow a four-phase process to solve problems:

Phase I: Identification of problems and development of solutions.

Phase II: Managerial review of the proposed solution and a decision on whether or not to implement it.

Phase III: Organizational implementation of the solution.

Phase IV: Evaluation of the success of the solution by the quality circle and the organization.

These phases of the typical quality circle process are presented in Figure 12–1.

Southern Pacific Railroad.   Southern Pacific Railroad was purchased by Philip Anschuty, and he immediately found out that his new company was not making money, had no strategic plan to cause a turnaround, was noncompetitive against other railroads and track transportation, and had a lot of customer hostility.[18] He also had to deal with organized labor craft unions that were very antagonistic. He evaluated the situation and decided to use a three-phase program. First, he wanted to hire a vice president for quality who could change the culture of the company by introducing a quality strategy. Second, he wanted to involve the 13 craft unions with whom Southern Pacific negotiated contracts and who were resistant to most changes that management introduced. Third, he wanted quality circles (called quality improvement teams) to be established. Eventually, 890 quality circles were formed.

The 890 quality circles have worked on problems that each face in the day-to-day operations. About 25 percent of the quality circles are cross-functional and include individuals from different units (e.g., marketing, manufacturing, and finance). The teams have worked on such issues as improving knowledge of customers, increasing scheduled-service reliability, meeting customer requirements, and identifying ways to improve revenue collection. Prior to the use of quality circles the percentage of uncontested bills was about 77 percent; now, after improvements in processing bills and serving customers, that percentage is over 90 percent. Quality circles (teams) are

---

FIGURE 12–1   The Quality Circle Process

Quality circles achieve results in terms of performance improvements and higher morale.

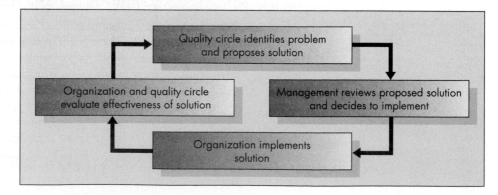

currently working on a host of invoicing problems, customer service problems, and scheduling problems.

Southern Pacific has learned how to use quality circles by involving employees, unions, and managers. The firm has complemented the quality circles with training that emphasizes learning about strategies that result in quality improvement and paying close attention to cost containment.

Southern Pacific hasn't yet turned the corner. It is still too early to determine whether the three-phase program will succeed. Despite a $43 million improvement in the firm's profitability, Southern Pacific will have to continue its quality improvement efforts and make them a part of the firm's culture for some time to be able to conclude that the firm is going to survive.

Some experts contend that quality circles often raise expectations that cannot be filled. Quality circle participants may want to change work flow, decision making, and procedures, but they are met with resistance in the way the company operates.[19] When brilliant recommendations in a quality circle face the reality of daily activities, they are often challenged and resisted. A quality circle program that demands more participative involvement of individuals may run right into managers who are not ready to change. This resistance can result in frustration, alienation, and even withdrawal from quality circle involvement.

A number of companies that have been using quality circles have recently decided to reduce their use of them and have instead started using ad hoc task forces or improvement teams.[20] These groups often make suggestions that management accepts, modifies, or rejects. These newer approaches are replacing more and more quality circles because managers feel that they have more control over an ad hoc group. Targeted improvement groups are expected to play an increasing role in helping make organizations more effective.

Self-Managed Teams

An increasingly popular approach to achieving group efficiency and effectiveness is the self-managed team. A self-managed team is an intact formal group responsible for a "whole" work process or segment that delivers a product or service to an internal customer. Individuals and groups can exercise self-control in achieving acceptable levels of performance; that is, instead of using an outside-initiated control system such as a manager to identify and direct appropriate behavior, the person or the group can exert the necessary influence. Self-managed teams facilitate behaviors that meet acceptable standards. Many organizations are beginning to discover that a self-managed team can be a super performing team.

Self-managed teams are *not* simply allowed to do whatever pleases them *whenever* it pleases them. Self-managed teams are groups of workers who are given some autonomy, with administrative review, to complete jobs and accomplish goals. Members of self-managed teams must plan, organize, head, and control their work.

The controversy surrounding self-managed teams is not that they are not effective in some cases, but that they threaten the notion of manager-initiated control. Because they manage themselves, the need for a manager is not obvious. The self-managed team can arrange schedules, set profit targets, hire and fire members, order materials, improve quality, and devise strategy. The self-managed team typically consists of between 3 and 30 members.

A key concept in self-managed teams is empowerment. The empowerment of an individual or a team is the passing on of authority and responsibility. Empowered individuals know that their jobs belong to them.[21]

A survey of 476 of the Fortune 1,000 firms shows that only 7 percent of the workforces are organized in self-managed teams. However, 50 percent of the firms state that they will use self-managed teams in the 1990s.[22] Some of the results from using self-managed teams have been outstanding. The following examples point out impressive improvements:

- At a weekly meeting at Federal Express Corporation, self-managed clerks spotted and solved a billing problem that was costing the firm $2.1 million a year.
- 3M Company turned around one division by creating self-managed teams that tripled the number of new products.
- At a General Mills cereal plant in Lodi, California, self-managed teams operate very effectively during the entire night shift without managers.

At Johnsonville Foods, a family-owned sausage company, President Ralph Stayer made a full commitment to self-managed teams. He decided to permit self-managed teams to operate the entire business.[23] The workers are their own bosses. When customer complaints come in, when a worker botches an order, when a forklift operator drops a pallet damaging items that must be shipped, the team handles the problem. If corrections must be made, if training has to be conducted, or if budgets must be submitted, the self-managed teams must do the job. After eight years of self-managed teams, Stayer believes his business is bigger and better than ever. Every six months, Johnsonville evaluates the performance of each employee and computes shares in the profit-sharing program. The evaluations are done by the employees themselves. The overall satisfaction with the system is very high, partly because fellow workers invented it, administer it, and constantly revise it to make it more equitable.[24]

The self-managed team approach appears to be appropriate when a job involves a high level of interdependence between three or more workers. Manufacturing and complicated service work in banking and telecommunications seem suited for self-managed approaches. The more complex the job tasks, the better suited they are for a self-managed approach. By working as a unit, individuals on a team can come up with ways to complete the job on schedule. The hierarchical approach of a manager directing a group or attempting to create a motivational climate is not always the most efficient.

Multicultural Work Groups: Managing Diversity

A culturally diverse workforce means that as the demographics of the population change, new group formation, effectiveness, and leadership challenges will occur. The implications of multiculturism in the workforce are already profound at companies such as Aramco in Dhahran, Saudi Arabia.[25] Professionals from 50 countries work together in work groups at all levels. Managing such groups requires that managers create a work atmosphere of respect for individuals from different cultural back-grounds.

A reevaluation of the organization's recruiting, training, motivation, and advance-ment programs will be especially important where multicultural work groups exist. Wang Laboratories has trained over 1,000 managers on how to value diversity among employees. Wang's program is centered around four important assessments: an awareness of one's own behavior, a recognition of one's own biases and stereotypes, a focus on job performance and an avoidance of assumptions.[26]

Managers must be aware of the concept of *acculturation*—that is, the transfer of culture from one ethnic group to another. Acculturation is the process of gradual adaptation to a new environment by a group, in situations where one or more minority groups are being merged with a majority group.[27] There are a number of degrees of acculturation. In *assimilation,* everyone is expected to conform to the values and norms of the dominant culture. In *separation,* the minority group is unable or unwilling to adapt to the dominant culture. In *pluralism,* acculturation is undertaken by both groups to accommodate each other's expectations.[28]

Managers need to understand each of the degrees of acculturation and work especially on understanding the preferences of workers in terms of acculturation. Immigrant workers are likely to vary in their preferences for acculturation. Organizations and managers are also likely to differ in what they consider to be the best degree of acculturation. Organizations can promote the understanding of acculturation through education and training programs. They can also alter reward systems so that managers who are effective in managing diverse workers and groups are rewarded.

Across the world, and in various cities of the United States, such as New York, Chicago, Miami, and Houston, immigrants make up a growing percentage of the workforce. In the 1980s, new waves of immigrants made up about 35 percent of the total US population growth.[29] The integration of immigrant workers is becoming almost a necessity in some industries, locations, and firms.

Oddou offers some positive suggestions for integrating foreign-born workers and groups that consist of a mix of people.[30] For example, communicating in as many languages as necessary could be very important. In recruiting, firms should use multilingual testing and advertising. Oddou also recommends cross-cultural mentoring in which co-workers would sponsor one or more of the foreign-born employees.

The concepts of multicultural work groups, degrees of acculturation, and integrating foreign-born immigrants have become extremely important. Unfortunately, many US-born managers and group members are not sufficiently knowledgeable about other cultures, work norms, and expectations. As increased global competition forces employers to use every skilled worker available, it will be important to achieve better cultural integration at work. The United States, Germany, and Canada have become magnets attracting skilled and educated immigrants. Managers in these countries will have to do a better job of managing the culturally diverse work groups that are producing the goods and services consumers purchase.

Development of Work Groups

Task groups, committees, or quality circles go through various stages of development. Initially, a group flounders while searching for an identity and a direction. Later, the group members begin to focus on helping one another and supporting the group's goals. Finally, the group is able to fully utilize the skills and abilities of members. These changes occur gradually and are often difficult to recognize.

Groups primarily develop along two main dimensions: member relationships and task and problem-solving activities. The development of work groups is distinctly related to learning—learning to work together, to accept one another, and to trust one another. These phases are referred to as the maturation of a group.[31] Various models of group development are available, such as Schutz's FIRO model, Whitaker's integrative model, and Hill and Gruner's model.[32] However, in terms of ease of managerial application, the use of managerial language, and the incorporation of organizationally relevant dimensions such as relationship development and task and problem-solving activities, the four-phase model is perhaps most insightful. The four-phase process outlined here clearly points out some characteristics and attitudes inherent in group development.[33]

1. *Mutual acceptance.* Members of a group are often hampered by their mistrust of one another, the organization, and their superiors. They are fearful that they do not have the necessary training or skill to perform the job or to compete with others. These feelings of insecurity motivate employees to seek out others in the same predicament and to express their feelings openly. After an initial period of uneasiness and learning about the feelings of others, individuals begin to accept one another.

2. *Decision making.* During this phase, open communication concerning the job is the rule. Problem solving and decision making are undertaken. The workers trust one another's viewpoints and beliefs; they develop strategies to make the job easier and to help one another perform more effectively.

3. *Motivation.* The group is reaching maturity and the problems of its members are known. Members have accepted that it is better to cooperate than to compete. Thus, the emphasis is on group solidarity.

4. *Control.* A group reaching this phase has successfully organized itself, and members are contributing according to their abilities and interests. The group exercises sanctions when control is needed to bring members into line with the group's norms.

As employees develop from a bunch to a mature group, they display and acquire personal trust, interactions, and friendships. Figure 12–2 illustrates the four phases of development.[34] Management needs to determine which phase of development a group

---

FIGURE 12–2   Four Phases of Group Development

A group matures as it moves through the four phases.

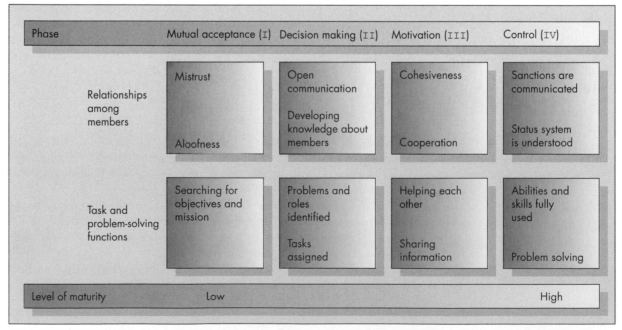

Source: L R Sayles and G Strauss, *Human Behavior in Organizations* (Englewood Cliffs, NJ: Prentice Hall, 1966). Reprinted with permission of Prentice Hall, Inc.

is in at any particular point. This is, of course, difficult but important, since it can provide answers about a group's capability.

There is also the need for managers to blend the talents of individuals and the group together. The accompanying Management Focus offers some hints for managers who want to encourage the evolution of "superteams."

Eastman Chemical, the $3.5 billion unit of Eastman Kodak Co., is mature and interested in problem solving and open communications. Self-managed teams have replaced a number of senior vice presidents.[35] Now managers serve on multicultural teams so that problems are identified and solved and individuals from different backgrounds communicate with one another. The abilities and skills of each member of the self-managed teams are used to focus on day-to-day operations. The success of manager depends to some extent on how well the self-managed teams function. The self-managed cross-functional teams run the business. This is a revolutionary change from the days when the long-standing functional departments operated the business.

Characteristics of Work Groups

The creation of a formal organization structure results in characteristics such as specified relationships between subordinates, superiors, and peers; leaders assigned to positions; communication networks; standards of performance; and a status rank order according to the position an individual is filling. Logically, if an organization is to accomplish its objectives, retain its personnel, and project a favorable image to the public, it must have structure and a favorable work atmosphere (that is, the employees must to some extent enjoy going to work). Work groups have characteristics similar to those of formal organizations that include standards of conduct, communication systems, and reward and sanction mechanisms. These and other characteristics of groups are discussed here.

Group Structure and Roles

As a group progresses through each developmental phase, structures emerge. Members begin to take on roles or engage in a set of activities and behaviors expected by others. The ability to carry out expected roles provides the group with an arrangement or a pattern for its members. If roles are not carried out according to the expectations of members, it is difficult to maintain a group structure.

Within groups, members tend to play specific roles. A **role** comprises the behaviors a person exhibits in a social context. In an organization, the person's position in the hierarchy has a major influence on the role behaviors exhibited. For example, the president of Xerox Corporation has a position that is supposed to carry out behaviors resulting in the firm's market, profit, and social responsibility successes. Whoever occupies the office of the president of Xerox is expected to behave in a manner that helps the firm be successful.

As groups in organizations develop, the members begin to play different roles within the structure. The process of taking on different roles is **role differentiation.** There are some individuals who take on task-oriented roles. These individuals attempt to initiate action, stimulate task-oriented discussions, and use important data and facts to help solve a group task. Researchers have found that within groups someone usually emerges to help the group achieve its task.

Table 12–2 summarizes three main roles that emerge within groups.[36] Each of these main roles—task-oriented, relations-oriented, and self-oriented—has a number of subrole behaviors being enacted. The subroles are played in each of the different types of groups (formal and informal) found in organizations.

TABLE 12-2   Roles and Subroles Enacted by Group Members

Task-Oriented Roles (Reaching the Goal)	Relations-Oriented Roles (Support, Encouragement)	Self-Oriented Roles (Self-Centeredness)
Initiators: Provide new ideas on how to proceed.	*Harmonizers:* Help relieve tensions and work through conflicts.	*Blockers:* Resistant, stubborn, and negative about issues and discussion.
Information seekers: Find the facts, data, and sources needed to solve the problem.	*Gatekeepers:* Get others involved in the discussions.	*Recognition seekers:* Boastful and egocentric; call attention to themselves.
Information providers: Provide accurate data and facts.	*Compromisers:* Shift opinions to achieve group harmony.	*Dominators:* Manipulative; assert authority to get their way.
Coordinators: Integrate facts, ideas, and opinions.	*Expediters:* Suggest ways the group can operate better.	*Avoiders:* Isolate themselves from fellow members.
Energizers: Provide a boost to get the group moving and to take action.		

Source: Based on K D Benne and P Sheats, "Functional Roles of Group Members," *Journal of Social Issues,* 1948, pp. 41–49.

Even though Benne and Sheats offered their view of role behaviors over four decades ago, their classification can still be applied today. Certainly, groups discussing new technology, environmental, human resource, and market decisions have task-oriented, relations-oriented, and self-oriented behaviors. Finding and using the right balance of each of these behaviors is a part of the group leader's decision-making domain. Those group leaders who can effectively orchestrate the right balance are likely to be a part of an effective and efficient group.

Group Goals

Work groups generally have two sets of goals. The organization's managers set goals for work groups. These *manager-assigned* goals reflect the reason for the group's formation. A second set of goals is the *group goals.*[37]

Within the groups, *achievement goals* provide the group with direction and an end-result target. *Maintenance goals* sustain the group and maintain its existence. Of course, not all members always agree with either the achievement or maintenance goals. On occasion, conflict with group goals is why members drop out and form new groups or join other groups.

As a group develops, the goals become clearer and more meaningful to members. Research indicates that a number of factors increase a person's commitment to the achievement and the maintenance of group goals. Some of these factors are participating in group activities, tying incentives to goal achievement, providing feedback on goal accomplishment, and training group members in the goal-setting process.[38]

Leadership

As a group attempts to accomplish an objective such as producing a product without a single defect, and as individual members get acquainted, one or more of the many group roles become filled. One of the most important is that of the group leader, who emerges from within and is accepted by the informal group. In the formal organization, however, the leader is appointed.

The Ingredients for Superteams

One of the best examples of how well teams can perform is a group of scientists at Data General Corporation who became the heroes of Tracy Kidder's book *The Soul of a New Machine*. Working late at night, "borrowing" resources, and avoiding the scrutiny of senior management, the team developed a new minicomputer way ahead of competitors.

As it turns out, most real teams—such as Data General's "skunkworks" team—get formed without top management's attention or encouragement. In fact, when managers try to form teams, they usually fail. The reason is that they assume individual performance is what really counts and that teams should be formed to improve morale or to build "openness."

Too many executives reorganize their companies around self-managing teams and make the number of officially designated teams the objective function instead of real improvements in performance. Of course, executives insist, "Naturally we want performance; we would never build teams for the sake of teams!" Yet, some leaders have literally set the number of teams established as the primary goal.

Teams are a means to an end—and that end is performance superior to what team members would achieve working as individuals. This applies to teams that recommend things, teams that make or do things, and teams that run or manage things.

Teams that make or do things often need to develop new skills for managing themselves. Teams that recommend things often find their biggest challenge comes when they make the handoff to those who must implement their findings. And groups that run or manage things must overcome hierarchical obstacles and turf issues more often than groups that recommend, make, or do things. But notwithstanding such differences, any team will deliver results well beyond what individuals acting alone can achieve as long as the focus is on performance.

A real team needs both a common purpose and specific goals. A common, meaningful purpose sets the tone and gives teams direction, momentum, and commitment. Setting specific and measurable performance goals is the surest first step for a team trying to shape a common purpose meaningful to its members.

Specific goals such as getting a new product to market in less than half the normal time, responding to all customer complaints within 24 hours, reducing ad errors by 50 percent, or achieving a zero defect rate while cutting costs by 40 percent, provide tangible footholds for teams. In contrast, fuzzy goals, such as introducing more products, reducing errors, or improving quality, provide no such footholds for teams.

When a team is given a clear mandate by top management (e.g., to determine how to improve customer delivery times or to design a better compensation plan), it helps teams perform rather than constraining them. During Procter & Gamble's performance turnaround between 1985 and 1991, management made expectations clear to teams and yet provided them with considerable freedom in meeting these challenges.

Most state-of-the-art models of the organization of the future—"networked," "clustered," "nonhierarchical," "horizontal," and so forth—are based on the notion that teams should surpass individuals as the primary performance unit in critical parts of the company. This seems to be a premature suggestion, especially in countries like the United States that still place a lot of faith on individual initiative, entrepreneurship, and freedom of individual choice. The real challenge for management then seems to be in deciding how to *balance* the roles of individuals and teams—not in deciding to favor one over the other.

Sources: "GM's German Lessons," *Business Week,* December 20, 1993, pp. 67–68; J Katzenbach, "The Right Kind of Teamwork," *The Wall Street Journal,* November 9, 1992, p. A10; T Kidder, *The Soul of A New Machine* (New York: Atlantic Monthly Press, 1981).

The leaders in formal organizations are followed and obeyed because employees perceive them as possessing the power and influence to reward or punish them for not complying with requests. The formal leaders possess the power to regulate the formal rewards of the members of a work group. On the other hand, informal group leaders do not possess this power.

The informal leader typically serves a number of facilitating functions. First, any group of individuals that does not have a plan or some coordination becomes an ineffective unit. The individuals are not directed toward the accomplishment of objectives, and this leads to a breakdown in group effectiveness. The leader serves to initiate action and provide direction. If there are differences of opinion on a group-related matter, the leader attempts to settle the differences and move the group toward accomplishing its objectives. Second, some individual must communicate to nonmembers the group's beliefs about policies, the job, the organization, the supervision, and other related matters. In effect, the group leader communicates the values of the group.

Norms and Control   Once a group addresses specific task goals, a pattern of behavior begins to emerge. The pattern becomes a regular feature of the group dynamics and is called a **norm,** which is an "attitude, opinion, feeling, or action—shared by two or more people—that guides their behavior."[39] The more an individual complies with norms, the more that person accepts the group's standards of behavior. Work groups utilize norms to bring about job performance acceptable to the group. In the workplace, a number of different production-related norms can exist. For example: don't agree with management in its campaign to change the wage structure; present a united front to the supervisor concerning the displeasure of the group about the firing of Mr. Jones; resist the suggestions of the new college graduate assigned to the group's work area; do not produce above the group leader's level of production; help members of the group achieve an acceptable production level if they are having difficulty and if you have time; and don't allow the union steward to convince you to vote for his favorite union presidential candidate.

Three specific social processes bring about compliance with group norms: group pressure, group review and enforcement, and the personalization of norms.

Group Pressure.   In groups, pressure can be applied to members to conform to group norms. Pressure is excessive when it interferes with the group's goal accomplishment. On the other hand, pressure is inadequate when lack of conformity to group norms is detrimental to a member, the group, or the organization. Conformity is optimal when it results in cooperation, efficiency, and the accomplishment of group goals.[40]

A number of factors influence the level of conformity in a group. **Task characteristics,** such as the nature of a particular job, affect conformity. An employee faced with a difficult, unfamiliar, and ambiguous task is more inclined to conform to a group norm.

The **personality** makeup of an individual influences that person's conformity behavior. A person who lacks self-esteem is more likely to conform than one who has the opposite personality traits.[41] Also, the more intelligent the individual, the less likely she is to conform to group norms.

The name Roger Boisjoly probably doesn't register with most readers. He was the engineer of the ill-fated Challenger flight that exploded in mid-air in 1986 costing the lives of seven US astronauts. He attempted to stop the flight because of flaws and problems but was not listened to or acknowledged. He was being a nonconformist and was saying things about safety that management didn't want to hear.[42] He felt helpless as a nonconformist and eventually stopped pressing the case. The result was a disaster.

Group characteristics affect conformity. For example, as size increases, pressures to conform increase. Also, when the majority of a group strongly supports a position, a member is more inclined to conform than when he has one or more partners who disagree with the majority view.[43] There is a tendency to conform when the consequence for deviance is social isolation by the group.

Conformity at Borden, Inc., is illustrated when the company's top executives have teamed together to form a contract called the people pills. The top executives all signed three-year contracts. They agreed to resign en masse if any new owner (takeover) fires or changes the responsibilities of any one of them. The agreement says the acquirer must pay the managers $10 million to $30 million, depending on when the offending action occurs, to buy out their contracts if they resign. Each manager is a part of the group conforming to the contractual agreement. The takeover specialist now has to deal with a tightly knit group that has protected itself with the people pill defense.

Group Review and Enforcement.   When individuals become members of a group, they quickly become aware of group norms. The group position on such matters as production, absenteeism, and quality of output is communicated. The group members then observe the actions and language of new members to determine whether the group norms are being followed.

If individual members, both old-timers and newcomers, are not complying with generally accepted norms, a number of different approaches may be employed. A soft approach would be a discussion between respected leaders and those persons deviating from the norm. If this does not prove effective, more rigid corrective action is used, such as the membership scolding the individual or individuals both privately and publicly. The ultimate enforcement would be to ostracize the nonconforming members, which might take the form of not communicating with them.

These are only a few of the numerous strategies to bring deviants into line. Other, more severe techniques, such as sabotaging the nonconformer's performance, have also been utilized. Review and enforcement occur at managerial levels in a form similar to that in nonmanagerial ranks.

Cohesiveness

Cohesiveness is another important group characteristic. **Group cohesiveness** (Figure 12–3) is defined as the attraction of members to the group and the strength of forces on the individual member to remain active in the group and resist leaving it.[44]

All of the characteristics of groups are influenced to some degree by the cohesiveness within the group.[45] For example, the greater the attraction within the group, the more likely it is that the membership adheres closely to a group norm.

Highly cohesive groups appear to have greater member satisfaction than groups with low cohesiveness. There is also more member communication in high- versus low-cohesiveness groups.[46]

Ford Motor Company, after suffering years of decreased sales and shrinking profit margins, instituted what was called the Team Taurus approach.[47] Designers, assembly workers, and marketing and finance people were brought together to develop the best car possible. In the usual sequential team approach, designers worked on a design and then "tossed their work over the wall," or passed their work to engineering; the engineers "tossed their work over the wall" to production; and so forth. The "not invented here" (NIH) syndrome took hold. NIH refers to the fact that most people are not likely to accept ideas or recommendations that other people have initiated. Tossing something to the next group meant that a lot of reinventing occurred.

Team Taurus was a large group, but all the voices were heard in the same room. The team came up with a want list of 1,401 items suggested by Ford employees. In an Atlanta setting, drawings and sketches were spread across the wall and on flip charts. This was a contrast to the secrecy often found in the automobile industry. The team was able to incorporate about 80 percent of the want list items. The result of the Team Taurus approach: *Motor Trend* picked the Ford Taurus as the car of the year.[48]

FIGURE 12–3   Some Factors That Influence Group Cohesiveness

Many factors can promote or hinder cohesiveness in a group.

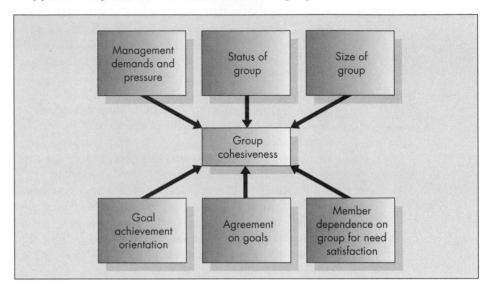

Psychologist Irving Janis proposed what is called the groupthink phenomenon.[49] The core to the groupthink concept is cohesiveness. The phenomenon occurs when highly cohesive groups lose their ability to critically evaluate situations or information. In a groupthink situation, there is unanimous public acceptance of decisions made by the group. The groupthink symptoms proposed by Janis include:[50]

- *Illusion of invulnerability.* Group members are overconfident and willing to take risks (e.g., President Kennedy and his advisors deciding to give the go-ahead for the Bay of Pigs invasion in Cuba).
- *Illusion of morality.* Group believes that they are morally correct to take a course of action (e.g., the various warring factions—Croats, Serbs, Muslims—in Bosnia and Herzegovina fighting one another).
- *Stereotypes of outsiders.* Group constructs unfavorable stereotype of those outside the group who are the targets of their decisions (e.g., hate groups who attack those people who are stereotyped as outsiders).
- *Pressure for conformity.* Members pressure one another to fall into line and maintain the group norms or views (e.g., the highly cohesive Hawthorne study groups).
- *Self-censorship.* Group members convince themselves to avoid holding opinions contrary to the group's (e.g., politicians in the party of the president who do not want to display a lack of agreement on an issue such as NAFTA or health care reform to the public).
- *Illusion of unanimity.* Group members perceive that unanimous support exists for a course of action (e.g., a product development team that has worked long and hard to develop a new product; differences of opinion become quieter as the team moves further into the project).

Groupthink can result in inappropriate decisions because of the unrealistic view that group members embrace.[51] The design and marketing of the disastrous Edsel automobile in 1958 has been attributed to groupthink. The 1986 Challenger disaster that killed seven American astronauts probably also illustrates how groupthink lowered the safety requirements and checks. In order to prevent cohesive groups from drifting into groupthink, leaders need to listen to all viewpoints, have group members test their views with outsiders, assign or welcome devil's advocates to test the points and issues being discussed, and even when a consensus is reached ask the group to rethink everything and to meet again to reach a second-time consensus.

Size

One important and necessary condition for the existence of a group is that members interact and communicate with one another. If the group is so large that members do not get to know one another, there is little likelihood that the group can become very cohesive. Research studies indicate an inverse relationship between size of group and group cohesiveness.[52] Smaller groups coalesce faster than larger groups.

In addition to affecting cohesiveness, a group's size can influence how much effort members apply to a task. A phenomenon called **social loafing** has been identified.[53] This involves the tendency of individuals in a group not to work hard, because there are others around to carry the workload. In cohesive groups, social loafing would not be tolerated once it was identified. Also, there are more opportunities for social loafing in large groups. A person not doing an equal share of work is often hard to identify. If a group leader is able to point out each member's contribution, the tendency to loaf would be reduced. Social loafing is found not only in the workplace but also within family units, student groups, and volunteer groups.[54]

Why don't people do their share of work? Perhaps if a person sees someone in the group not working hard, there is a tendency to slow down, stop pushing hard, or simply reduce one's effort. Coasting behind others or reducing effort is possible, especially when a group is larger and there are opportunities to become lost in the crowd. In offices or production lines, on large committees, or in large departments, individuals can become lost; they can indulge in social loafing.

Intragroup Conflict

Conflict is an everyday occurrence in life. *Conflict results when there are incompatible goals, cognitions, or emotions within or between individuals or groups that lead to opposition or antagonistic interaction.*[55]

Conflict among members of a group can arise in a variety of ways. In the mutual acceptance and decision-making phases of group development, there are likely to be disagreements over member roles, plans, schedules, and standards. These disagreements can cause the group to be ineffective and fragmented. Coalitions and power centers emerge and create anxiety for the membership. Management needs to be alert for these types of conflicts, especially in the relatively immature group.

Interpersonal conflict among members always is present to some extent. Differences in opinions, attitudes, values, and beliefs create tension. We tend to like people with values, beliefs, and opinions similar to our own. The personality clash happens not only between superiors and subordinates but also among members of groups. Individuals who are in a state of conflict with other members are also likely to be dissatisfied with the interpersonal features of the group. In addition, the member who is having interpersonal conflicts is likely to withdraw from most group activities.

Of course, if group performance is affected by intragroup conflict, management has a stake in determining the reasons for the problems. However, before managerial prescriptions are implemented, it is necessary to fully understand the reasons. This requires careful diagnostic work: observation, discussions, and reviews of performance records. Management's intent is not to eliminate intragroup conflict but to minimize it so that individual and organizational goals can be achieved.

Intergroup Conflict   Management prefers that groups cooperate and work toward the accomplishment of organizational and individual goals. However, conflicts often develop between groups. If the groups are working on tasks that are interdependent (i.e., department A's output flows to department B, and B's output flows to department C), the coordination and effectiveness of working together are crucial managerial issues. The relationships can become antagonistic and so disruptive that the entire flow of production is slowed or even stopped.

As an employee-owned company, Weirton Steel Corporation has generally performed better than its competitors. The company's owners now want to keep receiving their profit-sharing payments.[56] Management, however, wants the employees to give up some of the payments to keep the company competitive. There is a conflict between the need for strong management and employee desires to keep profit-sharing payments coming at the rate expected.

Although conflict exists between management and labor at Weirton Steel and in many firms, cooperation is the most desirable result of group interaction. For example, two groups can cooperate because they both oppose the introduction of new equipment. The equipment is being introduced to improve cost control, but the groups working together can make the period of testing the new equipment a bad experience for management.

Determinants of Intergroup Conflict.   Conflict develops between groups for many reasons.[57] Some of the more important ones relate to limited resources, communication problems, differences in interests and goals, different perceptions and attitudes, and lack of clarity about responsibilities.

- *Limited resources.* Groups that possess an abundance of materials, money, and time are usually effective. However, when a number of groups are competing for limited resources, there is a good chance that conflict will result. The competition for the limited equipment dollars, merit-increase money, or new positions can become fierce.

- *Communication problems.* Groups often become very involved with their own areas of responsibility. Each tends to develop its own vocabulary or jargon. Paying attention to an area of responsibility is a worthy endeavor, but it can result in communication problems. The receiver of information must be considered when a group communicates an idea, proposal, or decision. Often this is not the case, and misinformed receivers become irritated and hostile.

- *Different interests and goals.* A group of young workers may want management to do something about the inadequate promotion system. However, older workers are accusing management of ignoring improvements in the company pension plan. Management recognizes the two different goals but believes that the pension issue is the more pressing and addresses it. The groups may want management to solve both problems, but this is not currently possible. Thus, one group becomes hostile because it is ignored.

- *Different perceptions and attitudes.* Individuals perceive differently. The groups to which they belong also can have different perceptions. Groups tend to evaluate in terms of their backgrounds, norms, and experiences. Since each of these can differ, there is likely to be conflict among groups. Most groups tend to overvalue their own worth and position and undervalue the worth and position of other groups.

- *Lack of clarity.* Job clarity involves knowing what others expect in terms of task accomplishment. In many cases, it is difficult to specify who is responsible for a certain task. This difficulty exists in most organizations. Who is responsible for listing a talented management trainee—the personnel department or the training department? Who is responsible for the increased interest in the product line—marketing, advertising, or research and development? The inability to pinpoint positive and negative contributions causes groups to compete for control over those activities that are recognized.

The causes of conflict just cited are common. Each needs to be managed. The management of intergroup conflict involves determining strategies to minimize such problems.

Intergroup Conflict Management Strategies.   Management's reaction to disruptive intergroup conflict can take many different forms.[58] In a typical sequence of events, management first tries to minimize the conflict indirectly; if this fails, it becomes directly involved.

Indirect Approaches.   Initially, managers often avoid direct approaches to solving conflict between groups. *Avoidance* is easy in the short run, since the causes of conflict are unknown, and giving attention to conflict admits that it exists. Unfortunately, avoidance does not always minimize the problem. Matters get worse because nothing seemingly is being done about the problem, and the groups become more antagonistic and hostile.

Another indirect strategy is to encourage the groups to meet and discuss their differences and work out a solution without management involvement. This strategy can take the form of bargaining, persuasion, or working on a problem together.

Bargaining groups find ways to trade advantages and to agree on what each will get and give to the other. A group may agree to give another group quick turnaround time on the repairs of needed equipment if the other group agrees to bring complaints about the quality of repairs to them before going to management. Bargaining can be successful if both groups are better off (or at least no worse off) after an agreement is reached.

LKAB is a government-owned firm in Sweden that mines iron ore. Management (all except very top level) and operating employees are members of a variety of unions.[59] A wildcat strike spread to 5,000 employees. After almost two months on strike, the various groups decided to use consolidation and joint bargaining to end the strike. Group meetings and a joint counsel of management and labor met frequently. Ombudspeople were used, but the use of numerous committees from the joint counsel brought the conflict to an end.

Through *persuasion* groups find common areas of interest. They attempt to find points of agreement and show how these are important to each in attaining organizational goals. Persuasion is possible if clashes between group leaders do not exist.

A problem can be an obstacle to a goal. For groups to minimize their conflicts through *problem solving,* they must generally agree on the goal. Then the groups can propose alternative solutions that satisfy the parties involved. One group may want the company to relocate the plant in a suburban area, and the other group may want better working conditions. If both agree that a common goal is to maintain their jobs, then building a new facility in an area that does not have a high tax rate may be a good solution.

A number of indirect approaches to minimize conflict have been used to improve union–management relationships. The workforce of the steel industry decreased from 453,000 in 1979 to 169,000 in 1989, while the average employment in the auto industry dropped from 990,000 to 859,000 in the same period.[60] Thus, union and management decided that it would be better to work together than to destroy each other. The Management Focus points out some union–management cooperative work.

Direct Approaches.   Management may use *domination* to minimize conflict. It may exercise authority and require that the problem be solved by a specific date. If management uses authority, the groups may unite and resist the domination. Management becomes a common enemy, and they forget their differences in order to deal with their new opponent.

Another direct approach is to *remove the key figures* in the conflict. If two individuals are in conflict because of personality differences, this may be a possible alternative. Three problems exist with this approach: First, the figures who are to be removed may be respected leaders of the groups. This could lead to more antagonism and greater conflict. Second, it is difficult to pinpoint accurately whether the individuals in conflict are at odds because of personal animosities or because they represent their groups. Third, removal is not always good, because of a danger that martyrs will be created. The causes of the removed leaders will be remembered and fought for even though the persons themselves are gone.

A final, direct strategy to minimize conflict is that of finding *superordinate goals.* These goals are desired by two or more groups but can be accomplished only through cooperation of the groups. Studies have shown that when conflicting groups are faced with the necessity of cooperating to accomplish a goal, conflict can be minimized and cooperation increased.[61] For example, a companywide profit-sharing plan may be used to encourage groups to work together. At the end of the year, a percentage of company profits will be distributed equally to each employee. Conflict among groups can reduce the amount of profits each person receives. Thus, the superordinate goal, generating optimal profits, takes precedence.

Consequences of Group Membership

Two potential end results, or consequences, of group membership are the satisfaction of members and effective decision making. Behaviorists and managers have increased their efforts to understand the causes of member satisfaction and decision making within groups.

Member Satisfaction   One survey of 37 studies showed specific relationships between work group member satisfaction and perceived freedom to participate, perceived goal attainment, and status consensus.[62]

Perceived Freedom to Participate.   A member's perception of freedom to participate influences need satisfaction. Individuals who perceived themselves as active participators reported themselves more satisfied, while those who perceived their freedom to participate to be insignificant typically were the least satisfied members in a work group.

The freedom-to-participate phenomenon is related to the entire spectrum of economic and sociopsychological needs. For example, the perceived ability to

Labor–Management Conflict Reduction

Continued conflict would be likely to result in both a weaker union and weaker management in some American industries attempting to keep foreign competition from taking over. Consequently, problem solving, bargaining, and persuasion are being used in a number of labor–management partnerships. At the New United Motor Manufacturing Inc. (NUMMI), a Toyota–GM venture in Fremont, California, there are quarterly union–management meetings. These meetings have resulted in a more cooperative atmosphere and increased respect for both groups.

The labor–management relationship at NUMMI resembles similar relationships in Japan. The unions in Japan are considered part of the company.

At Saturn, a GM subsidiary in Spring Hill, Tennessee, the union has a seat on the plant's governing board. Saturn's president and the union coordinator have offices in the same suite and do business together. All major decisions, including which suppliers and dealers to use, how to proceed with product development, and what equipment and machinery investments to make, are made by consensus.

Honda's nonunionized plant in Marysville, Ohio, recognizes that workers must be given responsibility and that egalitarian practices result in less conflict. Here, increased work effort and loyalty are stressed.

AT&T and the Communications Workers of America and International Brotherhood of Electrical Workers formed a joint nonprofit corporation, which provides training and job placement and finances employees' education. About 66,200 AT&T employees have participated in the programs.

Northwest Aluminum Co., in Dalles, Oregon, uses a labor–management ownership team to operate the firm. The team interviews prospective employees, union meetings are held on company property, and management attends union meetings at the beginning to answer questions. The emphasis throughout the company is on the team—labor and management. Conflict within the team has been kept to a minimum.

Sources: Adapted from H Deresky, *International Management* (New York: HarperCollins, 1994), pp. 322–34; "Union, Management Talk It Out," *Houston Post,* December 9, 1990, pp. D1 and D7.

participate may lead individuals to believe that they are valued members of the group. This assumption can lead to the satisfaction of social, esteem, and self-actualization needs.

Perceived Goal Attainment.   A number of studies indicate that a group member's perception of progress toward attaining desired goals is an important factor in satisfaction.[63] Groups that progressed toward the attainment of goals indicated higher levels of member satisfaction, while members of groups not adequately progressing showed a lower satisfaction level.

The importance of measuring and rewarding group and team performance is becoming an area of managerial interest. Achievement of goals can result in specific rewards attached to the goals attained by the group or team. Hewlett-Packard's Medical Group maintains an emphasis on individual performance as the principal determinant of employees' compensation.[64] However, the firm uses a team recognition and reward program to reward the entire team when specific criteria such as goals, timelines, and team spirit are achieved. The "Gold" teams are provided with cash, savings bonds, "getaway" weekends, and time off.

Status Consensus.   This concept is defined as agreement about the relative status of all group members. Several studies indicate that when the degree of status consensus is high, member satisfaction tends to be high; where status consensus within the group is low, member satisfaction tends to be low. Status consensus is more readily achieved in groups where

- The group task specialist is perceived by the membership to be competent.
- A leader emerges who plays a role that is considered an important group task.
- A leadership role emerges and is filled by an individual who concentrates on coordinating and maintaining the activities of the group.

This research suggests that the perceptions of the membership concerning freedom to participate, movement toward goal attainment, and status consensus significantly influence the level of need satisfaction attained by group members. Research also clearly indicates that when an individual member's goals and needs are in conflict with the goals and needs of the overall group, lower levels of membership satisfaction result.

Health and welfare agency employees' degree of satisfaction toward their place of work was the focus of one study.[65] Researchers measured the flow of communication among staff members in formally scheduled meetings as well as in informal contacts. The total communication among colleagues was not associated with satisfaction. But the direction of the flow, whether it was up or down the hierarchy or among peers at the same level, was correlated with satisfaction. That is, when most of the informal talk was from subordinates to supervisors, more unfavorable views of the workplace existed. And when most of the informal messages were directed from superiors to subordinates, favorable workplace attitudes were the rule.

Group Decision-Making Effectiveness

A number of research studies have raised the question of whether group decision making is superior, inferior, or equal to individual decision making. Norman Maier, instead of developing an exact answer to the question, discussed assets and liabilities of group decision making.[66]

Group Assets.   In a group, there is greater total knowledge and information. Thus, decisions that require knowledge should give groups an advantage over individuals. This additional information is helpful in reaching the best decision possible.

Many problems require making decisions that depend on the support of other group members. More members accept a decision when a group solves the problem than when one person solves it. A person reaching a decision must persuade others in the group who may resist being told what the best solution is for the problem. Individuals, by working on the problem, believe that they are more responsible for the solution. This feeling of shared responsibility is satisfying to some people.

A decision that is made by an individual and that is to be carried out by others needs to be communicated to those who must execute it. Thus, the individual decision maker must communicate effectively before positive action is taken. The chances for communication breakdowns are reduced when the individuals who must execute the decision have participated in making it. They were involved in reaching the decision and are aware of how it was reached, which improves understanding.

Group Liabilities.   Making a decision in a group exerts pressure on each member. The desire to be an accepted and cooperative group member tends to silence individual disagreement and favors agreement. If the majority is forceful enough, its decision is usually accepted regardless of whether the quality is adequate.

In some groups, a dominating individual takes over. This person, because of a strong personality, organizational position, reputation, or status, can dominate the group. None of these traits or characteristics is necessarily related to decision-making skill. Further, the characteristics of this kind of person can inhibit group discussion, reduce creativity among other members, and stop members from making positive contributions.

"Stand taking" may hinder a group in reaching a good solution. Most problems have more than one possible solution, and individual group members may have personal preferences. Sometimes, a member may take a stand on his preference and feel that a defeat means loss of face. Thus, the member becomes more concerned with winning than with finding the best group decision.

Summary of Key Points

- Work groups (also referred to as teams) are formed formally and informally in organizations. Groups are extremely important because they influence individual and organizational goals and performance.
- Groups are formed because of physical proximity and the desire to satisfy needs.
- There are numerous and overlapping groups in organizations. Employees are members of multiple groups at the same time. Formal groups include command and task groups. Informal groups include interest and friendship groups.
- Committees are special kinds of task groups. Committees exist to accomplish such purposes as resolving conflict, recommending action, generating ideas, and making decisions.
- The term quality circle originated in Japan in 1962. The evolution of quality circles can be broken into three phases: studying statistical quality control, adapting the technique, and forming quality circles.
- A quality circle is a small group of employees and their supervisor, who voluntarily meet on a regular basis to study quality control and productivity improvement techniques and to identify and solve work-related problems.
- Groups move through various phases of development to maturity. Development occurs along two dimensions: relationships among members and task and problem solving. The four phases of development are mutual acceptance, decision making, motivation, and control.
- Group characteristics have a potential impact on how groups function. Their main features are summarized in Table 12–3. Groupthink is a negative phenomenon that occurs especially in cohesive groups when individual members lose their ability to think critically in evaluating situations or information.

TABLE 12–3   Summary of Key Group Characteristics

What makes groups tick: another reminder.

Characteristics	Major Point(s)
Roles	The behaviors that a person exhibits in a social context.
Group goals	Groups typically have two sets of goals: manager-assigned goals and group goals.
Leadership	In informal groups, leaders emerge from within. In the formal organization, the leader is appointed.
Norms	Work groups utilize norms to affect dress, language used, and job performance.
Cohesiveness	High group cohesiveness aligned with high performance goals is associated with high group performance.
Intragroup conflict	There is likely to be disagreement among different members because of plans, schedules, and standards.
Intergroup conflict	A few of the crucial reasons for intergroup conflict are limited resources, different perceptions, different interests, and lack of clear communication channels.

- Groups perform better than individuals in some situations and equal to or worse than individuals in others. Groups usually outperform individuals when complex and large-scale tasks must be completed.

Discussion and Review Questions

1. What did Lewin mean when he stated "it's easier to affect the personality of 10 people if they can be melted into a group than to affect the personality of any one individual separately"?

2. This chapter focuses on groups and the crucial role they play in organizations. Is it possible for managers to use both the advantages of teamwork and individualism to accomplish goals? Explain.

3. Informal groups exist in organizations and are very important to their members. If an organization has a number of informal groups, is this an indication that the company is being poorly managed? Why or why not?

4. What should a manager look for in determining whether a group is beginning to use a groupthink process in analyzing situations?

5. How is the concept of group norms and control used by weight-reduction clinics and stop-smoking clinics?

6. Why is role differentiation likely to occur in groups?

7. How would a group's structure influence the members' behavior and attitudes?

8. Explain how a group's influence on an individual can be positive or negative.

9. How can managers improve their understanding and ability to deal with the acculturation process among a culturally diverse work group?

10. How can one individual dominate the discussion or activities of a group attempting to reach decisions?

CASE 12–1
SAN DIEGO ZOO'S TEAM APPROACH

Employees at the San Diego Zoo used to have very narrow and very well-defined job responsibilities. Keepers did the keeping and gardeners did the gardening. Employees in construction and maintenance constructed and maintained. This system worked as long as there were clearly defined boundaries between animal exhibits, public areas, and horticultural displays.

Four years ago the zoo began to develop bioclimatic zones, in which plants and animals are grouped together in ageless enclosures that resemble their native habitats. Instead of viewing the exhibits from afar, visitors now walk into and become part of these zones in what the zoo calls an immersion experience. Bioclimatic zones, such as the humid, 3.5-acre Tiger River exhibit, not only provide a healthier environment for plants and animals, they provide a better way to educate visitors about conservation issues and to increase their enjoyment of the zoo experience.

Because the zones themselves are more interdependent—plants are there to be eaten, not just admired—the employees who manage them must work together more closely. This is why, instead of maintaining the new exhibits with employees from traditional functional areas, the zoo has assigned self-directed, multidisciplinary teams to manage the bioclimatic zones.

Tiger River, for example, is run by a seven-member team of mammal and bird specialists, horticulturists, and maintenance and construction workers. The team tracks its own budget, and members are jointly responsible for the display.

Before, the gardener may not have cared about trash on the ground because that was the groundskeeper's job. But today, the horticulturist may spend a morning cleaning the paths, helping the birdkeeper chase down some geese, and answering questions from curious visitors without ever looking at the plants.

Tiger River team members received extensive cross-training, and together they analyzed the work required, set goals for themselves, and gradually built a sense of mutual responsibility and ownership for the exhibit.

The move to self-directed teams met with problems and some resistance, but the process is now paying off. Zoo attendance is up, despite the depressed southern California economy. Workers' compensation claims are down, and employees report a much higher quality of work life. As one team member explained, "Until I was cross-trained and became responsible for a whole area, I had little regard for other job classifications. Tiger River has taught me to respect and help others for the benefit of the entire Zoological Society. This, in turn, gave me pride, which enriched my work."

Self-directed teams like those implemented at the San Diego Zoo are getting a lot of attention these days. In a survey conducted by Development Dimensions International, a human resources consulting firm in Pittsburgh, 27 percent of respondents reported that their organizations currently use self-directed teams, and half of those individuals predicted that the majority of their workforce will be organized in teams within the next five years.

This interest in self-directed teams is nothing short of phenomenal, since it's such a new concept. The same DDI survey revealed that most respondents have two years' or less experience with self-directed teams. As corporate executives and small-business owners alike embrace the total quality movement, they're finding that self-directed teams represent potentially one of the most productive forms of employee involvement.

Self-directed teams require an enormous amount of thought and planning, and no organization should implement them without first understanding what self-directed teams are—and aren't. Self-directed teams aren't teams of co-workers from the same functional department who join together to foster team spirit. Self-directed teams also aren't cross-functional groups of employees who come together to solve a particular problem and then return to their regular jobs. Neither of these two approaches represents self-direction because it doesn't change the way the organization is structured or the way work gets done.

The adoption of self-directed teams not only requires changing the attitudes of people; it requires changing the organizational structure, information patterns, rewards and compensation systems, and the whole concept of career paths. With self-directed teams, employees require a lot of training in team skills. They need cross-training in different functions, and they require much greater business training so that they can understand the impact of their actions on the entire organization.

Questions for Analysis

1. Should leaders at the San Diego Zoo have feared the loss of power when the self-directed teams were established? Why?

2. Was the San Diego Zoo move to self-directed teams automatically self-directing?

3. Why is the management of change so much a part of the transition to self-directed teams?

Sources: S Caudron, "Are Self-Directed Teams Right for Your Company?" *Personnel Journal,* December 1993, pp. 76–84; H Allender, "Self-Directed Work Teams: How Far Is Too Far?" *Industrial Management,* September–October 1993, pp. 13–15.

VIDEO CASE
QUALITY TEAMWORK AT THE UNIVERSITY OF MICHIGAN HOSPITALS

Foreign competition is increasing in almost every industry, and so are operating costs. Many industries have found that quality management is the solution to both of these challenges. As a result, a quality movement is sweeping across America. Teamwork is a significant part of this movement. Originally embraced by manufacturing industries, quality management and teamwork are now being used in many service industries as well. Service businesses appreciate the positive effect these practices have on employee morale, productivity, and customer satisfaction.

The University of Michigan Hospitals adopted quality management as a way to attract and keep top people in the health care profession. John Forsyth, Executive Director of the University of Michigan Hospitals, explained, "The three reasons the University of Michigan has become involved in total quality are: number one, to become the provider of choice; number two, to become preeminent in education in the medical sciences; and number three, to become the employer of choice. The key here is to have a diverse and motivated workforce, and we believe total quality will empower people to that end."

The development of problem-solving teams composed of both managers and employees is one highly effective aspect of a quality program. Team problem-solving techniques are proving to be a simple, effective catalyst to organizational creativity, quality improvement, and a higher quality of work life. But team building in the United States requires a major culture change. Working in groups is somewhat unnatural to Americans, who are instilled with a philosophy of individual achievement beginning in elementary school and continuing throughout their academic and business careers. Larry Warren, an administrator at the University of Michigan Hospitals, expressed his personal reservations about changing to a team-oriented culture: "To suggest that we change the way we do business to one of team approach to everything that we do and do in the future, stressed me out a little bit."

For teamwork to be effective, new work relationships must be based on trust. One important way to establish this trust is through extensive training and team skills. Ellen Gaucher, Senior Associate Hospital Director, said, "We were very concerned about pushing people too hard. We thought they might think this was just another thing administration had up their sleeve for making them work harder. So we got involved with developing a training program that we thought would be the hook for us, would get them excited about total quality. And it has worked very well."

When a quality team is initially selected, it should include decision makers from several key groups: employees, peers, senior managers, customers, suppliers, and staff support. The common characteristics of any team member are interest in the team and the ability to make decisions and commitments on behalf of the team. Joan Robinson, Director of Ambulatory Care Nursing, said, "Our nurses are next to the action. They know what our problems are, and they have been schooled on a scientific process of how to address problems. The total quality approach gives us some of the answers in terms of tools that they can use, and working with other people to solve problems, both clinical and some of the problems in the systems of how we get things done here."

Leadership is crucial for a team approach to be effective. The biggest part of a team leader's job is to keep the team together while its members solve the problem. This means developing critical thinking skills in other team members by asking open-ended questions, or by providing business information so decisions can be made. A team leader must know when to intervene and when to stand back. The leader must avoid the temptation to jump in with solutions, allowing the team to solve the problem it has been charged with. Essentially, there are seven ground rules for effective teamwork:

1. **Time control:** Each team should have a clear, achievable deadline for resolving the problem.

2. **Be sensitive:** Each team member should be sensitive to the other members' needs and expressions.

3. **Relaxed atmosphere:** An informal, relaxed atmosphere should be fostered.

4. **Be prepared:** Material needed for team meetings should be prepared in advance.

5. **Qualified and interested members:** All team members should be qualified and have an interest in the problem the team has been assigned to solve.

6. **Keep good records:** Minutes should be kept of all team meetings.

7. **Assess team performance:** Each team should periodically stop and assess its performance.

When a company develops a quality management program, it's important to implement it slowly and in stages. Widespread team mania at the start-up of a quality program can be dangerous. Leadership by example, employee involvement, and team-building pilot projects make the transition to team problem-solving easier. After training began at the University of Michigan Hospitals, for example, management looked for an area of the hospital to pilot the new team approach. The admitting/discharge unit was selected because of its convoluted system. After examining the problem, the quality team came up with a solution: use a computer link between admitting and housekeeping. Mary Decker Staples, Associate Hospital Administrator, said, "It was successful enough that when we initiated measuring how long it was taking us to admit patients we were averaging two hours after the patient was ready to go up to the room to actually get to the room. Last year the average was 24 minutes—a 65 percent reduction in the amount of time it takes to admit a patient."

This early success with the team approach built momentum for the future. Employees gained confidence that the approach was effective. Sally Ellis, Clinical Nurse, remarked, "I think the pilot program that we had with the admissions/discharge team has definitely helped. Some of the things that have come out after it is that we've all had an understanding now of what people do. It takes away some of the myths or perceptions of why something didn't happen. I think that prior to this it was easy to blame someone else why something didn't get done or why a patient didn't get out of here on time."

Once a pilot program has been implemented and employees begin to get excited about the new approach, quality teams can effectively solve all kinds of problems. At the University of Michigan Hospitals, another team tackled problems in accounts receivable. It found that the accounting department was receiving 200 to 300 calls a day—a volume so large that staff members were able to answer less than 50 percent of all calls. The quality team developed more effective means of bookkeeping, which freed up the staff so they were able to handle more calls. Pamela Chapelle, Assistant Manager of Financial Services, said, "For June, the number of calls that we answered was 74 percent. We have never, in the four years that I've been in this department, answered 74 percent of the calls that have come in."

Another quality team helped open up communication between departments for more effective patient care. A pharmacy team was reviewing the administration of drugs by the medical staff when it found that one drug could be administered on an eight-hour basis instead of the current six-hour basis. The team organized educational sessions with the medical and pharmacy staffs. Michael Ryan, Assistant Director of Pharmacy, said, "What we find now is that 97 percent of prescribing is being done on an eight-hour basis. This has resulted in savings of labor for staff that have to compound and administer the extra dose as well as the expense of the drug, which is a savings of about $30,000 per year."

The key element in effective team problem solving is employee empowerment. Teams cannot be effective if management changes or ignores the team's final recommendations. In a team situation, management must give employees wide latitude in how they go about achieving the company's goals. This requires turning the organizational chart upside down, recognizing that management is there to aid the worker in overcoming problems that arise. True employee empowerment enables an employee to achieve his or her highest potential, which benefits the company and the customer.

The success of quality teams at the University of Michigan Hospitals has been recognized throughout the health care profession. In 1990, Witt and Associates, Inc., and the Health Care Forum awarded the University of Michigan Hospitals with the Commitment to Quality Award. The award was established in 1987 to recognize health care professionals committed to quality health care services. The success of the teamwork approach at the University of Michigan Hospitals has convinced many managers that it is a worthwhile endeavor. Staples said, "I think one of the biggest advantages and positive aspects of total quality is our opportunity to use the knowledge that people who are working at the front line have about what works and what doesn't work. So often we as managers sit back thinking we know what's going on. And when you begin to ask employees what's going on you get a very different picture of the process."

The employees at the University of Michigan Hospitals have embraced the philosophy of quality management, and the use of teams for solving problems, increasing work effort, and developing good employee attitudes. Not only do teams solve problems more effectively, but they allow the employees to focus on improving the processes that affect them. The result? Smoother working relationships, streamlined procedures, and reduced costs.

Critical Thinking Questions

1. Producing quality services through the use of teamwork has proven an effective approach for the University of Michigan Hospitals. Why do you think team problem solving has proven to be so effective? How do teams differ from committees or task forces?

2. As discussed briefly in the video, some employees will initially resist organizational transformation to a team approach. Why do you think employees would resist this change? What are some techniques a manager might use to help overcome this resistance?

3. Teams are very effective in solving problems related to the process flow of an organization. Try to think of some organizational problems or issues that are not likely to be resolved using a team approach. Explain why you think so.

EXPERIENTIAL EXERCISE
GROUP BRAINSTORMING IN ACTION

Purpose

The purpose of this exercise is to provide experience in group brainstorming—to learn to use and pool the ideas, good and bad, of group members.

The Exercise in Class

The rules of the group brainstorming session are:

- Each group member is to contribute at least two ideas. The ideas must be written on a sheet of paper.
- The instructor (or group leader) will write each idea on a chalkboard or flip chart.
- Every idea will be recorded, no matter how unrealistic.
- While ideas are being recorded, there must be NO evaluation by other group members. This is an important part of brainstorming, the freedom to simply "say it like it is" and have no fear of being evaluated.

1. The instructor will form groups of six to eight persons. A group leader, who serves mainly as a recorder of ideas, will be elected. The leader should also contribute ideas.

2. The groups will brainstorm and develop solutions to this problem:

   The midwest region of the United States is known as the "rust bowl" of America. Steelworkers and autoworkers have been losing their jobs. Today, there are only 169,000 steelworkers in the United States, while in 1977 there were 460,000. Most of the job loss has occurred in the rust bowl states—Illinois, Indiana, Michigan, Ohio, and Pennsylvania. The dire prediction is that those who have lost their jobs will never again work in steel mills or auto plants. The jobs are lost forever. Assume that this prediction is basically correct. Using a brainstorming method, develop some solutions that labor, management, and government can take to ease the social, emotional, and psychological pain of job-loss victims. What should and can be done?

3. Each group member is to independently develop two solutions for the job-loss problem. After about 20 minutes, begin recording the solutions.

4. Discuss the brainstorming procedure in the group. If it were being done in an organization, what would be the next step to take once brainstorming has been completed?

Notes

1. Eric Sundstrom, Kenneth P. De Meuse, and David Futrell, "Work Teams," *American Psychologist,* February 1990, p. 120.

2. Alvin Zander, "The Psychology of the Group Process," *Annual Review of Psychology,* 1979, p. 418.

3. Dorwin Cartwright and Ronald Lippitt, "Group Dynamics and the Individual," *International Journal of Group Psychotherapy,* January 1957, p. 88.

4. Council on Japan–United States Economic Relations, "The Japan–United States Partnership in a New Age: A Challenge for the 21st Century," *Business and the Contemporary World,* Spring 1993, pp. 10–37.

5. Susan Caminiti, "What Team Leaders Need to Know," *Fortune,* February 20, 1995, pp. 93–100.

6. This is the widely used and insightful framework offered by Leonard R Sayles, "Research in Industrial Human Relations," *Industrial Relations Research Association* (New York: Harper & Row, 1957), pp. 131–45.

7. Daniel R Denison, Stuart L Hart, and Joel A Kahn, "From Chimneys to Cross-Functional Teams: Developing and Validating A Diagnostic Model," *Academy of Management Journal,* August 1996, pp. 1005–23.

8. A Donnellon, *Teamtalk* (Boston: Harvard University Press, 1995).

9. Originators of these comments are unknown. Individuals working in organizations often used more colorful descriptions to portray committees. It should be noted, however, that committees in some situations have been very productive and that jokes are not used to describe the effective committee arrangement.

10. Brian Dumaine, "Procter & Gamble Shoots for the Top," *Industry Week,* January 6, 1992, pp. 24–25.

11. Kenneth L Berttenhausen and J Keith Muinigham, "The Development of an Intragroup Norm and the Effects of Interpersonal and Structural Challenges," *Administrative Science Quarterly,* March 1991, pp. 20–35.

12. G M Prince, "How to Be a Better Chairman," *Harvard Business Review,* January–February 1969, pp. 98–108.

13. Norman B Sigband, "The Use of Meetings," *Nation's Business,* February 1987, p. 28.

14. Ibid.

15. Izumi Nonaka, "The History of the Quality Circle," *Quality Progress,* September 1993, pp. 81–83.

16. Izumi Nonaka, "Origin of Japanese Quality Control," *Quality Control,* March 1990, pp. 55–62.

17. IAQC-*International Association of Quality Circles,* Summer 1987, p. 3.

18. James M Carman, "Continuous Quality Improvement as a Survival Strategy: The Southern Pacific Experience," *California Management Review,* Spring 1993, pp. 118–32.

19. Edward E Lawler III, *The Ultimate Advantage* (San Francisco: Jossey-Bass, 1992), pp. 129–32.

20. Edward E Lawler III, Susan A Mohrman, and G E Ledford, *Employee Involvement and Total Quality Management* (San Francisco: Jossey-Bass, 1992), pp. 18–27.

21. Richard S Wellins, William C Byham, and Jeanne M Wilson, *Empowered Teams* (San Francisco: Jossey-Bass, 1991), pp. 21–22.

22. Brian Dumaine, "Who Needs a Boss?" *Fortune,* May 7, 1990, pp. 52–60.

23. Sharon Cohen, "Run-It-Yourself Idea One That Is Growing," *Post-Courier of Charleston,* December 2, 1990, pp. G1–2.

24. Ralph Stayer, "How I Learned to Let My Workers Lead," *Harvard Business Review,* November–December 1990, pp. 66–68, 80–83.

25. Robert Hayles and Armeda Mendez Russell, *The Diversity Directive* (Burr Ridge: Richard D. Irwin, 1997).

26. J Braham, "No, You Don't Manage Everyone the Same," *Industry Week,* February 6, 1989, pp. 28–35.

27. J W Berry, "Cultural Relations in Plural Society: Alternatives to Segregation and Their Sociopsychological Implications," in N Miller and M Bruner, eds., *Groups in Contact* (New York: Academic Press, 1984), pp. 75–98.

28. Taylor Cox and Joycelyn Finley-Nickelson, "Models of Acculturation for Intra-organizational Cultural Diversity," *Canadian Journal of Administrative Sciences,* June 1991, pp. 80–96.

29. Charles Marmer Solomon, "Managing Today's Immigrants," *Personnel Journal,* February 1993, pp. 56–65.

30. G Oddou, "Unlocking a Hidden Resource: Integrating the Foreign Born," in M Mendenhall and G Oddou, eds., *Cases in International Human Resource Management* (Boston, MA: PWS-Kent, 1991), pp. 118–22.

31. Warren G Bennis and Herbert A Shephard, "A Theory of Group Development," *Human Relations,* Summer 1963, pp. 415–57.

32. John P Wanous, Arnon E Reichers, and S D Malik, "Organizational Socialization and Group Development: Toward an Integrative Perspective," *Academy of Management Review,* October 1984, pp. 670–83.

33. This discussion of the development of groups is based largely on Bernard Bass, *Organizational Psychology* (Boston: Allyn & Bacon, 1965), pp. 197–98. A number of alterations have been made by the authors.

34. Fremont E Kast and James E Rosenzweig, *Organization and Management* (New York: McGraw-Hill, 1979), p. 290.

35. "The Horizontal Corporation," *Business Week,* December 20, 1993, pp. 76–81.

36. Original source of the role and subrole partition was found in K D Benne and P Sheats, "Functional Roles of Group Members," *Journal of Social Issues,* 1948, pp. 41–49. A more current arrangement of this original source is found in Don Hellriegel, John W Slocum, Jr., and Richard M Woodman, *Organizational Behavior* (St. Paul, MN: West, 1989), pp. 212–14.

37. Jerry C Wofford, *Organizational Behavior* (Boston: Kent, 1982), p. 311.

38. John M Ivancevich, "Different Goal Setting Treatments and Their Effects on Performance and Job Satisfaction," *Academy of Management Journal,* September 1977, pp. 406–19.

39. Robert R Blake and Jane S Mouton, "Don't Let Group Norms Stifle Creativity," *Personnel,* August 1985, p. 28.

40. L A Rosenberg, "Conformity as a Function of Confidence in Self and Confidence in Partner," *Human Behavior,* Spring 1963, pp. 131–39.

41. Ibid.

42. Pasul Mulvey, John F Veigh, Priscilla M Elsess, "When Teammates Raise a White Flag," *Academy of Management Executive,* February 1996, pp. 40–49.

43. Solomon E Asch, "Opinions and Social Pressures," *Scientific American,* November 1955, pp. 31–35.

44. This definition is based on the group cohesiveness concept presented by Stanley E Seashore, *Group Cohesiveness in the Industrial Work Group* (Ann Arbor: Institute for Social Research, University of Michigan, 1954).

45. Leonard R Sayles and George Strauss, *Human Behavior in Organizations* (Englewood Cliffs, NJ: Prentice Hall, 1966), p. 101.

46. Jeff Spingston, "Redefining Cohesiveness in Groups," *Small Group Research,* May 1990, pp. 234–54.

47. Robert Waterman, *The Renewal Factor* (New York: Bantam, 1987), pp. 81–83.

48. Lynn Adkins, "Such a Grand Design," *Business Month,* December 1987, pp. 30–31.

49. Irving Janis, "Groupthink," *Psychology Today,* November 1971, pp. 43–46.

50. Irving Janis, *Victims of Groupthink* (Boston: Houghton Mifflin, 1982), pp. 17–45.

51. Ann Reilly Dowd, "How Bush Manages the Presidency," *Fortune,* August 27, 1990, pp. 68–70.

52. Seashore, *Group Cohesiveness,* pp. 90–95; also see, Robert C Cummins and Donald C King, "The Interaction of Group Size and Task Structure in an Industrial Organization," *Personnel Psychology,* Spring 1973.

53. Brenda Paik Sunoo, "The Employee May Be Loafing: Can You Tell? Should You Care?" *Personnel Journal,* December 1996, pp. 54–62.

54. Robert Albanese and David D Van Fleet, "Rational Behavior in Groups: The Free-Riding Tendency," *Academy of Management Journal,* April 1985, pp. 244–55.

55. Hellriegel et al., *Organizational Behavior,* p. 109.

56. "Has Weirton's ESOP Worked Too Well?" *Business Week,* January 23, 1989, pp. 66–68.

57. Merv Singer and Susan Lazer, "Who's in Charge Here?" *NationsBank,* January 1995, p. 37.

58. Robert R Blake and Jane S Mouton, *Solving Costly Organizational Conflicts* (San Francisco: Jossey-Bass, 1984), pp. 7–10.

59. Olle Hammarstrom, "Joint Worker–Management Consultation: The Case of LKAB Sweden," in Louis E Davis and Albert B Cherns, eds., *The Quality of Working Life: Cases and Commentary* (New York: Free Press, 1985), pp. 66–79.

60. "Union, Management Talk It Out," *Houston Post,* December 9, 1990, pp. D1, D7.

61. M Sherif and C W Sherif, *Groups in Harmony and Tension* (New York: Harper & Row, 1953).

62. Richard Heslin and Dexter Dunphy, "Three Dimensions of Member Satisfaction in Small Groups," *Human Relations,* May 1964, pp. 99–112.

63. Clovis R Shepherd, *Small Groups: Some Sociological Perspectives* (San Francisco: Chandler, 1964), p. 101.

64. Douglas G Shaw and Craig Eric Schneier, "Team Measurement and Rewards: How Some Companies Are Getting It Right," *Human Resource Planning,* 1996, pp. 34–47.

65. C B Bagley, J Hage, and M Aiken, "Communication and Satisfaction in Organizations," *Human Relations,* October 1975, pp. 611–26.

66. Norman R F Maier, "Assets and Liabilities in Group Problem Solving," *Psychological Review,* July 1967, pp. 239–49.

13 LEADING PEOPLE IN ORGANIZATIONS

Chapter Learning Objectives

After completing Chapter 13, you should be able to:

- **Define** what is meant by the term *leadership*.
- **Describe** the importance of being able to lead an increasingly multicultural workforce.
- **Discuss** the power bases that leaders can use to influence the work behavior of followers.
- **Compare** the similarities and differences in the University of Michigan, Ohio State University, and Managerial Grid personal–behavioral explanations of leadership.
- **Identify** important differences among situational theories of leadership.

Leaders: Similarities and Differences

The search for the right mix to be a successful leader continues unabated. The sport of finding the activities, style, values, and whatever else explains successful leaders has played on for over five decades. A look at three individuals whom experts refer to as admired leaders gives some insight into what makes leaders tick.

Jack Welch, the CEO at General Electric, usually receives high leadership grades. He is considered to be a taskmaster, a hard driver, and a results-oriented person. He articulates his vision as emphasizing the go-forward and grow-it-large philosophies. He has a need to articulate this vision in a passionate manner and to build trust among others. As the discussion in this chapter will show, Welch is a transformational leader. The success of GE is tied to Welch's unrelenting drive. "A leader can and does make a difference," could be a motto of GE. Welch has reshaped GE and indicates that he is still not done making changes and leading from the front of the team.

Paula Marshall-Chapman is the CEO of Bama Pies, Limited, which is based in Tulsa. She admits to being both a workaholic and a quality fanatic. She has stressed 100 percent customer satisfaction. Bama Pies is McDonald's supplier of pies in the United States and its apple producer for restaurants in China and Korea. A tireless worker who wants to satisfy every customer and supplier, Marshall-Chapman serves as a role model and as a strategic thinker. She does not tolerate sloppiness and discourteous behavior. Her view is that if Bama Pies doesn't react to customer needs this time, there might not be a next time.

Sandy Sandbutte is the CEO at Minnesota Power Company. Sandbutte practices what is discussed in the chapter as empowerment. Minnesota Power empowers its employees to make decisions, feel free to make suggestions, and create the type of work culture that encourages and supports growth. Sandbutte believes that a leader plays a major role in creating a culture that develops many other leaders. Sandbutte works constantly to assure employees that empowerment is the rule rather than the exception at Minnesota Power.

These three leaders succeed by working hard and by practicing the style that best fits them and their situations. Though their styles may differ somewhat, all three appear to be good listeners, to possess tremendous drive, to have reputations for integrity, and to *want* to be leaders. As this chapter will clearly illustrate, there is no one best leadership approach. Some leaders succeed with an autocratic, hard-driving, do-it-my-way approach. Other leaders succeed by completely empowering followers to accomplish the job. There is no gender, race, country, or morality-based model of leadership. As Peter Drucker so aptly states, leadership is work.

Sources: Adapted from Tim Smart, "Jack Welch's Encore," *Business Week,* October 28, 1996, pp. 155–60; Marshall Loeb, "Jack Welch Let's Fly on Budgets, Bonuses, and Buddy Boards," *Fortune,* May 29, 1995, pp. 145–47; J F McKenna, "America's Most Admired CEOs," *Industry Week,* December 6, 1993, pp. 22–23; A Sandbutte, "Leadership," *Industry Week,* November 1, 1993, pp. 16–18; and P F Drucker, "Leadership More Doing than Dash," *The Wall Street Journal,* January 6, 1988, p. 16.

Interest in the subject of leading others has existed as long as people have been studying human behavior. Behavioral scientists in the past 50 years have scientifically analyzed leadership in organizational settings; they have found leadership is a complex process that can be explained by various theories and models.[1] Many of the available theories and models, however, are contradictory or overlap.[2]

Jack Welch, Paula Marshall-Chapman, and Sandy Sandbutte do not fit any particular theory or model. They lead by working at their jobs every single day. Peter Drucker is certainly an astute observer in stating that leadership is work. As you learn from this chapter, Drucker is that specific in how he views leadership. Cute gimmicks and buzzwords do not make a leader. Hard work every day is what it takes to be and to remain a leader in any country.

What Is Leadership?

Some writers have given the impression that leadership is a synonym for management. This assumption is not correct.[3] Leaders are found not only in the managerial hierarchy but also in informal work groups. The difference between leadership and management has been stated as follows:

> Leadership is a part of management but not all of it . . . Leadership is the ability to persuade others to seek defined objectives enthusiastically. It is the human factor which binds a group together and motivates it toward goals. Management activities such as planning, organizing, and decision making are dormant cocoons until the leader triggers the power of motivation in people and guides them toward goals.[4]
>
> Figure 13–1 shows graphically that managers are not always effective leaders. Of course, organizations of all sizes prefer to have or attempt to develop managers who are also leaders.

An important feature of the preceding definition of leadership is that leadership is a process whereby one individual exerts influence over others. Several attempts have been made to clarify and depict the basis on which a superior might influence a subordinate or a group of subordinates. One of the most concise and insightful approaches was offered by John French and Bertram Raven.[5] In addition to defining influence in terms of **power**—the control a person possesses and can exercise on others—they propose five different bases for such power:

1. *Coercive power.* Coercive power is based on fear. A subordinate perceives that failure to comply with the wishes of a superior would lead to punishment (for example, an undesirable work assignment, a reprimand). Coercive power is based on the expectations of individuals that punishment is the consequence of not agreeing with the actions, attitudes, or directives of a superior. In the 1993 strike between American Airlines and the Flight Attendants Union, leaders used coercive power: threats, intimidation, anxiety. Unfortunately, it took the intervention of President Clinton to settle the conflict.[6]

2. *Reward power.* Reward power is the opposite of coercive power. A subordinate perceives that compliance with the wishes of a superior will lead

---

FIGURE 13–1   The Preferred Leader–Manager Mix

Leaders = managers only in some cases, since leadership is only one part of management.

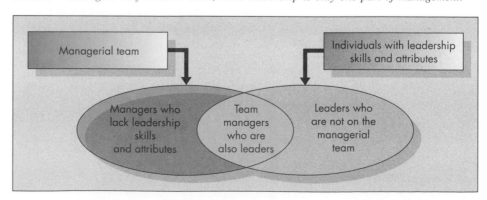

to positive rewards. These rewards could be monetary (increases in pay) or nonmonetary (a compliment for a job well done).

3. *Legitimate power.* Legitimate power comes from the position of a superior in the organizational hierarchy. For example, the president of a corporation possesses more legitimate power than the vice president, and the department manager has more legitimate power than the first-line supervisor.

4. *Expert power.* An individual with expert power is one with expertise, special skill, or knowledge. The possession of one or more of these attributes gains the respect and compliance of peers or subordinates. In some cases, individuals with expert power are placed in managerial positions and are expected to lead. This seems to be true in professional sports. Great athletes with superior skills are assumed to be potential leaders.

5. *Referent power.* Referent power is based on a follower's identification with a leader. Individuals want to identify with the powerful person; therefore, they grant the person power because of attractiveness or because the leader is perceived to have desirable resources.

A research study identified the meaning of each of these five power bases to individuals.[7] Table 13–1 summarizes these meanings.

The French and Raven power model has been criticized on a number of factors. Critics point out the lack of distinction between the five power bases. For example, supervisors' control of rewards and punishments correlates with their legitimate power.[8] Student found that referent and expert power were "incremental influence" factors, whereas the other three power bases were organizationally derived. He found

---

TABLE 13–1   Scale That Describes "My Supervisor Can . . ."

1. *Coercive power*
   Give me undesirable job assignments.
   Make my work difficult for me.
   Make things unpleasant here.

2. *Reward power*
   Increase my pay level.
   Provide me with special benefits.
   Influence my getting a promotion.

3. *Legitimate power*
   Make me feel that I have commitments to make.
   Give me the feeling I have responsibilities to fulfill.
   Make me recognize I have tasks to accomplish.

4. *Expert power*
   Give me good technical suggestions.
   Share with me his considerable experience and training.
   Provide me with sound job-related advice.

5. *Referent power*
   Make me feel valued.
   Make me feel like she approves of me.
   Make me feel important.

Source: Adapted from T R Hinkin and C A Schriesheim, "Development and Application of New Scales to Measure the French and Raven (1959) Bases of Power," *Journal of Applied Psychology*, August 1989, p. 567.

that expert and referent power were significantly related to the quality of a group's performance and to a reduction in costs. But average earnings decreased with the use of reward power, and the maintenance costs of the group increased when coercive power was used.[9]

The Leadership Job: A Mutual-Sharing View

Unquestionably, managers have the legitimate power to influence decisions as granted by the organization. However, influence should be viewed as a mutual exercise. To influence, one must *be* influenced to some degree. That is, the leader must be influenced by followers.

A leader who attempts to influence through coercion or fear eventually faces problems. This is not to say that the leader should be stripped of the right to discipline followers in an equitable manner. It does suggest, however, that employees should view the leader as approachable, equitable, and considerate. The leader can exert more influence if viewed as being open to influence in some situations.

This mutual-sharing view of leadership has an important message: Influence can be divided or shared and both parties can gain. A leader, by sharing influence with followers, can benefit from establishing better interaction and more respect. The followers can benefit by learning more about the leader. Managers and employees in effective organizations. perceive themselves as having greater influence. The greater the total influence leaders and followers have in the organization, the better seems to be the performance of the total system.[10]

The objective of what is referred to as the "reverse performance review" is to build a mutual relationship between managers and subordinates. It is designed to encourage them to talk to one another as equals.[11] And some of its original skeptics seem to be changing their tune. Frank Fuggine, vice president of human resources, stated: "I was skeptical when the reverse review was proposed. But it's been a real eyeopener. I learned more about myself . . . I found people in general were very candid and in most cases welcomed the opportunity. That really surprised me."

Empowering subordinates is growing in popularity. The logic is that by sharing more power with followers, the leader's power capabilities actually increase.

Empowerment is defined as providing employees at all levels the authority and responsibility to make decisions on their own. Empowerment occurs when power goes to employees who then experience a sense of ownership and control over their jobs. Empowered individuals believe that they have a say in how their jobs are to be done.

Max DePree, the president of Herman Miller, suggests that empowerment appears to be simple but is, in fact, challenging.[12] Asking leaders to permit others to share in decision making, problem solving, and job design is difficult. Many leaders have been told to take the lead and provide answers to followers. Empowerment requires a mutual sharing and even a handing over of some authority and responsibility to followers.

Jan Carlson, CEO at SAS, encouraged empowerment from the day he took over the top job. He believes a leader has to let people bear the weight of responsibility.[13] He stated that an employee's "self-confidence comes from success, experience, and the organization's environment. The leader's most important role is to instill confidence in people." Carlson wanted his subordinates to understand that they were empowered to do their jobs. His style, communications, and actions supported his empowerment-as-power viewpoint.

What empowerment means at Hampton Inn is presented in the accompanying Management Focus. The SAS and Hampton Inn examples illustrate how empowerment can make a difference in the way employees view their jobs.

Leader Attitudes: Important Assumptions

Douglas McGregor introduced the concept that the attitudes managers hold about the nature of people greatly influence their behavior. Managers who view subordinates as lazy, uncooperative, and possessing poor work habits treat them accordingly.[14] Likewise, managers who see their employees as hardworking, cooperative, and possessing positive work habits treat them in this manner. McGregor referred to this attitude–behavior link as the **self-fulfilling prophecy.**

McGregor's views about manager attitudes were presented in terms of assumptions. McGregor distinguished between what he called Theory X and Theory Y managers. Theory X managers behaved according to the following assumptions:

- The average employee inherently dislikes work and avoids it whenever possible.
- Most employees must be coerced, directed, and closely supervised to get them to put forth the effort to achieve organizational objectives.
- Most employees have little ambition and prefer job security above all other outcomes.
- Most employees avoid taking on responsibilities.

The Theory X manager making these assumptions would use an authoritarian and directive style of leadership.

On the other hand, Theory Y managerial behaviors would be based on the following assumptions and would reflect a less authoritarian leadership style:

- The expenditure of physical and mental effort in work is as natural as play or rest.
- Most people prefer to exercise self-direction and self-control.
- People learn, when encouraged, to accept and seek responsibilities.
- People are interested in displaying imagination, ingenuity, and creativity to solve organizational problems.

Under a Theory X manager, the employee having difficulty meeting standard output levels is seen as lazy and as one who needs to be closely supervised. However, the Theory Y manager would view this employee as perhaps needing further training, more support, or more autonomy to do the job. The self-fulfilling prophecy of managing and leading can be described as: What a manager expects of his subordinates and the way he treats them largely determine their performance and career progress. A unique characteristic of superior managers is their ability to create high performance expectations that subordinates fulfill.

Women versus Men as Leaders

Recently interest has renewed in studying male and female managers to determine differences in Theory X or Theory Y or sensitivity orientations. Prominent female government and social leaders have dotted the pages of history books. Eleanor Roosevelt, Jane Addams, Elizabeth I of England, Catherine the Great of Russia, and past prime minister of England Margaret Thatcher are a few of the female world

Management Focus

Empowerment at Hampton Inn

In October 1989, Hampton Inn became the first national hotel chain to create a formal, ongoing policy of "guaranteed" customer satisfaction. The company's 100% Satisfaction Guarantee simply states that if guests are not completely satisfied with their stay at a Hampton Inn, they are not expected to pay.

The effectiveness of Hampton Inn's guarantee is based upon a strong program of employee empowerment. Employees at every level of hotel operations—from housekeeping staff to front desk personnel—are empowered to use the guarantee as a tool to deliver total guest satisfaction without asking the general manager for permission in advance. All employees receive extensive training regarding the concept behind the 100% Satisfaction Guarantee and how to implement it in specific situations.

The guest services manager at the Hampton Inn Atlanta–Cumberland Mall explains how empowerment works:

A few years ago, while working as a guest services representative at a Hampton Inn hotel, I overheard a guest at our complimentary continental breakfast complaining quite loudly that his favorite cereal was not available. Rather than dismiss the person as just another disgruntled guest, I looked at the situation and saw an opportunity to make this guest happy. I gave him his money back—not for the continental breakfast, but for the cost of one night's stay at our hotel. And I did it on the spot, without checking with my supervisor or the general manager of the hotel, and without making the guest fill out a long complaint form.

Some people might be surprised to hear this story, or they might not believe it could happen. After all, how could a front-desk employee give a guest his money back without getting permission from the boss? And why would the hotel support this action for something simple like a bowl of cereal?

The answer is Hampton Inn's 100% Satisfaction Guarantee. This guarantee is a promise our hotels make to every one of our guests, which is that if they are not completely satisfied with every aspect of their stay, they're not expected to pay. What's more, the guarantee empowers every Hampton Inn employee to do whatever it takes to satisfy guests—including giving them their money back.

In early 1989, the company decided to launch the 100% Satisfaction Guarantee at every hotel nationwide beginning that October. At first, many employees thought this program would have very little effect on their jobs. But when we learned that every employee would go through a three-day training program, we knew that the guarantee was something special. It became more and more apparent that the new Hampton Inn guarantee would affect all of our jobs, and we would have to change the way we thought about performing our routine duties.

The company scheduled a series of training sessions at every hotel, involving videos, classroom-style teaching, open discussions, and role-playing. Through this training, we learned what to do if a guest asked to invoke the guarantee. We also learned how to identify situations when we, as employees, should invoke the guarantee for guests before they even complain. This training taught us the concept of empowerment and reinforced the message that employees at every level should use this responsibility to make sure guests are satisfied.

Many employees—including myself—were skeptical at first. Although we were proud of our hotels and the service that we offered, we thought that guests might take advantage of the guarantee as a way to get something for free. But the training emphasized that, although any reason given by a guest is a valid reason to invoke the guarantee, most guests would not take advantage of us. The company even provided research to back up this claim. Still, we felt we would have to find out for ourselves.

Now, after more than three years of experience with the 100% Satisfaction Guarantee in place, I believe that our entire corporate culture has changed for the better.

While the goal of the 100% Satisfaction Guarantee is to give every guest a satisfying stay, the guarantee has made employees more satisfied as well. When Hampton Inn tells employees that they can do whatever it takes to make a guest happy—without needing approval from a manager—they're telling employees that they trust them to do their jobs. Most employees have never worked for a company that will unconditionally back them up for refunding a guest's money, no matter how small the problem was to begin with.

Source: Adapted from R Thompson, "An Employee's View of Empowerment," *HR Focus*, July 1993, pp. 14–15.

leaders often cited. Today, researchers are studying female business leaders and learning about their styles, attitudes, and effectiveness.[15]

Leadership opportunities for women up to the 1980s tended to be limited to women's issues and a small range of occupations. Women in business have indicated in surveys that they have had to struggle more to succeed, and that they have suffered from job discrimination. Today, as more women enter the workforce, graduate from business school programs, and start their own businesses, there is a new interest in learning about leadership and how it applies to females.[16] Contrary to what may be expected from comments in the popular press, the preponderance of available empirical evidence shows no clear pattern of differences in styles of female and male leaders.[17]

Are female leaders different from male leaders? The popular press is warning "Mr. Hard-Driving, Competitive, Type A" that he and his style of leadership are on the way out. The gentler, more sensitive, and less-concerned-about-power "Ms. Consensus Builder" is being labeled what the doctor ordered to turn companies around.

The *Harvard Business Review* reported on a study undertaken for the International Women's Forum (IWF). The results intrigued the researcher Judy Rosener because they contradict some of the data reported in the press.[18] She found:

- Women are much more likely than men to use power based on charisma, work record, and contacts, as opposed to power based on organizational position.
- Women are more likely than men to use transformational leadership or to motivate others by transforming their self-interest into the goals of the organization.
- Women who describe themselves as predominantly "feminine" or "gender neutral" report a higher level of followership among their female subordinates than women who describe themselves as masculine.
- The women executives earn the same amount of money as their male counterparts. (Most studies have shown a wide gap between men's and women's earnings.)

Despite the new wave of reports and suggestions that women have better leadership styles, the hard data and facts indicate that in some situations one particular style is more effective than another style. Labeling a style as feminine or masculine doesn't seem to be a productive way to proceed in understanding leadership. The leaders who succeed in our rapidly changing world are not likely to have leadership characteristics based primarily on gender.[19] "Can the man or woman adapt to the situation?" The IWF survey results are interesting, but they shouldn't be used as a final verdict on which leadership style is best. Like men, some women are great leaders while others are disastrous failures. Which of these theories has the most use to practitioners?

The Leader as Coach

There is an increasing call for leaders to serve as coaches. Coaching involves working closely with subordinates and helping them change behaviors that prevent them from performing at the highest level. Coaching is difficult, time consuming, and still somewhat of a mystery in the discussion of leadership.[20] However, the goal of coaching is to improve performance. Whether one is suited to coach is not easy to assess.

Anecdotal and case examples of coaching such a number of relevant behaviors. Apparently, an effective leader engaged in coaching behavior needs to be introspective, a teacher, and supportive. Many leaders have difficulty with each of these

Gender Bias: Stop the Nonsense

In the 700 largest public companies, only 2 percent of top executives and only 0.5 percent of the highest-paid officers and directors are women. In Britain, women hold 8 percent of the top jobs, and in Japan women hold only 0.12 percent of the top jobs. Is there a glass ceiling? Perhaps so, but maybe there is, unfortunately, gender bias. The "glass ceiling" is a transparent or invisible barrier that prohibits women from rising above a certain level in the organization's ranks.

Gender bias refers to stereotyping and preconceptions that result in the unequal treatment (e.g., fewer promotion opportunities) of women. Overt bias would include differences in salaries or sex-segregated selection for leadership positions. Covert bias may come in the form of being given a promotion but not given the support or cooperation needed to be successful.

If the best leaders are to be available in an increasingly competitive world, gender bias is going to have to be overcome. Women leaders, men leaders, and leaders from culturally diverse backgrounds will be needed. Companies such as Dayton-Hudson, CBS, Avon, and Merck have acquired reputations as being firms that recognize the shortage of talented leaders. These firms pride themselves on not having glass ceilings, eliminating gender bias, and supporting their leaders. Women and minorities are reaching significant positions of power in these firms. These firms have especially guarded against the type of gender bias outlined in the following organizational practices.

Recruitment: Bias in how, where, and when positions are advertised; the nature of advertisements, job specifications, initial screening of applicants.

Selection: Bias in who conducts interviews, questions and format of interviews; criteria and methods used in assessment.

Task assignment: Differential assignment of men and women to visible divisions, jobs within divisions, tasks within jobs, bosses, clients, and customers.

Performance appraisal: Bias in the goals and objectives of performance, measures and criteria of performance, training of evaluators; poor collection of feedback and supporting performance information.

Salary allocation: Bias in the translation of performance appraisals into salary and bonuses; use of factors not formally assessed in compensation decisions.

Management development: Unequal access to formal training both in-house and externally; unequal opportunity for international positions or other posts essential to promotion; unequal access to mentors and informal networks of development.

Benefits: Lack of benefits such as flextime, flexiplace, day care, maternity, elder care.

Promotion: Differential assignment of men and women to career ladders with access to higher levels of the organization; bias in the criteria and characteristics required for promotion, and the evaluation and assessment of candidates; bias stemming from previous decisions related to task assignment and training opportunities.

Informal culture: Lack of recognition of sexism and/or unwillingness to confront and eliminate norms and values that foster sexism.

The rationale for supporting the elimination of gender bias, although motivated to some extent by competitive payoffs, needs a moral tone. It is morally corrupt to impose glass ceilings and other artificial barriers. It makes no sense to take into account gender, skin color, religious preference, or other factors not related to performance. *Can the man or woman lead and perform the job?* This is all that should count. The firms that practice this philosophy are going to be successful in an increasingly culturally diverse world.

Sources: Adapted from E R Austin, "Demystifying the Glass Ceiling: Organizational and Interpersonal Dynamics of Gender Bias," *Business and the Contemporary World,* Summer 1993, pp. 47–68; R J Burke, "Women in Corporate Management: Introduction," *Business and the Contemporary World,* Summer 1993, pp. 3–9; and M J Davidson, *Shattering the Glass Ceiling: The Woman's Manager* (London: Paul Chapman, 1992).

behaviors. Hard-charging leaders are competitive, judgmental, and so engaged that being supportive, which is time-consuming, is difficult.

Coaching requires confronting some unpleasant truths about other people. Suspending judgment in order to help a person is not easy. The imperfections of the person being coached can be very irritating to the coach. He or she must struggle with the irritation and the need to help the person.

A few helpful suggestions have been provided to improve coaching situations for the coach:

1. Be an active listener.
2. Move from easy to more difficult problems.
3. Engage in role-playing or have the person play out possible scenarios.
4. Have the person provide more positive feedback to his colleagues or subordinates.

The leader who is considered an effective coach appears to be one who is creative, patient, and dedicated to looking for a variety of solutions to help the person being coached. Coaching is complex because it means that behaviors must be changed. Behavioral change takes time, requires persistence and self-discipline, and often involves an occasional slip backward.[21] Leaders who can coach effectively are likely to become highly valued as the complexity of an internationally connected world and diverse workforce become more pronounced in the 21st century.

Trait Theories of Leadership

The first systematic attempt to understand leadership was the research to identify the particular characteristics of leaders that predict success. The theme of this research originally was that leaders are born, not made. However, the comparison of leaders by various physical, personality, and intelligence traits has resulted in little agreement among researchers.

At the beginning of the twentieth century, leaders were generally assumed to possess distinct traits such as intelligence, physical stature, and self-confidence. The search for the best combination of traits continued for the next 40 years, resulting in little agreement about which traits and abilities characterized successful versus unsuccessful leaders.

Reviews of the literature and research on traits suggest a number of desirable characteristics of leaders such as the following:[22]

Drive: Willingness to take initiative, high energy, and seeking achievement.

Motivation: A strong desire to lead and influence others.

Integrity: Honesty and truthfulness in dealing with others.

Self-confidence: Being decisive, assertive, and confident.

Intelligence: Verbal and quantitative competence and the ability to process and use complex information.

Knowledge: A solid understanding of the job, organization, and industry.

Even this set of desirable characteristics doesn't fit every situation or every leader. A successful leader is a person who is able to achieve the results desired. No specific set of characteristics can fit every person who achieves results.[23]

Personal–Behavioral Theories

Because a trait explanation could not be substantiated, other theorists and researchers emerged offering various explanations about leadership. Researchers attempted to identify specific behaviors characteristic of effective leaders. Thus, a set of personal–behavioral theories emerged. Personal–behavioral (P–B) theories contend that leaders may best be classified by personal qualities or behavioral patterns (styles). P–B theories of leadership focus on what the leader does in carrying out the managerial job. Of these, no specific style is universally accepted.

A Continuum of Leadership

Robert Tannenbaum and Warren Schmidt propose that managers often have difficulty deciding which action is most appropriate for handling a particular problem.[24] They are not sure whether to make the decision or to delegate the decision-making authority to subordinates.

To provide insight into the meaning of leadership behavior with regard to decision making, Tannenbaum and Schmidt suggest the continuum presented in Figure 13–2. Leadership actions are related to the degree of authority used by managers and to the amount of freedom available to the subordinates in reaching decisions. The managerial actions depicted on the left characterize managers who maintain a high degree of control, while those actions on the right indicate managers who delegate decision-making authority. Along the continuum, there are a number of leadership styles. According to this theory, effective leaders would be those who are adaptable, that is, who can delegate authority effectively because they consider their capabilities, subordinates' capabilities, and the objectives to be accomplished. Thus, Tannenbaum and Schmidt imply that leaders should not choose either a strictly autocratic or democratic style but should be flexible enough to cope with different situations.

FIGURE 13–2   Continuum of Leadership Behavior

Autocratic to democratic: Relating decision-making behaviors to styles of leadership.

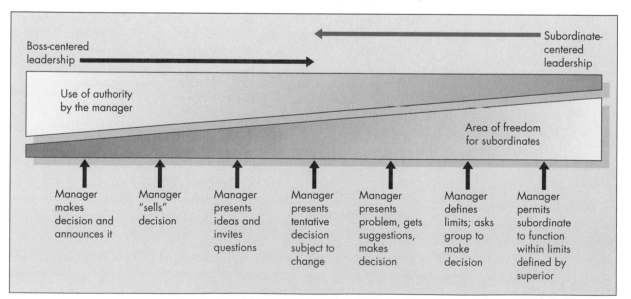

*Michigan Studies:
Job-Centered and
Employee-Centered
Leaders*

From 1947 on, Rensis Likert and a group of social researchers at the University of Michigan conducted studies of leadership.[25] They studied leaders in industry, hospitals, and government, obtaining data from thousands of employees.

After extensive analyses, they classified the leaders studied as job centered or employee centered. The *job-centered leader* structures the jobs of subordinates, closely supervises to see that designated tasks are performed, uses incentives to spur production, and determines standard rates of production based on procedures such as time study. The *employee-centered leader* focuses attention on the human aspects of subordinates' problems and on building effective work groups with high performance goals. Such a leader specifies objectives, communicates them to subordinates, and gives subordinates considerable freedom to accomplish their jobs.

The University of Michigan research showed that the majority of high-producing groups were led by supervisors who displayed an employee-centered style. A study of clerical workers described the employee-centered manager as a general supervisor and the job-centered manager as a close supervisor. Once again, productivity data clearly indicated that the general supervision (employee centered) was more effective than the close supervision style (job centered).

*Ohio State Studies:
Two-Dimensional
Theory*

In 1945, a group of researchers at Ohio State University began extensive investigations of leadership, focusing on the study of leader behavior. Their efforts uncovered many provocative insights and changed the conceptual foundation of leadership research from a trait-based approach to a behavior base.

Perhaps the most publicized aspect of the studies was the isolation of two dimensions of leadership behavior, identified as "consideration" and "initiating structure."[26] These two dimensions described leadership behavior in organizational settings. The researchers assessed how supervisors think they should behave in leadership roles. They also attempted to ascertain subordinates' perceptions of supervisory behavior. The findings allowed the Ohio State researchers to classify leaders on consideration and initiating-structure dimensions.

Leaders who scored high on the consideration dimension reflected a work atmosphere of mutual trust, respect for subordinates' ideas, and consideration of subordinates' feelings. Such leaders encouraged good superior–subordinate rapport and two-way communication. A low consideration score indicated that leaders were more impersonal in their dealings with subordinates.

A high initiating-structure score indicated that leaders structured their roles and those of subordinates toward the attainment of goals. They were actively involved in planning work activities, communicating pertinent information, and scheduling work.

One early research study attempted to compare supervisors having different consideration and initiating-structure scores with various performance measures.[27] The first measure was obtained from proficiency ratings made by plant management. Other measures were unexcused absenteeism, accidents, formally filed grievances, and employee turnover. Indexes for each of these measures were computed for each supervisor's work group for an 11-month period.

Supervisors who worked in production divisions were compared to supervisors in nonproduction divisions on consideration scores, initiating-structure scores, and proficiency ratings. In the production divisions, the supervisors who were rated by their superiors as most proficient scored high on structure and low on consideration. In the nonproduction division, the relationships were reversed.

After comparing the leadership scores and proficiency ratings, the researchers compared leadership scores to the other performance measures: unexcused absenteeism, accidents, formally filed grievances, and employee turnover. In general, it was determined that high structure and low consideration were related to more absenteeism, accidents, grievances, and turnover.

Managerial Grid Theory

Another P–B theory is the Managerial Grid® originally published by Robert Blake and Jane Mouton, who proposed that leadership style could be plotted on a two-dimensional grid.[28] The Managerial Grid® (republished as the Leadership Grid® in 1991 by Robert R Blake and Anne Adams McCanse) is used as a framework to help managers learn what their leadership style is and to track their movement toward the ideal management style. This Leadership Grid® is presented in Figure 13–3. Five specific leadership styles are used to highlight different approaches to leading others.

FIGURE 13–3   The Leadership Grid

After responding to questions, a person's leadership style is plotted on a grid with (9,9) being the ideal.

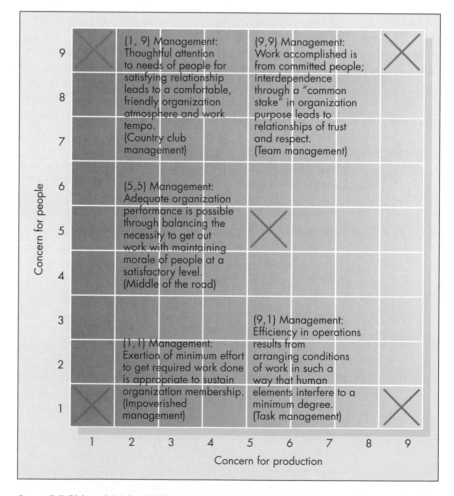

Source: R R Blake and A Adams McCanse (formerly the Managerial Grid Figure by RR Blake and J S Mouton), *Leadership Dilemmas—Grid Solutions* (Houston: Gulf Publishing, 1991), p. 29. Copyright © 1991, by Scientific Methods, Inc. Reproduced by permission of the owners.

Of course, these are only five of the many possible styles of leadership that can be, and are, utilized.

(1,1) *Impoverished:* A minimum effort to accomplish the work is exerted by the leader.

(9,1) *Task:* The leader concentrates on task completion but shows little regard for the development and morale of subordinates.

(1,9) *Country club:* The leader focuses on being supportive and considerate of employees. However, task completion is not a primary concern of this easygoing style.

(5,5) *Middle of the road:* Adequate task completion and satisfactory morale are the goals of this style.

(9,9) *Team:* The leader facilitates production and morale by coordinating and integrating work-related activities.

Blake and Mouton assume that the leader who is a 9,9 individual would be using the most effective style; however, defining a 9,9 leader for every type of job is very difficult. Blake and Mouton imply that a managerial development program can move leaders toward a 9,9 style. They recommend six management development phases (laboratory seminar groups, team building, intergroup processes, goal setting, goal feedback, and evaluation) to aid managers in acquiring concern for fellow employees and the expertise to accomplish objectives such as productivity and quality. Prior to undertaking these phases, research indicates that more than 65 percent of managers consider themselves 9,9. After a seminar on what constitutes a 9,9 manager (participation, openness, trust, consensus building, and mutual respect) only 16 percent of the managers believed they really fit the description.[29]

The Leadership Grid® is an attitudinal approach that measures a person's values, opinions, and feelings. It relates task effectiveness and human satisfaction to a formal managerial development program. This program is unique in that line managers, not academicians or consultants, run the program; a conceptual framework of management (the grid) is utilized; and the entire managerial hierarchy undergoes development, not just one level such as first-line supervisors.[30]

Synopsis of the Personal–Behavioral Approach

Examination of the various P–B theories presented in this section indicates that similar concepts are discussed but different labels are utilized. For example, the continuum, Likert, the Ohio State researchers, and the Leadership Grid approaches all utilize two broadly defined concepts summarized in Table 13–2.

Each approach in Table 13–2 focuses on two concepts; however, some differences should be emphasized:

- The continuum theory is based primarily on personal opinions. Although the opinions of the originators are respected, they should be supported with research evidence before much faith can be placed in this particular theory.

- Likert's supportive theory implies that the most successful leadership style is employee centered. He suggests that we need look no further. However, the critical question is whether the employee-centered style works in all situations. Some studies dispute Likert's claim.

- The Ohio State researchers found that, from a production standpoint, the leader with a high initiating-structure score was preferred by the executives of

TABLE 13–2   Personal–Behavioral Theories of Leadership

The four personal–behavioral theories have similar concepts but use different labels.

Theories	Two Concepts	Derivation	Theory Development
1. Leadership continuum theory	Boss centered Subordinate centered	Opinions of Tannenbaum and Schmidt	By authors' description
2. Supportive theory	Job centered Employee centered	Research at the University of Michigan—Likert	By field research studies
3. Two-dimensional theory	"Consideration" "Initiating structure"	Research at Ohio State University—Fleishman	By field research studies
4. Leadership grid	Concern for people Concern for production	Research by Blake and associates	By description and limited research

the company. Thus, Likert's claim, or any other claim, that one best leadership approach has been discovered is subject to debate.

· Blake and McCanse's Leadership Grid is an intuitively sound proposal. However, only limited research has been reported to test the grid. Also, it is not safe to assume that a (9,9) leader will always be successful. The need is obvious for research testing (9,9) in different settings, with various types of leader–follower situations and with diverse sets of constraints (e.g., time, monetary resources, technology).

Situational Theories of Leadership

After years of discussion and study, most managers today question the premise that a particular leadership style is effective in all situations. They believe that a manager behaving as a considerate leader, for example, cannot be assured of effective results in every situation. As noted earlier in this chapter, the Ohio State researchers found that supervisors who scored high on initiating structure were relatively more proficient when managing production rather than nonproduction workers. Thus, even in the current leadership literature, evidence exists on personal–behavioral theories to support the view that effective leadership depends on the interaction of the situation and the leader's behavior.

The identification of key situational factors and the determination of their relative importance are difficult undertakings. In this section we review four theories that take into account certain situational factors. They are contingency theory, path–goal theory, leadership-style theory, and tridimensional theory.

Contingency Theory   With a considerable body of research evidence behind him, Fred Fiedler developed a situational, or contingency, theory of leadership.[31] Three important situational dimensions are assumed to influence the leader's effectiveness:

1. *Leader–member relations:* The degree of confidence the subordinates have in the leader. It also includes the loyalty shown the leader and the leader's attractiveness.

2. *Task structure:* The degree to which the followers' jobs are routine as contrasted with nonroutine.

3. *Position power:* The power inherent in the leadership position. It includes the rewards and punishments typically associated with the position, the leader's formal authority (based on ranking in managerial hierarchy), and the support that the leader receives from supervisors and the overall organization.

Fiedler measures leadership style by evaluating leaders' responses to what is called a least-preferred co-worker (LPC) questionnaire. The leaders who rate their least preferred co-worker in more positive terms (high LPC) are assumed to be people oriented and supportive. Those leaders who give low LPC ratings are more task oriented.

In developing his theory, Fiedler uses the term *situational favorableness,* defined as the degree to which a situation enables a leader to exert influence over the group. In other words, leader–member relations can be either good or poor, task structure can be high or low, and position power can be either strong or weak. The various combinations of these three dimensions can be favorable, moderate, or unfavorable.

According to Fiedler, we should not talk simply about good leaders or poor leaders. He implies that there is no one best way to lead. A leader who achieves effectiveness in one situation may or may not be effective in another. The logic is that managers should think about the situation in which a particular leader performs well or badly.

The situational leadership logic is extended in Table 13–3. The examples represent the various combinations of the three dimensions. Furthermore, suggestions on what leadership action to take in the eight situations are indicated.

As suggested by Fiedler in his contingency theory and by Table 13–3, there may be a need to change the situation to fit the leader's style. Fiedler offers some pragmatic procedures for improving a leader's relations, task structure, and position power:

- *Leader–member relations* could be improved by restructuring the leader's group of subordinates to be more compatible in background, education level, technical expertise, or ethnic origin. Note that this would be extremely difficult in a unionized group, since they may assume that this restructuring is a management plan to weaken the union.

- The *task structure* can be modified in either direction. The task can be made more structured by spelling out the jobs in greater detail. It can be made less structured by providing only general directions for the work that is to be accomplished. Some workers like minimal task structure, while others want detailed and specific task structure.

- *Position power* can be modified in a number of ways. A leader can be given a higher rank in the organization or more authority to do the job. A memo can be issued indicating the rank change or the authority a leader now possesses. In addition, a leader's reward power can be increased if the organization delegates authority to evaluate the performance of subordinates.

Fiedler's suggestions may not be feasible in every organizational setting. Such factors as unions, technology, time, and costs of changes must be considered. For example, a unionized company that has a highly routine technology and is currently faced with intense competition in new product development may not have the

TABLE 13–3   Situational Leadership Applied to Eight Situations

Situation	Leader–Member Relations	Task Structure	Position Power	Most Effective Leadership	Reason(s) for Effectiveness
1. First-line supervisor at Ford Motor Company	Good	High	Strong	Task oriented	Employees respect task expertise, recognize power, and permit supervisor to lead.
2. Chairperson of college department	Good	High	Weak	Task oriented	Faculty member elected because he possesses group values. Understands what the group needs to do and pushes for task completion.
3. Sales manager at Procter & Gamble	Good	Low	Strong	Task oriented	Manager has formal authority and power, but salespeople work all over territory. They must have some autonomy because of unstructured nature of job.
4. Committee chairperson	Good	Low	Weak	About equally task and relationship oriented	Chair has little power and must rely on both types of leadership to accomplish job.
5. Middle-level manager at IBM	Poor	High	Strong	Relationship oriented	Manager is not well liked but has power to motivate. Can accomplish more if relationship approach is used.
6. Supervisor at General Mills	Poor	High	Weak	Relationship oriented	Employees know what they're supposed to accomplish. Supervisor is unpopular and has little say-so. More effective to use relationship style instead of creating more hostility.
7. Operating-room nurse supervisor at Massachusetts General Hospital	Poor	Low	Strong	Almost equally task and relationship oriented	Difficult to control unstructured activities through use of power. Because person is unpopular, it is best to use relationship orientation when appropriate and task orientation if necessary.
8. Detective in charge of other detectives working on a case in Washington, DC	Poor	Low	Weak	Task oriented	Detective has little power, is not well liked, and case in unstructured. Concentrate on solving the case.

patience, time, and energy to modify the three situational dimensions so that its leaders become more effective.

Interestingly, Fiedler's suggestions do not include leadership training.[32] In fact, he believes that training is not an effective approach, reporting that his own research has shown disappointing results from training. On the average, people with training perform about as well as people with little or no training.

Critics question Fiedler's methodology for measuring LPC, the subjects he used in some of his research (e.g., basketball teams, the Belgian Navy, and students), and the fact that only high and low LPC scores are considered.[33] Despite critics and some glaring shortcomings, Fiedler provided a starting point for situational leadership research.

Path–Goal Theory   A leadership approach that draws heavily on the expectancy theory of motivation is the path–goal theory.[34] It proposes that the leader is a key individual in bringing about improved subordinate motivation, satisfaction, and performance. The theory suggests that four leadership styles can be, and are, used:

1. *Directive.* The leader directs, and there is no subordinate participation in decision making.
2. *Supportive.* The leader is friendly and is interested in subordinates as people.
3. *Participative.* The leader asks for, receives, and uses suggestions from subordinates to make decisions.
4. *Achievement oriented.* The leader sets challenging goals for subordinates and shows confidence that they can achieve the goals.

The path–goal theory, unlike Fiedler's theory, suggests that these four styles are used by the same leader in different situations.[35]

The important key in this theory is the way the leader affects the paths between subordinate behavior and goals. In a sense, the leader is the coach who charts out realistic paths for the team. The leader can affect the paths by doing the following:

- Recognizing and stimulating subordinates' needs for rewards over which the leader has some control.
- Rewarding goal achievement.
- Supporting subordinates' efforts to achieve the goals.
- Helping reduce frustrating barriers to achieving goals.
- Increasing the opportunities for personal satisfaction for subordinates.

Basically, the leader attempts to help the subordinate find the best path, to set challenging goals, and to remove stressful barriers along the way.

Since the path–goal theory was proposed, a limited number of studies have tested its assumptions. A study by J Indvik examined leadership behaviors, expectancies, and satisfaction. He found that subordinates' preferences for structure and need for achievement had significant effects on whether directive, supportive, participative, or achievement-oriented leadership resulted in positive subordinate outcomes.[36]

Another study of 10 different samples of employees found that supportive leadership has its most positive effect on satisfaction for subordinates who work on stressful and frustrating jobs. Another study determined that in three separate organizations, subordinates doing nonroutine job tasks working for achievement-oriented leaders were more confident that their efforts would result in better performance.[37]

A comprehensive path–goal model that integrates theory and research suggests that

- Managers stimulate subordinate efforts by offering valid rewards and linking them to the effort and performance.
- Whether effort results in performance depends on subordinates' knowledge, skills, and abilities as well as the lack of obstacles in performing the job.
- If the rewards received by subordinates are valued and equitable, the recipients are satisfied and have less tendency to quit the job.[38]

Leader-Style Theory   Another situational leadership theory was originally provided by Vroom and Yetton and modified by the work of Vroom and Jago.[39] The theory attempts to identify the appropriate leadership style for a given set of circumstances, or situations. Five leadership styles are suggested by the leader-style theory:

AI: The leader solves the problem or reaches a decision using available information.

AII: The leader obtains the information from followers, then decides on the solution to the problem. The leader may or may not inform followers what the problem is in acquiring information from them. The role of followers is to supply information.

CI: The leader shares the problem with subordinates individually, getting their ideas and suggestions without bringing them together as a group. The leader makes the decision, which may or may not reflect followers' influence.

CII: The leader shares problems with subordinates as a group, obtaining their ideas and suggestions. The leader then makes a decision that may or may not reflect followers' influence.

GII: The leader shares a problem with followers as a group. Together the group generates and evaluates alternatives and attempts to reach consensus on a solution. The leader acts as a chairperson. The solution that has the support of the entire group is accepted and implemented.

The letters in the code identify the leadership practice: A stands for autocratic; C stands for consultative; and G stands for group. The appropriate style of leadership (AI, AII, CI, CII, GII) depends on the attributes of the problem situation. The attributes, along with diagnostic questions, are considered by the leader. The leader, if interested in, say, the importance of the quality of a decision (the first problem attribute), could ask the diagnostic question: "Is there a quality requirement such that one solution is more likely to be rational than another?"

The theory uses a decision tree for determining the best leadership style for a problem situation. Figure 13–4 illustrates how the seven diagnostic questions are asked and where a yes or no answer takes a person along the tree. The person using the decision tree works across it as the questions are answered. In this way, a leader can identify the appropriate situation and leadership style.

A study by Arthur Jago found that managers higher in the management hierarchy tend to use more participative styles than managers lower in the hierarchy.[40] Another study indicated that managers of retail franchises who more closely conformed to the style identified by the Vroom-Yetton decision tree were more successful and had employees who reported higher amounts of job satisfaction.[41]

Vroom, Yetton, and Jago have used such examples to train leaders in decision-making skills. An example can illustrate how the Vroom-Yetton-Jago model works.

You are the head of a research and development laboratory in the nuclear reactor division of a large corporation. Often it is not clear whether a particular piece of research is potentially of commercial interest or merely of "academic" interest to the researchers. In your judgment, one major area of research has advanced well beyond the level at which operating divisions pertinent to the area could possibly assimilate or make use of the data being generated.

Recently, two new areas with potentially high returns for commercial development have been proposed by one of the operating divisions. The team working in the area referred to in the previous paragraph is ideally qualified to research these new areas. Unfortunately, both the new areas are relatively devoid of scientific interest, while the project on which the team is currently engaged is of great scientific interest to all members.

FIGURE 13–4   **The Vroom-Yetton-Jago Model**

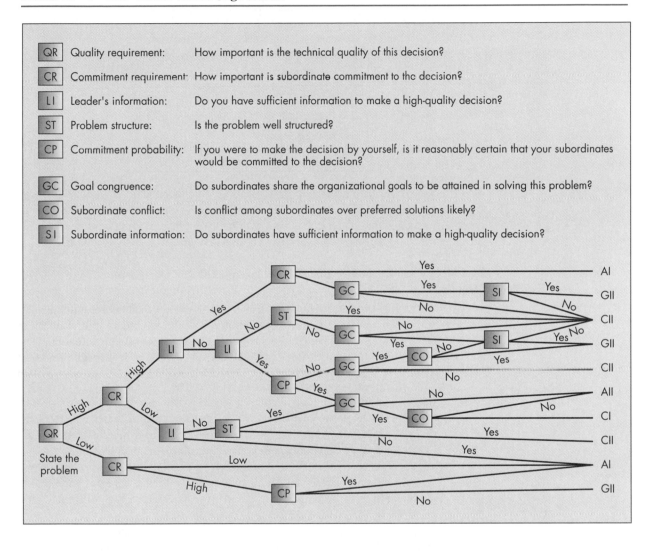

QR	Quality requirement:	How important is the technical quality of this decision?
CR	Commitment requirement:	How important is subordinate commitment to the decision?
LI	Leader's information:	Do you have sufficient information to make a high-quality decision?
ST	Problem structure:	Is the problem well structured?
CP	Commitment probability:	If you were to make the decision by yourself, is it reasonably certain that your subordinates would be committed to the decision?
GC	Goal congruence:	Do subordinates share the organizational goals to be attained in solving this problem?
CO	Subordinate conflict:	Is conflict among subordinates over preferred solutions likely?
SI	Subordinate information:	Do subordinates have sufficient information to make a high-quality decision?

At the moment, this is, or is close to being, your best research team. The team is very cohesive, has a high level of morale, and has been very productive. You are concerned not only that they would not want to switch their effort to these new areas, but also that forcing them to concentrate on these two new projects could adversely affect their morale, their good intragroup working relations, and their future productivity both as individuals and as a team.

You have to respond to the operating division within the next two weeks indicating what resources, if any, can be devoted to working on these projects. It would be possible for the team to work on more than one project but each project would need the combined skills of all the members of the team, so no fragmentation of the team is technically feasible. This fact, coupled with the fact that the team is very cohesive, means that a solution that satisfies any team member would very probably go a long way to satisfy everyone on the team.

Analysis	
Quality requirement	High importance
Commitment requirement	High importance
Leader information	Probably yes
Problem structure	Yes
Commitment probability	No
Goal congruence	Probably no
Subordinate conflict	Probably no
Subordinate information	No
Highest overall effectiveness:	CII

The Vroom and Jago model appears to be more valid than the original model.[42] They have attempted to address the criticism that having yes–no responses to diagnostic questions is too limiting by replacing them with five-point ratings. Other improvements in the outcomes, choices, and conditions have been made and empirically examined.

Tridimensional Leader-Effectiveness Theory

Paul Hersey and Kenneth H Blanchard (a coauthor of *The One Minute Manager*) have identified two leadership behaviors similar to those the Ohio State researchers discovered.[43] The two types of behaviors are task and relationship. *Task behavior* is defined as the extent to which leaders are likely to organize and define the roles of the followers, explain what must be done, and direct the flow of work. *Relationship behavior* is defined as the extent to which leaders are likely to maintain personal relationships with members of their group through being supportive, sensitive, and facilitative.

Since the effectiveness of leaders depends on how their leadership style interrelates with the situation, an effectiveness dimension is added to the task and relationship base. This results, according to Hersey and Blanchard, in the integration of leadership style and situation demands. When the style of a leader is appropriate in a given situation, it is effective; when the style is inappropriate in a given situation, it is ineffective.

Effective and ineffective styles are represented on a continuum, because effectiveness is a matter of degree. Hersey and Blanchard use an effective scoring range of +1 to +4 and an ineffective scoring range of −1 to −4. Figure 13–5 illustrates the tridimensional leader-effectiveness model.

To determine a leader's preferred style, Hersey and Blanchard use leaders' effectiveness and adaptability description (LEAD) questionnaires. First developed for use in training programs, the LEAD-self questionnaire contains 12 leadership situations in which respondents are asked to select from four alternative actions—a high-task/low-relationship behavior, a high-task/high-relationship behavior, a high-relationship/low-task behavior, and a low-relationship/low-task behavior—the style they believe most closely would describe their own behavior in the situation. For example:

Situation	*Leader Actions*
Your subordinates, usually able to take responsibility, are not responding to your recent redefinition of standards.	A. Allow group involvement in redefining standards but don't push. B. Redefine standards and supervise carefully. C. Avoid confrontation by pressure. D. Incorporate the group recommendations but see that new standards are met.

FIGURE 13–5   Hersey-Blanchard Tridimensional Leader-Effectiveness Model

Whether a leadership style is effective or ineffective will depend on the environment (circumstances) in which the leading will take place.

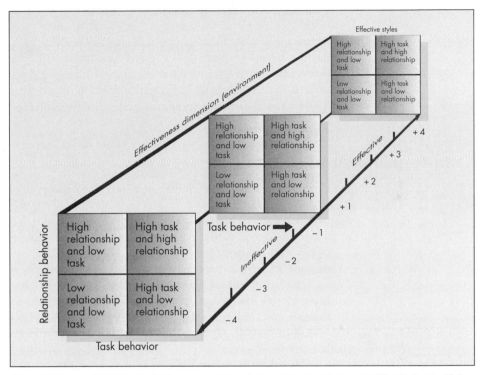

Source: P Hersey and K H Blanchard, *Management of Organizational Behavior* (Englewood Cliffs, NJ: Prentice Hall, 1993), p. 131.

The LEAD-self yields a self-perception picture of the leader's style, style range, and style adaptability. A LEAD-other questionnaire is completed by subordinates, superiors, or associates of leaders.

Hersey and Blanchard call specific attention to a leader's range, or flexibility. Each leader differs in the ability to vary her style in different situations. Flexible leaders have the potential to be effective in a number of situations. In structured, routine, simple, and established work flow situations, leadership flexibility is not that important.

To date, a handful of studies have reached rather ambiguous conclusions on the Hersey and Blanchard theory.[44] Critics state that this model has no logical or theoretical foundation.[45] However, the popularity of the Hersey and Blanchard explanation and leadership training approach seems to be growing around the world. BankAmerica Corporation, Shell Oil Company, Tenneco, Caterpillar Tractor Company, IBM, and Xerox Corporation are some of the training and assessment users of the tridimensional leader-effectiveness model.

Practicing managers and leaders of management training programs generally comment that other leadership explanations are much too theoretical and abstract. They prefer the straightforward presentation of the Hersey-Blanchard model. The model is simple, interesting, and relevant, which may give managers a sense of learning. Whether the manager actually learns or is able to apply those principles of flexibility in style suggested by the model has not been substantiated.

Comparison   There certainly are a growing number of situational theories of leadership. However, each approach is valuable because it adds insight into a manager's understanding of leadership. Table 13–4 contains a brief explanation of the four popular leadership theories that stress the importance of situational variables. Although the Fiedler theory has the largest research base and has been around for years, the Vroom-Yetton-Jago theory appears to offer the most promise for managerial training. At present, however, there is not enough evidence available to say how effective training is in applying the Vroom-Yetton-Jago theory to managerial problem solving and decision situations.

Transformational Leadership

German sociologist Max Weber introduced the concept of charisma into discussions of leadership. He viewed charisma as an adaptation of the theological concept involving the possession of a divine grace.[46] Weber's view emphasized the magnetic behavior of a person to rise to the occasion to complete the task. The charismatic leader has significant influence over followers. The followers are attracted to the leader's magnetism, divine grace, powers, and exceptional ability to respond to crises.

Instead of talking about the mystical concept of charisma, Burns discussed the hero. Heroic leadership, according to Burns, was displayed by those leaders who excited and transformed followers.[47] Bernard Bass extended Burns's view and

---

TABLE 13–4   **Comparison of Popular Situational Theories of Leadership**

Theme, leadership style, research base, and application value are important points of comparison in the four major situational theories of leadership.

Points of Comparison	Contingency Theory (Fiedler)	Path–Goal Theory (House)	Vroom-Yetton Theory*	Hersey-Blanchard Theory
1. Theme	No best style. Leader success determined by the interaction of environment and leader personality variables.	Most successful leaders are those who increase subordinate motivation by charting out and clarifying paths to effective performance.	Successful leadership style varies with situation. Leader can learn how to recognize requirements of situation and how to fit style to meet these requirements.	Successful leaders adapt their styles to the demands of a situation.
2. Leadership styles (range of choices)	Task or relationship oriented.	Directive to achievement.	Autocratic to participative.	Task behavior to relationship behavior.
3. Research base (number of supportive studies)	Large, in many settings: military, educational, industrial. Some contradictory results.	Moderate to low. Generally supportive.	Low but increasing. Generally supportive.	Low but generally supportive.
4. Application value for managers	Moderate to low: leaders can't generally be trained.	Moderate.	High: leaders can be trained.	Moderate but increasing.

*The contributions of Arthur Jago to the refinement and testing of this model have led some to refer to this approach as the Vroom-Yetton-Jago theory.

indicated that a transformational leader is a person who displays or creates charismatic leadership, inspirational leadership, intellectual stimulation, and a feeling that each individual follower counts.[48] The Burns and Bass insights suggest that leaders are able to stimulate, shift, and use the values, beliefs, and needs of their followers to accomplish tasks. These leaders who do this in a rapidly changing or crisis-laden situation are transformational leaders. The other explanations of leadership such as personal–behavioral explanations, or situational approaches typically focus on transactional leadership or that involving an exchange relationship between leaders and followers.

Leaders who are described by followers as transformational are depicted as more charismatic and intellectually stimulating than leaders described as transactional.[49] A potential area of concern in discussing and learning more about transformational leadership characteristics is that the discussion and interpretations are beginning to resemble early trait approaches. Searching for what constitutes attraction, divine grace, and power to influence is like examining such traits as intelligence, self-confidence, and physical attributes to determine which produces success.

What can practitioners learn about leadership from examining the transformation leadership literature? This question is raised when concepts such as charisma and inspiration are presented. Is charisma a rare attribute that few understand and are fortunate enough to possess and/or develop? Can the charisma of a leader be improved? These questions must be answered before transformational leadership approaches can be applied and adapted to organization settings.

Four skills appear to be used and sharpened by transformational leaders. First, the leader has a vision that she is able to articulate. The vision may be a goal, a plan, or a series of priorities. Second, the leader is able to clearly communicate the vision. She is able to present a compelling image of the benefits that will result if the vision is achieved. Third, the leader is able to build trust by being fair, decisive, and consistent. Persistence, even against barriers and hardships, shows through. Finally, the transformational leader has a positive self-regard. She works to fully develop her skills so that success is achieved.[50]

Lee Iacocca, when he took over a failing Chrysler Corporation, is an example of a transformational leader who used the four skills. He created a vision for turning Chrysler around and clearly articulated it to employees and others. He built trust with even a skeptical autoworkers union, and, despite reducing the workforce by 60,000, employees considered him fair, decisive, consistent, and persistent. Iacocca clearly had a positive self-regard that was projected in private and in public settings.

Selected Factors Influencing Leadership Effectiveness

We have defined leadership as the ability to persuade others to seek defined objectives enthusiastically. We also have identified four approaches to the study of leadership: trait, personal–behavioral, situational, and transformational. The trait and personal–behavioral approaches indicate that effective leadership depends on a number of variables such as intelligence, decisiveness, and style. The transformational approaches emphasize the mystical notion of charisma and how it influences followers. Despite considerable ignorance about leadership as a role and a process, we can suggest some ideas regarding factors that seem to influence leadership effectiveness.

Perceptual Accuracy   McGregor indicated how perception plays a role in leadership. Managers who misperceive employees may miss the opportunity to achieve optimal results. If you believe someone is lazy, you tend to treat him as a lazy person. Thus, managerial perceptual accuracy is extremely important. It is important in each of the situational models.[51]

Background, Experience, and Personality

The Leader.   The leader's background and experience affect the choice of leadership style. A person who has had success in being relationship oriented probably will continue the use of this style. Likewise, a leader who doesn't trust followers and who has structured the task for years will use an autocratic style.

Despite Fiedler's opinion, the majority of leadership researchers believe that a leader's style can be altered. That is, a leader who perceives that her preferred style is not effective can change it accordingly. Of course, some individuals are so rigid in their preferences and personality makeup that alteration is extremely difficult.

The Follower.   Followers are an important factor in the leader's choice of style. As stated earlier, the leadership job is a mutual-sharing process. For example, a leader with technically proficient followers is best advised to be more participative and less autocratic. On the other hand, inexperienced, recent hirees with a minimum of work knowledge may prefer a leader who structures the task and is firm. In that case, an autocratic or job-centered leader works best.

Hersey and Blanchard stress the notion of the follower's maturity. They define *maturity* as the ability and willingness of people to take responsibility for directing their own behavior. The term has two components: job maturity and psychological maturity. *Job maturity* is the knowledge, skills, and experience to perform without close supervision. *Psychological maturity* is the willingness to do the job.

The astute leader attempts to determine the background and maturity of followers, which may signal the style that is most appropriate. In any event, the followers must be given serious consideration in making a judgment about which leadership style can achieve the desired results.

Superior's Expectations and Style

Superiors are comfortable with and prefer a particular leadership style. A superior who prefers a job-centered, autocratic approach encourages followers to adopt a similar approach. Imitation of the superior's example is a powerful force in shaping leadership styles.

Since superiors possess various power bases, their expectations are important. For example, many firms seek to improve the relationship skills of first-level supervisors and send these managers to an off-the-job training program. Research indicates that during and immediately after these programs, supervisors' relationship skills are improved. However, soon after returning to the job, the learned skills often disappear. Why? A reasonable explanation is that the supervisors' superiors prefer more task-oriented behaviors instead of relationship-oriented behaviors.

Task Understanding

The task of a group or an individual refers to what is to be done on a job. Tasks are imposed by management or self-generated by the employee. A task has physical properties and behavioral features. The physical properties are the stimuli surrounding the job; these stimuli may be a set of instructions from management or the way the employee interprets the job. The behavioral properties are the requirements or kinds of responses expected of a person doing the task.

The task may be very structured, such as the job duties of a worker on an assembly line. The worker is instructed by management what to do with the products being processed. The goal or requirement of this type of job is to produce as many units of good quality as possible.

Other tasks, such as those of a research and development engineer or planning expert, may be unstructured. In these jobs, the goals are not easily defined. Thus, the leader may have to work hard to display paths and goals for the employees.

Leaders must be able to assess correctly the tasks their followers are performing. In an unstructured task situation, directive or autocratic leadership may be very inappropriate; the employees need guidelines, freedom to act, and the necessary resources to accomplish the task. Leaders must properly diagnose the tasks of followers so that proper leadership style choices are made. Because of this requirement, a leader must have some technical knowledge of the job and its requirements.

Peer Expectations   Leaders form relationships with other leaders. These peer relationships are used to exchange ideas, opinions, experiences, and suggestions. A leader's peers can provide support and encouragement for various leadership behaviors, thus influencing the leader in the future. Often, for example, when peers inform a leader that he was too easy on an uncooperative follower, the leader may respond by becoming very harsh and restrictive. Peers are an important source of comparison and information in making leadership style choices and modifications.

Integrating   Figure 13–6 illustrates that these six important factors can influence leadership
Influence Factors   effectiveness. Leadership also influences these factors. Although many other factors also influence leadership effectiveness, these six seem to be as important as any and serve to illustrate concisely the reciprocal nature of leadership.

The emphasis in Figure 13–6 is on leaders' ability to diagnose themselves and their total leadership environment. Perhaps if leadership training programs are used, they should stress diagnostic skills. But it should not be concluded that individuals can be trained easily to accurately diagnose work situations and to develop appropriate leadership abilities. This type of training difficulty was summed up by Fiedler:

> Industrial psychologists and personnel men typically view the executive's position as fixed and immutable and the individual as highly plastic and trainable. When we think of improving leadership performance, we generally think first of training the leader. Yet, we know all too well from our experience with psychotherapy, our attempts to rehabilitate prison inmates, drug addicts, or juvenile delinquents—not to mention our difficulties with rearing our own progeny—that our ability to change personality has its limitations.[52]

FIGURE 13–6   Selected Factors That Influence Leadership Effectiveness

Leaders must diagnose themselves and the total leadership environment to effect good leadership.

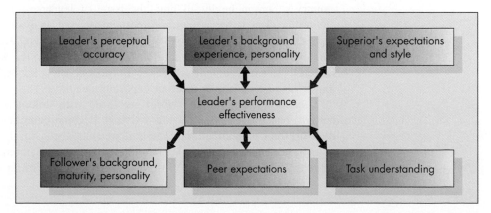

If leaders are to become skilled at diagnoses and flexible enough to adapt leadership styles to the circumstances at hand, patience is essential. The organization must be willing to plan and to fund development programs that are time-consuming. The approach we are suggesting is not applicable in those instances where changing the situation is less costly than changing the leader.

The clear message being received in executive suites around the United States is that America is losing its competitive edge in manufacturing, electronics, steel, and some service industries. There is a consensus that we must continue to revise many managerial, industrial, and leadership practices to remain competitive in the international arena. Managers and leaders must be part of the rededication to become more competitive.[53]

American management is at a crossroads in terms of leadership. Managers must be open to new styles of managing, new methods of leadership, and new competitive practices and procedures that are emerging from other countries. In the past, when little competition existed in world markets, American managers tended to ignore how others in the world managed work, people, and operations.[54] Ignoring positive examples of leadership makes little sense today. Managing- and leading-as-usual strategies are not going to solve international marketplace, global relationship, and foreign-competition problems.

Consumers and clients throughout the world are demanding quality, value, and service. It does not matter if a person lives in the United States, Singapore, Italy, New Zealand, South Korea, Kenya, or Poland.[55] As consumers, we write with Cross, Waterman, Mont Blanc, or Scripto pencils or travel with Samsonite, Gucci, or Louis Vuitton suitcases because of the kind of value we can afford and desire. At the cash register, the country of origin of the product or service is becoming less and less important. The fact that a British sneaker by Reebok (now owned by an American firm) was made in Korea is becoming less and less important. Customers care only about quality, price, design, value, and appeal.

Multicultural Leadership

As globalization speeds along and as international joint ventures increase at a frantic pace, we have to learn more about leadership outside the United States. For the most part, the research discussed to this point in this chapter has been dominated by samples of American leaders. It is likely that cultural differences must be considered in unraveling the mysteries of leadership. As major reforms occur in Eastern Europe and Latin America, as regional trading blocs begin to emerge, and as the importance of country of origin begins to blur, the issue of leadership effectiveness in different cultural settings is becoming an important topic of analysis.[56] For example, can the Japanese leaders in the Toyota plant in Georgetown, Kentucky, get American employees to improve the quality of their work? Or, can the American engineer at the General Electric Company laboratory in Singapore get her Asian technicians to work longer hours each day to meet an important deadline?

Leaders throughout the world are faced with linking employees from diverse cultural backgrounds. Leadership activities become complicated in situations where the workforce is multicultural. The trait, personal–behavioral, and situational explanations of leadership paid little attention to multicultural differences. Stereotypes, biases, language differences, value differences, and a host of other factors have to be considered.

FIGURE 13–7   **Expectations about Managerial Authority versus Participation**

A. Relative agreement across countries to the statement:
"The main reason for hierarchical structure is so that everybody knows who has authority over whom."

United States	Germany	Great Britain	Netherlands	France	Italy	Japan	Indonesia
18%	24%	38%	45%	50%	52%	52%	86%

B. Relative agreement across countries to the statement:
"It is important for a manager to have at hand precise answers to most of
the questions that his subordinates may raise about their work."

Sweden	Netherlands	United States	Denmark	Great Britain	Switzerland	Belgium	Germany	France	Italy	Indonesia	Japan
10%	17%	18%	23%	27%	38%	44%	46%	53%	66%	73%	78%

Source: Based on A Laurent, "The Cultural Diversity of Western Conceptions of Management," *International Studies of Management and Organization* 13, nos. 1–2 (Spring–Summer 1983), pp. 75–96.

The national origin of the leader may play a role in exactly how he handles a multicultural group or situation. Laurent, a French researcher, conducted an interesting study of the role that expectations about the use of managerial authority versus participation play in leading. He studied nine Western European countries, the United States, Indonesia, and Japan.[57] He concluded that national origin did affect the perception of the leader of what constitutes effective leadership. Two of the reasons he reached his conclusion are presented in Figure 13–7.

According to Laurent, Americans and Germans were more inclined to participation than were Italians and Japanese. Indonesians are more comfortable with using a strict top-down hierarchical style. Managers in Sweden, the United States, and Great Britain believe that employees should participate in problem solving rather than be told exactly what to do. Laurent's research contradicts what has been written about Japan's very participative, decision-making methods.

The prevalent leadership style in any country is intertwined with norms, expectations, history, cultural makeup of employees, and even economic conditions. A study conducted in Nigeria and Taiwan of small and medium-sized countries pointed out the complexity of leadership.[58] The researchers wanted to know which pattern of leadership is most positively associated with the economic success of the company. They used the concepts of initiating structure and consideration first introduced by Ohio State researchers, and it was determined that for both countries economic success is more likely to result from a severe, top-down disciplinary initiating structure style and less consideration of individual needs. The conclusion reached by the researchers is that the often-recommended participative style, which emphasizes consideration, would have negative results in Nigeria and Taiwan. Simply transporting a leadership style from one country to another is the wrong way to achieve success, according to these researchers.

Summary of Key Points

- Leadership and management are not synonymous terms. Leadership is the ability to persuade others to seek defined objectives enthusiastically.
- Leaders possess five potential power bases to influence followers: coercive, reward, legitimate, expert, and referent.
- McGregor believed that a manager's attitudes and assumptions explain her behavior toward followers. These attitudes were categorized as Theory X and Theory Y. The attitude–behavior relationship generates a self-fulfilling prophecy. If a manager assumes a person is a winner, then the manager treats the person as a winner.
- Numerous attempts to study and understand leadership have been made. Three major approaches are trait, personal–behavioral, and situational.
- Trait theories attempt to discover various traits that describe or predict leadership success. Some of the more important traits are intelligence, self-assurance, and decisiveness.
- Personal–behavioral theories contend that leaders may be classified by personal qualities or behavior patterns. Re-

searchers use a continuum of leadership, two-dimensional models, and managerial grids to explain leadership in personal–behavioral terms.
- The situational factors that influence leadership are given prominence in Fiedler's contingency theory, the House path–goal theory, the Vroom-Yetton-Jago theory, and the Hersey-Blanchard tridimensional theory.
- A newer explanation of leadership is referred to as the transformational approach. The transformational leader expresses charismatic leadership, inspirational leadership, intellectual stimulation, and a feeling that each follower really counts.
- Leadership comes in many varieties and is practiced throughout the world. Some common traits among international leaders seem to be confidence, vision, and decisiveness.
- There is no one best leadership approach or style that fits every group, situation, or nation.

Discussion and Review Questions

1. How would a leader assess the maturity of his followers?
2. Does the Vroom-Yetton-Jago approach to leadership suggest that leaders can or cannot be trained to improve their effectiveness? Explain.
3. Which role is the leader expected to play in the path–goal leadership theory?
4. Why is the diagnostic skill of the leader so vital to the situational approach to leadership?
5. Women can lead just as effectively and as ineffectually as men. Comment.
6. Why is it inappropriate to assume that the leadership style that works best in a manufacturing company in

Marietta, Georgia, will be just as effective in Lagos, Nigeria?
7. Can charisma be enhanced or increased? Why?
8. What other factors not included in Figure 13–6 are important in the achievement of leadership effectiveness?
9. The four skills of a transformational leader involve vision, communication, building trust, and a positive self-regard. Can individuals be trained to improve these leadership skills?
10. Why would American leadership techniques probably have to be modified to be somewhat applicable in Poland?

Case 13–1

Harley-Davidson: A Leader on a Motorcycle

He'd have been perfect as a sidekick for Teddy Roosevelt and his Rough Riders. He is rough and gruff on the outside but a self-admitted softy on the inside. His company has been through the turmoil of near extinction, survival, and now growth and prosperity. Along the way he has learned invaluable lessons about manufacturing, management, and leader-

ship. He's Richard F Teerlink, president and CEO of Milwaukee-based Harley-Davidson, Inc., and a magnetic personality who talks with the speed of a Harley tachometer "revving to redline." He's a realist without the time for what he calls "pontificating." Instead he offers clear, simple, and distinct advice to managers who are looking around their organizations to find out what is wrong and who or what is causing it.

> We looked at ourselves, and the problem was *us*. "Quality gurus say if you look at sources of problems in your business, 85 percent of the time they are materials, machines, and management. The other 15 percent is direct labor.
>
> This 85 percent really bothers me. [But] it's not materials, machines, and management. It's management. Let's not run and hide. When we looked inside Harley-Davidson, we found out the problem was the white shirts and ties.
>
> Our competitive problem was management, not the typical excuses used by many executives: unions, employees, Japanese culture/wage rates, or automation.
>
> In my view companies in trouble today are in trouble because they find someone else to blame rather than themselves. The solution isn't rocket science: It's knowing your business, knowing your customers, and paying attention to detail. All parts of the business must function well and together. If you have world-class manufacturing and Third World marketing, you are going to fail.

In the early 80s, Harley's reputation for reliability and quality had fallen as steeply as its market share, which had dropped from 100 percent of the domestic market to a low of 23 percent. Brand-new Harleys sitting on the dealership floor had to have cardboard put down beneath them to sop up the leaking oil.

Today, Harley is a dramatically different company. Demand for its products exceeds supply even though Harley has increased production from 150 units a day in 1986 to about 350 a day currently. Profits are enviable, and motorcycle-division sales have grown at an impressive 21 percent compound annual rate during the last five years. That's because the company restored quality, introduced the less-expensive Sportster line, and increased ownership loyalty through its motorcycle-owners group.

Market share is *only* 64 percent because Harley doesn't have the manufacturing capacity to make more motorcycles. The company literally controls the size of the domestic motorcycle market. The Harley Owners Group (HOG) at 185,000 members is a roaring marketing success and in another year will be larger than the American Motorcycle Association.

Teerlink offers some interesting views of leadership:

> As I see it, leaders have three responsibilities. One is to ensure that you define the *reality,* and the other two are to be a *servant* and to say *"thank you."* A leader's only real success comes through the efforts of others. The day that leaders think they deserve the gold stars is the day they should leave their companies. At Harley, I hope [our] leaders understand that they don't get the gold stars; their teams get them.
>
> This is one reason why most CEOs don't like me—because I think CEOs are the problem . . . including me, by the way. I didn't make Harley-Davidson a success. Thousands of people did. I *represent* them.

Harley keeps its values simple: Tell the truth, keep your promises, be fair, respect the individual, and encourage intellectual curiosity. "Mother, God, and country, right?" observes Teerlink. "If everybody knows this is right, why don't we live it? Think what would happen if everybody in your organization lived these values. Think of all the procedural manuals you could throw away. Let's understand why we have procedures. In most cases [company policies and procedures] protect us against the 5 percent who are abusers and abuse the 95 percent who do it right."

Teerlink stresses a participative environment where:

> [Empowered employees] must be able to make decisions, but they need fences. Dr. [Benjamin] Spock says, "If you want to raise good kids, you should raise them with freedom and fences." How do you build strong corporations? Provide fences so people can understand their individual level of authority. Then give the authority to them and let them do it. And if they don't do it, *don't shoot them.* Let's all learn from them and support them in a life-long learning environment.
>
> Our style is not management by committee. It's not consensus or majority rule; it's an opportunity to make a difference and an environment that is open to influence.
>
> I have people coming to me all the time and saying, "Rick, you aren't walking the talk." And 90 percent of the time they are right.

In the productivity arena, Teerlink throws out what he calls the "silly" definitions of productivity. "If we can get people to focus on doing the *right thing* and then doing the *thing right,* Harley will be in good shape on the productivity issue." The motorcycle maker invested heavily in hard tooling for its manufacturing line 15 years ago and is still in the midst of getting rid of the $4.8 million 22-station transfer line because its customers no longer want that product. So his advice is to be flexible in your approach to manufacturing equipment and investment decisions.

Harley has also shown flexibility in management during the last 18 months. It is making a transition from an informal to a more formal organization—complete with a corporate-office look from what once had been cubicles in converted manufacturing space. It is also learning to manage the expectations of Wall Street and is becoming more directly involved in foreign markets. Last year, for the first time in the company's 90-year history, marketing staff from around the globe gathered in Milwaukee to share ideas and information. (The company's globalization has also landed it in Japan, where Harley has three boutiques that sell clothing and collectibles, but no motorcycles, to HOG "wannabees.")

Even though he offers a recipe for success, Teerlink discourages the "cookbook"-for-success type of thinking.

"If anybody thinks we have a cookbook, they are wrong," he explains. "We have a *path* to follow, and we have a long way to go. We must continue to focus on the drivers of change—responsive product development, manufacturing excellence, and marketing innovation."

Questions for Analysis

1. Discuss Teerlink's critique of management. Why do you think he doesn't receive praise for his critique from corporate managers?

2. What aspects of empowerment does Teerlink practice?

3. Teerlink emphasizes quality at Harley-Davidson. Do you think that the culture of the firm has really changed to embrace the CEO's vision of quality?

Sources: Adapted from B S Moskal, "Born to Be Real," *Industry Week*, August 2, 1993, pp. 14–18; J F McKenna, "America's Most Admired CEOs," *Industry Week*, December 6, 1993, pp. 22–32.

VIDEO CASE
MOTIVATION AND LEADERSHIP AT BERNARD WELDING EQUIPMENT COMPANY

Leadership is a concept that is frequently discussed, but its meaning is unclear. What distinguishes a manager from a leader? What is power? How can a manager develop leadership skills and use power in a manner that will motivate and inspire employees to go beyond their job description? In the workplace, leadership can be defined as the application of personal attributes and abilities, such as insight, energy, and knowledge, to create a shared vision of the future. A manager must deal with the pressures of the moment, and is responsible for organizing and controlling the workforce. The means by which a manager creates lasting meaning or purpose for employees defines the manager's "leadership style."

Bernard Welding Equipment Company has garnered a large share of the world's welding accessories business. The company's success may be attributed to the application of a new style of leadership and a quality management approach to every stage of its operation. Reflecting on the important role of leadership at Bernard, company president Pat Cunningham said, "The leader of a company becomes the personality of the company. Very often, in the old days, he was an autocratic person. If you view old-time manufacturing, you've got one guy in the corner office barking out orders and people running around doing his bidding day in and day out. Well, in today's environment, where people are much more informed and communications can happen much more rapidly, that style of management is no longer effective."

Jim Therrien, Bernard's vice president of operations, noted in the video that his company began a continuous quality improvement journey in the early 1990s. The first step in the journey involved reviewing and refining the company's mission. Therrien explained the role of leadership in the mission review process: "The only constant in life is change, and the same is true in business. People who can capture change and run with it will be tremendously successful. Those that don't won't be in tune with the ever-changing markets and will be left behind. If management is efficiently climbing the ladder, then leadership is making sure the ladder is against the right wall. Our right wall is the customer need. Starting with that, and backing into the plant and moving through the organization gives you the wherewithal and the

master plan to effect the kinds of changes that we've had at Bernard. As people become part of a team, they feel like they're accomplishing something. When people are in that mode, it's very easy to lead them in the right direction. And the right direction is always based on what the customer need is. And when you're filling those customer needs, there's less of those complaint calls, there's less people coming down on people and more people being up with people and helping to move things in the proper direction."

After reviewing the mission, the second stage of Bernard's continuous improvement process was to examine its manufacturing operations. The company's assembly line was improved through the participative leadership style. Training for both the managers and the workforce was key to the change. Managers needed to learn how to delegate and empower their workforce, and the workers needed to learn how to accept their new responsibilities.

Production supervisor Kathy Yates enthused about the changes in the workforce that resulted from Bernard's new participative leadership style: "In the past when we had problems on the assembly line the operators would come to me and ask 'What should we do?' We're doing things a lot different now. When problems arise on the assembly line we get together as a group, we talk it out, and we decide what the best solution is to that problem. We didn't do that in the past. We're more of a team effort now and it really shows up in the results. Our production is up, our quality is up, the morale of the people is up. It really has paid off."

Bernard's continuous improvement process has also focused on reducing costs. Using employee-driven quality improvement teams, the company changed its practice of maintaining a supply of precut, assembled cables for its welding guns because it incurred unnecessarily high inventory costs. Bernard now uses a delayed, differentiated quick response system. With this new approach, the cable needed to fill each order is cut to the customer's specifications from the spools of cable as needed. Reduced inventory lowers costs and benefits the customer through lower prices and quicker turnaround times.

Workers on the shop floor have embraced their new decision-making authority. Randy Warren, manufacturing engineer, noted another example of employee-led cost reduction: "We've been able to reduce setup time across 65 percent of our head volume. A good example is our head forming process. A process that used to take a good setup person 30 to 40 minutes to accomplish can now be done by the operator in less than a minute. We recognize that our most important resource is our people out there. By empowering the people to make decisions on their own we've been able to generate a lot of input right at the floor level where the process takes place. These are the experts in the manufacture of our products. They see things that we can't anticipate on the tooling side or on the process side."

Bernard's new participatory leadership style has motivated the employees to reach new levels of quality and customer satisfaction, as Kathy Yates elaborated: "We find that, on a daily basis, when problems come up, we get together as a team and we solve them. I have found that [the line workers] are the experts, they are the ones who are out there building this product day after day after day. They know more about the product than I do. So, when problems arise, we get together, we sit down, we talk it out, we brainstorm it, whatever it takes to come up with a solution. I think this has really helped the quality of our product. I think people are dedicated to their work areas, and they feel an ownership. They're very concerned about what they're putting out and how they're doing it. If they have a question they go to whoever they need to talk to to get the answer, and they want it now, they're very strong on that they feel that they've got to make the highest-quality product."

Therrien explained how his own leadership style has changed in the continuous quality improvement culture: "As I've transitioned from managing to leading in this organization, and I think the same holds true for most managers here, I've learned to listen better than I've ever listened before. I only thought I was listening. People have a lot to say. You don't always want to hear it. But when you sit quietly, and gather data from many directions, then the decisions that you make are better decisions because they're based on more information. When you have everyone in one room, then you are going to hear from all sides, and you will gather information in the same manner that it goes through the organization. Most large organizations are vertically structured, and most of the information that the customer needs, and the product, goes through horizontally. Once you have your people in tune with that the product and the information flow moves horizontally, you will be able to look down on it and see where the bottlenecks are. Then you can bring your resources to bear to help the people do a better job."

Cunningham summarized the new leadership style being practiced at Bernard: "One of the benefits of the longer-term view that we've taken of improving the managerial capability of our people is their ability to make better decisions on improving productivity in a given product line. I can recall, some years ago, in sitting in meetings with our people, they looked upon myself and a couple of others to answer the key questions and communicate the direction of the company, to solve all of the problems, to take just about everything that needed to be decided and decide it. That doesn't make sense. For the CEO of a business or the top manager of a fairly sizable organization to think that he has the knowledge and capability to make all of the minute decisions that need to be made on a daily basis is kind of foolhardy. That may have been appropriate in a very small business 50 years ago, but it surely isn't appropriate in today's' environment. We now bring customers and distributors right into our factories and sit them down with employees and let them communicate, let them get a better understanding of exactly what's going on in our business and what the needs of our customers are right from the horse's mouth. We provide each of our employees with access to all of our financial information regularly on exactly how this company is doing. Our employees actually have access to every piece of financial data that I have. And I'm proud to say that I think it's helped them become more informed employees, who are willing to recognize faster when change needs to be made. I think that our growth in our industry in the last couple of years, in terms of sales, earnings and profit margins, and all the other places where you can measure the financial performance of a company, has outstripped all of our competitors as best we can judge that. And in many cases we can judge that very accurately. We think we do a better job, and the numbers are starting to prove that we do."

Critical Thinking Questions

1. Continuous quality improvement processes, like the approach being used at Bernard, call for authority and power to be pushed down from the management to employee level. Why do you think this is an important part of continuous improvement?

2. Bernard president Pat Cunningham stated that all employees have access to every bit of financial data pertinent to the company's performance. What are the possible advantages of sharing these data? What are the possible disadvantages?

3. Jim Therrien, vice president of operations, said that he has learned to listen better to employees. What role do you think listening should play in leadership? What steps can you take to become a more effective listener in your life?

EXPERIENTIAL EXERCISE
ARE YOU A TRANSFORMATIONAL LEADER?

Purpose

The purpose of this exercise is to assess your leadership orientation.

The Exercise in Class (15 minutes)

Complete this exercise by simply assigning points and adding up the totals. For each of the following 10 pairs of statements, divide five points between the two according to your beliefs, perceptions of yourself, or according to which of the two statements characterizes you better. The five points may be divided between the A and B statements in any one of the following ways: 5 for A, 0 for B; 4 for A, 1 for B; 3 for A, 2 for B; 1 for A, 4 for B; 0 for A, 5 for B, but not equally $2\frac{1}{2}$ between the two. Weigh your choice between each two according to the one that better characterizes you or your beliefs.

1. _____ A As leader, I have a primary mission of maintaining stability.
   _____ B As leader, I have a primary mission of change.
2. _____ A As leader, I must cause events.
   _____ B As leader, I must facilitate events.
3. _____ A I am concerned that my followers are rewarded equitably for their work.
   _____ B I am concerned about what my followers want in life.
4. _____ A My preference is to think long range: What might be.
   _____ B My preference is to think short range: What is realistic.
5. _____ A As a leader, I spend considerable energy in managing separate but related goals.
   _____ B As a leader, I spend considerable energy in arousing hopes, expectations, and aspirations among my followers.
6. _____ A While not in a formal classroom sense, I believe that a significant part of my leadership is that of teacher.
   _____ B I believe that a significant part of my leadership is that of facilitator.
7. _____ A As leader, I must engage with followers at an equal level of morality.
   _____ B As leader, I must represent a higher morality.
8. _____ A I enjoy stimulating followers to want to do more.

_____ B I enjoy rewarding followers for a job well done.
9. _____ A Leadership should be practical.
   _____ B Leadership should be inspirational.
10. _____ A What power I have to influence others comes primarily from my ability to get people to identify with me and my ideas.
    _____ B What power I have to influence others comes primarily from my status and position.

Scoring Sheet for Leadership Questionnaire

Transformational Your Point(s)	*Transactional Your Point(s)*
1. B _____	1. A _____
2. A _____	2. B _____
3. B _____	3. A _____
4. A _____	4. B _____
5. B _____	5. A _____
6. A _____	6. B _____
7. B _____	7. A _____
8. A _____	8. B _____
9. B _____	9. A _____
10. A _____	10. B _____
Column Totals _____	_____

Note: The higher column total indicates that you agree more with, and see yourself as more like, either a transformational leader or a transactional leader.

Discussion (30 minutes)

Divide the class into people who scored highest on transformational leadership and those who were highest in transactional leadership. Is there any relationship between your own leadership score and your evaluations of the leaders you have studied?

The Learning Message

The self-assessment attempts to have students rethink the discussion of transformational leadership and how it compares with transactional leadership.

Source: W W Burke, PhD. Reprinted by permission.

Notes

1. William E Rothschild, "Avoid the Mismatch between Strategy and Strategic Leaders," *Journal of Business Strategy,* September 1993, pp. 37–42.

2. Glenn Rifkin, "Leadership: Can It Be Learned?" *Forbes ASAP,* April 8, 1996, pp. 100–3, 106.

3. Arthur Shriberg, Carol Lloyd, David L. Shriberg, and Mary Lynn Williamson, *Practicing Leadership* (New York: John Wiley, 1997).

4. Keith Davis, *Human Relations at Work* (New York: McGraw-Hill, 1967), pp. 96–97.

5. John R P French and Bertram Raven, "The Bases of Social Power," in Dorwin Cartwright and Alvin F Zander eds., *Group Dynamics* (Evanston, IL: Row, Peterson, 1960), pp. 607–23.

6. The president of the United States has the power to intervene if it's decided that the nation's commerce or safety is in jeopardy.

7. M A Rahim, "A New Measure of Bases of Leader Power" (paper presented at National Academy of Management, Chicago, 1986).

8. Timothy R Hinkin and C A Schriesheim, "Development and Application of New Scales to Measure the French and Raven (1959) Bases of Social Power," *Journal of Applied Psychology,* August 1989, pp. 561–67.

9. K Student, "Supervisory Influence and Workgroup Performance," *Journal of Applied Psychology,* 1968, pp. 188–94.

10. For two classic studies, see D C Pelz, "Influence: A Key to Effective Leadership in the First-Line Supervisor," *Personnel,* 1952, pp. 201–21; and M Rosier et al., "Worker Participation and Influence in Five Countries," *Industrial Relations,* 1973, pp. 200–12.

11. Timothy D. Schellhardt, "It's Time to Evaluate Your Work and All Involved Are Groaning," *The Wall Street Journal,* November 19, 1996, pp. 1B and 3B.

12. Herman DePree, "How Green Is My Factory?" *Business Week,* December 16, 1991, pp. 54–56.

13. Ronald A Heifetz and Donald L Laurie, "The Work of Leadership," *Harvard Business Review,* January–February 1997, pp. 124–34.

14. Douglas McGregor, *The Human Side of Enterprise* (New York: McGraw-Hill, 1960). This is McGregor's original work.

15. Suzanne Oliver, "How Katherine Hammer Reinvested Herself," *Forbes,* August 12, 1996, pp. 98–103; Crystal L Owen and William D Todor, "Attitudes toward Women as Managers: Still the Same," *Business Horizons,* March–April 1993, pp. 12–16.

16. Ellen P Kelly, Amy Oakes Young, and Lawrence S Clark, "Sex Stereotyping in the Workplace: A Manager's Guide," *Business Horizons,* March–April 1993, pp. 23–29.

17. Bernard M Bass, *Handbook of Leadership* (New York: Free Press, 1990), pp. 707–37.

18. Judy B Rosener, "Ways Women Lead," *Harvard Business Review,* November–December 1990, pp. 119–25; Jaclyn Fierman, "Do Women Manage Differently?" *Fortune,* December 17, 1990, pp. 115–18.

19. Becci Robbins, "25 Milestones in Women's History," *Career Woman,* Winter 1993, pp. 41–43, 54.

20. James Waldroop and Timothy Butler, "The Executive as Coach," *Harvard Business Review,* November–December 1996, pp. 111–17.

21. Perri Capell, "Behavioral Coaching Can Help Troubled Executives," *Houston Chronicle,* December 26, 1996, p. 23.

22. Gary Yukl, *Leadership in Organizations* (Upper Saddle River, NJ: Prentice-Hall, 1995).

23. Jay A Conger, "The Brave New World of Leadership Training," *Organizational Dynamics,* Summer 1993, pp. 46–58.

24. Robert Tannenbaum and Warren H Schmidt, "How to Choose a Leadership Pattern," *Harvard Business Review,* May–June 1973, pp. 162–80.

25. Rensis Likert, *New Patterns of Management* (New York: McGraw-Hill, 1961). For a discussion of the history of Likert's work, see Rensis Likert, "From Production-and Employee-Centeredness to Systems 1–4," *Journal of Management,* Fall 1979, pp. 147–56.

26. See any of the following for excellent presentations of the two-dimensional theory: E A Fleishman, "The Measurement of Leadership Attitudes in Industry," *Journal of Applied Psychology,* June 1953, pp. 153–58; E A Fleishman and D A Peters, "Interpersonal Values, Leadership Attitudes, and Managerial Success," *Personnel Psychology,* Summer 1962, pp. 127–43; Abraham K Korman, "Consideration, Initiating Structure, and Organizational Criteria—A Review," *Personnel Psychology,* Winter 1966, pp. 349–61; C A Schreisheim and Barbara J Bird, "Contributions of the Ohio State Studies to the Field of Leadership," *Journal of Management,* Fall 1979, pp. 135–45.

27. E A Fleishman, E F Harris, and H E Burt, *Leadership and Supervision in Industry* (Columbus: Bureau of Educational Research, Ohio State University, 1955).

28. Robert R Blake and Anne Adams McCanse, *Leadership Dilemmas—Grid Solutions* (Houston: Gulf, 1991).

29. Robert R Blake and Jane S Mouton, *The Managerial Grid* (Houston: Gulf, 1964).

30. Robert R Blake and Jane S Mouton, *The Managerial Grid III* (Houston: Gulf, 1985).

31. Fred E Fiedler and Joseph E Garcia, *New Approaches to Effective Leadership: Cognitive Resources and Organizational Performance* (New York: John Wiley, 1987); Fred E Fiedler, *A Theory of Leadership Effectiveness* (New York: McGraw-Hill, 1969).

32. Fiedler, *A Theory of Leadership Effectiveness;* Fred E Fiedler and Martin M Chemers, *Leadership and Effective Management* (Glenview, IL: Scott, Foresman, 1975).

33. An early review article critical of the situational, or contingency, model of leadership is George Graen, Kenneth Alvaris, James B Orris, and Joseph A Martella, "Contingency Model of Leadership Effectiveness: Antecedent and Evidential Results," *Psychological Bulletin,* October 1970, pp. 285–96.

34. For two early works, see Martin G Evans, "The Effect of Supervisory Behavior on the Path–Goal Relationship," *Organizational Behavior and Human Performance,* May 1970, pp. 277–98.

35. Robert J House, "A Path–Goal Theory of Leader Effectiveness," *Administrative Science Quarterly,* September 1971, pp. 321–38.

36. J Indvik, "A More Complete Testing of Path–Goal Theory" (paper presented at National Academy of Management, Anaheim, CA, 1988).

37. See Alan C Filley, Robert J House, and Steven Kerr, *Managerial Process and Organizational Behavior* (Glenview, IL: Scott, Foresman, 1976), pp. 256–60.

38. L L Neider and C A Schriesheim, "Making Leadership Effective: A Three-Stage Model," *Journal of Management Development,* 1988, pp. 10–20.

39. Victor Vroom and Philip Yetton, *Leadership and Decision Making* (Pittsburgh: University of Pittsburgh Press, 1973). Much of the validation of this model and some of the refinements were initiated by Arthur Jago of the University of Houston.

40. Arthur G Jago, "Hierarchical Level Determinants of Participative Leader Behavior," PhD diss., Yale University, *Dissertation Abstracts International 30* (1977), p. 2921B; Arthur G Jago and Victor H Vroom, "An Evaluation of Two Alternatives to the Vroom-Yetton Normative Model," *Academy of Management Journal,* June 1980, pp. 347–55.

41. G Margerison and R Glube, "Leadership Decision-Making: An Empirical Test of the Vroom and Yetton Model," *Journal of Management Studies,* February 1979, pp. 45–55.

42. Victor H Vroom and Arthur G Jago, *The New Leadership: Managing Participation in Organizations* (Englewood Cliffs, NJ: Prentice-Hall, 1988), pp. 164–65.

43. P Hersey and K H Blanchard, *Management of Organizational Behavior* (Englewood Cliffs, NJ: Prentice Hall, 1993), pp. 152–60.

44. Robert P Vecchio, "Situational Leadership Theory: An Examination of a Perspective Theory," *Journal of Applied Psychology,* August 1987, pp. 444–51.

45. C L Graeff, "The Situational Leadership Theory: A Critical View," *Academy of Management Review,* April 1983, pp. 285–91.

46. Max Weber, *The Theory of Social and Economic Organizations* (New York: Free Press, 1947).

47. J M Burns, *Leadership* (New York: Harper & Row, 1978).

48. Louis Kraar, "Daewoo's Daring Drive into Europe," *Fortune,* May 13, 1996, pp. 145–52.

49. L Atwater and F J Yammarino, *Predictors of Military Leadership: A Study of Midshipmen Leaders of USNA (ONR Technical Report)* (Binghamton, NY: State University of New York, Center for Leadership Studies, 1989).

50. Bernard M Bass, "From Transitional to Transformational Leadership: Learning to Share the Vision," *Organizational Dynamics,* Winter 1990, pp. 140–48; Warren Bennis and Burt Nanis, *Leaders* (New York: Harper & Row, 1985), pp. 18–32.

51. Douglas McGregor, "On Visionary Leadership," *New Management,* Winter 1985, pp. 46–52.

52. Fiedler, *Theory of Leadership,* p. 247.

53. Charles M Farkas and Phillippe de Backer, "There Are Only Five Ways to Lead," *Fortune,* January 15, 1996, pp. 109–12.

54. Stephen S Roach, "The Hollow Ring of the Productivity Revival," *Harvard Business Review,* November–December 1996, pp. 81–89.

55. James F Moore, *The Death of Competition* (New York: Harper Business, 1996).

56. Douglas T Hall and Victoria A Parker, "The Role of Workplace Flexibility in Managing Diversity," *Organizational Dynamics,* 1993, pp. 5–18.

57. Andre Laurent, "The Cultural Diversity of Western Conceptions of Management," *International Studies of Management and Organizations,* Spring–Summer 1983, pp. 75–96.

58. Diether Gerbert and Thomas Steinkamp, "Leadership Style and Economic Success in Nigeria and Taiwan," *Management International Review,* Summer 1992, pp. 161–71.

14 COMMUNICATION AND NEGOTIATION

Chapter Learning Objectives

After completing Chapter 14, you should be able to:

- **Define** each element in the process of communication.
- **Describe** communication and negotiation in organizations.
- **Discuss** nonverbal communication and its importance in organizations.
- **Compare** situations in which informal and formal channels of communication would be utilized.
- **Identify** the major reasons why communications break down.

Communicating in a Diverse Organization

In today's global business environment, success in business depends, to a large degree, on an organization's ability to effectively manage a diverse workforce. Successful management of diversity requires companies to engage in productive communication aimed at promoting employee harmony. Managerial communication can be defined as communication in a management setting undertaken to achieve a desired result.

In taking a proactive approach to head off possible problems associated with a diverse workforce, leading-edge companies have successfully implemented programs to promote better communication throughout their organizations. What follows is a brief description of some of the programs in place at various companies.

- Avon encourages employees to organize cultural communication networks. These networks help new employees adjust, arrange cultural events, and provide feedback to a top-level council that includes the CEO.

- Apple Computer has taken several actions. First, the company established a managerial position, the responsibility of which includes developing and overseeing multicultural and affirmative-action programs. Second, the company started a mentor program whereby new minority employees are introduced to the company's culture. Third, Apple offers diversity-management workshops, which allow managers to explore the meaning of being a minority in a majority society. Finally, a multicultural board has been established to monitor Apple's overall diversity efforts.

- Digital Equipment Company celebrates Black History Month, Hispanic Heritage Week, and other various cultural events. The company also encourages the discussion of multiracial issues in support networks and design exercises to help employees put themselves into others' shoes. One such exercise has employees using a wheelchair for a day.

- At the Prudential Insurance Company, The Diversity Game is used as a learning tool. The Diversity Game is a board game similar in concept to Trivial Pursuit. Teams compete to answer multiple-choice questions about anything from legislation to real workplace situations. There is also The Global Diversity Game, which is geared toward teaching employees how to operate in a global marketplace. Prudential executives believe the games are an excellent way of allowing management and associates to learn more about other people and cultures in a nonthreatening manner.

Not difficult to implement, each of these programs has proved successful. For companies striving to effectively communicate the message to employees that they all are equally important, such programs can make a world of difference.

Sources: Bill Busbin, "New Technologies Enable Worldwide HRM," *HR Focus*, November 1996, p. 15; D Elmuti, "Managing Diversity in the Workplace: An Immense Challenge for both Managers and Workers," *IM*, July–August 1993, pp. 19–22; M Munter, "Cross-Cultural Communication for Managers," *Business Horizons*, May–June 1993, pp. 69–77; and M Wahl, "Diversity Training—The Fun Way," *Executive Female*, March–April 1993, p. 20.

Managing people effectively requires an understanding of several behavioral factors. Communication is surely one of them. Surveys clearly show that communication is one of the most vital skills that managers need.[1] Managers rarely work with things but rather with *information* about things. Thus, communication pervades the management functions of planning, organizing, leading, and controlling.

But what is communication? How do we communicate with one another? And how do we know when we have? "Telling isn't teaching, and listening isn't learning." This old adage known to instructors expresses in a few words the essence of poor and ineffective communication. In the context of our discussion, it can be restated as: "Writing isn't communicating, and reading isn't understanding." Why not? There are many reasons for ineffective communication. The one cited most often is that we tend to think in too-simple terms about this very complicated process. Communicating involves the emotional, psychological, and mental characteristics of individuals, as well as the technical characteristics of the medium used to communicate. The understanding that the speaker intended to express may be far different from what was actually imparted to the listener.

Recognizing the ever-growing importance of communication, more and more organizations are implementing programs designed to assess managerial communication skills and to provide follow-up training to overcome any communication deficiencies. Managers who have participated in such programs have been found to possess significantly stronger interpersonal skills and problem-solving abilities—leading to higher productivity levels—than those who have not.[2] The Management in Action section highlighted some of the efforts being taken by leading companies to improve both management's and employees' ability to communicate. Effective communication is so important for the management of people that we hope that our discussion of what it is and how it is achieved illustrates fully its complexity.

The Importance of Communication

The following statements, or ones very similar, are heard on a regular basis in most organizations: "The purchase order has not been sent because you never said it was a rush request." "I really never thought she was serious about resigning." "When the president says as soon as possible, he means now." In these and similar situations, we often hear, "What we have here is a failure to communicate." That statement communicates clearly to everyone, because all of us have faced situations in which the problem was poor communication. Whether it be on a person-to-person basis, nation to nation, in large organizations, or in small groups, breakdowns in communication seem to be pervasive.

Oral communication preceded written communication. In ancient Greece and Rome, it was necessary to communicate well on one's feet in the courts and in the government assemblies. Socrates, Plato, and Aristotle are part of the same history of communication that today is still very important to the very existence of organizations and to the career progress of individuals.[3]

It is difficult to find an aspect of a manager's job that does not have the potential for communication breakdowns. Problems arise when directives are misunderstood, rumors spread, informal remarks by an executive are misinterpreted or distorted, or casual kidding in a work group leads to anger. Thus, the real issue is not whether managers communicate but whether they do it effectively or ineffectively. Everything a manager does, or in many cases doesn't do, communicates something to some person or group. The only question is: With what effect? The accompanying Management Focus shows the importance of and potential payoffs from not only promoting effective communication within the organization but also extending this focus to other internal beneficiaries.

An example of what can be communicated and how to communicate is illustrated in a Mellon Bank annual report. Accompanied by photos of four successful managers is a report explaining how each spends time at work.[4] One manager is shown at his desk at 7 AM reviewing documents, at a 5 PM meeting with a client, and at 8 PM studying more documents. Another senior bank officer is shown starting the day at 7:30 AM and going home at 8 PM. Each of the other two have long 11-hour days. What was the message? The nine-to-fiver will not succeed at Mellon. The company wanted to communicate that at Mellon, effort counts.

Communicating with the Customer Yields a High Payoff

Effective communication should not be viewed as a management tool solely to be utilized within the confines of the organization. Businesses, both large and small, should also continually communicate with their customers. One of the most valuable means by which companies can receive customer feedback is through the monitoring of customer satisfaction. And, while many companies are diligent about responding to customer complaints, they could be doing more. In a recent survey of 259 companies with revenues of $40 million or less, a majority of respondents said they use standard methods of gaining customer feedback such as employing 1-800 call-in numbers and enclosing customer surveys with purchase orders. These methods rely on the customer to initiate action. Few companies take a proactive approach to getting feedback.

Companies that excel in customer intimacy are able to combine detailed customer knowledge with operational flexibility so they can respond to the needs of the customer before their competition strikes. Hanna Andersson of Portland, Oregon, is an example of a small but growing company that discovered the hefty benefits to be derived from paying closer attention to the wants and needs of the customer. The business, a $40 million mail-order catalog company specializing in children's clothes, has transformed the order-taking process into a two-way communications forum.

Hanna Andersson employs 120 order takers and customer service representatives who not only track but also actively solicit comments, suggestions, and complaints

from callers. These representatives subtly encourage customers to volunteer information regarding the company's products and service while they are in the process of placing orders for merchandise. Karen Johnson, the company's call center manager, believes the openness that Hanna Andersson employees promote helps establish a special bond with their customers. Every detail, from catalog copy to the order taker's spiel is designed to encourage customers to communicate their likes and dislikes.

Last year, for example, the company sold a type of shorts whose length they subsequently found customers were unhappy with. This valuable knowledge would not have been acquired if the company had been content to rely on customer-initiated complaints, because there were none. Rather, the information was acquired during conversations held with customers who were in the process of ordering additional merchandise. As a result of this intelligence gathering, Hanna Andersson added a few inches to the hem of the shorts. They then made sure all customers knew about this action by adding a byline to their new catalog, which stated, "By request, shorts are slightly longer than last year." Through actively seeking customer input, Hanna Andersson ensures itself a loyal following for years to come.

Sources: J C McCune, "Whether You're Large or Small, Entrepreneurship Is Staying . . . Close to the Customer," *Success,* October 1993, pp. 38–41; M Treacy and F Wiersema, "Customer Intimacy and Other Value Disciplines," *Harvard Business Review,* January–February 1993, pp. 84–93; "How Do You Get Customer Feedback?" *Inc.,* January 1993, p. 31.

Understanding the Process of Communication

Communication is *the transmission of common understanding through the use of symbols.* The term is derived from the Latin *communis,* meaning "common." In other words, unless a common understanding results from the transmission of verbal or nonverbal symbols, there is no communication.

Numerous examples of communication in international settings illustrate the importance of understanding. For example, in restaurants in the United States, a waiter is called "Sir" or "Waiter," and customers don't snap their fingers. In Europe, a customer clinks a glass with a spoon to get attention. In Singapore, customers extend their right hand, palm down, and rapidly open and close their fingers.[5]

Elements of Communication

Figure 14–1 presents our model and the key elements of communication.[6] It identifies the basic elements of communication as the communicator, perception/interpretation, encoding, the message, the channel, decoding, the receiver, feedback, and noise. In simple terms, an individual or group (the communicator) has an idea, message, or understanding to transmit to another individual or group (the receiver). To transmit the idea, the communicator must translate the idea into a meaningful form (encoding) and send the message by verbal, nonverbal, or written means (the channel). The message is received through the senses of the receiver and translated into a form meaningful to the receiver (decoded). With a nod of the head, a facial expression, or some other action, the receiver acknowledges whether understanding has been achieved (feedback). The intended message can be distorted by the presence of distractions in each element (noise).

Let's examine each element more closely in an organizational setting.

Communicator (Person). Communicators in an organization can be managers, nonmanagers, departments, or the organization itself. Managers communicate with other managers, subordinates, supervisors, clients, customers, and parties outside the organization. Nonmanagers likewise communicate with managers and nonmanagers, clients, customers, and external parties. People in sales departments communicate with people in production departments, and engineering personnel communicate with product design teams. Communications within the organization are important means for coordinating the work of separate departments. And more and more organizations communicate with employees, unions, the public, and government. Each of these communicators has a message, idea, or information to transmit to someone or some group.

FIGURE 14–1   Communication Model with Feedback

Communication is a multistep process, with movement in both directions necessary for a successful interchange.

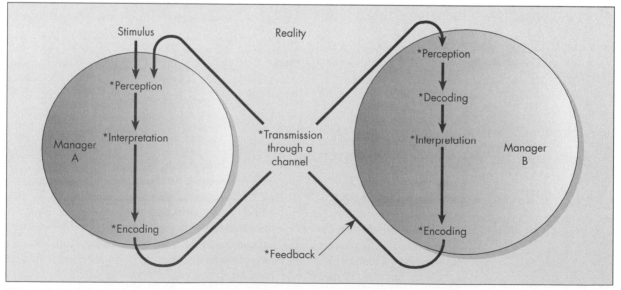

*Noise (and miscommunication) can occur here.

Source: Adapted from K O Locker, Business Administrative Communication (Burr Ridge, IL: Richard D. Irwin, 1989), p. 45.

Perception and Interpretation.   A person's view or perception of what is being communicated is crucial. Perception is reality to the person. It is how the person views the message. In perceiving, a person often must make an interpretation: What does the communicator mean?

Interpretation played a crucial role when two Boeing 747 jumbo jets collided on the ground in Tenerife in the Canary Islands. The two pilots were given specific instructions from the control tower.[7] The KLM pilot was told to taxi to the end of the runway, turn around, and wait to be cleared but didn't interpret the order to wait as an order he needed to follow. The Pan Am pilot interpreted his order to turn off at the third intersection as meaning the third unblocked intersection. He didn't count the first blocked ramp, so while he was on the main runway, the KLM plane plowed into his plane at 186 miles per hour. Fatal errors by two experienced pilots were caused by misinterpretation.

The Tenerife disaster resulted from a series of misunderstandings. Also, it should be noted that the air traffic controllers were communicating in a second language—English. Nonetheless, a series of communication gaps cost the lives of 576 people.[8]

Encoding.   Within the communicator, an **encoding** process must take place that translates the communicator's ideas into a systematic set of symbols expressing the communicator's purpose. The major form of encoding is language. For example, accounting information, sales reports, and computer data are translated into a message. The function of encoding is to provide a form in which ideas and purposes can be expressed as a message.

Message.   The result of the encoding process is the message—either verbal or nonverbal. Managers have numerous purposes for communicating, such as to have others understand their ideas, to understand the ideas of others, to gain acceptance of ideas, and to produce action. To be effective, it is essential that a message contain all the facts communicators deem necessary for the desired effect.[9] The message, then, is what the individual hopes to communicate, and the exact form that the message takes depends to a great extent on the medium used to carry it. Decisions relating to the two are inseparable.[10]

Channel.   The channel is the carrier of the message. Organizations provide information for their members by a variety of channels, including face-to-face communication, telephone, group meetings, computers, memos, policy statements, reward systems, production schedules, sales forecasts, and videotapes.

Less obvious, however, are *unintended* messages that can be sent by silence or inaction on a particular issue, as well as decisions about which goals and objectives are *not* to be pursued and which methods are *not* to be utilized.

Nonverbal Communication.   Communication that doesn't use words is a part of everyday life.[11] Try as they might, people cannot refrain from behaving nonverbally. A friendly smile, a worried expression, the seating arrangements at a committee meeting, the size and location of an office, the reception area, furniture—all are nonverbal communicators. They indicate a person's power, status, position, or friendliness. The interpretation of nonverbal cues is important. However, nonverbal cues are as easily misinterpreted as verbal messages (words).

Body language is fascinating nonverbal communication. Open body positions include leaning forward with uncrossed arms and legs. Closed, or defensive, body positions include leaning back with arms and legs crossed. Open positions are assumed to suggest acceptance and openness to what is being discussed. Closed positions suggest that people are physically or psychologically uncomfortable.

Americans see eye contact as a signal, a body language that connotes sincerity, interest, and honesty. In Korea, however, prolonged eye contact is considered rude. Arabs dislike talking to someone wearing dark glasses or while walking side-by-side; it is considered impolite not to face someone directly. In Muslim countries, women and men are not supposed to have eye contact.[12]

Emblems or gestures are a form of body language. For example, in the United States, the "thumbs-up" sign means good work, the "V" sign signals victory or peace, and the "high-five" denotes significant achievement. However, in Greece, the "thumbs-up" sign is a vulgar insult.[13]

The formation of a circle with the thumb and the index finger in the United States means OK. Imagine a manager gesturing this way to a recent French immigrant to the United States working as a technician! (In France, this gesture would mean you're worth nothing.)

Paul Ekman has conducted extensive research on facial expression.[14] He believes that proper training can allow a manager, for example, to link facial expression and emotion. Emotions linked with facial features in nonverbal communications include the following:

Fear: Eyes.

Sadness: Brows, forehead, eyes.

Disgust: Nose, cheeks, mouth.

Happiness: Cheeks, mouth, eyes.

Surprise: Any area of face.

Anger: Forehead, brows.

At one extreme, facial threat displays, such as lowered brows, staring, and lip drop, may act as signals of impending attack or aggression, and even if these behaviors are not followed by aggressive acts, they are clearly understood as precursors to potential aggression with the perceivers often avoiding interaction with the displayer.[15] At the other extreme, research has also found that speakers are perceived as more credible when they maintain eye contact, smile, and use other friendly facial expressions and gestures.[16] Indeed, these same factors are associated with the delivery characteristics of charismatic leaders.

Decoding.   For the process of communication to be completed, the message must be decoded by the receiver. **Decoding** is a technical term for the thought processes of the receiver. Thus, it involves interpretation. Receivers interpret (decode) the message in light of their own previous experiences and frames of reference. The closer the decoded message is to the intent of the communicator, the more effective is the communication. In a business organization, if the message that the chief executive receives from the marketing research department includes technical terms known only to marketing researchers, no communication exists. An often cited complaint in organizations that employ staff specialists is that they frequently cannot communicate. Each staff group (e.g., accountants, personnel, and marketing research) has a unique language and symbols that persons outside the group cannot decode.

Organizations should take steps to ensure that all employees possess the skills necessary to effectively decode messages, for regardless of the communicator's intent, it is the interpretation of the receiver that will dictate ensuing actions.[17]

Receiver (Person). Communication requires a communicator and a receiver. The foregoing discussion of decoding difficulties underlines the importance of taking the receiver into account when a communicator attempts to transmit information. "Telling isn't teaching" when the teacher uses language that the student cannot understand (cannot decode). Engineers cannot expect to communicate to nonengineers if the symbols they use are beyond the receivers' training and ability to comprehend. Effective communication requires the communicator to anticipate the receiver's decoding ability, to know where the receiver comes from. Effective communication is receiver oriented, not media oriented.

Feedback. One-way communication processes do not allow receiver-to-communicator feedback. Two-way communication processes provide for such feedback.[18] It is desirable to make provision for feedback in the communication process.[19] Managerial behavior such as dominating conversations and failing to listen to others will lead to situations where the potential exists for distortion between the intended message and the received message.[20] Productive managers effectively communicate by not only sending messages, but by drawing out employees' thoughts, ideas, and feelings.[21] A feedback loop provides a channel for receiver response, enabling the communicator to determine whether the message has been properly received and has produced the intended response. For the manager, communication feedback may come in many forms. In face to face situations, *direct* feedback is possible through verbal exchanges as well as through such subtle means as facial expressions that indicate discontent or confusion. In addition, communication breakdowns may be indicated by *indirect* means, such as declines in productivity, poor quality of production, increased absenteeism or turnover, and conflict or a lack of coordination between units. By actively encouraging feedback, managers not only increase employee job satisfaction but also ultimately facilitate increased organizational productivity.[22]

Noise. In the framework of communications, noise is any interfering factor that, if present, can distort the intended message. Noise can be present in any element (as seen in Figure 14–1). Later in this chapter, a number of sources of noise are identified.

Information Technology and Communications

Rapid technological changes and advances are changing the method, flow, and type of communications in organizations. Fax machines, cellular phones, video telephones, voice mail, E-mail, the "NET" and other technologies are available, used, and have become a part of communicating.[23] These advances mean that work, discussions and debates, meetings, and decisions can occur at widely dispersed locations.

Internet

Ever since the Internet ("NET") became available, it has changed the way business is transacted and communication occurs. Started by the US Defense Department's Advanced Research Project Agency, this "network of networks" now connects over 30,000 computer systems.[24] It is predicted that by the year 2000 there will be 100 million US Internet users.

Already one can exchange mail, documents, pictures, books, photographs, voice, music, video and television images and programs, and films on the Internet. Huge databases located at research institutes, government agencies, and universities are accessible at no or minimum costs.

There is no quarrel with the claim that the Internet is the main and most important part of the "Information Highway." There is no central authority running the Internet, which means that information is not filtered. Thus, the accuracy, validity, and value of the information must be determined by the user. A number of commercial computer networks such as CompuServe, America Online, Genie, and Prodigy have started to help people and companies get connected to the Internet for a fee.

There are four functions that can be accomplished on the Internet. One is to use it as an electronic (E-mail) system for communication. Everyone connected to the Internet receives a mailbox code. By typing in your code on a keyboard, E-mail messages can be sent. These messages travel over telephone lines and into the computer. The owner of the computer turns on his or her E-mail system to read the message and can transmit a message back to the sender and others.[25]

The second use of the Internet is as a source of information. Databases are available on almost any subject. Databases of newspapers, medical procedures, management tips, laws, and of other databases are available.[26]

The third use of the "Net" is to serve as a public forum of ideas. This is accomplished by using what is called the Usenet. The Usenet is a collection of over 10,000 discussion groups, each devoted to a different subject. The Usenet groups, called "Newsgroups," actually operate less like discussions and more like electronic bulletin boards. A person will submit a message to the group. Then, anyone who tunes in to read what is posted can view other postings and respond.

The fourth use of the Internet is for talking and chatting. This Internet function operates like a big conference call on the telephone. A person can talk with anyone else who happens to be on the same channel simply by typing a message into the computer. The typed-in communication appears on all of the monitors tuned in and a response can be made.

The world is quickly moving toward the time when anyone can get any kind of information to almost anyone else, anytime. In reality, information now moves instead of people. The global network of computers acts much like the body's nervous system. Discussion groups, databases, short communication notes or memos, ideas, product shapes, and a host of other communication products can be exchanged easily.[27]

Future economies are now described as being "knowledge based." As information becomes more important in the success of an organization, the most significant resource becomes knowledge. The information network is the tool that will allow managers and nonmanagers to use the databases to perform their jobs.

An example of the power of computers and knowledge is provided by Guisseppe Delean, a vehicle design chief working at a Ford Motor studio in Turin, Italy. He sits at his computer and shares ideas with his staff in the United States. The staff and Guisseppe look at their computer monitors as they scribble notes and turn a graphic of an automobile. The 100 percent interactive work meeting between designers in Italy and the United States is made possible by workstation computers.[28]

Another example of computer power involves the case of William Herndon, vice president of Technology for Bank America Corp.'s mortgage group. He gave up his office and oversees 125 technicians around the United States who maintain the mortgage group's computer networks. William Herndon does everything on the road using a laptop computer, wireless modem, cellular telephone, and personal 800 number. His style of telecommunicating allows him to move around freely as he sends and receives about 200 E-mail messages a day. When he can't take the laptop he uses a Hewlett-Packard palmtop handheld computer to communicate with technicians, customers, and colleagues at headquarters.[29]

Communication in Organizations

The design of an organization should provide for communication in four distinct directions: downward, upward, horizontal, and diagonal.[30] These four directions establish the framework within which communication takes place in an organization. Examining each of them enables the manager to better appreciate the barriers to effective organizational communication and the means for overcoming those barriers. Figure 14–2 illustrates the four directions in which organizational communication flows. While these are the major communication flows, many others can and do exist.

Downward Communication

Downward communication flows from individuals at higher levels of the hierarchy to those at lower levels. The most common downward communications are job instructions, official memos, policy statements, procedures, manuals, and company publications. Researchers have identified the most common downward organizational communications as job instructions; job descriptions; organization policies, procedures, and practices; employee performance feedbacks; and indoctrination of company goals.[31]

In many organizations, downward communication is both inadequate and inaccurate, as reflected in the often-heard statement among organization members that "we have absolutely no idea what's happening." Such complaints are indicative of inadequate downward communication and the need individuals have for information

---

FIGURE 14–2   Communication in Organizations

Communication in organizations flows in four distinct directions, and, in the design of the organization, channels must be provided for this flow.

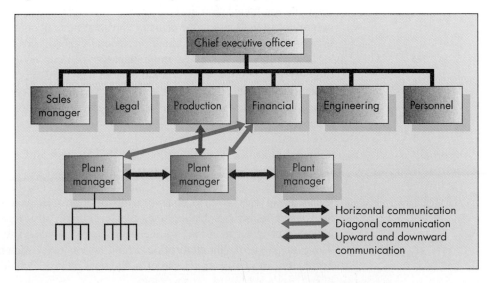

relevant to their jobs. The absence of job-related information can create unnecessary stress among organization members.[32]

In large organizations, communicating with employees is often undertaken by a trained staff of communication experts. The usual function of the staff is to produce a publication aimed at fulfilling three purposes: to explain the organization's plans and programs as they are implemented, to answer complaints and criticisms, and to defend the existing strategy and those who are responsible for it. The medium often selected to accomplish these purposes is a periodic publication such as a newsletter. The publication's intended messages present the organization's side of issues.

Upward Communication

A high-performing organization needs effective upward communication as much as it needs effective downward communication. Effective upward communication is difficult to achieve, especially in larger organizations. However, it often is necessary for sound decision making. Widely used upward communication devices include suggestion boxes, group meetings, reports to supervisors, and appeal or grievance procedures. In the absence of these flows, employees find ways to adapt to nonexistent or inadequate upward communication channels. The accompanying Management Focus describes how one company effectively utilizes upward communications.

Effective upward communication channels are important because they provide employees with opportunities to have a say. In fact, varying forms of upward communication play a key role in the successful operation of many Japanese business organizations.[33]

The Japanese place a strong emphasis on face-to-face communication between top-level managers and rank-and-file employees. It is common practice for nonmanagerial levels to talk directly to top-level executives regarding work-related issues. Often, top-level managers participate in orientation and training programs, so as to provide for employee access to them. In addition, both formal and informal mechanisms to actively solicit suggestions from employees are often put in place with rewards being given when these suggestions are implemented.

Lateral Communication

Often overlooked in the design of most organizations is provision for the horizontal flow of communication. When the supervisor of the accounting department communicates with the director of marketing concerning advertising budget expenditures, the flow of communication is horizontal. Although vertical (upward and downward) communication flows are the primary considerations in organizational design, effective organizations also need functional horizontal channels for communication.

According to a survey, more than 60 percent of employees in a variety of organizations say that lateral communication is ineffective.[34] This often results in a lack of understanding of other areas and functions. A consequence of this lack of understanding is that strategic decision making, planning, and coordination are hampered.

Diagonal Communication

Although diagonal communication probably is the least used channel of communication in organizations, it is important in situations in which members cannot communicate effectively through other channels. For example, the comptroller of a large organization may wish to conduct a distribution cost analysis, and one part of the analysis may involve having the salesforce send a special report directly to the comptroller rather than through the traditional channels in the marketing department. Thus, the flow of communication would be diagonal rather than upward and then horizontal. In this case, the use of a diagonal channel would minimize the time and effort expended by the organization.

Management Focus

Upward Feedback: An Old but Effective Communication Tool

Some organizations are discovering that an old and often unused form of corporate communications is greatly enhancing their ability to effectively incorporate employee knowledge into the planning and control processes. Upward feedback, employed as a means for implementing employee advice, helps create an environment of shared leadership in which managers actively solicit, listen to, and act on employees' suggestions. This method, when properly utilized, allows employees to augment their supervisors' management skills and provides a framework for setting in motion productive change throughout the organization.

Reflexite Corporation is a reflective plastics manufacturing company located in Stamford, Connecticut, that has taken an interesting approach to achieving successful upward feedback. Reflexite has implemented a version of the employee suggestion box that does more than just track complaints; it promotes companywide awareness of problems, their costs, and their potential solutions.

Matt Guyer, a Reflexite manufacturing manager, with assistance from representatives of various other departments, designed the Employee-Assistance Request form, which led to the creation of an upward feedback program that is commonly known around the company as EARS. Once a problem is identified by any employee through the EARS system, money is then allocated to solve the problem. If necessary, teams of employees can be as- sembled to attack problems that cross departmental boundaries. As for self-discipline, motivation is engineered into the system. Progress, on solving problems is charted on bulletin boards, and meetings are held each week to find out what's causing roadblocks to progress.

In the year since the EARS method has been implemented, every employee has attended classes to learn the steps and skills necessary to solve a problem correctly. The focus of the training has been on getting employees who identify problems to step back and quantify the magnitude of the problem and its impact on the entire company prior to offering a solution. Creation of the EARS program has helped both Reflexite management and employees pay attention to all of the small problems that have a long-term, cumulative effect on morale and the bottom line.

As the Reflexite example shows, upward feedback systems help managers to "walk the talk" by providing a means for effectively incorporating and acting on employee suggestions as part of the daily management process. Regardless of whether an "EARS" or other approach is utilized, upward feedback systems can lead to a more productive organization.

Sources: M Moravec, H Gyr, and L Friedman, "A 21st Century Communication Tool," *HRM Magazine,* July 1993, pp. 77–81; K Ludeman, "Upward Feedback Helps Managers Walk the Talk," *HRM Magazine,* May 1993, pp. 85–94; T Lammers, "The Effective Employee-Feedback System," *Inc.,* February 1993, pp. 109–11.

Interpersonal Communications

Communication flows from individual to individual in face-to-face and group settings. Such flows, called interpersonal communications, vary in form from direct orders to casual expressions. The primary manner in which managers relate to and learn from people in their environment is through interpersonal communication—information the managers receive from and transmit to individuals with whom they interact. And the way in which managers receive and transmit information depends in part on how they relate to two very important *senders* of information: themselves and others.

Regions of Information

Information is held by oneself and by others, but each of us does not fully have or know that information. The different combinations of knowing and not knowing relevant information are shown in Figure 14–3. The figure identifies four regions of information known and unknown by the self and others.[35]

1. *The arena.* The region most conducive for effective interpersonal communication is called the arena. In this setting, all the information

---

Figure 14–3   **Regions of Information Influencing Communication**

The four regions of information known and not known by the self and others can be modified by two improvement strategies.

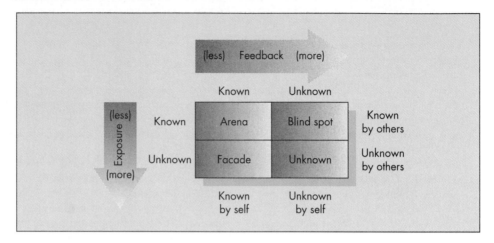

necessary to carry on effective communication is known to both the communicator (self) and the receivers (others). For a communication attempt to be in the arena region, the parties involved must share feelings, data, assumptions, and skills. The arena is the area of common understanding.

2. *The blind spot.* When relevant information is known to others but not to the self, a blind spot results. In this context, one is at a disadvantage when communicating with others, because one cannot know their feelings, sentiments, and perceptions. Consequently, interpersonal communications suffer. The blind spot presents an interpersonal handicap for the self, since one hardly can understand the behaviors, decisions, or potentials of others without having data on which these are based. Others have the advantage of knowing their own feelings, while the self is unaware of these.

3. *The facade.* When information is known to the self but unknown to others, a person (self) may resort to superficial communications—that is, present a false front, or facade. This situation is particularly damaging when a subordinate knows and an immediate supervisor does not know. The facade, like a blind spot, diminishes the arena and reduces the possibility of effective communication.

4. *The unknown.* This region, the unknown, constitutes that portion where the relevant information is not known by the self or by other parties to the relationship: "I don't understand them, and they don't understand me." It is easy to see that under such circumstances, interpersonal communication will be poor. The unknown area often occurs in organizations when individuals in different specialties must coordinate what they do through communications.

Improvement Strategies

Figure 14–3 indicates that an individual can improve interpersonal communications by utilizing two strategies, exposure and feedback:

1. *Exposure.* Increasing the arena by reducing the facade requires that the individual be open and honest in sharing information with others. The

process that the self uses to increase the information known to others is called exposure because it leaves the self in a sometimes vulnerable position. Exposing one's true feelings, "telling it like it is," often involves risk.

2. *Feedback.* When the self does not know or understand, more effective communications can be developed through feedback from those who do know. Thus, the blind spot can be reduced with a corresponding increase in the arena. Of course, whether the use of feedback is possible depends on the individual's willingness to hear it and on the willingness of others to give it. The individual is less able to control the obtaining of feedback than the provision of exposure. Obtaining feedback is dependent on the active cooperation of others, while exposure requires the active behavior of the self and listening of others.

Management Styles Interpersonal style refers to *the way in which an individual prefers to relate to others.* The fact that many of the relationships among people involve communication indicates the importance of interpersonal style.

The day-to-day activities of managers place a high value on effective interpersonal communications. Managers provide information, which must be understood, they give commands and instructions, which must be obeyed and learned, and they make efforts to influence and persuade, which must be accepted and acted on. Thus, the way in which managers communicate, both as senders and receivers, is crucial for obtaining effective performance.

Theoretically managers who desire to communicate effectively can use both exposure and feedback to enlarge the area of common understanding, the arena. However, realistically, managers aren't always able to utilize these two methods; their abilities differ in this regard. At least four different managerial styles can be identified:

1. *Type A:* Managers who use neither exposure nor feedback are said to have a Type A style. The unknown region predominates in this style because the manager is unwilling to enlarge the area of his or her own knowledge or the knowledge of others. Such managers exhibit anxiety and hostility and give the appearance of aloofness and coldness toward others. If an organization has a large number of Type A managers in key positions, then we would expect to find poor and ineffective interpersonal communications and a loss of individual creativity. Type A managers often display the characteristics of autocratic leaders.

2. *Type B:* Some managers desire a degree of satisfying relationships with their subordinates, but because of their personalities and attitudes, these managers are unable to open up and express their feelings and sentiments. Consequently, they cannot use exposure, and they must rely on feedback. The facade is the predominant feature of interpersonal relationships when managers overuse feedback to the exclusion of exposure. The subordinates are likely to distrust such managers, because they realize that these managers are holding back their own ideas and opinions. Type B behavior is often displayed by managers who desire to practice some form of permissive leadership.

3. *Type C:* Managers who value their own ideas and opinions but not the ideas and opinions of others use exposure at the expense of feedback. The consequence of this style is the perpetuation and enlargement of the blind spot. Subordinates soon realize that such managers are not particularly interested in communicating, only in telling. Consequently, Type C managers

usually have subordinates who are hostile, insecure, and resentful. Subordinates soon learn that such managers are mainly interested in maintaining their own sense of importance and prestige.

4. *Type D:* The most effective interpersonal communication style is one that uses a balance of exposure and feedback. Managers who are secure in their positions feel free to expose their own feelings and to obtain feedback from others. To the extent that the manager practices Type D behavior successfully, the arena becomes larger, and communication becomes more effective.

To summarize, the primary force in determining the effectiveness of interpersonal communication is interpersonal style, the attitude of managers toward exposure and feedback.

Why Communications Break Down

Why do communications break down? On the surface, the answer is relatively easy. We have identified the elements of communication as the communicator, perception/ interpretation, encoding, the message, the channel, decoding, the receiver, feedback, and noise. If noise exists in any other element in any way, clarity of meaning and understanding are impaired. A manager has no greater responsibility than to develop effective communications. A necessary first step toward developing effective communications is becoming aware of and understanding barriers that impede organizational communication.[36] In this section, we discuss some of the more common barriers: differing frames of reference, selective perception, poor listening skills, value judgments, source credibility, semantic problems, filtering, time pressures, and overload. These sources of noise can exist in both organizational and interpersonal communications.

Differing Frames of Reference

Individuals can interpret the same communication differently, depending on their previous experience. The result is variations between the *encoding* and *decoding* processes. When the processes are alike, communication is most effective. When they are different, communication tends to break down. In interpersonal communication, the arena is relatively small when compared to blind spots, facades, and unknown areas. To the extent that individuals have distinctly different frames of reference, effective communication among those individuals is difficult to achieve.[37]

One result of different frames of reference is that communications become distorted. For example, teenagers have different experiences from their parents'; district sales managers have different perceptions from salespersons'. In an organization, the jobs that people perform create barriers and distortions in communications. A pricing problem is viewed in different ways by the marketing manager and by the plant manager. An efficiency problem in a hospital is viewed by the nursing staff from its frame of reference and its experiences; this may result in interpretations that differ from those of the staff physicians.

Different levels in the organization also have different frames of reference. First-level supervisors have frames of reference that differ in many respects from those of vice presidents because they are in different positions in the organization's structure. As a result, the needs, values, attitudes, and expectations of these two groups differ, and this often produces unintentional distortions of the communications between them. Neither group is wrong or right.

In any situation, individuals choose that part of their own past experiences that relates to their current experiences and is helpful in forming conclusions and judgments. Unfortunately, this may create incongruities in encoding and decoding that result in barriers to effective communication. Ultimately, effective managerial problem solving depends on the manager's adopting the appropriate frame of reference to guide the search for solutions. If the problem is mislabeled or the wrong frame of reference is used, the chances for success diminish.[38]

Selective Perception

Each of us "catalogs" the world in his or her own way. Selective perception occurs when people block out new information, especially when it conflicts with what they believe. Thus, when people receive information, they are apt to hear only those parts that conform to or reaffirm their beliefs. Information that conflicts with preconceived notions is either not processed or is distorted to confirm our preconceptions.

For example, a notice may be sent to all departments that costs must be reduced if the organization is to earn a profit. Such a communication may not achieve its desired effect because it conflicts with the reality of the receivers. Employees may ignore or be amused by the notice in light of the large salaries, travel allowances, and expense accounts of some managers. Whether these expenditures are justified is irrelevant; what is important is that such preconceptions result in a breakdown in communication.

Finally, selective perception results in **stereotyping.** When an individual has preconceived ideas about other people and refuses to discriminate between individual behaviors, that person is applying selective perception to relationships with other people. Stereotyping is a barrier to communication because those who stereotype others use selective perception in their communications and tend to hear only those things that confirm their stereotyped images. For example, some managers stereotype union stewards, some men stereotype successful females, and some women stereotype aggressive men.

Poor Listening Skills

Listening should consume about half the time that a superior and subordinate spend together; it doesn't, because one or both persons fail to listen.[39] For example, a meeting between a boss and employee might go something like this: "Boss, I'm really having a problem finishing the report." "Is that so, Bob? Well, sit down a minute and let me hear about it." However, before Bob can even start his story, the boss begins to cite his current problem. "I've got to do something about the production unit. It is producing at 15 percent below standard rate. I am really on the carpet with the chief." As the boss finishes, he says: "Sorry, Bob, I've got a meeting to attend, so come on back tomorrow, and we can get to your problem." Bob leaves completely frustrated, his problem still on his mind and no one to talk to about a solution.

The boss simply failed to listen. He heard what Bob said, but he really wasn't listening. Failing to listen may result from a host of personal habits. We speak at rates of 100 to 200 words a minute, read at two or three times our speaking rate, and think several times faster than we read. As a result, a listener can move through a discussion much faster than can a speaker. Because of the speed involved, we typically develop poor listening habits. Bad listening habits are of particular interest in work settings. For example, if either a manager or a subordinate fails to listen to the other, the objectives of the discussion, feedback session, or job instruction are not accomplished.

Value Judgments

In every communication situation, receivers make value judgments by assigning an overall worth to a message prior to receiving the entire communication. Such value judgments may be based on the receiver's evaluation of the communicator, the receiver's previous experiences with the communicator, or the message's anticipated meaning. Thus, a hospital administrator may pay little attention to a memorandum from a nursing-team leader because "she's always complaining about something." An employee may consider a merit evaluation meeting with the supervisor as "going through the motions," because the employee perceives the supervisor as being concerned about administrative matters to the exclusion of performance.

Source Credibility

Source credibility refers to the trust, confidence, and faith that the receiver has in the words and actions of the communicator. The level of credibility that the receiver assigns to the communicator directly affects how the receiver views and reacts to the words, ideas, and actions of the communicator.

Thus, how subordinates view a communication from their manager is affected by their evaluations of the manager. The degree of credibility they attach to the communication is heavily influenced by their previous experiences with the manager. Hospital medical staff members who view the hospital administrator as less than honest, manipulative, and not to be trusted are apt to assign negative motives to any communication from the administrator. Union leaders who view managers as exploiters, and managers who view union leaders as inherent enemies, are likely to engage in little real communication.

In one incident involving source credibility, nutrition experts issued a message that pesticide residue on fresh fruits (especially apples) put children at increased risk of cancer.[40] The reaction to the message was alarm. Was this an overreaction? The National Defense Council, which issued the warning, is a litigation group, not a scientific organization. Even the council believes that people overreacted. How credible is the council? The US Environmental Protection Agency believes that the council's warning was just that—a warning. However, when the health of children is mentioned, the credibility of the source is usually not the first area of concern.

Semantic Problems

Communication is the transmission of information and understanding through the use of common symbols. Actually, we cannot transmit understanding. We can transmit only information in the form of words, which are the common symbols. Unfortunately, the same words may mean entirely different things to different people. The understanding is in the receiver, not in the words. Therefore, managers must pay careful attention to how they describe, both in verbal communication and in written communication, desired actions they want to see take place.[41]

When a plant manager announces that a budget increase is necessary for the growth of the plant, the manager may have in mind the necessity for new equipment, an expanded parts inventory, and more personnel. To the existing personnel, however, growth may be perceived as excess funds that can be used for wage and salary increases.

Again, because different groups use words differently, communication can often be impeded. This is especially true with abstract or technical terms and phrases. "Cost–benefit study" would have meaning to persons involved in the administration of the hospital but probably would mean very little to the staff physicians; in fact, it might even carry a negative meaning to the latter. Such concepts as trusts, profits, and Treasury bills may have concrete meaning to bank executives but little or no meaning to bank tellers. Because words mean different things to different people, it is possible for a communicator to speak the same language as a receiver but still not transmit understanding.

In some cultures, saying no is not acceptable. Koreans are taught not to say no. Chinese trade negotiators avoid saying no directly. They say "it is possible." In Japan, ways to avoid saying no include silence, counterquestions, changing the subject, or delaying answers.

Occupational, professional, and social groups often develop words and phrases that have meaning only to group members. Such special language can serve many useful purposes. It can provide group members with feelings of belonging, cohesiveness, and (in many cases) self-esteem. It also can facilitate effective communication within the group. The use of in-group language can, however, result in severe semantic problems and communication breakdowns when outsiders or other groups are involved. Technical and staff groups often use such language in an organization not for the purpose of transmitting information and understanding but rather to communicate a mystique about the group or its function.

Filtering

Filtering is a common occurrence in upward communication in organizations. It amounts to manipulating information so that the information is perceived as positive by the receiver. Subordinates cover up unfavorable information in messages to their superiors. The reason for such filtering should be clear. Upward communications carry control information to management. Management makes merit evaluations, grants salary increases, and promotes individuals based on what it receives by way of the upward channel. The temptation to filter is likely to be strong at every level in the organization.

The design of the organization determines the extent to which information can be filtered. An organizational design with many levels of management (a tall organization) experiences more information filtration than one with fewer levels (a flat organization). The reason is fairly simple: The more levels through which upward communications must flow, the greater is the opportunity for each successive layer of management to take out what it does not want the next level to know. An advantage of flat organizational designs is that they minimize the problem of filtration.

Time Pressures

The pressure of time is an important barrier to communication. An obvious problem is that managers do not have the time to communicate frequently with every subordinate. Time pressures can often lead to serious problems. *Short-circuiting* is a failure of the formally prescribed communications system that often results from time pressures. What it means simply is that someone who normally would be included has been left out of the formal channel of communication.

For example, suppose that a salesperson who needs a rush order for a very important customer goes directly to the production manager with the request, since the production manager owes the salesperson a favor. Other members of the salesforce get word of this and become upset over this preferential treatment and report it to the sales manager. Obviously, the sales manager would know nothing of the deal, since the sales manager has been short-circuited.

In some cases, going through formal channels is extremely costly or impossible from a practical standpoint. Consider the impact on a hospital patient if a nurse had to report a malfunction in some critical life-support equipment in an intensive care unit to the nursing-team leader, who in turn had to report it to the hospital engineer, who then would instruct a staff engineer to make the repair.

Communication Overload

One of the vital tasks performed by a manager is decision making. One of the necessary ingredients for effective decisions is information. The last decade has been described as the Information Era, or the Age of Information. Because of the advances in communication technology, difficulties may arise, not from the absence of information but from excessive information. Managers are often deluged by information and data. As a result, they cannot absorb or adequately respond to all of the messages directed to them. They screen out the majority of messages, which in effect means that these messages are never decoded. Thus, the area of organizational communication is one in which more is not always better.[42] Rather, the goal of organizations should be to implement communication systems that ensure that the proper information flows to those who need it and not to those who don't.[43]

The barriers to communication discussed here, though common, are by no means the only ones that exist. Upon examining these barriers, it is clear that they are either *within individuals* (e.g., frame of reference, value judgments) or *within organizations* (e.g., in-group language, filtering). This point is important because *attempts to improve communications must focus on changing people and/or changing the organization structure.*[44]

Improving Communication in Organizations

Managers striving to become better communicators have two separate tasks. First, they must improve their messages—the information they wish to transmit. Second, they must improve their own understanding of what other people are trying to communicate to them. They must become better encoders and decoders; *they must strive not only to be understood but also to understand.* Techniques for improving communication are following up, regulating information flow, utilizing feedback, empathy, simplifying language, listening effectively, and utilizing the grapevine.

Following Up

Following up involves assuming that you may have been misunderstood and, whenever possible, attempting to determine whether your intended meaning was actually received. As we have seen, meaning is in the mind of the receiver. An accounting unit leader in a government office forwards notices of openings in other agencies to the accounting staff members. Although this may be understood among longtime employees as a friendly gesture, a new employee might interpret it as a negative evaluation of performance and a suggestion to leave.

Regulating Information Flow

Regulating the flow of communications ensures an optimum flow of information to managers, thereby eliminating the barrier of communication overload. Both the quality and quantity of communications are controlled. The idea is based on the *exception principle* of management, which states that only significant deviations from policies and procedures should be brought to the attention of managers. In terms of formal communication, then, managers should be communicated with only on matters of exceptions and not for the sake of communication.

Certain types of organizational designs are more amenable to this principle than are other types. Certainly, in neoclassical organization, with its emphasis on free-flowing communication, the principle would not apply. However, classical organizations would find the principle useful.

Utilizing Feedback

Feedback is an important element in effective two-way communication. It provides a channel for receiver response, enabling the communicator to determine whether the message has been received and has produced the intended response.

In face-to-face communication, direct feedback is possible. In downward communication, however, inaccuracies often occur because of insufficient opportunity for feedback from receivers. Thus, a memorandum addressing an important policy statement may be distributed to all employees, but this does not guarantee that communication has occurred. One might expect that feedback in the form of upward communication would be encouraged more in neoclassical organizations, but the mechanisms discussed earlier that can be utilized to encourage upward communication are found in many different organizational designs. A healthy organization needs effective upward communication if its downward communication is to have any chance of being effective. Table 14–1 presents some of the major characteristics of effective and ineffective feedback.

All too often, managers perceive conversations with their employees to be more frequent than do their subordinates.[45] A poll by the American Productivity and Quality Center pointed out the need for more feedback. More than 85 percent of workers rated their bosses good or excellent when it came to giving employees autonomy on the job, but only 32.8 percent said their bosses were good to excellent about giving them regular feedback. An employee with no knowledge about how she is doing tends to become tentative, uncertain, and anxious about the job.[46]

Empathy

Empathy is the ability to put oneself in the other person's role and to assume the viewpoints and emotions of that person. This ability involves being receiver oriented rather than communicator oriented. The form of a communication should depend largely on what is known about the receivers. Empathy requires communicators to place themselves in the receivers' positions for the purpose of anticipating how the message is likely to be decoded.

It is vital that a manager understand and appreciate the process of decoding. Decoding involves perceptions, and the message is filtered through the perceptions of the receiver. For vice presidents to communicate effectively with supervisors, for faculty to communicate effectively with students, and for government administrators to communicate effectively with minority groups, empathy is often an important ingredient. Empathy can reduce many of the barriers to effective communication discussed earlier. The greater the gap between the experiences and background of the

---

TABLE 14–1   Characteristics of Effective and Ineffective Feedback

Feedback from management is ineffective if it does not promote improved employee performance.

Effective Feedback	Ineffective Feedback
1. Intended to help the employee	1. Intended to belittle the employee
2. Specific	2. General
3. Descriptive	3. Judgmental
4. Useful	4. Inappropriate
5. Timely	5. Untimely
6. Willingly heard by employee	6. Makes the employee defensive
7. Clear	7. Not understandable
8. Valid	8. Inaccurate

Source: F Luthans and M J Martinko, *The Practice of Supervision and Management* (New York: McGraw-Hill, 1979), p. 183.

communicator and the receiver, the greater is the effort that must be made to find a common ground of understanding—ground on which there are overlapping fields of experience.

Simplifying Language

Complex language has been identified as a major barrier to effective communication. Students often suffer when their instructors use technical jargon that transforms simple concepts into complex puzzles.

Colleges and universities are not the only places, however, where complex language is used. Government agencies also are known for their often incomprehensible communications. We have already noted instances in which professional people attempt to use their in-group language in communicating with individuals outside their group. Managers must remember that effective communication involves transmitting understanding. If the receiver does not understand, then there has been no communication. In fact, techniques discussed in this section have as their sole purpose the promotion of understanding.

Effective Listening

Just listening is not enough; one must listen with understanding. Can managers develop listening skills? Numerous pointers for effective listening are useful in organizational settings. For example, one writer cites the "Ten Commandments for Good Listening": stop talking, put the speaker at ease, show the speaker you want to listen, remove distractions, empathize with the speaker, be patient, hold your temper, go easy on argument and criticism, ask questions, and stop talking. Note that "stop talking" is both the first and last commandment.[47]

Such lists of guidelines can be useful for managers. However, more important than these lists is the *decision to listen*. The preceding guidelines are useless unless the manager makes the conscious decision to listen. The realization that effective communication involves being understood as well as understanding probably is far more important than lists of guidelines. Then and only then can such guidelines become useful.

Utilizing the Grapevine: Informal Communication Systems

The **grapevine** is an important informal communication channel that exists in all organizations. It basically serves as a bypassing mechanism and is often faster than the formal system it bypasses. If the formal organization is the skeleton of the company, the grapevine or informal channel can be viewed as the central nervous system.[48] In most cases, managers can count on the fact that the grapevine is fast, efficient, and accurate and fulfills people's need to communicate. Because it is flexible and because it usually involves face-to-face communication, the grapevine is capable of transmitting information rapidly. Through the grapevine, the resignation of an executive may become common knowledge long before it has been officially announced.

For management, the grapevine may frequently be an effective means of communication. It is likely to have a stronger impact on receivers because it is face-to-face and allows for feedback. Because it satisfies many psychological needs, the grapevine will always exist. No manager can do away with it.

If the grapevine is inevitable, managers should seek to utilize it or at least attempt to ensure its accuracy. One way to minimize the undesirable aspects of the grapevine is to improve other forms of communication. For example, companies can publish periodic employee newsletters.[49] If information exists on issues relevant to subordinates, then damaging rumors are less likely to develop.

Several consulting firms work to control or manage rumors, gossip, and grapevine messages. The Chatham Consulting Group of New York works to help firms manage communications. Citibank, American Express, and the New York Stock Exchange use Chatham when they make structural, personnel, and technological changes. The grapevine still exists and is active, but the communication of the changes and how they will occur is managed so that accurate information is sent to employees.[50]

Improving Group Communication through Negotiation

The previous section dealt with means by which managers can improve communication either through improving their own messages or through improving their understanding of what *others* are trying to communicate to them. A widely used yet often unrecognized method of enhancing organizational communication, especially between groups, is the process of negotiation. If done effectively, the negotiation process can be called a collaborative pursuit of joint gains and a collaborative effort to create value where none previously existed.[51]

Negotiation is a task in which two people or groups attempt to make joint decisions regarding the allocation of scarce resources.[52] The process entails having two sides, with differing or conflicting interests, come together to forge an agreement. Everyone is familiar with the importance of bargaining to settle union disputes, formulate trade pacts, handle hostage situations, and reach arms agreements.

Managers in organizations perform the same function on a continuing basis, negotiating with subordinates, superiors, vendors, and customers daily. In fact, any time two or more people share information with the intent of changing the relationship, they are negotiating.[53] For example, departments within an organization compete for new equipment and facilities. Likewise, individuals within a department compete for resources, including personnel and financial capital.

Group Negotiations

The most common form of organizational negotiations occurs between groups. Group negotiations take place whenever the work of one group is dependent on the cooperation and actions of another group over which the first group's manager has no control.[54] Negotiations between marketing and production functions regarding order deliveries, between finance and engineering over research and development funding, and between maintenance and manufacturing over machine maintenance are all examples of group negotiations.

Many managers or groups enter negotiations assuming that what's good for the other side must be bad for them.[55] Further, a myth exists that negotiating will result in a winning and a losing side. In truth, this is usually not the case. Negotiations differ from compromise in that the only really successful negotiations are those in which all the affected parties walk away feeling they have won.[56] Several tasks and tactics can be undertaken by managers as part of the negotiation process to improve communication between groups and increase the probability of achieving mutually beneficial results.

Prenegotiation Tasks

Understanding the Other Side.   Prior to sitting down and negotiating with other managers or representatives of other groups, managers must thoroughly understand the other side's needs and positions regarding the issues to be resolved.[57] For example, a product manager who desperately wants a customer order filled by manufacturing within the next two weeks should be aware of other obligations currently being placed on manufacturing.

To gain needed information, the manager must ask questions. Although positions are usually clear, underlying interests or problems often are not.[58] A manager's goal should be to come to the negotiations with a full appreciation of the values, beliefs, and wants that drive the other side's actions. By freely exchanging information with the other group and performing as much outside or third-party research as possible, the manager can come prepared for the process. The element of surprise, which can prove to be of value in many business tactics, serves only to delay and hinder the negotiation process.

Knowing All the Options.   Perhaps more important than the accumulation of information is its use in developing, understanding, and evaluating options available to forge agreement between parties to the negotiation process. Although the same issue may be negotiated over and over again, the outcomes may differ depending on the parties involved or the timing of the negotiations.

One instance of a negotiation between two groups in an organization would be the funding of a capital investment. For example, discussions between finance and manufacturing may lead to the funds' becoming available immediately, contingent on manufacturing's formulation of a detailed spending plan. A second outcome may consist of the funds' being allocated over time with the capital investment project being completed on a piecemeal basis. A third possible outcome would be the allocation of a certain percentage of the funding with the remainder coming from the sale of the assets being replaced. The important point is that the greater the number of options that can be identified, the greater is the likelihood that both groups can benefit from the negotiation process.

Negotiation Tactics   A countless number of specific negotiation tactics can be employed by managers involved in the process.[59] Several of the most often used ones are discussed.

- *Good-person/bad-person team.* Anyone who has read a detective story or seen a television police show is familiar with this tactic. The bad-person member of the negotiating group advocates positions so much out of line that whatever the good person says sounds reasonable.
- *The nibble.* This tactic involves getting an additional concession or perk after an agreement has been reached. An example would be the request for a new staff person by a marketing manager after an agreement was reached between his group and another marketing group regarding the division of market research duties.
- *Joint problem solving.* As mentioned previously, a manager should never assume that the more one side wins, the more the other side loses. For instance, can manufacturing provide earlier completion dates on products only if the sales department increases the order size and reduces the order frequency?
- *Power of competition.* Tough negotiators use competition to make opponents think they don't need them. For example, a line manager may use this tactic by threatening that her group will procure computer services outside the organization if the headquarter's staff doesn't comply with demands.
- *Splitting the difference.* This can be a useful technique when two groups come to an impasse. Managers should be careful, however, when the other group offers to split the difference too early. It may mean the other group has already gotten more than it thinks it deserves.

· *Lowballing.* Ridiculously low offers and concessions are often used to lower the other group's expectations. A manager should not let this type of offer lower his expectations or goals; nor should the manager walk out assuming the other group's position is inflexible. The communications process should continue.

Different situations call for different tactics. A manager should be aware of the options available and strive to understand the rationale behind the options.

The Impact of Personalities on the Negotiation Process

As evident in all communication, the process of negotiating is a very people-oriented experience. In addition to understanding the goals, needs, and wants of the other side, the successful negotiator tries to understand the relevant personality traits of the other individuals negotiating.[60] Negotiators come to the bargaining session from different backgrounds; their experiences, like their perspectives, differ. Their propensities to take risks vary, and their personalities and attitudes are quite diverse; all affect behavioral actions.[61] Managers must stop and look beneath the role that the other negotiating party is playing and ask what really motivates the individual(s).[62] Knowledge of these traits allows the manager to "read" and understand the other side—a valuable tool in negotiations.

The Role of Trust in Negotiations

There will be a greater likelihood of a beneficial outcome for the organization if a high degree of trust exists between the groups engaged in the negotiation process. Negotiators tend to regard making statements about their group's needs, wants, and priorities as risky and therefore are willing to make them only if there is mutual trust (i.e., if they believe that the other side is also cooperatively motivated).[63] A high level of trust between the two conflicting parties will lead to greater openness and sharing of information.

Managers tend to expect a little chicanery when they're negotiating.[64] Even relatively cooperative bargainers often inject straw issues or exaggerate the importance of minor problems to gain concessions on what really matters.[65] In nearly all bargaining encounters, a negotiator's key skill is the ability to communicate that she is firm on her (or her group's) position, when in fact, the negotiator is flexible—in short, bluffing about her intentions. However, bluffing does not constitute lying or fraud, and managers should be well aware of the difference.

In addition, a good negotiator will never place the other party in a position in which he can't move without losing face.[66] By offering choices between alternatives (sometimes done by following mild demands with stronger ones), the other side will be more likely to view the process as cooperative and thus be more willing to reach an agreement.

Finally, the negotiation process, if utilized correctly, can be an effective tool in improving communication between groups. Although the material in this chapter has focused on negotiations taking place within an organization, the same principles can be applied to negotiations with external entities.

Summary of Key Points

· The quality of managerial decision making depends in large part on the quality of information available. Communication is the process of achieving common understanding; for managerial purposes, it is undertaken to achieve an effect.

· A message must contain all the facts that communicators deem necessary for the desired effect. If the intended effect is not achieved, communication has not taken place.

· The elements of communication are the communicator, perception/interpretation, encoding, the message, the channel, decoding, the receiver, feedback, and noise. All of these elements must be in harmony if communication is to achieve understanding and effect.

- Nonverbal communication is a part of everyday life. Although in nonverbal communication words are not used, nonverbal signals or cues can be misinterpreted just as easily.
- A crucial factor in determining the effectiveness of communication in organizations is the way in which organizations are structured. Upward, downward, diagonal, and horizontal communication flows are more likely to occur in neoclassical than in classical organization structures. Upward communication channels are vitally important to an organization for they allow for employee input to enter into the decision-making process.
- The extent to which individuals share understanding depends on their use of feedback and exposure. People differ in this regard, with some preferring feedback and others

preferring exposure. A balanced use of both is the most effective approach.

- Numerous barriers exist that contribute to communication breakdowns. Managers must be aware of barriers relevant to their situations. Major barriers are differing frames of reference, selective perception, poor listening skills, value judgments, source credibility, semantic problems, filtering, time pressures, and communication overload.
- Improving communication in organizations involves following up, regulating information flow, utilizing feedback, empathy, simplifying language, listening effectively, and utilizing the informal communication system (the grapevine).
- Negotiation entails having two sides (usually groups) come together to forge an agreement. To be effective, managers involved in the negotiation process must know all the available options, understand and trust the other side, and be willing to share information.

Discussion and Review Questions

1. What types of barriers to communication exist in a classroom? How can they be overcome?

2. As American corporations hire increasing numbers of immigrants, what role will the assessment of nonverbal communication play in interviewing job candidates?

3. Based on your own experience, which element of communication has most often been the cause of your failures to communicate? How can you improve your communication effectiveness?

4. Are you a Type A, B, C, or D person when you engage in interpersonal communications? Are you satisfied to be what you think you are? Why? If not, how could you change?

5. How would you feed back information to employees about their performance?

6. Why is source credibility such an important trait for a manager to possess? How can one increase his own source credibility?

7. Describe a situation in which you heard a rumor through a grapevine. Did the rumor turn out to be true?

8. Why is accuracy of lateral information so important to employees working in different units?

9. Describe a situation in which you, as an individual or member of a group, were involved in a negotiation process. Did you consider the outcome of the process satisfactory to both sides? Why or why not?

10. How could a lack of trust between two departments in an organization lead to a breakdown in negotiations? Provide an example to back up your answer.

CASE 14–1
DO YOU KNOW WHAT I LIKE ABOUT YOU?

Jim McCabe, only 33, is a successful bloodstock agent in the highly volatile and competitive thoroughbred horse industry. He locates thoroughbred buyers and sellers for his clients, as well as breeding rights for stallions and mares. It is a complicated and risky business. His knowledge of thoroughbred horses and their bloodlines, along with much hard work, has enabled him to achieve success.

Educated in the physical sciences (master's degree), McCabe chose the thoroughbred industry because of his love of

horses. His firm, which he began alone five years ago, now employs five other agents, three researchers whose task it is to research thoroughbred bloodlines, three secretaries, an office manager, and me. My title, when I was hired four months ago, was assistant office manager, but no one ever told me what I was supposed to do. For a part-time job while in college, the pay is good, and I'm learning a great deal about a business I knew nothing about previously. In addition, there is always some kind of excitement around the office.

One day I stood by the door of McCabe's office. He was on the phone, and before I could knock, he motioned for me to come in and sit down. Every inch of his desk was covered by reports, memos, horse-sale catalogs, telephone messages, and racing results. Other reminders on bits of paper were taped to the wall, and a "to do" list with at least 10 entries on it was taped to the base of the telephone. Evidently these were things that he had to do immediately. While talking on the phone, he added another item to this list.

As he continued the phone conversation, he was shaking his head and signing letters at the same time. Finally, he put his hand over the phone and said to me, "This is Robinson in Florida on that two-year-old filly deal. All the tests on her leg are not in yet, but he insists on giving me every detail on the entire test procedure. The guy is going to drive me nuts."

Turning his attention back to the phone he removed his hand and resumed talking. "Right, Robbie, OK . . . Great . . . OK . . . Sure . . . Call me back on that . . . Terrific . . . 'Bye."

He hung up the phone with a sigh of relief and looked at me. "Do you know what I like about you, Tinsley?" I didn't have time to answer, nor did he, because the phone rang again. "Yeah . . . Fine . . . Terrific . . . Count me in . . . 'Bye."

At this point, his secretary looked in and said, "John Towne of Winthrop Farms is on hold. It sounds urgent."

McCabe shook his head again and went back to the telephone. After a few minutes of conversation, he put his hand over the receiver and called to his secretary. "Get Johnson and Burke in here, fast." Johnson was the office manager, and Burke was an agent. They arrived as he hung up the phone.

"Burke," he said, "you know that deal you put together for the syndication of that three-year-old, Ol' Blue? Well, they don't like it. Put this information into it and tell me what effect the changes will have on us. When you get it finished, bring it to me so I can call Towne back." Burke left.

"Johnson, I want all of the training fees, jockey expenses, and all other expenses on that horse. Don't give them to me by the month like you did last time. I need totals in *all* categories; and for crying out loud, this time break out the 'other' category a little better. I looked real good last week when Towne asked me what the $6,300 in 'other expenses' was for. I want all the information at my fingertips in case we've got to go to war with these people." Johnson left.

"Now, Tinsley, what did you need me for?"

"Just sign this bill of sale," I said. "No reason to spend a lot of time on it. It's for the sale of that yearling you asked me to take care of."

"That's what I like about you, Tinsley," he said as he leaned back in his chair and signed the bill of sale. "When I give you a job, you listen. Then you do it right the first time and tell me when it's done. You don't tell me how you did it, the problems you're having doing it, who you met while doing it, and every other Mickey Mouse detail. If the rest of the people around here had that ability, I might be able to get some work done. I think I got more work done five years ago when I had nobody working for me."

As I left his office, I didn't have time to thank him, because the phone began ringing.

Questions for Analysis

1. What is your impression of McCabe?

2. What is your opinion of his communications to the other employees of the firm?

3. What might be the reasons for his demands on employees?

4. Could this influence the effectiveness of the organization? In what ways?

Source: W V Haney, *Communication and Interpersonal Relations: Text and Cases* (Burr Ridge, IL: Richard D. Irwin, 1979), pp. 250–51.

EXPERIENTIAL EXERCISE
PERCEPTUAL DIFFERENCES

Purpose

The purpose of this exercise is to illustrate how people perceive the same situation differently through the process of selective perception.

The Exercise in Class

The instructor will divide the class into groups of four students each. Each group should then complete the following steps:

1. As individuals, complete the following quiz. Do not talk to your group members until everyone in the class has finished.

2. Your instructor will provide the answers to the 15 questions. Score your responses.

3. As a group, discuss your members' responses. Focus your discussion on the following questions:

    a. Why did perceptions differ across members? What factors could account for these differences?

b. Many people don't perform very well with this quiz. Why? What other factors beyond selective perception can adversely affect performance?

Quiz: The robbery.   The lights in a store had just been turned off by a businessman when a man appeared and demanded money. The owner opened a cash register. The contents of the cash register were scooped up, and the man sped away. A member of the police force was notified promptly.

Answer the following questions about the story by circling T *for true,* F *for false, or* ? *for unknown.*

1. Man appeared after the owner turned off his store lights.   T   F   ?

2. The robber was a man.   T   F   ?

3. The man who appeared did not demand money.   T   F   ?

4. The man who opened the cash register was the owner.   T   F   ?

5. The store owner scooped up the contents of the cash register and ran away.   T   F   ?

6. Someone opened a cash register.   T   F   ?

7. After the man who demanded money scooped up the contents of the cash register, he ran away.   T   F   ?

8. While the cash register contained money, the story does not state how much.   T   F   ?

9. The robber demanded money of the owner.   T   F   ?

10. A businessman had just turned off the lights when a man appeared in the store.   T   F   ?

11. It was broad daylight when the man appeared.   T   F   ?

12. The man who appeared opened the cash register.   T   F   ?

13. No one demanded money.   T   F   ?

14. The story concerns a series of events in which only three persons are referred to: the owner of the store, a man who demanded money, and a member of the police force.   T   F   ?

15. The following events occurred: Someone demanded money, a cash register was opened, its contents were scooped up, and a man dashed out of the store.   T   F   ?

A Learning Message

This exercise aptly demonstrates the wide variety of perceptual differences among people when considering a situation where little factual information is provided. The exercise should also indicate that most people selectively perceive the information they are comfortable with in analyzing a situation. Many will also subconsciously fill in gaps of information with assumptions they suppose are facts.

Notes

1. Chris Argyris, "Good Communication That Blocks Learning," *Harvard Business Review,* July–August 1994, pp. 77–85.

2. Dean Takabashi, "Why Hot Gadgets Won't Be in Santa's Sack," *The Wall Street Journal,* November 19, 1996, pp. B1 and B10.

3. Raymond Burke, "Virtual Shopping: Breakthrough in Marketing Research," *Harvard Business Review,* March–April 1996, pp. 120–31.

4. "Four Portraits with a Message," *The Wall Street Journal,* March 15, 1989, p. B1.

5. Andrew Tanzer, "Stepping-Stones to a New China?" *Forbes,* January 27, 1997, pp. 78–82.

6. The most widely used contemporary model of the process of communication has evolved mainly from the work of Shannan and Weaver, and Schramm. See Claude Shannan and Warren Weaver, *The Mathematical Theory of Communication* (Urbana: University of Illinois Press, 1948); Wilbur Schramm, "How Communication Works," in Wilbur Schramm, ed., *The Process and Effects of Mass Communication* (Urbana: University of Illinois Press, 1953), pp. 3–76.

7. Andrew D Wolvin and Caroline G Coakley, *Listening* (Dubuque, IA: Wm C Brown, 1985), p. 6.

8. Karl Weick, "How Small Things Lead to Disaster: The Tenerife Air Tragedy," *Research Beat,* Spring 1990, pp. 5–6.

9. For a discussion of the elements that a message needs in order to be effective, see Florence B Grunkemeyer, "Using C-Qualities in Communication," *Journal of Education for Business,* March–April 1993, pp. 247–51.

10. T L Griffith and G B Northcraft, "Distinguishing between the Forest and the Trees: Media, Features, and Methodology in Electronic Communication Research," *Organization Science,* 1994, pp. 272–85.

11. For a detailed review of research associated with nonverbal communication, see B M DePaulo, "Nonverbal Behavior and Self-Presentation," *Psychological Bulletin* 11 (1992), pp. 203–43.

12. Helen Deresky, *International Management* (New York: Harper Collins, 1994), pp. 441–42.

13. Ibid.

14. Pauline E Henderson, "Communication without Words," *Personnel Journal,* January 1989, pp. 22–29.

15. Tricia S Jones and Martin S Remland, "Nonverbal Communication and Conflict Escalation: An Attribution-Based Model," *The International Journal of Conflict Management,* April 1993, pp. 405–27.

16. Sherry Holiday and W Timothy Coombs, "Communicating Visions: An Exploration of the Role of Delivery in the Creation of Leader Charisma," *Management Communication Quarterly,* May 1993, pp. 405–27.

17. For an in-depth discussion of this topic, see Elmore R Alexander III, Larry E Penley, and I Edward Jernigan, "The Relationship of Basic Decoding Skills to Managerial Effectiveness," *Management Communication Quarterly,* August 1992, pp. 58–73.

18. The classic experiment comparing one-way and two-way communication is described in Harold J Leavitt and R A H Mueller, "Some Effects of Feedback on Communications," *Human Relations,* 1951, pp. 401–10. Also see Harold J Leavitt, *Managerial Psychology* (Chicago: University of Chicago Press, 1978).

19. R W Rasberry and L L Lindsay, *Effective Managerial Communication* (Boston: Wadsworth, 1994).

20. Christine Nolan, "Conflict Resolution: Guiding Members toward Agreement," *Association Management,* September 1993, pp. 32–37.

21. Michael P Thompson, "The Skills of Inquiry and Advocacy: Why Managers Need Both," *Management Communication Quarterly,* August 1993, pp. 32–37.

22. For a discussion on this topic, see Phillip G Clampitt and Cal W Downs, "Employee Perceptions of the Relationship between Communication and Productivity: A Field Study," *The Journal of Business Communication* 30 (1993), pp. 5–27; and Donald L Harville, "Person/Job Fit Model of Communication Apprehension in Organizations," *Management Communication Quarterly,* November 1992, pp. 150–65.

23. Deborah Spar and Jeffrey J Bussgang, "The Net," *Harvard Business Review,* May–June 1996, pp. 125–33.

24. Laurence A Canter and Martha S Siegel, *How to Make a Fortune on the Information Superhighway* (New York: Harper Collins, 1994), pp. 7–10.

25. Thomas A Stewart, "Managing in a Wired Company," *Fortune,* 1994, pp. 44–56.

26. "Beyond Bean-Counting," *Business Week,* October 28, 1996, pp. 130–32.

27. Peter Huaber, "Cyberpower," *Forbes,* December 2, 1996, pp. 142–47.

28. Oscar Suris, "Behind the Wheel," *The Wall Street Journal,* November 18, 1996, p. R14.

29. Dean Takahashi, "Road Warrior," *The Wall Street Journal,* November 18, 1996, pp. R27, R31.

30. James L Gibson, John M Ivancevich, and James H Donnelly, *Organizations: Behavior, Structure, Processes* (Burr Ridge: Richard D Irwin, 1997), p. 413–14.

31. Ibid.

32. John M Ivancevich and James H Donnelly, Jr., "A Study of Role Clarity and Need for Clarity in Three Occupational Groups," *Academy of Management Journal,* March 1974, pp. 28–36.

33. For a discussion of how Japanese organizations actively encourage employee communication, see M Erez, "Interpersonal Communication Systems in Organizations, and Their Relationship to Cultural Values, Productivity, and Innovation: The Case of Japanese Corporations," *Applied Psychology: An International Review,* 1992, pp. 43–64.

34. Valorie A McClelland and Richard E Wilmot, "Improve Lateral Communication," *Personnel Journal,* August 1990, pp. 32–38.

35. The discussion in this section is based on J Hall, "Communication Revisited," *California Management Review,* Fall 1973, pp. 56–67.

36. John Jensen, "Ten Days to Better Communication," *Executive Female,* March–April 1993, pp. 70–71.

37. For a related study, see J D Hatfield and R C Huseman, "Perceptual Congruence about Communication as Related to Satisfaction: Moderating Effects of Individual Characteristics," *Academy of Management Journal,* June 1982, pp. 349–58.

38. F W Nickols, "How to Figure Out What to Do," *Training,* August 1991, pp. 31–34, 39.

39. George D. Webster, "Internal Communication Issues," *Association Management,* May 1995, pp. 150–53.

40. Barbara Rosenvicz, "Pesticide Risk from Apples: Who's Right?" *The Wall Street Journal,* March 10, 1989, pp. B1, B3.

41. For a discussion on the influence that figures of speech have on receivers, see Robert J Marshak, "Managing the Metaphors of Change," *Organizational Dynamics,* Summer 1993, pp. 44–55.

42. Charles A O'Reilly III, "Individuals and Information Overload in Organizations: Is More Necessarily Better?" *Academy of Management Journal,* December 1980, pp. 684–96.

43. Robert Pelley, "The Shared Vision," *Management Review,* March 1993, p. 63.

44. Bill Richards, "The Business Plan," *The Wall Street Journal,* November 18, 1996, p. R10, R16.

45. Victor J Callan, "Subordinate-Manager Communication in Different Sex Dyads: Consequences for Job Satisfaction," *Journal of Occupational and Organizational Psychology,* 1993, pp. 13–27.

46. "Workers Empowered, Feedback Scares," *Personnel: HR Focus,* December 1990, p. 14.

47. Keith Davis, *Human Behavior at Work* (New York: McGraw-Hill, 1985), p. 387.

48. For a discussion on informal communication systems, see David Krackhardt and Jeffrey R Hanson, "Informal Networks: The Company behind the Chart," *Harvard Business Review,* July–August 1993, pp. 104–11.

49. J Mishra, "Managing the Grapevine," *Public Personnel Management,* Summer 1990, pp. 213–28.

50. "Stopping Those Nasty Rumors," *Personnel: HR Focus,* November 1990, p. 22.

51. T Anderson, "Step into My Parlor: A Survey of Strategies and Techniques for Effective Negotiation," *Business Horizons,* May–June 1992, pp. 71–76.

52. Leigh Thompson, "The Impact of Negotiation on Intergroup Relations," *Journal of Experimental Social Psychology,* 1993, pp. 304–25.

53. Jack W Kane, "Don't Fight—Negotiate," *Association Management,* September 1993, pp. 38–43.

54. Adam M Brandenburger and Barry J Nalebuff, *Co-Opetition* (New York: Carrency-Doubleday, 1996).

55. Dorian Burden, "Avoid This Negotiating Pitfall," *Executive Female,* January–February 1993, p. 14.

56. M Zetlin, "The Art of Negotiating," *Success!,* June 1986, pp. 34–39.

57. R Dawson, "Resolving Angry Disagreements," *Supervisory Management,* January 1989, pp. 13–16.

58. Harry J Sapienza and M Audrey Korsgaard, "Procedural Justice in Entrepreneur-Investor Relations," *Academy of Management Journal,* June 1996, pp. 544–78.

59. Zetlin, "Art of Negotiating."

60. James Musgrave and Michael Arness, *Relationship Dynamics* (New York: Free Press, 1996).

61. J A Wall, Jr., and M W Blum, "Negotiations," *Journal of Management,* 1991, pp. 273–303.

62. G Dangot-Simpkin, "Eight Attitudes to Develop to Hone Your Negotiating Skills," *Supervisory Management,* February 1992, p. 10.

63. Frederick F Reichheld and Thomas Teal, *The Loyalty Effect* (Boston: Harvard Business Press, 1996).

64. J D O'Brien, "Negotiating with Peers: Consensus Not Power," *Supervisory Management,* June 1992, p. 4.

65. Michael J Marquadt, *Building the Learning Organization* (New York: McGraw-Hill, 1996).

66. Valerie Frazee, "Keeping Up on Chinese Culture," *Global Workforce,* October 1996, pp. 16–17.

15   HUMAN RESOURCE MANAGEMENT

Chapter Learning Objectives

After completing Chapter 15, you should be able to:

- **Define** human resource management (HRM).
- **Describe** the activities conducted by various divisions of a human resource department: employment, training and development, wage and salary management, employee benefits and services, and labor relations.
- **Discuss** what is meant by sexual harassment.
- **Compare** HRM activities in large and small business organizations.
- **Identify** the impact that laws and executive orders have had on the management of human resources.

Managing Culturally Diverse Employees

More and more companies are searching for ways to train, educate, and convince employees that cultural diversity is a positive factor. However, as more companies experiment with ways to train people, they are finding out that the results of such training are difficult to measure. Some even believe that there are absolutely no results occurring because of training.

There are, however, a handful of companies that may just be on the right track. These firms are linking managers' pay to diversity effort or are using a mentoring pair program. By holding managers accountable, a serious message is being sent through the firm. At Colgate-Palmolive about 550 managers are in the pay–diversity plan. Two-thirds of managers' annual award is based on financial results. One-third is based on specific projects such as training more women and minorities for promotions, and assigning more women and minorities to more significant jobs. The manager who shows progress on these projects is rewarded monetarily.

At Corning, Inc., the ability to manage culturally diverse employees (as well as effectiveness in doing so) is one of the factors considered in the annual performance reviews of managers. Corning looks at whether minorities and women were adequately considered when filling job openings, and when promotions and salary increases were being decided. The firm also reviews the manager's complaint file and examines the type and source of complaints about the manager.

At Quaker Oats, each facility has a different set of diversity issues and goals. Recruitment, diversity, awareness training, and upward-mobility programs at each facility are monitored. Managers are asked to outline their specific diversity programs annually. These outlines are then evaluated at the end of the review period, and the results are weighed in making merit-based compensation decisions.

At St. Louis, Missouri-based Monsanto, a "consulting pairs" program is used. The firm trains facilitators who will help employees in conflict with one another solve their problems. The facilitators are trained in dealing with ethnic, gender, racial, and other types of conflict. The facilitator helps the people in conflict with one another improve their communication and awareness skills. Monsanto believes that as the workforce becomes more diverse, there is likely to be conflict, but it can be resolved if handled well. The "consulting pairs" program has served Monsanto well in terms of the reduced turnover of women and minorities. The "consulting pairs" approach has also been used in sexual harassment situations.

Since the workforce of the future will include more people of color, more women, more new immigrants, and more special-needs employees, the need to use new management approaches is obvious. Experimentation is likely to continue in managing cultural diversity. This chapter will illustrate progressive, as well as traditional, steps used to manage human resources.

Sources: Ron Stodghill II, "Get Serious about Diversity Training," *Business Week,* November 25, 1996, p. 39; J Laabs, "Employees, Managing Conflict and Diversity," *Personnel Journal,* December 1993, pp. 30–36; D T Hall and V A Parker, "The Role of Workplace Flexibility in Managing Diversity," *Organizational Dynamics,* 1993, pp. 5–18; S Overman, "A Measure of Success," *HR Magazine,* December 1992, pp. 38–40.

To meet the challenges of managing, managers must understand the potential of human resources and then secure, retain, and develop these resources. This requirement is the foundation of human resource management (HRM).

The management of any organizational unit or department—marketing, finance, accounting, or production—involves the accomplishment of objectives through use of the skills and talents of people. Thus, HRM is considered both a line-management responsibility and a staff function.[1]

In organizations of any size, human resources must be recruited, compensated, developed, and motivated.[2] The small organization typically cannot afford to have a separate HRM (sometimes called personnel or industrial relations) department that continually follows the progress of individuals and reviews the accomplishment of goals.[3] Instead, each manager is responsible for using the skills and talents of employees. Larger firms usually have an HRM department that can be a source of help to line managers. In either case, much of the work in recruitment, compensation, and performance appraisal must be finalized and implemented by managers.

Human Resource Management Function

The role of HRM in an organization's strategic management planning is extremely important in helping firms find ways to compete effectively at home and internationally. Chapter 1 described the competitive situation facing US companies and industries. A Gallup survey of executive perceptions identified the critical competitive issues facing US business. Of the eight issues on which the executives were questioned, they cited service and product quality and productivity as the most critical to their companies.[4] Quality and productivity constitute the core of managing work, organizations, people, and operations because they are critical to costs, sales, competitiveness, and profitability.

Survey takers also asked the executives how quality and productivity could be improved in organizations. The executives preferred human resource methods, such as employee motivation programs, employee training and education, and changing the organization's culture, rather than technology-oriented solutions.

The strategic importance of effective human resource management is likely to become more recognized. Improvements in the firm's competitive position can occur only if HRM is elevated and remains a crucial area in the strategic planning and implementation of plans. The expert in HRM has become a partner in helping shape strategy and implementing plans. Digital Equipment Corporation, General Electric Company, IBM, Revco, Liz Claiborne, Hewlett-Packard Company, Avon Products, and J. C. Penney Company are a few of the firms that have announced that HRM specialists will play an expanded role in their strategic planning.

Hallmark Cards is a firm that regularly accomplishes human resource objectives. It has gained a reputation for being a super company to work for because it clearly demonstrates that it values its employees. Because of its employee-friendly reputation, most individuals join the firm and never want to leave. The accompanying Management Focus illustrates only a small sample of some of the employee-friendly practices of Hallmark.

Human resource management can be defined as the process of accomplishing organizational objectives by acquiring, retaining, terminating, developing, and properly using the human resources in an organization. Accomplishing objectives is a major part of any form of management. Unless objectives are regularly accomplished, the organization ceases to exist.

The acquisition of skilled, talented, and motivated employees is an important part of HRM. The acquisition phase involves recruiting, screening, selecting, and placing personnel. Retaining competent individuals is also important to any organization. If qualified individuals regularly leave a company, it becomes necessary to continually seek new personnel, which costs money and time. The opposite of retention is, of course, termination, an unpleasant part of any manager's job. Employees occasionally must be terminated for breaking rules or failing to perform adequately, or because of job cutbacks. Procedures for terminations are usually specified by an HRM staff expert or are included in a labor contract.

Developing human resources involves training, educating, appraising, and preparing personnel for present or future jobs. These activities are important for the economic and psychological growth of employees. The need for personal growth cannot be satisfied in an organization that does not have an active employee development program.

The proper use of people involves understanding both individual and organizational needs so that the full potential of human resources can be utilized. This part of

Management Focus

Hallmark

Hallmark Cards Inc. is the world's largest greeting card company, producing 11 million greeting cards and 1.5 million other personal communications products each day and boasting annual sales of $3.8 million. The company readily admits to the strength behind its prominence in the global marketplace. Its corporate credo states: The people of Hallmark are the company's most valuable resource. As a result, the Kansas City, Missouri-based employer has an 87-year history of providing the best—from birthday cards to employee benefits.

One of the best ways Hallmark expresses its commitment to employees is through an employee profit-sharing and ownership plan. Founder Joyce C Hall began the plan in 1956 based on his philosophy that the company should share its profits with employees. Today, employees own one-third of Hallmark's stock, worth more than $20 billion in 1996.

Although the profit-sharing plan stands as the cornerstone of Hallmark's compensation and benefits package, it's only one of the many benefits highly regarded by employees. Hallmark also strives to help employees balance their work and family lives by offering a variety of generous family-friendly benefits. The following are just a few of the available benefits:

Parental leave. Workers can take up to six months of unpaid maternity and paternity leave.

Adoption assistance. Hallmark reimburses full-time employees up to $5,000 for the cost of an adoption. Only two other US companies—Syntex and Colgate-Palmolive—offer adoption aid up to $5,000, according to *The 100 Best Companies to Work for in America.*

Family care. The Family Care Choices program helps employees locate care for their children, aging parents, and family members with disabilities.

Sick child care. One of the most popular benefits, this program provides care for mildly ill children at one of six area hospitals.

Voyagers. This program provides an alternative care arrangement for children during school holidays.

The parents' exchange. Hallmark holds noontime seminars on a variety of parenting and elder care topics, such as "How to Talk so Kids Will Listen" and "Parenting in the '90s: New Answers to Old Problems." The lunch-and-learn seminars are very popular and generate a lot of positive feedback. Hallmark also offers seminars on the weekends.

In addition to these benefits, Hallmark provides flex-time and job-sharing programs. To encourage more managers to accept and use flexible arrangements, the company offers a course for anyone interested in looking at new ways to make the workforce more flexible. The course looks at options regarding flexible hours and discusses success stories.

Another of Hallmark's challenges is to make its benefits package more responsive and user friendly. One example of this responsiveness is the telephone access Benefits-Line known as "the B Line," which provides a convenient and confidential way for employees to get information about their benefits and to make changes in some of their accounts. Employees can now call the B-Line and complete push-button transactions or speak with customer service representatives who can answer questions about the savings and profit-sharing plans.

Hallmark not only talks about being employee friendly, it *acts* like the employee's best friend. The company has a reputation of being one of the best companies to work for in the United States. Hallmark pays attention to its number one asset—people.

Sources: Gillian Flynn, "Hallmark Cares," *Personnel Journal*, March 1996, pp. 50–58; K Mathes, "Greetings From Hallmark, *HR Focus*, August 1993, pp. 12–13.

human resource management suggests that it is important to match individuals over time to shifts in organizational and human needs.

HRM in larger organizations such as Alcoa, Bausch & Lomb, Polaroid Corporation, and Marriott Corporation is performed in a staff department like the one shown in Figure 15–1. At the Northbank Restaurant in La Jolla, California, HRM activities such as hiring employees, answering complaints about employees' service, sending a

FIGURE 15–1   **A Personnel Human Resource Management Department**

Human resource departments in large organizations are organized according to company needs and objectives.

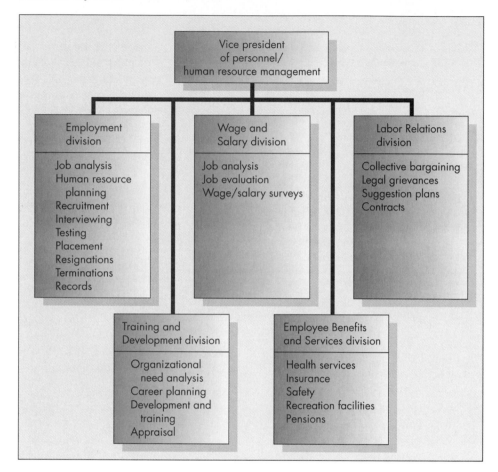

chef to school to learn how to prepare new seafood dinners, and properly developing an assistant manager to take over when the manager retires in six months are performed by the owner, Pablo Mazzeriti. He is responsible for HRM. Remember, each company organizes its department according to its own set of needs, objectives, and size.

Human resource management occurs in an environment in which laws and regulations must be followed. **The Civil Rights Act of 1964**[5] is an especially important piece of legislation in terms of human resources. Title VII of the act prohibits discrimination in hiring, compensation, and terms, conditions, or privileges of employment based on race, religion, color, sex, or national origin. Any organization with 25 or more employees is covered by the act. A landmark Supreme Court Case, *Griggs* v. *Duke Power*, states that any employment test must fairly increase the knowledge of skills required for a job or it cannot be used in making employment decisions.

By 1972, Congress realized that Title VII of the Civil Rights Act of 1964 could be interpreted in various ways. In 1972 an amendment created the **Equal Employment**

Opportunity Commission (EEOC). The EEOC was granted authority to effectively prohibit all forms of employment discrimination. The EEOC was given the power to file civil suits (individuals may also file a suit themselves if the EEOC declines to sue) against organizations if it was unable to secure an acceptable resolution of discrimination charges within 30 days.

Title VII, as it exists today, specifies that organizations must do more than discontinue discriminatory practices. Firms are expected to actively recruit and give preference to minority group members in employment decisions. This activist approach is designated **affirmative action**. Roosevelt Thomas, executive director of The American Institute for Managing Diversity, believes that the reasons for the development of affirmative action programs are that white males frequently made up the majority of workers in firms, US companies were still growing and able to accommodate more workers, minorities needed to be hired to correct past prejudice that has kept them from gaining employment, and legal and social coercion were necessary to bring about change.

On the one hand, affirmative action was one of the major vehicles that allowed the first significant wave of African–Americans to enter the workforce in important, well-paying jobs.[6] On the other hand, women, nonblack minorities, and disabled employees have also benefited from affirmative action policies. Despite some gains, there has been a backlash that has caused abandonment of minority employment goals linking affirmative action policies with unpopular quotas,[7] or the number of individuals in a class or group that must be hired, and setting aside scholarships for meritorious minority students while excluding majority (Caucasian) students in higher education.[8] The importance of affirmative action rests on the important principle of equal employment opportunities for everyone. The situation is still evolving.

The **Civil Rights Act of 1991** was passed because of the effect various court decisions had had in reducing employment oppotunities of minorities.[9] The Act of 1991 prohibits discrimination on the basis of race and prohibits racial harassment, returns the burden of proof that discrimination did not occur back to the employer, and reinforces the illegality of employers' making hiring, firing, or promoting decisions on the basis of race, ethnicity, sex, or religion. Individuals claiming they have been intentionally discriminated against can sue for damages.[10]

The **Americans with Disabilities Act of 1990 (ADA)** expands the Vocational Rehabilitation Act of 1973.[11] ADA includes in the disability category those employees afflicted with AIDS. Companies are required to make reasonable accommodations to provide a qualified individual access to the job as well as eliminate any post-job-offer medical examination. A company may also be required to provide technology to enable a disabled individual to complete his job. As of July 1994, all companies with 15 or more employees were covered by this act.

The EEOC is charged with investigating and enforcing ADA. Most companies have attempted to work within the guidelines of ADA.[12] There are, however, numerous complaints about the ambiguous language of ADA. Terms such as "reasonable accommodation" and "undue hardship" cause interpretation problems. The surprise is that, although job applicants with disabilities were expected to file complaints, about 80 percent of the cases have been entered by current employees claiming a prior disability or by recently disabled workers contending that their employers have not reasonably accommodated their needs.[13]

The **Family and Medical Leave Act of 1993 (FMLA)** guarantees 12 weeks of unpaid leave a year for family-related matters such as childbirth, adoption, or personal or family illness. Employees must have worked more than 1,250 hours, or at least 25 hours a week for more than a year, to be eligible. Companies with fewer than 50 employees are exempt.[14]

A key element of the FMLA is that a person taking leave must be restored to her position or an equivalent position with equivalent benefits, pay, and other terms and conditions of employment. The employer is also required to maintain health insurance benefits at the same level and under the conditions covered had the employee continued working.[15] Employers who violate the law will have to pay monetary damages in an amount equal to wages, salary, employment benefits, out-of-pocket money incurred to pay someone else to provide care, or other compensation denied or lost.[16]

A summary of the highlights of significant laws and presidential executive orders that have an impact upon human resources is presented in Table 15–1. The scope of the law affecting human resources has increased significantly since the Civil Rights Act of 1964 was passed.

Sexual Harassment   In San Francisco, a female secretary receives $3.5 million in a sexual harassment suit against the law firm of Baker & McKenzie.[17] In New York, Tiffany & Co. is ordered to pay $360,000 to a former employee who claimed that she was sexually harassed and

TABLE 15–1   **Laws and Executive Orders Affecting Human Resources**

Federal Law/Order and Year	*Main Provisions*
Civil Rights Act of 1964	Title VII prohibits employment discrimination in hiring, compensation and terms, conditions or privileges of employment based on race, religion, color, sex, or national origin.
Executive Order (E.O.) 11246, 1965	Prohibits discrimination on the basis of race, religion, color, and national origin by federal agencies as well as those working under federal contracts.
Executive Order 11375, 1965	Adds sex-based discrimination to Executive Order 11246.
Age Discrimination in Employment Act of 1967	Protects employees 40–65 years of age from discrimination. Later amended to age 70, then amended to eliminate age limit altogether.
Executive Order 11478, 1969	Amended part of Executive Order 11246, states that practices in the federal government must be based on merit. Also prohibits discrimination based on political affiliation, marital status, or physical handicap.
Occupational Safety and Health Act (OSHA), 1970	Established mandatory safety and health standards in organizations.
Equal Employment Opportunity Act of 1972	Established the EEOC.
Vocational Rehabilitation Act of 1973	Prohibits employers who have federal contracts greater than $2,500 from discriminating against individuals with disabilities, racial minorities, and women.
Veterans Readjustment Act of 1974	Provides equal employment opportunities for Vietnam War veterans.
Age Discrimination Act of 1978	Increased mandatory retirement age from 65 to 70. Later amended to eliminate upper age limit.
Pregnancy Discrimination Act of 1978	Affords EEOC protection to pregnant workers and requires pregnancy to be treated like any other disability.
Americans with Disabilities Act of 1990	Prohibits discrimination against an essentially qualified individual and requires enterprises to reasonably accommodate individuals.
Civil Rights Act of 1991	Nullifies selected Supreme Court decisions. Reinstates burden of proof by employer. Allows for punitive and compensatory damages through jury trials.
Family and Medical Leave Act of 1993	Permits employees in organizations of 50 or more workers to take up to 12 weeks of unpaid leave for family or medical reasons each year.

subsequently fired for complaining about the harassment. A male employee in Los Angeles wins a $1 million settlement claiming that his female chief financial officer made regular and unwelcome sexual advances. This chapter could be filled with example after example of similar lawsuits and rulings. Sexual harassment is one of the most serious problems that is constantly in need of attention and with which organizations must cope every day.[18]

In 1995 the EEOC processed more than 15,000 sexual harassment claims. The EEOC defines illegal sexual harassment as the following.

"Unwelcome sexual advances, requests for sexual favors, or other verbal or physical conduct of a sexual nature constitute sexual harassment when:

- Submitting to or rejecting such conduct is an explicit or implicit term or condition of employment.
- Submitting to or rejecting the conduct is a basis for employment decisions affecting the individual.
- The conduct unreasonably interferes with an individual's work performance or creates an intimidating, hostile, or offensive working environment."

The Anita Hill–Clarence Thomas hearings before a Senate subcommittee in 1991 and the Navy's "Tailhook" convention scandal made front page headlines. These headlines brought attention to the issue of sexual harassment that had been largely ignored by many employers. Sexual harassment is a serious liability that cannot be overlooked.

A significant case highlighting the sexual harassment issue was the 1986 case *Meritor Savings Bank* v. *Vinson.*[19] The case stemmed from a situation where Vinson initially refused the sexual advances of her boss. However, out of fear of reprisal, she ultimately conceded. But the sexual harassment continued in front of other employees. The creation of a hostile environment was the position taken by Vinson's lawyers. The Supreme Court said that any workplace conduct that is severe enough to alter the conditions of a person's employment (Vinson) is abusive and unlawful. The court further ruled that the fact that a sexual relationship is voluntary may be irrelevant. If the advances were unwelcome, they may be unlawful under Title VII. This case made it clear for the first time that women have a legal right to a harassment-free workplace.

Research shows that 90 percent of Fortune 500 companies have dealt with sexual harassment complaints. More than a third have been sued at least once, and about a quarter have been sued over and over again.[20] It is estimated that employers spend about $200,000 on each complaint that is investigated.

In most cases of sexual harassment, behavior is subtle and is difficult to prove. One study showed (from a survey of women nationwide) that only 34 percent of harassed women tell the harasser to stop and just 2 percent file a formal complaint. There is also the problem of overreaction. What happens if a man is falsely accused? At Pennzoil an anonymous letter was written charging a male vice president of sexual harassment. He denied the allegations but was fired. He sued and won $500,000 in damages for wrongful discharge. Pennzoil apparently relied on rumor and innuendo in building its case against the man. The judge declared the in-house investigation to be too superficial.

An increasing number of companies are providing policies regarding sexual harassment, as well as providing training for managers and employees for handling the harassment issue.[21] Examples of steps to follow in order to control and eliminate sexual harassment are shown here:

1. Develop a clear written policy describing what constitutes sexual harassment and making clear that it is prohibited.

2. Institute training programs for all employees.

3. Institute a clear process for filing and investigating sexual harassment complaints.

4. Thoroughly investigate every sexual harassment complaint immediately.

5. Take corrective action.

6. Follow up on the corrective action to determine if it is working and to make sure that no retaliation has occurred.

7. Periodically survey current employees and people leaving the organization about sexual harassment.

8. Assure commitment from the very top of the organization to freeing the workplace of sexual harassment.

Sexual harassment is a serious issue that needs to be addressed promptly, thoroughly, and fairly. The seriousness and complexity of the issue suggest that failure to pay attention to sexual harassment claims can be costly in terms of legal liability, reduced morale, and a loss of respect among employees.

Employment Activity

An organization can only be as effective as the people who operate the office, store, plant, or equipment. Thus, acquiring the necessary qualified people is the first phase of any HRM program. This phase is carried out by the employment division.[22] Recruitment, selection, placement, and other activities of the employment division stem from the human resource plans established by managers throughout the organization.[23]

Human resource planning involves estimating the size and makeup of the future workforce. This process helps the organization acquire the right numbers and kinds of people when they are needed. Experience indicates that the longer the period predicted, the less accurate the prediction. Other complicating factors include changes in economic conditions, fluctuations in the labor supply, and changes in the political environment.[24]

Both formal and informal approaches to human resource planning are used. For example, some organizations use mathematical projections. Data are collected on such topics as the supply of resources, labor market composition, demand for products, and competitive wage and salary programs. From these data and previous records, statistical procedures are used to make predictions. Of course, unpredictable events can alter past trends, but somewhat reliable forecasts can be made.[25]

Estimating from experience is a more informal forecasting procedure. For example, simply asking department managers for opinions about future human resource needs is an informal forecasting procedure. Some managers are confident in planning, whereas others are reluctant to offer an opinion or are just not reliable forecasters.

In the past decade, there has been a noticeable shrinkage of the auto, steel, rubber, and textile industries. This has resulted in the downsizing of many companies. In the 1990s, more than 3 million blue- and white-collar workers have lost their jobs. Human resource planning at firms that have downsized, such as IBM, General Motors,

Goodyear Tire and Rubber, and Allied Signal, has had to develop approaches to lay people off, reduce the number of hours worked by remaining employees, and institute early retirement programs. Each of these strategies has had an impact on the remaining employees, the image of the firm, and the human resource pool seeking employment.[26]

Recruitment

The primary objective of **recruitment**, an essential step in staffing an organization, is to attract the best-qualified applicants to fill vacancies.[27] However, even before acquiring applicants, it is necessary to understand clearly the job that needs to be filled. The methods and procedures used to acquire an understanding about jobs are called job analysis.[28] Through job analysis, managers decide what kind of people to hire.

Sources of Job Information.   Job analysis is the process of determining the tasks that make up a job and the skills, abilities, and responsibilities an employee needs in order to accomplish that job. Numerous methods are used to collect and classify job analysis information. Interviews, surveys, self-reports, and expert-observer rating scales are some of the more popular job analysis data collection procedures. The facts about a job are found in a **job description** and a **job specification**. Figure 15–2 shows a comparison of these.

Effective job analysis provides information used by every unit within the human resource management department. For example, to recruit and select effectively, qualified personnel must be matched with job requirements. Complete job information is provided by the description and the specification. Another example involves the establishment of proper rates of pay. If equitable pay systems are to be developed, complete job descriptions are necessary.

Two widely used systemic job analysis approaches are the functional job analysis (FJA) and the position analysis questionnaire (PAQ).[29]

Functional job analysis focuses on four dimensions of an individual job:

FIGURE 15–2   Sources of Job Information

Job analysis provides interviews with criteria for evaluating applicants.

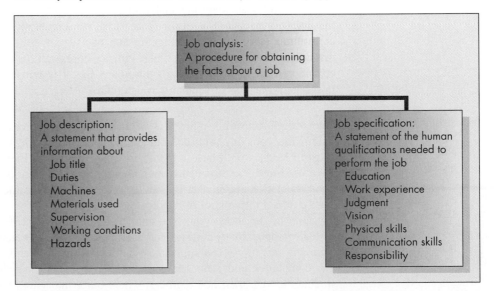

1. What the worker does in relation to data, people, and jobs.
2. Which methods and techniques the worker uses.
3. Which machines, tools, and equipment the worker uses.
4. Which materials, products, subject matter, or services the worker produces.

The first three dimensions relate to job activities, and the fourth relates to job outcomes. FJA provides a description of jobs that can be the basis for classifying them according to any one of the four dimensions. It can also be the basis for defining standards of performance. For example, managers can prescribe what an individual should do with what methods and machines to produce a standard level of output. FJA is the most widely used systematic job analysis method[30] and is the basis for the most extensive listing of occupational titles.[31]

The **position analysis questionnaire** focuses on the actual behavior of the individual in the performance of the job. PAQ has been the object of considerable attention by experts who believe that position analysis must take into account not only job-oriented dimensions but also worker-oriented dimensions.[32] A PAQ analysis attempts to identify six dimensions:

1. Information sources critical to job performance.
2. Information processing and decision making critical to job performance.
3. Physical activity and dexterity required by the job.
4. Interpersonal relationships required by the job.
5. Physical working conditions and the reactions of individuals to those conditions.
6. Other job characteristics, such as work schedule and work responsibility.

PAQ and FJA overlap considerably. Each attempts to identify work activities and outcomes. But PAQ includes the additional consideration of the employee's psychological responses to the job demands and context. Thus, PAQ attempts to acknowledge that job performance is a combination of job dimensions and human characteristics. It enables managers to set standards and obtain information about the individual, the performance of work, and the results of work.

Performing accurate job analysis is, for many jobs, a complex task. For example, the job of managing is difficult to analyze. Planning, organizing, leading, and controlling involve abstract thinking and decision making. And these activities are difficult to quantify. However, if performance appraisals are to be meaningful, fair, and comprehensive for the manager's job or any job, a systematic job analysis that results in the identification of standards is essential.

Recruiting Actions. When the needed human resources are not available from within the company, outside sources must be tapped. A well-known firm, such as General Mills, would have a file of previous applicants. Even though such applicants were not hired, they frequently maintain an interest in working for a company with a good reputation and image. By careful screening of these files, some good applicants can be added to the pool of candidates.

One of the most important sources for recruiting professional managers is the college campus. Many colleges and universities have placement centers that work with company recruiters. The applicants read advertisements and information provided by the companies and then are interviewed. Companies invite the most promising students to visit their home offices, where other interviews are conducted.

In locating experienced employees, organizations can use private employment agencies, executive search firms, or state employment agencies. Some are no-fee agencies, which means that employers pay any fees instead of the applicant. An organization is not obligated to hire any referred persons, but the agency is usually informed when the right person is hired.

Employee Selection and Placement

The selection and placement of personnel begin with a need for human resources and are also heavily influenced by legal requirements. Discriminatory practices in recruiting, testing, and job offerings are illegal, as stated in the Civil Rights Act of 1964, the Equal Employment Opportunity Act of 1972, and the Civil Rights Act of 1991. The selection process is a series of steps that starts with the initial screening and ends with orientation of newly hired employees. Figure 15–3 is a flow diagram showing each step in the process.

Preliminary Interview.   This screening weeds out unqualified applicants and is often the first personal contact an applicant has with a company.

Application.   The applicant who passes the preliminary screening usually completes an application blank. The application blank obtains information that can help in reaching an employment decision. Therefore, the questions on the blank should, at least in a general sense, help predict job success. HRM personnel usually develop the appropriate questions after completing a job analysis.

Interviews.   Even though interviews are used throughout the selection process, there are three basic interviewing steps.[33] First, interviewers must acquaint themselves with the job analysis. Second, they must analyze the information on application blanks. Third, interviewers need to ask questions that elicit information that can add to data on the application blank. While performing these three interviewing steps, the interviewer must be courteous, create a favorable atmosphere, and provide applicants with information and a positive image of the organization.[34]

Testing.   For years, companies have used selection tests to screen applicants.[35] Widespread testing started during World War II, when the Army Alpha test measured intelligence. Installation of a sound testing program is costly and time-consuming, and it must be done by experts.
    The advantages of a testing program include:

- *Improved accuracy in selecting employees.* Individuals differ in skills, intelligence, motivation, interests, and goals. If these differences can be measured and if they are related to job success, performance can be predicted to some extent by test scores.
- *An objective means of judging.* Applicants answer the same questions under the same test conditions, so one applicant's score can be compared to the scores of other applicants.
- *Information for present employee needs*. Tests given to present employees can provide information about training, development, or counseling needs. Thus, tests can objectively uncover needs.

Despite these advantages, tests have become controversial in recent years. Important legal rulings and fair-employment codes have resulted in strict procedures for developing tests. The following criticisms have been directed at testing programs.[36]

FIGURE 15–3   **Steps in the Selection Process**

The selection process requires input from the organization as well as the applicant.

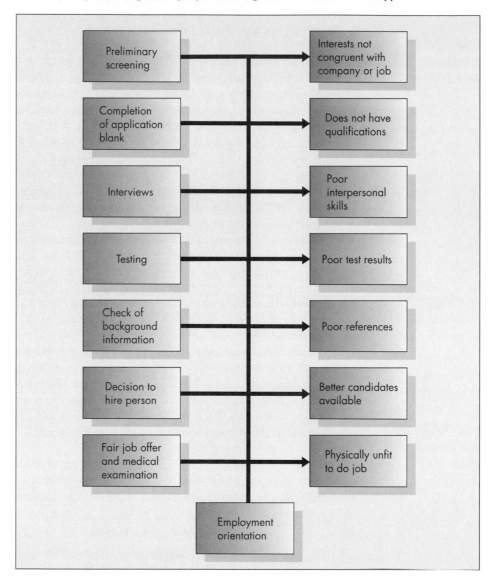

- Tests are not infallible. Tests may reveal what people can do but not what they will do.
- Tests are given too much weight. Tests cannot measure everything about a person; they can never be a complete substitute for judgment.
- Tests discriminate against minorities. Ethnic minorities, such as African-Americans and Mexican-Americans, may score lower than whites on certain paper-and-pencil tests.

Experts claim that alcohol and drug abuse cost American industry over $100 billion annually. As a result, alcohol and **drug testing** of job applicants is increasing.

A 1993 American Management Association survey found that 84 percent of the 630 respondent firms performed drug testing compared with 74 percent one year earlier (1992).[37] The survey also found that more companies are engaging in other antidrug initiatives such as drug education programs and supervisory training to help managers spot behaviors that might indicate a drug problem. Companies also sponsor employee assistance programs designed to help employees with chronic abuse or personal problems that hinder job performance and attendance.

Because some employers and employees are concerned about the accuracy of drug tests, a new alternative has surfaced. It is called performance testing, and it measures the ability of a person to do the job the very day the applicant or employee is tested.

The **Employee Polygraph Protection Act of 1988** prohibits private sector employers from using polygraph tests on applicants or employees with a few exceptions.[38] For example, a firm that manufactures and distributes controlled drugs may continue to use polygraph testing. Since polygraph testing is so limited, firms have increased their use of paper-and-pencil **honesty tests**. These tests attempt to have applicants provide information about their attitudes toward theft and toward dishonesty.[39] Sample questions might include "Compared with other people, how honest are you?"; "Should an employee be fired if caught taking home an unpaid-for product of the firm?"; and "Have you ever stolen anything from an employer?" Answers to this type of questions are checked for consistency.

Even the use of honesty tests will not help an organization in situations involving dishonesty such as stealing if careful procedures are not followed. The accompanying Management Focus discusses how Procter & Gamble incorrectly investigated and addressed an alleged theft. As the firm learned, carelessness can be very costly.

As of the early 1990s, it is estimated that over 6,000 firms are using some type of honesty test to screen job applicants. Results of research on the effectiveness and fairness of honesty tests have to date been mixed. Employers have to be careful in using any form of test that classifies a person as dishonest.

Despite the problems, controversies, and costs involved, tests are widely used.[40] Testing is a part of the employment process—one of the tools that can help managers make selection decisions. In summary, test results provide some usable information, but they do not provide a total picture of how well the person will perform.[41]

Steps in the Hiring Decision.   After the preliminary steps—screening, evaluating the application form, interviewing, and testing—the company may consider making an offer. If so, a background check is often done to verify information, usually by letter, by telephone, or in person. One important group of references consulted is previous employers; the company tries to gather facts about the applicant's previous record of job performance. Under the **Fair Credit and Reporting Act** (1971), the prospective employer is required to secure the applicant's permission before checking references.

When the reference check yields favorable information and the decision to hire is made, the line manager and the human resource department representative meet to decide what the offer will be. The job offer is usually made contingent on successful completion of a physical examination. The objective is to screen out people whose physical deficiencies might lead to expensive liabilities and to place people in jobs they are physically able to handle. The orientation of a new employee is fully discussed in the next section. As Figure 15–3 shows, orientation is part of the selection process in that rejection is still possible if orientation is not successfully accomplished.

Management Focus

Even Honesty Tests Do Not Help a Flawed Investigation

A Texas jury awarded a fired employee $15.6 million. Procter & Gamble (P&G) had fired the employee after publicly accusing him of stealing a $35 company telephone. The employee claimed that the telephone was his property and that P&G libeled him by posting notices on company bulletin boards.

The P&G case sends the loudest message to date that management had better be careful in how an alleged theft is investigated and how the findings are announced. Security guards at the P&G plant stopped the employee and searched his tote bag. The employee informed the guards and his manager that he had purchased the phone after a flood damaged a telephone on his desk in the plant. He said that he hadn't been reimbursed by P&G because he had lost the receipt and that his immediate supervisor had told him he could keep the telephone.

P&G fired him after a six-day investigation and posted notices on 11 bulletin boards and on the plant's electronic mail system. The message named the employee and the work rule he had violated. The employee had a co-worker defend him at the trial, claiming that he had accompanied the fired worker to a mall where the telephone was purchased with cash.

The fired employee has applied for more than 100 new jobs, only to be rejected when prospective employers learned that he had allegedly stolen a telephone. The $15.6 million jury award was broken down as follows: $1.3 million for damage to the person's character,

$200,000 for mental anguish, $100,000 for physical injury (high blood pressure after the firing), and $14 million in punitive damages.

Ex-employees of other companies are also using defamation lawsuits to fight firings. For example, the New Jersey Supreme Court ruled that Bell Laboratories fired a manager for allegedly misusing funds. An anonymous letter had accused the manager of embezzling funds, and after an internal investigation, the manager had been fired. The manager claimed that she had been defamed, and she won.

The lesson to be learned from court-settled firing and defamation cases is that companies should follow these guidelines:

- Be certain of the facts.
- Avoid innuendos.
- Tell only those who need to know.
- Do not make an example of a fired employee.

Some employees who have stolen property should be fired. However, the burden of proof must be placed on the employer in any theft and firing case. Also, managers need to learn more about the issue of defamation before making any rash decisions in these kinds of situations.

Sources: G Stern, "Companies Discover That Some Firing Backfired into Costly Defamation Suits," *The Wall Street Journal*, May 5, 1993, p. B1.

Training and Development

Training and development programs include numerous activities that inform employees of policies and procedures, educate them in job skills, and develop them for future advancement. The importance of training and development to the organization cannot be overemphasized.[42] Through recruitment and placement, good employees can be brought into the company, but they need orientation and continual education and development so that their needs can be met and the objectives of the organization can be achieved simultaneously.

Training Programs   Training is a continual process of helping employees perform at a high level from the first day they start to work. Training is designed to improve a person's skills to do the current job. Whether it occurs at the place of work or a special training facility, training should always be supervised by experts in the educational process.[43]

To be effective, a training program must accomplish a number of goals. First, it must be based on organizational and individual needs. Training for training's sake is not the aim. Second, the training objectives should spell out which problems will be solved. Third, all training should be based on sound theories of learning; this is a major reason that training and management development are not tasks for amateurs. Finally, training must be evaluated to determine whether the training program is working and is cost effective.[44]

Developmental Methods

Training is generally associated with operating employees; development is associated with managerial personnel. **Management development** refers to the process of educating and developing selected personnel so that they have the knowledge and skills needed to manage in future positions. The process starts with the selection of a qualified individual and continues through that individual's career.[45]

The objectives of management development are to ensure the long-run success of the organization, to furnish competent replacements, to create an efficient team that works well together, and to enable each manager to use her full potential. Management development may also be necessary because of high executive turnover, a shortage of management talent, and our society's emphasis on lifelong education and development.

Employees can acquire the knowledge and skills necessary to become successful managers in two main ways.[46] One is through formal development programs; the other involves on the job development. On-the-job development includes the following:

- *Understudy programs*: A person works as a subordinate partner with a boss so that eventually he can assume the full responsibilities and duties of the job.
- *Job rotation*: Managers are transferred from job to job on a systematic basis. The assignment on each job generally lasts about six months.
- *Coaching*: A supervisor teaches job knowledge and skills to a subordinate. The supervisor instructs, directs, coaches, and evaluates the subordinate.

These on-the-job development plans emphasize actual job experience. They increase the manager's skill, knowledge, and confidence. The Center for Creative Leadership believes that managers must also develop mental toughness.

Formal management development programs are often conducted by training units within organizations or by consultants in universities and specialized training facilities around the country. In the very large corporations (e.g., General Electric Company, Westinghouse Electric Corporation, and AT&T), full-time training units conduct regular management development courses. For example, General Electric's advanced management course is designed for the four highest levels of management. Conducted over a period of 13 weeks, course content includes strategic planning, economics, social issues, and management principles.

Performance Appraisal

Performance appraisal involves the formal evaluation of an individual's job performance. It includes feedback to the individual and determination of whether and how the performance can be improved.[47] As a control technique, effective performance appraisal requires standards, information, and corrective action. The standard in performance evaluation is prior specification of acceptable levels of job performance. Information must be available to measure actual job performance in comparison to standard job performance. Finally, managers must be able to take corrective action to restore any imbalance between actual and standard job performance. Recall from

Chapter 8 that standards, information, and corrective action are the three elements of the management function of control.

Because performance appraisal involves individuals judging the quality and quantity of job performance of other individuals, the process is often emotional; it brings into play ideas and perceptions of fairness and equal treatment. The human element of performance appraisal must be taken into account if it is to serve individual and organizational purposes.[48]

As shown in Figure 15–4, a performance appraisal system has the characteristics of all feedback control methods. Through the system, managers can obtain information related to inputs (employees), activities (job performance), and outputs (outcomes). Corrective action is directed toward changing employees' knowledge and skills, as well as job performance, activities, and behaviors. The effectiveness of a performance appraisal system depends on the quality of the three elements of all control techniques: standards, information, and corrective action.

Standards.   The most crucial aspect of performance appraisal is identifying the standard of effective performance. In performance evaluation systems, it is customary to refer to standards as criteria—ways of identifying success in an activity. For example, a criterion for a student is the grade earned in a course or the grade point average after one year at college.

Information.   Managers must decide three issues regarding performance information: the source, the schedule, and the method.

Sources of Information.   Five possible parties can provide appraisal information: the supervisor or supervisors of the appraisee, the peers, the appraisee, subordinates of the appraisee, and individuals outside the work environment. In most situations, the appraiser is the appraisee's immediate supervisor, who should be most familiar with the employee's performance.

Some organizations use group ratings to appraise managerial personnel; members of the group could include superiors, subordinates, and peers. Although some

FIGURE **15–4**   **Performance Appraisal**

Effective performance appraisal requires effective feedback control.

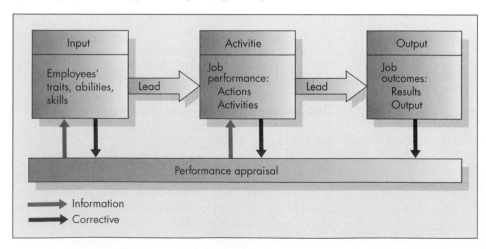

companies use peer appraisal systems, lack of success with this method is not unusual. Peers need mutual cooperation to do their jobs, and performance appraisal undermines the spirit of cooperation.

There is some interest in using self-appraisals. The major claims in support of this approach are that it improves the employee's understanding of job performance, increases the personal commitment of employees because of their participation in the performance appraisal process, and reduces the hostility between superiors and subordinates over ratings. Some employers fear that self-appraisals would be unusually high and not sufficiently critical of current performance.

There is some support for the use of multiple appraisers. The major advantage of using superior, peer, and self-ratings is that this provides a great deal of information about the appraisee. In making decisions about promotion, training/development, and career planning, as much information as possible is needed to suggest the best alternative courses of action for the employee.

Schedule of Appraisal.   In general, long-term employees receive one formal appraisal a year. Recent hires are usually appraised more frequently than other employees. The time to appraise depends on the situation and on the intent of the appraisal. If performance appraisals are either too far apart or occur too frequently, the appraisee may not be able to use the feedback to make improvements.

An appraisal program conducted solely for the sake of appraising employees will soon lose impact unless it becomes integrated with the main emphasis of the organization.[49] The performance appraisal program should be considered a continual process that focuses on task accomplishment, personal development, and the organization's objectives.

Appraisal Methods.   At one extreme, the most simplistic method of information gathering consists solely of the manager's periodic observations of the subordinate's performance. At the other extreme are complex systems—the manager completes forms documenting the subordinate's performance during the period covered by the appraisal. A number of performance evaluation systems have been developed.

Graphic Rating Scales.   The oldest and most widely used performance evaluation procedure, the graphic-scaling technique, appears in many forms. Generally, the rater is supplied with a printed form, one for each subordinate to be rated. The form contains a number of job performance criteria. The rating scales are distinguished by how the criteria are defined, the degree to which the person interpreting the ratings can tell what response was intended by the rater, and how carefully the performance criteria are defined for the rater.

Some common **graphic rating-scale** formats are depicted in Figure 15–5.

Behavioral Anchored Rating Scales.   Behavioral anchored rating scales (BARS) are constructed through the use of critical incidents.[50] Once the important areas of performance are identified and defined by employees who know the job, *critical-incident* statements are used as criteria to discriminate among levels of performance. The form for a BARS usually covers 6 to 10 specifically defined job behaviors, each uniquely described. Each description is based on observable behaviors and is meaningful to the employees being evaluated.

An example of a BARS for engineering competence is presented in Figure 15–6. The criterion is defined for the appraiser; the descriptions defining the particular

FIGURE 15–5   **Samples of Rating-Scale Formats**

Performance criteria must be carefully defined on rating scales.

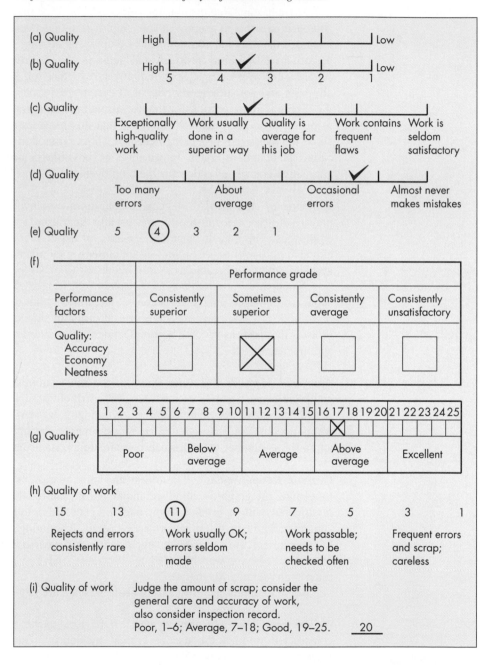

response categories are easy to interpret. The feedback provided by the BARS is specific and meaningful. For example, if the appraisee is given a 1.50 on this criterion, the individual is provided with the specific performance incident that the appraiser used to make the rating.

Despite the time, cost, and procedural problems of developing and implementing BARS, this system possesses some advantages. Specifically, a BARS program could

FIGURE **15–6   A BARS Performance Dimension**

BARS focus on actual behavior to discriminate among levels of performance.

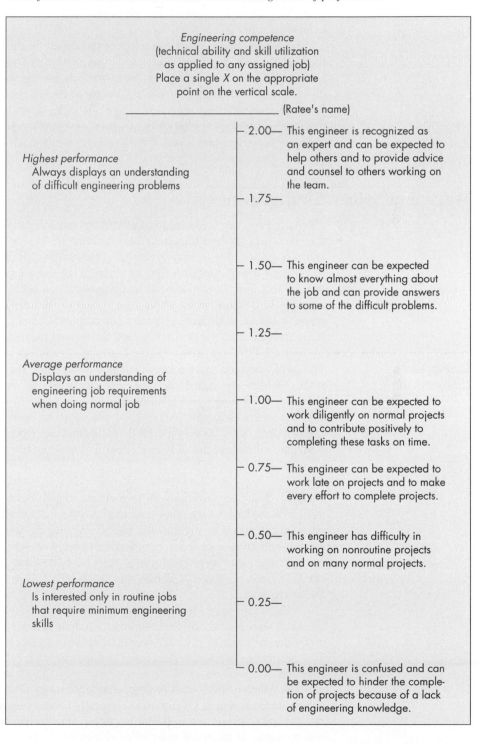

minimize subordinate or superior defensiveness toward evaluation. By being involved in the development of BARS, subordinates have input into how they are to be appraised. The BARS development steps could include both superiors and subordinates. In a sense, then, all of the parties involved can contribute to the creation of the evaluation criterion.

Since job-knowledgeable employees participate in the actual development steps, the final BARS rating form is assumed to be reliable and valid and to cover all aspects of the job. (A common problem of many performance appraisal techniques is that they do not evaluate all aspects of a job.) The use of BARS also provides valuable insights for developing training programs. The skills to be developed are specified in actual behavioral incidents rather than abstract or general skills. Trainees could learn expected behaviors and how job performance is evaluated.

Wage and Salary Management

Money is important, both economically and psychologically. Without it, we cannot buy the goods and services that make life comfortable. Money is also equated with status and recognition. Many employees are quite sensitive about the amount of pay they receive and how it compares to what others in the company and in society are earning. We can see, then, how money, or compensation, can strongly affect the motivation of employees. Because of its importance, employee motivation was the subject of an earlier chapter. As Chapter 11 points out, employees must believe that they are being fairly compensated for the time, effort, and results they provide the employer.[51]

Employee Compensation

The most common system by which nonmanagerial employees are compensated is **wages**, which are based on time increments or the number of units produced. Nonmanagerial employees traditionally have been paid at an hourly or daily rate, although some are now being paid biweekly or monthly. Employees who are compensated on a weekly or longer schedule are paid **salaries**. Hewlett-Packard Company eliminated the daily rate of pay and now considers all personnel at all levels to be salaried employees.[52]

Wages.   Some organizations try to motivate employees to improve performance by paying on the basis of the number of units produced. This is a piecework system. Piece rates are calculated by dividing the hourly wage for the job by the number of units an average employee is expected to produce an hour. For example, if the rate of pay is $5 per hour and the average employee is expected to produce 25 units per hour, the piece rate is 20 cents per piece. A worker who produced 40 pieces under this plan would earn $8 for the hour.

A daily rate of pay is easier than a piece rate to understand and use because time standards and records of the employee's output are not needed. Unions generally prefer the daily rate of pay over systems that involve piecework or incentive payments. This preference is based on the belief that a piecework system tends to reduce group cohesion.

The existing wage rates in competing companies or in the community also help determine wage scales. Organizations typically conduct wage surveys to assess hourly rates, piecework or other incentive rates, and fringe benefits offered by other organizations. If the wage rates of an organization are too low, it may be unable to attract qualified personnel.

Many organizations determine the relative worth of a job and the wage adjustments for it by using **job evaluation** systems. A job is compared with others within the organization or with a scale. Under the ranking method, all jobs are ranked from highest to lowest, on the basis of skill, difficulty, working conditions, contribution to goods or services, or other characteristics. This simple plan is not totally objective. The personalities of the current jobholders often distort rankings. Nor are unions enthusiastic about job evaluation. With such a system, the union negotiator has almost no role to play.

Full-time nonexempt employees must be paid at least $4.25 per hour. Since the first minimum wage law enacted in 1938, the rate has risen more than 1,000 percent, from 25 cents to $4.75 as of February 1, 1997. In addition, the **Fair Labor Standard Act** (1938) forbids the employment of minors between 16 and 18 years of age in such hazardous occupations as coal mining, logging, and woodworking.

The **Equal Pay Act** (1963) forbids employers to pay employees differently on the basis of sex. Women performing the same work as men must receive the same wage or salary. AT&T was required to pay $6.3 million to 6,100 women employees whose pay had suffered because of their gender.[53] The act does not prohibit compensation differences based on seniority, merit, or performance.

There is a debate about what is referred to as **comparable worth**. The argument is that while the true worth of jobs may be similar, some jobs (usually held by women) are paid at a lower rate than other jobs (usually held by men). The resulting differences in pay are claimed to be wage discrimination. Each year the Bureau of Labor Statistics reports on the difference between women's and men's median incomes. The earnings gap has remained at about 30 percent for the past decade. That is, full-time women employees earn about 70 percent of what full-time men earn.[54] The earnings gap across occupations is shown in Figure 15–7.

There may be a number of reasons for the earnings gaps displayed in Figure 15–7. Seniority, work performance, or the credentials of the jobholders may be the cause of the earnings gaps. However, none of these reasons may be the cause, and a gender bias may be the explanation. If there is a gender bias and it can be proven, there will have to be some form of redress.

To handle legal cases involving comparable worth most courts have relied on Title VII of the Civil Rights Act. The courts have generally concluded that Title VII incorporates the equal pay for equal work principle along with four affirmative defenses for pay differentials (seniority, merit, quality or quantity of work, or any condition other than gender). Comparable worth is likely to remain an emotion-laden issue until there is either a reduction in the earnings gap between men and women or until the courts become more sympathetic to comparable worth claims. Even though Title VII has been applied in most comparable worth cases, the courts have in most instances rejected the claims of plaintiffs.

Salaries.   Salaried employees are assumed to have more influence over the way they perform their jobs than are employees paid wages.[55] In developing an equitable compensation system for executives, managers use a similar approach: Comparisons are made, surveys are conducted, and both the supply and demand of candidates and the job duties and responsibilities are analyzed.

The consulting firm of Hay Associates developed one method specifically to evaluate middle and top management positions. First, analysts evaluate each position from information provided in the job description. Three factors are analyzed: job know-how, problem solving, and accountability. Second, through a statistical proce-

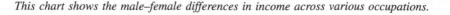

FIGURE 15–7   **A Comparison of Median Income of Male and Female Year-Round, Full-Time Workers for 1990**

This chart shows the male–female differences in income across various occupations.

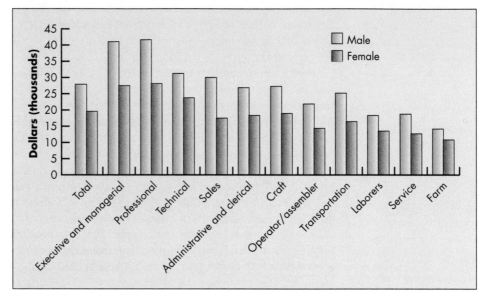

Source: US Bureau of the Census, *Money Income of Households, Families, and Persons in the United States: 1990,* Current Population Reports, Series P-60, No. 174 (US Government Printing Office: Washington, DC, 1991).

dure, the evaluations for the jobs in a particular company are converted to Hay control standards, a special ranking system. Hay Associates publishes annual surveys showing the compensation practices of a number of companies for similar jobs. All Hay clients use the same evaluation method, so they can compare management salaries.

Benefits and Services

Benefits and services are forms of supplementary compensation. They represent monetary and nonmonetary payments over and above wage and salary rates. **Benefits** are financial in nature, whereas **services** are employer-supplied programs, facilities, or activities, such as parks, gymnasiums, housing, or transportation, that are considered useful to employees.

Two additions to some benefit packages are elder care and day care provisions. The US population 80 years old and older is expected to increase from 6 million in 1990 to more than 23 million in 2040. An estimated 12 percent of women who care for aging parents are forced to quit their jobs to do so. Some organizations help employees pay for dependent care through pretax salary deductions. The Internal Revenue Code permits excluding up to $5,000 of employer payments for dependent care expenses from an employee's annual taxable income. As the population ages, it is likely that **elder care** will become a more important human resource issue.[56] Some companies are banding together with public agencies to provide elder care services. For example, American Express, J P Morgan, and Philip Morris use the New York City Department for the Aging to provide employees referrals, counseling, seminars, and other elder care programs.[57]

More than 50 percent of all adult women work; 80 percent of these women are of childbearing age, and 90 percent will become pregnant during their working lives. Thus child care is becoming an increasingly important issue.

The first day care center in the United States opened in New York City in 1827. It was founded to "relieve parents of the laboring classes from the care of their children."[58] Recognizing the importance of **child care** in the 1990s, an increasing number of employers are providing child care assistance to their employees. The help ranges from on-site child care facilities, to the arrangement of part-time work schedules, to work-at-home programs.

Despite pioneers in child care such as Campbell Soup, it appears that not enough US employers are addressing this issue. A survey by the Gallup Organization of 710 full- and part-time employees showed that only 11 percent received child care benefits.[59] If employers are going to attract female employees, much more attention is going to have to be directed toward child care benefits. As labor shortages become more acute, the need to integrate more females and single parents into all levels of organizational hierarchies is going to make child care an important benefit for recruiting, selecting, and retaining employees.

The concept of being a family-friendly company in terms of benefits has been developed. Figure 15–8 presents a type of index (score) developed to pinpoint the kind of policies followed by a firm. Note that dependent care benefits receive the most points in calculating the family-friendliness score.

Labor Relations

Many managers must deal with organized employees who have elected to form a **union**. Under labor laws, employees have the right to form unions for the purpose of improving wages, hours of work, benefits, working conditions, and management practices of dealing with workers. When unions did not exist, employers set all conditions of work, performance evaluation, and rewards. Unions in the United States attempt to improve the life of union members through a process called collective bargaining. The union is recognized as a certified (voted in by members) representative of employees.

The rapid expansion of mass production facilities in the United States created a growing class of unskilled and semiskilled workers. This led to the formation of the Congress of Industrial Organizations (CIO) in 1938. Unions affiliated with the CIO organized workers in such industries as steel, rubber, and automobile.

Union strength and membership grew dramatically from 1935 to 1955. In 1955, the American Federation of Labor and the CIO merged to become the AFL-CIO. Approximately 36 percent of the workforce was unionized in 1952. Today about 16 percent of 17 million workers belong to unions. Membership is still relatively high in the transportation and communication industries and rather low in the service and finance industries.

Although union membership is declining, the union movement has an impact on nonunionized employees and employers. The nonunion affiliated people and firms tend to copy the human resource management practices of unions. Therefore, managers should observe and learn about union goals, programs, and demands.

The majority of US employees have decided not to join a union. There may be a host of reasons why employees have decided not to join unions, such as having to pay union dues, the reputation of the union or its leaders, sound and fair human

---

FIGURE 15–8   The Family-Friendly Index and the Top Ten Companies

If 610 is the maximum score, it appears that even these family-friendly companies have a long way to go.

Company Program or Benefit	*Maximum Score*
Flexible work arrangements: Variable starting and quitting times, part-time work.	105
Leaves: Length of parental leaves, who's eligible, job guarantees.	40
Financial assistance: Flexible benefits, long-term care insurance, child care discounts.	80
Corporate giving/Community service: Funding for community or national work/family initiatives.	60
Dependent care services: Child care and elder care referral, on-site centers, sick-child programs.	155
Management change: Work/family training for managers, work/family coordinators.	90
Work–family stress management: Wellness programs, relocation services, work/family seminars.	80
Total possible: Because all policies may not fit every company, the ideal score is probably below the maximum.	610

Top Scoring Companies

Company	*Score*
Johnson & Johnson	245
IBM	223
Aetna	195
Corning	190
AT&T	178
John Hancock	175
Warner–Lambert	175
U.S. West	165
Du Pont	163
Travelers	158

Sources: E Galinsky, D Friedman, and C Hernandez, *The Corporate Reference Guide to Work—Family Programs* (New York: Families and Work Institute, 1991); "Corporate America Is Still No Place for Kids," *Business Week*, November 25, 1991, pp. 234–38.

---

resource-oriented management practices that resulted in safe and clean working conditions and competitive wages, and management programs to keep unions out.

Collective Bargaining

When a union is present and certified, a process called **collective bargaining** is used. The union has the right to approach management for the purpose of negotiating a contract for members of the collective bargaining unit. There are a number of possible labor–management bargaining relationships.

Four types of collective bargaining dominate labor–management discussions about contracts and issues.[60] First, in **distributive bargaining**, the parties are in conflict over a resource or issue. When they argue about resources, there is usually a fixed amount; if the union wins, management loses or vice versa. Second, in

integrative bargaining, more than one issue is resolved. There is usually give and take and an attempt to reach decisions in which both parties can benefit.

Third, **concessionary bargaining** has occurred more frequently because of economic slowdowns. To survive and remain in operation, employers have sought givebacks or concessions from the unions.

Fourth, there is **continuous bargaining**. A joint labor–management committee meets on a regular basis to explore and solve problems and issues. The committee uses this problem-solving and regular-meetings approach over the life of the contract.

The Bargaining Issues

The **Labor Management Relations Act of 1947** (also called the Taft–Hartley Act) specifies that wages, hours, conditions of employment, and safety are *mandatory* issues for bargaining. Labor and management must in good faith discuss and bargain over these issues. *Permissive* issues are matters that both parties may negotiate if they both agree to do so. For example, the creation of new jobs and who within the firm is eligible to bid for the job may be negotiated if both parties agree. There are also *prohibited* issues that are not negotiable and are not permitted within the collective bargaining structure. For example, a request that the employer use only union-produced goods or that the union not permit a woman to be a representative is prohibited and considered illegal.

Conflict Resolution

The desired result of collective bargaining is a contract that is beneficial to both union members and management. However, there are impasses that result in various tactics being used. When a union is unable to get management to agree to a request, it may **strike** the firm. A strike is the refusal of employees to come to work. The membership of the union votes to strike when negotiations are not successful. Management may decide to prohibit employees from working and resort to a **lockout**. In the spring of 1990, professional baseball team owners decided to lock the players out of training camps in Florida and Arizona.

Employees may resort to a work slowdown to make a point in contract negotiations. They just work a little slower, a little more deliberately, to illustrate to management that they have power and want their demands met.

Mediation is a method in which a neutral third party is called in to help the union and management resolve their impasse. The mediator makes suggestions and attempts to facilitate a cooperative relationship. The US government operates the Federal Mediation and Conciliation Service (FMCS) to make experienced mediators available.

Arbitration is a method in which a third party listens to both sides, analyzes the arguments, and makes a decision that is binding on the union and management. The arbitrator determines the agreement, and the decision is final.

Usually disagreements occur over the life of a contract. Collective bargaining contracts provide a grievance procedure for resolving these conflicts. Table 15-2 presents a typical grievance step-by-step approach. If resolution is not reached at Step 1, the next step is initiated and so forth. Most grievances are resolved in Steps 1 and 2. However, if Step 5 is initiated, an arbitrator makes the decision to settle the conflict.

Unions have attempted to temper their adversarial approach to management through increased cooperation.[61] When unions attempt to cooperate they also want something in return from management. For example, some unions want companies to open the books more to them, particularly cost and profit data.

An example of a long-existing cooperative effort is Xerox and the clothing workers' union. At one time Xerox was losing market share to the Japanese and

Table 15–2   Steps in the Grievance Process

Step 1	The employee and the departmental steward, if the employee desires, shall take the matter up with his [or her] foreman. If no settlement is reached in Step 1 within two working days, the grievance shall be reduced to writing on the form provided for that purpose.
Step 2	The written grievance shall be presented to the foreman or the general foreman and a copy sent to the production personnel office. Within two working days after receipt of the grievance, the general foreman shall hold a meeting, unless mutually agreed otherwise, with the foreman, the employee, and the departmental steward and the chief steward.
Step 3	If no settlement is reached in Step 2, the written grievance shall be presented to the departmental superintendent, who shall hold a meeting within five working days of the original receipt of the grievance in Step 2 unless mutually agreed otherwise. Those in attendance shall normally be the departmental superintendent, the general foreman, the foreman, the employee, the chief steward, departmental steward, a member of the production personnel department, the president of the UNION or his representative and the divisional committeeman.
Step 4	If no settlement is reached in Step 3, the UNION COMMITTEE and an international representative of the UNION shall meet with the MANAGEMENT COMMITTEE for the purpose of settling the matter.
Step 5	If no settlement is reached in Step 4, the matter shall be referred to an arbitrator. A representative of the UNION shall meet within five working days with a representative of the COMPANY for the purpose of selecting an arbitrator. If an arbitrator cannot be agreed upon within five working days after Step 4, a request for a list of arbitrators shall be sent to the Federal Mediation and Conciliation Service. Upon obtaining the list, an arbitrator shall be selected within five working days. Prior to arbitration, a representative of the UNION shall meet with a representative of the COMPANY to reduce to writing wherever possible the actual issue to be arbitrated. The decision of the arbitrator shall be final and binding on all parties. The salary, if any, of the arbitrator and any necessary expense incident to the arbitration shall be paid jointly by the COMPANY and the UNION.

Source: J A Fossum, *Labor Relations: Development, Structure and Process*, 5th ed. (Burr Ridge, IL: Richard D. Irwin, 1992), p. 377.

closing plants. Union leaders offered ways to improve quality and efficiency.[62] The union also agreed to a "no fault" termination procedure. (If a worker was absent on four occasions for two or more hours per year, he could be terminated. Hospitalization and vacations were not included.) Xerox has now turned its situation around, and jobs have increased. The union worked with management to bid for parts contracts and won. For over a decade labor and management at Xerox have found that cooperation can be good for both parties.

Summary of Key Points

- Human resources management (HRM) is the process of accomplishing organizational objectives by acquiring, retaining, terminating, developing, and properly using the human resources of an organization.
- Human resource management has become a strategic issue and concern of organizations. Increasing costs, international competition, changing demographics, and more com-

plex legislation are some of the main reasons for the emerging status bestowed on managing human resources.
- The human resource department in a medium-sized or large firm typically includes areas handling employment, training and development, wage and salary, employee benefits and services, and labor relations functions.

- Laws and regulations affect how human resources are managed. Title VII of the Civil Rights Act of 1964 has set the tone for 30 years of laws and regulations that must be followed. Table 15-1 highlights some of the most significant legislation including the Civil Rights Act of 1991, the Americans with Disabilities Act of 1990, and the Family and Medical Leave Act of 1993. Human resource planning is an important activity that involves estimating the size and makeup of the future workforce.
- Job analysis is an important process used in HRM to determine both the tasks that make up the job and the skills, knowledge, and responsibilities an employee needs to successfully accomplish the job.
- Selection for employment is a process with a number of steps. The steps in the process include preliminary screening, application blank, interviews, testing (e.g., performance, drug, alcohol, and AIDS), background check, the decision to hire, job offer and medical examination, and orientation.

- Training and development programs inform employees of policies and procedures, educate them in job skills, and develop them for future advancement.
- Management development refers to the process of educating and developing selected personnel so that they have the knowledge and skills needed to manage future positions.
- Performance appraisal requires managers to make decisions about how well individuals perform their jobs.
- Performance appraisal requires standards of acceptable job performance. These standards are criteria, and they measure aspects of the job critical to effective job performance.
- Nonmanagerial employees are usually paid wages on the basis of time worked. Managerial employees are usually paid salaries on the basis of a weekly or monthly rate.
- Benefits and services are forms of supplementary compensation. Benefits are financial (insurance protection); services are programs provided by the employer (a gymnasium).

Discussion and Review Questions

1. Discuss with a small business owner the types of human resource management in which the owner engages. What did you find out?
2. Why has honesty testing grown in popularity?
3. Does the Family and Medical Leave Act of 1993 seem fair? Can small businesses afford this type of law? Why?
4. Some persons refer to comparable worth as an emotional issue. What do they mean when referring to it as emotional?
5. Is drug testing an invasion of a person's right to privacy? Discuss.
6. Why is job analysis such a vital step in the development of a performance appraisal technique or method?
7. An engineer stated, "My job is so complex and dynamic that it is virtually impossible to find criteria for assessing job performance." What do you think about this claim? Why?
8. It seems as though every action in a firm is referred to as a strategy. Why is the management of human resources referred to as a strategic requirement of an organization?
9. Do you believe that affirmative action policies are still needed? Why?
10. It is stated that in most situations sexual harassment is subtle. What does this mean?

CASE 15-1
PINKERTON: A SCREENING LESSON

Alan Pinkerton founded the Pinkerton's National Detective Agency in 1850. The company's logo is "The eye that never sleeps." Pinkerton's business was the first national detective agency in the United States, and as fate would have it, its first client was the Illinois Central Railroad Company. The railroad's attorney, Abraham Lincoln, and Alan Pinkerton developed a relationship that proved mutually beneficial to the two

men, especially when Pinkerton uncovered a plot to assassinate the president-elect on the way to his inauguration. As a result, Pinkerton was hired to help protect Lincoln, and his business became the forerunner to today's Secret Service.

After the Civil War, Alan Pinkerton returned to private life and served clients in business and industry. The company's reputation flourished toward the end of the nineteenth century when his men pursued Wild West "bad guys" such as Frank and Jesse James and Butch Cassidy and the Sundance Kid.

In this century, the company turned to more routine private security jobs, including policing office sites and school campuses, but it continued to grow and prosper. By the 1980s, the industry that Pinkerton created had spawned some 10,000 competitors, and Pinkerton Security remained one of the largest, boasting 135 offices in the United States, 20 in Canada, and 1 in the United Kingdom.

In its own hiring practices, Pinkerton practices the security measures that it preaches. Would-be Pinkerton employees undergo thorough background investigations and in-depth preemployment testing to corroborate experience, skills, and integrity. Tom Wathen, chairman and CEO, believes that this program has helped Pinkerton recruit the best people internally, and in turn, Pinkerton offers its extensive screening and assessment program to its industrial, commercial, and retail clients.

Each year, the company screens more than 1 million job applicants, both for its own operations and for its clients'. Other services, such as crisis management, executive protection, public record searches, and even coupon verification, help complement Pinkerton's core competencies of contract security and investigations.

Wathen's strategy has been to expand only into operations that offer synergy to the core businesses of uniformed security and investigation services. Technology, in turn, has played a major role in Pinkerton's growth as a company. Pinkerton has developed an advanced, multistep approach. The first step in this approach—asking candidates to fill out job applications and go through initial interviews—is a routine recruitment practice. But the second step signals the beginning of a more in-depth evaluation; job applicants take a pencil-and-paper questionnaire designed to measure a person's attitude toward honesty and willingness to follow company rules. It takes about 30 minutes for an applicant to complete the integrity test.

In the past year, all tests have been reviewed and revised to comply with employment guidelines under the Americans with Disabilities Act and the Civil Rights Act of 1991. In addition, responding to a Massachusetts state law outlawing integrity testing in the pre-employment process, Pinkerton administers a different test that meets the state law and is designed to help Massachusetts firms better determine if candidates have the potential to meet job requirements.

In the third step, applicants are introduced to IntelliView, a structured interview session conducted via a touch-tone telephone. The recruiter dials the telephone access number, punches in a code number, and leaves the room. From there, the applicant responds to about 100 questions asked by a computerized voice system. Applicants respond to each question by pushing one number for yes or another number for no. The process takes about 10 minutes to complete.

IntelliView offers clients a consistent and structured interview session. The computerized voice system asks the same questions to each applicant in the same neutral tone. There are, however, different types of interviews designed for various industries. Specific IntelliView interview sessions have been designed for retail, health care, child care, and systems and application development, as well as one that was developed with and endorsed by the National Wholesale Druggists' Association. Clients can also use IntelliView to conduct exit interviews or customize it for employee surveys or customer service studies.

Each question is very straightforward and requires a yes or no response. For example, applicants may be asked, "For you, is it too troublesome to help co-workers?" or "Do you dislike detail work?" Respondents can even skip a question and return to it once all questions have been asked.

IntelliView results are not scored, which avoids the potential for negligent hiring claims or lower ratios for statistical EEOC analysis. The benefits of IntelliView are in its ability to help recruiters pinpoint areas in which to follow up with applicants during the fourth phase of the application process—the face-to-face interview.

Within minutes after an applicant completes the IntelliView session, the recruiter can call Pinkerton's information services office in Charlotte, North Carolina, and get the results. Those results actually list the questions that had the least desirable responses. For example, if an applicant answered that she thought it was too much trouble to help her co-workers, the interviewer would be able to follow up with the applicant to find out why she felt that way. The same would hold true for the individual who responded yes to the question about disliking detail work. The interviewer would delve more into why the applicant has an aversion to detail work. In every situation, responses to questions are considered in relation to the job requirements.

The overall recruitment process, according to Pinkerton, is often not complete without a background investigation. The intensity of background investigations also depends on the level of responsibility of the individual being hired. But when the position warrants it, Pinkerton can uncover information that often remains hidden when client companies conduct their own investigations.

Social Security numbers are checked to uncover any possible use of invalid numbers. Criminal checks in superior and municipal courts ferret out possible felonies and misdemeanors. Motor vehicle records are reviewed not only for status of driving privileges and previous offenses, but as a character reference as well. A search can reveal if individuals were responsible and paid their fines or appeared in court.

Civil checks are conducted if warranted, such as when prospective employees will have control over company funds or work directly with clients. A check of credit history reveals the timeliness of payments for transactions. Consumer public filings uncover any tax liens, notices of default in leases, bankruptcy, and small claims experience.

A new addition to Pinkerton's investigative services is its National Verification Network. Pinkerton has developed a network of individuals across the country who will do the legwork for public records searches. The only legal criminal background search for human resources is a public records search. That requires going to the municipal courthouse and pulling records or reviewing microfiche.

Questions for Analysis

1. What lessons should a student of management learn about background checking from reviewing the Pinkerton case?

2. What should a pre-employment check provide a company?

3. Is the cost of the type of screening conducted by Pinkerton too prohibitive? Why?

Sources: B Smith, "The Evolution of Pinkerton," *Management Review,* September 1993, pp. 55–58; E Carlson, "A Business of Background Checking Comes to the Force," *The Wall Street Journal,* August 31, 1993, p. B2.

Video Case
Southwest Airlines: Competing through People

For some organizations, the slogan "focus on customers" is merely a slogan. At Southwest Airlines, however, it is a daily goal. For example, Southwest employees responded quickly to a customer complaint: Five students who commuted weekly to an out-of-state medical school notified Southwest that the most convenient flight got them to class 15 minutes late. To accommodate the students, Southwest moved the departure time up by a quarter of an hour.

Southwest Airlines is an organization that has built its business and corporate culture around the tenets of total quality management. Focus on the customer, employee involvement and empowerment, and continuous improvement are not just buzz words to Southwest employees or to Herb Kelleher, CEO of Southwest Airlines in Dallas. In fact, Kelleher has even enlisted passengers in the effort to strengthen the customer-driven culture. Frequent fliers are asked to assist personnel managers in interviewing and selecting prospective flight attendants. Focus groups are used to help measure passenger response to new services and to help generate new ideas for improving current services. Additionally, the roughly 1,000 customers who write to the company every week generally get a personal response within four weeks. It's no surprise that in 1994, for the third consecutive year, Southwest won the U.S. Department of Transportation's Triple Crown Award for best on-time performance, best baggage handling, and fewest customer complaints.

The Airline Industry

Southwest has been posting hefty profits in an industry that lost $4 billion between 1990 and 1993. Since the 1978 Airline Deregulation Act, constant fare wars and intense competition have contributed to a turbulent environment for the industry. Under deregulation, the government no longer dictates where a given airline will fly and which cities should have service. Rates and service are now determined through competitive forces. The impact on the industry has been tremendous. In 1991 alone, three carriers went through bankruptcy and liquidation, and in early 1992, TWA sought protection from its creditors. Very few airlines, such as Southwest, American, and Delta, have continued to grow into the 1990s.

In 1994, when industry earnings were only $100 million (on revenues of $54 billion), Southwest earned $179 million while spending an industry-low 7 cents a mile in operating costs. The following year, despite facing new competition from upstart low-cost airlines, Southwest had record earnings of nearly $183 million.

Both external factors, such as the price of jet fuel and the strength of the economy, and internal factors, including routing system designs, computerized reservation systems, and motivated, competent employees, help to determine success. The airline industry is capital intensive, with large expenditures for planes. In addition, carriers must provide superior customer service. Delayed flights, lost baggage, overbooked flights, cancellations, and unhelpful airline employees can quickly alienate an airline's passengers.

Southwest's Corporate Strategy

Herb Kelleher has been the primary force in developing and maintaining a vision and strategy which have enabled Southwest Airlines to grow and maintain profitability. Created in the late 1960s as a low-fare, high-frequency, short-haul, point-to-point, single-class, noninterlining, fun-loving airline, it expands by "doing the same old thing at each new airport," Kelleher reports.

"Taking a different approach" is the Southwest way, which has allowed the airline to maintain a 15 percent annual growth rate even during a period of drastic change. Although reservations and ticketing are done in advance of a flight, seating occurs on a first-come, first-serve basis and is only one illustration of the company's nonconformist practices. Turnaround times are kept to an industry low of 15 minutes with the help of pilots and crew who clean and restock the planes. Refreshments are limited to soft drinks and peanuts, except on its longer flights when cookies and crackers are added to the menu. Southwest does not exchange tickets or baggage with other carriers. Kelleher has noted that if Southwest adopted an assigned-seating and computerized, interlining reservation system, ground time would increase enough to necessitate the purchase of at least seven additional airplanes. At a cost of $25 million apiece, the impact on the fares customers pay would be high. Currently, Southwest charges significantly less than its competitors.

Corporate Philosophy, Culture, and HRM Practices

How does Southwest maintain its unique, cost-effective position? In an industry in which antagonistic labor-management relations are common, how does Southwest build cooperation with a workforce that is 83 percent unionized? Led by Kelleher, the corporation has developed a culture that treats employees the same way it treats passengers—by paying attention, being responsive, and involving them in decisions.

According to Elizabeth Pedrick Sartain, vice-president of People (the company's top HRM person), Southwest's corporate culture makes the airline unique. "We feel this fun atmosphere builds a strong sense of community. It also counterbalances the stress of hard work and competition." As Kelleher has stated, "If you don't treat your own people well, they won't treat other people well." So, Southwest's focus is not only on the customer but on the employees, too.

At Southwest, the organizational culture includes a high value on flexibility of the workforce. Employees take pride in their ability to get a plane ready to go in only 15 minutes, less than half the industry average. A cultural refrain is "Can't make money with the airplane sitting on the ground." Ramp agents unload baggage, clean the lavatories, carry out trash, and stock the plane with ice, drinks, and peanuts. Flight attendants prepare the cabin for the next flight, and pilots have been known to pitch in when they have time. Working hard is not just an obligation at Southwest; it is a source of pride. Ramp agent Mike Williams brags that in a conversation with an employee for another airline, the other man

explained Southwest's fast turnaround by saying, in Williams's words, "The difference is that when one of [the other company's] planes lands, they work it, and when one of our planes lands, we *attack* it."

In addition to the high motivation and expectations for performance, evidence of the company culture can be seen in the recruitment and selection process. Southwest accepts applications for ground operations positions or as flight attendants all year round. Many of the applicants are Southwest customers who've seen recruitment ads like the one featuring Kelleher dressed as Elvis. In 1994, Southwest received more than 126,000 applications for a variety of positions; the People Department interviewed more than 35,000 individuals for 4,500 positions. The expanding company was off to an even faster start the next year; in the first two months of 1995, it hired 1,200 new employees. This large labor pool allows the company to hire employees who most closely fit a culture in which they are asked to use their own judgment and to go beyond "the job description."

Kelleher's philosophy of "fun in the workplace" can be seen in a number of company practices. Company parties can be triggered by many events, including the CEO's birthday, when employees dress in black. The annual company chili cook-off, Southwest's annual awards dinner, and the every Friday "Fun Day," when employees wear casual clothes or even costumes to work, illustrate the company credo that a sense of humor is a must and that relaxed people are productive people. Kevin Krone, area manager of marketing in the Detroit office, described efforts by the Detroit area airport employees to set up get-togethers to foster both fun and the commitment to the Southwest family that supports the airline's culture.

Employee involvement in decision making is another key tenet of organizational culture at Southwest. An active, informal suggestion system and all types of incentives (cash, merchandise, and travel passes) serve to reward employees for their ideas. Both teams and individuals are expected, as part of their role at Southwest, to contribute to the development of customer service improvements and cost savings.

Corporate responses to difficult issues are consistently formulated around the company philosophy. As the cost of benefits has risen, cost-conscious Southwest redesigned the employee benefits program into a flexible plan. However, the company went a step further a few years ago, when Sartain was director of benefits and compensation. She believed that for the effort to succeed and satisfy employees, communication was critical. After seeking the advice of more than 700 employees in seven different cities, a promotional program that parodied newspapers and morning new shows was presented. Horoscopes, advice columns, and advertisements all promoted the new program, BenefitsPlus. Employees found this format was more fun and less intimidating than the traditional benefits brochure. In fact, the effort won Southwest first place in the 1990 Business Insurance Employee Benefits Communication Awards competition. More importantly, employees understand their benefits options and appreciate the willingness of their organization to communicate openly.

Many human resource practices have been designed to support the company culture. Compensation programs are designed to increase the connections between Southwest and its employees, who enjoy the benefits of a profit-sharing program. Southwest employees own roughly 11 percent of the company's outstanding stock. The company's union contracts have avoided overly restrictive work rules in order to support the efficient operation of the company. Part of the company credo is that employees need to be able (and want to able) to step in wherever they are needed, regardless of job title or classification. Southwest has not laid off an employee since its founding in 1971; annual employee turnover, at 7 percent, is the industry's lowest. A recently signed 10-year contract with the pilots includes stock options in lieu of guaranteed pay increases during the first five years, demonstrating the trust between the employees and the organization. Kelleher wanted a time frame that would give the pilots enough time to hold on to and exercise the stock options; the pilots' outside investment experts agreed. Also, in 1996 Kelleher voluntarily agreed to freeze his pay at its 1992 level through 1999 to match the pilots' wage freeze. Such shared sacrifice helps build morale and organizational commitment even further.

The combined focus on customers and employees has led to an increase in the diversity of Southwest's workforce. To serve passengers in the southwestern United States more effectively, the company has been recruiting Spanish-speaking employees as well as offering a Spanish Berlitz course at a discount to current employees.

The employees of Southwest are actively involved in numerous community-based service projects at Ronald MacDonald house and the Junior Olympics, among others. This commitment to service is encouraged and demonstrated within the organization, too. A catastrophe fund, initiated by employees, supports individual employees during personal crises. Departments frequently show appreciation to other departments by giving awards and parties.

Kelleher claims that it is hard for Southwest to expand through the purchase of other airlines because the difficulty of merging two corporate cultures, particularly when one is so strong, it too great. In fact, the company's recent difficulties in the Pacific Northwest bear this out. Its expansion into that market was accomplished through the purchase of Morris Air. But Southwest continues to compete. In 1996 it expanded routes into Tampa, Houston, Las Vegas, and secondary routes in the Northeast.

"We tell our people that we value inconsistency," Kelleher explains. "By that I mean that . . . I can't foresee all of the situations that will arise at the stations across our system. So what we tell our people is, 'Hey, we can't anticipate all of these things, *you* handle them the best way possible. *You* make a judgment and use *your* discretion; we

trust you'll do the right thing.' If we think you've done something erroneous, we'll let you know—without criticism, without backbiting."

Employees offer a large number of what they consider to be "everyday examples" of ways they provide high-quality service to their customers. When a California customer service agent was approached by a harried man who needed to catch a flight to meet his vacationing family, the man wanted to check his dog onto the flight. Because Southwest does not fly animals, this could have caused him to miss the flight and his family. The service agent involved volunteered to take the dog home, care for it, and bring the dog back to meet the man two weeks later, upon his return. A torn-up back yard and a very appreciative customer were the outcomes.

Critical Thinking Questions

1. How has Southwest dealt with the competitive challenges in the airline industry today? Rank, in order of importance, the various human resource practices and business practices (such as the low-price strategy) that Southwest Airlines has developed to successfully meet its competitive challenges.

2. Do you think that Southwest's success is more a result of business practices, human resource practices, or the interaction between the two? Can good HR practices help a company be successful without good business practices?

3. How might a ground crew supervisor at Southwest describe her job, given the corporate culture and practices of this organization?

4. Which Southwest HRM strategies directly support total quality management?

5. What aspects of work life at Southwest do you think you would most enjoy and least enjoy? Why?

6. Would the HRM practices used at Southwest Airlines work in other organizations? Why or why not?

Sources: Scott McCartney, "Southwest Airlines Net Sets Record for 4th Quarter," *New York Times,* January 26, 1996, p. A4; Brenda Paik Sunoo, "How Fun Flies at Southwest Airlines" *Personnel Journal,* June 1995, pp. 62–73; Scott McCartney, "Salary for Chief of Southwest Air Rises after Four Years," The Wall Street Journal, April 29, 1996, p. A24; "Southwest Air to Add Routes," *The Wall Street Journal,* April 4, 1996, p. C20; "Southwest Air to Add at Least One City before the Year Ends," *The Wall Street Journal,* May 17, 1996, p. C11; National Public Radio, "Morning Edition," June 30, 1994; J. Castelli, "Finding the Right Fit," *HRMagazine,* September 1990, pp. 38–41; D. K. Henderson, "Southwest Luvs Passengers, Employees, Profits," *Air Transport World,* July 1991, pp. 32–41; J. E. Hitchcock, "Southwest Airlines Renovates Benefits System," *HRMagazine,* July 1992, pp. 54–56; C. A. Jaffe, "Moving Fast by Standing Still," *Nation's Business,* October 1991, pp. 57–59; J. C. Quick, "Crafting an Organizational Culture: Herb's Hand at Southwest," *Organizational Dynamics* 21 (1992) pp. 45–56; R. S. Teitelbaum, "Southwest Airlines: Where Service Flies Right," *Fortune,* August 24, 1992 pp. 115–16. For more information on Southwest Airlines, including the latest press releases, tour of a Boeing 737, or the most recent flight schedule, visit the Southwest Airlines home page on the World Wide Web at http://www.iflyswa.com.

EXPERIENTIAL EXERCISE
A CONTROL PROCEDURE: YOUR PERSONAL PERFORMANCE APPRAISAL

Purpose

The purpose of this exercise is to apply performance appraisal guidelines to your own activities and objectives.

The Exercise in Class

1. Write a paragraph (150 words or less) describing a successful you. What would make you successful? Select your school, job, family, or personal life as a reference point. In your paragraph, list the outcomes (results) that would mean you were successful (e.g., school—grade point average 3.3, graduating with honors, receiving highest grade on a final; job—promotion to next level in two years, receiving recognition, receiving large merit increase).

2. For the reference point (choose one), select five areas of major concern and the measure of success you would use. Determine whether the measures of success are subjective or objective. Do they have a time frame?

Major area of concern	How is success measured?	Subjective/ objective	Time frame yes/no
1. _____	_____	_____	_____
_____	_____		
2. _____	_____	_____	_____
_____	_____		
3. _____	_____	_____	_____
_____	_____		
4. _____	_____	_____	_____
_____	_____		
5. _____	_____	_____	_____
_____	_____		

3. Develop the major areas of concern into specific personal objectives—one for each major area of concern. Each objective should be one single sentence, clearly stated, with a time period specified. Rank the objectives from the most important to the least important.

Ranked Objectives

1. _____
2. _____
3. _____
4. _____
5. _____

4. The instructor will form groups of three students to share their success stories, measures of success, and objective statements. Are there differences in what are considered success measures, objectives, and priorities?

The Learning Message

Even self-appraisal of performance is a control procedure. It serves to direct individual behavior toward objectives that are meaningful, clear, comprehensive, and challenging. Explicit objectives that are well stated must be carefully worked on. Skill in developing objectives can be improved with practice. Good objectives can be helpful in planning, organizing, and controlling behavior and attitudes.

Notes

1. John M Ivancevich, *Human Resource Management: Foundations of Personnel* (Burr Ridge, IL: Richard D. Irwin, 1995), pp. 12–20.
2. Raymond A Noe, John R Hollenbeck, Barry Gerhart, and Patrick M Wright, *Human Resource Management: Gaining a Competitive Advantage* (Burr Ridge, IL: Austen Press, 1994), pp. 3–5.
3. Jennifer J Laabs, "The Personal Side of Global HR," *Global Workforce,* January 1997, pp. 14–15.
4. Y K Shetty and Paul F Buller, "Regaining Competitiveness Requires HR Solutions," *Personnel,* July 1990, pp. 8–12.
5 Civil Rights Act of 1964 (401 FEP Manual 1); 401 FEP Manual II.
6. Alfred Edmond, Jr., "25 Years of Affirmative Action," *Black Enterprise,* February 1995, pp. 156–57.
7. Tim W Ferguson, "Dear Stan," *Forbes,* September 1996, pp. 47–48.

8. Mark Lowery, "The War on Equal Opportunity," *Black Enterprise,* February 1995, pp. 148–54.

9. Fred S Stungold, *The Employers Legal Handbook* (Berkeley, CA: Nolo Press, 1996), pp. 8/4–8/24.

10. "The New Civil Rights Act of 1991 and What It Means to Employers," *Employment Law Update 6,* December 1991, pp. 1–12.

11. "President Signs Act into Law," *Human Resource Management: Ideas and Trends,* no. 227 (Chicago: Commerce Clearing House, August 8, 1990), p. 133.

12. Karen Matthes, "ADA Update: The First Year in Review," *HR Focus,* August 1993, p. 18.

13. "ADA Complaints Are Not What Experts Predicted," *HR Focus,* November 1993, pp. 1, 6.

14. "The Family and Medical Leave Act," *HR Focus,* May 1993, pp. 1, 4.

15. David I Shair, "The Family Medical Leave Act: May Lower Your Costs," *HR Focus,* August 1993, p. 23.

16. Nancy D Weatherholt, David W Cornell, and Cynthia Jeffrey, "The Family and Medical Leave Act," *Management Accounting,* November 1993, pp. 31–33.

17. Sharon Nelton, "Sexual Harassment Reducing the Risks," *Nation's Business,* March 1995, pp. 24–26.

18. Jonathan A Segal, "The World May Welcome Lovers," *HR Magazine,* June 1996, pp. 170–79.

19. *Meritor Savings Bank* v. *Vinson,* 106 US 2399 (1986).

20. Judith L Lichtman, "How Can We Fight Harassment?" *USA Today,* October 14, 1993, p. 13A.

21. Jan Bohren, "Six Myths of Sexual Harassment," *Management Review,* May 1993, pp. 61–63.

22. Patrick Wright and G McMahan, "Theoretical Perspectives for Strategic Human Resource Management," *Journal of Management,* June 1992, pp. 295–320.

23. Shari Caudron, "Staffing Drought," *Personnel Journal,* November 1996, pp. 58–67.

24. For complete discussions of human resource planning see D W Jarrell, *Human Resource Planning: A Business Planning Approach* (Englewood Cliffs, NJ: Prentice Hall, 1993).

25. "Industry Report," *Training,* October 1996, pp. 37–47.

26. Jacky Fierman, "What Happened to the Jobs?" *Fortune,* July 12, 1993, pp. 40–41.

27. James A Breaugh, *Recruitment: Science and Practice* (Boston: PWS-Kent, 1992).

28. R Harvey, "Job Analysis," in Marvin M Dubnette and L Hough, eds., *Handbook of Industrial and Organizational Psychology* (Palo Alto, CA: Consulting Psychologists Press, 1991), pp. 71–164.

29. Ivancevich, *Human Resource Management,* pp. 171–73.

30. Ibid.

31. US Department of Labor, *Dictionary of Occupational Titles,* 4th ed. (Washington, DC: US Government Printing Office, 1989).

32. E T Cornelius II, A S De Nisi, and A G Blencoe, "Expert and Naive Raters Using the PAQ: Does It Matter?" *Personnel Psychology,* Autumn 1984, pp. 453–64.

33. Robert L Diploye, *Selection Interviews: Process Perspectives* (Cincinnati, OH: South-Western, 1991).

34. Wayne E Barlow, "Pre-employment Interviews: What You Can and Can't Ask, " *Personnel Journal,* January 1996, p. 99.

35. Anne Anastasi, *Psychological Testing* (New York: Macmillan, 1982), p. 12.

36. Charlene Marmer Solomon, "Testing at Odds with Diversity Efforts," *Personnel Journal,* April 1996, pp. 131–40.

37. "Fewer People Fail as Workplace Drug Testing Increases," *HR Focus,* June 1993, p. 24.

38. Paul Sackett, Laura R Burris, and Christine Callahan, "Integrity Testing for Personnel Selection: An Update," *Personnel Psychology,* Autumn 1989, pp. 491–529.

39. "Companies Pay a Big Price for Employee Theft," *HR Focus,* January 1992, p. 14.

40. Gillian Flynn, "Will Drug Testing Pass or Fail in Court?" *Personnel Journal,* April 1996, pp. 141–44.

41. Jerry Flint, "Can You Tell Applesauce from Pickles?" *Forbes,* October 9, 1995, pp. 106–8.

42. *Training Partnerships* (Washington, DC: The American Society for Training and Development and US Department of Labor Employment and Training Administration, March 1990), pp. 1–46.

43. Brian O'Reilly, "How Execs Learn Now," *Fortune,* April 5, 1993, pp. 52–58.

44. Rich D Arvey, Scott E Maxwell, and E Sales, "The Relative Power of Training Education Designs under Different Cost Configurations," *Journal of Applied Psychology,* April 1992, pp. 155–60.

45. Thomas A Stewart, "The Organizational Chart: You Inc., " *Fortune,* January 15, 1996, pp. 66–75.

46. Alan Farnham, "Are You Smart Enough to Keep Your Job?" *Fortune,* January 15, 1996, pp. 34–48.

47. Timothy D Schellhardt, "It's Time to Evaluate Your Work, and All Involved Are Groaning," *The Wall Street Journal,* November 19, 1996, pp. A1, A5.

48. Dirk D Steiner, Jeffrey S Rain, and Mary M Smalley, "Distributional Ratings of Performance: Further Examination of a New Rating Format," *Journal of Applied Psychology,* June 1993, pp. 438–42.

49. Brenda Paik Sunoo, "This Employee May Be Loafing," *Personnel Journal,* December 1996, pp. 54–62.

50. M Piotroroski, J Barnes-Farrel, and F Erig, "Behaviorally Anchored Bias: A Replication and Extension of Murphy and Constans," *Journal of Applied Psychology,* October 1989, pp. 823–26.

51. Thomas P Plannery, David A Hofrichter, and Paul E Platten" *People, Performance, and Pay* (New York: Free Press, 1996).

52. George Milkovich and Jerry M Newman, *Compensation* (Plano, TX: Business Publications, 1987), pp. 188–212.

53. Edward E Lawler III, "The New Pay," *New Management,* Summer 1985, pp. 52–59.

54. Joan E Rigdon, "Three Decades after Equal Pay Act, Women's Wages Remain Far from Parity," *The Wall Street Journal,* June 9, 1993, p. B3.

55. 1995 Hay Compensation Conference Participant Study.

56. Sue Shellenbarger, "Firms Try Harder, but Often Fail to Help Workers Cope With Elder Care Problems," *The Wall Street Journal,* June 23, 1993, pp. B1, B6.

57. "Employees Band Together for Better Elder Care," *The Wall Street Journal,* June 23, 1993, p. B1.

58. "Child Care an Old Issue," *Heritage,* May–June 1990, p. 50.

59. "Checking up on Childcare," *Personnel,* August 1990, p. 7.

60. John Fossum, *Labor Relations* (Burr Ridge, IL: Richard D. Irwin, 1992).

61. Bill Vlasic, "The Saginaw Solution," *Business Week,* July 15, 1996, pp. 78 and 80.

62. Peter Nulty, "Look What the Unions Want Now," *Fortune,* February 8, 1993, pp. 128–33.

16 ORGANIZATION CHANGE, DEVELOPMENT, AND INNOVATION

Chapter Learning Objectives

After completing Chapter 16, you should be able to:

- **Define** the term *organization development.*
- **Describe** a five-step model or framework that displays the organization change process.
- **Discuss** four major reasons why people resist change.
- **Compare** specific techniques that are used to bring about structural, people, and technological changes.
- **Identify** some of the productivity and human resource advantages and disadvantages associated with robotics in work settings.

New Management Styles to Manage Diversity

American managers in the twenty-first century will have to change the way they manage in order to deal with diversity in both the workplace and the marketplace. They will also have to deal with different world cultures, as a consequence of the globalization of business. In response to changing demographics in the American workforce, some companies have increased their diversity-management activities, some have become bogged down not knowing what to do, and others have chosen to do nothing. Roosevelt Thomas, Jr., president of the American Institute for Managing Diversity, defines *managing diversity* (MD) as the process of creating and maintaining an environment that naturally enables all organizational members to reach their full potential in pursuit of the enterprise's objectives. He offers the following guidelines for change in order to manage diversity:

- Begin by asking yourself if you truly understand what MD is. Do you see it as a strategically important issue for your business or is it merely a legal requirement?

- Accept the role of a change agent. MD will require advocates to ensure its success.

- Develop an MD strategic plan. What is the "big picture" facing the company in regard to the change required to manage a diverse workforce?

- Use the "umbrella approach," taking into account the necessity to combine the contributions of human resource systems, affirmative actions, and sensitivity training to manage diverse employees and markets.

- Develop a strategic business rationale for launching MD. Change leaders must make others aware of the strategic importance of MD.

- Foster shifts of mindset. Ultimately, for MD to be successful, organizational members must change their way of thinking about diversity.

- Audit and modify the culture. The cultural audit is an essential element of MD for the purpose of identifying hindrances to and facilitators of the desired MD state. Only after the existing culture is understood can changes be made that support MD.

- Adopt a long-term MD perspective. The change required to institutionalize MD will require several years.

- Adopt a pioneering attitude. The thinking of a pioneer is different from that of one who prefers the well-trodden path.

Change leaders must be willing to assist others in dealing with the rigors of changing in order to manage diversity. The overriding issue for management in the twenty-first century may well be change itself. Change in response to diverse employees and markets is but one manifestation of management's responsibility. Equally compelling are changes in response to technology, politics, and social demands.

Sources: M Wilson, "Diversity in the Workplace," *Chain Store Age Executive,* June 1995, pp. 21–23; L Morris, "Diversity Effort Links to Climate Study Results," *Training and Development,* January 1994, pp 64–66; Anonymous, "Is Diversity Training Worth Maintaining?" *Business and Society Review,* Spring 1994, pp. 47–49; and R Thomas, Jr., "Managing Diversity: Utilizing the Talents of the New Work Force," in A R Cohen ed., *The Portable MBA in Management* (New York: John Wiley, 1993), pp. 315–39.

Twenty-first century managers will face inescapable and inevitable pressures from many sources to change their organizations. We have already witnessed significant and irreversible changes in organizations during the 1980s and 1990s as managers have sought to respond to global competition, diversity in the workplace, the drive for quality and competitiveness, and ethical dilemmas. The Management in Action that introduced this chapter describes some guidelines for possible reactions to the increasingly diverse nature of the workforce. Throughout this chapter we will suggest other specific pressures for change and describe the variety of responses available to managers.

That the word *change* has become a daily part of conversations throughout the world was well documented during the 1994 federal and local elections. Indeed, change was the most obvious promise of candidates for office during those election campaigns, and change is certainly the most frequently used word on the business pages of every newspaper in the world. Not only have entire countries and empires gone through dramatic and wrenching changes in their political, economic, and social institutions, but so have large companies such as IBM, General Motors, and Ford. Some large organizations, such as Pan-American Airlines, have simply ceased to exist. So it makes a great deal of sense to devote a significant portion of this text, which is devoted to the preparation of future managers, to the issues associated with managing change.

Well-known business writers state that contemporary business organizations confront changing circumstances that put all previously experienced eras of change to shame by comparison. The combination of global competition, computer-assisted manufacturing methods, and instant communications has implications that are more far-reaching than anything since the beginning of the industrial revolution.[1] Popular literature and best-sellers warn managers that their organizations' futures depend upon their ability to master change.[2] The professional literature states that change is a pervasive, persistent, and permanent condition for all organizations.

Effective managers must view managing change as an integral responsibility, rather than a peripheral one.[3] The reality is that not all organizations will successfully make the appropriate changes. The ones that have the best chance for success are relatively small and compete in industries in which research and development expenditures have traditionally been relatively high and barriers to entry are relatively low. Firms in various industries have had to change to survive, and they are likely to be the survivors in the twenty-first century.[4]

Before beginning our discussion of the processes of organizational change and development, we must explain the manner in which we use the terms *change* and *development*. As even the casual reader of management literature soon must realize, the term *organization development* (OD) implies a variety of meanings and management strategies. In its most restrictive sense, it refers specifically to some form of sensitivity training; in a larger and more encompassing sense, it refers to any systematically planned effort to improve the effectiveness of an organization through the application of behavioral science concepts, theories, and approaches. The change effort may focus on the way in which the organization is structured, the behavior of employees, or the technology that is used in getting the work done. Therefore, *OD is a method for facilitating change and development in structures and processes (e.g., relationships, roles), people (e.g., styles, skills), and technology (e.g., more routineness, more challenge).*[5]

The growing realization that organizations can be changed and made more effective through managerial applications of behavioral science has created a wealth of literature.[6] This chapter presents some of the established ideas from this literature, in the context of practical management. To provide a theme, we present the material in a model describing the important factors of the change and development process. For simplicity, we use the phrase "the management of change" to include the concept of organization development in its broadest sense.

Resistance to Change

Most organizational change efforts eventually run into some form of employee resistance. Change triggers rational and irrational emotional reaction because of the uncertainty involved.

Why Do People Resist Change?

Instead of assuming that employees resist change or act in a particular manner, it is better to consider in a general way the reasons why people resist change. Four common reasons have been found.[7] As you read about each of them, think about your own reasons for resisting change. Do any of the reasons fit you?

Parochial Self-Interest.   One reason some people resist organizational change is the fear of losing something they value. Individuals fear the loss of power, resources, freedom to make decisions, friendships, and prestige. In cases involving fear of loss, individuals think of themselves and what they may have to give up. The fearful individual has only his parochial self-interest in mind when resisting change. The organization and the interests of co-workers are not given much priority.

Misunderstanding and Lack of Trust.   When individuals do not fully understand why change is occurring and what its implications are, they resist change. Misunderstanding about the intent and consequences of organizational change is more likely to occur when trust is lacking between the individual and the person initiating the change. In organizations characterized by high levels of mistrust, misunderstandings probably accompany any organizational change.

Different Assessments.   Since individuals view change—its intent, potential consequences, and personal impact—differently, there are often different assessments of the situation. Those initiating changes see more positive results because of the change, while those being affected and not initiating the changes see more costs than benefits involved with the change. Take, for example, the introduction of robots. Management might view the change to robots as a benefit, while subordinates may consider the robot introduction as a signal that they will lose their jobs.

The initiators of change frequently make two overly broad assumptions: (1) They have all the relevant data and information available to diagnose the situation and (2) those to be affected by the change also have the same facts. Whatever the circumstances, the initiators and the affected employees often have different data and information. These differences lead to resistance to change. However, in some cases, the resistance is healthy for the firm, especially in the situation where the affected employees possess more valid data and information.

Low Tolerance for Change.   People resist change because they fear they will not be able to develop the new skills necessary to perform well. Individuals may understand clearly that change is necessary, but they are emotionally unable to make the transition. For example, this type of resistance was found in offices that introduced computerized word-processing systems. Some secretaries and even their bosses resisted these changes, which were clearly needed if office productivity was to be improved.

A low tolerance for change is also found in individuals who resist change to save face. Making the necessary adjustments and changes would be, they assume, an open admission that some of their previous behavior, decisions, and attitudes were wrong.

Resisting change is a human response, and management needs to take steps to minimize such resistance. Minimizing resistance can reduce the time it takes for a change to be accepted or tolerated. Also, the performance of employees can rebound more quickly if resistance is kept at a minimal level.

Minimizing Resistance to Change

Given that resistance to change can be a normal human response to unknown futures, how can managers overcome it? Generally they have access to six different strategies that can reduce, if not eliminate, resistance to change.[8]

1. *Education and communication.* One of the most common ways to reduce resistance is to communicate and educate before the change occurs. This helps people prepare for the change. Paving the way, showing the logic, and keeping everyone informed helps cut down resistance.

2. *Participation and involvement.* Having those to be affected help design and implement the change increases their commitment to the change. If individuals feel their ideas and attitudes are being included in the change effort, they tend to become less resistant and more receptive.

3. *Facilitation and support.* Being supportive is an important management characteristic when change is implemented. It is especially important for managers to be supportive (e.g., show concern for subordinates, be a good listener, go to bat for subordinates on an issue that is important) and to help facilitate the change when fear and anxiety are at the heart of resistance.

4. *Negotiation and agreement.* Negotiation can reduce resistance. Discussion and analysis can help managers identify points of negotiation and possible agreement. Negotiated agreement involves giving something to another party to reduce resistance. For example, getting a person to move to a less desirable work location may require paying him a bonus or increasing her monthly salary. Once this agreement is negotiated, others may expect the manager to grant them the same concessions in the future.

5. *Manipulation and co-optation.* Manipulation involves the use of devious tactics to convince others that a change is in their best interests. Holding back information, playing one person against another, and providing slanted information are examples of manipulation. Co-opting an individual involves giving him a major role in the design or implementation of the change. The ethical problems associated with manipulation and co-optation are obvious and should preclude the widespread use of these techniques.

6. *Explicit and implicit coercion.* Using explicit and/or implicit coercion, the manager engages in threatening behavior. She threatens the employees with job loss, reduced promotion opportunities, poor job assignments, and loss of privileges. The coercion is intended to reduce a person's resistance to the management-initiated change. Coercive behavior can be risky because of the bad feelings and hostility generated.

Each of these six approaches has advantages and drawbacks that need to be carefully considered. Managers can use them in different situations and in various combinations. Use of any of the six approaches depends on a systematic analysis of the particular situation. Often this involves the use of a model, or framework, to help provide guidelines and an overview of the situation.

A Model for Managing Change

The management of change can be broken down into subprocesses or steps. A model describing this process is illustrated in Figure 16–1 and consists of five steps linked in a logical sequence. The prospects for initiating successful change and minimizing resistance are enhanced when the manager explicitly and formally goes through each successive step. For this reason, each step and process is discussed in a separate section of this chapter.

FIGURE 16–1   The Process of Managing Organizational Change

Managers will manage change with greater success by explicitly and formally following each successive step in the process.

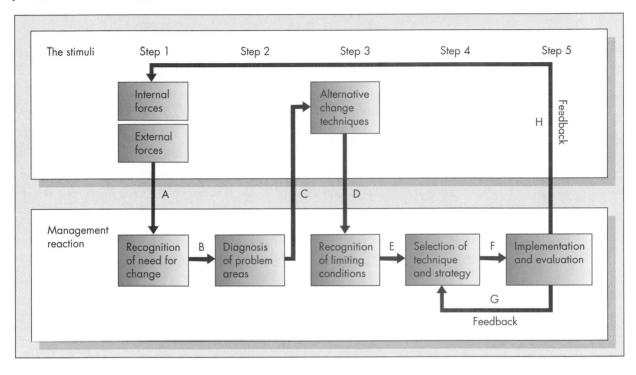

The knowledgeable manager recognizes the multiplicity of alternatives and is not predisposed toward one particular approach to the exclusion of all others.[9] At the same time, the effective manager avoids the pitfall of stagnation.

A flexible, forward-looking stance for managers is an essential attribute for using the change model (see Figure 16–1). The model assumes that forces for change continually act on the firm, reflecting the dynamic character of the modern world. At the same time, it is the manager's responsibility to sort out the information received from the firm's control system and other sources that reflect the magnitude of change forces (A). This information is the basis for recognizing the need for change; it is equally desirable to recognize when change is not needed. But once the problem is recognized, the manager must diagnose the problem (B) and identify relevant alternative change techniques (C). The change technique selected must be appropriate for solving the problem, as constrained by limiting conditions (D). One example of a limiting condition discussed in an earlier chapter is the prevailing character of group norms. A work group may support some of the change techniques but may sabotage others.

The fact that a change program can be thwarted underscores the truth that the choice of change strategy is as important as the change technique itself (E). Finally, managers must implement the change and monitor the change process and change results (F). The model includes feedback to the selection-of-strategy phase and to the forces-for-change phase. These feedback loops (G and H) suggest that the change process itself must be monitored and evaluated. The implementation strategy may be faulty and lead to poor results, but prompt action could correct the situation. Moreover, the feedback loop to the initial step recognizes that no change is final. A new situation is created within which other problems and issues will emerge; a new setting is created that will itself become subject to change. The model suggests no final solution. Rather, it emphasizes that managers operate in a dynamic setting where the only certainty is change itself.

Step 1: Stimuli—Forces for Change

The forces for change (stimuli) can be classified into two groups: external and internal forces. **External change forces** include changes in the marketplace, technology, and environment; they are usually beyond the control of the manager. **Internal change forces** operate inside the firm and are generally within the control of management.

External Forces

Managers of business firms historically have been concerned with reacting to changes in the *marketplace*. Competitors introduce new products (Diet Pepsi versus Tab), increase advertising (General Motors versus Toyota), reduce prices (Delta Airlines versus United Airlines), or improve customer service (Apple versus IBM). In each case, a response is required unless the manager is content to permit the erosion of profit and market share. At the same time, changes occur in customer tastes and incomes. The firm's products may no longer have customer appeal; customers may be able to purchase less expensive, higher-quality forms of the same product.

The second source of external change forces is *technology*. The knowledge explosion since World War II has introduced new technology for nearly every management function. Computers have made possible both high-speed data processing and the solution to complex production problems. New machines, new processes, and robots have revolutionized the way many products are manufactured and distributed.[10]

A new technology tool is transforming organizations like never before. Information technology—the capabilities offered by computers, software applications, and telecommunications—has the potential to redesign many business processes.[11] Effective implementation of information technology systems can lead to competitive advantages resulting from lowered costs, time reduction, increased output quality, improved learning, and enhanced quality of work life.

Finally, the third external force consists of *environmental changes*. Managers must be tuned in to great movements over which they have no control but that, in time, affect the firm's fate. Worldwide changes in international markets and competition are occurring rapidly. Japan, Korea, Taiwan, Germany, and Hong Kong have become major economic forces. Within these countries are firms that are competing worldwide for human resource talent, market share, and technology. The great movement of the 1990s and beyond will be the continued internationalization of the business world, which will create intensified environmental forces for change.

The transformation of the former USSR from a controlled to a market economy has been the subject of great interest throughout the world. The struggle of organizations in the former USSR to cope with changes in their environment has caught the attention of the world. The outcome of this transformation is of great importance for all of us. One of the more difficult concepts for managers of enterprises within Russia and other republics to grasp is that of the firm related to the marketplace.

Internal Forces

The forces for change occurring within the organization can be traced to *processes* and *people*. Process forces include decision making, communications, and interpersonal relations. Breakdowns or problems in any of these processes can create forces for change. Decisions are either not being made, are made too late, or are of poor quality. Communications are short-circuited, redundant, or simply inadequate. Tasks are not undertaken or not completed because the person responsible did not "get the word." Because of inadequate and/or nonexistent communications, a customer order is not filled, a grievance is not processed, an invoice is not filed, or a supplier is not paid. Interpersonal and interdepartmental conflicts reflect breakdown in the interaction between people.

Low levels of morale and high levels of absenteeism and turnover are symptoms of people problems that must be followed up. A wildcat strike or a walkout may be the most tangible sign of a problem; such tactics are usually employed because they arouse management to action. There is in most organizations a certain level of employee discontent; a great danger is to ignore the complaints and suggestions. The spring 1989 machinists union strike at now defunct Eastern Air Lines illustrates what can occur when problems are not recognized.[12] The machinists refused to take the company-recommended 20 percent pay cut, and pilot complaints and requests for job security were not heeded by management. Ultimately, this failure to heed warnings of needed change led to Frank Lorenzo's loss of control at Continental Air Lines and the resulting demise of Eastern Air Lines.

In the five-step process of change, the first step is the recognition phase. It is at this point that management must decide whether to act or not to act.

Step 1: Reaction—Recognition of the Need for Change

Information helps managers comprehend the magnitude of the change forces. Some of the important sources of information were discussed earlier. Certainly, the most important information comes from the firm's preliminary, concurrent, and feedback control data. Indeed, the process of change can be viewed as a part of the control function, specifically the corrective action requirement. Financial statements, quality control data, budgets, and standard cost information are important media through which both external and internal forces are revealed. Declining profit margins and market shares are tangible signs that the firm's competitive position is deteriorating and that change may be required. Spiraling hospital costs may be a sign of inefficient hospital management. Because of their crucial importance, these sources of feedback-control information are highly developed in most organizations.

Intel microchips, which power every IBM personal computer and most of the machines compatible with them, are constantly being challenged.[13] A new technology has emerged that has been threatening Intel's dominance in the market. Recognizing the technology and deciding to produce the new technology itself, Intel is now in the business of producing ultrafast processors based on a design called RISC (reduced instruction set computing). Intel has recognized a need to change its product to stay on top and has taken action.

Several European companies, most notably Unilever and BMW, early on recognized and implemented the necessary changes in organizational structure, policies, and procedures required for successful marketing efforts in Japan.[14] Adaptation of distribution systems was a critical first step undertaken by these companies. Unilever engaged scores of small wholesalers to get products to the tens of thousands of neighborhoods in the rural regions of Japan. BMW built a new distribution system from scratch by selling dealerships to Japanese entrepreneurs who had the money and banking connections to finance operations at no cost to BMW. In addition BMW invested more than $20 million to improve previously inadequate facilities. Through recognition of the need for change, these companies are now dispelling the notion that European companies can't survive in Asia.

Step 2: Reaction—Diagnosis of the Problem

Before appropriate action can be taken, the symptoms of the problem must be analyzed to discover the problem itself. Experience and judgment are critical to this phase unless the problem is readily apparent to all observers. However, managers often disagree as to the nature of the problem. There is no magic formula, but the objectives of this phase can be met by answering three questions:

1. What is the problem, as distinct from the symptoms of the problem?
2. What must be changed to resolve the problem?
3. What outcomes (objectives) are expected from the change, and how will such objectives be measured?

The answers to these questions can come from information ordinarily found in organizations, such as financial statements, department reports, or attitude surveys. Or it may be necessary to generate ad hoc information through the creation of committees or task forces. Meetings between managers and employees provide a variety of points of view that can be sifted through by a smaller group. Technical operational problems may be diagnosed easily, but more subtle human relations problems usually entail extensive analysis.

One approach to diagnosing the problem is the attitude survey. Attitude questionnaires such as shown in Figure 16–2 can be administered to the entire workforce or to a sample of it. Such surveys permit the respondents to evaluate and rate management, pay and pay-related items, working conditions, equipment, and other job-related items. The appropriate use of such surveys requires that the data be collected (usually by questionnaires) from members of an organization, analyzed in detail, and communicated to various organization members. The objective of the survey is to pinpoint the problem or problems as perceived by the members of the organization. Subsequent feedback discussions of the survey results at all levels of the organization can add additional insights into the nature of the problem.

The accompanying Management Focus describes the approaches two banks took to manage significant changes. These approaches exemplify many of the principles discussed thus far.

Step 3: Stimuli—Alternative Change Techniques

The choice of the particular change technique depends on the nature of the problem management has diagnosed. Management must determine which alternative is most likely to produce the desired outcome. As we have noted previously, diagnosis of the problem includes specification of the outcomes management desires from the change. In this section, we describe a number of change techniques. They are classified according to the major focus of the technique: structure, people, or technology. This classification of organizational change techniques in no way implies a distinct division among the three types. On the contrary, the interrelationships of structure, people, and

Figure 16–2   Employee Attitude Survey (sample)

Attitude surveys can provide management with a wealth of information within a short time.

Instructions

This is a survey of the ideas and opinions of Baker Company salaried employees. WHAT YOU SAY IN THIS QUESTIONNAIRE IS COMPLETELY CONFIDENTIAL. We do not want to know who you are. We do want to know, however, how employees with different interests and experience and doing different kinds of work feel about their jobs and Baker.

This is not a test. There are no right or wrong answers. Whether the results of this survey give a true picture of the Baker Company depends on whether you answer each of the questions in the way you really feel. The usefulness of this survey in making Baker a better place to work depends on the honesty and care with which you answer the questions.

Your answers will be compiled with many others and summarized to prepare a *report* for Baker. Your identity will always be protected. We do not need your name, only your impressions. Your written comments will be put in typewritten form so that your handwriting will not even be seen by anyone at Baker.

Please complete each part of the survey so that all of your impressions can be recorded. Remember, your honest impressions are all that we are asking for.

Part 1: The Job and Conditions

The statements below are related to certain aspects of your job at Baker. Please circle the response number that best describes how you feel about each statement.

1—strongly disagree   2—disagree   3—undecided   4—agree   5—strongly agree

Pay	*Strongly Disagree*	*Disagree*	*Undecided*	*Agree*	*Strongly Agree*
My pay is all right for the kind of work I do.	1	2	3	4	5
I make as much money as most of my friends.	1	2	3	4	5
My pay allows me to keep up with the cost of living.	1	2	3	4	5
I am satisfied with the pay I receive for my job.	1	2	3	4	5
Most employees at Baker get paid at least what they deserve.	1	2	3	4	5
I understand how my salary is determined.	1	2	3	4	5
What changes, if any, should be made with the Baker pay system?					

Fringe Benefits	*Strongly Disagree*	*Disagree*	*Undecided*	*Agree*	*Strongly Agree*
Our major fringe benefit plan provides excellent coverage.	1	2	3	4	5
I understand what our fringe benefits at Baker are.	1	2	3	4	5
I am satisfied with our fringe benefit plan.	1	2	3	4	5
What, if anything, should be done with the Baker fringe benefit plans?					

Management Focus

Managing Change in the Banking Industry

In early 1981, BankAmerica Corporation was the largest and one of the most successful bank holding companies in the world. In the ensuing six years, the corporation was unable to respond quickly enough to changes brought about by deregulation, fierce new competition, and an unstable world economy. By 1986, BankAmerica was losing money (net losses of $1.8 billion for 1985–1987), had suspended payment of stock dividends, was in danger of hostile takeover, and was facing a serious capital reserve shortage. In sum, serious questions were being raised about BankAmerica's ability to survive.

Between 1986 and today, BankAmerica has returned to profitability. It has cut costs dramatically, increased revenue and marketshare, reinstated a dividend, improved its capital ratios, and been aggressively pursuing its markets. The dramatic turnaround is a direct result of a concerted effort on the part of management to fully understand BankAmerica's distinctive strengths in a new competitive environment and to develop specific strategies to put BankAmerica's future back into its own hands.

Five fundamental management steps were taken to make BankAmerica's recovery a reality. First, a management team of proven winners was assembled—people who understood that the company's survival depended on how well each job was done. Second, the entire business was reassessed. Both the organization and the approach to banking at BankAmerica was restructured. Third, a focus was placed on developing means to generate maximum shareholder value. For example, a determination was made that size and geographical presence were not of critical importance unless they led to improved profitability.

Fourth, the business was managed to produce immediate results. Concentration was placed on actions that would have immediate impact, yet not handcuff the future. Fifth, communication was stressed—both inside and outside the company. The company undertook efforts to consistently underpromise and overperform. The key to BankAmerica's successful turnaround was the realization that success results from melding and motivating a team approach to problem solving.

BankAmerica is not the only bank that has battled back from adversity. Since 1984, Continental Bank Corp. has operated under the watchful eye of the Federal Deposit Insurance Company, which stepped in when Continental was close to going under. Since then, Continental has followed a strategy of growth through subtraction. Through product by product reviews, the poorer performers such as foreign trading activities were cut. By picking its targets carefully, Continental succeeded in effecting change for the better. The situation at Continental improved dramatically. By 1990, Continental was fully in control of its own destiny, with the FDIC making plans to sell its remaining shares in the bank.

Sources: Adapted from S Zuckerman, "New Man Atop the Pyramid," *Business Week,* January 22, 1996, pp. 76–77; R D Hylton, "BankAmerica: Go Where the Money Is," *Fortune,* March 21, 1994, p. 70; A W Clausen, "Strategic Issues in Managing Change: The Turnaround at BankAmerica Corporation," *California Management Review,* Winter 1990, pp. 98–105; and D Greising and L J Nathans, "The Remake of the Remake at Continental Bank," *Business Week,* August 13, 1990, pp. 40–44.

technology must be acknowledged and anticipated. The majority of literature on organizational change indicates the relative weakness of efforts to change only structure (e.g., job design), only people (e.g., sensitivity training), or only technology (e.g., introducing new equipment or a new computer).[15]

Changes in the structure of the organization ordinarily follow changes in strategy.[16] Logically, the organizing function follows the planning function since the structure is a means for achieving the goals established through planning. A publicly announced major structural change occurred at AT&T when 6 major businesses were restructured into 19 smaller units. Seven regional companies (e.g., Bell Atlantic, Pacific Telesis Group, Nynex) were created after Judge Harold Green ordered the structural breakup of AT&T.[17] General Electric Company cut the number of management layers from nine to four. To make the company feel small, McDonald's Corporation added a position in its structure called the vice president for individuality.[18]

Structural change in the context of organizational change refers to managerial action that attempts to improve performance by altering the formal structure of task and authority relationships. At the same time, we must recognize that the structure creates human and social relationships that gradually can become ends for the members of the organization. These relationships, when they have been defined and made legitimate by management, introduce an element of stability.[19] Members of the organization may resist efforts to disrupt these relationships.

Structural changes alter some aspect of the formal task and authority definitions. As we have seen, the design of an organization involves definition and specification of jobs, grouping of jobs in departments, determination of the size of groups reporting to a single manager, and delegation of authority. Within this framework, the communication, decision-making, and human interaction processes occur.

Changes in the Nature of Jobs.   Changes in the nature of jobs originate with the implementation of new methods and new machines. Job enrichment, work simplification, and job enlargement are examples of methods changes. Scientific management introduced significant changes in the way work is done, through the use of motion and time studies. These methods tend to create highly specialized jobs. Job enrichment (see Chapter 11 for a discussion of motivation and job enrichment), however, moves in the opposite direction, toward despecialization.

An interesting example of attempted job enrichment took place in the stock transfer department of a large metropolitan bank.[20] The department was responsible for transferring the ownership of securities from one owner to another and recording the transfer. To remain competitive with other banks in the area, the entire stock transfer had to be completed within 48 hours. At the time of the study, 300 employees worked in the department.

Each employee reported to a work coordinator, who was responsible for 8 to 12 employees performing the same function. A job enrichment plan was developed in which the work of the department was divided into 13 modules. The modules focused on total responsibility for a group of corporations whose stock was handled by the bank. Under the old arrangement, employees arbitrarily handled whatever work was assigned.

Researchers hoped that the assignment of a specific set of corporations to each group working on a module would increase the employees' identification with and commitment to the work. These feelings were to be strengthened by allowing the workers in the module to leave work together when the security transactions from their assigned companies had been completed.

Modules were scheduled to be introduced one at a time. The researchers collected data on the nature of the jobs themselves, employee performance, and the change process by use of questionnaires, interviews, company records, and actual observations.

Employees reported almost no impact from the changes in the characteristics of the jobs. Researchers concluded that the type of changes in structure that, if performed, should have increased performance and effectiveness were not initiated as planned. For example, it was planned that employees would experience more autonomy in the modules because each module would be making its own decision. In fact, however, no structural changes were made to encourage the module members to take more responsibility. Moreover, managers continued to give orders and to supervise rather closely. In effect, management did not delegate as had been planned. And employees had the same feeling as before the modules were started—namely, that they had little autonomy.

FIGURE 16–3   Saab Engine Assembly Line before Enlarging Jobs

---

In Saab's traditional assembly line, an engine spent, on average, 1.8 minutes at each of seven workstations.

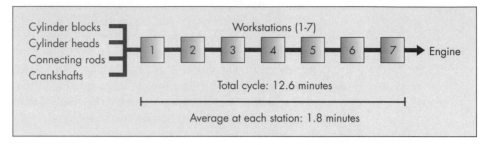

This example illustrates the value of research even on unsuccessful job changes. In a "pure" sense, this change in the job did not occur. However, it provided a valuable lesson about the interrelationships between people and structure. It also indicated that job enrichment is not always a simple solution to managerial work-related problems.

Job Enlargement.   Job enlargement involves making a job larger by increasing the number of tasks to perform. A traditional assembly line can be converted to a line with enlarged jobs. The assembly line is created by breaking down the total product (a television set, an automobile, a clothes dryer) into specialized stations. Each station has tools and workers that do a specific job. Stations are connected to one another by a work flow plan. At a General Motors Corporation assembly plant in Lordstown, Ohio, the average time cycle that a worker performs on a job at a station is 36 seconds. Thus, a worker faced a new automobile part over 700 times in each eight-hour shift.

Saab Automobile Company in Sweden decided to build a new automobile engine assembly plant and considered alternative ways of setting up jobs on the assembly line.[21] The engineering team working on the problem decided that the typical system of assembly, with a cycle of 12.6 minutes to put an engine together (1.8 minutes per station at seven workstations), could be improved. The traditional assembly system is presented in Figure 16–3. Rather than have seven specialists (one at each workstation on the line), Saab management elected to have one person follow an engine from start to finish. The new arrangement is presented in Figure 16–4. The average time a worker spends on the assembly of an engine is about 30 minutes, as opposed to the 1.8 minutes spent at the old workstation. By assembling an entire engine, a worker might find the work more interesting and challenging. Of course, whether the work becomes more interesting and challenging depends on the person and the change. Adding tasks that are meaningless may be enlargement, but it may also have negative effects on performance and morale.

Changes in Line—Staff Relationships.   The usual approach in changing line–staff relationships is to create staff assistance as either an ad hoc or permanent solution. An illustrative case is a company that had grown quite rapidly since its entry into the fast-food industry. Its basic sources of field control were area directors who supervised the operations of sales outlets of particular regions. During the growth period, the area directors had considerable autonomy in making the advertising decisions for their

FIGURE 16-4   Saab Engine Assembly Line after Enlarging Jobs

In the new work flow at Saab, each worker has a total job.

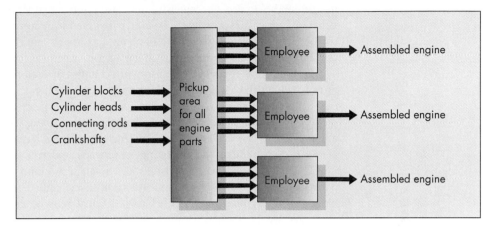

regions. They could select their own media, formats, and budgets within general guidelines. But as their markets became saturated and as competitors appeared, corporate officials decided to centralize the advertising function in a staff unit located at corporate headquarters. Consequently, the area directors' freedom was limited, and an essential job aspect was eliminated.[22]

A second illustration of changes in line–staff relationships is based on the case of a large insurance company that hired a management consulting firm to analyze the problem created by a deteriorating market position.[23] The consulting company recommended changing a staff position to a line manager. The consultants' belief was that the company must have its best personnel and resources available at the branch office level to increase premium income. Accordingly, the consultants recommended that assistant managers be converted to first-level supervisors reporting to branch managers. The transformation required a significant change in the work of both assistant managers and managers throughout the organization.

Changes in Sociotechnical Systems.   The term *sociotechnical systems* is identified with research originally done by the Tavistock Institute in Great Britain. Change efforts have attempted to develop a better fit between the technology, the structure, and the social interaction patterns of a unit, department, or office.[24]

While jobs, rewards, physical equipment, work schedules, and other factors may be altered in sociotechnical change, none of these is the central focus of the change activities. Instead, employees, union members, nonunion members, and managers examine all aspects of the work operation. Potential changes emerge from the collaboration and discussion of employees. A distinct feature of sociotechnical systems change is that groups of employees share the responsibility for initiating changes.

One of the earliest studies of sociotechnical change was in British coal mining. A team approach was used to develop enlarged jobs and team pay incentive plans. This study indicated improved productivity, safety, and morale after the team initiated changes.[25] Using the British results, a study was conducted at the Rushton Coal Mine in Phillipsburg, Pennsylvania. A steering committee comprising management and local union officials met to consider methods for improving mine safety. It was decided that crew members should be trained in all jobs in a section, trained in state and federal mine laws and in group problem solving, and made responsible for the production of coal and any initial handling of grievances.[26]

The results after one year indicated fewer violations of federal laws by the crews in the study, lower absenteeism, increased job satisfaction and cooperation, and generally better performance. The crews involved in recommending and initiating the sociotechnical changes were overall better performers and reported higher morale than counterparts not collaborating in changing the system.

Despite some reported successes with changes in sociotechnical systems, there are problems with the approach. Sociotechnical system change approaches have, in many cases, ignored individual differences in how people react to various changes. Some people do not want the sociotechnical aspects of their jobs or work environment altered. There are also union representatives who claim that collaborative efforts between management and operating employees undermine the union's influence on rank-and-file members. Likewise, some managers claim that collaborative efforts permanently undermine management's right to manage. These types of problems will be addressed by managers and behavioral scientists who are learning more about the strengths, weaknesses, and future uses of changes in sociotechnical systems.

People Change

The early efforts to engage in people change date back to scientific management-work improvement and employee-training methods. These attempts were directed primarily at improving employee skills and knowledge. The employee counseling programs that grew out of the Hawthorne studies were (and remain) primarily directed at improving employee attitudes. Equally important as the attitudes of those being changed are the attitudes of those bringing about change, and some individuals seem to be better than others at bringing about change. The accompanying Management Focus profiles one individual who has been credited with much success as a change agent.

Training and development programs for managers typically have emphasized supervisory relationships. These programs attempt to provide supervisors with basic technical and human relations skills. Since supervisors are primarily concerned with overseeing the work of others, the content of these traditional programs emphasizes techniques for dealing with people problems: how to handle the malcontent, the loafer, the troublemaker, or the complainer. The programs also include conceptual material dealing with communications, leadership styles, and organizational relationships. The vehicles for training include role-playing, discussion groups, lectures, and organized courses offered by universities.[27]

Training continues to be an important technique for introducing people changes. Training has taken on quite a different form in some applications from that which developed in classical management theory.[28] Among some managers, a popular behavioral change approach is sensitivity training.

Sensitivity Training.   This change technique attempts to make the participants more aware of themselves and of their impact on others. "Sensitivity" in this context means sensitivity to self and to relationships with others. An assumption of sensitivity training is that the causes of poor task performance are the emotional problems of people who must collectively achieve a goal. If these problems can be removed, a major impediment to task performance is eliminated. Sensitivity training stresses the "*process* rather than the *content* of training and . . . *emotional* rather than *conceptual* training."[29] We can see that this form of training is quite different from traditional forms stressing the acquisition of a predetermined body of concepts with immediate application to the workplace.

Bell Atlantic's Change Agent

When Raymond Smith became CEO of Bell Atlantic in 1989, he confronted the imperative of changing an organization that had become a slow-to-act bureaucracy to a fast-response entrepreneurial entity. The driving force behind the change was the deregulation of the communications industry, which had resulted in the breakup of AT&T into small operating units. Rather than rely on outside consultants for transforming the organization, Smith took on the role of champion of change himself with a full understanding of all the demands that the role would place on him. He immediately set about the process of fact gathering and consensus building through discussions with managers and nonmanagers throughout the organization. His intent was to demonstrate by word and deed that Bell Atlantic had to change in fundamental ways if the company was to survive in the competitive, deregulated environment.

Some of the signs of progress that demonstrate Smith's impact include the breaking down of barriers between departments, the sharing of resources, and the development of attitudes that encourage teamwork and idea sharing. He attributes much of this success to the creation of the sense of empowerment among Bell employees. They believe that if they act for the good of the company and succeed, both they and the company prosper. But if failure is the outcome, the failure is shared by all. Thus Smith has apparently managed to play the roles of both internal and external change agent: He has reoriented the company to its environment and revised the internal structure of the company to be consistent with the new environmental demands—competition.

Sources: R W Smith, "Driving Change at Bell Atlantic," *Planning Review,* September–October 1994, pp. 25–27; and R M Kanter, "Championing Change: An Interview with Bell Atlantic's CEO Raymond Smith," *Harvard Business Review,* January–February 1991, pp. 119–30.

The process of sensitivity training includes a group of managers (training group or T group) that, in most cases, meets at some location other than their place of work. Under the direction of a trainer, the group usually engages in a dialogue with no agenda and no focus. The objective is to provide an environment that produces its own learning experiences.[30] The unstructured dialogue encourages one to learn about self in dealing with others. One's motives and feelings are revealed through behavior toward others in the group and through the behavior of others. The T group is typically unstructured. As Alfred Marrow points out in a report of his own sensitivity training, "It [sensitivity training] says, 'Open your eyes. Look at yourself. See how you look to others. Then decide what changes, if any, you want to make and in which direction you want to go.' "[31]

The role of the trainer in the T group is to facilitate the learning process. According to organization researcher Kelly, the trainer's mission is "to observe, record, interpret, sometimes to lead, and always to learn."[32] The artistry and style of the trainer are critical variables in determining the direction of the T group's sessions. The trainer must walk the uneasy path of unobtrusive leadership, able to interpret the roles of participants and encourage them to analyze their contributions without being perceived as a threat. Unlike the group therapist, the T-group trainer is dealing with people who are not having emotional problems but who have come together to learn. The ordinarily prescribed role of the trainer is that of "permissive, nonauthoritarian, sometimes almost nonparticipative" leadership.[33]

A critical test of sensitivity training is whether the experience itself is a factor leading to improvement in task performance. It is apparent that even if the training induces positive changes in the participant's sensitivity to self and others, such behavior may be either not possible or not permissible back in the workplace. The participant must deal with the same environment and the same people as before the training. The open, supportive, and permissive environment of the training sessions is not likely to be found on the job. Even so, proponents of sensitivity training would reply that it makes the participant better able to deal with the environment. We should also recognize that sensitivity training may well induce negative changes in the participant's ability to perform organizational tasks. The training sessions can be occasions of extreme stress and anxiety. The capacity to deal effectively with stress varies among individuals, and the outcome may be dysfunctional for some participants.

The research evidence to date suggests mixed results on the effectiveness of sensitivity training as a change technique.[34] A detailed review of 100 research studies found that sensitivity training was most effective at the personal level.[35] The studies compared the influence of 20 or more hours of training on the participants' attitudes or behaviors. The review concluded that sensitivity training:

- Stimulated short-term improvement in communication skills.
- Encouraged trainees to believe that they controlled their behavior more than others.
- Was likely to increase the participative orientation of trainees in leadership positions.
- Improved the perceptions of others toward the trainee.

Managers should critically examine this technique in terms of the kinds of changes desired and those that are possible. Our model suggests the existence of conditions that limit the range of possible changes. In this light, managers must determine whether the changes induced by sensitivity training are instrumental for organizational purposes and whether the prospective participant is able to tolerate the potential anxiety of the training.

A major limitation of sensitivity training is the assumption that when people are aware of themselves, positive changes will be made. This assumption evolves from principles of psychotherapy, where individuals are encouraged to confront their emotions, values, and experiences. Of course, each person has a different capacity to confront values, emotions, and experiences, and some simply refuse.

Team Building.   Team building is a change technique that involves an entire group (e.g., a unit, a department) that works on a problem facing the members.[36] Figure 16–5 presents the events that typically occur in team building. First, the problem is identified. Then, the full group participates in diagnosing the problem. The main contributing reasons to the problem are identified. After the problem and reasons are clarified, alternative solutions and their positive and negative features are discussed. A solution is selected and then implemented.

An important potential benefit of team building as an organizational change approach is that through interaction in solving problems, the group members become more familiar with one another and the solution. This results in an increased commitment to the solution and its implementation.

A number of barriers to effective team building have been concisely outlined for managers to consider before they adopt it as a change strategy. For team building to have a chance at being successful, it must meet four conditions:

FIGURE 16–5   Team Building: Sequence of Events

Team building places an entire group in close contact in order to work on solving a specific problem.

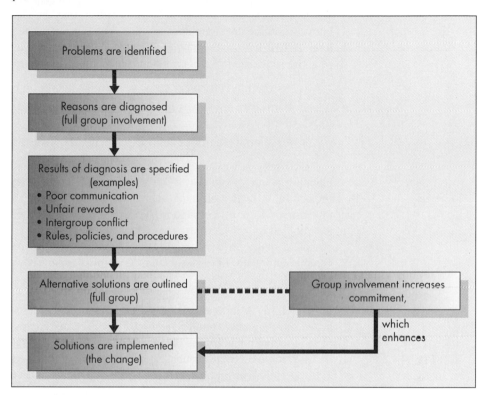

1. The group must have a natural reason (e.g., task completion) for existing.
2. Group members must be mutually dependent on one another in task experience and abilities. If dependence is not present, there is less commitment.
3. Group members must have similar status.
4. Group communications must be open and trusting.[37]

General Motors Corporation reopened a Fremont, California, plant as a joint venture with Toyota Motor Corporation. The company was called New United Motor Manufacturing, Inc. (NUMMI). Labor and management worked to develop a team approach at the plant, aiming at high productivity levels, low levels of defects, low absenteeism, and more satisfied employees. For four years, the results have looked excellent. But opponents of the labor–management team-building approach claim that team building is a management device to substitute peer pressure for traditional management practice; a number of employees have criticized their union leadership as being too close to management. At NUMMI, the majority of employees appear to be pleased with the team concept; however, there are signals that dissension, disappointment, and jealousy are not entirely eliminated by team building.[38]

Life and Career Planning.   Company-sponsored programs for life and career planning are growing in popularity. These programs use formal classroom or counseling settings. Participants are asked to focus on their past, present, and future[39] and to work out their life and career plans. Typically plans are developed after some self-assessment and self-study.[40] These plans may be discussed with colleagues, a human resource development specialist, or a manager. The objective is to have people look at their lives and career plans in a systematic and thorough manner.

The sequence of steps in many life and career-planning programs is as follows:

1. Assess life and career paths up to now, noting highlights.
2. Formulate objectives for both desired lifestyle and career path, and forecast the future.
3. Develop a plan of action for achieving the goals and schedule target dates.

Generally, life planning and career planning are done concurrently because career planning is but one subset of life planning. Whether life and career planning has any impact on individual attitudes and behaviors has not been scientifically determined at this time. Most of the support for this type of program is found in the form of testimonials of those who have participated in life and career planning. Those who complete such exercises enthusiastically claim that they understand themselves, their careers, and their lifestyles better. They also report having less anxiety about the future.

Total Quality Management (TQM).   This important change approach has emerged as the most significant and widespread approach to change in the 1990s. One measure of its growing popularity is the increasingly voluminous literature on the subject. Prior to 1989, the ABINFOR database contained fewer than 40 citations on the subject; from 1990 to 1992 that number grew to over 300. Books and articles on TQM proliferate. The contemporary and future manager must be familiar with the ideas of the proponents of TQM.[41]

We will not attempt a full description of all aspects of TQM here. Our point is that implementation of TQM in organizations involves a near-total transformation of their structural and people components including the underlying culture.[42] Moreover, the ideas of the experts who propose TQM as a solution to America's declining competitiveness in global markets emphasize the necessity of organizational development principles, particularly employee involvement, as the means for implementing TQM.[43]

Motorola, Ford Motor Company, Procter and Gamble, IBM, and Xerox are but a few of the important large and small organizations that have implemented TQM and, consequently, brought about profound transformations of their organizations.[44] It cannot be said that these organizations have totally recovered from the problems that beset them during the 1980s, however. For example, IBM has yet to regain its position as the global leader of the computer industry. Nevertheless, IBM remains committed to TQM as its best chance. On a larger scale of endorsement, the United States government has acknowledged the importance of TQM by establishing the Baldrige Award competition to recognize firms that make the greatest progress toward implementing TQM.[45]

TQM has as many meanings and definitions as organizations that have decided to implement it. But the overriding sense of TQM endorses the importance of fact-based decision making, quality products and services, and employee-centered management through empowerment and participation.[46] At the formal level of the organization,

TQM requires complete job redesign to include self-directed work teams where possible, organic organization structure, and cross-functional coordinative groups. At the informal level, TQM requires trust and commitment to the organization and its mission, cooperativeness rather than competition among individuals and groups, and honesty in the reconciliation of differences.

Technological Change

This category of change includes any application of new ways to transform resources into the product or service. In the usual sense of the word, technology means new machines—robots, lathes, presses, computers, and the like. But we expand the concept to include new techniques, with or without new machines. From this perspective, the work improvement methods of scientific management can be considered technological breakthroughs.

Robots.   The word *robot* conjures visions of complex machines that both look and perform like human beings. C3PO in the popular *Star Wars* movies helped create these viewpoints. In reality, robots are quite different; they scarcely resemble people and perform a limited range of job tasks.[47] However, robots are a technological force that is creating resistance and fears among many people—namely, workers in the automobile and electrical-component industries.

The Robotics Institute of America defines a robot as a "reprogrammable multifunctional manipulator designed to move material, parts, tools, or specialized devices through programmed motions for the performance of a variety of tasks."[48] The more sophisticated robots are called intelligent, while their less sophisticated counterparts are labeled dumb, slaves, grasshoppers (an automobile industry term), and CAM (computer-aided manufacturing).

Robot use is expected to continue to grow throughout the remainder of this century because of wage inflation and the development of the microprocessor, a computer small enough to act as the brains of a robot.[49] In the 1960s, a typical assembly-line robot cost $4.20 an hour (averaged over its lifetime), which was slightly higher than the average factory worker's wages and fringe benefits. Today, the robot can be operated for less than $4 an hour, while the employee now makes between $25 and $30 an hour.

One of the earliest countries to realize the economic benefits of robots was Japan. Although most of the original research and development on robotic technology occurred in the United States, Japan has over 40,000 of the world's 60,000 robots. Not content to rest on their laurels, Japanese companies today are aiming to wrest the lead away from American companies in developing microrobots—motors, sensors, and other devices so small they barely span the breadth of human hair.[50] These microrobots have the potential to be used in everything from medicine to nuclear power plants.

Some American firms realize that for them to be competitive in various manufacturing industries, robots are mandatory. General Motors has formed a joint-venture robotics company, GM Fanus Robotics Corp., which is the largest robotics manufacturer in the United States. At an engine plant in Romulus, Michigan, 40 percent more engines are produced per day than prior to the introduction of robots.[51]

The changes in organizational efficiency brought about by a new machine or robot are calculable in economic and engineering terms. Whether the robot or machine is a good investment is a matter of estimating its future profitability in relation to its present cost. These calculations are an important part of the managerial control function. Here, however, we are interested in the impact of the machine or robot on the structure of the organization and on the behavior of the people in the organization.

As some scholars have observed, technology is a key determinant of structure.[52] They tentatively conclude that firms with simple and stable technology should adopt a structure that tends toward classical organization, whereas firms with complex and dynamic technology ought to move toward the more open and flexible neoclassical structure.[53] Thus, it would appear that the adoption of new technology involves a concurrent decision to adapt the organizational structure to that technology.

Organizations must be willing to use technology to change their systems rather than just be content to mechanize old ways of doing business.[54] Leaving existing processes intact and simply utilizing technology to speed up these processes fails to address fundamental performance deficiencies. Many companies' job designs, work flows, control mechanisms, and organizational structures came of age in a different competitive environment and before the advent of the computer and robots. They are geared toward efficiency and control. Yet the watchwords of the 1990s are innovation, speed, service, and quality.

Impact of Robots.   The most recognizable impact of robot technology is likely to be on the behavior of groups and individuals. In the short run, robots have displaced some employees. This displacement creates feelings of insecurity, uncertainty, and fear, which lead to resistance on the part of workers.[55] Some organizations have attempted to minimize this resistance by having workers participate in planning the introduction of robots.

To catalog the impact of technological change on structure and behavior, organization researcher Mann analyzed a number of actual cases and concluded that the adoption of new machines in the factory involves:[56]

- Major changes in the division of labor and the content of jobs.
- Changes in social relations among workers.
- Improving working conditions.
- The need for different supervisory skills.
- Changes in career patterns, promotion procedures, and job security.
- Generally higher wages.
- Generally higher prestige for those who work.
- Around-the-clock operations.

The degree and extent of these observed changes in structure and behavior depend on the magnitude of the technological change. Obviously, the introduction of a new offset printing press will not cause the great dislocations and changes that Mann observes, but the introduction of robots on a previously human-paced manufacturing process would include many, if not all, of them.

Figure 16–6 portrays the three approaches to organizational change, the types of programs in each approach, and the anticipated outcomes. The potential and actual accomplishment of such outcomes is why managers search out, test, and evaluate various change techniques.

Step 3: Reaction—Recognition of Limiting Conditions

The selection of the change technique is based on diagnosis of the problem. But the choice is tempered by certain conditions that exist at the time. Three sources influence the outcome of management change efforts. They can be generalized to cover the

FIGURE 16–6   **Selected Programs, Techniques, and Outcomes of Organizational Change**

Manangers seek change techniques in the hope of making improvements in many areas of production and performance.

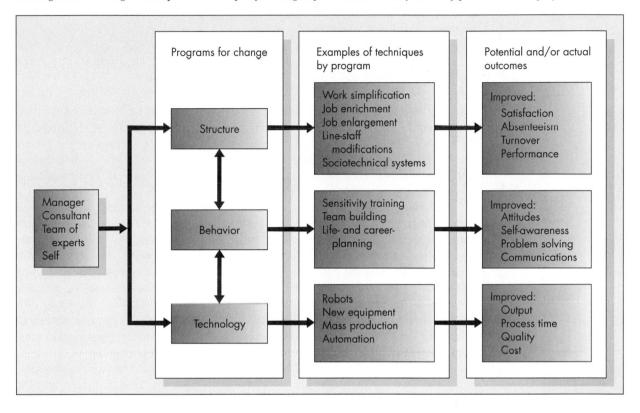

entire range of organizational change efforts, whether structural, behavioral, or technological. They are leadership climate, formal organization, and organizational culture.

Leadership climate refers to the nature of the work environment resulting from the leadership style and administrative practices of superiors. Any change program that does not have the support and commitment of management has slim chance of success; managers must be at least neutral toward the change. The style of leadership itself may be the subject of change. For example, sensitivity training is a direct attempt to move managers toward a certain style—open, supportive, and group centered. But the participants may be unable to adopt styles that are not compatible with their own superiors' styles.

The *formal organization* must be compatible with the proposed change. This includes the effects on the environment that result from the philosophy and policies of top management, as well as legal precedent, organizational structure, and the system of control. Of course, each of these sources of impact may be the focus of the change effort; the important point is that a change in one must be compatible with all others. For example, a change in technology that eliminates jobs contradicts a policy of guaranteed employment.

The *organizational culture* refers to the impact on the environment resulting from "group norms, values, philosophy, and informal activities."[57] The importance of traditional behavior, sanctioned by group norms but not formally acknowledged, was first documented in the Hawthorne studies. A proposed change in work methods or the installation of an automated device can run counter to the expectations and attitudes of work groups. The concept of culture is rooted in theories of group dynamics and group growth. Such being the case, the change strategist must anticipate the resulting resistance that can evolve from the group.[58]

Step 4: Reaction—The Strategy for Change

Selection of a strategy for implementing the change technique has consequences in the final outcome. Larry Greiner analyzes a number of organization changes to determine the relationship of various change strategies to the relative success of the change itself.[59] He identifies three approaches, located along a continuum, with unilateral authority at one extreme and delegated authority at the other extreme. In the middle of the continuum are approaches he calls shared authority.

Unilateral approaches can take the form of an edict from top management describing the change and the responsibilities of subordinates in implementing it.[60] *Shared approaches* involve lower-level groups in the process of either defining the problem and alternative solutions or defining solutions only after higher-level management has defined the problem. In either case, the process engages the talents and insights of all members at all levels. Finally, *delegated approaches* relinquish complete authority to subordinate groups. Through freewheeling discussions, the group ultimately is responsible for the analysis of the problem and proposed solutions. According to Greiner, the relatively more successful instances of organizational change are those that tend toward the shared position of the continuum.

Why would this be the case? As has been observed, most instances of organizational change are accompanied by resistance from those involved in the change. The actual form of resistance may range in extreme from passive resignation to deliberate sabotage. The objective of shared approaches is at least to minimize resistance and at most to maximize cooperation and support. The manner in which the change is managed from beginning to end is a key determinant of how employees and lower-echelon managers react.

Step 5: Reaction—Implementation and Evaluation

The implementation of the proposed change has two dimensions: timing and scope. *Timing* is the selection of the appropriate time to initiate the change. *Scope* is the selection of the appropriate scale of the change. The matter of timing is strategic and depends on a number of factors, particularly the company's operating cycle and the groundwork preceding the change. Certainly, if a change is of considerable magnitude, it is desirable that it not compete with ordinary business operations. Thus, it might well be implemented during a slack period. On the other hand, if the problem is critical to the survival of the organization, immediate implementation is in order. The scope of the change depends on the strategy. The change may be implemented throughout the organization and become an established fact in a short time. Or it may be phased into the organization, level by level, department by department. The strategy of successful changes, according to Greiner, makes use of a phased approach, which limits the scope but provides feedback for each subsequent implementation.

Evaluation is an important and often overlooked step in organizational change programs. Essentially, evaluation should be made by comparing the results (the benefits) with the objectives of the organizational change program. It is difficult to evaluate the effectiveness of most change efforts. But it is crucial to know what has resulted in terms of attitudes, productivity, and behavior.

The three criteria for evaluating organizational change programs are internal, external, and participant reaction. *Internal criteria* are directly associated with the basis of the program. For example, did the sociotechnical change result in increased frequency of employee exchange of job information, or did the employees in the job enrichment seminar learn the core dimensions of the job? *External criteria* are related to the effectiveness of employees before and after the change is implemented. Possible external criteria include increased number of units produced per work hour, increased sales volume, and better quality of workmanship. *Participant reaction criteria* attempt to determine how the individuals affected by the change feel about it.

One useful device encourages the use of multiple and systematic assessment. Figure 16–7 presents a guideline for managers to use. The costs and benefits of any organizational change effort can be determined only if evaluation programs are used. Simply asking individuals if they like the sensitivity training program or the job enlargement changes is not very thorough. It would be more systematic and thorough to monitor changes in structure, people, and technology over long periods.

FIGURE 16–7   An Evaluation Matrix: Issues to Consider

Systematic evaluation programs enable managers to more accurately assess the costs and benefits of organizational change.

Relevant Issues to Cover and Evaluate	Examples of What to Measure	Who or What to Examine for Answers	How to Collect Data to Answer Issue Questions
1. Are the employees learning, changing attitudes, and improving skills?	Employees' attitudes and skills before and after (even during) training or development sessions	Comments Method of participation Co-workers Superiors	Interviews Questionnaires Records Observation
2. Are organizational change materials used on the job?	Employees' on-the-job performance, behavior, and style	Subordinate performance, attitudes, and style	Records Interviews Questionnaires Critical incidents Observation
3. What are the costs of organizational change programs and techniques?	The fixed and variable costs of conducting the change programs	Cost of consultants Participant time Travel expenses Training aids Rent Utilities	Budget records
4. How long does the organizational change program have an affect on employees?	Employees' on-the-job performance, behavior, and style over an extended period	Subordinate performance, attitudes, and style	Records Interviews Questionnaires Critical incidents Repeated observation

Summary of Key Points

- Organization development (OD) is a method for facilitating change and development in structures and processes (e.g., relationships, roles), people (e.g., styles, skills), and technology (e.g., more routineness, more challenge).
- Employees have numerous reasons for resisting change. Some of the most commonly cited are parochial self-interest, misunderstanding and lack of trust, different assessments, and a low tolerance for change.
- Managers can take some steps to minimize resistance: education and communication, participation and involvement, facilitation and support, negotiation and agreement, manipulation and co-optation, and explicit and implicit coercion.
- A five-part model presented in Figure 16–1 provides some order and a framework for the study of organizational change and development. Step 1 includes stimuli such as internal and external forces that trigger a reaction or recognition of the need for change. Step 2 involves the diagnosis for problem areas. Step 3 involves stimuli in the form of alternative change techniques that can be selected and a reaction by managers in that limiting conditions are recognized. In Step 4, a decision is made on the strategy and the technique to use. Step 5 involves the implementation and evaluation of the change.

- The choice of a particular change technique depends on the nature of the problem management has diagnosed. We classify the change techniques according to the major focus of the change technique: structure, people, or technology. Techniques to change structure include changes in the nature of jobs, job enlargement, changes in line–staff relationships, and changes in sociotechnical systems. Techniques to change people include sensitivity training, team building, life and career planning, and TQM. Techniques to change technology include any application of new ways to transform resources into the product or service, such as new technology (e.g., robots).
- Strategies for introducing change are *unilateral* (an edict for change comes from top management), *delegated* (control for the change is relinquished to those being affected by the change), and *shared* (participation is shared between the initiators and recipients of change in deciding on the problem or solution).
- In many cases, not enough time and effort are spent on the evaluation of change. Evaluation of behavior, results, and attitudes is needed to examine the costs and benefits of any structural, people, or technological change effort.

Discussion and Review Questions

1. How could team building enhance commitment to a structural change in an organization?

2. In which situations might change be undesirable? Use examples in answering this question.

3. Why is it important to focus on problems rather than symptoms of problems?

4. Can you present an example that you are familiar with in which a job can be enlarged? Use the Saab example to help you think through the necessary features for job enlargement.

5. It has been claimed that as the tasks performed by humans become more complex, the probability of robots replacing human labor increases. Do you agree?

6. Using an organization that you are familiar with, present an example of a situation where change was resisted. Looking back, what possible solutions could have been pursued to overcome the resistance to change?

7. As an individual or group project, interview academic officers in the university or college you attend. These officers can be chairs, deans, presidents, or their representatives. From these interviews, obtain an understanding of what forces are acting on the institution to bring about change and what responses the institution is undertaking to meet these forces.

8. Why has total quality management (TQM) become such a popular response to change in the 1990s? What forces have made quality in goods and services necessary for becoming and remaining competitive?

9. What particular factors that cause people to resist change generally would cause them to resist TQM? Explain your answer.

10. Explain why the strategy for implementing change can have such a significant impact on the potential success of organizational change.

CASE 16–1
IMPLEMENTING TOTAL QUALITY MANAGEMENT AT THIOKOL CORPORATION

Background

The Huntsville Division of Thiokol Corporation consists of approximately 700 employees and has been located in northern Alabama since 1949. It now occupies 256 buildings totaling over 1 million square feet of sheltered research, engineering, and production space. Products are primarily small to mid-size rocket motor propulsion systems for tactical and space applications, including Patriot, Maverick, HELLFIRE, Sidewinder, TOW, MK 70, Castor, and other rockets. The Huntsville Division is part of the Thiokol Corporation, a Utah-based $1-billion-plus company with eight operating divisions and 11,500 employees.

Getting Started

Thiokol/Huntsville Division (THD) formally embarked on implementation of a total quality management process in mid-1989. The working definition of total quality that was developed for application throughout the business unit is as follows: *Doing the right things right, the first and every time, in a mode of continuous improvement, focused on customer satisfaction.* As part of an off-site executive total quality workshop, this definition was used as a basis for developing the following vision statement, which would provide direction for other business decisions and practices: *To be a recognized leader in our industry, working with pride, integrity and teamwork to provide products and services of unmatched quality and value to our customers.*

Part of the executive team's challenge was to "walk the talk" and show employees that our total quality/continuous improvement (TQ/CI) process was not just another program. We had had a lot of them, including "value management" and "zero defects" in the 1960s, "quality thinking" and "error-cause removal" in the 70s, and "quality circles" and "productivity teams" in the 80s.

One of the formal ways to ensure that our TQ/CI process was indeed not just another program was to establish measures of success. To define success, however, it became obvious quite early that the executive staff should have input from the employee population. An attitude and opinion survey was generated using Tom Peters's Excellence Audit Kit, which is based on his book, *Thriving on Chaos*.

The audit was developed using input from a team of 10 employees, representing a diagonal cross-section of the population, and was then administered to all 1,000 employees in small groups on company time during September 1989. The survey contained approximately 50 business practices/philosophy areas, asking the following questions for each one: How much are we like this? and How important is it to

be like this? A numerical rating scale was used, and we were able to use the data to determine the areas that were deemed very important but where we were not doing as well as we needed to. Additionally, a section of the survey included traditional human-resource "climate" questions about how employees feel about their own jobs. An extract from that portion of the survey and the results are shown in Exhibit 1. On a rating scale of 1 to 5, we considered 4 to be acceptable. We were encouraged that although a lot of areas were identified as needing improvement, basically employees felt that THD was "a good place to work." Data from the various parts of the survey were summarized and shared with employees through company newsletters and during interactive TQ/CI workshops.

Additionally, initial action plans were provided for the areas needing improvement. In this way, we were able to prioritize and publicize the first improvement targets within the business unit. Publicizing also put our management commitment to the test since we were putting in writing a major part of what we intended to do, and how we intended to do it. If we didn't "walk the talk" and follow through, the "new way" would have no credibility.

Adding Structure

A Total Quality/Continuous Improvement Executive Steering Council was established and chaired by the vice president/division manager and included all of his direct reports. This group meets regularly to discuss issues related to the improvement process in a forum separate from other routine business issues. The steering committee provides prioritization, guidance, monitoring, sponsorship, and leadership for the improvement teams and other elements of the process.

To ensure that the TQ/CI process is consistent with business direction, the five-year strategic business plan was modified to add a section for total quality. In this plan, which is updated annually, the TQ/CI strategy is laid out, objectives and time frame established, and goals set. Long- and short-range improvement project plans are included from all functional organizations. The TQ/CI Executive Steering Council monitors activities of the plan and directs and manages changes as appropriate.

Training

Early on, it was decided that the traditional approach to training for total quality would not produce the desired results in THD's culture and structure. A training plan was established for TQ/CI and was later expanded and integrated

Exhibit 1   Some of the Employee Survey Results

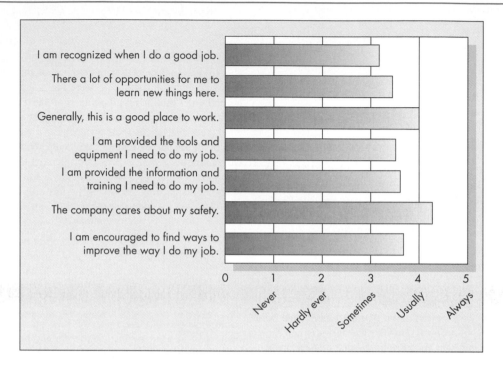

with THD's overall training plan. Within the first seven months after the initial attitude survey, all employees participated in a TQ/CI workshop. This workshop, representing Phase I of the TQ/CI training program, was normally eight hours, conducted in groups of 15 to 25 from a natural work group, and broken into two half-day sessions. Eight hours is generally considered "light weight" for training that is supposed to effect a major cultural change, but it was supplemented in a unique way that will be discussed shortly.

The workshops were conducted top-down with most supervisors going through them twice: once with their peers and their boss, and then again with their subordinates. Two complementary sets of the basic materials were developed so that the viewgraphs, videos, and exercises had enough diversity to keep the supervisors interested. Further, the supervisors kicked off the session for their subordinates, providing a constancy of purpose and support down through the organization.

Each eight-hour workshop was tailored to the work group in attendance, so that groups consisting primarily of supervisors were provided leadership/people-skills training to reinforce the change from a traditional, authoritarian style, to one of encouraging employee involvement without threat. Each eight-hour workshop covered the essentials of the TQ philosophy—effective organizations, visioning, human resource implications of TQ/CI, prescription for excellence (employee survey results), and implementation at the Hunts-

ville Division. Statistical process control (SPC), on which alone many companies spend days of training, was only briefly touched on, giving an overview of the common SPC terms and charting methods so that employees would be familiar with them when at some future point they were needed in their work environment.

One of the unique aspects of THD's TQ/CI training program is "just-in-time" training. Not just-in-time (JIT) in the sense of inventory management, but rather training that is provided *just in time* for when it will be applied. When an employee is selected or volunteers to participate in a process improvement team (discussed later), the team receives additional training as Phase II. Team participants are trained in the tools to implement the fundamentals of total quality on the process they are working on. This tailored training includes issues of customer focus, problem solving/process analysis (including more detailed SPC than in Phase I), measurement/feedback, team building, effective meetings, and goal setting.

As teams review their systems and processes, special courses/modules are provided to fill the needs for specific skills that have to be developed, such as Design of Experiments or Quality Function Deployment. This just-in-time training has proved not only to be cost-effective, but also to have the maximum possible impact on the employees' retention of the learned skills for application back in the normal workplace (when employees are not working on a specific process improvement team).

Process Implementation Teams

Implementation of TQ/CI at THD is through two types of teams: departmental teams and critical process improvement teams. Departmental teams are designed around existing organizational structure and are based on the concept that every person is a member of the team made up of the department/group in which he or she works. This is in contrast to early implementation of quality circles in which participation was optional. Managers are members of departmental teams at two levels: the department team they manage and the team consisting of their peer group reporting to the next level manager. Mission statements are developed and improvement opportunities identified at all levels, as presented in Exhibit 2. Department teams are tasked with determining their supplier–customer relationships, defining customer expectations, mapping and reviewing departmental processes, establishing improvement opportunities, providing both internal and external feedback and measurement to monitor for continuous improvement, and reporting status to cognizant management.

When employees and management identify processes that are multiorganizational in nature and high in impact, a critical process improvement team is formed of a group of individuals whose background and experience allow them to evaluate specific processes for restructure and improvement opportunities. As multifunctional groups similar to ad hoc task forces, these teams are brought together as needed by the steering council and are given special training to aid them in their responsibility to map out selected major processes, identify root causes of problems and waste, select solutions, and, most important, oversee the effective implementation of those changes.

Measures of Progress

To assess the effectiveness of the total quality process, a variety of measures are used at both local and macro levels. Thiokol believes that "what gets measured, gets improved." At the macro level, it was found to be very difficult to design a single, overall productivity measure for the business unit, so instead, several measures are used that are easy to collect and that link tangibly to day-to-day activities. Measures are posted on special performance boards throughout the business unit, and each manager is required to work with her or his people to establish improvement measures for key activities and to keep progress charts visible in the work area. These measures are usually associated with specific process improvement projects, and serve to stimulate new ideas and often friendly competition between organizations that have similar goals.

Measurement is also key to the process analysis that is done by the process improvement teams. As they map out

EXHIBIT 2   Process Improvement Structure

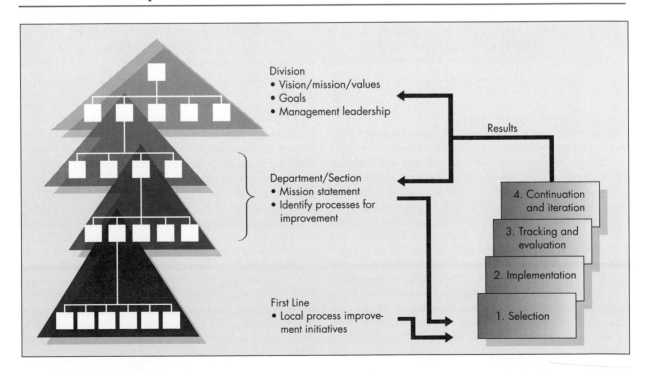

Exhibit 3   **Improved Process**

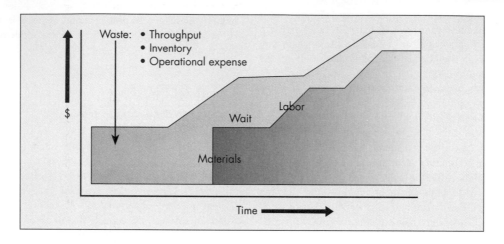

Exhibit 4   **Measures of Success—Other Areas of Impact**

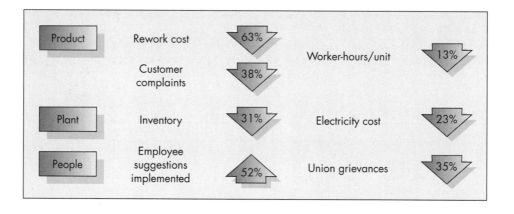

their existing process, they assess the amount of time and cost associated with each step in the traditional approach. While Thiokol/Huntsville uses this method extensively, some small, local processes are not treated to the full mapping; those processes may simply have a time/cost profile established as a baseline and then be reprofiled after the improvement project has been completed. The simple model used for this profile was established by the Westinghouse Corporate Quality/Productivity Center and is shown in Exhibit 3. It has also been an excellent tool to "roll up" a number of subprocesses to determine overall improvement. Any area under the curve is considered to be a waste of throughput, materials, inventory, and time and thus costs extra. While not easily quantified in hard dollars, the removal of any area under the curve is removal of waste and is considered worthy.

Examples of macro measures used by THD are shown in Exhibit 4, and indicate the level of success of the overall TQ/CI process. In a comparison of the most recent two fiscal years, all key areas show double-digit improvement. The 63 percent improvement in scrap, rework, and repair costs follows a 34 percent improvement the year before, indicating that the improvement curve need not flatten out after the first year of the improvement process, but rather can accelerate. The same is true of most of the other indicators shown in Exhibit 4, proving that a company need not wait the traditionally espoused five years to have substantial results in the improvement process.

While it may be true that it does traditionally take about five years to change a company culture—the way people think—in the near term, management can strongly influence and even dictate if necessary, the way people *act,* and that is where the immediate improvement comes from. As success breeds success, the desired culture change is reinforced and follows naturally.

EXHIBIT 5   Targeted Processes—Examples

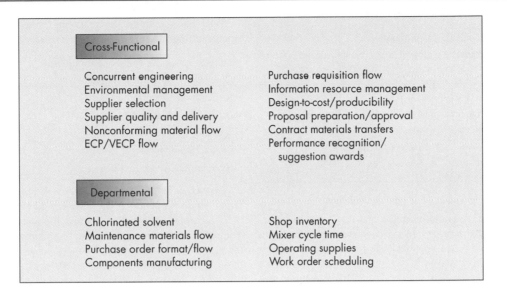

Cross-Functional

Concurrent engineering	Purchase requisition flow
Environmental management	Information resource management
Supplier selection	Design-to-cost/producibility
Supplier quality and delivery	Proposal preparation/approval
Nonconforming material flow	Contract materials transfers
ECP/VECP flow	Performance recognition/ suggestion awards

Departmental

Chlorinated solvent	Shop inventory
Maintenance materials flow	Mixer cycle time
Purchase order format/flow	Operating supplies
Components manufacturing	Work order scheduling

EXHIBIT 6   1990 Manufacturing Improvement Projects

Partial Listing			
Project	*Program*	*Implementation Cost*	*Savings*
Insulation wiping sequence	Castor	None	18.6 worker-hours per motor
Move chemlock control panel	Castor	3 hours	6 worker-hours per motor
Use of disposable tubing	Castor	$35 per motor	3.8 worker-hours per motor
Modified pot liner sleeve	Mk70	1 hour plastic shop	1.5 worker-hours per motor
Case unpacking location	Mk36	None	16 worker-hours per mix
Insulation cutting and installation	Mk36	None	32 worker-hours per mix
Rebalance inspection coverage	HELLFIRE	None	46 worker-hours per mix

Process Improvement Examples

The outstanding results shown in the previous section are, in effect, a rollup of processes being improved at all levels across the business unit. The previously mentioned Employee Attitude Survey, along with opportunity targets developed in the TQ/CI workshops, formed the basis for the initial process-improvement team activities. Examples of departmental and cross-functional processes addressed are shown in Exhibit 5. Many of the processes are specific to our industry, but the listing provides the reader with a feel for the type and range of processes being attacked.

An initial concern of management was that teams would recommend grandiose changes to processes that required investment in time and capital well in excess of near-term return. As it turned out, team-generated improvements of

processes usually result in low- or no-cost solutions to problems through streamlining and restructure. Some typical improvements in manufacturing and nonmanufacturing areas are shown in Exhibits 6 and 7.

External Customer/Supplier Involvement

To be successful, any process improvement effort must include a focus on external elements of the product and service chain—namely, external customers and suppliers. THD involves both customers and suppliers in our "concurrent engineering" of new products. Suppliers are brought in during the preliminary design phase to ensure producibility of the final requirements. Likewise, frequent communication with external customers ensures that integration and performance requirements will meet their expectations.

EXHIBIT 7   **Process Improvement Examples**

Nonmanufacturing

Deficiency Reporting/Dispositioning
- Average processing Cost of 8 worker-hours reduced to one-half worker-hour on low-cost Items (20 percent of all DRs).

Procedure Review/Approval Process
- Average cycle time of 66 days reduced to 14 days.

Contract Materials Transfers
- 4,000 CMTs per year reduced by 50 percent.
- 1,800 worker-hours per year savings.

To optimize the communication and day-to-day management of supplier issues, THD is aggressively pursuing a reduction of our active supplier base by at least 10 percent per year in each of the next five years. It may sound a bit cliché, but "only the best will survive." This pressure is also being applied by our customers toward us in their striving for excellence and cost-effectiveness. To this end, a cost-based supplier rating and certification system was developed that allows buying decisions to be made based on historical true cost of doing business with a supplier, rather than awarding a contract primarily based on bid price. "Certified" suppliers are given an additional cost advantage of up to 10 percent when evaluating competitive bids, recognizing that there are additional cost benefits of developing long-term business relationships with proven performers.

Management Action Areas for Change

Where do we go from here? Any business enterprise that has been so successful in achieving improvement goals must be careful not to rest on its laurels. It has become evident that a number of areas need continued diligence to improve. Although significant results have been achieved at the bottom line in a short time, certain support systems need to be changed from the traditional approaches to ensure continued improvement.

THD has identified the following areas as targets for significant improvement over the next two years or so:

- Integration across functional boundaries.
- Compensation/reward system.
- Recruitment/selection.
- Individual job structure.
- Training/skill development.
- Organization structure.
- Evaluation and recognition.

Experience at the Huntsville Division of Thiokol Corporation has shown that it is not necessary to wait five years or more to achieve substantial bottom-line results from TQM. Through a commitment to integrating continuous improvement into all aspects of the business on an ongoing basis, these results come from implementation of a well-thought-out, comprehensive plan with top-management support and involvement. In the beginning, near-term results are achieved by dictating behavior and allowing the internalized "culture change" to follow in the longer term.

Questions for Analysis

1. What are the factors for success in the Thiokol case? What did the firm do that led to improvements in performance?
2. What strategy for change did the company use? Did the strategy for change have anything to do with the program's success?
3. Can the increases in performance be sustained if the culture does not change? Explain your answer.

Source: M P Charness, Director of TQM, Thiokol Corporation, Huntsville Division, Huntsville, Alabama (case presented at the 1992 ASQC Quality Congress, Nashville, Tennessee). Reproduced here by permission of Michael P Charness.

VIDEO CASE
MANAGING CHANGE AND DEVELOPING ORGANIZATIONS AT MARSHALL INDUSTRIES

The manager's job increasingly requires knowing how to manage change. But most change efforts fail because of inadequate preparation and attention to process. On the other hand employees want and seek change they see as improving their lives. They resist change when they doubt its usefulness. Marshall Industries is one of the five largest distributors of industrial electronic components in America. From its warehouses and corporate offices near Los Angeles, Marshall supplies 30,000 computer-related customers in the United States and Canada with a broad range of semiconductors, connectors, tool kits, and work stations. How did the management of Marshall Industries diagnose, plan, and implement useful changes? How did they overcome resistance to change? And how did they measure and modify the changes?

This video examines those questions, focusing on Marshall's so-called "Red Letter Days" when major systems and organizational structure systems are changed, overhauled, revised, or, in one case, completely done away with.

One common way of labeling phases of change in human behavior are unfreezing, changing, and refreezing. Unfreezing involves initiating actions and attitudes to help employees see that change is in fact needed, and in their best interest. Sometimes this means helping people learn that the old way no longer works. The manager's goal is to instill an openness to change. The second phase involves actually making the change and changing behavior. Refreezing means reinforcing the changes made. Ideally, the newly created and desired behavior will become a natural, self-reinforcing pattern over time. Continuous improvement calls for continuous cycles of change. Successful managers know that nothing ever stays frozen.

Robert Rodin, Marshall Industries' president, commented on his company's approach to managing change: "We plan our approach. We do a little trial, we study the results of that trial, and then we act on it. We then continually cycle through that over and over again. Improvement continually is one of the goals, but innovation is the breakthrough that gets us to a new learning curve and allows us to be a better company."

But how does a manager recognize when change is necessary? Many businesses flourish on the principle that if it's not broken, don't fix it. Obvious change is called for when results are not in line with expectations, or staff morale is low, or the bottom line is sinking lower. Some companies miss signals for change when they neglect to monitor both their internal and external environments.

Marshall's director of quality, Jacob Kuryan, said, "Primarily trying to live our mission statement has really helped us reduce waste in our system. Let me give you an example. Making employees think about how they add value to the customer has allowed each and every individual at Marshall Industries to focus on customer service. If you don't know how to do something, you can't accomplish it. If you can't learn on a daily basis about customer requirements, about people, about what affects and motivates people, then you can't improve it. The only way to acquire customer knowledge is to be able to invite it from outside your organization and maybe examine your organization through an entirely different set of lenses."

Once a need for change is acknowledged, one process for diagnosing and planning for change is called "force field analysis." This process identifies and assesses the strength of forces driving change and those which are restraining it. From force field analysis managers can take action regarding which forces to change, who to do it, when, and how. It's important to decide in advance how success will be determined. Rodin said, "We realized that we were going to go through an awful lot of changes over the last four years. So we set a schedule together because people get nervous in a company when there's a lot of changes. Every 90 days we

met with out executive team. Every two weeks we had a conference call. In this way people got to expect regular communications. But they weren't done in a haphazard way—it was predictable."

There's nearly always a learning period when change is introduced and implemented. During this period there may be a strong desire to return to the old ways of doing things. To stabilize change, management must be ready to increase support, encouragement, and resources to help people weather the transitional storm and internalize their newly learned behaviors. Monitoring change means creating objective standards and goals with reasonable time tables while retaining the flexibility to adjust to surprises and setbacks. Using these guideposts, a successful manager knows when the broken machine has been fixed in order to terminate change. How do these principles work in a real world environment? Managers at Marshall have gone through each phase of change repeatedly on "Red Letter Days" when major systems and organizational structures are changed.

Robert Rodin explained the concept of Red Letter Days: "We would always brief people on the Fridays before the conference calls and frequently roll out these programs on a Monday. After every meeting the field operations knew that they would have a meeting the following Monday. After every conference call the field knew that they would be updated that evening. And in this predictable way people didn't have a chance to come up with a lot of rumors, and nervous sensation about what might happen in the event that some special meeting was planned in the middle of a time that they weren't expecting."

Although in-depth year-long preparations were made, the sales division and its 500 sales people nationwide will never forget the day that individual commissions were abolished and replaced with quarterly bonuses based on overall company performance. Robert Caldarella, general manager of corporate sales, said, "I remember the day we cut over to the incentive plan and moved away from the commission plan. Sales people came forward with their problem accounts, saying, 'Geez, I don't really think that this is a great account for us,' or 'I really don't think that this is a good Marshall account.' They become honest with themselves and they became honest with us as managers. Now we are one organization with people aligned in one direction."

Another Red Letter Day at Marshall was when automated retrieval machines went on line in the warehouse—an example of technology impacting both people and their task. Adrian Quintana, Jr., warehouse supervisor, said, "I think there was a lot of fear and uncertainty coming down here not knowing what working with an automated system was going to be like. Fear that it was going to eliminate a lot of jobs. You know they always hear that automation eliminated a lot of human jobs. But once we got down here and became accustomed to it and learned the system people found that it didn't eliminate jobs, it actually created new jobs. And I like working with the automated system. I think it's been really interesting learning the automation and it's eliminated a lot of the human errors that came from the conventional type environment."

On December 7, 1995, Marshall implemented its biggest single change: new computer software for its operating and financial systems. Richard Bentley, executive vice president, said, "The computer change is probably the one that sticks most in my mind because I couldn't sleep and I came back in and it was like 4:00 in the morning here, which means the east coast was coming up. As the company came across the country and the machine was still running we felt very good and we were able to conduct business. So that's probably what sticks in my mind the most."

Marshall Industries, like most dynamic companies, is in a constant state of change. What sets it apart is how its managers approach change from the inside out, and from the bottom up. Marshall's management is very aware that they are part of an interrelated, interactive system where change is not random, but planned and anticipated. Caldarella said, "There are a couple of stories that we use commonly to teach our organization how to think about processes and systems within organizations. The first one is the hamburger story. It's a busy day and you've been working very hard in the morning. At noon have to go out to lunch. You drive up to the hamburger stand and you tell them you're having a really busy day and you need your lunch really quick and he says 'Hey no problem,' and then the hamburger doesn't come for an hour. When you walk out the door you don't give the waiter or the waitress a tip. Whose fault was it that the hamburger was late? There could be any number of reasons

why the hamburger was late. But the one that you punish was that waiter or the waitress. So the lesson that we teach, using that example, is that when you look at why something went wrong you have to understand the process. You have to look at the people, method, equipment, materials, and the environment—all those factors that fall into that category to understand what you have changed to improve that process."

The people at Marshall have learned to expect change. Although sometimes stressful, they know firsthand how change is essential to success and survival. Donald E. Elario, Jr., vice president of operations, said, "Continuous improvement goes hand in hand with everything. It's everybody's role. It doesn't stop for anybody or anything. It's not just for operation, it's not just for automation. It's for sales, it's for accounting, it's for fixed assets, it's for everybody. Continuous improvement means you are truly never satisfied with whatever level you reach and one secret that we found is that's the way we function. No matter what we do we continue to look. As we're implementing the present, we're looking to the next and to the future and it just never stops. It absolutely never stops."

Critical Thinking Questions

1. One method of changing an organization is unfreeze, change, refreeze. Explain this approach.

2. What techniques can a manager use to ensure that organizational changes are permanent?

3. What is the purpose of Marshall's Red Letter Days?

Experiential Exercise
Are You Receptive to Change?

Purpose

The purpose of this exercise is to help students determine how open- or closed-minded they are to change.

The Exercise in Class

1. Take a few minutes and complete the questionnaire that follows in Exhibit 1. For each question, circle one response that best reflects your opinion. There are no right or wrong answers.

2. Then see the scoring format. Add your scores up and answer the question: Are you open- or closed-minded? Compare your scores with others in the class. How do your results match your self-image of your willingness to accept change?

Interpretation: A high score indicates a tendency to resist change because of fixed or rigid attitudes. A rigid person is called closed-minded. The most rigid person would have the highest score: + 36. A totally open-minded person would score a − 36.

The Learning Message

Resisting change is almost a fact of life. The way a person thinks indicates how resistant to change she or he will be when faced with changes in structure, technology, and personnel. This exercise provides some insight into a person's openness toward change.

EXHIBIT 1   Questionnaire: Are You Receptive to Change?

Statement	Agree Very Much	Agree in General	Agree Somewhat	Disagree Somewhat	Disagree in General	Disagree Very Much
1. The main thing in life is for a person to want to do something important.	1	2	3	4	5	6
2. Most people don't care about others.	1	2	3	4	5	6
3. Most ideas found in the press are worthless.	1	2	3	4	5	6
4. Compromising with Russia* is dangerous.	1	2	3	4	5	6
5. Our way of living and doing business is proven and should be the world model.	1	2	3	4	5	6
6. I would love to become a famous person like Einstein.	1	2	3	4	5	6
7. The United States and Russia* have nothing in common.	1	2	3	4	5	6
8. Freedom of speech is generally great, but some restrictions should be placed on radical groups.	1	2	3	4	5	6
9. I become very angry when a person refuses to admit he is wrong.	1	2	3	4	5	6
10. I would like to find someone to tell me how to solve my personal problems.	1	2	3	4	5	6
11. It is best to reserve judgment about what's going on until one hears the opinions of respected people.	1	2	3	4	5	6
12. Most people don't know what's good for them.	1	2	3	4	5	6

*Changed from the Soviet Union to reflect present situation.

Source: Adapted from V C Troldahl and F A Powell, "A Short-Form Dogmatism Scale for Use in Field Studies," *Social Forces,* December 1965, p. 213.

Scoring Format: Are You Receptive to Change?			
Response	Number of Responses ×	Weight =	Score
(1) Agree very much	_____	+3	_____
(2) Agree in general	_____	+2	_____
(3) Agree somewhat	_____	+1	_____
(4) Disagree somewhat	_____	−1	_____
(5) Disagree in general	_____	−2	_____
(6) Disagree very much	_____	−3	_____
Total score			_____

Notes

1. Rosabeth M Kanter, Barry A Stein, and Todd Jick, *The Challenge of Organizational Change: How Companies Experience It and Leaders Guide It* (New York: Free Press, 1992).

2. Leon Martel, *Mastering Change* (New York: New American Library, 1987).

3. Frederick M Zimmerman, *The Turnaround Experience: Real-World Lessons in Revitalizing Organizations* (New York: McGraw-Hill, 1991).

4. Laurie W Pant, "An Investigation of Industry and Firm Structural Characteristics in Corporate Turnaround," *Journal of Management Studies,* November 1991, pp. 623–43.

5. Frank Friedlander and L Dave Brown, "Organization Development," *Review of Psychology,* 1974.

6. Michael Beer, *Organization Change and Development* (Santa Monica, CA: Goodyear Publishing, 1980); Wendell L French and Cecil H Bell, Jr., *Organization Development* (Englewood Cliffs, NJ: Prentice Hall, 1978); Edgar Huse, *Organization Development* (St. Paul, MN: West, 1980).

7. Four reasons are discussed in John P Kotter and Leonard A Schlesinger, "Choosing Strategies for Change," *Harvard Business Review,* March–April 1979, pp. 106–14. Our discussion of resistance to change is based on this article.

8. Ibid.

9. See the range of change strategies in Wendell L French, Cecil H Bell, Jr., and Robert A Zawacki, *Organization Development* (Plano, TX: Business Publications, 1987).

10. Leon Martel, *Mastering Change* (New York: Simon & Schuster, 1986).

11. For a detailed discussion of the benefits derived from information technology, see Thomas H Davenport and James E Short, "The New Industrial Engineering: Information Technology and Business Process Redesign," *Sloan Management Review* Summer 1990, pp. 11–27.

12. "Lorenzo Is Running Out of Choices—and Time," *Business Week,* March 20, 1989, pp. 37–38.

13. Carrie Gottlieb, "Intel's Plan for Staying on Top," *Fortune,* March 27, 1989, pp. 98–100.

14. For a further discussion of these and other European companies prospering in Japan, see Michael Berger, "European Winners," *International Management,* February 1990, pp. 54–56.

15. Clayton P Alderfer, "Change Processes in Organization," in Marvin D Dunnette ed., *Handbook of Industrial and Organizational Psychology* (Skokie, IL: Rand McNally, 1976).

16. Alfred Chandler, *Strategy and Structure* (Cambridge, MA: MIT Press, 1962).

17. Kenneth Labich, "Was Breaking Up AT&T a Good Idea?" *Fortune,* January 2, 1989, pp. 82–86.

18. "Is Your Company Too Big?" *Business Week,* March 27, 1989, pp. 84–94.

19. R K Ready, *The Administrator's Job* (New York: McGraw-Hill, 1967), pp. 24–30.

20. Linda L Frank and J Richard Hackman, "A Failure of Job Enrichment: The Case of the Change That Wasn't," *Journal of Applied Behavioral Science,* October 1975, pp. 413–36.

21. W F Dowling, "Job Design in the Assembly-Line: Farewell to the Blue-Collar Blues?" *Organizational Dynamics,* Spring 1973, pp. 51–67; P G Gyllenhammer, *People at Work* (Reading, MA: Addison-Wesley, 1977).

22. See Herbert A Simon et al., *Centralization versus Decentralization in Organizing the Controller's Department* (New York: Controllership Foundation, 1954), for a classic discussion of the key issues to be resolved in deciding where to locate staff units—in this case, an accounting unit.

23. Jeremiah J O'Connell, *Managing Organizational Innovation* (Burr Ridge, IL: Richard D Irwin, 1968).

24. Fred Emery, "Participative Design: Effective, Flexible and Successful, Now!" *Journal of Quality and Participation* January–February 1995, pp. 6–9.

25. William Fox, "Sociotechnical System Principles and Guidelines: Past and Present," *Journal of Applied Behavioral Science,* March 1995, pp. 91–105.

26. T Mills, "Altering the Social Structure in Coal Mining: A Case Study," *Monthly Labor Review,* October 1976, pp. 3–10.

27. Ernest Dale and L C Michelon, *Modern Management Methods* (New York: World, 1966), pp. 15–16.

28. A survey of alternative training methodologies is presented in Edward C Ryterband and Bernard M Bass, "Management Development," in Joseph W McGuire, ed., *Contemporary Management* (Englewood Cliffs, NJ: Prentice Hall, 1974), pp. 579–609.

29. L This and G L Lippit, "Managerial Guidelines to Sensitivity Training," *Training and Development Journal,* June 1981, pp. 141–50; Henry C Smith, *Sensitivity to People* (New York: McGraw-Hill, 1966), p. 197.

30. L P Bradford, J R Gibb, and K D Benne, *T-Group Theory and Laboratory Method* (New York: John Wiley & Sons, 1964).

31. Alfred J Marrow, *Behind the Executive Mask* (New York: AMACOM, 1964), p. 51.

32. Joe Kelly, *Organizational Behavior,* 3d ed. (Burr Ridge, IL: Richard D Irwin, 1980), p. 569.

33. See Harold J Leavitt, "Applied Organizational Change in Industry: Structural, Technological and Humanistic

Approach," in James G March, ed., *Handbook of Organizations* (Skokie, IL: Rand McNally, 1965), pp. 1144–68.

34. Robert Golembiewski and A Blumberg, eds., *Sensitivity Training and the Laboratory Approach: Readings about Concepts and Applications* (Itasca, IL: F. E. Peacock, 1977).

35. P B Smith, "Controlled Studies of the Outcome of Sensitivity Training," *Psychological Bulletin,* July 1975, pp. 597–622.

36. S Jay Liebowitz and Kenneth P DeMeuse, "The Application of Team Building," *Human Relations,* January 1982, pp. 1–18.

37. P Palleschi and P Heim, "The Hidden Barriers to Team Building," *Training and Development Journal,* July 1980, pp. 14–18.

38. John Holersha, "Labor Pains in a U.S. Utopia," *Herald International Tribune,* February 1, 1989, pp. 9, 12.

39. Margaret Butteress and Karl Albrecht, *New Management Tools* (Englewood Cliffs, NJ: Prentice Hall, 1979), pp. 57–62.

40. William F Rothenback, "Career Development: Ask Your Employees for Their Opinions," *Personnel Administrator,* November 1982, pp. 43–51.

41. Philip B Crosby, *Quality Is Free: The Art of Making Quality Certain* (New York: McGraw-Hill, 1977); W Edwards Deming, *Out of the Crisis* (Cambridge, MA: MIT Center for Advanced Engineering Study, 1986); Kaoru Ishikawa, *What Is Total Quality Control? The Japanese Way* (Englewood Cliffs, NJ: Prentice Hall, 1985); Joseph M Juran, *Juran on Leadership for Quality* (New York: Free Press, 1989).

42. Marshall Sashkin and Kenneth J Kiser, *Total Quality Management* (Seabrook, MD: Ducochon Press, 1992); Richard D Hames, "Managing the Process of Cultural Change," *International Journal of Quality and Reliability Management* 8, no. 5 (1991), pp. 14–23.

43. Edward E Lawler III, Susan Mohrman, and Gerald E Ledford, Jr., "The Fortune 1,000 and Total Quality," *Journal of Quality and Participation,* September 1992, pp. 6–10.

44. United States General Accounting Office, *Management Practices: U.S. Companies Improve Performance Through Quality Efforts* (Washington, DC: GAO Printing Office, 1991).

45. David A Garvin, "How the Baldrige Award Really Works," *Harvard Business Review,* November–December 1991, pp. 80–93.

46. Warren H Schmidt and Jerome P Finnigan, *The Race without a Finish Line: America's Quest for Total Quality* (San Francisco: Jossey-Bass, 1992).

47. Jeffrey G Miller and Thomas E Vallmann, "The Hidden Factory," *Harvard Business Review,* September–October 1985, pp. 142–50.

48. George L Whaley, "The Impact of Robotics Technology upon Human Resource Management," *Personnel Administrator,* September 1982, p. 61.

49. Robert A Pierson, "Automation," *Management Review,* July 1985, pp. 33–35.

50. Karen Lowry Miller, Neil Gross, and John Carey, "Japan Pours Big Bucks into Very Little Machines," *Business Week,* August 27, 1990, p. 83.

51. *General Motors Public Interest Report,* 1988.

52. For example, see, Joan Woodward, *Industrial Organization* (New York: Oxford University Press, 1967); Frank J Jasinski, "Adapting Organization to New Technology," *Harvard Business Review,* January–February 1959, pp. 79–86.

53. Tom Burns and G M Stalker make this point in their analysis of the ways Scottish electronics firms responded to technological change. They use the terms *mechanistic* to refer to relatively tight, highly structured organizations and *organic* to refer to relatively loose, flexibly structured organizations. Tom Burns and G M Stalker, *The Management of Innovation* (London: Tavistock, 1961).

54. Michael Hammer, "Reengineering Work: Don't Automate, Obliterate," *Harvard Business Review,"* July–August 1990, pp. 104–12.

55. Vandra L Huber and Geri Gay, "Channeling New Technology to Improve Training," *Personnel Administrator,* February 1985, pp. 49–57.

56. Floyd C Mann, "Psychological and Organizational Impacts," in John T Dunlop, ed., *Automation and Technological Change* (Englewood Cliffs, NJ: Prentice Hall, 1962), pp. 50–55.

57. Edgar H Schein, *Organizational Culture and Leadership* (San Francisco: Jossey-Bass, 1985).

58. Lawrence A Benningson, "Managing Corporate Cultures," *Management Review,* February 1985, pp. 31–32; Ralph H Kilman, *Beyond the Quick Fix* (San Francisco: Jossey-Bass, 1984), pp. 21–124.

59. Larry E Greiner, "Patterns of Organization Change," *Harvard Business Review,* May–June 1967, p. 119.

60. Greiner identifies replacement of key personnel and structural changes as two other forms of unilateral change. For our purposes, personnel and structural changes are change techniques, not strategies for implementing change. Techniques specify *what* is to be done; strategies specify *how* it is to be done.

IV   MANAGING PRODUCTION AND OPERATIONS: PLANNING, ORGANIZING, LEADING, CONTROLLING

17   PRODUCTION AND OPERATIONS MANAGEMENT

Chapter Learning Objectives

After completing Chapter 17, you should be able to:

- **Define** the term *quality*.
- **Describe** the steps that managers must take to develop a system of quality control.
- **Discuss** the importance of managing production and operations to achieve maximum levels of productivity and quality.
- **Compare** the four production/operations management functions: design, scheduling, operations, and transformation control.
- **Identify** the main factors that affect quality.

US Companies Improve Competitiveness through the Implementation of Total Quality Management

The most widely circulated publication in the history of the United States General Accounting Office (GAO) deals with the issue of how American companies have implemented total quality management (TQM). The GAO undertook the 1991 study at the request of Congressman Donald Ritter with the endorsement of 29 colleagues. Ritter wanted a study that would determine the impact of TQM practices on the performance of US companies. In particular, the congressman wanted to know what TQM companies actually achieved, how they improved quality, and what lessons could be learned for general application.

The GAO research team studied a sample of firms that had received the highest scores on the written portion of the Malcolm Baldrige Award competition. The Baldrige awards go to firms that demonstrate the greatest progress toward implementing TQM processes and achieving quality products and services. The criteria for the award require each applicant to demonstrate what it does to achieve the following objectives:

- Understand and act on the ideas that customers have the final say in what quality is and that the organization produces products and services to satisfy customers' expectations. This aspect of TQM requires applicants to have methods and procedures for obtaining and using customer information when designing and producing products and services.
- Exhibit strong leadership throughout the organization to develop the commitment to quality and to overcome impediments to the development of that commitment. Top-management leadership counts heavily on this criterion.
- Continuously improve all business operations and work activities to achieve higher and higher levels of efficiency. Improvement in production methods, processes, and organization must be an ongoing commitment in the organization.
- Demonstrate that decision making reflects facts, data, and analysis, not rule of thumb and habit. The firm that practices TQM commits to fact-based decision making as the standard throughout the organization.
- Enable and empower employees to participate in the achievement of quality outcomes. TQM begins with the idea that people closest to the place where

work is done are the most knowledgeable individuals for doing what must be done to achieve higher levels of quality.

Winners of the Baldrige Award demonstrate high levels of commitment to these five aspects of TQM. Since 1987, when President Bush signed the Malcolm Baldrige National Quality Award, many firms have applied for the award. For example, in 1990 alone over 180,000 firms requested applications from the US Department of Commerce, which administers the competition. In 1988 and 1989, only 22 firms received on-site visits from the Baldrige Award evaluation team, and 20 of these firms agreed to share information with the GAO to become part of the study.

The study includes a relatively small sample size—20 firms—and some of the results of these firms' efforts to implement TQM are positive. The most important of the positive results are as follows:

- The companies reported the attainment of lower costs and improved quality. Indicators of improved quality included increased product reliability and on time delivery, and decreased errors and lead times.
- They reported increased customer satisfaction, as indicated on customer surveys, as well as increased customer retention rates and decreased number of complaints.
- They reported increased employee satisfaction, as indicated on attitude surveys, and decreased absenteeism and turnover.

These results would seem to indicate that TQM holds great promise for improving outcomes that have importance in determining competitiveness in the global marketplace. That TQM has become the most widespread management practice since scientific management should not then come as a surprise.

Sources: United States Government Accounting Office, *Management Practices: U.S. Companies Improve Performance through Quality Efforts* (Washington, DC: GAO/NSIAD, 1991). Copies of this report can be obtained by calling (202) 512-6000. Other reports of successful TQM implementation include: L Struebling, "GAO Symposium Uncovers Eight Principles for Managing People," *Quality Progress,* April 1996, pp. 21–25; K Bemowski, "1994 Baldrige Award Recipients Share Their Expertise," *Quality Progress,* February 1995, pp. 35–40; and M Brown, "Measuring Up against the 1995 Baldrige Criteria," *Journal of Quality and Participation,* December 1994, pp. 66–72.

The terms *manufacturing management, production management,* and *operations management* are used interchangeably to refer to the functional field of production and operations management (P/OM). Traditionally, the word production brings to mind smokestacks, assembly lines, and machine shops. However, P/OM refers to the broader idea of the producing activities of all kinds of organizations—manufacturing or service, public or private, large or small, profit or nonprofit.[1]

P/OM as a field of study and practice uses concepts and principles from scientific management and management science. It also uses ideas from the behavioral sciences. As a part of management, P/OM is quite eclectic and application oriented.[2] As the Management in Action indicates, the implementation of quality improvement methods involves applications of ideas from the full range of management theory, including production and operations management. The point is that managing production and operations involves managing organizations and people as well.

In this chapter, the nature and area of influence of P/OM will be surveyed. We will emphasize the analytical side of P/OM while acknowledging the importance of people-related issues. We will place a special emphasis on the attainment of quality because of the increasing importance of quality in competing successfully in the global marketplace.

The Nature of Production and Operations Management

P/OM goes well beyond manufacturing operations involving the assembly of products. It also covers the operation of banks, transportation companies, hospitals and clinics, school systems, insurance companies, and high-technology firms. Any system that generates tangible products (e.g., a Ford automobile, a Sunbeam shaver) or intangible services (e.g., a flight on American Airlines, advice on computer programming) is part of the domain of P/OM.

A Systems View

P/OM practitioners view organizations in terms of systems.[3] A *system* is a collection of objects united by some form of regular interaction and interdependence. We noted in Chapter 2 that organizations themselves are systems made up of interacting subsystems. One of the significant subsystems of many organizations is the production and operation management department. Figure 17–1 illustrates the organization as a system that takes in and transforms inputs and then provides outputs that are consumed or demanded. The transformation portion of Figure 17–1 is the point at which P/OM activities, or processes, are conducted. According to this representation, organizations can be thought of in terms of being productive transformation systems. The P/OM executive gives special attention to the creation of goods and services—that is, the productive transformation work that occurs within an organization.

P/OM is a specific function that affects the behavior and performance of other major functions like marketing and accounting. The interrelationships of these three main functions of any organization can be better understood by thinking of an organization as a system. The marketing subsystem deals primarily with the demand side of business; the accounting subsystem addresses the control side of business; the P/OM subsystem centers around converting inputs into outputs, or the supply side of business. No matter how great the demand is for a product or service, there must be a supply available. Producing enough goods and services to meet demand is the primary task of organizations, according to the P/OM viewpoint.[4]

FIGURE **17–1**   **Scope of Production and Operations Management**

P/OM activities can be understood in the context of systems theory concepts such as inputs, outputs, transformation, and feedback.

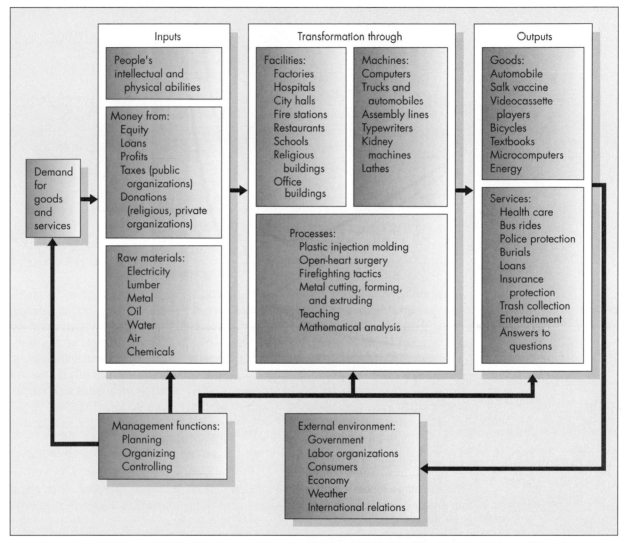

Source: Adapted from F G Moore and T E Hendrick, *Production/Operations Management,* 9th ed. (Burr Ridge, IL: Richard D. Irwin, 1985), p. 11.

Goods and Services   According to P/OM managers, the term **product** is a generic label for the output of a productive system. A product can be a good or a service. In economic terms, **goods** are defined as movable personal property; examples include autos, home computers, desks, and microwave ovens. A capital good is immovable personal property, such as a house or factory. A **service**—an activity required by a customer or a client or work done for another person—is another production output.[5]

Economists refer to the transformation of inputs into goods and services as the "production function." Managers are aware of the fact that simply moving goods and services from input to transformation to output is often affected by unpredictable or

FIGURE 17–2   **Transformation Process on a Farm**

A wide variety of situations, including farms, can be viewed as P/OM systems.

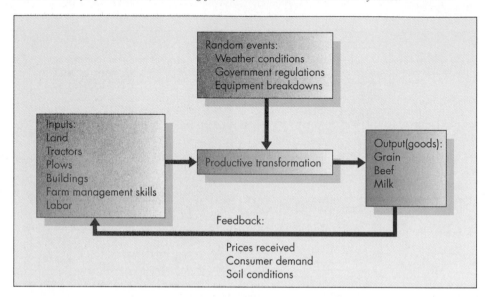

random events. For example, a farm manager takes land, equipment, labor, and skills and transforms them into goods such as grain, beef, and milk. However, the weather, government regulations, and equipment breakdowns affect the transformation or productive work activities. Figure 17–2 illustrates this example in terms of a systems framework. The framework reflects the P/OM viewpoint, paying particular attention to inputs, transformation, outputs, and feedback cycles. Table 17–1 highlights the variety of productive systems in society by examining a few of the various input transformations, random events, and outputs of some typical organizations.

Managing the Transformation Process

When managing the transformation process, P/OM managers pay particular attention to four specific functions: design, scheduling, operation, and transformation control.[6]

Design

Designing the transformation process involves making decisions on equipment selection, type of production process, and work flow patterns.[7] Contemporary technology has developed manufacturing capability to readily shift from product to product and from machine to machine in response to changes in product demand and machine availability. This flexible manufacturing technology has increased tremendously the ability of firms to respond to change.[8]

Transformation processes are usually either continuous, intermittent, or "one-shot" projects. Continuous processes are generally very specialized, producing one type of product (for example, Oldsmobiles) or service (for example, H&R Block tax services). Intermittent processes are more general and utilize a variety of equipment; for example, an intermittent process is used in a job shop (i.e., a shop that produces

---
TABLE 17–1   Productive Systems and Their Characteristics

All organizations can in fact be viewed as production systems.

System	Main Inputs	Transformation Activities	Random Events	Main Outputs
Chrysler Corporation	Steel, glass	Assembly of autos	New government regulation, new competing car	Automobiles
Methodist Hospital, Houston, Texas	Patients	Diagnosis, surgery, rehabilitation	Reduction in Medicare payments	Well people
Apple Computer	Electrical circuits, computer languages	Assembly of personal computers and development of software	Competitive product from IBM	Computers and software
Tadich's Grill, San Francisco, California	Lobsters, hungry customers, waiters	Preparation of food	Price increase for lobsters, strike by waiters	Satisfied customers who want to come back
University of Kentucky	High school graduates	Classroom instruction, lecture enrichment, discussions with alumni who return to the campus, use of library	Missing books in library, cancellation of course with outstanding instructor	Educated and employable graduates

a product to meet a customer's specifications). The one-shot project is found in building, bridge, and highway construction. The decision as to which process to utilize is based on economic considerations, volume required, and labor resources and skills available.

Scheduling

Once the optimal process is designed, it must be scheduled to produce the desired product or service at the right time. Scheduling in P/OM terms covers both long and short runs. In long-range scheduling, forecasts and estimates of product or service demand are developed so that labor, capacity, raw materials, and other input needs can be met. Scheduling also can involve the management of projects over time. Short-range scheduling involves employees' daily or weekly work activities: the sequencing of work flow, raw materials, patients, or other similar inputs.[9]

Operation

Operating the transformation process involves the actual implementation of P/OM procedures. The planning, organizing, and controlling of operations directly affect the output of a productive system. The operating function also involves such activities as purchasing, redesigning the process if necessary, and forecasting requirements.

Control

The transformation control function requires some method of measuring the product or service before it is sold or used. For example, computers are used to monitor sales in Kroger and Safeway stores. By using the computer, the store manager can monitor inventory levels so that stock reorders can be placed and outages minimized. Another means of control is inspection. For example, inspectors monitor the waterproof protection of upholstery in Ford automobiles in the Chicago assembly plant.

Effective Management of the Transformation Process

What then are the key differences between good plants and poor plants? What distinguishes factories that year-in and year-out manufacture high-quality goods and services without sacrificing productivity from factories that do not do as well? These questions and their answers are of great importance to the American economic system and to the managers of firms that make up that system. Remaining competitive in an increasingly international marketplace requires American managers to evaluate every avenue of potential productivity and quality gains. To obtain some answers to these questions, *Fortune* magazine examined the 10 best factories in America with the intent of seeing what they had in common.[10] Included in the 10 were factories bearing logos of well-known firms—AT&T, GE, IBM, and Hewlett-Packard. The 10 plants were selected because of their records of high productivity, high product quality, or both.

According to the author of the study, these plants tended to do many things the same way. They all made use of the most current production-management methods for planning and controlling the transformation process. But in addition to those technically oriented practices, these plants did some other things. They all began by reducing the barriers between product design and manufacturing. In the typical plant, considerable friction and even hostility exist between the group that designs the product and the group that manufactures the product. The most successful plants, on the other hand, manage to design the product and to design the required manufacturing process concurrently rather than sequentially. This means merging the two groups into a single unit from the initial idea for the product to the final production layout to make the product.

Another characteristic of the excellently managed factories is the ability to create working conditions that allow employees to make quality products. The conditions include enabling employees to stop the production line to correct defects and to continue to hold the line until the source of the product defect is discovered. In effect, these factories have turned every employee into a quality inspector. To obtain employee commitment to quality, the competitors' products are displayed prominently on the factory floor so as to demonstrate what is at stake.

Excellently managed factories do things to help employees understand that their enemy is competition, not management. This is not to say that these plants are free of employee complaints and union grievances. But it is fair to say that managers of these factories do a better job of substituting trust and communication for strife and confrontation. The basic idea is to get managers and nonmanagers to think of themselves as teams having a common stake in the outcome of their daily work activities. With this kind of atmosphere in place, production-management methods and techniques can be implemented to achieve their maximum potential.

Designing and managing these plants involves managers in many diverse issues. The extent to which managers resolve these issues can be difficult to evaluate, yet one standard for evaluation that has taken on considerable importance in recent years is **quality.** The remainder of this chapter is devoted to a discussion of quality as an attribute of products and services.

The Management of Product and Service Quality

Quality as an attribute of products and services is often ignored in favor of an emphasis on *quantity* of products and services. Why? While outputs, such as assembled autos, manufactured pipes, or tons of grain processed, can easily be quantified by counting or weighing, it is generally more difficult to evaluate their quality. And often quality is judged on subjective opinions rather than on objectively based data. But emphasizing quantity may lead to a lack of concern for quality.

Quality is important. Fine-quality products lead to customer goodwill and satisfaction that manifest themselves in the form of repeat sales, loyal customers and clients, and testimonials to prospective customers or clients. Certainly, to achieve total customer satisfaction would not only be cost prohibitive but would also lead to unrealistic expectations.[11] Nonetheless, even though total customer satisfaction is not attainable, a reasonable record of quality must be established.

Quality has often been defined as the "totality of features and characteristics of a product or service that bear on its ability to satisfy stated or implied needs."[12] Although many people may evaluate quality, the customer is the key perceiver of quality because her purchase decision determines the success of the organization's product or service and often the fate of the organization itself. As the world markets become more interrelated and as American firms must compete throughout the world, managers will become more and more aware of the effects of cultural differences on the meaning of quality. The accompanying Management Focus suggests cultural differences in the meaning of quality.

Management Focus

The Meaning of Quality in Different Cultures

Quality means different things in the United States, Japan, and Russia and the countries once part of the Soviet Union. These different meanings of quality have important implications as the global marketplace replaces national marketplaces. If a firm is to be a successful competitor in the global marketplace, its management must know how to meet quality expectations in all the countries in which it hopes to sell its products and services.

The views of quality that dominate American business practice reflect the writings of Deming, Juran, and Crosby. Each of these individuals has an international reputation that has grown in substance in recent years, and the influence of each in the United States has pervaded at least the discussion, if not the practice, of quality management. These three writers and consultants define quality in terms of how well the product or service meets consumers' needs (Deming); is fit for use (Juran); and conforms to requirements (Crosby). Generally Deming and Juran emphasize quality in terms of the user while Crosby emphasizes quality in terms of manufacturing.

Contrast these views of quality with that of the Japanese consultant, Taguchi, who defines quality in terms of closeness to an ideal state, which brings maximum well-being to the society that consumes it. This view

of quality has a philosophical origin, but, in practical terms, it emphasizes the absence of product variability and social cost. Thus, the Japanese view of quality (as reflected in Taguchi's view) provides a more stringent test of quality than do the American views.

The views of quality in countries once part of the Soviet Union are relatively underdeveloped. The effect of nearly 70 years of state-controlled manufacturing to state-determined standards of quality has been to leave these countries with little understanding of quality as either user determined or value determined. To counter this lack of quality understanding, governments in these countries have established systems of awarding "Marks of Quality" to products that have the same apparent quality as competitive products in advanced, non–ex-Soviet countries. Thus, until a stronger sense of quality can develop as an inherent part of their thinking, the countries of the former Soviet Union will use whatever they find in the products of their competitors.

Sources: T Gylfason, "Reforms in Eastern Europe," *Journal of World Trade,* June 1995, pp. 107–33; Z D Radovilsky, "Managing Operations in the Former Soviet Union," *International Journal of Operations and Productions,* 14, no. 2 (1995), pp. 43–50; L B Forker, "Quality: American, Japanese, and Soviet Perspectives," *Academy of Management Executive,* November 1991, pp. 63–74; and K Bemowski, "Quality American Style," *Quality Progress,* February 1993, pp. 65–68.

Many well-known American corporations have established reputations for excellence. For example, a *Fortune* magazine article surveyed quality experts, management consultants, securities analysts, industry representatives, academics, consumers, unions, and other informed observers of world commerce to identify American firms with reputations for quality.[13] *Fortune* established a stringent set of criteria to qualify a product as world champ. The item had to be the most durable, the innovative and technological leader, a value for the price, and a world market-share leader.

Not surprisingly *Fortune* found a wide mixture of high- and low-technology American products. In over 100 categories, American products lead the field. In aerospace (General Dynamics), agricultural equipment (John Deere), personal computers (Apple), pharmaceuticals (Genetek), and medical instrumentation (Medtronic), these and other US companies produce products that are tops. The United States also gets superior marks for craftsmanship in dishwashers (General Electric), ballpoint pens (A T Cross), clothes dryers (Whirlpool), jeans (Levi Strauss), and hunting boots (L L Bean).

Fortune found that American quality leaders totally commit to meeting and exceeding standards for excellence year after year. In addition to surpassing customer expectations, the elite American products suit their function. The unequaled managements constantly improve their products and listen to anyone who has something to say about their products.

A consumer's perception of a product or service's "excellence" is generally based on the degree to which the product or service meets his specifications and requirements. Specifically, a consumer perceives "excellence" by evaluating one or more dimensions of quality, which are summarized in Table 17–2. In judging the quality of a Sony television set, for example, a prospective buyer may examine performance: how well the TV set performs its primary function (is the picture sharp, the color vivid, the sound clear?).

TABLE 17–2   Dimensions of Quality

Quality, a relatively abstract term, has some rather specific dimensions when we stop to consider it.

Dimension	Example
Performance: Product/service's primary operating characteristics.	Sony TV's richness of color, clarity of sound.
Features: Secondary, extra characteristics.	Hyatt Regency's complimentary breakfasts.
Reliability: Consistent performance within a specific period.	Honda Acura's rate of repair in the first year of purchase.
Conformance: Degree to which design and characteristics meet specific standards.	Apple computer's compatibility with IBM software.
Durability: Length of a product/service's useful life.	Average 17-year life of Kirby vacuum cleaners.
Serviceability: Speed, courtesy, competence, and ease of repair.	Caterpillar Tractor's worldwide guarantee of 48-delivery of replacement parts.
Aesthetics: Looks, taste, feel, sound, smell of a product/service.	Flavor, texture of Baskin-Robbins ice cream.
Perceived quality: Quality conveyed via marketing, brand name, reputation.	Bose's reputation in stereo speakers.

Source: Reprinted by permission of *Harvard Business Review,* from "Competing in the Eight Dimentions of Quality," by D. A. Garvin, November–December 1987. Copyright © 1987 by the President and Fellows of Harvard College, all rights reserved.

The set's extra features, such as automatic fine tuning, may be evaluated. The rate of repair or reliability may be a factor as well as serviceability—the convenience and quality of repair should a breakdown occur. Conformance—the set's compatibility with a VCR of another brand, durability—the typical life span of the set, and the visual appeal of its design (aesthetics) may also be examined. Sony's reputation for product quality may also influence the consumer's evaluation of the set's overall quality (perceived quality).[14]

Two points are noteworthy concerning a consumer's "perception of excellence" or quality. First, consumers emphasize different dimensions of quality when judging a product or service. For example, some prospective car buyers value performance above all; others may be more influenced by the car's appearance (aesthetics). Because of these differences in consumer preferences, a company may choose to emphasize one or a few dimensions of quality rather than compete on all eight dimensions. For example, Tandem Computers emphasizes superior reliability in its computer systems. The company achieved this dimension of quality by designing and building dual processors into its computers. If one processor fails (which would shut down most computers), work automatically shifts to the second processor and no operations time is lost. This quality feature has provided tremendous sales growth for Tandem.[15]

Second, perceiving "excellence" can be highly subjective. Some dimensions, such as reliability or durability, can be quantified by simply reviewing the product's records. However, other dimensions such as aesthetics depend on personal likes and dislikes, which are highly subjective. Differences in preferences and the subjectivity of perceptions underscore the need for organizations to obtain accurate market information concerning consumers' views.[16] The accompanying Management Focus illustrates the importance of timely market information.

One other important element of the quality concept concerns the relationship between quality and price. In many cases, if quality increases, so will the price (given that price reflects the cost of providing the product or service). This relationship is

---

Management Focus

The Japanese Raise the Ante Again

Just when Detroit automakers thought they had caught on to the idea of quality, the Japanese introduced cars that redefined the concept. In addition to the usual characteristics defining quality, the Japanese now include the notions of "fascination," "bewitchment," and "delight" in their idea of quality. As one representative of Mitsubishi Motor Sales stated, "We've entered the second phase of quality. Now it's the personality of the product that dictates quality." The personality of the product! What can that mean? People have personalities. Cars have fenders.

Nissan surveyed its customers to find out the small things that make the difference when the total image has improved. Nissan engineers have made improvements like reducing the obtrusiveness of pop-up head-lights.

Similarly, Honda engineers have designed every manually operated button and switch to yield to the same pressure, and their customers told them that these were the characteristics of a Honda's personality. One need only watch the television promotions for the Infiniti and Lexus to understand the subtle but real changes taking place in the minds of auto buyers as they reflect on the meaning of quality.

Sources: A Dunkin and L Armstrong, "Japan Swings into the Sport-Utes," *Business Week,* April 1996, pp. 128–29; M Matzer, "Misubishi Looking for a Position Beyond Price," *Brandweek,* April 1, 1996, p. 10. R Pastore, "A Virtual Shopping Spree," *CIO,* August 1993, pp. 70–74; R Higurashi, M Ito, and J Fukuda, "The Japanese Auto Industry: Where Is It Headed?" *Tokyo Business Today,* April 1993, pp. 8–12. "Nissan Develops a Practical In-Vehicle Multiplexing System," *Japan 21st,* May 1993, pp. 16–17.

particularly strong when an organization produces a product or service that rates high on all eight dimensions of quality. However, a higher level of quality does not *always* result in a higher price; sometimes improving quality actually reduces the cost of quality.

To understand this relationship, it is first necessary to understand the concept of cost of quality and its component parts. An organization's cost of quality is the total expense involved in ensuring that a product or service meets established quality standards. The cost of quality comprises three types of costs. *Prevention costs* are the costs of preventing product or service defects—the precontrol aspect of quality control. Examples of prevention costs are the expenses of effective employee training, reengineering the product's manufacturing process, or working with suppliers to ensure that materials are of high quality. *Appraisal costs* are all expenses involved in directly evaluating quality such as the costs of quality inspection and testing. *Failure costs* occur once a defect is produced and identified. If the defect is found before the product leaves the plant, the failure costs are internal (e.g., the costs of scrap material or of reworking the defective part or product). If the defect is found by the customer, external failure costs are incurred (the costs of recalled products, customer complaints, and a damaged product image).[17]

Each of these three cost components make up a different proportion of the total cost of quality largely because they are incurred at different points in the production process. Figure 17–3 represents what is often referred to as the quality funnel principle. According to the principle, the nearer to the start of the production process, the lower the cost of quality. Such is the case because, as the product or service progresses through the process, more resources, such as labor, time, and materials, are

FIGURE 17–3   The Quality Funnel Principle

Managers need to identify poor quality before the product/service gets too far into the process—certainly before the customer receives it.

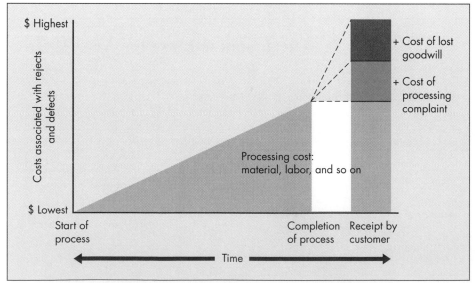

Source: Adapted from D Bain, *The Productivity Prescription: The Manager's Guide to Improving Productivity and Profits* (New York: McGraw-Hill, 1962), p. 120.

invested. The greater the amount of resources invested, the higher the cost of rejection (and quality). Applying this principle, prevention costs are incurred primarily at the beginning of the production process and are the least expensive component (5 to 10 percent of total quality costs). Failure costs are incurred mostly at the end of the process and thereafter and are the most expensive component (65 to 75 percent). Appraisal costs are incurred primarily during the production process and are larger than prevention but smaller than failure cost (20 to 25 percent of total quality costs).[18]

Many companies are wisely shifting their quality control emphasis to prevention (precontrol). They are increasing prevention costs of quality by focusing more on such preventive mechanisms as employee training and the design of the manufacturing process. Over time, this increase in prevention quality costs produces larger returns. Quality is improved. Appraisal costs are reduced because improved prevention reduces the need for inspection and testing activities. Above all, failure costs—the most costly quality component—are reduced because the service or product is produced right the first time. Overall quality costs thus decline.

Factors That Affect Quality

Quality depends on a number of factors: policy, information, engineering and design, materials, equipment, people, and field support. An integrated quality control system must focus on these factors.

Policy

Management establishes policies concerning product quality. These policies specify the standards or levels of quality to be achieved in a product or service; they can be an important precontrol and concurrent control means for ensuring quality.[19]

Management considers three factors in determining its policy for quality: the product or service's market, its competition, and image. An evaluation of the market provides an indication of customer expectations of quality and the price consumers are willing to pay for the product or service. Quality expectations and price, for example, widely differ in the luxury car (Mercedes) and economy car (Geo) markets within the auto industry. Quality levels provided by the competition also affect policy because the company's products or services must be competitive to succeed in the marketplace.

Besides considering the market and competition, management must also consider the organization's image. Long-term interests may be damaged by making a product of quality inconsistent with the firm's image. For example, marketing a low-priced Porsche or a new, low-priced Ben & Jerry's ice cream flavor might create a backlash from regular customers. Customer images of these products (and their loyalty) may be tarnished if they associate a lower-priced product or service with lower quality.

Information

Information plays a vital role in setting policy and ensuring that quality standards are achieved. Concerning policy, accurate information must be obtained about customer preferences and expectations and about competitor quality standards and costs. Competitive benchmarking is one effective approach to obtaining valuable information about a competitor's quality standards and costs.[20] Also, new computer technology is enabling organizations to quickly obtain and evaluate information about the quality of products while they are being produced.

Engineering and Design

Once management has formulated a policy concerning quality, it is the engineer or designer who must translate the policy into an actual product or service. The engineer or designer must create a product that will appeal to customers and that can be produced at a reasonable cost and provide competitive quality.

Materials

A growing number of organizations are realizing that a finished product is only as good as the materials used to produce it. In this regard, many manufacturing companies are implementing a new precontrol strategy with material suppliers. They are reducing their number of suppliers (weeding out the lower-quality vendors and focusing on developing effective, long-term relationships with the better ones). Ford, General Motors, and Chrysler use this approach.

Equipment

The ability of equipment, tools, and machinery to accurately and reliably produce desired outputs is important, especially in manufacturing industries. If the equipment can meet acceptable tolerances, at competitive costs and quality, an organization will have the opportunity to compete in the marketplace.[21]

People

Materials, design, and equipment are important ingredients in quality products. But people are the vital contributors.[22] Working individually or in teams, employees take the ingredients and process them into the final product or service. Managers must therefore not only provide the proper training to produce quality, but also enable people to develop attitudes that value quality.[23]

Field Support

Often, the field support provided by the supplier determines a product's quality image (perceived quality). IBM, General Electric, and Sears have reputations for providing strong field support for their products. Many customers select IBM computers, General Electric refrigerators, and Sears dishwashers for that reason. This is not to say that the products of these firms are necessarily the best in their industries; an excellent field-support reputation, however, can have a positive impact on a product's quality image.

Many American manufacturers have been proponents of Japanese methods, which bring together in one system all the elements of a quality management. The system features such practices as just-in-time (JIT) production, JIT supply of purchased parts, statistical process control (SPC), and systems of production control such as kanban. Most American manufacturers, regardless of size and location, have heard about these methods, and many have adopted one or more of them. The promise of these methods is that they increase productivity at the same time that they increase quality. It isn't any wonder then that manufacturing managers all over the world have evaluated their potential

The Basic Elements of a Quality Management System

A system to reduce the chances that poor-quality output will get to the customer involves the following five elements, as shown in Figure 17–4.[24]

Develop Quality Characteristics

The first step in establishing a quality control system is to define the quality characteristics desired by the customer or client. Examining customer preferences, technical specifications, marketing department suggestions, and competitive products provides quality-characteristic information. As previously noted, the preferences of the customer—the key perceiver of quality—are especially important. These preferences will greatly influence the dimensions of quality an organization will choose to emphasize and the level of quality to be achieved for each dimension.

FIGURE 17–4   Five Key Steps in Developing a Quality Control System

Managers who want to improve quality must take five specific, sequential actions.

Action	Purpose
1. Develop quality characteristics	Quality control systems must ensure that products deliver what customers expect.
2. Establish quality standards	Standards of quality must pertain to customer-defined characteristics.
3. Develop quality review program	Quality control is realized only through the implementation of specific procedures.
4. Build commitment to quality	Employees make the product—their commitment is necessary to achieve quality standards.
5. Design reporting system	Product quality information must be channeled to employees who can take corrective actions.

Establish Quality Standards

Once the quality characteristics have been defined, the next step is to determine the desired quality standards. These standards quantify the specific quality requirements for the organization's output. Quality standards serve as the reference point for comparing what is "ideal" to what actually "is."

In many organizations, quality standards are coupled with objectives concerning the organization's cost of quality. Often the objective is to reduce the failure costs of quality (both internal and external). These costs make up 15 to 40 percent of a company's sales.[25] Tennant Co. of Minneapolis confronted substantial quality problems in the maintenance equipment it produces for industrial floors. The company's failure costs of quality averaged 17 percent of sales. Tennant launched a companywide program to reduce the failure costs to less than 9 percent of sales in four years. It planned to further cut failure costs to less than 3 percent thereafter.[26] DuPont's polymer products department faced a similar problem; internal and external failure costs were running $400 billion each year, about double the department's yearly profits. The department launched a quality campaign designed to reduce failure costs by 10 percent each year.[27]

Develop a Quality Review Program

Management must establish methods for quality review and decide where the reviews will be conducted, by whom, when they will occur, and how the review will be reported and analyzed by managers. One important management decision involves determining how many products will be checked for quality. Will all products be inspected or will there be a representative sampling? Representative sampling is less costly than inspecting all products manufactured. But inspecting only a sample (not every product) for quality creates some problems: the risk that a greater number of low-quality products will get into the hands of customers; more likelihood that customer goodwill will be tarnished; and the need to decide what constitutes an acceptable number of defects or low-quality products.

Representative sampling in manufacturing firms can take one of many forms. Some organizations use a random spot check. A number of products (e.g., cars, generators, computers) are randomly selected from a sample and are inspected for quality. When a formal random spot check is used, the results can be meaningful and can provide adequate control. Other forms of sampling plans using statistical analysis also are available.[28] In each case, the decision about which plan to use will involve making inferences about the entire production based on samples. Representative sampling thus means that defective products will occasionally slip through the quality-check network.

Build Quality Commitment

A commitment to quality among all employees is essential to an effective quality control system.[29] Management can encourage this commitment through four actions:

1. *Communicating the need for quality.* Effective quality control systems require a communication program designed to demonstrate to employees the importance of quality to the consumer, the company, and ultimately its workforce.[30] These programs use videotapes, seminars, and discussions to illustrate the impact of quality on organizational sales and profits and on compensation and benefits for the workforce.

2. *Training employees in the skills and knowledge of quality.* Inadequate training can be a major barrier to quality; the Tennant Co. found that poor training was a primary source of its quality problems. Management had not effectively trained assembly workers to correctly install certain product parts. The company's engineers were not instructed in the latest technology concerning relevant circuitry. To avoid these problems, companies focus training on providing the skills and abilities needed to achieve the organization's quality standards. And training is not limited to nonsupervisory employees. At Tennant Co., every manager completed at least five courses in quality control during the initial years of the company's quality campaign.

3. *Securing employee involvement in quality.* Some organizations train employees in problem-solving techniques and skills and encourage them to use what they've learned in identifying and solving quality-related problems.[31] One indicator of employee involvement in quality at Toyota is the number of suggestions employees provide management concerning productivity and quality.

4. *Rewarding for quality.* Management boosts employee motivation and involvement in the quality effort by rewarding employees for their contributions to meeting and especially surpassing quality standards. To motivate its managers, Ford Motor Co. includes quality objectives as part of its executive compensation plan. In 1986, for example, Ford based 40 to 65 percent of a manager's annual bonus on contributions to quality. IBM extends rewards for quality to its suppliers; the company pays premiums for materials that exceed a certain quality standard. IBM also penalizes suppliers for materials of lesser quality via reductions in the prices it pays for those materials.[32]

Design Reporting Systems

To control and improve product or service quality, management requires information in the form of quality measurements and progress reports. Measures of inputs entering the process are important indicators of how good, questionable, or poor these inputs are. Input measures prepare management for possible process and output problems. Measures of quality at the point of processing are also valuable. Concurrent control information can indicate the need to alter, regulate, or shut down the process. And making these changes or decisions could prevent faulty outputs from reaching customers or clients. The final outputs must be checked and the results reported. Measures taken prior to shipment can result in last-minute corrections. Measures and reports from customers or clients also can provide crucial data.

Without a measurement and reporting system, critical quality problems can be overlooked. The consequence of such faulty control can mean the loss of customers or clients.

When customers or clients perceive that quality meets their expectations, the image of the product or service is enhanced. It is these perceptions that the five-step quality program attempts to influence.

Total Quality Management

In response to competitive pressures, a growing number of organizations are adopting a unique philosophy concerning quality termed *total quality management* (TQM). Motorola, Hewlett-Packard, IBM, Milliken & Co., and other companies who have adopted this philosophy generally follow three principles concerning quality.[33]

First, the objective of quality control is to achieve a constant and continual improvement in quality. Meeting the same quality standards year after year is not sufficient. Instead, the goal is to provide more and better quality for customers.[34]

Second, the focus of quality improvement and quality control extends beyond the actual product or service that an organization provides. The focus of quality is on every process in the organization. Accounting systems, product promotion activities, R&D processes, and virtually all other activities in the organization are the focus of quality improvement.

Third, employees bear a major responsibility for quality improvement. Quality becomes an integral element of every job in the organization.

Implementing total quality management *involves the same four elements of a quality control system as described in the preceding section.* However, the breadth of the quality focus and the challenge of continual improvement require extra efforts. For example, an integral part of the TQM system is the quality audit, a careful study of every factor that affects quality in an activity or process. Audits are conducted in every department and division to identify existing and potential contributors to quality problems and to discover new ways to further improve quality.[35]

Like the traditional quality control system, employee training is emphasized. However, because employees are key participants in quality improvement efforts, training focuses on problem-solving skills and techniques such as data collection methods, statistical analysis, and group brainstorming. The CEO and the top-management team are often the first to receive training in quality concepts and quality control. Employees put their newly acquired skills to work in project teams in their divisions. These teams tackle specific assignments such as improving customer service and the manufacturing work flow or making the performance of a certain job more efficient. Team members come from the division's various departments. Projects of wider scope are handled by cross-functional teams with representatives from the organization's different divisions.[36]

To help implement and maintain total quality management, an organization often creates a staff of managers trained in TQM principles and techniques. Staff members direct employee training in problem-solving techniques, coordinate quality audits, assist in the development of quality standards and measurements, and perform other functions in the TQM effort. Total quality management councils or committees are also often created at the division and top-management level to oversee the organizationwide TQM effort.

Total Quality Management at Corning

Corning Glass Works, an industrial glass manufacturer, is one company that has successfully implemented a total quality management system. In the mid-1980s, Corning's international competitors were making substantial gains in product quality. To keep its competitive edge, Corning launched the total quality management system to improve quality in every company operation and to involve all of its 28,000 employees in the effort.

Among Corning's objectives in the TQM effort were to identify the key quality "errors" in every department and reduce those errors by 90 percent, to manufacture new products that equal or beat the competition in quality, and to substantially reduce the company's failure cost of quality (its total cost was estimated to be 20 to 30 percent of sales).

Employee training is a major element of Corning's system. To provide effective training, Corning established the Corning Quality Institute, which is staffed by 10 veteran employees specially trained in quality concepts and techniques. Every salaried employee has completed courses in quality awareness and skills at the institute. Corning also trained 150 local line employees as instructors. These trainers have provided quality training to more than 12,000 production and maintenance people in Corning's plants worldwide. Training has focused on overall quality awareness and on statistics, problem-solving skills, communications, and group dynamics.

To provide employees the opportunity to use the skills they've acquired, Corning organized quality improvement teams in every department. Some of the teams are cross-functional; for example, the customer financial services and information services departments formed a joint corrective action team to find ways to reduce computer-processing costs of accounts receivable. These efforts help achieve quality implementation goals. All departments—and all employees—have quality goals. Corning also received valuable ideas and suggestions from responses to "99 Questions," Corning's worldwide employee survey conducted to identify barriers to total quality.

Corning appointed a top-level executive to head the quality system and created a quality council, staffed by representatives from each division, to monitor the overall effort. To date, Corning has substantially reduced its cost of quality and boosted product quality.[37]

Post–Total Quality Management at Xerox

Xerox, another firm that has experienced considerable success implementing TQM, has moved beyond the fundamentals of quality and productivity improvement to a higher level of commitment.[38] According to Paul Allaire, Xerox's chairman and CEO, the company is not content with having won a Baldrige Award and now seeks a new initiative, which he terms "rugged groupism.

Rugged groupism involves developing a sense of community around the precepts of creativity and individual contribution within the context of diverse groups of people. The initiative involves many of the principles of management introduced throughout this text, but focuses on the issues of production and operations management. For example, Xerox plans to redesign work around complete task units, embodying the principles of job enrichment. The idea of self-management plays a large part in the Xerox system and relies on the ideas of management by objectives through which individuals learn to set their own goals.

In addition, Xerox encourages employees to learn multiple skills and rewards those who do so. The company understands that narrowly trained individuals are less capable of responding to change and innovation than are multiskilled people. We can see the influence of organic organization design principles at work in this initiative.[39] The company also encourages diversity—in culture, attitudes, and orientation as well as in race, religion, and gender. Diversity and differences are recognized as strengths to be cultivated and encouraged.[40]

The experiences of Corning and Xerox demonstrate that production and operations management involves more than attention to machines and material. Indeed, the improvement of America's capability to compete in the modern global market requires attention to all organizations, small as well as large, and to people as well as production and operations.[41]

Looking Ahead

The remaining two chapters in this part of the book will examine some of the specific tools and techniques used by P/OM managers. Tools and techniques such as linear programming, PERT, inventory control, and material requirements planning (Chapter 18) are the basis for making P/OM decisions and for performing the functions of management. Decision support systems (Chapter 19) provide information for making the difficult and important production and operations decisions. It will become clear that whether we discuss Burger King, Methodist Hospital, the Tennessee Valley Authority, or New York University there is a need to study and understand the production process of organizations. It is P/OM that brings into clear focus the importance of design, scheduling, operation, transformation control, and quality. Very few organizations can survive for long without these factors' being properly managed.

Summary of Key Points

- Any productive system that generates tangible products or intangible services is within the sphere of influence of production and operations management.
- P/OM views organizations in terms of systems or a collection of objects united by some form of regular interaction and interdependence. Thus, according to this view, organizations are a productive transformation system.
- Managing a productive transformation system involves the planning, organizing, and controlling functions. However, some specific P/OM functions must also be performed: design, scheduling, operation, and transformation control.
- A primary responsibility of P/OM is assuring quality. Customer/client satisfaction and goodwill are affected by quality. In managerial terms, quality is measured in terms of accuracy and timeliness.
- Specific factors that affect quality include policy, engineering/design, equipment, and field support.

- Management can, through the development of a quality-control program, improve quality. A five-step program to achieve quality improvement includes defining quality characteristics, establishing quality standards, developing a quality-review program, building quality commitment, and the design and use of quality measurements and a reporting system.
- Total quality management (TQM) involves the organization in an all-out effort to improve its performance by improving its quality through fact-based decision making, continuous improvement of all processes and activities, customer-determined quality standards, and employee involvement. TQM is presently the fastest-growing management practice in the United States and the world.

Discussion and Review Questions

1. Explain how international events affect the inputs required for a production process. Provide examples from recent events that have appeared in the media.

2. Describe the transformation processes that are required in a large grocery chain such as Kroger Company or Safeway Supermarkets. Consider these organizations at both the store and corporate levels of the system.

3. What does a city produce, and what are the elements of the system that a city uses to produce its output?

4. What inputs, transformation elements, and outputs does a university use to do its work? How does your university or college rate in your opinion as a production/operations management system?

5. Explain why the assurance of quality involves not only the design of the product but also the design of the production process that will manufacture the product.

6. Why do organizations not inspect 100 percent of all inputs and outputs to assure quality at both these points in the production system?

7. What is your understanding of total quality management (TQM)? Is it just another management fad that will be history by the time you finish this course or begin your own career in business?

8. Using the quality funnel principle as the basis for your discussion, explain how TQM minimizes quality assurance costs.

9. What seem to be the bases for the successes that Corning has achieved in its quality management efforts?

10. Explain why the management of quality and productivity involves all functions of the business, not just the production/operations function.

CASE 17–1
A VISIT TO BURGER KING

Burger King Corporation is a wholly owned subsidiary of the Pillsbury Company. Burger King fast-food restaurants prepare and serve hamburgers, ham and cheese sandwiches, chicken sandwiches, fish sandwiches, french fries, onion rings, soft drinks, shakes, apple pies, and frozen desserts. In general, a Burger King restaurant is square in design, stands on about one acre of land, and is constructed largely of brick and glass. The restaurant seats about 100 customers.

Making sandwiches and filling orders at Burger King can be viewed as an assembly-line operation. All burgers follow a straight path from the back of the kitchen to the front (order) counter; along this assembly line are a series of workstations. A "board" is used as one workstation. The board is where buns and meat (inputs) are transformed into Whoppers and other sandwiches and products. The board is a long table on which pickles, onions, cheese slices, plastic squeeze bottles of ketchup and mustard, sliced tomatoes, shredded lettuce, mayonnaise, and tartar sauce are kept.

Each Burger King workstation is staffed differently, depending on the pace of demand at the restaurant. At any time, the preferred ratio of front-counter hosts to backroom production workers (cooks, preparers) is about 1 to 1.5. During a peak period, the crew in a Burger King often increases from about 5 to about 13 workers.

The typical Burger King employee works part-time and is a high school student. Wages are paid for hours worked. The days and hours to be worked are scheduled in advance. The use of high-school labor permits day-to-day and peak-to-slow time adjustments.

Most Burger King restaurants have a manager and two assistant managers. Since the week contains 14 shifts and each manager works about 5 shifts a week, one of the three managers is always present in the restaurant.

Management's primary responsibility is to ensure that a quality product is promptly served in a clean environment. Quality is stressed in every part of the production process. While management's abilities to control costs are valued, meeting the Burger King Corporation service goals always comes first. Achieving service goals requires management to motivate and develop the workforce. Thus, managers at Burger King have line responsibilities, and this means that they need to effectively manage work, people, the organization, and the production process.

Other specific responsibilities of Burger King management include ordering materials, receiving and checking deliveries, checking on standards of performance (e.g., how much time it takes to service a customer at the order counter and at the drive-in window), supervising the cleanup and maintenance work, and scheduling the work assignments. One of the most difficult managerial tasks is scheduling work assignments because labor is the chief controllable cost. More labor is scheduled when there are higher sales, longer hours of operation, and more service provided (such as a drive-in window).

EXHIBIT 1

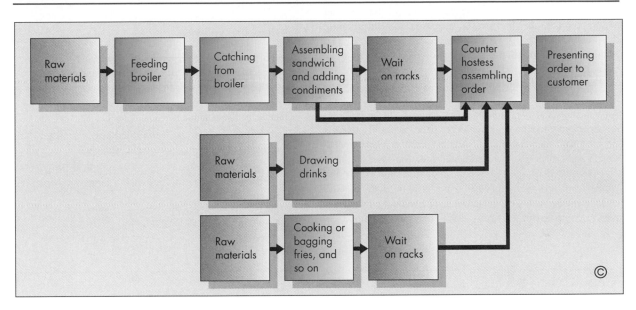

EXHIBIT 2

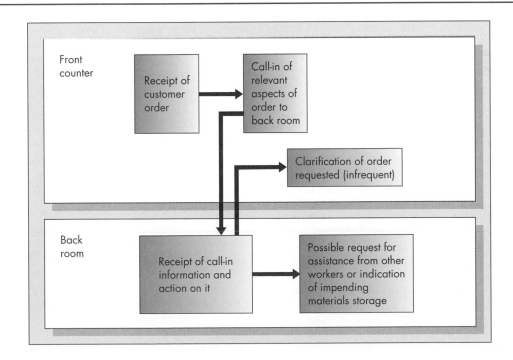

In most service industries, the time delay between service requests (placing an order) and service consumption (receiving the order) must be short. In other words, service is rarely put in an inventory. A doctor's recommendation, tips for making investments, or a hot, tasty Whopper cannot be inventoried. It is one of Burger King's service objectives to customize its services to fit customer needs—to make the sandwich the way the customer wants it.

The production process flow for assembling a Burger King order is depicted in Exhibit 1. Responsibilities are clearly specified, and yet the famous Burger King customizing can be done by the workers at the main assembly point—the board (shown as the "assembling sandwich and adding condiments" box on the diagram). The information flow at a Burger King is displayed in Exhibit 2. The free-flowing information permits rapid changes in the work being performed.

The customizing feature of Burger King requires flexibility from the workforce. The job content and production pace vary throughout any worker's shift during the day. What management encourages on a worker-paced assembly line (as opposed to a machine-paced assembly line) is a team atmosphere and effort. Each worker depends on the other workers.

Managers at Burger King plan, organize, and control the work. They are also expected to perform the four specific P/OM functions: design, scheduling, operation, and transformation control. Burger King's status as a service operation

heightens the importance of quality, and this goal always requires special management attention.

Questions for Analysis

1. Describe how Burger King could implement a TQM management system including specific methods and procedures associated with the Baldrige Award criteria as described in the Management in Action at the opening of the chapter.

2. Discuss how each of the factors that affect quality would apply in a typical Burger King.

3. What special problems, if any, does a typical Burger King face because it employs such a large number of part-time workers?

VIDEO CASE
THE PRODUCTION PROCESS AT WASHBURN GUITARS

When you think of manufacturing firms, names like GM and IBM come to mind. But there are thousands of smaller manufacturers in the marketplace providing us with many of the products that make life more enjoyable. Certainly guitars are one of those products. Washburn guitars in Chicago, Illinois, is a manufacturing company that uses the *intermittent process* of production. That is, they make a few of one model of guitar and then shift production to a different one. They call it *small batch production.*

Even though Washburn makes only a few products each day (about fifteen guitars), they still need to use the latest in production techniques to stay competitive. For example, they use *flexible manufacturing.* They have a machine that is capable of doing many different tasks: building guitar necks, drilling holes for the fretboard, and so on.

Washburn also follows the total quality concepts that other, larger firms follow. When planning the production process, the company also keeps in mind the need for profits. Therefore, popular, more-expensive guitars take precedence over less-expensive items. Today, all of Washburn's acoustic guitars are made overseas, but they have plans to make them in a new facility in Nashville, Tennessee. Total quality management and modern production techniques now make it

possible to manufacture them in the United States and still stay competitive on price.

When making career plans, it is important to include smaller firms like Washburn Guitars in your thoughts. It is often more exciting to work in a smaller, more intimate work environment, especially if the firm practices participative management and other modern techniques.

Critical Thinking Questions

1. What small manufacturing facilities are located in or near your city or town? Visit them and see for yourself what it's like working for a small manufacturer.

2. Do you think that guitars are the kind of item that lends itself well to continuous process manufacturing? Why?

3. One of the more important aspects of small-batch manufacturing is scheduling. What kinds of scheduling techniques have you learned in this chapter that you could use in a business similar to Washburn?

4. Does a career in production management seem attractive to you? Why or why not?

EXPERIENTIAL EXERCISE
DIVERSITY OF QUALITY CONTROL SYSTEMS

Purpose

The purpose of this exercise is to enhance the students' understanding of actual quality control systems in different organizations.

The Exercise in Class

The instructor will divide the class into groups of four to six students each. Each group will complete the following steps:

1. Select a quality control system in a particular organization that you would like to learn more about. The choices are numerous, including the control of student quality, faculty quality, instructional quality, graduate quality, and administrative quality at any college; the control of materials quality, employee quality, process quality, output quality at any local business; the control of treatment quality, care quality, and physician and nurse quality at any local hospital; or any other organization that interests you.

2. Interview the individual who manages the respective control system. Your objective is to develop a written profile of the system. The interview should last approximately 30 minutes. Some suggested questions:

   a. What are the objectives of the control system?

   b. How are standards set and information collected to determine whether standards have been met?

   c. How has the control system changed over the years? What factors led to the changes?

   d. In what ways have you fine-tuned the system to meet your organization's particular needs and constraints?

   e. What are the challenges in implementing and managing the system?

3. Prepare a five-page written report on your findings. The paper should focus on presenting an overall profile of the objectives, makeup, and function of the system. You should also address how the system has evolved over the years and how the system is designed to meet the organization's particular needs. Be sure to include any system problems you identified and to suggest solutions.

The Learning Message

This exercise illustrates that quality control systems differ widely across organizations, even when the same variable, such as input, is the focus of the system.

Notes

1. Valarie A Zeithaml, A Parasuraman, and Leonard L Berry, *Delivering Quality Service* (New York: Free Press, 1990). Leonard L Berry and A Parasuraman, *Marketing Services: Competing through Quality* (New York: Free Press, 1991).

2. Numerous texts survey the field of production/operations management. See Lee J Krajewski and Larry P Ritzman, *Operations Management* (Reading, MA: Addison-Wesley, 1993); James A Gardner, *Common Sense Manufacturing* (Burr Ridge, IL: Business One Irwin, 1992).

3. Robert D Klassen, "The Integration of Environmental Issues into Manufacturing: Toward an Interactive Open-Systems Model," *Production and Inventory Management Journal,* First Quarter 1993, pp. 82–88.

4. Robert O Knorr, "Strategic Restructuring for the 1990s," *Journal of Business Strategy,* May–June 1990, p. 59.

5. Sue P Siferd, W C Benton, and Larry P Ritzman, "Strategies for Service Systems," *European Journal of Operational Research,* February 10, 1992, pp. 291–303.

6. Eugene F Finkin, "Use Technology to Reduce Manufacturing Costs," *Journal of Business Strategy,* May–June 1990, pp. 51–54.

7. Roy L Harmon and Leroy D Peterson, "Reinventing the Factory," *Across the Board,* March 1990, pp. 30–38.

8. Harry Boer and Koos Krabbendam, "The Effective Implementation and Operation of Flexible Manufacturing Systems," *International Studies of Management and Organization,* Winter 1992–93, pp. 33–48.

9. Richard Schonberger and Edward Knod, *Operations Management* (Plano, TX: Business Publications, 1988), pp. 200–41.

10. Gene Bylinsky, "America's Best-Managed Factories," *Fortune,* May 28, 1984, pp. 16–24.

11. Madhav Sinha and Walter O Willborn, *The Management of Quality Assurance* (New York: John Wiley & Sons, 1985).

12. Ross Johnson and William O Winchell, *Management and Quality* (Milwaukee, WI: American Society for Quality Control, 1989), p. 2.

13. "Victory in the Quality Crusade," *Fortune,* October 10, 1988, pp. 80–86. "What America Makes Best," *Fortune,* March 28, 1988, pp. 40–53.

14. David A Garvin, "Competing on the Eight Dimensions of Quality," *Harvard Business Review,* November–December, 1987, pp. 101–9.

15. Ibid., p. 108.

16. Ibid., p. 107.

17. W Jack Duncan and Joseph G Van Matre, "The Gospel According to Deming: Is It Really New?" *Business Horizons,* July–August 1990, pp. 3–9.

18. A V Feigenbaum, *Total Quality Control* (New York: McGraw-Hill, 1983), pp. 112–13.

19. Samuel Walthen, "Production Processes and Organizational Policies," *International Journal of Operations and Production* 13, no. 1 (1993) pp. 56–70.

20. Bernard Taylor, "Corporate Planning for the 1990s: The New Frontiers," *Long Range Planning,* December 1986, pp. 13–18.

21. Tamara J Erickson, John F Magee, Philip A Roussel, and Kamal N Saad, "Managing Technology as a Business Strategy," *Sloan Management Review,* Spring 1990, pp. 73–78.

22. Frank T Adams, "Motivation and the Bottom Line," *Human Capital,* July 1990, pp. 19–22.

23. John Dupuy, "Flexible Jobs: Key to Manufacturing Productivity," *Journal of Business Strategy,* May–June 1990, pp. 28–32.

24. David Bain, *The Productivity Prescription: The Manager's Guide to Improving Productivity and Profits* (New York: McGraw-Hill, 1982), p. 114.

25. Tom Peters, *Thriving on Chaos* (New York: Harper & Row, 1987), p. 74.

26. Ed Bean, "Causes of Quality Control Problems Might Be the Managers—Not Workers," *The Wall Street Journal,* April 10, 1985, p. 31.

27. Thomas C Gibson, "The Total Quality Management Resource," *Quality Progress,* November 1987, pp. 62–66.

28. Sherie Posesorski, "Here's How to Put Statistical Process Control to Work for You," *Canadian Business,* December 1985, pp. 163ff.

29. E. Ted Prince, "Human Factors in Quality Assurance, *Information Systems Management,* Summer 1993, pp. 78–80.

30. Allen E Puckett, "People Are the Key to Productivity," *Industrial Management,* September–October 1985, pp. 12–15; Philip E Atkinson and Brian W Murray, "Managing Total Quality," *Management Services,* October 1985, pp. 18–21.

31. Richard L Bunning, "Modules: A Team Model for Manufacturing," *Personnel Journal,* March 1990, pp. 90–96.

32. Peters, *Thriving on Chaos,* p. 75.

33. David A Garvin, "How the Baldrige Award Really Works," *Harvard Business Review,* November–December 1991, pp. 80–93.

34. Anonymous, "The Cracks in Quality," *The Economist,* April 18, 1992, p. 67.

35. John H Farrow, "Quality Audits: An Invitation to Management," *Quality Progress,* January 1987, pp. 11–13.

36. Harry W Kenworthy, "Total Quality Concept: A Proven Path to Success," *Quality Progress,* July 1986, pp. 21–24.

37. Tim R V Davis, "Benchmarks of Customer Satisfaction: Honeywell, Toyota, and Corning," *Planning Review,* May–June 1994, pp. 38–41; Eric Sandelands, "Bringing Equality Back to Quality at Corning," *Management Decision* 32, no. 5 (1994), pp. 61–62; William W Wagel, "Corning Zeros In on Total Quality, *Personnel,* July 1987, pp. 4–9.

38. Richard L Lee, "Xerox 2000: From Survival to Opportunity," *Quality Progress,* March 1996, pp. 65–71; Judd Everhart, " 'Beyond Quality' at Xerox," *At Work: Stories of Tomorrow's Workplaces,* July–August 1992, pp. 1, 24.

39. E Craig McGee, "The Convergence of Total Quality and Work Design," *Journal of Quality and Participation,* March 1993, pp. 90–96.

40. Pamela Bloch-Flynn and K Vlach, "Employee Awareness Paves the Way for Quality," *HRMagazine,* July 1994, pp. 78–80; James A Anderson, "Thinking about Diversity," *Training and Development,* April 1993, pp. 59–60.

41. Suzanne Axland, "Small Wonders," *Quality Progress,* November 1992, pp. 29–34.

18   Production and Inventory Planning and Control

Chapter Learning Objectives

After completing Chapter 18, you should be able to:

- **Define** the terms *production planning* and *inventory control.*
- **Describe** the applications and limitations of linear programming, program evaluation and review technique, economic order quantity, material requirements planning, and just-in-time models.
- **Discuss** the importance of production and inventory planning and control in product- and service-providing organizations.
- **Compare** the circumstances that would determine whether linear programming or program evaluation review technique is the appropriate production planning model.
- **Identify** the characteristics of inventory that enable a firm to use economic order quantity, material requirements planning, and just-in-time models for inventory control.

Linear Programming Saves Money for Montreal's Urban Transport System

Montreal's urban transport system saved $4 million a year through the application of linear programming to schedule buses and assign operators. One of the 10 largest systems in North America, Montreal's public transport system employs 8,000 and has an annual budget of $577.5 million. Such large systems present extremely complex problems for managers to solve. As service organizations, large public transport systems must meet customers' demand for transportation to and from specific locations at particular times of the day.

The nature of the demand for public transportation places extreme burdens on the system at specific times of the day. During rush-hour traffic in the early mornings and late afternoons, public buses, taxis, subway cars, and commuter trains are crowded. At other times during the day, these same vehicles are relatively empty.

During a typical day, the Montreal system places in service as few as 200 to as many as 1,450 buses to meet the peak demand for transportation. The system also operates the city's subway service, its commuter train line, and a special taxi service for the handicapped. The management problem is straightforward: How many of these different vehicles (along with their operators) should be scheduled at specific times of the day to meet the expected demand for service at that time of day? In production/operations management terms, Montreal's transit company's management faced a scheduling prob lem that lent itself to the linear programming model for feasible solutions.

Effective scheduling of transportation service should improve service quality, reduce costs, and improve employee morale. For example, the linear-programming service schedules reduced the necessity to impose last-minute, unwanted overtime by 67 percent; this alone accounted for considerable cost savings and improved employee morale. The linear programming model that enables managers to make scheduling decisions also enables them to estimate effects of changes through the use of what-if analyses. In this respect, the linear programming approach plays much the same role as a well-developed decision support system. All in all, the linear programming applications in Montreal's public transportation system have brought about significant improvement in the system's operations.

Sources: Adapted from D Dooling, "Technology 1996: Transportation," *IEEE Spectrum*, January 1996, pp. 82–86; J Y Blais, J Lamont, and J M Rousseau, "The HASTUS Vehicle and Manpower Scheduling System at the Societe de transport de la Communaute urbaine de Montreal," *Interfaces*, January–February 1990, pp. 26–42.

Production planning and inventory control issues recur routinely in all organizations. Whether the organization produces products or services, management must decide how many of each and which products or services to produce, and what inventories to keep in stock. As we noted in the Management in Action, the managers of Montreal's public transportation system have to determine the number and types of vehicles to schedule at different times of the day. A manufacturer makes similar decisions: which products and how many to produce, with which resources and how much of them allocated to each product.

Montreal's public transportation managers as well as managers in nearly all organizations must decide how many items to keep in inventory. Inventories as we will see include materials to be processed, goods in process, and finished goods, as well as maintenance supplies and support items. We will discuss both production planning and inventory control methods in this chapter. We will begin the discussion with a presentation of production planning.

Production Planning

For our purposes, we will present production planning in two contexts. The first context is a manufacturer of multiple products that are demanded by large numbers of consumers who are willing to buy them at particular prices. Manufacturers of autos, home products, appliances, and textiles are representative. Here, the production planning decision requires managers to determine the specific number of each product to produce given the resource constraints of the firm and the relative profitability of each product.

The second context is the firm that takes on few, but large-scale, construction or product development projects. These projects are typically one of a kind. The firm may never again produce an identical or even similar product. Builders of roads, buildings, ships, missiles, spacecrafts, and dams are but a few examples of firms that produce under these circumstances. In this second context, the production planning decision requires managers to determine the combination and sequence of activities to complete the project given the cost and time constraints of each activity.

In this chapter, we will describe two of the more widely used techniques—linear programming and program evaluation review technique. These two are representative of the vast array of techniques available to managers who must confront the production and operations planning issue. Our presentation will emphasize the applications of these two techniques.

Planning Repetitive Production: Linear Programming

Determining which specific combination of products to manufacture during a time period becomes more complex as the number of products increases. To assist management in making this decision, a class of techniques called programming methods is available. The simplest of these methods is linear programming (LP). Since World War II, linear programming models have increasingly been used to solve management problems. With the growth of the electronic computer, complex linear programming models are now being utilized on a wide scale.[1]

The model is called linear because the mathematical equations employed to describe the particular system under study and the objective to be achieved are in the form of linear relations between the variables. A linear relationship between two or more variables is directly and precisely proportional.

A linear programming model enables managers to maximize an objective (such as profits) or minimize an objective (such as costs) by determining the future value of certain variables affecting the outcome. These variables are ones that the manager can control.

Specific Applications of Linear Programming

Linear programming has been applied to a number of specific management problems:

1. *Production planning.* In production planning (the specific interest of this chapter), a manager must determine the levels of a number of production activities for the planning period. If a firm manufactures two products, both of which must go through the same three production processes, the manager faces a problem of this nature. The two products compete for time in the three production processes, and the task of the linear programming model would be to allocate the limited resources (available time in the three processes) in such a way as to produce the number of each product that maximizes the firm's profit. Linear programming is a general tool of analysis that managers have adapted to numerous production problems, such as inventory problems,[2] and to workforce allocation decisions.[3]

2. *Feed mix.* Large farming organizations purchase and mix together several types of grains for different purposes. For one situation, the production manager must mix the different grains to produce feed for livestock. Each grain contains different amounts of several nutritional elements. The mixture must meet minimal nutritional requirements at the lowest cost. Linear programming is used to allocate the various grains so that the resulting mixture meets both nutritional and dietary specifications at the minimum cost. A number of different problems in agriculture lend themselves to application of linear programming.[4]

3. *Fluid blending.* This variation of the feed-mix problem requires the manager to blend fluids such as molten metals, chemicals, and crude oil into a finished product. Steel, chemical, and oil companies make wide use of linear programming models for problems of this type.[5] Computing the right mixture of octane requirements in the blending of different gasolines is an example of such a problem in the oil industry.[6]

4. *Transportation.* The managers at many manufacturers and large retail chains must select transportation routes that minimize total shipping costs, given a number of supply sources (e.g., warehouses) and destinations (e.g., customers) and the cost of shipping a product from the source to each destination. This problem becomes even more complex if the firm has many warehouses and thousands of customers in different parts of the country.[7] Other interesting transportation-related applications of linear programming include scheduling ports of call of oceangoing tankers[8] and scheduling optimal routes for school buses.[9]

5. *Advertising media mix.* In most organizations, a manager must sooner or later face a media mix problem. Given an advertising budget, how can the funds be allocated over the various advertising media to achieve maximum exposure of the product or service? Linear programming enables the manager to make these decisions regarding a number of media (e.g., five magazines) all competing for limited resources (the advertising budget). In fact, many advertising agencies use linear programming for problems of this type.

Although the preceding examples represent the most common applications, linear programming has also proved its worth in handling many other practical problems. In British Columbia, water resource experts use linear programming to regulate water levels of lakes controlled by dams. The experts found that more electricity is generated by a dam when the lake behind it is full; however, when the lake overflows after rain, much generating power is lost. Linear programming boosted electricity generation from dams by 5 percent by telling when and how to open and close the gates of the dam.[10] In other applications, linear programming has aided allocation of tax dollars to public projects,[11] space and time to tree development,[12] credit to customers,[13] dollars to investments,[14] hospital resources to patients,[15] and military funds to repair operations.[16]

Applications of linear programming are widespread in large and small firms. The accompanying Management Focus describes applications of linear programming in textile mills of a relatively small firm with foreign and domestic locations.

The Value of Linear Programming

Properly constructed linear programming models provide managers with three specific benefits:

Management Focus

Linear Programming in a Small North Carolina Textile Mill

Textile mills throughout the world face the identical problem of allocating scarce capacity in their knitting machines to meeting the demand for different types of cloth. The problem in linear programming terms requires a solution that maximizes the value of the cloth that can be produced within the constraints imposed by the knitting machines. All textile mills confront this decision.

Applications of linear programming usually bring about increases in productivity and decreases in idle machine time. More important, the profitability of each knitting machine increases because each produces an optimal quantity of the most profitable fabrics. These positive results are very encouraging because they demonstrate the superiority of linear programming over the more traditional manual planning systems that have dominated the textile industry.

Moreover, the positive social and economic consequences of increasing productivity in developing regions cannot be overestimated. Improved production planning can contribute to productivity gains, which can, in turn, improve the national and regional standards of living.

Sources: C Saydem and W D Cooper, "Dye Machine Scheduling and Roll Selection," *Production & Inventory Management Journal,* Fourth Quarter 1995, pp. 64–70; B L Carr, "Modern Garment Manufacture and the Role of Work Study," *Management Services,* December 1995, pp. 16–18; and U Akinc, "A Practical Approach to Lot and Setup Scheduling at a Textile Firm," *IIE Transactions,* March 1993, pp. 54–64.

Improved Planning.   Linear programming can, with the aid of a computer, quickly solve a problem containing over 500 equations and 1,000 variables. This incredible capability means that linear programming can expand the analytic ability and, therefore, the planning ability of a manager. It permits an exhaustive search of numerous alternative solutions and systematically searches for the optimum one. Previously, time constraints might have permitted examination of only a few possible alternative solutions when numerous potential solutions actually existed.

The production planning decision is crucial in manufacturing. The outcome of the decision determines how the scarce resources are to be allocated to the alternative products. The LP method is a very flexible method that has general applicability. As the service sector of the American economy becomes more important, managers of service organizations have discovered LP as a way to improve efficiency. The banking industry in particular has found LP to be especially useful.[17]

Improved Decisions.   Linear programming models can also improve management decisions by quickly finding the optimal solution for a problem under a variety of conditions. For example, after a solution has been selected using an LP model, the manager may alter or add a constraint or change the objective. The computer can quickly provide a new solution under the revised set of conditions. Only a manager, however, can determine which of the two solutions is better.

Improved Understanding of Problems.   Since linear programming models are highly efficient ways of analyzing very complex problems, they also improve a manager's comprehension and appreciation of these complex problems. By structuring a problem, LP models enable the manager to comprehend more easily the effects of alternative assumptions. They not only provide a solution but also enable the manager to understand the problem.

Planning Nonrepetitive Production: PERT

Techniques used to combine resources or to control activities so that plans are carried out as stated are called *network models*. Such models are especially suited to projects that are not routine or repetitive. Coordination is needed for these projects, to ensure that prerequisite tasks are completed before subsequent tasks are started. For nonrepetitive projects, some method is needed to avoid unnecessary conflicts and delays by keeping track of all events and activities—and their interrelationships. Network models provide the means to achieve these purposes. As such, they are valuable aids in managerial planning and controlling.

Program evaluation and review technique (PERT) is a network model that minimizes conflicts, delays, and interruptions in a project by coordinating the various parts of the overall job. PERT's goal is to complete the job on schedule. It does not solve a manager's problems, but it does help identify what the problems are and what solutions are realistic, as well as aid in anticipating problems. PERT is especially useful for nonrepetitive projects—ones that the manager has not previously encountered and is not likely to encounter again. Nonrepetitive projects pose a special problem: How can the manager learn to manage work that is done only once? Such projects have two major characteristics: First, they are extremely complex in that hundreds or thousands of interdependent tasks must be accomplished; second, most of the tasks are single-occurrence tasks that are not likely to be repeated. In contrast to repetitive processes (such as the mass production of a product or the periodic reorders of inventory for which management has past experience, standards, and costs), historical data are not available for nonrepetitive projects. However, each task in a one-of-a-kind program must be performed on time and be of the necessary quality, just as with routine work. In other words, management must still plan and control nonroutine operations. PERT is extremely helpful in such situations because it enables a manager to think through a project in its entirety. As such, it usually results in a more optimum utilization of resources.

Specific Applications of PERT

PERT (and variations of it) is probably one of the most widely used production planning models. It was developed through the cooperation of the US Navy and the management consulting firm of Booz Allen & Hamilton Inc. Introduced by the Special Projects Office of the US Navy in 1958 on the Polaris missile project, PERT was widely credited with helping to reduce by two years the time originally estimated for the completion of the engineering and development programs for the missile. By identifying the longest paths through all of the tasks necessary to complete the project, it enabled the program managers to concentrate efforts on those tasks that vitally affected the total project time. PERT has spread rapidly throughout the defense and space industries. Today, almost every major government agency involved in the space program utilizes PERT. In fact, many government agencies require contractors to use PERT and other network models in planning and controlling their work on government contracts.

While the aerospace business faces peculiar problems, one-of-a-kind development work is also an important element in many other kinds of organizations and industries. In addition to developing space vehicles and putting a man on the moon, PERT has also been utilized successfully in:

· Constructing new plants, buildings, and hospitals.
· Designing new automobiles.

- Coordinating the numerous activities (production, marketing, and so forth) involved in managing a new product or project.[18]
- Planning and scheduling space probes.[19]
- Managing accounts receivable.[20]
- Coordinating the installation of large-scale computer systems.
- Coordinating ship construction and aircraft repairs.

In addition to engineering-oriented applications, PERT has been used to coordinate the numerous activities associated with mergers and acquisitions and with economic planning in underdeveloped countries. The technique has also contributed to planning large conventions and meetings.

Properly constructed, PERT and other network models provide direct aid to managers in two important areas.[21]

Improved Planning.   Network models help managers handle the uncertainties involved in projects where no standard cost and time data are available. Because it shows the manager the interconnections of tasks and provides estimated times, PERT increases the manager's ability to plan an optimum schedule before starting work.[22] In other words, while a project is still in the planning stage, management can take a number of steps to reduce the total time needed to complete the project. Time reductions can be brought about in a number of ways:

- By reducing the expected time on the longest path through the network (the critical path) by transferring resources or additional funds from those activities that can afford it since they do not take as long to complete.
- By eliminating some part of the project that previously might have been considered desirable but not necessary.
- By adding more resources—people or machines.
- By purchasing a component if the time required to produce the component is too long.
- By changing some work to parallel activities that had previously been planned in a series.

Better Control—A Major Advantage.   The planning necessary to construct the network contributes significantly to the definition and ultimate concurrent control of the project. In the case of PERT, the construction of the network is a very demanding task that forces the planner to visualize the number, different kinds, and sequence of all the necessary activities. This kind of thinking cannot help but be a benefit in and of itself in most cases.

Throughout the early days of space exploration, Goddard Space Flight Center (GSFC) made extensive use of PERT as its principal schedule planning and control tool in flight projects.[23] Each project was assigned a schedule team of from two to four PERT analysts to draft and update PERT networks. However, budget and personnel reductions forced Goddard to reduce the size of schedule teams and the use of PERT. Goddard was forced to substitute less detailed methods of schedule planning and control. One result was a loss of monitoring information necessary for controlling key activities in a project.

A number of computer graphic programs have the capability of producing high-quality and accurate PERT network drawings in a few hours. PERT analysts simply sketch out a network, put the information in a proper format, submit the data for computer processing, and in a few hours receive a complete, finished network. The critical paths are identified and highlighted in the computer-produced network, and any subsequent updates or corrections can be quickly processed.

Since the development of computer-graphic programs, the use of PERT has exceeded its use in the early 1960s. The time-consuming aspects of PERT have been virtually eliminated. A PERT analyst can now handle five times more PERT networks than was possible using manual methods. The availability of computer software has increased the applicability of PERT to any organization that can afford a personal computer.

Used effectively, PERT can be valuable as both an internal and external control device. For internal control, it provides time schedules for each activity. Networks can therefore be revised if unforeseen difficulties arise. Resources can be shifted and activities rescheduled with minimal delay in the outcome of the project.

Financial controllers in a variety of organizational settings have applied PERT to their operations problems. Hospitals, in particular, have found PERT a useful technique for controlling costs because the rising cost of health care encourages health care managers to search for ways and means to manage resources more efficiently.[24] The more efficiently they manage resources, the more competitive they are in obtaining clients for their hospitals and clinics. One opportunity for efficient management of resources is the collection of patients' accounts receivable. The sooner an account is collected, the sooner the cash is available for other uses. Hospital managers have discovered that PERT enables them to identify the events and activities related to accounts receivable collection cycles for different types of patients. The PERT network for the cycle begins when the patient is physician-referred or self-referred and ends when the bill for services rendered is collected. Between the beginning and ending events are other events and activities for which critical times can be estimated.

Program evaluation review technique is a powerful technique that has numerous applications in production/operations management. It and linear programming are the bases for more sophisticated techniques that have enabled managers to deal with the complex issues associated with the production/operations function in business.

Inventory Control

A key factor in managing production/operations is inventory control. In its broadest sense, inventory control implies securing and maintaining the optimal quantities and types of physical resources required by the organization's strategic plan. The importance of inventory in production/operations management is underscored when we visualize a manufacturing process as a flow of materials through a process that changes the form of those materials into finished goods. Thus inventory control is at the heart of production control.

Inventory Management as a Strategic Factor

Organizations such as Black and Decker Manufacturing Company (BD) fully realize the relationships among inventory, production, and profit.[25] This global corporation has annual sales in excess of $1 billion. BD is the world's largest manufacturer of power tools and its product line includes drills, saws, sanders, grinders, hedge trimmers, and lawn mowers as well as appliances. If it's powered by an electric motor, chances are that BD makes it. The largest BD plant, located in Hampstead, Maryland, assembles some 120 major product groups requiring 20,000 inventory items. Because of the large required investment in inventory and the costs associated with such a large inventory, managers at the Hampstead plant are always on the alert for ways to control inventory.

Over time BD management has developed an effective inventory control system that has attracted much industry attention. The system, which combines the latest computer technology and control techniques, has four essential features:

1. *A sound materials plan* controls quantities ordered, order dates, and reorder dates in coordination with changes in specifications caused by product or production changes. This materials plan is the foundation of the entire system; the other three elements build on it.

2. *A commitment to executing the plan* requires adherence to the specified order dates and lead times. Through adherence to the discipline of the plan, BD avoids the unnecessary inventory costs associated with administrative mistakes.

3. *Constant evaluation* of ways to reduce inventory levels commits BD managers to continuous review of the inventory system. Through the commitment to continuous review, the company instills the attitude that proaction to potential problems is preferable to reaction to actual problems.

4. *Insistence on maintaining accurate records* of inventory levels and characteristics reflects BD's understanding that a major challenge in any inventory control system is keeping accurate records. The 20,000 different inventory items that the Hampstead plant must keep records on indicates the importance of this part of the plan.

These four elements come together in a unified system that Black and Decker managers believe to be an effective inventory control system. The acronym for the system is PACE, planned action and constant evaluation; it aptly expresses the philosophy of inventory management at this important international corporation.

The development of this system required BD managers to consider all of the issues that we address in this chapter: What are the types and purposes of inventory? How much of each is required? When should inventory be acquired? How can we control inventory cost? The responses to these questions involve many considerations that can best be managed through the use of inventory planning and control methods such as economic order quantity (EOQ), material requirements planning (MRP), the advanced version of MRP—manufacturing resource planning (MRP II), and just-in-time purchasing (JIT). These four contemporary inventory management methods are discussed in this chapter. But first, let us turn to a description of inventories and the purposes inventories serve in organizations.

Types of Inventories

The particular inventories that must be managed depend on the nature of the particular business. The following inventory types are generally found in all businesses:

Raw Materials.   Raw materials are the ingredients that go into the final product. Raw materials are the adhesive, gauze, and paper required to make sanitary bandages; the grains, sweeteners, preservatives, paper, and adhesive required to make and box breakfast cereals; the paper, ink, and binding required to make books. The exact form of the raw material depends on the manufacturing process.

Some manufacturers take nature's own resources and convert them to a product. Steel-making firms must have iron ore and coal to produce steel, which is then sold to auto manufacturers. For them, steel becomes a raw material. Other manufacturers assemble component parts into a final product. Their raw materials inventory consists of many different components supplied by other manufacturers. Corning Incorporated makes more than 60,000 different products, but its largest facility doesn't manufacture a thing. The company's Greencastle, Pennsylvania, facility packages, warehouses, and distributes some 1,250 finished goods items from eight different manufacturing plants.[26] Despite the fact that the Greencastle plant doesn't manufacture a product, it has a considerable inventory of raw materials.

Supplies. Every business requires materials that do not become part of the final product. These materials, termed MRO (maintenance, repair, and operating) items, are usually small in number and expense, compared with other inventories. Nevertheless, they are essential to the operation of the plant. Examples of MRO items include stationery and other office-related materials, repair tools and parts, lubricants, and cleaning supplies.

Work in Process. Raw materials moving through the stages of production are termed *work in process.* Depending on the length and complexity of the production process, work-in-process inventory can be relatively large or small. Controlling work-in-process inventory is an important element of scheduling goods through the various stages of production as rapidly as possible and in order of priority. Multiproduct manufacturers must determine not only how many of each product to make but also when to produce each product.

Finished Goods. Finished goods inventory consists of final, unsold products. Finished goods are stored at the manufacturing facilities or at some point in the distribution channel—at warehouses or retailers, for example. Job order manufacturers carry little, if any, finished goods inventory, since their products are made to customer specifications. Process and assembly manufacturers typically carry large finished goods inventory. Automobile manufacturers, for example, must produce large quantities in *anticipation of* rather than in *response to* customer demand.

The relative size of the inventory depends on the relative certainty of customer demand. Firms in the fortunate position of having unmet demand have no finished goods inventory except that being transported to customers. When electronic games first appeared on the market, manufacturers such as Atari and Coleco Industries experienced demand beyond their ability to supply. Consequently, their investment in finished goods was minimal.

Inventory exists in all organizations, whether business or nonbusiness, in one form or another. Although we usually think of inventory in the context of manufacturing and distribution firms, other types of businesses have inventory as well. Banks, for example, must maintain an inventory of cash to meet customer demand. Hospitals are examples of *non*businesses with inventories; they have inventories of medicine, surgical supplies, and all kinds of housekeeping items. Schools have instructional supplies, and government agencies have inventories of office supplies (and red tape, some would say).

Inventory is costly. The organization must store it, move it from place to place, and safeguard it. The organization also incurs the opportunity cost of having funds that are tied up in inventory and therefore unavailable for other, profit-making, investments.

We will have more to say about inventory costs later. The point is that inventory is costly, and organizations would prefer to do other things with their funds. In most instances, firms consider inventory to be a major source of cost. Managers in these firms seek approaches to controlling inventory cost. One of the most widely used approaches is the economic order quantity (EOQ) model.[27]

EOQ Method

The **economic order quantity (EOQ) model** enables managers to make a number of key inventory decisions. Managers who order goods from a supplier can use EOQ to decide how many units to order and how often to order them. If used to determine the size of batches to produce and when, the method is called the economic lot size (ELS) model. The principles of the model are the same whether the goods are ordered or produced. Here, we emphasize the EOQ variation. EOQ involves balancing the costs of having too much inventory and the costs of having too little inventory.

Cost Factors in Inventory Control

To control inventory, the manager must initially identify cost factors. First, there are the **ordering costs** of getting a particular item into the actual inventory. These costs are incurred each time an order is placed. They are the clerical and administrative costs per order, which also include the cost of receiving the goods and placing them into inventory.[28]

Second, there are the **carrying costs.** These include the interest on money invested in inventory; the cost of storage space, rent, obsolescence, and taxes; and the cost of insurance against theft, fire, and deterioration. Carrying costs are usually expressed as an annual figure and as a percentage of the average inventory.

To reduce inventory costs, a manager must minimize both ordering and carrying costs. Unfortunately, these two costs are related to each other in opposing directions, as shown in Figure 18–1. As the size of each order increases, the number and cost of orders decrease; but since larger quantities are being ordered and placed in inventory, the cost of carrying the inventory increases. (The total cost curve, which is the summation of the other two curves, is discussed in a later section.)

Computing ordering costs is relatively simple. The number of orders for a given period of time is equal to demand (D) for the period divided by the size of each order quantity (Q). The total ordering cost per period (week, month, or year) is equal to the cost of placing each order (J), multiplied by the number of orders per period. Thus, the formula for computing ordering costs reads (D/Q)J, or DJ/Q. As the order size increases, fewer orders are required to meet the demand for a period; consequently, ordering costs decrease, illustrated by the downward sloping order-cost curve in Figure 18–1.

Carrying costs for one item in inventory are calculated by multiplying the value of the item (V) by a percentage figure (E), which is management's estimate of taxes, insurance, and so forth, per period as a percentage of the value of inventory. Total carrying costs are equal to the cost of carrying one item (VE) multiplied by the average inventory $Q/2$. Thus, the formula for calculating total costs is ($Q/2$)VE. For the sake of simplicity, carrying cost is shown as a straight line in Figure 18–1.

Limitations of the EOQ Model

The most obvious limitation of the EOQ model is that conditions of certainty rarely exist in the real world. In our problem, we have assumed that the correct time to order is known. But transportation problems, order requisition difficulties, and other related problems often make the lead time a highly unpredictable phenomenon.[29]

FIGURE 18-1   Ordering and Carrying Cost Relationship

As the size of the order increases, carrying costs increase and ordering costs decrease.

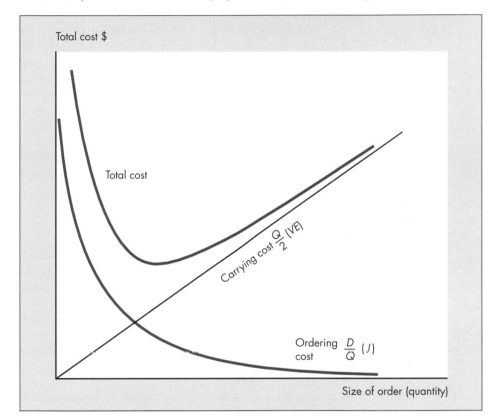

Estimating demand is another problem. Throughout our discussion, demand is known with certainty. But the demand for any item in the real world can at best be only roughly estimated. Many variables—competitors' prices, economic conditions, social conditions, and substitutable items—can influence demand.[30]

A final limitation of the EOQ model is that it is most useful for controlling inventory that has independent demand. That is, the demand is unrelated to the sale or usage of other items. Finished goods and supplies are examples of inventories that have independent demand. Inventory errors for these items are isolated and have no cumulative effects. Therefore, the EOQ model can be applied to these inventories, given its inherent limitations.

Material Requirements Planning

Raw material, component, subassembly, and work-in-process inventories have dependent demand. The demand for these inventories depends on the demand for the finished goods. The EOQ model is much less applicable to these inventories because errors, such as shortage, compound forward. In recent years, an inventory control method termed **material requirements planning (MRP)** has been developed to control inventories with dependent demand. MRP uses sophisticated computer software to plan and control inventory costs. This method enables management to combine a vast number of interlocking decisions related to ordering, scheduling, handling, and using inventories of parts and supplies that are components of the final product. MRP, certainly a contemporary production/operations technique, applies advances in decision support systems, materials-handling technology, and decision making to the difficult problem of planning and controlling.

The popularity of MRP has increased significantly since the early 1970s. The firms that have been quickest to adopt MRP are in the transportation equipment, instruments, and electrical machinery industries. Firms in these industries must carry a complex and expensive array of materials and components. At the other extreme, firms in continuous-process industries (e.g., paper, petroleum, lumber and wood) have not rushed to adopt MRP. Generally, MRP is more applicable in firms that manufacture to order and whose manufacturing process includes both assembly and fabrication.[31] But what is MRP and how does it work?

The Basics of MRP   Material requirements planning involves breaking down a product into its components and subassemblies. Management can then coordinate the ordering and delivery of components and the production start date of all subassemblies.[32] MRP is applicable to a wide range of problems related to producing an end product with numerous components. For example, the method has been successfully applied to the management of NASA's space operations.[33]

The basic tools of MRP are the master production schedule, bills of materials, and inventory records. Although most manufacturing firms have some form of these schedules and records, MRP requires greater detail and sophistication than is usually present in a manual system.

Master Production Schedule.   The **master production schedule** details the planned quantities of finished goods to be produced during a particular time period. The master production schedule is based on the company's strategic plan and the production plan.[34] The strategic plan identifies the product market strategies that propel the firm toward its long-run objectives. The production plan details the production volume of each product or class of products. The optimum product mix must reflect product demand, resources, and overall profitability. Linear programming or more complex programming models can assist managers in determining what combination of products is optimal. In any case, the master schedule depends on prior determination of a production plan.

The master schedule takes the information from the production schedule and adds the timing element; it details what will be produced and when it will be produced. Thus, the master schedule provides the bases for controlling the amount and type of work-in-process inventory during a specified period.

Bill of Materials.   The **bill of materials** defines the required components—those items of inventory that have dependent demand—for each subassembly and finished good. The required quantity, quality, and timing of components depend on the production schedule for the final products.

Figure 18–2 shows the relationship between the master production schedule and two bills of materials. In MRP terms, bills of materials are the result of "exploding" each final product into its subassemblies and components. As shown in the figure, the requirement for wheels depends on the production schedule for baby carriages. The

---

FIGURE 18-2   **The Relationship between the Master Schedule and Bills of Materials**

Bills of materials and master schedules enable managers to see the types and amounts of inventory required to produce a particular volume of output for a specified time period.

Master Production Schedule for Week of November 20, 1993:

Product:	Bicycles	Baby carriages	Playpens
Quantity:	100	50	25

→ **Bill of Materials: Baby Carriage:**

Part Number	Description	Amount
1.	Body assembly	1 each
2.	Wheel assembly	2 each
3.	Handle and frame assembly	1 each

→ **Bill of Materials: Wheel Assembly:**

Part Number	Description	Amount
2/A	Wheels	2 each
2/B	Axle	1 each

→ Inventory requirements for wheel, Part 2/A, for week is 50 (carriages) × 2 (wheel assemblies) × 2 (wheels) = 200 wheels.

---

material requirements are determined by exploding the bill of materials for 50 baby carriages into subassemblies and components. The information could be expanded to include the bills of materials for the subassemblies and components of bicycles and playpens.

It should be obvious that the master schedule and supporting bills of materials become considerably more complex as the number of products increases. To control the scheduling by manual and intuitive means becomes unwieldy and unproductive.

Inventory Records.   The current status of each component subassembly and finished good item must be available. This information requirement necessitates developing and maintaining records that are updated to reflect current usage and replenishment. Thus, perpetual rather than periodic **inventory records** are parts of an MRP system.

The Complete MRP System.   A complete MRP system is diagrammed in Figure 18-3. The simplicity of the diagram should not disguise the complexity of the system. To fully implement the system requires managerial commitment, adequate decision support systems, and computer facilities.[35]

One apparently successful MRP system is operating at the IPE-Cheston Company, which has integrated inventory control with computer capability.[36] The company produces equipment used for heat treating steel, aluminum, copper, and other metals. The company's customers are firms in the forging and metalworking industries. The company experienced rapid growth from 1976 into the early 80s; one effect of that growth was that the number of items in inventory increased from 3,000 to 6,000. The

---

FIGURE 18–3   Elements of an MRP System

The master production schedule, the key element of the MRP system, integrates information from all other elements of the system.

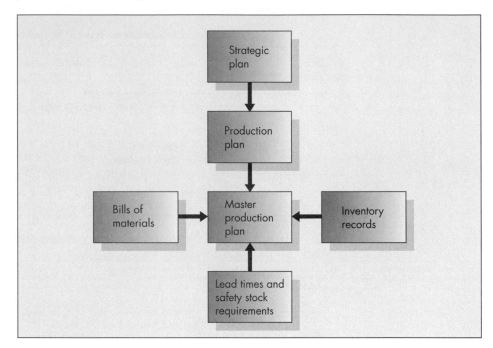

company's method of inventory control was unable to deal with the increased complexity. The old method, primarily a manually operated reorder point and tracking system, permitted numerous errors; inventory on hand and production orders became badly imbalanced. A change was required.

Under the direction of John W. Stoll, director of materials, IPE-Cheston switched to an MRP inventory control system. The switch was greatly facilitated by the use of existing computer hardware, a Wang VS80. The MRP system (produced by Computer Technology Inc.) that IPE-Cheston adopted is compatible with the Wang. The new system increased customer service and reduced inventory by 34 to 40 percent (about $500,000). If carrying costs are 2 percent per month, the savings represents a profit increase of $120,000 per year. "A good investment," states Stoll.

The MRP system at IPE-Cheston contributes to productivity increases because it is adaptable to unexpected changes. For example, bills of materials change as a consequence of engineering and technical improvements. The development of a welding technique can make obsolete a bill of materials that includes bolts and nuts that previously attached the components. Lead times and safety stock determinations can be altered by changing supplier capabilities. A key supplier may suffer a work stoppage that upsets the entire ordering schedule. The ability to adapt to these changes depends on quickly accessing and entering the required data. Thus, the importance of computer capability is underscored.

Another example of inventory control underscores the plantwide effort required to make a system effective. Norton Company's construction products division in Gainesville, Georgia, has been a case study in the successful application of a manufacturing resource planning system.[37] The division's managers implemented a broad-based effort to reverse the upward trend of costs caused by late deliveries, downtime, excessive inventory, and record-keeping. The implementation of the effort involved the application of computers, the education of employees, and the commitment of top management—the usual three ingredients of successful efforts to implement new systems of inventory control.

Manufacturing Resource Planning (MRP II)

Since its original inception as a means for controlling inventory, material requirements planning has evolved into a complete production planning system. This advanced version of MRP, termed manufacturing resource planning (MRP II), integrates production planning, inventory control, and strategic planning. As such, MRP II involves a great deal more detail than MRP.[38]

In application MRP II expands the concept of the bill of materials to include all resources required of a product. Such a bill of resources would specify required materials and labor, machines, capacity, managerial and technical skills, energy, capital, and cash. In this system, planning and controlling inventory is, in the final analysis, planning and controlling the organization itself. The driving force in the system is the forecast of demand for products and services, which activates manufacturing, marketing, engineering, and all other relevant processes.

MRP II has worked best in lot and batch manufacturers. These types of manufacturing firms can better forecast customer demand because of the specific nature of the manufactured output. Mass producers must instead rely on forecasts of economic factors rather than direct forecasts of customer intentions. Digital Equipment Corporation uses MRP II to plan and control the production of its minicomputer line.[39] The firm produces these computers in relatively small quantities to customer specifications that DEC knows in advance. Firms that mass-produce PCs are less likely to be able to implement MRP II.

Just-in-Time Inventory Control

Another advanced version of MRP is **just-in-time inventory control (JIT).** As its name implies, JIT provides the raw material or component part on the very last day, or even hour, before it is needed.[40] JIT attempts to eliminate the need for inventory by altering some of the basic conditions of manufacturing. The JIT approach originated in Japan and is one of the keys to that country's manufacturing success. The Japanese believed that if the underlying reason for inventory could be eliminated, inventory could be eliminated. American industry soon discovered the advantages of JIT, and over 100 major US firms and countless small firms have adopted it.[41]

The Basic Elements of JIT

The underlying reason for inventory is the existence of uncertainty in the production system. Rather than being a smooth-flowing, integrated process, production systems are loosely coupled subsystems producing component parts at different rates. The component parts do not arrive at assembly points at reliable, predictable times. Thus, it is necessary for faster-moving subsystems to have inventories of slower-moving subsystems' outputs so that production proceeds without interruption. The mismatch in the production rates of interdependent production units combines with other factors to create uncertainty, which management usually copes with by investing in inventory.

Another important factor contributing to production uncertainty is unreliable deliveries of acceptable materials from vendors.[42] If a vendor's shipment contains unacceptable units or if it is not on time, production comes to a halt unless a safety stock of inventory is on hand. Equipment breakdowns and insufficiently skilled or trained employees can also contribute to production uncertainty and the need for inventory. The flow of components is interrupted by unacceptable quality or quantity of components whether internally produced or externally supplied. Even the most reliable vendors, well-maintained equipment, and skilled employees cannot overcome poorly designed production layouts or incompetently drawn production plans. When everything is done competently, however, JIT can have remarkable success.

One example of JIT success is the way American automakers now control their inventory of parts for assembling auto seats.[43] Before JIT, carmakers would maintain a cushion room next to the assembly line. In this room, carmakers stored foam, fabric, nuts and bolts, frames, and motors supplied by up to 20 separate vendors. Since JIT, this entire inventory and assembly line no longer exist in many plants.

Today, at General Motors Corporation's Willow Run plant in Michigan, a single supplier, Lear Siegler, makes the seats in the same sequence as GM assembles its cars. Three to four hours before assembly, GM electronically tells Lear Siegler—at its Romulus plant 15 miles away—not only the number, color, style, and options needed on each seat, but also the sequence in which seats are needed. Lear Siegler then assembles the seats that hour and loads them in reverse order on special trucks. Every hour a truck leaves Romulus for Willow Run. When the truck arrives, robots assist unloading the seats as needed on GM's line.

Both firms benefit from the arrangement. For GM, seating inventories at Willow Run are minimal. GM has a reliable supplier almost at its back door. Because GM commits to a steady order schedule, Lear Siegler's inventory is one-fifth of pre-JIT levels. Despite the tight delivery schedules, GM and Lear Siegler have not experienced a single delay. The closest instance came when police seized a truck for a short time to block off traffic. Even under JIT, one cannot guard against all contingencies.

Japanese and American manufacturers who have successfully implemented JIT have done so by eliminating both the human and technical reasons for inventory. The Japanese are notable for their success in developing cooperation among interdependent groups. Japanese managers, as discussed in previous chapters, use participative management and quality circles to encourage communication among groups connected in the work flow. They also invest heavily in employee training and development, including management.[44] On the technical side, JIT requires effective quality control, preventive maintenance, and vendor relations programs. A full-scale, all-encompassing evaluation of the production system must precede the installation of JIT inventory control. American firms such as General Electric Company, Goodyear Tire & Rubber, Ford Motor Company, Chrysler Corporation, and General Motors Corporation have had some success with JIT.[45] It is no coincidence that these same firms face the stiffest competition from the Japanese.

Many American companies have found that developing effective supplier relationships under JIT requirements is the most challenging aspect of JIT implementation. Demands on suppliers are considerable; they must make frequent deliveries of high-quality materials and make them on time. Daily, even hourly deliveries are not uncommon. Under the JIT concept, late or defective materials can shut down the production process, as there are no safety stocks to cushion the effects of such problems.

Successful implementers of JIT usually follow three steps in developing relationships with suppliers. They first communicate the technique's benefits for themselves and their suppliers (who benefit from a stable, long-term purchasing relationship). Second, they train the suppliers in JIT concepts; many companies encourage suppliers to adopt JIT in their own operations and help them implement the concept to reap the same benefits in productivity, costs, and quality. Third, they help the suppliers find ways to simplify their own production processes to make frequent deliveries easier.[46]

Applications of just-in-time inventory can be found throughout manufacturing organizations. In addition to the applications of JIT in specific organizations, the idea of JIT has taken hold in other contexts. For example, training and development managers have begun to apply the idea of JIT to the timing of training experiences. The accompanying Management Focus describes how JIT principles are applied to the training required to undertake total quality management (TQM).

Some Problems and Limitations of JIT	Not all organizations can successfully implement JIT. To ensure JIT's effectiveness, management must overcome several obstacles. One survey of firms using JIT reported four problems that were most difficult to overcome: coordinating the buyer's delivery requirements with the suppliers' production schedules, securing and maintaining the agreed-on levels of quality from suppliers, convincing suppliers of the benefits of JIT, and coordinating information flows between the buyer and the suppliers.[47] A close examination of these four problem areas indicates that they are the very essence of JIT. The more important concern is the underlying causes of these problems.

One critical assessment of JIT's potential indicates that certain market and industry characteristics limit its usefulness.[48] In particular, firms facing considerable aggressive competition find it difficult to keep inventories at a minimum and at the same time respond to their competitors' moves and countermoves. A firm that has zero inventory has no way of responding immediately to opportunities to sell additional goods. Competition increases as firms are able to enter freely and compete in the industry. Successful applications of JIT have the built-in hazard of actually inviting new competitors: JIT lowers costs and increases profits; profit potential invites

---

Management Focus

JIT and TQM: Variations on an Idea

Trainers and educators have long recognized that people are most likely to learn something when they need to know it. Thus if the interval between formal training and real application is too long, the effects of training can deteriorate. To counteract this tendency, managers who schedule training have learned the basics of JIT; they schedule the training *just in time* to meet the need for the learning.

In most organizations that adopt TQM as a management approach and philosophy, the training of line managers to be team leaders and team facilitators poses special difficulties. Line managers have been brought up in organizations that encouraged them to be decisive and to take action; team leadership on the other hand requires

group consensus-building, problem-centered decision making, as well as conflict management. Effective utilization of the new skills has the best chance when the training is presented right as the line managers need to know. Thus the training information is scheduled to coincide with the specific stage of team development that the line managers and their team members are experiencing.

Sources: J H Im, S J Hartman, and P J Bondi, "How Do JIT Systems Affect Human Resource Management?" *Production & Inventory Management Journal,* First Quarter 1994, pp. 1–4; R Sisco, "What to Teach Team Leaders," *Training,* February 1993, pp. 62–67; E R Nutwell, "TQL at Sea," *US Naval Institute Proceedings,* September 1993, pp. 86–88.

competition from firms not now in the industry. Finally, the nature of JIT is to increase the buyer's dependence on the suppliers for timely shipment of quality products. Suppliers can exercise the power they derive from this dependency by insisting that the buyer share the increased costs of shipping smaller and less economical lots (as noted in the EOQ model). The buyer may have no choice except to pay the higher cost and, as a result, lose some of the benefits of JIT.

Managers who wish to implement JIT for some of its benefits should recognize these limitations. They can counteract some of the limitations by acknowledging the need for a level of safety stock and building that level into the inventory strategy.[49] They can also recognize that JIT is no substitute for management and no salvation to all the problems of inventory. It is a way to control inventory costs and nothing more than that. If it does not serve that purpose, it has no place in inventory strategy.

JIT is a powerful tool for lowering inventory costs and investment, cutting labor costs, and boosting product quality and plant capacity/productivity. By eliminating delays in the production process, JIT makes a company's production more flexible. Because the process is quicker, the company can respond more swiftly to customer demand for product variations.[50] However, because it is a challenging concept to implement, many companies first establish JIT on a small scale before making a plantwide commitment to the concept. For example, Hewlett-Packard Company's computer systems division first implemented JIT in the last two steps of the production process before implementing the concept back through the factory to the first step in the process.[51] JIT works best in companies where inventory and product demand can be accurately forecast, the production processes are repetitive, and high-quality suppliers are located nearby.[52]

Summary of Key Points

- Production planning involves determining the quantity of each product to manufacture, given the relative profitability of each product and the availability of scarce resources. It is a recurring decision that managers make with the aid of information, knowledge, and methods such as linear programming and program evaluation review technique.

- Linear programming (LP) is widely used to determine optimal production schedules when management must allocate scarce resources to alternative products. Each product competes, in a sense, with other products for the productive resources of the firm.

- Linear programming has applications for a variety of settings in which resources must be allocated. Production planning is the focus of this chapter, but LP can be applied to decisions involving optimal feed mixes, fuel blendings, transportation routes, and advertising media mix.

- The value of linear programming is to improve managerial decisions, plans, and understanding of the problem. The process of setting up LP solutions requires the manager to thoroughly analyze the elements of the problem under study.

- Many firms produce a single, nonrepetitive product or project. Unlike the multiproduct firm, the single, nonrepetitive product firm must find the optimal allocation of resources to activities that are necessary to complete the product or project.

- A class of management science techniques termed *network models* is applicable to nonrepetitive production planning. Of this class of models, program evaluation review technique (PERT) has enjoyed the greatest popularity among production planners.

- PERT has been a useful aid in planning and building new plants, dams, and other such large-scale construction projects. It is also useful for planning new product developments, sales campaigns, computer installations, and other projects that involve sequences of activities.

- The value of PERT is that it assists management in planning and controlling large-scale projects. A completed network of activities enables management to know better how resources should be allocated among the activities. The network also provides standards for gauging progress toward project completion.

- A key to increased productivity in P/OM is inventory control. Inventory control methods attempt to reduce the costs of inventory by maintaining a balance between the cost of having too much inventory and the cost of having too little.

- The management science approach has long recognized the importance of inventory control. That recognition has resulted in an impressive array of ideas, theories, and methods of inventory management. Economic order quantity (EOQ) methods, material requirements planning (MRP) systems, management resource planning (MRP II), and just-in-time (JIT) are the most widely used.
- The economic order quantity (EOQ) method is appropriate for controlling independent demand inventories, whose demand is relatively constant over time and known with certainty. EOQ controls inventory cost by determining the size of an order (or lot size, if manufactured rather than bought) that minimizes the total inventory cost.
- EOQ is most applicable in organizations whose product or service is consumed in fairly constant rates and has relatively few dependent items in the bills of materials.

- Material requirements planning (MRP) is applicable for dependent demand inventory, in which the demand or usage of inventory is discontinuous, such as job-lot or batch manufacturing. MRP stresses the control of the dependent inventory through computer-based ordering and scheduling.
- In its most fully developed state, MRP has evolved into a general P/OM technique: manufacturing resource planning (MRP II). At this point, MRP II is a way of managing the business.
- Just-in-time (JIT) inventory control owes much to the Japanese for its popularity. JIT involves creating relationships with suppliers to deliver materials at the precise time when needed for production.

Discussion and Review Questions

1. Explain the two general types of production systems and give examples of each one.
2. Why is it useful to think of production planning as a problem that involves the allocation of scarce resources to alternative products or services?
3. The text discusses a number of different production planning problems for which linear programming solutions are available. Describe what these problems have in common that makes them amenable to linear programming.
4. Illustrate the practical value of linear programming by relating the benefits to the planning and controlling functions of management.
5. Helene Manufactures, Inc., produces two different models of professional hair dryers. Dryer A contributes $20 profit, and dryer B contributes $10. Each dryer must go through three manufacturing processes: X, Y, and Z. Dryer A requires four hours in department X, five hours in department Y, and five hours in department Z. Dryer B requires nine hours in department X, six hours in department Y, and 14 hours in department Z. The available time in departments X, Y, and Z are 180 hours, 150 hours, and 175 hours

respectively. Which of the production management methods would be helpful for determining the optimal production schedule for Helene Manufactures? Explain.
6. What are the specific characteristics of production problems for which PERT is an applicable technique?
7. Under which circumstances is MRP preferable to EOQ as an inventory control method? Are EOQ and MRP mutually exclusive? That is, must a firm use one or the other for all inventory items? Explain.
8. Define the basic tools and decisions making up an MRP system. Which decisions are pivotal for determining the relative effectiveness of an MRP system?
9. Explain why MRP usually requires computer utilization. Does the computer requirement place limits on the kinds of firms for which MRP is applicable? Explain.
10. What are the important economic and ethical issues associated with obtaining the necessary supplier relationships to make JIT a successful method for controlling inventory costs?

CASE 18–1

JUST-IN-TIME INVENTORY CONTROL AT THE TOYOTA TRUCK PLANT

Long Beach, California, is the site of a truck bed manufacturing facility owned and operated by Toyota Motor Company. The plant has attracted considerable attention because

of its successful application of Japanese inventory control procedures. The Long Beach plant fabricates, assembles, and paints four models of truck beds for Toyota light trucks. It has a capacity of 150,000 units per year and an annual payroll of $10 million. The plant is a significant economic factor in the Long Beach community, as well as an enlightened user of modern inventory control methods.

The Long Beach plant's mission is to supply truck beds of appropriate style, size, and color to each of the eight ports of entry receiving truck cabs from Toyota plants in Japan. The cabs are shipped from Japan without beds, which are added on arrival. Close coordination is required to ensure that cabs and beds match at the eight ports. The system puts a high premium on production scheduling, inventory management, and shipping. At the heart of the Long Beach system is a practice and philosophy termed just-in-time (JIT) inventory control.

JIT involves a complete commitment to the idea that whatever is being done now can be done in a better way. Consequently, there is never a sense of acceptance of the status quo. As soon as a practice or procedure is implemented in response to a problem, it itself becomes the focus of scrutiny. This critical attitude is necessary to attain the ideal inventory situation: lot sizes of one unit and zero work in process. At that point, the cost of raw materials and work-in-process inventories is at its absolute minimum.

The JIT system takes its name from the idea that a required inventory part or unit should arrive at the point where it is needed at the split second before it is needed. Thus, a brace for a truck bed would arrive on the assembly line at the precise moment when the worker is ready to weld it in place. As we move on down the line, we can see that the truck bed is completed at the precise instant when it is to be painted; it comes off the line at the precise moment when it is to be loaded and shipped to one of the eight ports of entry; it arrives at the port of entry precisely on time to coincide with the arrival of the cabs from Japan.

The ultimate purpose of JIT is to eliminate the need for inventory. But that requires the elimination of defects, late arrivals of component parts from outside vendors, assembly-line breakdowns, and work stoppages in general. The focus of JIT, then, is more than inventory; the focus is the entire manufacturing process from beginning to end.

The managers of the Long Beach plant had the advantage of knowing what to expect when they decided to adopt JIT.

Toyota plants in Japan had adopted the method. The difference at Long Beach was that American, not Japanese, workers and managers would be responsible for planning, implementing, and operating the system. Could Americans do the job as well as the Japanese? Could Americans be retrained to expect perfect quality rather than acceptable quality? Could they be motivated to accept the idea that nothing is perfect, that anything can be improved? Could they be expected to develop and implement procedures that would mean the elimination of their jobs, if the company promised to relocate them to other jobs? Could they work effectively in problem-solving groups, called quality circles, rather than working as individuals to solve knotty problems?

Apparently they not only could—they did. Some of the early performance improvements included a reduction by 45 percent of the work-in-process inventory and a reduction of 24 percent in raw materials inventory in the first year. The warehousing costs of material were reduced by 30 percent. In the production area, the labor cost savings were 20 percent and productivity increased by 40 percent, absenteeism and turnover decreased, and interdepartmental conflicts went down.

These gains stirred considerable pride of accomplishment among the employees of the plant. Their successes were publicized throughout the Toyota organization and the community. The company believes that JIT is no longer a Japanese management tool. JIT is as American as management by objectives and could be adopted by any American manufacturing plant that seeks productivity improvements in manufacturing.

Questions for Analysis

1. Do you believe that JIT can be applied in plants that do not have a Japanese connection? What, if anything, is there about JIT that is peculiarly Japanese?

2. Why is it necessary to consider the entire manufacturing process to make improvements in inventory control?

3. What feature of the JIT approach can apply in organizations that do not have inventories, such as banks, professional firms, and the like?

EXPERIENTIAL EXERCISE
APPLICATIONS OF INVENTORY CONTROL

Purpose

The purpose of this exercise is to reinforce students' understanding of the technical aspects of inventory control, as well as their appreciation of information and assumptions as vital parts of inventory control.

The Exercise in Class

The instructor will divide the class into groups of four to six students in order for each group to consider a hypothetical firm in a specific industry. The choice of firms is at the instructor's discretion. (The exercise works best when the firms chosen relate to those in the surrounding community.) Assigning the same firm to more than one group will facilitate useful comparisons, during class discussion, of the underlying assumptions and knowledge used by each group as the bases for its report. After receiving its assigned business, each group will do the following:

1. Evaluate the applicability of inventory control in the hypothetical firm.
2. Prepare a report that describes the features of the system, including the underlying technique (EOQ, MRP,

JIT, etc.) and the expected costs of the system (e.g., record-keeping and administration).

3. Present the report to the rest of the class, and answer questions about its content.

The Learning Message

Inventory systems are technical applications, but they also depend on the knowledge base of those who develop them. In the absence of knowledge, assumptions become even more important.

Notes

1. Frederick H Murphy, "Making Large-Scale Models Manageable: Modeling from an Operations Research Perspective," *Operations Research,* March–April 1993, pp. 241–52.
2. Gabriel R Bitran and Li Chang, "A Mathematical Programming Approach to a Deterministic Kanban System," *Management Science,* April 1987, pp. 427–41.
3. Robert P Crum and Mohammad Namazi, "Multi-Objective Linear Programming Techniques in Manpower Staff Assignments," *Akron Business and Economic Review,* September 1987, pp. 95–109.
4. Keith Butterworth, "Practical Applications of Linear Programming in US and Canadian Agriculture," *Journal of the Operations Research Society,* January 1985, pp. 99–108.
5. T N Sear, "Logistics Planning in the Downstream Oil Industry," *Journal of the Operational Research Society,* January 1993, pp. 9–17.
6. Cornelis van de Panne, "The Organizational Interaction between Oil Refineries," *Journal of the Operational Research Society,* December 1992, pp. 1159–71.
7. Joao N Climaco, C Henggeler Antunes, and Maria J Alves, "Interactive Decision Support for Multiobjective Transportation Problems," *European Journal of Operational Research,* February 19, 1993, pp. 58–61.
8. Raymond F Boykin and Reuven R Levary, "An Interactive Decision Support System for Analyzing Ship Voyage Alternatives," *Interfaces,* March–April 1985, pp. 81–84.
9. A J Swersey and W Ballard, "Scheduling School Buses," *Management Science,* July 1984, pp. 844–53.
10. William M Buckley, "The Right Mix: New Software Makes the Choice Much Easier," *The Wall Street Journal,* March 27, 1987, p. 24.
11. Colin O Benjamin, "A Linear Goal Programming Model for Public-Sector Project Selection," *Journal of the Operations Research Society,* January 1985, pp. 13–24.
12. T H Mattheiss and S B Land, "A Tree Breeding Strategy Based on Multiple Objective Linear Programming," *Interfaces,* September–October 1984, pp. 96–104.
13. John D Stowe, "An Integer Programming Solution for the Optimal Credit Investigation/Credit Granting Sequence," *Financial Management,* Summer 1985, pp. 66–76.
14. Gordon J Alexander and Bruce G Resnick, "Using Linear and Goal Programming to Immunize Portfolios," *Journal of Banking and Finance,* March 1985, pp. 35–54.
15. William L Hughes and Soliman Y Soliman, "Short-Term Case Mix Management with Linear Programming," *Hospital and Health Services Administration,* January–February 1985, pp. 52–60; Eugene W Grant, Jr., and Fred N Hendron, Jr., "An Application of Linear Programming to Hospital Resource Allocation," *Journal of Health Care Marketing,* September 1987, pp. 69–72.
16. John Moffat, "Three Case Studies of Operations Research for the Royal Air Force," *Journal of the Operational Research Society,* October 1992, pp. 955–60.
17. Thomas O Davenport and H David Sherman, "Measuring Branch Profitability," *Bankers Magazine,* September–October 1987, pp. 34–38.
18. Hal Jackman, "State-of-the-Arts Project Management Methodology: A Survey," *Optimum* (Canada) 20, no. 4 (1990), pp. 24–27.
19. James E Zerega, "Down and Up with PERT at Goddard," *Astronautics and Aeronautics,* February 1976, p. 65.
20. Ann Wiles and Ronald M Horowitz, "PERT Charts Pinpoint Problems in Accounts Receivable Management," *Healthcare and Financial Management,* September 1984, pp. 38–40.
21. D M Dougherty and D B Stephens, "The Lasting Qualities of PERT," *R&D Management,* January 1984, pp. 47–56.

22. Mitchell H Goldstein, "Project Management Systems," *National Productivity Review,* Summer 1986, pp. 290–92.

23. Zerega, "Down and Up," p. 65.

24. Wiles and Horowitz, "PERT Charts," p. 39.

25. John J Kanet, "Inventory Planning at Black and Decker," *Production and Inventory Management,* Third Quarter 1984, pp. 9–21.

26. Bruce Horovitz, "Why Corning Is Sticking with MRP," *Industry Week,* January 25, 1982, p. 46.

27. Kailash Joshi, "Storage Space Costs and the EOQ Model," *Journal of Purchasing and Materials Management,* Summer 1990, pp. 37–41.

28. Joseph R Biggs, Emil A Thies, and James R Sisak, "The Cost of Ordering," *Journal of Purchasing and Materials Management,* Summer 1990, pp. 30–36.

29. C A Ntuen, "Physical Resource Availability Figured into EOQ Formulations Cuts Warehouse Logistics Cost," *Industrial Engineering,* May 1990, pp. 20–23.

30. William M Bassin, "A Technique for Applying EOQ Models to Retail Cycle Stock Inventories," *Journal of Small Business Management,* January 1990, pp. 48–55.

31. John C Anderson, Roger G Schroeder, Sharon E Tupy, and Edna M White, "Materials Requirements Planning Systems: The State of the Art," *Production and Inventory Management,* Fourth Quarter 1982, pp. 51–66; R Dave Garwood, "Explaining JIT, MRP II and Kanban," *Production and Inventory Management Review,* October 1984, pp. 72–74.

32. Charles J Anton and Charles J Malmborg, "The Integration of Inventory Modeling and MRP Processing: A Case Study," *Production and Inventory Management,* Second Quarter 1985, pp. 79–90.

33. Earl Steinberg, William B Lee, and Basheer M Khumawala, "MRP Applications in the Space Program," *Production and Inventory Management,* Second Quarter 1982, pp. 65–77.

34. Sam Tomas, "Material Requirements Planning: A Better Way to Plan Material," *Hospital Materials Management,* August 1990, pp. 30–33.

35. Thomas M Maloney, "What's Wrong with MRP II Systems and How to Maximize Their Effectiveness," *Production and Inventory Management Review,* June 1990, pp. 38–40.

36. "MRP System Cuts Inventory, Improves Services, Productivity," *Industrial Engineering,* July 1982, p. 80.

37. Richard L Thompson, "How to Achieve and Maintain Inventory Accuracy," *Production and Inventory Management,* First Quarter 1985, pp. 38–44.

38. David Tanaka, "MRP II Pulls Stanley Out of a Severe Tailspin," *Computing Canada,* March 29, 1993, pp. 1–6; William Wassmeiller, "Know the MRP II Fundamentals That Support Remanufacturing," *Manufacturing Systems,* January 1993, pp. 52–55;

Philip E Quigley, "MRP II: Growing Business Solves Big Business Problems," *Industrial Engineering,* November 1992, pp. 22–24.

39. Alan Luber, "Living in the Real World of Computer Interfaced Manufacturing," *Production and Inventory Management,* September 1991, pp. 10–11.

40. Richard J Schonberger, "The Transfer of Japanese Manufacturing Management Approaches to US Industry," *Academy of Management Review,* July 1982, p. 480; Richard J Schonberger, "Just-in-Time Systems Focus on Simplicity," *Industrial Engineering,* October 1984, pp. 52–63.

41. R Anthony Inman and Satish Mehra, "The Transferability of Just-in-Time Concepts to American Small Business," *Interfaces,* March–April 1990, pp. 30–37.

42. Fuchiao Chyr, Tsong M Lin, and Chin-Fu Ho, "Comparisons between Just-in-Time and EOQ," *Engineering Costs and Production Economics* (Netherlands), January 1990, pp. 233–40.

43. Ernest Raia, "JIT in Detroit," *Purchasing,* September 15, 1988, p. 74.

44. Nick Oliver, "Human Factors in the Implementation of Just-in-Time Production," *International Journal of Operations and Production Management* (UK) 10, no. 4 (1990), pp. 32–40.

45. Richard J Schonberger and Marc J Schniederjans, "Reinventing Inventory Control," *Interfaces,* May–June 1984, pp. 76–83; Mehran Sepehri, "Kanban and JIT: American Style," *Manufacturing Systems,* June 1985, pp. 49–50.

46. Larry C Giunipero, "Motivating and Monitoring JIT Supplier Performance," *Journal of Purchasing and Materials Management,* Summer 1990, pp. 19–24.

47. Paul A Dion, Peter M Banting, and Loretta M Hasey, "The Impact of JIT on Industrial Marketers," *Industrial Marketing Management* 19, no. 3 (1990), pp. 41–46.

48. Ernest H Hall, Jr., "Just-in-Time Management: A Critical Assessment," *Academy of Management Executive,* November 1989, pp. 315–17.

49. S Subba Rao and Hamid Bahari-Kashani, "Economic Order Quantity and Storage Size—Some Considerations," *Engineering Costs and Production Economics* (Netherlands), May 1990, pp. 201–4.

50. Bruce D Henderson, "The Logic of Kanban," *Journal of Business Strategy,* Winter 1986, pp. 6–12.

51. Richard C Walleigh, "What's Your Excuse for Not Using JIT?" *Harvard Business Review,* March–April 1986, pp. 38ff.

52. Ranga V Ramasesh, "Recasting the Traditional Inventory Models to Implement Just-in-Time Purchasing," *Production and Inventory Management,* First Quarter 1990, pp. 71–75.

19   MANAGING INFORMATION FOR DECISION MAKING

Chapter Learning Objectives

After completing Chapter 19, you should be able to:

- **Define** decision support systems.
- **Describe** the different sources of information.
- **Discuss** the functions of decision support systems.
- **Compare** the advantages of the central data bank with those of an information center.
- **Identify** the important issues associated with managing information.

Without Appropriate Information, Quality Management Is Impossible: An Australian Approach

Managing production and operations to achieve high levels of productivity and quality requires information. The required information includes cost data, projected revenues, setup times, lead times, parts requirements, employee availability and capability, machine capabilities and capacities, vendor reliability, and competitor intelligence. We can get a grasp of the information requirements for effective production/operations management by simply reviewing the methods discussed in previous chapters: LP, PERT, EOQ, MRP, MRP II, and JIT. Each of these methods requires reliable information if managers are to use them in decision making.

Throughout the discussion of production/operations management we have indicated the increasing popularity of total quality management (TQM) as a management philosophy. Although TQM can connote many different meanings, most of its adherents and practitioners will agree that it emphasizes (perhaps insists on) managers' making rational decisions based on scientific, reliable data rather than opinion. Other aspects of TQM, including process improvement, continuous improvement, team-based job design, and employee empowerment, are rendered ineffective in the absence of information that supports and makes possible rational decision making.

Some of the more difficult settings for applications of TQM are hospitals and other organizations that emphasize care giving and services that have a subjective outcome. For example, whether one is "cured" of a disease or "restored to a previous life-sustaining status" is largely a subjective judgment. Thus applications of TQM in health care organizations have a special challenge when it comes to developing reliable information to measure progress, improvement, and effectiveness.

The Australian health system has undertaken a large-scale data collection program that will collect, on a national basis, information such as in-patient visits and clinical performance data. These data will enable hospitals and clinics to access the data as bases for their quality improvement efforts and programs. The data sets facilitate the development of standards for benchmarking through comparisons across hospitals and clinics. Thus the externally generated data enable hospital managers to develop internal information systems that measure the patient and treatment processes and outcomes that have relevance to the particular setting. In the absence of these national, external data, individual hospital efforts to improve quality of care would necessarily be undertaken without the benefit of data; the decisions would reflect opinion not fact.

Sources: S M Neysmith, "Would a National Information System Promote the Development of Canadian Home and Community Care Policy? An Examination of the Australian Experience," *Canadian Public Policy*, June 1995, pp. 159–73; D Johnson and P Kenton, "Economics and Health Care," *Australian Economic Review*, Second Quarter 1994, pp. 69–72; P Fahey and S Ryan, "Quality Begins and Ends with Data," *Quality Progress*, April 1992, pp. 75–79.

The Management in Action touches on the compelling management issue that we will address in the following discussion: What information do managers need to make a decision, and how can managers design systems that enable them to obtain that information? As pointed out in the Management in Action, managers can obtain relevant information from external as well as internal sources. In fact, were it not for the Australian government's efforts to obtain national data pertaining to health, individual hospital managers would be hard-pressed to develop standards to guide their process improvement efforts.

As organizations grow in complexity, managers depend more heavily upon various internal and external sources of information. Growing complexity also increases the number of points at which decisions must be made, ranging from individual decision makers at the lowest operating levels to strategic decision makers at the top. The need to manage information and to make it available to decision makers is certainly not a recent realization. In fact, we can trace information-management efforts to the very earliest days of the development of accounting systems. In addition to accounting systems, many firms have marketing information systems, customer information files, warehouse information systems, and others. Generally we use the term *management information systems* to refer to all these different types and sources of information. But in recent years, one very important idea moves beyond the management information system: the decision support system.[1]

This chapter presents the major issues that managers must take into account when designing a system to manage information to support decisions. First we examine the sources of information that flow into and out of organizations; next we discuss the need for decision support systems; then we examine the specific functions of decision support systems; and finally we review issues related to the design of decision support systems.

Sources of Information

The first step in designing a DSS is to develop a clear understanding of the various information flows that managers must manage. Generally we can distinguish between external and internal sources of information flows as shown in Figure 19–1.

FIGURE 19–1   Information Flows and Types of Information

Information flows both to and from the organization; once inside the organization, it moves both vertically and horizontally.

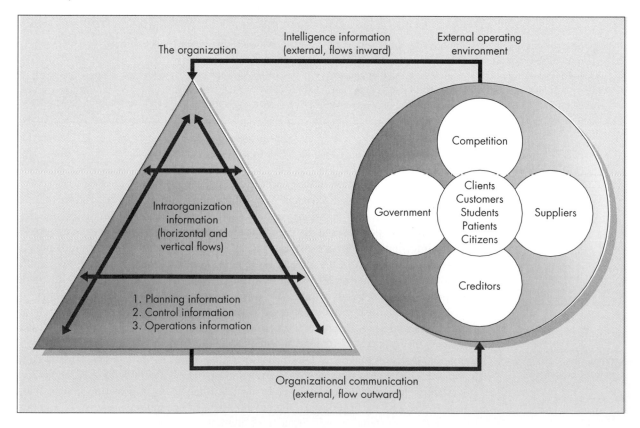

*External
Information Flows*

These flows proceed from the organization to its environment and/or from the environment to the organization. The inward flow is referred to as intelligence information and the outward flow as organizational communications.

Intelligence Information.   These flows relate to the various elements of the organization's operating environment—such as clients, patients, customers, competitors, suppliers, creditors, and the government—for use in evaluating short-run, strategic-planning information on the economic environment—such as consumer income trends and spending patterns for a business organization—as well as tracing developments in the social and cultural environment in which the organization operates. This type of information has long-run significance to the organization and aids in long-range strategic planning. Increasingly technological advancements in computer and computer-related hardware have eased the burden of gathering intelligence information, as Frito-Lay discovered.

In 1989, Frito-Lay Inc. completed installation of a sophisticated DSS that management is counting on to keep the company from losing a step to competition.[2] The system uses information gathered daily from supermarket checkout scanners to identify local trends and problems. Early in 1990 the system alerted management that a problem was developing in the San Antonio and Houston markets. Sales were down in these areas' big supermarkets.

CEO Robert Beeby turned on his computer and quickly isolated the problem and its cause: A regional competitor had recently introduced a white corn tortilla chip. The new product was getting good sales and more shelf space, at the expense of Frito-Lay's traditional product, Tostitos tortilla chips. With this information as backup to the decision, Beeby instructed product design personnel to develop a similar product. Within three months the product was on the market, and Frito-Lay had regained its market share in the troubled areas.

The breakthrough that enabled Frito-Lay and eventually other food manufacturers to develop the DSS was software developments that enabled analysts to use the vast amount of information gathered by checkout scanning devices. The breakthroughs came in response to the volumes of information that scanning devices made available, but not accessible except by the application of considerable human energy. Now with the software, Frito-Lay Inc. can gather important intelligence information efficiently.

Organizational Communications.   These flows move outward from the organization to the various components of its external operating environment. Advertising and other promotional efforts are considered organizational communications. Whatever the type of organization, the content of this information flow is controlled by the organization. Although an important information flow, it nevertheless is an outward flow, with which we will not be concerned in this book.

*Intraorganization
Flows*

This term means exactly what the name says: information flowing within an organization. To be useful, intelligence information must, along with internally generated information, reach the right manager at the right time. Within every organization, there are vertical (both upward and downward) as well as horizontal information flows.[3] The rationale of a DSS is that all information flows must become part of a master plan and not be allowed to function without a formal scheme and direction. The objective of the master plan is to circulate information to the proper person at the right time.

Managing Information for Better Decision Making

As we have seen throughout this book, the quality of a decision depends greatly on understanding the circumstances surrounding an issue and selecting the strategy appropriate to the issue. The better the information, the better the resulting decision, because there is less risk and uncertainty. If new, advanced information technology is to support management decision making, organizations must plan now. The need for comprehensive decision support systems has resulted from three factors: the importance of information in decision making,[4] mismanagement of current information,[5] and the increased use of personal computers by individual decision makers.[6]

Although the specific issues associated with managing production and operations are the focus of this chapter, we should understand that decision support systems are critical for decision making in all aspects of management. Strategic planning, designing jobs and organizations, selecting, placing, and appraising personnel are all assisted by the development of effective decision support systems. An effective decision support system integrates decision making throughout the organization and provides means for managing rivalry among the units which make up the organization.[7]

The Importance of Information in Decision Making

Information is really a fuel that drives organizations. A major purpose of a manager is to convert information into action through the process of decision making. Therefore, a manager and an organization act as an information-decision system.[8]

Information-decision systems should be considered in conjunction with the fundamental managerial functions: planning, organizing, and controlling. If organization is to implement planning and control, if organization is tied to communication, and if communication is represented by an information-decision system, then the key to success in planning and controlling any operation lies in the information-decision system.

Viewing an organization as an information-decision system points out the importance of generating only information that is necessary for effective decision making. If management converts information into action, then how effective the action is depends on how complete, relevant, and reliable the information is. The effectiveness of an organization is more often than not at the mercy of the information available to its managers.[9]

Mismanagement of Current Information

The ability of organizations to generate information is really not a problem, since most are capable of producing massive amounts of information and data. In fact, the last decade has often been described as the Age of Information. Why then do so many managers complain that they have insufficient or irrelevant information on which to base their everyday decisions?

Specifically, most managers' complaints fall into the following categories:

- There is too much of the wrong kind of information and not enough of the right kind.
- Information is so scattered throughout the organization that it is difficult to locate answers to simple questions.
- Vital information is sometimes suppressed by subordinates or by managers in other functional areas.
- Vital information often arrives long after it is needed.

Historically managers did not have to deal with an overabundance of information. Instead they gathered a bare minimum of information and hoped that their decisions would be reasonably good. In fact, in some business organizations, marketing research came to be recognized as an extremely valuable staff function during the 1930s and 1940s because it provided information for marketing decisions when previously there had been little or none.

Today, by contrast, managers often feel buried by the deluge of information and data that comes across their desks. This deluge of information, much of which is not useful, has led to the mismanagement of current information. The management of "information overload" requires managers to distinguish between data and information, as suggested in the accompanying Management Focus.

The Increased Use of Personal Computers

Many experts believe that before this decade is over, most managers will be sharing their desk space with a personal computer. Personal computers have the capability of increasing both the productivity of managers and the quality of their decisions.[10] First, the capacity of computers to extract, process, and analyze data swiftly and accurately is awesome. Second, computers have become smaller, faster, and smarter in a shorter period of time than any other technological innovation in history. A common desktop personal computer can solve ordinary arithmetic problems 18 times faster than the world's first large-scale computer (weighing 30 tons) built only 38 years ago. Present-day computers have become extremely inexpensive compared to earlier models. Just 30 years ago, a medium-sized computer cost a quarter of a million dollars. A firm can now buy a desktop computer with three times the memory capacity for less than $2,000. Consequently, many firms are now making personal computers widely available to their employees.

Management Focus

Managing Information Overload in a Sales Force

No sales force confronts the necessity to respond to changing product developments and customer requirements to a greater degree than those who sell computers and computer-related adjuncts. Computers and related products change rapidly as technological upgrades appear on a weekly if not daily basis. Customer requirements change correspondingly as organizations and individuals discover new ways to exploit the computer's capability. In response to these circumstances, computer manufacturers flood their sales personnel with enormous amounts of information—product specification sheets, brochures, flyers, and updates.

The typical computer salesperson spends a great deal of time sifting through the data to obtain the information critical to the job—selling the product to a satisfied customer. But when the salesperson closes a deal based on out-of-date information and the deal subsequently falls through, the chances of doing the job disappear.

In response to this kind of information overload, one organization shifted away from a paper-based information system for its sales force and developed an electronic information system that sales personnel can tap into through their laptop computers. By the simple expedient of centralizing the source of information and decentralizing the access to the information, the organization enabled its sales force to escape from information overload.

Sources: J Arlen, "Information Overload," *Discount Store News,* February 5, 1996, p. 3; R Tetseli, "Surviving Information Overload," *Fortune,* July 11, 1994, pp. 60–65; M Wheatley, "An Escape from Information Overload," *At Work: Stories of Tomorrow's Workplace,* May–June 1991, pp. 9–10.

The computer has changed the ways information is utilized. Through computer networks, managers can instantly access information sources and communicate directly with other managers who have appropriate information.

Westinghouse Electric Corporation, for example, has made considerable progress in the development of systems to facilitate information utilization.[11] Westinghouse adopted advanced electronic mail and voice-message systems to facilitate greater output. Westinghouse's centerpiece of management productivity is its electronic mail (E-mail) system. Personal computers link 10,700 managers and over 1,000 top customers. Managers can exchange and store ideas and information far more rapidly than before. Message exchanges that heretofore took days now take place in only minutes.

Westinghouse Electric's president, Paul Lego, is a strong believer in E-mail. Because Lego can connect his home IBM-PC AT to the system at Pittsburgh headquarters, Lego can send or respond at home to anyone in the 38-country network. Lego says, "It makes it possible both at home and at work for me to have continuous access to important information." Lego recently purchased a laptop computer. Now, wherever he treks in the world he can stay in constant contact with Pittsburgh as well as locations around the globe.

The E-mail system has generated some shocking results. Westinghouse presently has a permanent and secure record of who said what to whom and when. Telephone tag is a thing of the past. Overseas E-mail is 90 percent less expensive than a personal call. E-mail is 75 percent less costly than a telex letter and far more time effective. Lego credits management productivity increasing over 2 percent annually since 1980 solely to E-mail. He feels that E-mail gives Westinghouse Electric a competitive edge.

The means necessary to produce information are available. Still, managers complain of information losses, delays, and distortions. Apparently many managers have been so concerned about advancing technology and the ready availability of computers that they have overlooked the planning necessary for their effective use.[12] To enable managers to make swift and effective decisions, present management information systems must be developed into more effective decision support systems.

The Need for Decision Support Systems

Decision support systems satisfy one primary managerial need: to provide the manager with the necessary information for making intelligent decisions. The critical point here is that not just any information will do. A system is needed that converts raw data into information that management can actually use. To accomplish this purpose the information system must take into account the information needs of specific managers and the information requirements of specific types of decisions.

The Needs of Managers

Thus, a DSS is a specialized information system designed to support a manager's skills at all stages of decision making—identifying the problem, choosing the relevant data, picking the approach to be used in making the decision, and evaluating the alternative courses of action. A DSS must produce information in a form managers understand— and at a time when such information is needed—and place the information under the managers' direct control.

In short, a DSS shapes information to management's needs. Thus, a DSS provides support for programmable and nonprogrammable decisions under conditions of certainty, risk, and uncertainty. By way of summary, we can see that an effective DSS will do the following:[13]

- Support but not replace management decision making.
- Assist management decision making throughout the organization, but primarily at the middle- and top-management levels.
- Enable the decision maker to interact with the computer to examine the effects of alternative decisions.
- Gather, store, and make available data and decision models relevant to specific types of decisions.
- Invite usage (i.e. be "user-friendly").

The types of problems faced and the procedures used for dealing with them vary according to a manager's level in the organization. The same factors—level in the organization and the type of decision being made—also affect managerial information requirements. To ensure that the types of information match the types of decisions being made, appropriate information must be directed to the proper decision points.

Need for Specific Information for Specific Decisions

The types of information needed are classified by the types of decisions being made: planning decisions, control decisions, and operations decisions. Decision support systems must generate the right types of information for particular types of decisions.[14] Planning, control, and operations decisions require planning, control, and operations information.

Planning Decisions.   These decisions involve formulating objectives for the organization, the amounts and kinds of resources necessary to attain these objectives, and the policies that govern the use of the resources. Much of this planning information comes from external sources and relates to such factors as the present and predicted state of the economy, availability of resources (nonhuman as well as human), and the political and regulatory environment. Effective planning is crucial for effective performance, in public as well as private organizations.[15] Planning information forms the input for nonprogrammed types of decisions made at this top level in the organization.[16]

Often the planning decision is complicated by the very size and complexity of the organization. Of particular concern is the quality of planning that must take place during periods of rapid and considerable growth. The accompanying Management Focus describes the approach that Bell Canada took to provide timely information to planners in a dynamic environment.

Other examples of public organizations using DSS for planning decisions have been noted in the management literature. For example, the Egyptian government has recently reported the results of developing a DSS to provide information for a variety of important public decisions. The Egyptian government's DSS assisted the development of an appropriate tariff policy, a revised debt-management policy, and an innovative energy-pricing policy.[17]

The United States Army has made great progress in its development of a decision support system to assist its human resource planning decisions. The system uses many of the models we discussed in the previous chapter, such as PERT and linear programming, to forecast and plan for human resource needs such as skills and staffing requirements. The DSS takes on some of the characteristics of an MRP system as it breaks down the aggregate requirements into successively smaller units of analysis (e.g., division and company levels).[18]

Management Focus

Bell Canada Develops a DSS System to Integrate Activities

Bell Canada is Canada's major telephone company. During the 80s the company experienced rapid and considerable growth with the effect that management now has to plan and integrate the activities of over 100 departments. Like many other companies that have had a similar experience, Bell Canada found itself with a great need for information to support planning and budgeting for all its far-flung departments. Existing systems were on different hardware and software and usually not compatible with one another.

To address the problem, top management developed a single integrated financial information system based on DSS software. Once developed and installed, the new system enabled uniform plans and budgets to be prepared across departments with results analyzable on a monthly basis. The integrated system contains considerable corporatewide as well as department-specific information on employee head count, as well as operating and financial data. The important development in Bell Canada was the role that the integrated DSS played in melding the organization into a more cohesive whole.

Sources: J Shoesmith, "Networks Now Business Model for the '90s," *Computing Canada,* August 2, 1995, p. 33; Anonymous, "Bell Canada Improves Customer Service with Management Software," *Industrial Engineering,* July 1994, pp. 25–26; J P Stamen, "Decision Support Systems Help Planners Hit Their Targets," *Journal of Business Strategy,* March–April 1990, pp. 30–33.

Control Decisions.   Middle management makes control decisions to ensure that the organization's performance is consistent with its objectives. Control information comes mainly from internal sources (often interdepartmental) and involves such problems as developing budgets and measuring performance of first-line supervisors. The nature of problems faced may either be programmable or nonprogrammable.[19]

Control decisions take on many forms and in some instances involve providing information to customers using the company's products. Manufacturers of chemicals, for example, must be concerned with how the customers use their products. In a sense, the manufacturer must control the customers' usage of the chemical. To accomplish this purpose customers must have information that enables them to make informed decisions about the product.

Olin Chemical faced exactly this problem when Congress passed the Superfund Amendment and Reorganization Act.[20] To comply with the provisions of the act, Olin and other manufacturers of dangerous materials were required to prepare and maintain detailed technical descriptions on how to handle each of their thousands of chemicals under normal as well as adverse situations. These detailed material safety data sheets (MSDS) cost between $10,000 and $20,000 per chemical to prepare.

Ross Ahntholz, Olin Chemical's chief information officer, dealt with this situation by developing an information system. He first established a four-person task force to oversee the creation and maintenance of an MSDS system. Next, through Olin's computerized mail system, Ahntholz simultaneously linked technical service people in Kentucky, Tennessee, Louisiana, and Connecticut; environmental engineers and transit authorities in New Jersey, Kansas, and Connecticut; and medical technicians from five different cities. Together these people wrote, edited, verified, and centrally stored in one database detailed MSDSs for all of Olin's toxic chemicals.

Once positioned, Ahntholz linked the MSDS database to Olin's order system. First, all persons and agencies who recently came in contact with any of Olin's chemicals, or anyone who needed an initial MSDS, received one under a mass mailing.

Next, Ahntholz attached the database to new orders. Today, when an order leaves Olin, appropriate MSDSs shadow Olin's toxic chemicals wherever they go.

Operations Decisions.   These decisions focus on the day-to-day activities of the organization and how efficiently its resources are being used. Operations information comes from routine and necessary sources, such as financial accounting, inventory control, and production scheduling.[21] This information is generated internally, and since it usually relates to specific tasks, it often comes from one designated department. First-line supervisors are the primary users. Since decision making at this level in the organization usually involves programmed types of problems, many problems at the operations level are stated as mathematical models.[22] Some examples of such models and the information they require were discussed in Chapter 18.

The Functions of a Decision Support System

An effective DSS should provide managers with four major services: determination of information needs, information gathering, information processing, and utilization (see Figure 19–2).

Determination of Information Needs

At the start, the manager must attempt to answer questions such as the following: How much information is needed? How, when, and by whom will it be used? In what form is it needed? In other words, the manager begins with an examination of the output requirements. Questions helpful for identifying a manager's information needs are presented in Table 19–1.

FIGURE 19–2   The Functions of a Decision Support System

The outcomes from decisions based on DSS information become inputs in the system to determine future informational needs.

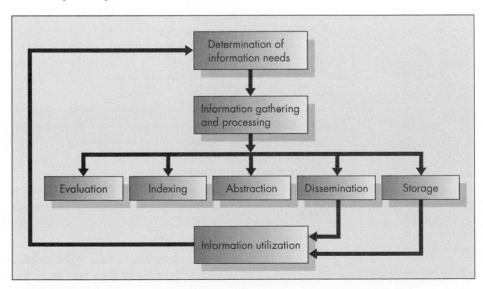

TABLE 19–1   Checklist for Manager's Information Needs

Knowing the right questions can assist the design of an information system.

1. What types of decisions do you make regularly?
2. What types of information do you need to make these decisions?
3. What types of information do you regularly get?
4. What types of information would you like to get that you are not now getting?
5. What information would you want daily? Weekly? Monthly? Yearly?
6. What types of data analysis programs would you like to see made available?

Source: Adapted from P Kotler, *Principles of Marketing,* 3d ed. (Englewood Cliffs, NJ: Prentice Hall, 1986).

As discussed earlier in this book, research and practical experience have demonstrated the need to involve people in changes that affect them. The same is true if a decision support system is being installed: Managers who are expected to use it should be involved in implementing it.[23] Thus, output requirements are based on answers to such questions as the following: What information is necessary for planning and controlling operations at different organizational levels? What information is needed to allocate resources? What information is needed to evaluate performance?

These types of questions recognize that a different kind of information is needed for formulating organizational objectives than for scheduling production. They also recognize that too much information may actually hinder a manager's performance. The manager must distinguish between "need-to-know" types of information and "nice-to-know" types of information. More information does not always mean better decisions.

Determining what information a manager needs for decision making is a useless exercise unless that information can be obtained. For example, any production manager would like to know exactly how many employees are going to show up each day. With that information, the production manager could always schedule the use of part-time temporary employees. But such information is seldom available.

Other information that a manager might need is likely to be found in the minds of experts who have done a particular task for many years but are unable to articulate what it is that they do.[24] For example, Campbell Soup Company recently faced the problem of replacing an employee who was retiring after 44 years with the company. This particular employee knew more about operating the company's huge soup kettles than anyone in the organization. To replace him was next to impossible.[25]

In response to the problem of obtaining information about the kettle operation, Campbell Soup developed an *expert-decision system.*[26] The system incorporates the latest in decision-system technology and includes computer software that simulates the thought processes that the retired employee had used when running the kettles. Other companies are also engaged in the development of these systems for application in production management.[27]

Yet the field of artificial intelligence is just now beginning to develop.[28] It promises to be an exciting extension of decision support systems.[29]

Information Gathering and Processing

The purpose of this service is to improve the overall quality of the information. It includes five component services:

1. *Evaluation* involves determining how much confidence can be placed in a particular piece of information. Such factors as the credibility of the source and reliability of the data must be determined.

2. *Abstraction* involves editing and reducing incoming information in order to provide the managers with only information relevant to their particular task.

3. *Indexing* provides classification for storage and retrieval purposes once information has been gathered.

4. *Dissemination* entails getting the right information to the right manager at the right time. Indeed, this is the overriding purpose of a DSS.

5. *Storage* is the final information-processing service. As noted earlier, an organization has no natural memory, so every DSS must provide for storage of information so that it can be used again if needed. Modern electronic information-storage equipment has greatly improved the "memory" capabilities of organizations.

Information Utilization

How information is used depends greatly on its quality (accuracy), presentation (form), and timeliness. Effective utilization is possible only if the right questions to determine information needs are asked in the beginning and if the system is planned carefully. The major goal of a DSS is to provide the right information to the right decision maker at the right time. To this end, timeliness may take precedence over accuracy.[30] If information is not available when it is needed, then its accuracy is not important. In most cases, however, both accuracy and timeliness are critical.

Timeliness is not the same for every manager; it is determined by the nature of the decisions that must be made. For example, a sales manager may find accurate reports of sales for each company product to be adequate weekly, while an investment manager may need accurate information every few minutes.

Designing a Decision Support System

In most organizations, many different independent information systems exist for different organizational functions. Along with the development of accounting information systems, other line and staff groups in businesses have developed management information systems uniquely suited to their own needs. While management information systems are critical for effective performance within functional areas, what happens when a decision maker requires information from other functional areas? Designing a DSS requires a system perspective.[31] The system perspective means developing a central data bank and an information center, as well as viewing information as an important organizational resource.

The Central Data Bank

A central data bank is the core of a decision support system. Information in one area of an organization is made readily available for decision making in other areas through use of a central data bank. Recent developments in computer and communications technology have made such decision support systems both possible and affordable. And the idea is simple: Centralizing information means that sales data would not have to be stored separately in accounting, marketing, and production but would be available in one central data bank. Since its data can be accessed at will by any decision maker needing it, the central data bank increases both the quality and timeliness of decisions.[32] Figure 19–3 presents the central data bank concept, illustrating two subsystems in more detail.

The Information Center

The information *requirements* of most managers have greatly changed in the past decade, while the information *arrangements* within most organizations have remained

FIGURE 19–3   **The Central Data Bank in a DSS and Two Component Information Systems**

A central data bank enables information in one area of the organization to be available to other areas of the organization.

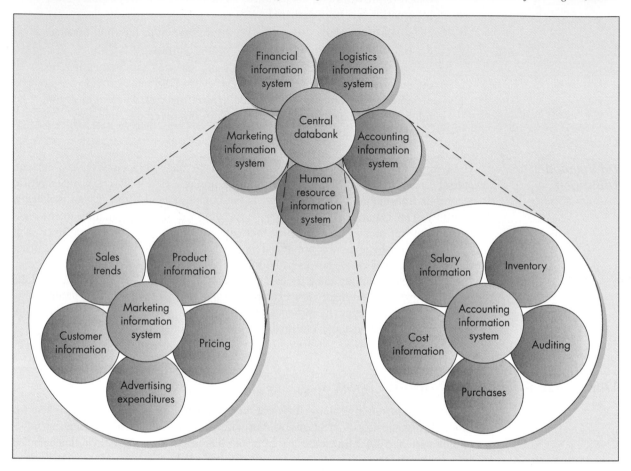

essentially the same. Because both users and suppliers of information are scattered throughout an organization, some unit is needed to oversee the operation of the central data bank. In fact, a basic weakness in most organizations has been the absence of a central entity—known as the information center—for the gathering and processing of information.

To develop an information center, three tasks are necessary:

1. Dispersed information activities must be identified throughout the organization.
2. These activities must be viewed as parts of a whole.
3. These activities must be brought under the management of a separate, centralized information center.

The information center is a consultant, coordinator, and controller for the functions of a DSS—determination of information needs, information gathering and processing, and information utilization. In order to justify its existence, it must facilitate improved managerial performance through more, as well as better, information availability and use.[33]

Many "information-oriented" organizations have developed a separate, centralized, companywide information office. The use of such an office is probably more widespread in highly competitive, volatile consumer-goods industries. However, the need is becoming greater in both private industry and the public sector.[34] This organizational arrangement offers several advantages, such as increased efficiency and more effective use of information, because all computer facilities, knowledge, and storage and retrieval facilities become available to all other functions in the organization.

Information as an Organizational Resource

Developing a central data bank and an information center does not guarantee that information will be used wisely. A frequent problem in many organizations is that a great deal of information is generated for no real purpose and should be eliminated. The tendency to generate large quantities of information is based on the assumption that a direct relationship exists between the amount of information and the quality of decisions. But as we have seen, the quality rather than the quantity of information is more important for decision making.[35] To promote effective utilization of a DSS is to see information as a basic resource of the organization, just as we do money, materials, personnel, and plant and equipment. Thus, as a basic resource, information:

- Is vital to the survival of the organization.
- Can be used only at a cost.
- Must be at the right place at the right time.
- Must be used efficiently for an optimal return on its cost to the organization.

Each user of information should consider the cost of the information relative to its utility for decision making. For example, the cost of compiling complete information for a decision must be weighed against the expected value of a decision made with incomplete information. Many information-system planners do not adequately consider the cost of obtaining the basic information that the system requires.[36]

While the concept of a DSS is relatively new, we have seen in this chapter that it is a reality in small[37] and large[38] organizations. Certainly, one of the major reasons for the increased interest in and the development of DSS has been the growth in information technology. However, the development of DSS is more than technology; its purpose is more effective management decision making.

Summary of Key Points

- More comprehensive decision support systems are necessary because of the importance of information in decision making, mismanagement of current information, and the increased use of personal computers by decision makers.
- Designing a DSS involves understanding information flows as well as the functions of such a system. The functions of a DSS are determination of information needs, information gathering and processing, and information utilization.
- A DSS must be designed to support a manager's skills at all stages of the decision-making process—from identifying and defining problems to evaluating alternative courses of action.
- The types as well as sources of information required for management decisions will vary by level in the organization. We identify three types of information—planning, control, and operations—based on the types of decisions made.
- Organizing a DSS involves developing a central data bank and an information center, as well as viewing information as an important organizational resource.

Discussion and Review Questions

1. What reasons account for the growing importance of information in management decision making? Can a manager make a decision without information? Explain.

2. Explain how a DSS can be designed to provide information for each step in the decision-making process. For which steps would the development of information be most difficult?

3. Explain how the use of personal computers and laptop computers can ease the sense of information overload.

4. What kinds of information would a manager need to make the following decisions?
   a. Hiring a new employee.
   b. Promoting an employee.
   c. Purchasing a computer system.
   d. Assigning salespersons to regions.
   e. Assigning shelf space to a product.

5. Provide examples of decisions, other than the ones listed in Question 4, to illustrate the differences between planning, control, and operations decisions.

6. Interview a member of the college admissions office and determine the kinds of decisions made in the office and the kinds of information required for each decision. Design the basic elements of a DSS that could provide the appropriate information.

7. What are the different functions of a decision support system? How do these functions differ in manufacturing as compared with service organizations?

8. Explain how a manager could make sure that the centralized information center does not become overly powerful in the organization by virtue of its position as monopolist of information.

9. If information is a resource, as suggested by the chapter discussion, should it be valued in the balance sheet like other assets? Why or why not?

10. In the modern age of information, is the study of information little more than the study of computer technology, including hardware and software? Explain your answer.

Case 19–1

Information Systems Development to Compete for the Baldrige Award

Joseph Arthur was an entrepreneur who started a hugely successful restaurant chain throughout Kentucky and Tennessee. He had 12 sit-down, family-style restaurants in the two states, all of which he had personally started from scratch. He managed the enterprise from Lexington, Kentucky, with the help of a small group of dedicated office personnel who researched the restaurant industry, market, and technological developments to provide information for the local restaurant managers' decision making.

The key to Arthur's success was a carefully developed reputation for quality food at prices comparable to fast-food restaurants. His strategy was to use fast-food methods to deliver a diverse menu served at the table. Each restaurant had a menu that appealed to the market, and the food was prepared from products secured from local suppliers. Thus, Arthur's approach to the business was similar to that of Burger King and McDonald's, precluding the use of standardized ways to prepare the main dishes.

In every respect except the order-placing counter, the kitchen and food preparation areas of each of Arthur's restaurants were much like what one would find in a typical Burger King restaurant (see Case 17–1 for details). The restaurants featured sit-down service, a complete menu of locally popular dishes, and servers taking orders and providing service.

As 1994 was approaching, Arthur decided that he had a good enough organization to compete for the Baldrige Award in the small business competition. As he read about the award and its categories, he was particularly concerned about the information and analysis category. This category requires applicants to document the ways in which they go about selecting, securing, and using information related to the production of customer-oriented, high-quality products and services. Despite the fact that Arthur had developed a skilled headquarters staff that provided information to him and the store managers, he believed that much of his success was due to instinct and hard work.

Arthur read the application form and noted that the information and analysis category consists of three sections, each of which identifies specific areas of concern that applicants must address in their application for the award. The three sections and areas of concern are as follows:

1. *Scope and management of quality and performance data and information:* Describe the company's base of data and information used for planning, day-to-day

management, and evaluation of quality. Describe how data and information reliability, timeliness, and access are assured. The key areas of concern for this section are:

a. Describe criteria used for selecting types of data and information to be included in the quality-related data and information base. Data and information related to customers, internal operations, company performance, and cost should be included.

b. Describe how the company ensures reliability, consistency, standardization, review, timely update, and rapid access to data and information throughout the organization.

c. Describe the key methods and key indicators the company uses to evaluate and improve the scope and quality of its data and information and how it shortens the cycle from data gathering to access. Describe efforts to broaden company units' access to data and information.

2. *Competitive comparisons and benchmarks:* Describe the company's approach to selecting data and information for competitive comparisons and world-class benchmarks to support quality and performance planning, evaluation, and improvement. The key areas of concern for this section are:

a. Describe the company's criteria for seeking competitive comparisons and benchmarks including key company requirements and with whom to compare—within and outside the company's industry.

b. Describe the scope, sources, and uses of competitive and benchmark data, including company and independent testing or evaluation of product and service quality, customer satisfaction, internal operations, and supplier performance.

c. Describe how the firm uses competitive and benchmark data to encourage new ideas and to improve the production/service providing process.

d. Describe how the firm evaluates and improves the scope, sources, and uses of competitive and benchmark data.

3. *Analysis and uses of company-level data:* Describe how quality and performance-related data and information are analyzed and used to support the company's overall operational and planning objectives. The key areas of concern for this section are:

a. Describe how customer-related data are aggregated, analyzed, and translated into information to support developing priorities for prompt solutions to customer-related problems, determining relationships between product and service quality and customer satisfaction, customer retention, and market share, and identifying key trends in customer-related performance.

b. Describe how operational performance data are used to develop priorities for short-term performance in company operations such as improved cycle time, productivity, and waste reduction.

c. Describe how cost, financial, and market data are used to support improved customer-related and company operational performance.

d. Describe the methods and indicators the company uses to evaluate and improve its analysis in terms of (1) reduced time between gathering and using data and (2) integration of all sources and uses of data and information.

The amount of detail required to document the information and analysis category seemed overwhelming to Arthur. He took the description of the areas of concern to his data processing staff at the Lexington office and asked them to advise him whether to continue the application process. Initially the staff were frustrated by the apparent complexity of the category, but they eventually recommended that Arthur continue the application, and they began to work on obtaining the required information.

Questions for Analysis:

1. Where in the organization would the data processing staff be likely to find the answers to each of the questions posed in the category?

2. Which of the specific areas of concern would be the most difficult one for which to develop an answer? Explain and indicate what you would do to get the answer.

3. In your personal opinion, what do you think of the amount of detail required to document this category of the Baldrige Award? Could a firm be likely to spend a lot of time completing the applications and get little in the way of return? What would be the reasons to go through the exercise even if the chances of winning are very low?

Video Case
Information for Managers

At the turn of the century few would have guessed how dependent we would become on the horseless carriage. This "high-tech" device was considered a novelty and was dismissed as having little use. But those who did guess right had the advantage. The business community would never be the same. Today, our future is electronic: microprocessors, computers, information systems. Like the horseless carriage of yesterday, computer technology has arrived.

Information systems open new horizons and offer exciting ways of looking at information. They can make our jobs easier and reduce the monotony in our lives. Information systems allow organizations to make information work for them, giving them the competitive advantage they need. What skills will the manager of the future need to survive? The manager of the future will need to be computer literate and have a sensitivity for human qualities that are best complemented by information systems.

The telecommunications industry is being transformed by companies that are taking advantage of new computer technology. To maintain its leadership, AT&T understands that it needs to stay on the cutting edge of technology. The company offers examples of how telephone technology might change our lives through video phones, voice recognition, intelligent agents, and phones that are sophisticated computers. While the tools the company develops might be important, the people it employs are its most valuable asset.

To protect this asset, human resource departments in many companies are offering on-site multimedia systems and sophisticated phone networks that provide instant benefits information. Companies are providing their employees with more choices: choices of health plans, insurance plans, and retirement options. Managing these plans and explaining the options to employees have become such a large task that companies are hiring outside firms to manage their benefits programs. Hewitt Associates is one such firm. It uses a sophisticated information system with around-the-clock staff linked to a database ready to answer questions and provide service by phone.

The benefits center provided by Hewitt combines an interactive voice-response system with an account representative to provide 24-hour benefits assistance for its client's employees. An automated voice response system will either answer participants' questions or forward the call to an account representative. Plan participants can have questions answered, update personal records, or complete transactions at their convenience. This allows the client to reduce overhead for benefits processing and focus on its business.

Another industry that has benefitted from information systems is manufacturing. Computer integrated manufacturing, or CIM, is being used by Nucor Steel to help it with its manufacturing process. After years of decay the steel industry is seeing a rebirth in small companies like Nucor. Vincent Schiavoni, a Nucor mill manager, said, "Our one mill operator controls the entire mill from the time it enters the furnace about 600 feet downstream until the time it exits at the end of our line as a coil about 300 feet in the other direction. He has control of the furnaces, mills, and everything in between. Computer screens provide him with the information he needs to monitor that process."

The integration of computer technology into the manufacturing process has allowed Nucor to compete in the global market. This has provided the means for reestablishing the United States in a leadership position in the steel industry.

Marketing products is as important to a company's success as the quality of their product. Two companies, SoftAd and Navistar, have taken unique approaches to marketing through the use of computers. Navistar has constructed an elaborate database to help it target potential customers. Through an on-line system it can show customers how its trucks compare to competitors' trucks.

SoftAd has taken a completely new approach to advertising by harnessing the computer's power to communicate. SoftAd advertised via computers through floppy disc mailers, multimedia systems, kiosks, and presentation systems. Paula George, president of the SoftAd Group, said, "There is no mass market, not at least in the way we used to think of it. It's getting less and less efficient to put ads on television, at least network television, and clients across the land are looking for new ways to influence their target audiences. We're now looking at niche audiences, specialized audiences—and computer enthusiasts represents a tremendous potential audience." Many traditional advertisers are waiting to see what will become of this new media. But SoftAd has embraced the new technology and has nearly doubled its profits each year.

The investment community has learned that getting the right information at the right time can be extremely valuable. Computer technology allows traders to profit from information. This technology has also turned the world into a single global market. C. Fred Bergsten, director of the Institute for International Economics, said, "I think it's fair to say that the new technology has linked the world into virtually a single, efficient, capital market. New instruments and further advances in the technology will probably enhance that capability even further. We will ultimately be living in a world that is not only financially interdependent but financially almost a single unit."

Telerate is a financial information network that links global financial centers electronically. Through the use of computers and satellite communications, Telerate has created a real time, 24-hour, seven-days-a-week financial trading system that has revolutionized financial management.

The training process has also benefitted greatly from information systems. Allstate Insurance and United Airlines are two examples of successful companies that have employed multimedia technology in training their employees. Allstate implemented its world-class training program using a mix of computer technologies to keep its employees trained. Training workstations throughout the company provide current and consistent training. This reduces the cost of travel and downtime from sending employees to a central location.

United Airlines uses multimedia work stations at airports around the world to train flight attendants on the features of the Airbus A320, a new addition to its fleet. This technology provides valuable training to a workforce that is geographically diverse, saving time and money.

Another way to travel besides flying is virtual travel on the information highway. The Internet may change the way we communicate, the way we keep in touch, the way we do research. It can make us more social and at the same time keep us at home. Friendships form over the Internet without even meeting and we can easily exchange ideas with people around the world. Accessing, downloading, uploading, navigating—all of the basic information needed to begin surfing on the cyber freeway can be acquired through the Internet. The information highway has the potential to become the central form of communicating, much like the telephone of today.

Stop and Shop, Mannington Mills, Microdynamics, and Speigel are all companies that have information systems as part of their retail efforts. Mannington Mills uses multimedia kiosks located in flooring stores throughout the country to position its product above the competition. These systems free up sales staff and provide in-depth information on their products.

Microdynamics supplies computer-assisted design, or CAD, systems for the fashion industry. The fashion industry uses these systems to reduce the amount of samples needed to sell clothing lines. Microdynamics' CAD systems also allow store buyers to instantly modify styles and patterns to fit their particular needs.

Speigel is one example of a company that uses Microdynamics' CAD systems in its retail business. Not only does Speigel use the CAD system in its retail efforts, but it has networked and integrated the systems with every other department in this completely computerized company.

For many years computers were the domain of programmers who could decipher the thousands of lines of codes. Computers today are much less intimidating. One technology that capitalizes on this is multimedia. Multimedia technology is rapidly emerging as a new field and it promises to be a huge industry in its own right. Businesses are demanding multimedia presentations, training applications, market tools, etc. Electronic data interchange (EDI), CD ROM, and laser disc are some of the different mediums that are being used. Medicine, education, aerospace—it's hard to find an industry that's not employing multimedia applications. An example of multimedia is a doctor's office application that features digital video and patient input to reduce paperwork. This system can even help patients diagnose and understand their illnesses by carefully questioning the patients on the reason for their visit.

IBM has created a multimedia kiosk for use at large expositions and public events. The kiosks are designed to help guide visitors, inform them of daily events, make reservations, and even allow for recording voice messages for other members of their party. "About Your Diabetes" is the title of a compact disc interactive or CDI multimedia application for newly diagnosed diabetics. The multimedia program uses touch screen or mouse input to provide general information about diabetes. This program is currently in use at medical institutions around the country.

These are just a few of the business applications being used today. The horseless carriage was an invention that changed our lives and business forever. Today's horseless carriage is the computer and now we are faced with the challenge of taking advantage of the opportunities it can provide.

Critical Thinking Questions

1. The video uses the analogy of the invention of the automobile to illustrate the potential impact of the invention of computer technology. What are some ways in which this analogy is accurate? What are some ways in which it is a misleading analogy?

2. The video referred to CIM and CAD systems. What do these abbreviations refer to?

3. What skills will managers need in the information-rich workplace of the future?

EXPERIENTIAL EXERCISE
DSS DESIGN IN A CAMPUS BOOKSTORE

Purpose

The purpose of this exercise is to enable students to experience the difficulty of developing an information system that provides pertinent and timely data for decision making.

The Exercise in Class

Scenario.   The manager of the campus bookstore has requested that the class determine the essential features of a decision support system that would enable its book buyers to do their jobs—specifically, make decisions about how much should be paid for used books brought in by the students at the end of a particular semester, how many of each book they should buy at different prices, and what price they should charge students who purchase the books for use in subsequent semesters. The manager indicates that the system should be compatible with the store's personal computer system, which enables each of the six book buyers to have access to a common database through the network. The manager envisions a system that would enable the book buyer to call up all the pertinent information on the personal computer whenever an individual comes into the store with a book to sell.

Activity.   The instructor will divide the class into groups of 8 to 10 students. Each group will complete the following steps:

1. Consider the problem as outlined in the scenario.
2. Develop ideas for the design of a decision support system to meet the bookstore manager's needs.
3. Present to the class a report that outlines:

   a. The specific informational needs of the book buyers, as well as the needs of other jobs in the bookstore that the group believes can be satisfied by its decision support system.
   b. Internal and external sources of pertinent information.
   c. The means by which the system will be updated.

The Learning Message

The exercise will reinforce the students' understanding of decision support systems in the context of an organization that they know very well, since they are all likely to have bought and sold books at the campus bookstore.

Notes

1. Hyun B Eom and Sang M Lee, "Decision Support Systems Applications Research: A Bibliography (1971–1988)," *European Journal of Operations Research,* June 1990, pp. 333–42.
2. "How Software Is Making Food Sales a Piece of Cake," *Business Week,* July 2, 1990, pp. 54–55.
3. Thomas H Davenport and James E Short, "The New Industrial Engineering: Information Technology and Business Process Redesign," *Sloan Management Review,* Summer 1990, pp. 11–27.
4. Cornelius H Sullivan, Jr., "Systems Planning in the Information Age," *Sloan Management Review,* Winter 1985, pp. 3–12.
5. C Wood, "Countering Unauthorized Systems Accesses," *Journal of Systems Management,* April 1984, pp. 26–28.
6. E W Robak, "Toward a Microcomputer-Based DSS for Planning Forest Operations," *Interfaces,* September–October 1984, pp. 105–11; W L Fuerst and M P Martin, "Effective Design and Use of Computer Decision Models," *MIS Quarterly,* March 1984, pp. 17–26.
7. Hyun B Lee and Sang M Lee, "A Survey of Decision Support System Applications," *Interfaces,* May–June 1990, pp. 65–79.
8. George P Huber, "A Theory of the Effects of Advanced Technologies on Organizational Design, Intelligence, and Decision Making," *Academy of Management Review,* January 1990, pp. 47–71.
9. Thomas H Davenport and James E Short, "The New Industrial Engineering: Information Technology and Business Process Design," *Sloan Management Review,* Summer 1990, pp. 11–27.
10. Robert T Sumichrast, "Using a Microcomputer Decision Support System for Production Planning," *Production and Inventory Management,* First Quarter 1990, pp. 59–61.
11. "At Westinghouse, 'E-Mail' Makes the World Go Round," *Business Week,* October 10, 1988, p. 110.

12. Raul Espejo and John Watt, "Information Management, Organization, and Managerial Effectiveness," *Journal of the Operational Research Society,* January 1988, pp. 7–14.

13. Jack T Hogue and Alan J Greco, "Developing Marketing Decision Support Systems for Service Companies," *The Journal of Services Marketing,* Winter 1990, pp. 21–30.

14. L Mann, "User Profiles for Systems Planning and Development," *Journal of Systems Management,* April 1984, pp. 38–40.

15. Robert P McGowan and Gary A Lombardo, "Decision Support Systems in State Government," *Public Administration Review,* Winter 1986, pp. 579–83.

16. Robert Fildes, "Quantitative Forecasting—The State of the Arts," *Journal of the Operations Research Society,* July 1985, pp. 549–80; Kelvin Cross, "Manufacturing Planning with Computers at Honeywell," *Long Range Planning,* December 1984, pp. 64–75.

17. Hisham El Sherif, "Managing Institutionalization of Strategic Decision Support for the Egyptian Cabinet," *Interfaces,* January–February 1990, pp. 91–114.

18. Henry S Weigel and Steven P Wilcox, "The Army's Personnel Decision Support System," *Decision Support Systems,* April 1993, pp. 281–306.

19. John Murdoch, "Forecasting and Inventory Control on Micros," *Journal of the Operations Research Society,* July 1985, pp. 607–8.

20. "Olin Computerizes Safety Data," *Management Review,* October 1988, pp. 60–61.

21. H G Heymann and Robert Bloom, *Decision Support Systems in Finance and Accounting* (New York: Quorum Books, 1988).

22. John Bowers, "Network Analysis on a Micro," *Journal of the Operations Research Society,* July 1985, pp. 609–12; A C McKay, "Linear Programming Applications on Microcomputers," *Journal of the Operations Research Society,* July 1985, pp. 633–36.

23. William J Doll, "Avenues for Top Management Involvement in Successful MIS Development," *MIS Quarterly,* March 1985, pp. 17–36; Thomas H Davenport, Michael Hammer, and Tauno J Metsisto, "How Executives Can Shape Their Company's Information System," *Harvard Business Review,* March–April 1989, pp. 130–34.

24. Ole Fadum, "Expert Systems in Action," *Pulp & Paper,* April 1993, pp. 86–99.

25. Emily T Smith, "Turning an Expert's Skill into Computer Software," *Business Week,* October 7, 1985, pp. 104, 108.

26. N A Connell and P L Powell, "A Comparison of Potential Applications of Expert Systems and Decision Support Systems," *Journal of the Operational Research Society* (UK), May 1990, pp. 431–39.

27. Keith Denton, "Decision-Making Technology," *Production and Inventory Management Review,* January 1988, pp. 35–37.

28. Sheila M Jacobs and Robert T Keim, "Knowledge-Based Decision Aids for Information Retrieval," *Journal of Systems Management,* May 1990, pp. 29–34.

29. Brian McNamara, "An Appraisal of Executive Information and Decision Support Systems," *Journal of Systems Management,* May 1990, pp. 14–18.

30. Kenneth M Drange, "Information Systems: Does Efficiency Mean Better Performance?" *Journal of Systems Management,* April 1985, pp. 22–29.

31. Charles R Necco, Carl L Gordon, and Nancy W Tsai, "Systems Analysis and Design: Current Practices," *MIS Quarterly,* December 1987, pp. 461–78.

32. Ernest M von Simson, "The 'Centrally Decentralized' IS Organization," *Harvard Business Review,* July–August 1990, pp. 158–62; Kenneth E Kendall and Barbara A Schuldt, "Decentralized Decision Support Systems," *Decision Support Systems,* April 1993, pp. 259–68.

33. Clinton E White, Jr., and David P Christy, "The Information Center Concept: A Normative Model and a Study of Six Installations," *MIS Quarterly,* December 1987, pp. 451–60; Gail L Cook and Martha M Eining, "Will Cross-Functional Information Systems Work?" *Management Accounting,* February 1993, pp. 53–57.

34. John C Henderson and David A Schilling, "Design and Implementation of Decision Support Systems in the Public Sector," *MIS Quarterly,* June 1985, pp. 157–70.

35. T Hirouchi and T Kosaka, "An Effective Database Foundation for Decision Support Systems," *Information and Management,* August 1984, pp. 183–95.

36. Brian L Dos Santos and Vijay S Mookerjee, "Expert System Design—Minimizing Information Acquisition Costs," *Decision Support Systems,* February 1993, pp. 161–81.

37. Stewart C Malone, "Computerizing Small Business Information Systems," *Journal of Small Business Management,* April 1985, pp. 10–16.

38. G Nigel Gilbert, "Decision Support in Large Organizations," *Data Processing,* May 1985, pp. 28–30.

V SPECIAL MANAGEMENT TOPICS

20   ENTREPRENEURSHIP

Chapter Learning Objectives

After completing Chapter 20, you should be able to:

- **Define** the term *entrepreneur.*
- **Describe** the characteristics and motivations of entrepreneurs.
- **Discuss** why entrepreneurship is a concept that fits people from around the world.
- **Compare** the managerial tasks of the entrepreneur with those of the nonfounder CEO of a large, ongoing corporation.
- **Identify** the benefits that result from developing a business plan.

Women Who Mean Business

Throughout the past decade, women have emerged as key players in the realm of entrepreneurship. In fact, the number of female-owned business start-ups has continued to increase at a record-setting pace during the 1990s. In starting their own businesses, many of these female entrepreneurs have left behind successful careers at large corporations. Primary reasons why these women have decided to strike out on their own include the desire to pursue the fulfillment of personal dreams of entrepreneurship, be their own boss, achieve success in business ownership, and have a meaningful impact on society. The rapid expansion of female-owned enterprises is significant because small business, in the past, has proved to be the major source of new job growth. In fact, some financial institutions who recognize that women entrepreneurs are an emerging force in business have begun to set up organizational units designed to specifically meet the financing needs of women who have been initiating business start-ups at twice the rate of men.

A prime example of a nontraditional company started by a woman entrepreneur is Aegir Systems, Inc., which is based in California. This small, well-respected engineering and computer services company was started by Ella Williams in 1981. Williams who is an African-American, began her business with funds acquired by placing a $65,000 second mortgage on her home. From this humble beginning, Aegir has enjoyed continual growth. Today, Aegir Systems employs 69 people and generates more than $5 million in annual revenues. Aegir has become one of the nation's top small-business contractors, performing safety and reliability assessments on everything from high-tech missiles to commuter railcars. In recognition of her company's efforts, Williams has twice been named the Small Business Prime Contractor of the Year by the US Small Business Administration.

Williams believes that one of the most satisfying rewards of entrepreneurship has been the opportunity to contribute back to the community in which she lives. Financially secure after years of struggling, Williams, with profits from Aegir Systems, is opening a bakery, Ella's World-Class Cheesecakes, Breads, and Muffins, in inner-city Los Angeles. Williams plans to sell the baked goods in stores throughout the greater Los Angeles area, and as part of the business plan, she intends to employ minority youths to help run the bakery and retail outlets.

Responsible for more than 5 million businesses with a net worth exceeding $477 billion, female entrepreneurs carry a lot of clout in today's business and social environment. More and more, successful women business owners are finding themselves in the fortunate position of being able to not only make money but do so in a way that helps others. Williams is a wonderful example of entrepreneurial success and social responsibility in action.

Sources: J Phillips, "Marketing: Lending to Women Entrepreneurs," *Commercial Lending Review,* Fall 1996, pp. 65–70; P A Frishkoff and B M Brown, "Women on the Move in Family Business," *Business Horizons,* March–April 1993, pp. 66–70; and E H Buttner, "Female Entrepreneurs: How Far Have They Come?" *Business Horizons,* March–April 1993, pp. 59–65.

Peruse the latest issues of *The Wall Street Journal, Inc., Success, Fortune, Business Week,* and other major business periodicals; watch the evening's national news broadcast. The impression is clear: Big businesses provide the foundation of the US economy. Exxon, Microsoft, Wal-Mart, Ford, Philip Morris, Citicorp, and other huge corporations generate the jobs, revenues, and financial strength central to our economic well-being.

However, this clear impression is actually misleading and woefully incomplete. The vital, missing contributor is small business. The gas stations, corner florist shops, record stores, restaurants, medical clinics, and any number of other small businesses you see everywhere produce a great portion of the nation's gross national product. For example, retail companies with fewer than 100 employees account for 98.6 percent of the retail industry's sales.[1]

In 1992, nearly 500,000 new small businesses were started by individuals who made the career decision to leave traditional wage-earning jobs and go out on their own.[2] Further, small businesses ship over 30 percent of the nation's exports, a percentage that is continually growing.[3] Indeed, results of a survey revealed that small businesses (with 19 or fewer employees) represented the majority of job growth in the United States during a recent five-year period.[4] Yet the majority of Americans still do not recognize the importance of small businesses to the economy. In total, America's small business community is the world's fourth greatest economic power behind the economies of the entire United States, Japan, and the republics constituting the former Soviet Union.[5]

At the helm of many, if not most, of these companies is the **entrepreneur:** the individual who, propelled by an idea, personal goals, and ambition, brings together the financial capital, people, equipment, and facilities to establish and manage a business enterprise. As the creators and navigators of small business, entrepreneurs are a dominant force in the US economy.

In starting and managing businesses, entrepreneurs face unique challenges different from those of their big business counterpart, the nonfounder chief executive officer (CEO) of a large, ongoing corporation. Unlike the corporate CEO, entrepreneurs are deeply and personally involved in every aspect of the enterprise, at least in the early stages of the business. They apply the management functions in creating, building, and shaping the business. As a result, the organization significantly reflects the entrepreneur's needs, goals, and values.[6] Entrepreneurs also cope with far greater personal and professional risk. In most cases, personal financial resources are lost if the business fails. Unlike large corporations, there are no resources to cushion the effects of mistakes or unexpected developments. Most small businesses are initially run on a shoestring budget that heightens the importance as well as the stresses of the entrepreneur's decision making. Entrepreneurs are also strictly and singularly accountable for their businesses' success or failure. There is usually no board of directors to share the burden of responsibility.

This chapter's discussion of entrepreneurship focuses specifically on the entrepreneur. We devote much of the chapter to the tasks of entrepreneurship, which are presented in the three functions of managing work and organizations (planning, organizing, and controlling) and the entrepreneur's activities involved in managing people, specifically leadership. We also discuss three special challenges that confront many entrepreneurs today.

We devote a chapter to this topic because of the entrepreneurs's considerable economic and social importance in the United States and because of the growing prevalence of entrepreneurship. As seen in the Management in Action that opened this chapter, each year many individuals are assuming the challenge and risks of creating a business. At some point in your career, you may well become an entrepreneur.

Entrepreneurs are active around the world. Honda Motor Company, Toyota Motor Company, and Sony Corporation in Japan were founded by entrepreneurs. New entrepreneurs in Taiwan, Singapore, and South Korea are creating new jobs and becoming financially powerful. For instance, Symon Chang of Tyan Computer is a Taiwanese who now operates a plant in Sunnyvale, California, and has plans to expand his business worldwide.[7]

The Entrepreneur

Management scholars and observers differ in their definitions of an entrepreneur. Many view an entrepreneur as the creator, owner, and chief executive of a business enterprise. Some have emphasized financial risk as a key characteristic of the entrepreneur. A more recent perspective distinguishes between the small business owner and the entrepreneur. The small business owner establishes and manages a business to attain personal objectives. The business is an extension of the owner's needs, goals, and personality, and growth may not be a primary objective. In contrast, entrepreneurs create a business to build the enterprise for growth and profit. They use a deliberate, planned approach that applies strategic management concepts and techniques. The entrepreneur is also highly innovative, creating new products and markets and applying creative strategies and ways of managing.[8]

Our perspective assumes the more general definition of the entrepreneur as the creator and manager of a business. Toward this end, an entrepreneur should not be viewed as a specific type of individual. Rather, entrepreneurship can be considered a behavior encompassing an individual's pursuit of opportunity without regard to the resources the individual currently controls.[9] However, this chapter's discussion emphasizes the innovative, growth-oriented entrepreneur.

Risks

At least during the early stages of the enterprise, the entrepreneur works in a small business. Combining definitions provided by the Small Business Administration and the Committee for Economic Development, a small business is an organization that is privately owned (usually by top management), is not dominant in its market, maintains local operations (though it may serve a much larger market), and employs fewer than 500 people.[10] Half of the small businesses in the United States have annual sales of less than $500,000 and employ 10 or fewer individuals.

In launching a small business, the entrepreneur usually faces substantial *business risk.* Although well over 1 million new businesses are started each year, the failure rate of young companies is disturbingly high.[11] According to research by the Small Business Administration, from 25 to 33 percent of all independent small businesses fail during the first two years of operation.[12] Eight of every 10 businesses end within 10 years.[13]

Besides considerable business risk, entrepreneurs face significant *financial risk,* as they typically invest most if not all of their financial resources in the business. They take a *career risk* when leaving a secure job for a venture with a highly uncertain future. They incur *family and social risks* because the demands of starting and running a young business consume 60- to 80-hour workweeks that leave little time for attention to family and friends. The demands of entrepreneurship often strain marriages and friendships. Entrepreneurs also assume a *psychological risk*—the risk of a deep sense of personal failure if the business does not beat the odds and succeed.[14] The highly successful entrepreneur succinctly summed up the considerable personal risks of entrepreneurship by describing the emotions of launching a business as "entrepreneurial terror."[15]

Motivations

Given the sizable risks, time, and energy requirements of entrepreneurship, why do so many individuals take the entrepreneurial plunge every year? Entrepreneurs are motivated to launch businesses for a number of reasons. While the potential costs are high, the rewards can also be substantial.

Independence. Corporate reorganizations have resulted in the layoff of many managers and professional employees. Rather than seeking employment at other large firms, these individuals are using their education, experience, and skills to start their own businesses.[16] "Being my own boss" is a powerful motivator for many entrepreneurs who seek the freedom to act independently in their work. As heads of businesses, regardless of size, they enjoy the autonomy of making their own decisions, setting their own hours, and determining what they will do and when they will do it. Just as important, these individuals' careers are not dependent on the decisions of others.

Robert Levin is the 32-year-old CEO of Cabletron, a $105 million computer products manufacturer.[17] He believes that being able to make decisions quickly is important to continued success. He proudly states that at Cabletron "we write our own rules to do things."

Personal and Professional Growth.   The challenges of building a business virtually require individual growth. To be successful, an entrepreneur must be able to cope with risk, uncertainty, and stress, handle many different interpersonal relationships, and manage a business with limited resources. Many individuals become entrepreneurs to experience this growth and the fulfillment gained from building a business into a purposeful, productive entity.

Ateeco is a fast-growing family business in Shenandoah, Pennsylvania. It is an ethnic food business that sells pierogies. These are Eastern European pasta pockets—small squares of pasta dough filled with cheddar cheese and mashed potatoes.[18] Ted Twardizik started the business in 1952 and feels that he has grown something of value to pass on to his sons. The sons are interested in experiencing growth and taking on the competition that is now beginning to appear.

The pierogy has tremendous potential because it tastes good and is inherently a healthy food—low in fat and high in carbohydrates. Ateeco now turns out 20,000 an hour—4 million a week—on three production lines. The feeling of personal growth that Twardizik experienced is now becoming a reality for his two sons, Tim and Tom. For entrepreneurs like the Twardiziks, personal as well as professional growth becomes an obsession, with the goal being to grow their business into a large organization able to withstand marketplace competition.[19]

A Superior Alternative to an Unsatisfying Job.   Many entrepreneurs are former executives and employees of large corporations who, while in no danger of being terminated, became dissatisfied with their jobs.[20] For example, there have been a significant number of successful members of the financial community who have chosen to leave Wall Street to pursue a totally different line of work ranging from starting up a nonprofit organization to launching a ski school.[21] Common reasons cited by CEOs of the Inc. 500 (the 500 fastest-growing private companies in the United States) for leaving corporate positions include boredom, corporate noninterest in their work, and slow decision-making processes associated with larger firms.[22]

Other executives, plateaued in their jobs, have launched businesses as a second career, becoming late-bloomer entrepreneurs.[23] The accompanying Management Focus describes how one company is trying to retain managers and other workers by attempting to create for employees a feeling of working in an entrepreneurial environment.

Many female entrepreneurs report poor advancement opportunities as their major reason for launching a business.[24] For example, although many women have found success in middle- or top-management jobs, very few have become CEOs of large retail businesses.[25] One-third of the female members of the Inc. 500 (twice the percentage of male members) cite their inability to move up as a major motivator for becoming an entrepreneur.[26] Other women have tired of the corporate grind, which can be exceptionally difficult for women with children. They view running a business as ultimately providing the needed flexibility for having both a professional career and children. These trends have contributed to a boom in female entrepreneurship. By the year 2000, it is expected that women will own one-half of all the small businesses in the United States.[27]

Management Focus

Building an Entrepreneurial Spirit in Large Organizations

The number of small business start-ups continues to grow at a rapid pace in today's business environment. A substantial number of employees of large companies are voluntarily leaving their jobs and using their education, experience, and skills to launch their own businesses. To combat this growing phenomenon, some large organizations are trying to create an internal atmosphere that emulates the one typically found in small businesses. Toward this end, the concept of employee empowerment has become an integral part of corporate strategy, for, in a small business, employee empowerment is a necessity for survival and growth. In fact, there are those who believe that employee empowerment and teams in the workplace are two of the major forces that will shape the role of the corporate leader in the 21st century.

Employee empowerment is the process of instilling a sense of ownership and pride in employees regarding their jobs and responsibilities. The process is aimed at creating an entrepreneurial spirit within the large company. This spirit builds a feeling in employees that they are working for themselves, in addition to working for a large corporation. Those with an entrepreneurial spirit feel they have a large stake in the success/failure of their business and, further, firmly believe they can directly affect the probability of success. Employee stock option plans (ESOPs) and profit sharing are two of the most popular incentives that companies offer employees in an attempt to stimulate this entrepreneurial spirit.

PepsiCo, Inc., the large soft drink marketer, which also owns Kentucky Fried Chicken, Pizza Hut, and Taco Bell is an example of one company that has gone to great lengths to instill a sense of ownership among its employees. In the true spirit of entrepreneurship, PepsiCo decided to delegate decision making to lower levels, create a greater sense of team spirit, and make it easier for employees to identify with the company.

Through liberal use of its employee stock option program, PepsiCo provided the financial motivation needed to institute changes leading to increased productivity and longer employment stays among PepsiCo people. As the program's name, SharePower, implies, stock options provide employees with the opportunity to purchase company stock. In many companies, stock options are solely reserved for executive personnel and are considered quite a status symbol. However, PepsiCo's innovative approach offers stock options to all of its employees who work an average of at least 30 hours a week. In total, over 100,000 employees, ranging from truck drivers to pizza makers, can participate in the program.

Today, many small businesses are struggling to implement the latest management trends (including reengineering and total quality management) that are sweeping through large corporations. At the same time, many large businesses, such as PepsiCo, are working hard to create a small business atmosphere within their organization. Somewhat ironically, this just underscores the theory that businesses, both large and small, have much they can learn from each other.

Sources: W H Miller, "Leadership at a Crossroads," *Industry Week,* August 19, 1996, pp. 42–56; C R Barnes, "Full Team Ahead: A Team Building Checklist," *Human Resource Professional,* March–April 1996, pp. 15–17; G Fuchsberg, "Small Firms Struggle with Latest Management Trends," *The Wall Street Journal,* August 26, 1993, p. B2; and D K Denton, "Entrepreneurial Spirit," *Business Horizons,* May–June 1993, pp. 79–84.

Income. Many entrepreneurs are enticed by the hefty profits of a highly successful business, although the odds in favor of such considerable success are slim. Others are motivated by making back their own investment in the business. Surprisingly, however, many entrepreneurs do not rate money as a primary motivator for starting a business. The surveyed Inc. 500 entrepreneurs, for example, ranked money fourth in importance (behind frustration, independence, and controlling one's life). However, money is a major factor among part-time entrepreneurs, those who work full time for a company and maintain a one-person business during off-hours. According to recent statistics, the number of these microbusiness entrepreneurs is increasing significantly.[28]

Security. Given the substantial risks and uncertainty of entrepreneurship, personal security may seem an unlikely motivator. However, in a time of corporate downsizing

FIGURE **20–1   Personal Characteristics: Comparing Entrepreneurs with Corporate Executives**

Entrepreneurs' personal traits tend to move them away from the corporate structure and toward independence.

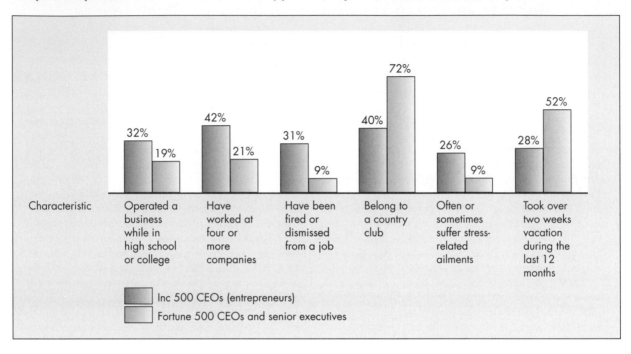

and layoffs, some entrepreneurs view running their own businesses as a more secure alternative, especially those in the middle and later stages of their corporate careers.

Characteristics Researchers have conducted a number of studies to determine whether entrepreneurs differ distinctly from managers and the public at large in personality and other characteristics. Drawing generalizations from this body of research is difficult because studies differ in their definitions of an entrepreneur. However, assuming a general definition of the term, some research support exists for a number of characteristics.[29]

Studies have found that entrepreneurs possess a significantly greater need for independence and autonomy, compared with managers. Studies also picture the entrepreneur as having a substantial need to achieve and as having a tolerance for ambiguity—the ability to handle uncertain and ambiguous situations. Many entrepreneurs also have high energy and endurance, substantial self-esteem, and strong dominance, that is, a need to take charge and to control and direct others. Several studies also find that the entrepreneur has a lower need for social support, compared with managers. He is not a team player or joiner. Figure 20–1 shows some distinct differences in the characteristics of Inc. 500 CEOs and the CEOs and senior executives of Fortune 500 companies.

The Entrepreneur's Tasks

Creating and building a successful enterprise requires, above all, effectively managing work, the organization, people, and production/operations. As research clearly indicates, both poor management and inexperienced management are the primary causes of new venture failure.[30] Thus, knowing the principles of management and applying them well are critical to new venture success. By now, you are well versed in the three primary functions in managing work and organizations (which apply in managing production/operations) and in the dynamics of managing people. Therefore, our discussion in this section focuses on how they apply to the special task of launching a small business.

Before we begin, however, we must briefly discuss the first entrepreneurial task—the critical first step that precedes planning. The first step is the *entrepreneur decision:* specifically deciding whether to become an entrepreneur. Making the right decision requires a clear understanding of entrepreneurship and the requirements for success. Above all, the decision should be based on an accurate self-assessment of individual skills, abilities, and shortcomings, because initially the entrepreneur *is* the business. She makes all the decisions, initiates critical business relationships, and performs the management functions. The entrepreneur's strengths and limitations directly and profoundly affect the enterprise. Take a minute and answer the questions in Table 20–1 for a brief self-assessment of your entrepreneurial potential.

Many management observers agree that success requires certain entrepreneurial attributes. The entrepreneur must be motivated to make a profit, because profitability (not self-fulfillment, independence, or other motivations) is essential for survival. The entrepreneur must be an effective planner, organizer, problem solver, and decision maker and be able to manage people well. Experience in the business is a virtual must, as are a talent for getting along with people and the ability to handle stress. The entrepreneur must have nerve, be prepared to bounce back from inevitable setbacks, and be willing to devote long hours to the business.[31] Now, count the number of your

---

TABLE **20–1**   **Taking Stock of Your Entrepreneurial Potential**

Your answers to these questions can provide some indication of your potential as an entrepreneur.

	Yes	No
1. Are you a self-starter?		
2. Do you like to take charge and see things through?		
3. Can you tolerate hard work for long periods of time?		
4. Can you make up your mind in a hurry and not regret the decisions you have made?		
5. Can people trust what you say?		
6. Do you have the energy to do most of the things you want to do?		
7. Can you look at a problem and see opportunity?		
8. Can you maintain organization?		
9. Do you have confidence in your ability to solve problems as they arise?		
10. Can you explain your ideas to people and have them adopt your point of view?		
11. Are you willing to delegate authority as well as responsibility?		
12. Can you maintain that positive attitude day in and day out?		

Source: Adapted from G Brenner, J Evans, and H Custer, *The Complete Handbook for the Entrepreneur* (Englewood Cliffs, NJ: Prentice Hall, 1990), p. 4.

affirmative answers to the self-assessment quiz. If you gave eight or more uncondi-
tional yes responses, you have definite entrepreneurial potential.

Planning

Of the three functions of managing, planning probably contributes the most to new
venture performance. Planning provides a well-thought-out blueprint of action for the
critical first months of the new business. This activity is vital because mistakes can be
costly, even fatal, when resources are so slim in the early days of the business. Careful
planning reduces the chances of major mistakes; it also forces the entrepreneur to
examine the business's external environment, competition, potential customers, and
strengths or limitations.[32] However, despite the importance of planning, many entrepreneurs don't like to plan because they believe planning hinders their flexibility.[33]

The entrepreneur performs two types of planning. *Start-up planning* occurs before
the enterprise opens for business. Thereafter, the entrepreneur performs *ongoing
planning,* which provides further strategic and operational direction for the established
business. (We discussed this latter type of planning in Chapters 5 and 6.)

Start-up planning essentially involves providing comprehensive, carefully
thought-out answers to the following five questions:

1. What product or service will the business provide?
2. What market will be served?
3. How will the business be established?
4. How will the business be operated?
5. How will the business be financed?

**What Product or Service Will the Business Provide? What Market Will Be
Served?**   We consider these two questions jointly because answering one requires
consideration of the other. Doing so also avoids a classic flaw of many new product
entrepreneurs: the assumption that a good product automatically sells itself and that a
ready-made market exists. The entrepreneurial graveyard is filled with unique, creative
products that died for lack of customers.[34]

Many entrepreneurs address the product question by first conducting a widespread
information search to identify opportunities. Numerous resources exist for this task:
the business section of the newspaper, business magazines, and trade journals that
focus on one industry are a few published sources of ideas. The Small Business
Administration provides free, informative publications on many types of businesses.[35]
Trade shows and discussions with bankers, business consultants, and large businesses
can also provide direction.

Once a large list of prospective businesses is developed, the list is reduced by
considering each business's feasibility and compatibility with the entrepreneur's goals
and strengths. For instance, does the entrepreneur want a business that is relatively
easy to establish, one with few barriers to entry? Or is stability (long-term survival) or
profit growth the primary objective? These considerations are critical because few
businesses satisfy all three criteria. In a study of 1.4 million ventures (236 types of
businesses), researchers found that businesses with relatively easy start-ups ranked low
on long-term survival; those with high survival rates were the ones that were less
frequently launched. High-growth ventures (such as basic steel and electronic component manufacturers) ranked low on both stability and ease of start-up.[36]

Concerning personal strengths, the entrepreneur compares each prospect's key
ability requirements with his own strengths. For example, people skills are essential in
a clothing retail store, while technical abilities are vital in a computer repair service.

Effectively answering the first two questions requires an analysis of each business's market, assessing four factors: the market's size—assessing past and projected sales trends, the life-cycle stage of the product/service, and business survival rates; the competition—determining the bases of competition (price, quality, image, customer service) and the strengths and limitations of competitors; customers— assessing average income; and market share—determining the share of the market that a new business can reasonably obtain.[37]

Many free sources of information exist for this analytical task. The chambers of commerce in the prospective market area can provide data; other census and valuable market information is available in the local library. For example, US census data indicate that in the next 20 years, the 50-plus segment of the population will increase from 64 million to 97 million people.[38] Businesses that are developed to cater to this segment's desire for convenience, quality, and service should prosper. Once market information is obtained, entrepreneurs must gain an in-depth understanding of the competition. To acquire such knowledge, some prospective entrepreneurs scan trade journals, newspaper articles, and government filings for information on their prospective competitors. Because business computer databases are also becoming cheaper and easier to use, many prospective entrepreneurs are tapping these bases for competitors' annual reports, financial statements, patent information, and even in-depth profiles of corporate managers.[39]

Most entrepreneurs launch a business that offers a product or service already available in the market. In this case, the entrepreneur must devise an effective positioning strategy for the product or service. Positioning requires the entrepreneur to devise a certain product or service characteristic that will be considered unique by potential customers.[40] However, some new businesses are based on a totally new product or service idea. These ideas sometimes produce the largest business successes; consider, for example, the Weed Eater, personal computer, garage door opener, and microwave oven. (Some other successful new product/service ideas are summarized in Table 20–2.) Market analysis is more challenging in this case. Because the product or service is new, there is no market data on demand or pricing. The entrepreneur must determine whether demand exists and, if so, what customers would pay. Market surveys are essential to answering these questions.[41] (Entrepreneurs of new ideas must also realize that marketing a new product or service requires additional spending just to explain what the new product or service is.)[42]

Regardless of whether the product or service is new or already exists, the entrepreneur should select a business that has a healthy market, is financially feasible, and matches her or his own objectives and abilities.

How Will the Business Be Established?   In other words, how will the entrepreneur enter the business? Three strategies are available: buyout, start-up, and franchise.[43]

The entrepreneur may *buy out* and acquire an existing company in the chosen business and market. This strategy affords a speedy entry into a business and market; the staff, facilities, and supplier and distribution networks are immediately provided, once the buyout contract is signed. A company with a solid track record and consumer image provides advantages that normally require years to develop. However, companies for sale can possess major, sometimes hidden problems. Entrepreneurs must deal with what they have purchased; they can't develop all aspects of the business exactly as they prefer. An effective buyout requires careful selection of a company, a thorough evaluation of the company's strengths and weaknesses, and obtaining a fair price for the business.

TABLE 20–2   Successful New Product/Service Ideas

Area	Idea
Health/fitness	An exercise studio for large women. Women at Large Systems Inc. (Yakima, Washington) found a successful market niche—overweight women who feel uncomfortable at regular aerobics classes. The company also offers fashion shows, makeup, and hair design. National franchise is coming soon.
Healthy eggs	Eggs that taste good and have low cholesterol. Feeding chickens a special diet of kelp, rice bran, alfalfa meal, and Vitamin E results in healthier eggs. C. R. Eggs (King of Prussia, Pennsylvania) charges about $1.89 a dozen.
Evening wear	Evening gown rentals for big occasions. Gowns priced at $500 to $5,000 rent for $75 and up, plus a $200 minimum deposit (three-day rental). One Night Stand (New York City) carries 600 gowns, sizes 4–18.
Baby products	Toddler casseroles are microwave dinners for children, ages nine months to three years. Kid-sized servings in beef, turkey, and chicken with grains and vegetables. Cost: $2.50 each. Growing Gourmet Inc. (Walnut Creek, California).
Auto parts	An Alter-Break device automatically adjusts an auto carburetor. About the size of a cigarette package, it attaches to the carburetor. A microchip inside detects when to make the adjustment. Cost is about $50. Nutronics Corp. (Longmont, Colorado).
Paintings	Custom ceiling designs. Using phosphorescent paint, Stellar Vision (Portland, Oregon) paints star constellations on bedroom ceilings. Sleep under the stars for a cost of $49.95 per ceiling. Service in seven states.
Portable cold drinks	A five-gallon backpack and uniform, worn by vendors at sports stadiums and concert halls, keeps drinks frosty while vendors work the aisles. A backpack stores up to 100 drinks that lose only 1 degree of temperature per hour. Manufactured by Thirstenders International Corp. (Houston, Texas).
What-if hairdos	The New Image Salon System allows customers to try new hairstyles or hair colors by using a computer, camera, and interactive video with a memory of hundreds of cuts and colors. A stylist takes a "before" photo of the customer, superimposes the suggested hairstyle, and projects the results on the monitor.

Source: Adapted from S Losee, "Innovation," *Fortune,* January 14, 1991, p. 87; "100 Ideas for New Businesses," *Venture,* November 1988, p. 35ff; "Exercise Studios—and More for Larger Women," *Venture,* March 1988, pp. 40–41; "Yard Cards Inc: A Giant Surprise for All Occasions," *Venture,* April 1988, p. 11. "Dresses Perfect for a One Night Stand," *Venture,* May 1988, p. 14; "Dialing for Diapers," *Venture,* May 1988, p. 15.

In the *start-up,* the entrepreneur creates the business from scratch. He has the freedom to define and build the business largely according to preference. However, as previously discussed, the time, effort, requirements, and risks of start-ups are usually high.

In the *franchise,* the entrepreneur (franchisee) provides a product or service under a legal contract with the franchise owner (franchisor). The franchisor provides the distinctive elements of the business (the name, image, signs, facility design, patents), an operating system, and other services. To obtain a franchise, the entrepreneur pays an initial fee and thereafter a percentage royalty on sales. The entrepreneur operates under the rights and restrictions of the contract.

Franchises are an increasingly popular form of new business. Over 500,000 franchise outlets currently operate in the United States.[44] Franchises are popular because they are less risky than start-ups or buyouts. During the first five years of operation, about 65 percent of all start-ups fail; only 5 percent of franchises close, according to the SBA.[45] This lower failure rate is substantially a result of the support the franchisor provides—usually management and employee training; operations and accounting systems; a recognized brand name; reputation; and financial, marketing, and management assistance.

Some entrepreneurs are not content with owning one franchise unit or even two.[46] For them, life as a franchisee means operating multiple units—either of the same or different concepts. According to a recent survey by Arthur Andersen & Co., an average of 20 percent of franchisees own more than one franchise unit. Among them, they own an average of 2.6 units. Among franchisors, slightly more than one-half allow multiunit ownership by their franchisees.

Franchising has been growing at a rapid rate in the European Community. It already accounts for 10 percent of retail sales in France and 11 percent in England.[47] In many cases, it is easier to put financing together in foreign countries than in the United States. The accompanying Management Focus describes franchise opportunities from a global perspective.

Although a franchise can provide substantial benefits, the strategy is not fault free. Major problems can arise when the franchisor does not provide the necessary guidance, reputation, and support. Consider, for example, the case of Dave Michael.[48] Michael bought a Pizza Pizza Ltd. franchise in the Toronto area. With his wife's help, working 12 hours a day, seven days a week, Michael managed to pay real estate fees, telephone fees, advertising fees, and cartage fees to Pizza Pizza, plus royalties (amounting to 6 percent of sales) and occasional fines to the company for infractions such as an employee's not wearing a name tag. His hard work paid off as the store's average sales increased in an eight-year period, from $3,000 to $13,000 a week. His reward? Pizza Pizza opened another store in the area, immediately cutting his delivery sales by 50 percent.

Because of this and other actions taken by the franchisor to seemingly limit franchisees' profit potential, Michael and 50 other owners of Canadian Pizza Pizza franchises banded together to sue the company for dealing in bad faith with the franchisees. Indeed, problems between franchisors and franchisees in the United States have become so prevalent that an association (The American Franchisee Association) has been formed with the sole purpose of protecting franchisee rights.[49]

Beyond inadequate franchisor support, the entrepreneur's creative freedom is usually inhibited by the franchise contract, which stipulates how the business is to be run.[50] Franchise contracts specify the products sold, retail quality standards, prices, hours of operation, and many other aspects of the business. Contracts also specify a starting date, the length of the franchise agreement, renewal periods, and termination clauses.

Ensuring a successful franchise requires carefully evaluating the prospective franchisor (growth rates, performance, reputation, degree of support) and the franchise contract. Many entrepreneurs obtain franchisor evaluations from the company's other franchisees and examine the franchisor's depth of management (e.g., McDonald's maintains one manager for every 20 franchisees).[51] Many entrepreneurs also conduct their own market analysis in addition to reviewing the franchisor's assessment.

How Will the Business Be Operated?   The entrepreneur answers this question by planning the business's various functions such as production, marketing, personnel, and research and development. Concerning production, for example, the entrepreneur determines who will supply materials and plans the layout of the production facilities. In marketing, the entrepreneur plans how the product will be distributed to retailers and promoted. Planning for operations also involves the other management functions (organizing and controlling).

How Will the Business Be Financed?   Successfully funding a new business requires financial planning, which comprises three steps: estimating the business's projected income and expenses, estimating the required initial investment, and locating sources of funding.[52] In estimating the new venture's income and expenses, the entrepreneur uses sales projections from the market analysis and approximates cost of production and other operating expenses, drawing from past experience and industry research. These projections are typically done for at least the first year of business.

The start-up costs are also calculated. These expenses are one-time-only costs of establishing the business (e.g., installation of equipment, beginning inventory, licenses and permits). Estimates of start-up costs and ongoing income and expenses provide a projection of the amount of funding needed to launch the business and cover costs until the business is profitable.

Management Focus

International Franchising Opportunities

More and more, budding entrepreneurs worldwide are reducing the risks associated with starting their own business by purchasing franchises. Entrepreneurs (in this case, franchisees) buy the right to use a franchisor's brand of products and brand name. As part of the franchise agreement, franchisees are provided with an array of support services that assure the value of the franchise. These support services typically include both start-up and ongoing assistance. Start-up assistance encompasses such activities as selecting a site, negotiating a lease, and field training for the franchisee. Once started, ongoing services such as central data processing, inventory control, and field operations evaluation are also usually provided to the franchisee.

The North American Free Trade Agreement, the fall of communism, and an increasingly unified Europe have brought about a surge in the growth of international franchising. Global expansion offers an attractive opportunity for franchisors to keep growth curves streaking upward in light of increasing domestic competition in the saturated US market. In fact, some believe that global franchising is an outstanding growth opportunity for many businesses because it is often less expensive and in many instances is not as highly regulated as the US franchise market.

When franchisors decide to go global and enter international markets, they are likely to discover that foreign governments offer a warm welcome. Unlike entrepreneurs who go to market with only a product to sell, franchisors export a total system of doing business. As a result, foreign governments view franchise operations as a viable means to build their economies without losing jobs to imported products. Even with government support, however, franchisors who seek international expansion face numerous problems and obstacles such as backward economies, unstable governments, and currency crises that must be overcome.

The race for success in the global franchise market has begun in earnest. The rewards will go to those franchisors that can quickly identify the right markets and then overcome the obstacles that go hand in hand with expansion to a foreign country. An integral part of this process involves finding and training capable foreign franchisees who share similar abilities, past experiences, and drives for success with the individual(s) who initially launched the franchise in the United States.

Sources: I Jones, "Where Everybody Knows Your Name," *World Trade,* June 1996, pp. 4–41; J Delaney, "Franchise Finds, Career Launcher," *Executive Female,* September–October 1993, p. 28; and D A Baucus, M S Baucus, and S E Human, "Choosing a Franchise: How Base Fees and Royalties Relate to the Value of the Franchise," *Journal of Small Business Management,* April 1993, pp. 91–114.

Many entrepreneurs rely substantially on their own personal savings to launch their businesses. Personal finances were used by almost three out of four founders of the Inc. 500 companies. Other funding alternatives are often available. Commercial and investment banks, savings and loan associations, and the Small Business Administration are all frequently used sources of new venture funding. Venture capitalists, groups of investors who provide funding in exchange for a share of ownership in the company, are a possibility for ventures with substantial profit potential.[53] And a number of communities provide loans to businesses they believe will boost the area's employment and contribute to the local economy.[54]

When approaching a prospective investor, the entrepreneur's chances of obtaining funding are enhanced by presenting a formal **business plan.** This document presents an overall analysis of the proposed business. It contains a description of the product/service, a thorough analysis of the market, the entrepreneur's strategic objectives, the plans for each of the business's functional areas, a profile of the firm's management team, and most important, the company's projected financial position and funding needs. Answers to the five questions of start-up planning provide the plan's content. Many successful entrepreneurs consider the business plan for launching a business the most important document an entrepreneur will ever write.[55] It is the formal blueprint for the development of the new venture. Prospective investors scrutinize it closely before making a funding decision. Other important parties (e.g., suppliers and prospective major customers) often ask to see the plan before establishing a relationship with the new business. The entrepreneur can also use the plan as a tool for communicating to employees her vision and concept of the company. The business plan is also an important guide for ongoing decision making as the company develops.[56]

Organizing

As we discussed in Chapters 8 and 9, the organizing function involves developing an organizational structure via job design, departmentation, determining span of control, and delegating authority. Ideally, these tasks provide a structure of relationships and authority that effectively coordinates the organization's efforts.

Organizational activities, obviously important, are often neglected by entrepreneurs in the early stages of the start-up. With limited resources and personnel, entrepreneurs focus on the immediate demands of generating sales and producing the product/service to meet the demand and to earn income. Organizational issues seem less important, especially when the business is so small.

When entrepreneurs do explicitly address organizational tasks, the results are often more informal and flexible than in larger organizations. This informality is often intentional. One study of successful growth-oriented entrepreneurs found that most of the founders intentionally avoided developing written job descriptions for their employees in the early stages of the firm's development; in more than two-thirds of the cases, oral descriptions were maintained through the company's first major expansion.[57] Written job descriptions were avoided because the entrepreneurs felt they would constrain the potential contributions and growth of employees while the firm was still small. None of the entrepreneurs wanted an employee's motivation and development to be hemmed in by the boundaries of a written description. The strategy also enabled the entrepreneurs to quickly change major job responsibilities when needed, which happens frequently when the organization is still taking shape.

Many of the entrepreneurs in the sample prepared an organization chart; however, the chart was viewed as a dynamic, continually changing picture of the company's structure. The chart also served an important purpose as a tool for continually assessing and reevaluating the company. The study's researcher summed up the entrepreneurs' use of the organization chart: "It was more a means of thinking through key activities. . . a way to identify gaps and new needs—a tool for *thought*."[58]

As the firm grows in the number of employees, functions, and size of work groups and departments, job design, descriptions, and the overall structure of the business gradually become more formalized. However, the emphasis of organizing is initially on informality and flexibility to accommodate the dynamic change and adjustments that usually occur in the early stages of a new enterprise.

Controlling

As we discussed in Chapter 10, the controlling function involves establishing standards, obtaining information that provides a comparison of actual with desired results, and taking actions to correct any adverse deviations from standards. In the small business, the controlling activities are particularly important because, in the initial stages of the venture, every aspect of the business is newly established. Given the newness of the business and its operations, mistakes are bound to be made. Because the business's resources are limited, it is essential that the entrepreneur detect and correct problems as quickly as possible. Effective controlling activities enable the entrepreneur to do so.

In the early stages of business, control systems are usually basic rather than sophisticated. However, most entrepreneurs develop financial, production, and inventory control systems to provide key indicators that they monitor weekly, even daily. These indicators include sales, production rates, inventory, accounts receivable, accounts payable, and, most important, cash flow and the cash flow outlook.[59] Ensuring that funds are on hand to pay immediate expenses is a particularly troublesome task, according to a survey of small business owners.[60]

A growing number of entrepreneurs are installing computerized control information systems to assist them in monitoring aspects of the company's performance and in conducting financial and production analysis. Many software firms are developing programs specifically designed for a small business's control needs; this development along with the decreasing costs of computer hardware is making computerized control information systems a reality for small businesses.

Managing People in the Small Business

Effectively managing and motivating employees is a critical ingredient of effective entrepreneurship. These activities make up the leadership function—encouraging employees to work to achieve the business's goals by effectively communicating the tasks to be done, rewarding good performance, and creating an environment that supports the employees' efforts and individual needs.

Significant differences exist between the small business entrepreneur and the corporate CEO in performing the leadership function. First, in the newly launched business, the entrepreneur is solely responsible for effective leadership. There is no cadre of managers who share leadership responsibilities. Usually, the entrepreneur is the organization's single boss. Leadership—effective or not—depends totally on the entrepreneur.

Second, although leadership is a critical activity of the corporate CEO, quality of leadership is even more vital for the entrepreneur because there are no extra resources to compensate for the adverse effects (employee absenteeism, poor workmanship) of poor leadership. Moreover, the entrepreneur's relationship with each employee has a considerable impact on the firm. Consider that in a 10-employee company, each employee proportionately provides 10 percent of the firm's output. Therefore, the quality of the entrepreneur's personal or business relationship with an employee can have a major effect on the overall venture. Every individual's effort is critical to the firm. Thus, training must not only include teaching employees job-related skills but also comprehensive education in management and organization.[61]

In performing the leadership function, entrepreneurs usually must deal with one primary disadvantage. Given the firm's very limited financial resources, they usually cannot offer employees the salary and benefits that larger, more established firms can provide. Given the uncertainty of any new business, neither is long-term job security assured. These disadvantages may prevent entrepreneurs from obtaining the quality of employees they prefer.

However, entrepreneurs often possess two important advantages: First, they are in a unique position to create an atmosphere in the company that promotes effective performance. Unlike the corporate CEO, the entrepreneur does not have to deal with prior company traditions and policies that may hamper motivation and performance. There are no established traditions, practices, or preexisting norms of behavior. The venture is new, and the entrepreneur is the firm's creator and—if he chooses—promoter and nurturer of employee excellence.

A second factor facilitates the entrepreneur's efforts in this regard. In the early days of a new, small business, the venture's employees are often a small group. Especially when the company's product is new and promising, camaraderie and cohesiveness develop among members. Under a strong leader, the company's purpose is clearly communicated: Make the product a success and put the venture on the map. In this type of highly challenging, stressful, and familial environment, employees can become highly motivated, driven by the sense that anything is possible.

Indeed, employee pride can be one of the greatest assets small businesses have.[62] Because resources and staff are limited when businesses are small, employee dedication resulting from their direct, personal interest in the creation of products and rendering of services can be considered the best quality control system of all. Such is particularly the case when part of the employee's income is tied to company performance. For example, Phelps County Bank of Rolla, Maryland, may not offer the highest employee salaries in the United States, but through a generous stock ownership plan provided by the bank, employees are able to save more.[63]

The entrepreneur can create a climate of excellence and productivity in large part by setting a personal example in the ways she works and approaches the business, customers, and employees. For example, some entrepreneurs encourage employees to take responsibility by allowing them to make any decisions deemed necessary to increase product or service quality and customer satisfaction.[64]

Although resources are limited, some entrepreneurs are creating innovative ways to facilitate effective leadership and motivation. Original Copy Centers Inc., a reproduction service in Cleveland, Ohio, assessed the needs of its 76 employees, who are mostly under 30 years of age and single. The company established a laundromat, exercise room, game room, and kitchen in its facility and provided employees with free coffee and private use of the company's personal computers. Although the company's compensation is no higher than the industry average, the workforce is productive and the quality of work is exceptional. During the business's first 12 years of operation, only three employees quit.[65]

Smith & Hawken, an importer of garden tools, uses a technique called the "5–15 report" for maintaining open communication with employees (5–15 stands for 15 minutes to write and 5 minutes to read). Each week, every employee completes the three-part report by telling what he did during the week, describing his morale and that of his department, and providing one idea for bettering his job, department, or company. Management takes no longer than one week to respond to each idea. The technique is one way that Smith & Hawken keeps tabs on each employee's development, finds ways to improve the business, and provides needed support for the employees to do their jobs.[66]

Special Challenges of Entrepreneurship

At some point in their careers, entrepreneurs encounter major challenges that test their abilities and character. Three particular challenges merit special mention at this point.

Growth of the Enterprise

Successful entrepreneurs who create a business for growth and profit inevitably discover that the business they are running is dramatically different from the one they created. Because of growth, the company is no longer a shop with a handful of employees, a one-page customer list, and a single supplier and distributor. Rather, the company now employs several hundred workers in many departments. There are networks of suppliers and distributors, and operations run on a much larger scale.

Successfully managing a company with this type of growth requires a transition in management tasks and focus. Because of the company's greater size and complexity, coordination and control must be emphasized. Professional managers must be hired, and more sophisticated and formal control systems and procedures must be developed and managed.[67]

The company's transition from a small shop to complex corporation also requires a major change in the entrepreneur's task and management style. To effectively lead the company, the entrepreneur can no longer make all decisions and maintain a hands-on involvement in all aspects of the business; the company is simply too big. Instead, she must, after examining the overall progress of the company, incorporate employees into management by delegating authority, provide thorough, personalized training to these individuals, and focus on coordinating their efforts.[68] In this situation, many entrepreneurs find the very skills that brought the company its early success are no longer effective. The company requires a new set of abilities from its CEO.

Do entrepreneurs effectively make this transition? Some, like Bill Gates of Microsoft, do. However, others have major difficulties in managing a much larger and more complex company.[69] Many have particular problems with delegating authority. As the creators of the business, they have a strong need to control its operations and find it extremely difficult to relinquish any decision making. ("It's my baby," said one entrepreneur.) Others find that they simply lack the professional management skills needed to run a complex business.

Some entrepreneurs, like Mitch Kapor, are uncomfortable with the environment of a big business. As founder of Lotus Development Corp., Kapor saw his computer software firm quickly grow from a small shop operation to a diversified, international corporation with more than 1,300 employees and $275 million in sales. Kapor found that "leading by coordinating" poorly matched his management skills, his desire to work with people in small groups, and his penchant for perfectionism.[70] Joseph Solomon, founder of Vidal Sassoon Hair Products, had similar problems when his company boomed in size. Solomon became frustrated because he missed the fast-moving, flexible, more spirited small-group environment that his smaller company had provided.[71]

Entrepreneurs resolve this dilemma in several ways. Many learn to delegate, often by being careful in selecting those to whom they delegate and by delegating gradually.

Some, like Mitch Kapor, resign from their company or, like Joseph Solomon, sell their firm and start all over, launching a new venture. Other entrepreneurs avoid the dilemma entirely by deliberately restricting the size of their companies.[72]

Entrepreneurial Stress

All CEOs experience stress from the burden of responsibility for managing a business. However, entrepreneurs, especially those who run small businesses, often experience particularly high levels of stress. The stress is partly caused by the risks the entrepreneur incurs in launching a business and his sense of total accountability for its success or failure.

According to a study of 210 small business owners, other factors contribute to entrepreneurial stress.[73] Loneliness is a major source (over half of the entrepreneurs reported they "frequently feel a sense of loneliness"); there is no one in the business or among friends or family with whom the entrepreneur can openly talk about the business and its problems and seek advice, especially in the early days of the company. No one is experiencing the same or even similar work activities or problems.[74]

Total immersion in the business, frustration with employee problems, and an overly high need for achievement can also contribute to entrepreneurial stress. Some entrepreneurs set unreasonable goals for themselves, push themselves too hard, and experience great frustration when they fall short of their expectations.[75]

There is no perfect cure for entrepreneurial stress. Indeed, many entrepreneurs believe that high stress is an inherent element of entrepreneurship, and many cope with and even thrive on it. However, entrepreneurs who do view stress as a problem have alleviated it with a number of strategies, such as making changes in their business routine (e.g., scheduling more time between meeting appointments and taking time off for exercise), setting time aside for social activities, and creating more opportunities for interacting with employees. Some entrepreneurs participate in local business organizations (such as the Rotary Club) that provide an opportunity to talk about their businesses with other CEOs of noncompeting companies.[76]

Selling the Company

Most US businesses acquired today are not large corporations; they are small, independent businesses, many of which were owned by entrepreneurs ready to sell their companies. Entrepreneurs decide to sell their businesses for several reasons. They may sell the company to retire and enjoy the financial returns the sale provides them or to use the profits to launch yet another company. Entrepreneurs may sell their firm because, on the verge of retirement, they realize that no qualified successor is available to assume leadership. (This problem often arises among family-owned and managed entrepreneurships.)[77] Or they may sell because the buyer can provide much-needed additional cash and other resources to fund the company's growth.[78]

Regardless of the motivation, the decision to sell the business introduces a complex acquisition process and new concerns. Most entrepreneurs want their businesses to continue to thrive after the sale, and many are well aware of the poor performance record of acquisitions: From one-half to two-thirds of all acquisitions ultimately fail.[79]

Entrepreneurs approach selling their companies with many objectives; three are particularly important:

1. *Locate the right buyer.* For entrepreneurs concerned about the company's future, this task involves finding a buyer whose objectives for the firm are compatible with those of the entrepreneur. Compatibility is particularly important for entrepreneurs who want to continue to head the company after the sale.

2. *Secure satisfactory terms of the sale.* These terms focus on price for the company, payment, and special conditions concerning the company's employees and other aspects of the business. An entrepreneur's bargaining position is strengthened if the company possesses valuable resources such as an impressive record of financial performance, a strong reputation with customers, and difficult-to-replace assets (such as exceptionally talented management and strong, specialized research and development capabilities).

3. *Obtain satisfactory autonomy.* Entrepreneurs who stay with the acquired firm usually seek to maintain as much autonomy as possible in managing the company after its sale. For those who continue with the acquired company, managing the firm after the acquisition requires major adjustments. The entrepreneur must cope with less independence in running the business. Regardless of the amount of autonomy promised by the new owners, the entrepreneur must still report to a senior manager in the parent company, provide ongoing, detailed reports of the business, and account for its performance. This is often a difficult adjustment for entrepreneurs, who previously answered only to themselves.[80] Also, the entrepreneur's salary is often reduced.[81] Many entrepreneurs have problems making these adjustments; consequently, many leave the acquired firm sooner than they had expected.[82]

The Future of Entrepreneurship

The trend toward new business creation will be likely to continue throughout the remaining years of this decade and well into the twenty-first century as more people assume the risks to achieve the personal and professional rewards of running a small business. Success requires the ability to effectively implement the important principles and functions of management—especially during the early stages of the new venture when mistakes can be costly. Success also requires that the entrepreneur take to heart the valuable lessons learned by others and avoid the mistakes that are so common to many new ventures.

Perhaps above all, successful entrepreneurship requires a keen understanding of personal assets and limitations and a strong commitment to the challenge. The adage "know thyself" aptly applies to anyone contemplating launching a business. If one day you seriously consider this important step, thoroughly examine your motivations for starting a business, and the personal strengths and shortcomings you would bring to the enterprise. Self-understanding greatly improves the odds of building a productive company and reaping the substantial rewards of entrepreneurship.

Summary of Key Points

• An entrepreneur is the creator and chief executive of a business enterprise. During recent times, small businesses headed by entrepreneurs have accounted for the majority of the job growth in the US economy.

• Entrepreneurship can be considered a behavior encompassing an individual's pursuit of opportunity without regard to the resources the individual currently controls. Entrepreneurs enjoy the autonomy of making their own decisions, setting their own hours, and determining what they will do and when they will do it.

• Despite the risks, many individuals launch new businesses each year for a number of reasons: to attain independence, personal and professional growth, income, and security or to achieve an alternative career, which they view as superior to remaining at a dissatisfying job.

• Success in entrepreneurship requires careful start-up planning. This activity involves determining the product or service to be provided, the market to be served, and how the business will be established, financed, and operated.

• Although many entrepreneurs perform organizing activities in the early stages of their businesses, they often keep job descriptions and other organizational aspects of the firm flexible because of the dynamic change that the firm frequently experiences.

• Although often financially unable to provide compensation packages strongly competitive with larger, more estab-

lished firms, the entrepreneur has a special opportunity to develop an organizational culture that promotes employee pride and empowerment, leading to high productivity and excellent operating results.

• Much of an entrepreneur's efforts in performing the controlling function centers on financial control, particularly ensuring that enough cash is on hand to cover immediate expenses.

• At some point in their careers, many entrepreneurs face the challenges of coping with entrepreneurial stress, of making the transition from small business manager to large-company CEO, and of dealing with the tasks and concerns that surround selling the company.

Discussion and Review Questions

1. Why is so little attention paid to small businesses even though these businesses constitute a significant portion of the US economy?

2. Do all individuals have the ability to someday become entrepreneurs? Why or why not?

3. Do you think you possess an entrepreneurial orientation? Frame your answer in the context of the entrepreneurial quiz.

4. Hewlett-Packard Company, Lands' End, David's Cookies, and Cuisinarts are all highly successful businesses that had no formal business plan when they were established. Does their success diminish the importance of a formal plan? Discuss.

5. Many managers, especially women, voluntarily leave large organizations to start their own businesses. Do you think this trend will continue? Why or why not?

6. What are the drawbacks of maintaining orally communicated and flexible job descriptions in the early stages of a new business?

7. Suppose you are the head of a young, fast-growing company (you pick the specific industry depending on

personal interests). How would you go about the process of beginning to delegate decision making and other authority to employees within your organization? At what stage of growth should this delegation process begin?

8. Beyond those noted in the chapter, identify other strengths and shortcomings of the franchising strategy for starting a new business. Which strength is the most valuable; which shortcoming is the most costly for a franchisee?

9. What special problems face the entrepreneur who needs highly skilled employees but lacks the financial resources to fund a strongly competitive compensation program? How can an entrepreneur deal with this problem?

10. Many entrepreneurs ultimately decide to sell their business, even though it is highly successful, so that they can start another one. What factors might influence this decision?

CASE 20–1
WILL THIS BUSINESS SUCCEED?

Todd LeRoy and Michael Atkinson have launched a franchise business that they are certain will be a winner. The business, Associated Video Hut Inc., franchises drive-through video rental outlets.

Each "Video's 1st" outlet is a small Fotomat-type kiosk that a franchise owner buys and can place in a small shopping mall parking lot or in some other suburban, high-traffic area. There, customers can drive up to the kiosk window, review

Exhibit 1   Competitive Analysis

	Industry Average Performance for Video Retailer	Video's 1st Performance Assumptions
Store size	2,089* square feet	48 square feet
Tapes stocked	3,478* tapes	300 tapes
Individual titles stocked	2,417* titles	30 titles
Tapes rented daily	185[†] tapes	120 tapes
Percent of stock rented daily	5.3%[†]	40%
Rental price	$1.80[†]	$2.95
Wholesale tape cost (new releases)	$50[†]	$60
Resale price of used tapes	$16[†]	$20
Full-time employees	3*	1
Part-time employees	4*	4

*Source of statistics: Video Software Dealers Association.
[†]Source of statistics: The Fairfield Group Inc.

Source: Reprinted with permission, *Inc.* magazine, (February 1988). Copyright (1988) by Goldhirsh Group, Inc., 38 Commercial Wharf, Boston, MA 02110.

the list of titles shown on the promo board, pay the rental fee, and obtain a videocassette without leaving their cars. The outlet specializes in hit movies, carrying only current top titles (10 to 25 copies of each title, for a total inventory of 300 to 750 tapes). Because several copies of each title are available, customers are virtually assured of obtaining the hit film they want.

Each film rents for $2.95 a day, more than the industry's average $2-a-day rental. The two founders believe that customers will pay more for the timesaving convenience (just as people do at convenience food stores) and for the selection (hit films are difficult to rent at other video stores that carry only one or two copies). The kiosks are portable so that, if one location doesn't net much business, the franchise owner can easily move the shop to another site.

LeRoy and Atkinson believe their venture will succeed for the following reasons:

- *The market is there.* In 1987, consumers nationwide spent more than $4 billion in videocassette rentals; in 1988, the rental revenues continued to climb for the several thousand video rental businesses in the industry. (By 1995, an estimated 90 percent of all homes with TVs had a videocassette recorder.) The founders believe that the rental industry should eventually top $15 billion in sales annually.

- *Low overhead.* Leroy and Atkinson believe that most video rental stores incur unnecessary costs because they carry tapes that aren't rented. As shown in the competitive analysis in Exhibit 1, the average video rental store carries 3,478 tapes but rents only 5.3 percent of its inventory each day. The remaining tapes are unused, incurring high inventory costs as well as costs of the storage space (rent, utilities). The Video's 1st concept eliminates this problem by keeping a limited inventory of high-volume tapes. Overhead is much lower. The two founders believe that their top competition is provided by the video superstores, which carry virtually all titles, and the "rack jobbers," which maintain limited inventory at gas stations, convenience stores, and other locations.

- *Franchise support.* The two entrepreneurs estimate that each kiosk will be highly profitable for a franchise owner (the pro forma statement is shown in Exhibit 2). These figures are estimates of an average month and annual totals for a kiosk's second year of operation. Given the pro forma projections, a franchise owner will earn $33,807, a pretax return on assets of at least 40 percent each year per kiosk if about 40 percent of a 300-tape inventory is rented every day. Franchise costs, which include kiosk, initial inventory, training, a grand opening, and sufficient working capital, will run about $88,000. The company will provide promotion materials (such as ads, four-color newsletters for the franchisee's customers, and a list of movie titles for insertion into local newspapers). The founders will realize a profit of $23,500 per kiosk franchise, excluding royalties.

Associated Video Hut has already opened two pilot stores and sold its first franchise to a group of investors in New York. They are negotiating with a Burger King multifranchise owner who wants to provide drive-through video rentals along with drive-through burgers. The founders' goal is to sell 5,000 kiosk franchises by the mid-1990s. To meet this objective, they are targeting individuals who want to set up at least three kiosks.

LeRoy and Atkinson recently presented their business plan to a group of experts on new ventures. "We keep asking people to shoot holes in the concept," asserted Atkinson, "and they can't do it." Some of the experts disagree.

EXHIBIT 2   Video's 1st Pro Forma Operating Statement per Kiosk*

	Monthly Average	*Yearly Total*
Revenues:		
Tape rental fees (116 rentals per day @ $2.95)	$10,260	$123,117
Used tape sales (55 tapes per month @ $20)	1,100	13,200
Popcorn	150	1,800
Other	100	1,200
Total revenues	11,610	139,317
Cost of sales:		
Prerecorded tapes (55 tapes per month @ $60)	3,300	39,600
Popcorn	93	1,116
Other	50	600
Total cost of sales	3,443	41,316
Gross profit	8,167	98,001
Operating expenses:		
Rent	500	6,000
Payroll (12 hours per day, seven days per week)	1,950	23,400
Payroll taxes	234	2,808
General (insurance, supplies, utilities, miscellaneous)	505	6,055
Royalty payment (7% gross receipts)	813	9,752
Local advertising (2% gross receipts)	232	2,786
Corporate advertising (1% gross receipts)	116	1,393
Note payable principal, and interest		
($45,000 note @ 12%, five-year term)	1,000	12,000
Total operating expenses	5,350	64,194
Net income before taxes	$ 2,817	$ 33,807

*Depreciation and amortization not included.

Source: Reprinted with permission, *Inc.* magazine, (February 1988). Copyright (1988) by Goldhirsh Group, Inc., 38 Commercial Wharf, Boston, MA 02110.

Questions for Analysis

1. Identify and assess the strengths and shortcomings of the concept behind Associated Video Hut.
2. Would you buy a "Video's 1st" franchise? Why or why not?

3. What suggestions can you provide to improve the business concept and operations?

Source: Adapted from T Richman, "Drive-In Movies," *Inc.*, February 1988, pp. 42ff.

EXPERIENTIAL EXERCISE
PORTRAIT OF AN ENTREPRENEUR

Purpose

The purpose of this activity is to enhance students' understanding of the entrepreneurial personality and the motivations, challenges, and rewards of entrepreneurship.

The Exercise in Class

The instructor will divide the class into groups of up to four students each. Each group should complete the following assignment:

1. Identify a successful entrepreneur in your community whom you can interview. Concentrate on identifying a successful small business that is directed by its founder. The business section of recent issues of your community's newspaper(s) or the local chamber of commerce should be helpful in locating an entrepreneur.

2. Interview the entrepreneur. Don't underestimate your chances of obtaining an entrepreneur's cooperation. Entrepreneurs typically enjoy talking about themselves and their businesses. The interview should take from 30 minutes to one hour. Here are some suggested questions:

   a. What motivated you to start your own business?

   b. How would you describe yourself to a stranger? Are you self-confident, energetic, independent? Are you an optimist, a realist, a pessimist?

   c. Which personality characteristics and abilities are essential for success as an entrepreneur?

   d. How would you describe your leadership style?

   e. Describe a typical workday.

   f. What aspects of your work do you find the most satisfying? The most frustrating?

   g. Which aspects of your work are the easiest for you? The most difficult?

   h. In which of your business's activities (operations, finance, marketing, personnel) are you most involved?

   i. How much emphasis do you place on motivating employees?

   j. What important lessons have you learned from your experience in creating and running your own business?

   k. What advice would you offer to a young, prospective entrepreneur?

3. After completing the interview, develop an oral report that profiles the entrepreneur.

4. Elect a spokesperson, who will present your group's findings to the class.

The instructor will lead an open discussion that draws together general, common characteristics of entrepreneurs, based on the interviews.

The Learning Message

This exercise should illustrate the common characteristics possessed by entrepreneurs, including substantial energy, optimism, a practical, nuts-and-bolts approach to business, and ambition. Among the profiles, entrepreneurial differences should also emerge, especially between the entrepreneurs driven by growth objectives and those with other goals.

Notes

1. Tracy Mullin, "Small Business Power," *Stores,* June 1993, p. 10.
2. "Making the Career Switch to Independence; Tips for Small Business Success," *PR Newswire,* July 7, 1993.
3. "America's Little Fellows Surge Ahead," *The Economist,* July 3, 1993, pp. 59–60.
4. Mullin, "Small Business Power," p. 10.
5. George Melloan, "Small Firms Brace for Legislative Attack," *The Wall Street Journal,* May 5, 1987, p. 37; "Millions of New Jobs to Be Created in '86, Survey Shows," *Mobile Register,* March 31, 1986, p. 3A.
6. Several studies have examined the impact of an entrepreneur's personal characteristics on the firm (e.g., firm growth, structure, flexibility). For two insightful examples, see Norman R Smith and John B Miner, "Type of Entrepreneur, Type of Firm and Managerial Motivation: Applications for Organizational Life Cycle Theory," *Strategic Management Journal* 4, no. 3 (1983), pp. 325–40; and Graeme Salaman, "An Historical Discontinuity: From Charisma to Routinization," *Human Relations* 30, no. 4 (1977), pp. 373–88.
7. Lourdes L Valeriano, "Other Asians Follow Japanese as Investors in US Firms," *The Wall Street Journal,* January 7, 1991, p. B2.
8. James W Carland, Frank Hoy, William R Boulton, and Jo Ann C Carland, "Differentiating Entrepreneurs from Small Business Owners: A Conceptualization," *Academy of Management Review,* April 1984, pp. 354–59.
9. For a discussion of what an entrepreneur is, see Michael Warshaw, "The Mind-Style of the Entrepreneur," *Success,* April 1993, pp. 28–33.
10. *Meeting the Special Problems of Small Business* (New York: Committee for Economic Development, 1974), p. 14; *The State of Small Business: A Report to the President* (Washington, DC: US Government Printing Office, March 1983), p. 28.
11. David L Birch, "The Truth about Start-Ups," *Inc.,* January 1988, pp. 14–15.
12. Jeremy Main, "Breaking Out of the Company," *Fortune,* May 25, 1987, p. 83.
13. Richard Greene, "Do You Really Want to Be Your Own Boss?" *Forbes,* October 21, 1985, pp. 86–87.

14. Patrick R Liles, *New Business Ventures and the Entrepreneur* (Burr Ridge, IL: Richard D. Irwin, 1974), pp. 14–15.

15. Wilson Harrell, "Entrepreneurial Terror," *Inc.*, February 1987, pp. 74–76.

16. Bruce Nussbaum, "Corporate Refugees: After the Pain, Some Find Smooth Sailing," *Business Week,* April 12, 1993, pp. 58–64.

17. Joshua Hyatt, "Born to Run," *Inc.*, January 1991, pp. 36–39.

18. Michael Barrier, "From the Pierogy Capital," *Nation's Business,* January 1991, pp. 11–12.

19. Wilson L Harrell, "Don't Call Me Small: To Entrepreneurs, Those Are Fighting Words," *Success,* June 1993, p. 12.

20. Walter Kiechel, "The Microbusiness Alternative," *Fortune,* October 24, 1988, p. 220.

21. Beth Selby, "Get a Life," *Institutional Investor,* March 1993, pp. 58–63.

22. Curtis Hartman, "Main Street, Inc.," *Inc.*, June 1986, p. 52.

23. Main, "Breaking Out," p. 83. See also Faye Rice, "Lessons from Late Bloomers," *Fortune,* August 31, 1987, pp. 87–91; Harry Bacas, "Leaving the Corporate Nest," *Nation's Business,* March 1987, pp. 14ff.

24. See Susan Fraker, "Why Women Aren't Getting to the Top," *Fortune,* April 16, 1984, pp. 40–44; Alex Taylor III, "Why Women Managers Are Bailing Out," *Fortune,* August 18, 1986, pp. 16–23.

25. Teresa Andreoli, "These Women Mean Business," *Stores,* June 1993, pp. 24–26.

26. Hartman, "Main Street," p. 54.

27. Shirley F Olson and Helen M Curtis, "Female Entrepreneurs: Personal Value Systems and Business Strategies in a Male-Dominated Industry," *Journal of Small Business Management,* January 1992, pp. 49–57.

28. Kiechel, "Microbusiness Alternative," p. 220.

29. The discussion that follows is drawn primarily from Donald L Sexton and Nancy Bowman, "The Entrepreneur: A Capable Executive and More," *Journal of Business Venturing* 1, no. 1 (1985), pp. 129–40.

30. For example, see *USA Today,* March 13, 1987, p. 13.

31. Harry Bacas and Nancy L Croft, "Go Out on Your Own?" *Nation's Business,* March 1986, pp. 18–21.

32. See Erik Larson, "The Best-Laid Plans," *Inc.*, February 1987, pp. 60–64; Bruce G Posner, "Real Entrepreneurs Don't Plan," *Inc.*, November 1985, pp. 129–35.

33. Richard L Osborne, "Planning: The Entrepreneurial Ego at Work," *Business Horizons,* January–February 1987, pp. 20–24.

34. Larson, "Best-Laid Plans," p. 63.

35. The Small Business Administration (SBA) publishes a *Starting Out* series on many types of businesses and a *Management Aids* series of booklets on marketing and all aspects of small business management. These booklets are available free at your regional SBA field office.

36. Birch, "Truth about Start-Ups," pp. 14–15.

37. Leon C Megginson, Charles R Scott, Jr., Lyle R Trueblood, and William L Megginson, *Successful Small Business Management* (Plano, TX: Business Publications, 1988), pp. 87–88.

38. Joan Delaney, "Franchise Finds: Tapping into the 50-Plus Market," *Executive Female,* January–February 1993, p. 30.

39. Mark Robichaux, " 'Competitor Intelligence': A Grapevine to Rivals' Secrets," *The Wall Street Journal,* April 12, 1989, p. B2.

40. "Positioning, Pricing, and Promotion: Three Keys to Successful Marketing," *Profit-Building Strategies for Business Owners,* January 1993, pp. 20–23.

41. For an excellent, down-to-earth approach for assessing the feasibility of a new product/service idea, see Wilson Harrell, "But Will It Fly?" *Inc.,* January 1987, pp. 85ff. Also, some insightful perspectives on the pitfalls of bringing a new idea to market (and suggested strategies) are provided in Doug Garr, "The Practical Inventor," *Venture,* October 1988, pp. 35ff.

42. Paul B Brown, "Mission Impossible?" *Inc.*, January 1989, pp. 109–10.

43. This discussion is based primarily on L Megginson et al., *Successful Small Business Management,* (Burr Ridge, IL: Richard D. Irwin, 1985) pp. 88–95, 130–44; and John G. Burch, *Entrepreneurship* (New York: John Wiley & Sons, 1986), pp. 101–26, 130–37.

44. Dennis Holder, "Franchise Fever Catches On," *Working Woman,* July 1986, pp. 35–36.

45. Ibid.

46. For further discussion on this topic, see Carol Steinberg, "Multi-Unit Owners: They're Hooked on Franchising," *USA Today,* September 9, 1993, pp. 8B–10B.

47. Michael Selz, "Europe Offers Expanding Opportunities to Franchisers," *The Wall Street Journal,* July 20, 1990, p. B2.

48. For a description of this and other misfortunes that have beset some franchisees, see Bruce McDougall, "Franchise Follies," *Report on Business Magazine,* August 1993, pp. 26–32.

49. "Franchises Gird for Battle," *Success,* May 1993, p. 64.

50. For a discussion of how to choose a franchise, see David A Baucus, Melissa S Baucus, and Sherrie E Human, "Choosing a Franchise: How Base Fees and Royalties Relate to the Value of the Franchise," *Journal of Small Business Management,* April 1993, pp. 91–104.

51. Jeannie Ralston, "Promises, Promises," *Venture,* March 1988, pp. 55–57.

52. Megginson et al., *Successful Small Business Management,* pp. 112–14.

53. For an insightful look at sources and requirements of venture funding, see Marj Charlier, "Patient Money," *The Wall Street Journal Reports on Small Business (Special Section),* February 24, 1989, p. R22; Jose De Cordoba, "Wanted: Good Managers," *The Wall Street Journal Reports on Small Business (Special Section),* February 24, 1989, p. R16; and Marie-Jeanne Juilland, "Alternatives to a Rich Uncle," *Venture,* May 1988, pp. 62ff.

54. Minneapolis is one community that provides substantial assistance for new businesses. A profile of the city's efforts is provided by Curtis Hartman, "Is It Easier than Ever to Start a Business?" *Inc.,* March 1987, pp. 69ff.

55. For excellent, in-depth advice on how to prepare and present a business plan, see Gary Brenner, Joel Evans, and Henry Custer, *The Complete Handbook for the Entrepreneur* (Englewood Cliffs, NJ: Prentice Hall, 1990), pp. 183–201.

56. Charles J Bodenstab, "Directional Signals," *Inc.,* March 1989, pp. 139ff; Roger Thompson, "Business Plans: Myth and Reality," *Nation's Business,* August 1988, pp. 16ff.

57. Thomas F Jones, *Entrepreneurism* (New York: Donald I. Fine, 1987).

58. Ibid.

59. Dan Steinhoff and John F Burgess, *Small Business Management Fundamentals* (New York: McGraw-Hill, 1986), p. 339.

60. *The Wall Street Journal,* November 2, 1986, p. 35.

61. Tom Ehrenfeld, "School's In: Teaching Job Skills Is One Thing," *Inc.,* July 1993, pp. 65–66.

62. For a discussion of this topic, see Alessandra Bianchi, "True Believers: Pride in, and Passion for, a Business's Product or Service Is One of the Most Powerful Workplace Enhancers Around," *Inc.,* July 1993, pp. 72–73.

63. Tom Ehrenfeld, "Cashing In," *Inc.,* July 1993, pp. 69–70.

64. Howard Rothman, "The Power of Empowerment," *Nation's Business,* June 1993, pp. 49–50.

65. Robert A Mamis, "Details, Details," *Inc.,* March 1988, pp. 96–98.

66. Paul Hawken, "The Employee as Customer," *Inc.,* November 1987, pp. 21–22.

67. See Neil C Churchill and Virginia L Lewis, "The Five Stages of Small Business Growth," *Harvard Business Review,* May–June 1983, pp. 30ff.

68. Jacquelyn Denalli, "Keeping Growth under Control," *Nation's Business,* July 1993, pp. 31–32.

69. For some interesting profiles, see Lucien Rhodes, "At the Crossroads," *Inc.,* February 1988, pp. 66ff; Lucien Rhodes, "Kuolt's Complex," *Inc.,* April 1986, pp. 72ff.

70. Keith H Hammonds, "Mitch Kapor's Well-Greased Dream Machine," *Business Week,* May 30, 1988, pp. 92–93; Michael W Miller, "Starting Over: High-Tech Entrepreneurs Who Have Left Their Old Firms Ponder Next Moves," *The Wall Street Journal,* September 8, 1987, p. 33.

71. Jones, *Entrepreneurism,* pp. 248–50.

72. For an interesting perspective from an entrepreneur who maintains a limited growth strategy, see Robert Mulder, "Sole Proprietor," *Inc.,* November 1986, pp. 96–98.

73. See David E Gumpert and David P Boyd, "The Loneliness of the Small-Business Owner," *Harvard Business Review,* November–December 1984, pp. 18ff; David P Boyd and David E Gumpert, "Coping with Entrepreneurial Stress," *Harvard Business Review,* March–April 1983, pp. 44ff.

74. Gumpert and Boyd, "Loneliness"; Boyd and Gumpert, "Coping."

75. Gumpert and Boyd, "Loneliness"; Boyd and Gumpert, "Coping."

76. For insightful profiles of how four founders dealt with stress by changing their managerial lifestyles, see Joshua Hyatt, "All Stressed-Up and Nowhere to Go," *Inc.,* January 1987, pp. 74ff; John Grossman, "Burnout," *Inc.,* September 1987, pp. 89ff.

77. For a look at the special problems (and some solutions) common in family entrepreneurships, see Patricia W Hamilton, "The Special Problems of Family Businesses," *D & B Reports,* July–August 1986, pp. 18–21; Curtis Hartman, "Taking the 'Family' Out of Family Business," *Inc.,* September 1986, pp. 70ff; Sharon Nelton, "Strategies for Family Firms," *Nation's Business,* June 1986, pp. 20ff.

78. See Suzanne Woolley, "Rule No. 1 for Selling Your Company: Don't Rush," *Business Week,* April 3, 1989, pp. 114–15; Beatrice H Mitchell and Michael S Sperry, "Selling Out," *Venture,* January 1988, pp. 25–26; Sandra Salmans, "Cutting the Deal," *Venture,* January 1988, pp. 27ff.

79. See S E Prokesch and W J Powell, Jr., "Do Mergers Really Work?" *Business Week,* June 3, 1985, pp. 88–94; Amanda Bennett, "After the Merger, More CEOs Left in Uneasy Spot: Looking for Work," *The Wall Street Journal,* August 27, 1986, p. 15.

80. R H Hayes and G H Hoag, "Post-Acquisition Retention of Top Management," *Mergers and Acquisitions,* Summer 1974, pp. 8–18.

81. See Sanford L Jacobs, "Unrealistic Expectations Pose Problems for Sellers of Firms," *The Wall Street Journal,* August 20, 1984, p. 17.

82. Hayes and Hoag, "Post-Acquisition Retention," p. 10.

21   CAREERS IN MANAGEMENT

Chapter Learning Objectives

After completing Chapter 21, you should be able to:

- **Define** the concept of career effectiveness and the criteria that determine career effectiveness.
- **Describe** the relationship between career stages and career paths.
- **Discuss** the positions supporting and opposing the creation of mommy track career paths in organizations.
- **Compare** the needs of individuals and organizations in career planning.
- **Identify** the potential benefits and pitfalls of mentoring relationships.

To Be or Not to Be a Manager

Who becomes managers? What are they like? What do they like? How did they become managers? And if they had it to do over again, would they still become managers? Throughout this textbook, we have presented ideas about management and managers. In fact, we have covered a great deal of information about a process termed *management* and about an occupation termed *manager*. This Management in Action suggests that anyone considering a managerial career should undertake that decision with considerable forethought.

Throughout the 1990s, managers have become prime candidates for dismissal and demotion as organizations have reduced managerial levels in the name of downsizing. So, in addition to the ordinary rigors of managerial work, the prospect of being dismissed by the organizations for which they work has been added to the list of managers' stressors.

A prime target for termination recently has been the middle managers in organizations. According to the reports of these matters, middle managers are facing obsolescence in the wake of information processing and computer-assisted decision making, team-oriented production, and worker self-pacing. Individuals doing the work no longer depend on the middle manager for technical support, information, or supervision. Middle managers have been found in the unemployment offices and outplacement services in proportionately larger numbers than so-called blue-collar workers.

Even the middle managers who retain jobs confront what some observers believe to be inevitable burnout, learned helplessness, and mid-career crisis as they attempt to make career progress in organizations that continually shrink opportunities for advancement. Particularly vulnerable to the loss of opportunity are individuals in the baby-boom set.

The contemporary organization seems to create conditions that produce alienation among managerial personnel. Organizations continue to insist on performance, productivity, and commitment, but no longer promise to return the manager's loyalty with protection from dismissal. Alienation in the workplace has long been studied as an outcome of routine, assembly-line work. But the idea that *managers* could also become victims of alienation has relatively recent currency in the business press.

So what does the future hold for individuals embarking on careers? Should they be thinking about trying the historically rewarding climb up the corporate ladder to higher-paying and more rewarding positions? Are the rungs on these ladders being eliminated? Are the ladders themselves disappearing? These are pessimistic thoughts indeed.

The fact is that Western economies and their organizations are going through irrevocable changes. Taking charge of one's career, whether at its beginning, middle, or end, makes a great deal of sense. To make conscious decisions about one's working life, including the development of a career plan with appropriate contingencies, seems the only choice.

Sources: W I Gordon, "People Should Be as Important as Profits: From Enchantment to Empowerment," *Vital Speeches of the Day,* February 15, 1996, pp. 285–88; B Ashforth, "Petty Tyranny in Organizations," *Human Relations,* July 1994, pp. 755–78. J W Hunt, "Alienation among Managers: The New Epidemic or the Social Scientists' Invention?" *Personnel Journal* 20, no. 3 (1991), pp. 34–40; and J Rogers, "Baby Boomers and Their Career Expectations," *Canadian Business Review,* Spring 1993, pp. 13–16.

The distinction between the concepts of careers *in* management and management *as* a career is more than a play on words. A career in management implies *descriptions* of *what* constitutes such careers and *where* such careers are acted out. Management as a career implies somewhat more personal issues, such as *why* one should pursue such a career, *who* should attempt such a career, and *how* an individual can increase the odds of having a successful and fulfilling career in management. This chapter explores both careers in management and management as a career.

Management Careers

The popular meaning of career reflects the idea of moving upward in one's chosen line of work. Moving upward implies larger salaries, more responsibility, status, prestige, and power. Although typically restricted to lines of work that involve gainful employment, we can certainly relate the concept of career to homemakers, mothers, fathers, volunteer workers, civic leaders, and the like. These people also advance in the sense that their knowledge and skills grow with time, experience, and training. Here we will restrict our attention to those who either choose careers in management or find themselves facing that career choice.

The definition of **career** as used in this discussion is as follows: the individually perceived sequence of attitudes and behaviors associated with work-related experiences and activities over the span of a person's life.[1] This definition emphasizes that career consists of both attitudes and behaviors in an ongoing sequence of work-related activities. Yet, even though the concept of career clearly relates to work, a person's nonwork life and roles play a significant part in it. For example, a mid-career manager who is 50 years old can have quite a different attitude about job advancement (involving greater responsibilities) from the attitude of a manager nearing retirement. A bachelor's reaction to a promotion involving relocation is likely to be different from that of a father of school-age children.

An individual's career involves a series of choices from among different opportunities. But from the organization's standpoint, a career involves processes by which the organization renews itself.[2]

Although definitions of careers have typically relied on upward mobility, recent ideas have enlarged the concept. For example, an individual can remain in the same job, acquiring and developing skills but without moving upward in an organizational or professional hierarchy.[3] It is also possible for an individual to move among various jobs in different fields and organizations.[4] Thus the concept of career must be broad enough to include not only traditional work experiences, but also emerging work and lifestyles. Contemporary career development practices recognize the diversity of individual choices and career alternatives.

As the emphasis on employee empowerment has gained acceptance in recent years, many organizations have undertaken career development programs that acknowledge the realities of the new workplace. The accompanying Management Focus describes some of these programs.

Career Effectiveness

In organizational settings, career effectiveness is judged not only by the individual, but also by the organization itself. But what is meant by career effectiveness? Under what circumstances will individuals state that they have had "successful" or "satisfying" careers? And will the organization share the individuals' views about their careers? Although numerous characteristics of career effectiveness could be listed, four are often cited: performance, attitude, adaptability, and identity.

Performance

Salary and position are the more popular indicators of career performance. Specifically, the more rapidly one's salary increases and one advances up the hierarchy, the higher the level of career performance. As one advances (is promoted), one's responsibilities increase in terms of employees supervised, budget allocated, and revenue generated. The organization is, of course, vitally interested in career performance since it bears a direct relation to organizational effectiveness. That is, the rate of salary and position advancement reflects in most instances the extent to which the individual has contributed to the achievement of organizational performance.

Management Focus

Career Development for the New Age Global Corporation

Organizations throughout the world have shed their centralized, bureaucratic practices. Many of these practices smacked of paternalism, and employees responded to them by taking on dependent, rather than independent, behaviors. They had no incentive and no interest in efforts to improve their employment situation. Therefore they had no interest in career development, an activity that inherently involves self-improvement. But enlightened management has begun to get rid of bureaucratic practices and in turn begun empowering employees to take control of their own futures in the organization.

Contemporary career development programs consist of self-assessment, goal setting, career planning, and implementation phases. These programs enable employees to have open and two-way communication with their supervisors throughout the four phases. To maintain the new sense of openness and trust, the career development program is voluntary; no employee is forced to undertake the phases. Nevertheless, through recognition and supervisory support, the organization encourages employees who do enter the program. Employees use the program to improve their skills and job performance. Moreover they use their development plans to market themselves within the organization. Throughout the process, organizations provide opportunity; employees must exploit the opportunity.

Sources: J Moad, "When the Career Ladder Crumbles," *Datamation*, January 15, 1995, pp. 44–47; R Bolton and J Gold, "Career Management: Matching the Needs of Individuals with the Needs of the Organization," *Personnel Review*, 23 no. 1 (1994), pp. 6–24; and R Tucker and M Moravec, "Do-It-Yourself Career Development," *Training*, February 1992, pp. 48–52.

Two points should be made here. First, to the extent that the organization's performance evaluation and reward processes do not fully recognize performance, individuals may not realize this indicator of career effectiveness. Thus, individuals may not receive those rewards, the salary and the promotions associated with career effectiveness, because the organization either does not or cannot provide them. Many employees discover that organizations often state that performance is rewarded when, in fact, other, nonperformance outcomes are rewarded.[5] Second, the organization may have expectations for the individual's performance that the individual is unwilling or unable to meet. The organization may accurately assess the individual's potential as being greater than her present performance, yet because she has other, nonjob interests (for example, family, community, religion), performance does not match potential. In such instances, the individual may be satisfied with career performance, yet the organization is disappointed. This mismatch occurs as a consequence of the individual's attitude toward the career.

Attitudes

The concept of *career attitudes* refers to the way individuals perceive and evaluate their careers. Individuals who have positive career attitudes will also have positive perceptions and evaluations of their careers. Positive attitudes have important implications for the organization because individuals with positive attitudes are more likely to be committed to the organization and to be involved in their jobs. The manner in which individuals come to have positive career attitudes is a complex psychological and sociological process; a full development of that process is beyond the scope of this discussion. However, it is evident that positive career attitudes are likely to coincide with career demands and opportunities that are consistent with an individual's interests, values, needs, and abilities.

Specific career attitudes such as *career commitment* and *job involvement* are associated with behaviors that concern organizations. For example, one study of career commitment among bank tellers found that high career commitment is related to low turnover.[6] The study distinguishes between career commitment and job involvement with commitment referring to attitudes about a career in banking, where the teller job is seen as a first step in that career, and involvement referring to attitudes specific to the teller job. Individuals can have positive attitudes about a career in banking but be little involved in the job, although the two should be positively associated for most individuals. Important to management is the recognition that career-committed individuals who leave the bank usually go to another bank and work there in a higher position; job-involved individuals who leave the bank usually go to another job with lower stress and demands.

Adaptability

Few professions are stagnant and unchanging. On the contrary, the condition of change and development more accurately describes contemporary professions. Changes occur in the profession itself requiring new knowledge and skills to practice it. For example, medicine and engineering have and will continue to advance in the utilization of new information and technology; other professions likewise have changed markedly. Individuals unable to adapt to these changes and to adopt them in the practice of their careers run the risk of early obsolescence and the loss of their jobs. Other individuals complain of "burnout" when they are unable to adapt to the constant demands of their job or career, particularly when the sense of burnout occurs late in their careers.[7]

The effects of job loss on individuals have taken on considerable importance as economic pressures of the 1980s and 1990s have caused organizations to reduce their managerial and professional staff.[8] Managerial personnel have been particularly vulnerable to downsizing as recent studies have documented. One study establishes that managers suffered proportionately greater job loss as organizations downsized.[9] This lack of employment security will doubtless cause managers to reconsider the wisdom of planning their careers within a particular organization.

It goes without saying that an organization benefits through the adaptiveness of its employees. An expression of the mutual benefits derived from career adaptability is the dollars expended by organizations for employee training and development. Thus career adaptability implies the application of the latest knowledge, skills, and technology in the work of a career.

Identity

Career identity includes two important components. First is the extent to which individuals have clear and consistent awareness of their interests, values, and expectations for the future. Second is the extent to which individuals view their lives as consistent through time, the extent to which they see themselves as extensions of their past. The idea expressed in this concept is, "What do I want to be and what do I have to do to become what I want to be?" Individuals who have satisfactory answers to this question are likely to have effective careers and to make effective contributions to the organizations that employ them.

Effective careers in organizations, then, are likely to occur for individuals with high levels of performance, positive attitudes, adaptiveness, and identity resolution. Moreover, effective careers are without doubt linked to organizational performance.

Career Stages

Individuals typically move through distinct stages during the course of their careers.[10] Although numerous descriptive labels have been proposed to identify these stages, we will use a four-stage model: establishment, advancement, maintenance, and withdrawal.[11] The establishment stage occurs at the onset of the career. The advancement stage is a period of moving from job to job, both inside and outside the organization. Maintenance occurs when one has reached the limits of advancement and the individual concentrates on the job he is doing. Finally, at some point prior to actual retirement, the individual goes through the withdrawal stage. The duration of each stage varies among individuals, but in general most people go through them in this same order.

Establishing a Career

A series of studies of American Telephone and Telegraph (AT&T) managers found they expressed considerable concern for security needs during the establishment phase.[12] During establishment, individuals require and seek support from others, particularly their managers. It is important for managers to recognize this need and to respond by assuming the role of mentor.[13]

Advancing a Career

During the advancement stage, the AT&T managers expressed considerably less concern for security-need satisfaction and more concern for achievement, esteem, and autonomy. Promotions and advancement to jobs with responsibility, as well as opportunity to exercise independent judgment, are characteristics of this stage. But those specific factors that explain why some individuals advance while others do not remain obscure.[14]

Maintaining a Career

The maintenance stage is marked by efforts to stabilize the gains of the past. In some respects, this phase is analogous to a plateau—no new gains are made, yet it can be a period of creativity since the individual has satisfied many of the psychological and financial needs associated with earlier phases. Although each individual and career will be different in actuality, it is reasonable to assume that esteem is the most important need in the maintenance stage. Many people experience what is termed the mid-career crisis during the maintenance phase. Such people are not successfully achieving satisfaction from their work and may, consequently, experience physiological and psychological discomfort. They may experience poor health and a heightened sense of anxiety. They no longer desire to advance and, consequently, they underperform. They then lose the support of their managers, which further intensifies the health and job problems.[15]

Managers in the maintenance stage are expected to become mentors of those in earlier stages. They also tend to broaden their interests and to deal more and more with people outside the organization. Thus, the central activities of managers in this stage are training and interacting with others. They assume responsibility for the work of others, a characteristic of this stage that can cause considerable psychological stress. An individual who cannot cope with this new and different requirement may decide to return to a previous stage. Others may be satisfied seeing some of their peers move on to bigger and better jobs. They are content to remain in the maintenance phase until their retirement.

As mentors, managers can make important contributions to the career development of their protégés. The mentor can help the protégé by sponsoring (recommending the protégé for promotion), providing visibility (creating opportunities for the protégé to demonstrate special skills and talents), coaching (suggesting ways to handle demanding and difficult tasks and situations), and protecting (steering the protégé away from controversial situations). Overall, the **mentor** counsels, guides, supports, and protects the less experienced protégé.[16]

Managers can mentor one or multiple protégés, and the mentor relationship can develop informally (initiated by the mentor or prospective protégé) or formally. In formal mentor programs, the organization matches mentors with protégés. At Bank America Corporation, for example, a manager may be asked to mentor three or four junior managers at a time for one year.[17] In a growing number of companies, formal mentor programs are being established to provide mentors for promising minority and female managers. Research indicates that these employees are often less likely to obtain an informal mentor.[18]

Successful mentor relationships can advance a beginning manager's career in the organization. In a study of 1,300 senior executives, mentors were ranked second only to education in positive impact on the executives' careers.[19] Some studies have found that managers with mentors earn more, are more likely to follow a career plan, and are more satisfied with their careers than are managers without mentors.[20]

However, the mentor relationship has potential pitfalls. A 25-year study of 3,000 mentor–protégé pairs found that many of the studied relationships were hindered by several problems. Protégés often resented their mentors and believed that they were overworked, too heavily scrutinized by the mentors, and too closely identified with them. Protégés also were frustrated when their mentors publicly reprimanded them for performance mistakes. The mentors, in turn, believed that heavy workloads and public criticism were necessary to avoid the criticism of playing favorites.[21] In sum, mentor relationships, while potentially beneficial for both mentor and protégé, can be delicate relationships to manage and maintain.[22] The accompanying Management Focus suggests difficulties women managers can experience in the mentoring relationship.

Besides mentoring, the maintenance-stage manager can enhance her career development by developing peer relationships. Kathy Kram and Lynn Isabella examined the nature of supportive and significant peer relationships at early, middle, and late career stages in a large manufacturing company.[23] The researchers interviewed managers and peers. Analysis of the interview data indicated that a continuum of peer relationships exists. The relationships were classified as information peer (information sharing), collegial peer (job-related feedback, friendship), and special peer (emotional support, confirmation).

The three types of **peer relationships** seem to be perceived somewhat differently by individuals at different career stages. For example, concerns about competence and professional identity often characterize the developmental needs of a person such as an engineer or an accountant at the initial, or establishment, stage. Individuals in their 20s use information peers to learn the ropes on how to get the job done, they use collegial peers to help define their professional role, and they use special peers to acquire a sense of competence and to help manage the stresses and anxieties of work and developing families. Kram and Isabella's interesting study suggests that peer relationships can be an adjunct to or used instead of a mentor relationship to support individual career development. For individuals without a mentor, peers can be a valuable source of help, support, and encouragement. It would be interesting to examine peer relationships in other than manufacturing settings. Would such relationships be able to mature in rapidly changing environments, such as those found in high-tech industries?

Withdrawing from a Career

The withdrawal phase follows the maintenance phase. The individual has, in effect, completed one career and may move on to another one.[24] During this phase the individual not moving on to another career may have opportunities to experience self-actualization through activities that were impossible to pursue while working.

Management Focus

The Benefits of Mentoring: Does Being a Woman Make a Difference?

Women continue to make significant progress in their quest for equal career opportunities in management. The idea of the "glass ceiling" has been much discussed by women and men alike. The glass ceiling refers to an unseen barrier that prevents women from advancing beyond a certain point up the managerial hierarchy. Surveys, testimonials, and rigorously designed research have identified the glass ceiling as real, and organizations have begun to implement plans to break that ceiling. Many of these plans include mentoring for women.

One study of women in organizations reported the factors that the participants identified as effective for their career progression. The women identified mentoring as one of the factors and, more often than not, the mentors were men rather than women. The women reported that, rather than depending on one mentor, they relied on several mentors who provided them with a number of benefits, including job opportunities that enabled them to demonstrate skills and abilities, feedback and advice, the sharing of expertise, and encouragement to meet high performance standards and acknowledgement when they did. The women in the study stated that without the support of their mentors, their career progress would have been hindered.

Despite the findings of the study cited above, other studies present less than positive endorsement of mentoring as an effective method of assistance for women who aspire to climb managerial hierarchies. For example, effective mentors are often in short supply in specific organizations, and every aspiring manager may not have equal access to an effective mentor.

Other barriers to effective mentoring may also be present in organizations, and aspiring managers, whether men or women, will have to overcome these barriers. One study reported that women perceive more barriers than men. Why should that be so? One suggestion notes that since most mentors for women are men, women find it harder to initiate mentoring relationships with men than with women. Until more women work their way into mentoring positions, this fact of organization life will remain unchanged.

M M Hale, "Mentoring Women in Organizations: Practice in Search of Theory," *American Review of Public Administration,* December 1995, pp. 327–39; R M Wentling, "Breaking Down Barriers to Women's Success," *HRMagazine,* May 1995, pp. 79–85. A Vincent and J Seymour, "Profile of Women Mentors: A National Survey," *SAM Advanced Management Journal,* Spring 1995, pp. 4–10 and B Ettorre, "Women at Work: Breaking the Glass. . . or Just Window Dressing?" *Management Review,* March 1992, pp. 16–22.

Painting, gardening, volunteer service, and quiet reflection are some of the many positive avenues available to retirees.

The importance of these career phases as reflecting different career stages cannot be overestimated. One study of scientists, engineers, accountants, and professors, for example, found that high performers go through each phase; they do not skip over them. Moreover, individuals in the study who had grown older *without* advancing to the appropriate phases are seemingly less valued than those who do. The interrelationships among career phases and life stages reflect milestones in individuals' lives and serve as bases for judgments of career effectiveness.[25]

Career Paths

Effective advancement through career stages involves moving along **career paths.** From the perspective of the organization, career paths are important inputs into personnel planning. An organization's future workforce needs depend on the projected passage of individuals through the ranks. From the perspective of the individual, a career path is the sequence of jobs which he desires to undertake to achieve personal and career goals. It is virtually impossible to completely integrate the needs of both the organization and the individual in the design of career paths, yet systematic career planning has the potential for closing the gap.

In the traditional sense, career paths emphasize upward mobility in a single occupation or functional area, as reflected in Figure 21–1. When recruiting personnel, the organization's representative will speak of engineers', accountants', or marketers' career paths. In these contexts, the recruiter will describe the different jobs typical individuals will hold as they work progressively upward in an organization. Each job, or rung, is reached when the individual has accumulated the necessary experience and ability and has demonstrated that she is ready for promotion. Implicit in such career paths are attitudes that failure results whenever an individual does not move on up after an elapsed period of time.

The idea of career path reflects the idea of moving upward in the organization along one "path." That path is usually the managerial, or line, path. Employees in staff positions are often prevented from moving upward unless they give up their specialty and move into a line position. Organizations are beginning to recognize the importance of multiple paths as well as career planning. For example Dow Corning established a "dual ladder" system for engineers who excell in technical achievement but do not desire managerial responsibility. In the early 1980s, the company updated its system to include all technical employees regardless of their educational or occupational backgrounds.[26]

An example of a career path for general management in a telephone company is depicted in Figure 21–1. According to the path, the average duration of a first-level management assignment is four years. It consists of two and a half years as a staff assistant in the home office and one and a half years as the manager of a district office

FIGURE 21–1   Career Path, General Management

Most jobs are stepping stones to other, more demanding positions.

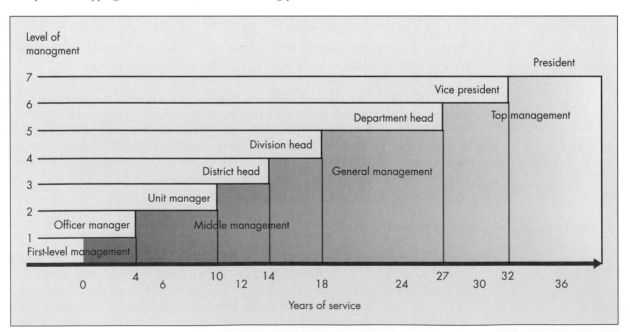

in a small city. By the 14th year, the average manager should have reached the fourth level of management. At this level, the assignment might be that of division manager of the commercial sales and operations division. Obviously, few managers reach the fifth level, much less the seventh (president). The number of openings declines, and the number of candidates increases as one nears the top of the organization.

The performance of businesses, universities, hospitals—indeed all organizations—depends on the effectiveness of managers. Their careers, similar to those in any occupation, follow the same general stages along appropriate career paths, although there is no single correct path to a successful management career.

Implicit in Figure 21–1 and, indeed, in the concept of the career path is that career progress occurs when you move up the organizational hierarchy to positions with progressively more responsibility, challenge, and rewards. Today, however, moving upward is becoming increasingly difficult for many employees, especially those in large organizations. During the 1980s, a wave of mergers and intensely competitive environments led to the major reorganization of many companies. These restructurings eliminated many management jobs (some 1 million jobs from 1980 to 1990).[27] Typically, the number of levels in the organizational structure was also reduced.

These moves made organizations leaner and more flexible. They also changed the nature of the traditional, upward career path. Today, there are simply fewer positions in the middle and upper levels of organizations for individuals who want to move upward, even if they are highly qualified to do so. This reality is continuing in the 1990s, given plans in many organizations to further restructure and reduce the size of their management workforces.[28]

Plateaus

As a result of current trends, more employees are reaching a plateau in their career paths—the point in a career where the likelihood of further movement up the hierarchy is very low.[29] The plateau becomes the final point of ascent in a person's career. Employees nowadays are also reaching the plateau sooner. One career management expert estimates that the average white male manager plateaus by age 40 to 42; minorities and women plateau at about age 38.[30] A career plateau is a frustrating dilemma for many employees who feel their careers are at a dead end; many also experience a sense of personal failure.[31]

Zigzag Career Paths

Some employees respond by adopting a zigzag career path; they leave the organization and try to move upward by switching from company to company, sometimes from industry to industry.[32] For example, Jon Rotensteitch first worked 18 years for Salomon Brothers, where he reached the position of managing director. Feeling stymied, Rotensteitch left his prestigious position and accepted the position of treasurer at IBM. In sharp contrast to most IBMers, Rotensteitch stayed only three years. He moved on to become president of Torchmark Corp., an insurance and financial services company. A zigzag career path (especially one across industries) involves risk because, with each job, the employee must learn a new culture and ways of doing business. However, its increasing popularity indicates that more managers are willing to take the risk for potentially greater professional growth and career rewards.[33]

Plateaued employees who remain with a company may accept a lateral transfer to broaden their managerial skills and to assume new challenges. Sometimes, a lateral transfer can open a new path upward. Some employees become more involved in training younger managers in their areas of expertise. Others focus more on improving their marketability by obtaining more education and on further developing their lives outside the job. For their part, more and more companies are developing career training and seminars that focus on improving a manager's satisfaction with her present job, in part by better matching aspects of the job to the manager's likes and talents and by giving the manager more responsibility.[34]

Dual Career Paths

Companies are also rejuvenating the **dual career path,** a concept first introduced in the mid-1970s. Dual career paths were designed to provide nonmanagerial professionals (e.g., scientists, engineers, R&D specialists) with the opportunity to progress up a career ladder, receiving the same rewards and prestige as their managerial counterparts while still working in their professional fields. The dual career path was intended to retain talented professionals who were frustrated by the lack of advancement opportunities in the organization unless they went into management (which many did not want to do).

However, with few exceptions, the dual career paths created in the mid-70s were ineffective. According to many management observers, the management path to achievement is so ingrained in organizational cultures that the dual career paths were not viewed as legitimate by either management or professionals in many organizations. Often, the dual ladders were poorly maintained; the rewards were not commensurate with those provided for employees on managerial career paths. However, in the late 1980s, a growing number of organizations began developing dual career paths for many types of professional employees (e.g., salespeople, bank loan officers, service representatives) and are now taking greater care to communicate the path options to professional employees and to ensure that the path's rewards correspond to those in managerial career ladders. In some organizations, plateaued managers with strong professional backgrounds are being given the opportunity to change to a dual career path. From that point, they resume their professional work and are no longer managers; however, opportunities still exist for upward advancement.[35]

The Mommy Track

In 1989, Felice Schwartz, president of Catalyst, a national research and advisory group on women's leadership, proposed the creation of a different career path for women managers and professionals in organizations. She suggested that organizations do the following:

- Identify two separate groups of women employees. One group, "career-primary" women, are individuals, most of whom are childless, who have made their careers their top priority. The second group, "career-and-family" women, are working mothers and mothers-to-be who want to combine family and career but require flexibility in work hours and responsibilities to do so.
- Provide career-primary women with the same career paths and opportunities as their male counterparts.
- For career-and-family women, create a separate career path that enables them to take time off or to work part-time during critical child-rearing years. In either case, the rate of advancement and pay is lower for those on the mommy track until they resume full-time work and responsibilities.[36]

Schwartz's proposal has stirred a storm of controversy. Proponents assert that the mommy track provides substantial benefits for both the organization and its female managers and professionals. The mommy track enables a company to keep many talented career-and-family women who would otherwise leave because of family demands. (According to one study, turnover among top-performing women managers occurs at over twice the rate of male managers; in many cases, the turnover occurs when a woman does not return to the company after maternity leave or returns and then leaves later.) By being flexible, the organization retains the contributions of these employees over the long term and avoids the substantial investment in training and development that is lost if they resign.[37]

For women, the mommy track provides the needed time to devote to family and the opportunity to later resume their careers with the company. It gives more women the flexibility to have children, an option many executive women have not taken because of the price they pay in their careers. According to one major study, 61 percent of female executives are childless, compared to less than 5 percent of male executives.[38]

However, critics respond that the mommy track legitimizes the view that women alone should bear the major responsibilities and make the professional sacrifices for bearing and raising children. Such, they argue, contradicts the growing trend of fathers assuming a greater role in raising their children. Second, the mommy track may legitimize the status of women as second-class employees and permanently derail women's careers. Once they're on the track, they may be on a slow track for the rest of their careers. Instead of implementing the mommy track, critics argue, organizations should provide parental support for both male and female employees, in terms of day care support, parental leave, and other programs.[39]

Whether the mommy track will proliferate in organizations remains to be seen. However, the controversial career path is another example of attempts by organizations to help employees balance the demands of family and career.

A related issue deals with problems associated with dual-income couples.[40] Today, there are approximately 29.4 million dual-income couples. While numerous books and articles have chronicled the arrival of women into high-ranking managerial positions, little mention has been made of the men they married. There exists confusion over the man's role in an executive marriage. Potentially, men's identities as the family providers can be threatened by wives who are also providers. Yet men, of course, want their wives to be happy and their marriages to be successful. The successful survivors of executive marriages point out that these marriages work best when no one keeps score regarding earnings, promotions, and other job-related factors.

Management as a Career

An individual striking out on a career has a vital interest in doing everything possible to make an informed job decision. Initial choices are reversible but not without some costs—lost time being the most obvious.[41] Although it is impossible to know at age 20 or so what one's interests, values, abilities, and needs will be when age 40, there are some things to consider. For example, the reader should have a general idea at this point of what managers do and are expected to do.

We know that managers are called on to manage work, people, and operations. They are expected to plan, organize, and control individuals, groups, and organizations. They are expected to motivate people and groups, to provide leadership, and to sense, recognize, and provide for change. They are expected to use information to make decisions that either directly or indirectly affect efficient production and operations.

• *Managing work and organizations:* The managerial issues associated with managing work and organizations are the focus of the classical approach. Planning, organizing, and controlling organizations were the first issues examined by management theorists and practitioners. Scientific management and classical organization theory made significant contributions that are now taken for granted in management practice, such as the principles of work measurement and simplification, principles of planning and organization, and basic control techniques.

• *Managing people:* The behavioral approach unites the ideas of the social and behavioral sciences and tests their applicability to management. Managing people to achieve effective levels of individual and group performance demands knowledge of individual differences, motivation, leadership, and group dynamics. Managing people is the most challenging and difficult aspect of the manager's job. People are unique; and while theories of motivation may be able to predict the behavior of most of the people most of the time, they cannot be counted on to predict what any individual will do in a specific situation. The art of management is to know the limitations of theory and to modify predictions when necessary.

• *Managing production and operations:* All organizations exist to achieve results, whether producing goods or providing services. The process of acquiring and combining the physical and human resources to achieve the intended results is the production and operations function. The management science approach—with the aid of mathematics, statistics, and computers—has made great strides in providing models that achieve effective and efficient performance of the production and operations function.

Management is an applied discipline. Unlike medicine and engineering, there is no science of management per se. Instead, management takes theories and concepts from all relevant sciences. Thus, effective managerial performance results from choosing an appropriate theory and technique for a particular problem or situation that arises in the manager's job.

Understanding the job of a manager, we can attempt to answer some questions about careers in management. Who should pursue a career in management? What are the characteristics needed to achieve career effectiveness as managers? How does one who has these characteristics plan a management career?

Who Should Pursue Management as a Career?

The trait theory of leadership does not provide precise answers to the question of who will become a leader. The same can be said of the question, "Who will achieve a successful career in management?" Predicting success is difficult because many factors play a role in an individual's management career.

Some factors, such as effective career planning and a strong educational background, are within a manager's control. However, other factors are often beyond an individual's influence. For example, a faltering organization may undergo a reorganization that eliminates a manager's job, thus prohibiting him from acquiring further management experience that contributes to improved skills. Or, as research has found, luck can substantially influence an individual's career. Luck—mere happenstance—is, of course, beyond a person's control.[42] However, we do know that certain individual characteristics significantly enhance a manager's probability of becoming an effective manager.

What Are the Characteristics of Effective Managers?	Although many characteristics contribute to managerial effectiveness, two are particularly important.

The Will to Manage.   The desire or need to influence the performance of others and the satisfaction derived from doing so is termed the "will to manage."[43] The fundamental characteristic of management is that managers achieve results through other people and that the setting for managerial work is an organization. Those who have studied the will to manage correlate it with several attitudes:[44] favorable attitude toward authority, desire to compete, assertiveness, desire to exercise power, desire to stand out from others in the group, and sense of responsibility.

John Miner devised questionnaires that measure the strength of these attitudes and found that individuals who score relatively high on each item are likely to select management as a career and are likely to achieve career effectiveness. One of his more important findings was that students' will to manage (as measured by the questionnaire) declined throughout the 1970s from the level of the 1960s. Miner predicted that this shift would contribute to the shortage of managerial talent during the 1980s. If Miner's ideas were correct, an individual with a strong will to manage should have had a competitive edge in pursuing a managerial career during those years.

Some evidence suggests that the will to manage can be strengthened through training. In a study of 116 college leaders at a major university, scores on the will-to-manage questionnaire increased in one group that underwent training. Scores of the comparison group, student leaders who did not take the training courses, remained unchanged during the study.[45] Similar studies of practicing managers also indicate that the will to manage can be developed.[46]

Supervisory Ability.   Supervisory ability is an important variable that distinguishes effective from ineffective managers.[47] Effective management involves utilizing the correct supervisory tactics required in a particular situation. The ability to use appropriate supervisory practices implies a contingency orientation toward management. Effective managers recognize and apply the relevant elements from each of the approaches of management, are responsive to changing social and economic conditions, and can motivate people.[48] As we have noted throughout this text, each approach to management contributes to the body of management thought and practice. Effective careers in management are related to the ability to select the appropriate idea for the situation.

Ability to Assess Potential for Effective Management Career.   Individuals can use personal initiative to discern whether they really want and are suited for a career in management. Both Miner and Edwin Ghiselli have devised measurements of will to manage and supervisory ability. With the assistance of a counseling professional, individuals can reach some *tentative* understanding of their potential. However, our knowledge of which variables predict managerial success is quite incomplete. Moreover, the measurements of those variables are not totally valid. The emphasis should be on *tentative* understanding of whether one wants to manage and has, or can develop, the ability to manage. Confronting these two issues is a first step in career planning.

How Does One Plan a Management Career?	**Career planning** involves matching an individual's career aspirations with the opportunities available in an organization. **Career pathing** is the sequencing of specific jobs associated with those opportunities. The two processes are intertwined.

Planning a career requires identifying the activities and experiences needed to accomplish career goals. Career path considerations include the sequence of jobs that results in reaching these career goals. Although still a relatively new practice, many organizations are turning to career planning as a way to be proactive about, rather than reactive to, problems associated with ineffective managerial careers.

The career planning and pathing process is described in Figure 21–2. Successful practice places equal responsibility on the individual and the organization. Individuals must identify their aspirations and abilities and, through counseling, recognize the training and development required for a particular career path. Organizations must identify their needs and opportunities and, through personnel planning, provide career information and training to their employees. Career planning cannot proceed unless information about career paths, expected vacancies, and position requirements is available to employees.[49]

Aspiring managers should note that opportunities differ across companies.[50] For example, there are many companies, including but not limited to US West, Square D Company, Pitney Bowes, Dayton-Hudson Corporation, IBM, Honeywell, and Corning, that are known for being woman friendly. These companies encourage and give active support to women pursuing career opportunities. They create environments where everyone has an equal shot at contributing, participating, and most of all, advancing. To do that, these companies are challenging the traditional practices, assumptions, and attitudes of corporate men. That can mean anything from setting goals for promoting women to awareness training for men.

Companies such as Weyerhaeuser, Gulf Oil, Exxon Corporation, and Eaton Corporation use career development programs to identify a broad pool of talent available for promotion and transfer opportunities. Career counseling is often restricted to managerial and professional staff, but IBM, General Electric Company, TRW, and Gulf provide career counseling for blue-collar as well as managerial personnel.

FIGURE 21–2   A Career Planning Process

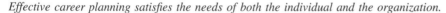

Effective career planning satisfies the needs of both the individual and the organization.

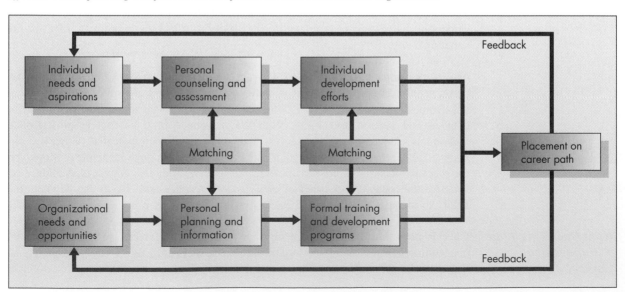

Matching individual and organizational needs can be done through a variety of personnel practices. An American Management Association survey revealed that the most widely used practices are informal counseling by the personnel staff and career counseling by supervisors. Less common, somewhat more formal practices involve workshops, seminars, and self-assessment centers.

Informal Counseling. The organization's personnel function often includes counseling services for employees who wish to assess their abilities and interests. The counseling process can also move into personal concerns, and it is proper to do so since these concerns are important factors in determining career effectiveness. In this context career counseling is viewed by the organization as a service to its employees, but not a primary one.

Supervisors often include career counseling during their performance evaluation sessions with employees. The question of the employee's future in the organization quite naturally arises in this setting. In fact, the inclusion of career information in performance appraisal predates the current interest in career planning. A characteristic of effective performance evaluation is to let the employee know not only how well she has done, but also what the future holds. Thus supervisors must be able to counsel the employee in terms of organizational needs and opportunities not only within the specific department, but throughout the organization. Since supervisors usually have limited information about the total organization, it is often necessary to adopt more formal and systematic counseling approaches.

Formal Counseling. Workshops, assessment centers, and career development centers are increasingly used in organization. Typically, such formal practices are designed to serve specific employee groups. Management trainees and "high-potential" or "fast-track" management candidates are two groups who have received most of the attention to date. However, women employees and minority employees are increasingly the targets for such programs. The adoption of career development programs for women and minority employees are indications of an organization's commitment to affirmative action.

All employees cannot be on the fast track and, by definition, all employees cannot be members of minority groups. Organizations have a vested interest in enabling all employees to continue their progress within the organization. Most employees will reach the limit of their progress up the organizational hierarchy; the number of jobs simply falls behind the number of employees, and with the advent of downsizing, the number of jobs per employee declines even further. But most employees should never reach the limit of their progress in developing skills and abilities to perform their existing jobs better. Thus there are two ways for employees to reach a "plateau" in their careers: one unavoidable for most, the other avoidable for most.

Other Human Resource Management Practices. Organizations can use a variety of personnel practices to facilitate their employees' career plans. One of the oldest, most widely used methods is some form of the *tuition aid program.* Employees can enroll in educational and training courses available at nearby schools, and the organization pays all or part of the tuition. J. I. Case, a Tenneco company with corporate offices in Racine, Wisconsin, is one of many organizations that provide in-house courses and seminars, plus tuition reimbursement for courses related to the individual's job.

Another practice is *job posting*. The organization publicizes job openings to employees. This requires more than simply placing a notice on the company's bulletin board. At minimum, effective job posting should meet the following conditions:[51]

- Posting should include promotions and transfers as well as permanent vacancies.
- Available jobs should be posted at least three to six weeks prior to external recruiting.
- Eligibility rules should be explicit and straightforward.
- Selection standards and bidding instructions should be stated clearly.
- Vacationing employees should be given the opportunity to apply ahead of time.
- Employees who apply but are rejected should be notified in writing, and a record of the reason should be placed in their personnel files.

Whatever counseling approach is used, the crucial element of its success will be the extent to which individual and organizational needs are satisfied.

Career Planning Benefits.   Career planning is becoming more widespread in organizations. Individuals who wish to make formal career plans should seek out those organizations that have demonstrated a commitment to career planning.

From the organization's perspective, who is most likely to benefit from career planning? Although this question has only recently been raised, it appears that some individuals gain little from the process. Recent studies, for example, indicate that career planning is most effective for people who have relatively high needs for growth and achievement, the skill to carry out their career plans, and a past history of career successes.[52] These results should not be interpreted to mean that career planning is for the select few; much more needs to be known about the issue before conclusions are drawn. But the findings do indicate that organizations should try to identify people who are most likely to take advantage of career planning programs.[53]

Individuals need not rely on company-sponsored programs, however. Nothing except lack of initiative prevents any of us from using our own resources to answer the key questions:

- Do I want to be a manager?
- Do I have the ability to be a manager?
- How do I go about having an effective career in management?

Summary of Key Points

- Management can be a challenging, rewarding career for those who have the knowledge, skills, attitudes, values, and opportunity to pursue it. Career effectiveness implies that one's performance, attitude, adaptability, and identity resolution are satisfying to both the organization and the individual.
- As a career, management progresses through stages that are more or less typical of all occupations. Career paths tend to be specific to individual organizations.

- Each career stage involves both career and personal demands. Both opportunities and problems arise when one's career and one's personal life conflict.
- In the 1980s, organizational mergers and restructurings reduced the number of upper- and middle-level management positions available for ambitious and qualified employees. As a result, many managers are experiencing career plateaus. They are responding in a number of ways, such as becoming more mobile, improving their market-

ability via education, and further developing their lives outside of work. Some companies are responding by developing dual career paths.

- Some organizations have mommy track career paths for female managers and professionals. These paths enable a woman with young children to take time off or work part-time during critical child-rearing years. She later resumes her full-time career with the company. The mommy track is a controversial strategy for helping women balance career and family demands.
- Individuals desiring a career in management should be encouraged to plan their careers. Career plans are tentative by nature, but they force individuals to consider their own strengths and weaknesses.
- Two factors are essential in management: Does one really *want* to manage (will to manage), and does the person have or can the person develop the *ability* to manage (supervisory ability)?
- More and more organizations are providing some form of career counseling and development for their employees.
- The potential for effective managerial careers is crucial. Failure to recognize and develop managerial talent will almost certainly affect an organization's performance adversely throughout the 1990s.

Discussion and Review Questions

1. How has the emergence of diversity in the workplace and the global market affected career planning?
2. Rank the relative importance of the four characteristics of effective careers from the perspective of the individual, the organization. Explain your rankings.
3. What has been your experience with job interviews and previews? Have they accurately described the job as you subsequently experienced it? What could the organization have done to more accurately depict the job as you experienced it?
4. Why has career counseling for preretirees emerged as an important issue in organizations? How does career counseling for pre-entry employees differ from preretirement employees?
5. Of what value to an organization is the mentor relationship?
6. How can you discover career paths in a particular organization? Is this the kind of information you would want to receive when you interview for a job? What questions would you ask to get this information?
7. As the CEO of a large company, would you implement a mommy track program in your firm? Why or why not? As a young female executive who plans to have a family, would you support a mommy track? Explain.
8. Many individuals leave their first jobs within the first two years. Why do you think this situation occurs?
9. How would you know that your career had plateaued in an organization? If you were frustrated by being plateaued, what actions would you take to alleviate your dissatisfaction?
10. In your opinion, what personal characteristic is most important for achieving success as a manager? Explain.

Case 21–1
Career Development as a Personal Responsibility

Assisting individuals with their career development plans and planning can be a powerful tool for integrating organizational and individual goals. But the managerial challenge is to design a program that will enable individuals to plan their careers with realistic information about career path opportunities that exist within a particular organization. At the most basic level individuals must know and understand how their goals fit with those of their supervisors and work groups. In the absence of such information, individuals cannot find their places in the organization and, consequently, will never be able to make optimal contributions to it.

One R&D organization implemented a career development program in one of its divisions. The management of the division initially perceived the program to be an attempt to get nonsupervisory employees to take responsibility for their own career development. Eventually, however, the program provided not only opportunities for individual growth, but also a way for supervisors to support employees' career goals and to disseminate organizational goals and objectives.

Another initial focus of the program was to improve peer relations among the nonsupervisory personnel. Managers and supervisors perceived poor peer relations to be a problem, but it was later discovered that the nonsupervisory personnel did not see the same problem. What they did see as a problem was the unfair way that supervisors assigned jobs and distributed rewards. Nonsupervisory employees perceived the problem to be poor employee–supervisor relations, not peer relations. The program then became a catalyst for managing employee–supervisor relations because effective career development can succeed only in workplaces that employees believe to be free of arbitrary job and reward assignments.

These changes in management's expectations for what a career development program can accomplish were the result of how the program was designed. Rather than imposing the program, management designed the program only after involving managers, supervisors, and nonsupervisory personnel in a needs-assessment phase. It was during this phase that it became obvious that an individual's career goals and strategies can be developed only with participation of the individual's supervisor who can represent the organization's goals and strategies. The information obtained in the design phase enabled management to think in terms of a program that could go beyond the usual expectations for a career development program. But what would be the features of the program?

The division's management decided on a workshop to include a series of related activities. Each of the activities was to accomplish certain objectives in the context of the entire program. The workshop's first activity was the division leader's presentation of the division's mission, goals, and overall strategy. The presentation outlined current and future major projects and anticipated job requirements as well as the division's philosophy of career development. Prior to attending the workshop, participants had received from their supervisors answers to some important questions, including: "What are the major goals for the work group and how can I support you to meet those goals? What do you see as the major results for my job in the next 12 months? How can you support me to achieve those results? What are my major competencies? What, in your view, is an outstanding employee?"

The workshop activity included group discussion of the division leader's presentation and the responses of supervisors to the key questions. The participants completed a variety of self-assessment inventories to help them discern their values and appropriate strategies for achieving those values. The participants took all this information as important input in the development of their own individual development plans (IDP).

The IDP identifies what each individual can and should do to achieve career aspirations. It identifies development needs for performance improvement and job competency and specific actions to take to improve any deficiencies. It also identifies the assistance required of the supervisor and other division-controlled support such as job assignments, training, and information. The IDP also identifies all of the obstacles that must be overcome if the individual is to accomplish the plan. Completing the IDP was the last activity of the workshop and all the other activities led up to this important exercise. Following the workshop, individuals discussed their IDPs with their supervisors.

Through the participation of all key individuals throughout the organization, the career development workshop became more than a career planning exercise. The workshop can be used as an important strategy for integrating organizational and individual goals. In addition it can serve as an important activity for identifying and managing key work-related problems that can stifle not only an organization's purposes, but an individual's ambitions as well.

Questions for Analysis

1. Explain how the R&D unit integrated the unit's objectives with its employees' objectives through the career development program.

2. What can you identify as potential sources of conflict among employees and their supervisors who participate in this kind of program?

3. In what ways could the IDP concept be used in the context of classrooms, students, and teachers?

EXPERIENTIAL EXERCISE
CAREER PLANNING THE TQM WAY

Purpose

The purpose of this exercise is to provide students with experience in thinking about their careers and in using the ideas of total quality management.

The Exercise in Class

Each student should complete the following steps:

1. Review understanding of basic elements of total quality management to include fact-based decision making,

customer-oriented measures of performance, and analysis of processes that produce customer-acceptable outcomes.

2. Review your life to this point to determine the primary customers whom you have sought to serve through your behavior, determine what each of them desires as acceptable behavior from you, examine how you have gone about satisfying those expectations, and evaluate the extent to which you have undertaken your career to this point through the use of fact-based decision making.

3. Project your life beyond this point in time to determine the potential customers having an interest in your career, what each of these customers will expect as acceptable performance, what you will do, the processes you will use to satisfy these customers, and the fact-based decision-making tools you can use to assist you with this career plan.

4. Identify the potential conflicts among all those customers who have interests in your career

performance and indicate the ways you think you can resolve these conflicting expectations.

After completing these four steps, each individual can share answers with the class to enlarge the scope of each student's understanding of career planning in the context of total quality management concepts.

The Learning Message

This exercise illustrates the difficulty of thinking about one's career plan. In particular it will cause students to think about the different expectations of other individuals—family members, co-workers, bosses, friends—and how those expectations can and will create conflicts that must be resolved one way or another. The total quality management concepts facilitate the exercise.

Notes

1. Douglas T Hall, ed., *Career Development in Organizations* (San Francisco: Jossey-Bass, 1986).

2. Hugh Gunz, "The Dual Meaning of Managerial Careers: Organizational and Individual Levels of Analysis," *Journal of Management Studies,* May 1989, p. 226.

3. Jeffrey A Sonnenfeld and Maury A Peiperl, "Staffing Policy as a Strategic Response: A Typology of Career Systems," *Academy of Management Review,* October 1988, pp. 588–600.

4. Meryl R Louis, "Career Transitions: Varieties and Commonalities, *Academy of Management,* July 1980, p. 330.

5. Roy J Lewicki, "Organizational Seduction: Building Commitment to Organizations," *Organizational Dynamics,* Autumn 1981, p. 9.

6. Gary Blau, "Testing the Generalizability of a Career Commitment Measure and Its Impact on Employee Turnover," *Academy of Management Proceedings,* 1989, pp. 53–57.

7. Cary Cherniss, "Long-Term Consequences of Burnout: An Exploratory Study," *Journal of Organizational Behavior,* January 1992, pp. 1–11.

8. Janina C Latack and Janelle B Dozier, "After the Ax Falls: Job Loss as a Career Transition," *Academy of Management,* April 1986, pp. 375–92.

9. Peter Cappelli, "Examining Managerial Displacement," *Academy of Management Journal,* March 1992, pp. 203–17.

10. Nigel Nicholson, "A Theory of Work Role Transitions," *Administrative Science Quarterly,* June 1984, pp. 172–91.

11. Lloyd Baird and Kathy Kram, "Career Dynamics: Managing the Superior/Subordinate Relationship," *Organizational Dynamics,* Spring 1983, p. 47.

12. Douglas T Hall and Khalil Nougaim, "An Examination of Maslow's Need Hierarchy in an Organizational Setting," *Organizational Behavior and Human Performance,* 1968, pp. 12–35; A Howard and Douglas W Bray, *Managerial Lives in Transition* (New York: Guilford Press, 1988).

13. David M Hunt and Carol Michael, "Mentorship: A Career Training and Development Tool," *Academy of Management Review,* July 1983, pp. 475–85.

14. John F Veiga, "Mobility Influences during Managerial Career Stages," *Academy of Management Journal,* March 1983, pp. 64–85.

15. Janet P Near, "Work and Nonwork Correlates of the Career Plateau," *Academy of Management Proceedings,* 1983, pp. 380–84.

16. Raymond A Noe, "Women and Mentoring: A Review and Research Agenda," *Academy of Management Review,* January 1988, p. 66.

17. Selwyn Feinstein, "Women and Minority Workers in Business Find a Mentor Can Be a Rare Commodity," *The Wall Street Journal,* November 10, 1987, p. 31.

18. Ibid.

19. Ibid.

20. See Gerald R Roche, "Much Ado about Mentors," *Harvard Business Review,* January–February 1979, pp. 14ff.

21. Srully Blotnick, "With Friends like These," *Savvy,* October 1984, pp. 42ff. Also see Donald W Myers and Neil J Humphreys, "The Caveats in Mentorship," *Business Horizons,* July–August 1985, pp. 9–14.

22. Some spouses in a dual career relationship look to each other for mentorlike support and guidance. For a look at these relationships and their benefits, see Anita Shreve, "Mutual Mentors," *Working Woman,* September 1988, pp. 128ff.

23. Kathy E Kram and Lynn A Isabella, "Mentoring Alternatives: The Role of Peer Relationships in Career Development," *Academy of Management Journal,* March 1985, pp. 110–32.

24. James B Shaw, "The Process of Retiring: Organizational Entry in Reverse," *Academy of Management Review,* January 1981, pp. 41–47.

25. Paul H Thompson, Robin Z Baker, and Norman Smallwood, "Improving Professional Development by Applying the Four-Stage Career Model," *Organizational Dynamics,* Autumn 1986, pp. 49–62.

26. Charles W Lentz, "Dual Ladders Become Multiple Ladders at Dow Corning," *Research-Technology Management,* May–June 1990, pp. 28–34.

27. Paul Hirsch, "The Management Purges," *Business Month,* November 1988, pp. 39–42.

28. Rosabeth Moss Kanter, "The Contingent Job and the Post-Entrepreneurial Career," *Management Review,* April 1989, pp. 22–27.

29. Douglas T Hall, "Career Plateauing and Subidentity Change in Midcareer," in Douglas T Hall ed., *Organizational Career Development* (San Francisco: Jossey-Bass, 1986).

30. Walter Kiechel III, "High Up and Nowhere to Go," *Fortune,* August 1, 1988, pp. 229ff.

31. See Lester Korn, "Plotting Your Next Career Move," *Working Woman,* January 1988, pp. 66ff.

32. See James Braham, "Managers on the Move," *Industry Week,* January 2, 1989, pp. 11–12; Neal E Boudette, "Jumping into Smaller Ponds," *Industry Week,* January 2, 1989, pp. 15ff.

33. Carol Hymowitz, "More Executives Finding Changes in Traditional Corporate Ladder," *The Wall Street Journal,* November 14, 1986, p. 25.

34. Larry Reibstein, "As Firms Try to Refocus Workers' Career Prospects," *The Wall Street Journal,* November 14, 1986, p. 25.

35. Mark L Goldstein, "Dual-Career Ladders: Still Shaky but Getting Better," *Industry Week,* January 4, 1988, pp. 57ff.

36. Felice N Schwartz, "Management Women and the New Facts of Life," *Harvard Business Review,* January–February 1989, pp. 65–76.

37. Ibid.

38. Elizabeth Ehrlich, "The Mommy Track," *Business Week,* March 20, 1989, pp. 126ff.

39. Ibid.; Janice Castro, "Rolling along the Mommy Track," *Time,* March 27, 1989, p. 72.

40. For further discussion, see Julie Connelly, "How Dual-Income Couples Cope," *Fortune,* September 24, 1990, pp. 129–36.

41 Meryl Reis Louis, "Managing Career Transitions: A Missing Link in Career Development," *Organizational Dynamics,* Spring 1982, pp. 68–77.

42. For an insightful perspective on the impact of luck on careers (and some interesting examples of its effect), see Daniel Seligman, "Luck and Careers," *Fortune,* November 16, 1981, pp. 60ff.

43. Sterling Livingston, "Myth of the Well-Educated Manager," *Harvard Business Review,* January–February 1971, pp. 79–89; John B Miner, *The Challenge of Managing* (Philadelphia: W. B. Saunders, 1975), p. 276.

44. Miner, *The Challenge of Managing,* pp. 220–23.

45. Timothy M Singleton, "Managerial Motivation Development: A Study of College Student Leaders," *Academy of Management Journal,* September 1978, pp. 493–98.

46. Miner, *The Challenge of Managing,* p. 296.

47. Edwin E Ghiselli, *Exploration in Managerial Talent* (Santa Monica, CA: Goodyear, 1971).

48. Lawrence A Armour, ed., *Managing to Succeed: Stories from The Wall Street Journal* (Burr Ridge, IL: Dow Jones-Irwin, 1979).

49. Kenneth B McRae, "Career-Management Planning: A Boon to Managers and Employees," *Personnel,* May 1985, pp. 56–60.

50. For a more detailed discussion and listing of woman-friendly companies, see Walecia Konrad, "Welcome to the Woman-Friendly Company," *Business Week,* August 6, 1990, pp. 48–55.

51. David R Dahl and Patrick R Pinto, "Job Posting: An Industry Survey," *Personnel Journal,* January 1977, pp. 40–42.

52. Sam Gould, "Characteristics of Career Planners in Upwardly Mobile Occupations," *Academy of Management Journal,* September 1979, pp. 539–50. John B Miner and Donald P Crane, "Motivation to Manage and the Manifestation of a Managerial Orientation in Career Planning," *Academy of Management Journal,* September 1981, pp. 626–33.

53. Mary Ann Von Glinow, Michael J Driver, Kenneth Brousseau, and J Bruce Prince, "The Design of a Career-Oriented Human Resource System," *Academy of Management Review,* January 1983, pp. 23–32.

INTERNET APPENDIX

Chapter 1

Out-of-Class Exercise: Exploring the Writing of Frederick Taylor

This exercise is designed to provide students with an opportunity to explore a classic paper written by Frederick Taylor about scientific management. The paper featured at the web site below was written by Taylor in 1911 in response to a growing perception that the country was experiencing a crisis in management, leading to a waste of natural resources. Students should read the entire document at the following web site:

http://www.cohums.ohio-state.edu/history/courses/ hist563/fwt5-29.htm

After reading the article, students should consider the following list of questions and be prepared to discuss during the next class:

1. What do you think is Frederick Taylor's view of the rank-and-file worker? What is his view of the business owner?

2. After reading the piece, think about what parts of Taylor's arguments you most strongly disagree with. Why do you disagree on these points? What parts of Taylor's arguments do you agree with?

3. What does Taylor mean by the term "soldiering?" Do you think that this phenomenon can be removed from the work place using the techniques Taylor endorses? Why or why not? What are some potential consequences of using Taylor's techniques to eliminate soldiering?

4. Taylor's scientific management revolves around his philosophy of getting maximum output from each individual and from each machine. Do you agree with this philosophy? Why or why not?

5. Compare and contrast Taylor's prescription that "almost every act of the workman should be preceded by one or more preparatory acts of the management which enable him to do his work better and quicker than he otherwise could" with current trends in management. Do you think this prescription would be well-received in today's work place?

In-Class Exercise: Visiting Frederick Taylor University

Frederick Taylor has a respected name in the annals of management theory. That good name has been appropriated by at least one private university. Frederick Taylor University offers undergraduate degrees in management and business administration, and the Masters of Business Administration.

Visit the following web site in class:

http://www.ftu.com

This is the home page for Frederick Taylor University. Explore with students the degree program offerings. Examine the curriculum for the various degrees. How much of Frederick Taylor's influence is evident in the curriculum? Would students be interested in obtaining their MBA from such a university? Does the name of the university influence their response?

Chapter 2

Out-of-Class Exercise: The Federal Government Seeks to Improve Customer Service

Over the past several decades companies all over the world have been paying increasing attention to their customers. This increased emphasis on customer service and customer satisfaction is driven in part by an increasingly competitive global economy. This factor is often cited as the principal driver of the changing orientation of companies. Equally important, however, is the fact that customers have more choices today than ever before. They are able to choose among companies for a wide variety of common services and products. Customers can choose to do business with companies who best cater to their particular tastes and needs. Thus, companies must not only look at what their competitors are doing; they must also be exceedingly interested in what their customers want.

The federal government in the United States undertook a program to "reinvent government" during the Clinton administration. This program involved importing management techniques from private industry, such as reengineering and TQM, into government units. One of the main components of the reinventing government program is a renewed commitment to improving customer service.

The web site listed below is a US government document on improving customer service in several units: the Internal Revenue Service, the Post Office, and the Social Security Administration. Students should visit the following web site outside of class:

http://www4.ai.mit.edu/npr/user/structure/improving-customer-service.html

Students should visit this web site and click on the "Improving Customer Service" overview. After reading that short piece, they should go back to the original page and click on the link to the Customer Service standards for the federal agency of their choice (either the IRS, Post Office, or Social Security). In preparation for discussion in class, the students should consider the following questions:

1. What does the agency say about the competitive environment in which it operates? What does it say about its "customers?"

2. How does the agency rate its current level of customer service? What improvements does it want to make?

3. How does the agency propose to measure its improvement in customer service and customer satisfaction?

4. If you have used any of the services from the agency you examined, have you noticed any improvements in customer service?

5. What are the obstacles to improving customer service and customer satisfaction that a manager of a federal agency faces? How do these differ from those faced by a manager of a private company?

Chapter 3

Out-of-Class Exercise: Exploring the US Trade and Development Agency

The decision to become a multinational company is a major one. Companies large and small face tremendous barriers to success when they attempt to establish operations in a foreign country. The questions faced by companies seeking to conduct business abroad range from "What products or services should we try to establish in the international market?" to "What are the laws and customs for conducting business in the international market?"

Both of these questions and many like them must be answered rigorously before a company invests valuable resources in the foreign market. There are many organizations that have been established to assist companies in their quest to establish overseas operations. One of these organizations is the US Trade and Development Agency. Its services can be explored at the following web site:

http://www.tda.gov/

Students should visit this web site outside of class. They should feel free to surf the web site according to their interests, but each should click on and read the "TDA Primer." Students should be prepared to discuss their findings to the following questions during the next class period:

1. What services does the TDA provide? How can businesses take advantage of these services?

2. What criteria does the TDA use to determine which projects it will undertake?

3. How does the TDA help small businesses? What are some current opportunities for small businesses in developing countries?

4. What are current areas of focus for the TDA? Do you agree that these are likely to be fruitful areas of investment?

In-Class Exercise: Linking to the **Multinational Monitor**

This exercise is designed to expose students to a valuable Internet resource concerning the global business environment. The *Multinational Monitor* is an Internet magazine that features articles, editorials, and commentary on multinational companies and global business practices. It tracks corporate activity, especially in the Third World, focusing on the export of hazardous substances, worker health and safety, labor union issues and the environment.

As the discussion in Chapter 3 evolves toward multinational companies, link to the following web site in class:

http://www.essential.org/monitor/

This takes you to the *Multinational Monitor* home page. This page will allow you to link to the recent or back issues, select an article, or search for specific topics. Link to an article of choice and enter a class discussion.

Chapter 4

Out-of-Class Exercise: Exploring Corporate Codes of Conduct and Ethics

At the core of many companies' efforts to establish ethical business practices is a corporate code of ethics. Typically established by top management, a code usually consists of a written statement of a company's values, beliefs, and norms of ethical behavior.

Ideally, a code of ethics should provide employees with direction in dealing with ethical dilemmas, clarify the organization's position regarding areas of ethical uncertainty, and achieve and maintain overall ongoing conduct that the organization views as ethical and proper.

The following web site provides links to a wide range of professional society and corporate codes of conduct:

http://condor.depaul.edu/ethics/ethb11.html#codes

Students should visit the site outside of class. They should select at least three *corporate* codes of conduct that they will review. Students should download and print the codes they review and bring them to the next class period.

For this exercise, students will compare the codes they examine, and address the following questions:

1. What issues do the various codes address that are common? Are quality standards addressed? Behavior standards? Customer service standards?
2. What issues do the codes not address that you think should be addressed?
3. Of the codes reviewed, which do you think would be the most effective in creating an ethical culture?

4. Are there any distinctive differences between codes from different industries?
5. Are there any distinctive differences between codes of companies headquartered in different countries?
6. Are the codes well written? What would you change? Why?

In-Class Exercise: Business Ethics Resources on the Web

This exercise is designed to expose students to a valuable link to a wide range of web-based business ethics resources. The following link goes to the business school at Nijenrode University, the Netherlands.

http://www.nijenrode.nl/nbr/eth/

The school has gathered a list of resources focusing on business ethics, the environment, and sustainability. Instructors may want to visit a few of the sites to explore them more in depth. Discussion should center on how the web can be used as a resource to help improve business ethics. Which of the resources at this site are useful to practicing managers? What else could be done on the web to help practicing managers with the ethical challenges they face?

The out of class exercise for this chapter will take students to a web site on "Codes of Ethics." Several codes of ethics links are featured at the Nijenrode site. Instructors may want to preview the exercise in class by examining one of these links prior to assigning the out-of-class exercise.

Chapter 5

Out-of-Class Exercise: Decision Making Techniques

Decision making is an important part of every manager's job. Making a decision is usually not something that happens at a single instant in time, but rather is a process that involves numerous stages and strategies. Researchers have developed a number of techniques that managers can employ to help them make better decisions. Three of those techniques are critical path analysis, brainstorming, and decision trees.

The web site listed below provides overviews of critical path analysis, brainstorming, and decision trees. Students can choose which of the three decision making techniques they'd like to explore, but they should start their search at the following web address:

http://www.mindtools.com/critpath.html

The above web site should be visited outside of class. The site is the page for critical path analysis. Students can choose to review the information on this page, or click on the buttons that will take them either to brainstorming, or decision trees.

For this exercise, students should choose one of the three decision making techniques for further study. They should review the entire site related to the technique and be prepared to discuss their findings during the next class period. Discussion should focus on the following questions:

1. What insights did you gain from reviewing the decision making technique that you chose?
2. What types of decisions would be amenable to the technique you chose? Give examples.
3. What types of decisions would not be amenable to your technique? Give examples.

4. Have you ever used this technique in decision making? What are the technique's strengths and weaknesses?

In-Class Exercise: Three Keys to Successful Meetings

This exercise will visit a web site that addresses three keys to successful meetings. It is appropriate for the section of the chapter dealing with group decision making.

Most students have probably already attended numerous meetings, some more effective than others. There's often nothing worse than spending several hours in a meeting with no decision reached or action plans established. The following web site has simple rules for decision making that can be easily read and reviewed in class:

http://openthis.com/secrets.htm

Review the three principles of effective meetings listed at this site. Discussion should focus on the students' experiences with meetings. Ask the students to tell stories about ineffective meetings they've attended. What made the meeting ineffective? What could have been done to make it more effective? How do the three principles discussed in this exercise apply?

Also ask the students to tell a story about an effective meeting they've attended. What made this particular meeting effective? Were the three principles followed? What additional principles might be added to the list of three?

Chapter 6

Out-of-Class Exercise: Planning for Tomorrow's Transportation Problems in Chicago

Planning focuses on the future: what is to be accomplished and how. The essence of planning is identifying future environmental conditions and preparing for them. The challenge of planning is undertaken by managers in organizations of all sizes, even organizations as large as an entire US city. The city of Chicago is the third largest metropolitan area in the United States. Its traffic problems are well known. Chicago commuters could relate many horror stories of being stuck for hours in traffic jams as a single fender-bender or other mishap can have day-long affects on traffic patterns.

Future prospects for the city's traffic problems are not bright. Continued degradation of the existing infrastructure as well as continued in-migration of new people means more cars, poorer roads, and bigger headaches. City officials have decided to meet their future problems head on. The web site listed below is an action plan developed by officials to alleviate some of the congestion and other problems related to Chicago traffic.

http://www.cnt.org/tsp/comm_pln.htm

Students should visit this web site outside of class. They should read the entire plan, taking special note of the milestones and actions that it suggests. After reading the plan, they should consider the following questions and be prepared to discuss their answers during the next class:

1. Does the plan focus on the future? How far into the future does the plan seem to consider?
2. Can you determine whether the plan focuses on the four dimensions of planning: objectives, actions, resources, and implementation? Explain how it addresses these dimensions.
3. Who has been included in the development of the plan? Should there have been others included?
4. What do you think are the weaknesses of this plan? Strengths?
5. Why do you think Chicago officials decided to display their plan on the web?

Chapter 7

Out-of-Class Exercise: Strategic Planning: How to Write a Plan to Plan

Strategic planning's origins are military. The term derives from ancient Greek, meaning, literally, general of the army. Strategoi were generals of Greek tribal armies who carried the day at Marathon, nearly 2,500 years ago. They were elected political leaders, who left battlefield tactics to troop leaders, but ruled on policy issues as a group.

Today, strategic planning is used by all types of for-profit organizations in their day to day "battles" against economic competitors. Strategic planning is also being used by non-profit and governmental agencies as they strive to run their operations "more like a business."

When President Clinton signed the Government Performance and Results Act of 1993 he set in motion a process that will help the federal government to operate more like a business. This Act will create standard goal-setting and performance measurement processes in all federal agencies. The Act requires all federal agencies to submit a strategic plan by September 30, 1997, an annual performance plan for fiscal year 1999, and a performance report by March 31, 2000.

The following web site is an overview of the strategic planning process that is being used by US governmental agencies to prepare their mandated strategic plans. It discusses definitions of key terms associated with strategic planning, describes the process of establishing a mission statement, and reviews the outcomes of a successful strategic planning process:

http://www.perfstrat.com/articles/ptp.htm#review

Students should visit the above web site outside of class. They should read the entire site and be prepared to discuss the following questions during the next class period:

1. How does the definition of strategic planning at the web site compare to the definition in the text? How does the process described at the web site compare to the process outlined in the text?
2. What new insights about strategic planning were you able to derive from reading the web site?
3. Do you agree with the "Strategic Planning Cycle" graphic at the web site. What elements are new you? What elements do you think are missing?

4. What is meant by the term "Plan to plan?" How does that fit with what you've now learned about organizational planning and strategic planning?
5. Do you think governmental agencies will be improved through use of this strategic planning process?

In-Class Exercise: The State of Texas Strategic Planning Template

This exercise visits a web site organized by the State of Texas to provide people with an overview of the state government's strategic planning process. The site contains graphical illustrations of the elements of the state government's strategic plan, and textual narrative to explain how all the elements fit together.

Instructors should visit the following web site in class:

http://www.lbb.state.tx.us/lbb/members/reports/strat/ SP2.htm

Discussion about the site should center on the first illustration which displays all the different elements of the Texas state government's strategic plan. This is a complex "template." Students should be asked to reflect on the document to elicit their input on how useful they think it is. Who would find it useful? Do they think state agencies will use the template? Does the template help in the strategic planning process? Instructors should ask students what, if anything, is missing from the template.

Chapter 8

Out-of-Class Exercise: Downsizing: How To's for the Employer and Employees

The widespread practice of downsizing and "flattening" organizational hierarchies is a continuing phenomenon in organizations of all types. While it has to some extent gone out of "fashion," many managers continue to use downsizing as a means of cutting costs and streamlining operations.

There is no easy way to go about corporate downsizing. Not only will there be dramatic effects on organizational structure and work flow, but also on those who are let go and those who are left behind. Throughout the downsizing trend of the last decade, managers and employees alike have learned many lessons about how to organize and survive downsizing. The following web site offers a variety of useful tips for employers on how to conduct a downsizing and avoid costly lawsuits. It also offers tips to employees on how to survive a downsizing in their firm:

http://www.princetoninfo.com/sgdown.html

Students should visit the above web site outside of class. They should read all of the material *except* that under the

heading "Turnaround Time," and be prepared to discuss the following questions during the next class period:

1. Do you agree with the tips offered to employers about how to behave during a downsizing? What issues would you take up with these tips?
2. Do you agree with the tips offered to employees about how to survive a downsizing? What do you think is the mindset of employees who survive a downsizing?
3. What obligations do you think employers have to employees when a company goes through a downsizing?

In-Class Exercise: The Object Oriented Organization

For as long as there have been formal organizations, managers have been seeking the best way to organize people and processes to maximize productivity and efficiency. The various types of organizational structures studied in Chapter 8 are just a snapshot of the evolving "science" of organizational design. It will probably come as no surprise that management theorists are busy dreaming up the next organizational design that will make workers more effective, productive, and satisfied.

One new type of organizational structure is discussed at the web site listed below. The structure described at the site is known as the Object Oriented Organization. The OO Organization, as it is called, is based on the new "object oriented programming" approach that has made it easier to develop complex software. The OO Organization is discussed at the following web site:

http://www.goodnews.net/oiintl/matrix.html

Instructors should visit this site in class. Although there is a fair amount of text, it isn't difficult to read and understand.

Instructors should read the text aloud to the class and discuss the material as one goes along. More important, instructors should discuss the illustrations. The illustrations attempt to make clear why the OO Organization is superior for the current organizational content.

Discussion should focus first on understanding the OO Organization. What makes this structure different from other structures? Would the OO Organization work for all types of organizations? What flaws does it have? What new challenge does it offer for managers?

Chapter 9

Out-of-Class Exercise: CALSTART: A Virtual Organization Building Successful Businesses

One of the fastest-developing practices in business throughout the world involves firms in cooperative relationships with their suppliers, distributors, and even competitors. These networks of relationships enable organizations to achieve both efficiency and flexibility—to exploit the advantages of the mechanistic and organic organizational designs. These network organizations have become so pervasive that some experts refer to them as the models of twenty-first century organizations.

CALSTART is a non-profit California-based organization dedicated to the creation of an advanced transportation technologies industry and related markets. CALSTART is made up of over 200 companies and organizations involved in the electric, hybrid electric, natural gas and intelligent transportation systems arenas. CALSTART participants range from large companies like Toyota and Hewlett Packard to small start-up technology businesses.

CALSTART serves as a "strategic broker" in linking people and ideas together, further accelerating the pace of growth in this expanding industry. The organization provides key industry services that bring together people, technologies, and resources to bridge the gap between technology development and the marketplace. CALSTART has created and is now managing over $90 million in 50 different technology development programs.

CALSTART offers its participants a variety of core services, including: strategic information (e.g. newsletter,

newsnotes, and Internet web site); marketing visibility, networking/partnering, notification of funding opportunities, and technical assessment and feedback. Its web site is at the following address:

http://www.calstart.org/about/anr94/anr94vir.html

Students should visit the CALSTART web site out of class. The page at the above address describes CALSTART's status as a "virtual" organization. Students should read and explore this web site, and follow links to other CALSTART pages to get a feel for the organization's services. They should be prepared to discuss the following questions during the next class:

1. What is a virtual organization? Why does CALSTART see itself as such an organization? Do you agree that it is a virtual organization?

2. What benefits can organizations realize by partnering with CALSTART? What are some potential disadvantages of partnering with CALSTART?

3. What role does the Internet play in making virtual organizations such as CALSTART more common? Could such an organization exist without the Internet?

4. What are the advantages of a virtual organization over other organizational structures?

5. What is the CALSTART "Knowledge Network?" How does it help CALSTART's partner organizations?

Chapter 10

Out-of-Class Exercise: Quality Control in the Service Industries

The controlling function in management refers to all activities the manager undertakes in attempting to ensure that actual results conform to planned results. Quality control has taken on increased visibility in management because it has become a major competitive factor in the global economy. That is to say, along with price, product features, and other attributes important to consumers, the quality of a product or service has become vitally important.

All institutions, whether for manufacture, service or other purposes, face problems of attaining quality. In the case of the manufacturing industries, extensive work has been done in the last three decades to identify the quality problems which are common to all manufacture, and to discover common solutions to these problems. This search for commonality has led to identification and successful application of various universals of quality control.

It is only recently that the service industries have taken an equally hard look at quality control. The Malcolm Baldrige award for quality, for example, has only in the past few years added an "education" category, making educational institutions eligible for recognition based on the quality of their operations.

The web site listed below looks for the universals of quality control for service organizations.

http://www.juran.com/juran/download/papers/ SP7316.html

Students should visit this web site outside of class. They should read the entire site *(be sure to stress that students must read both Part I and Part II)* and be prepared to discuss the following questions during the next class period:

1. How does a service company differ fundamentally from a manufacturing company? What unique quality control problems does the service company face?

2. What does the term "fitness for use" mean? How does it apply to a service company?

3. Why do consumers of service companies have a sense of self-importance? What should service companies do about this attitude?

4. To what extent should a service company be concerned with "internal conformance?"

5. In what ways can a service company measure its "external conformance?"

Chapter 11

Out-of-Class Exercise: Employee Motivation and Morale

Many management theorists focus on employee motivation and morale as key factors in an organization's overall productivity and effectiveness. Certainly, few of use would disagree that an organization is likely to be more effective if it has satisfied, even happy, employees.

Although thousands of theorists have developed models and techniques for motivating employees and improving morale, no perfect model or technique is likely ever to be discovered. Thus, business bookshelves are bursting with titles offering new perspectives, new tools, and new insights into how to motivate workers. The empowerment movement is a good example of how "trendy" motivation theory can become. Empowerment theorists argue that employees will be more motivated and perform at a higher level if they are given responsibility and authority to act according to their own ideas about what's best for the organization. This idea has some value, and has led to many changes in the work place. It also has some limitations that managers must watch out for.

This exercise is designed to expose students to a range of new ideas in employee motivation and morale. The following web site contains a list of articles in this topic area:

http://www.fed.org/motivation/

Students should visit the above web site and choose to read at least three of the eight short articles listed. They should be prepared to discuss what they've learned during the next class period. Some questions they might consider include:

1. Do these articles incorporate any motivation theories discussed in the text? If so, which ones and to what extent?

2. Do these articles seem to develop an alternative theory of motivation; i.e., one that's different from anything in the text?

3. Of the articles you read, which one seems to offer insights and suggestions that you find easy to agree with? Why? Which one offers insights and suggestions that you can't agree with? Why?

In-Class Exercise: The Three R's of Employee Motivation

This is a simple exercise intended to expose students to an easy-to-remember recipe for effective employee motivation. The web site listed below is a short human resources newsletter called "News and Views" electronically published by a management consulting firm. The Winter 1995/96 issue featured a short article on "the Three R's" of employee

motivation: Responsibility, Recognition, and Rewards. This simple recipe for effective employee motivation is easily recalled, yet it conveys important truths about people and what they will respond to in the work place.

The News and Views newsletter is available at the following web address:

http://www.kgn.com/news/v14n4/manage.html

Instructors should visit this site in class and review the "Three R's" of employee motivation with the class. Discussion should center on how these management principles mesh with the motivation theories discussed in the text. How do the Three R's fit with Maslow's hierarchy of needs theory? With Herzberg's theory? How do the Three R's fit with other contemporary motivation theories such as employee empowerment and the movement towards work place teams?

Chapter 12

Out-of-Class Exercise: When Teams Don't Work

Today's work place is increasingly focusing on employee teams rather than individuals as a means of achieving organizational goals. The challenges faced by managers who must organize, lead, and control employee teams are daunting. Most work places have not been structured in a way that makes teamwork the norm. Reward systems, geographic plant layout, and other factors have always favored the individual over the group. In fact, it still makes big business news when some new company decides to organize its office space in a way that emphasizes group work space and de-emphasizes individual offices. Most middle-level and upper manager just aren't prepared for these radical changes.

Besides the "culture shock" that many managers face when trying to introduce and lead teams in the work place, many don't know what techniques will lead to productive team work. The following web site contains an excerpt from a book titled *Why Teams Don't Work:*

http://www.bitwise.net/iawww/IAWWW-WP-LEADERSHIP.HTML

Students should visit the above web site and read the entire excerpt. They should be prepared to discuss the following questions during the next class period:

1. What is often the problem when a team is ineffective?

2. How does the traditional notion of "leadership" compare to the notion of leadership that is necessary for effective teams?

3. Do you agree with the problems of leadership as discussed in this excerpt? Explain. Have you ever experienced some of these problems in a team environment?

4. Did you see yourself in any of the ineffective team leader styles discussed in this excerpt? How can you go about changing your behavior?

Chapter 13

Out-of-Class Exercise: Building a Personal Mission Statement

One of the most popular books of the last decade is Dr. Stephen R. Covey's *Seven Habits of Highly Effective People.* Covey studied effective people (i.e., leaders) and identified seven habits or disciplines they commonly follow to achieve their effectiveness. As a result of the success of that book,

Covey founded the Covey Leadership Center. The center is involved in providing training programs, books, articles, and other tools to help managers become more effective leaders.

This exercise is designed to help students begin a journey of becoming a more effective leader. It uses a free product at the Covey Leadership Center web site to help students develop a personal mission statement. According to Covey: "Creating a Personal Mission Statement will be, without question, one of the most powerful and significant things you will ever do to take leadership of your life. In it you will identify the first, most important roles, relationships, and things in your life—who you want to be, what you want to do, to whom and what you want to give your life, the principles you want to anchor your life to, the legacy you want to leave. All the goals and decisions you will make in the future will be based upon it. It's like deciding first which wall you want to lean your ladder of life against, and then beginning to climb. It will be a compass—a strong source of guidance amid the stormy seas and pressing, pulling currents of your life."

Whether or not a personal mission statement is as important as Covey thinks, this exercise will help students think about areas of their life where they can make improvements. The free personal mission statement tool is available at the following web site:

http://www.covey.com/mission/

Students should visit the above web site outside of class. They will be asked to provide personal information to obtain the mission statement tool. Students should be encouraged to leave only required information, unless they wish to receive future mailings from the Covey Leadership Center. The process of building a personal mission statement should take 10 to 15 minutes. Students should bring their personal mission statements to the next class period to discuss.

In-Class Exercise: Test Your Leadership Skills

One way for individuals to learn more about their leadership potential is to take any one of a number of diagnostic tests that are available. These tests, while not foolproof, do offer important feedback to individuals that helps them better understand their own behavior. Managers often participate in training activities that involve diagnostic tests to determine their skill or attitude levels on certain scales.

The web site below provides users with an opportunity to explore their skills in three areas: creating vision, aligning a team, and leadership style. Each of these leadership areas offers a simple diagnostic test and feedback that can be completed in just a few minutes of time. The web site is at the following address:

http://www.leaderx.com/

Instructors should visit this web site in class. Discuss with the class which diagnostic test they would prefer to take (Recommendation: encourage "leadership style"). Click on that choice, and you will be taken to a page where you will be able to choose the diagnostic test. The test for leadership style requires that an individual answer just 15 simple questions. These questions are answered on-line and submitted for immediate feedback on leadership style.

Instructors should either answer the questions themselves to reveal their own leadership styles, or ask one of the students to step forward and respond to the questions. At the least, instructors should respond to the questions and submit the completed form to demonstrate the process to students so that they may undertake a self-examination of their own leadership styles in private.

Following the self-analysis, instructors should discuss the diagnostic process with students. What are the limitations of this process? What are the strengths? What can people learn from such a test? What actions should people take in response to such a test? What actions should they not take?

Chapter 14

Out-of-Class Exercise: Exploring the Journal of Computer Mediated Communication

Increasingly, communication in and out of organizations is taking place over a new and relatively unknown medium: the "net." The world wide web, the Internet, Intranets, and other new networks of computers and people have opened a vast new realm of communication, problem solving, and deal making. Managers are just beginning to discover productivity gains through "groupware" such as Lotus Notes and other software packages that link employees to one another.

This exercise is designed to expose students to a so-called electronic journal that is dedicated to articles concerning the use of computers in communications for work and play. The journal can be viewed at the following web site:

http://207.201.161.120/jcmc/index.html

Students should visit the journal outside of class. For this exercise, they are asked to select volume 2, number 4 titled "Network and Netplay." Students should click on the link to that issue and select the "Editor's Introduction" to read. They should read this entire article prior to the next class. WARNING: The article, and the journal in general, is fairly academic and uses technical language in some places. Students should be encouraged to read the article nonetheless and develop an understanding of the issues faced with computer-mediated communication.

Chapter 15

Out-of-Class Exercise: Compensation and Benefits—What Are the Options?

People decide to become employees of organizations for a number of reasons. One of the primary reasons is money. The way organizations compensate employees can have a profound effect on their motivation and productivity. Managers need to be able to match their approach to compensation with organizational goals and with employee needs. Different employees respond differently to alternative compensation schemes. In addition, different organizational goals are better achieved with alternative compensation schemes.

Besides monetary compensation, employees are also attracted to organizations based on the benefits they offer. Many organizations offer employees insurance and other types of benefits. As with compensation schemes, managers must be able to determine the benefits package that best meets organizational and employee needs.

The web site visited for this exercise provides students with in-depth information on employee compensation and benefits. It introduces different compensation schemes and when they should be applied, and discusses various benefit packages. Students should visit the following web site outside of class:

http://www.auxillium.com/contents.htm

Once at this site, they can review the different topics that are available for further exploration. For this exercise, students are asked to click on the heading *"Compensation and Benefits."* They should read the entire web site and be prepared to discuss the following questions during the next class period. However, students should be encouraged to review the other sites for more information on human resources management.

1. What is meant by the term "pay equity?" Why do managers need to be concerned with pay equity in the work place?

2. What is meant by the term "variable pay systems?" What are the factors that have led to increasing use of variable pay systems?

3. What are the different types of variable pay systems? Give an example of an organizational context where each type would be appropriate.

4. What are the retirement plan options that employers can offer employees? What are the insurance plan options?

In-Class Exercise: Dilbert Reflects on the Work Place

One of the more innovative comic strips dealing with the work place is Dilbert. Dilbert is an engineer with a slightly jaded view of the work place, managers, and fellow employees. The strip is written by cartoonist Scott Adams and is syndicated to major newspapers around the world. The following web site is sponsored by United Media, Dilbert's publisher:

http://www.unitedmedia.com/comics/dilbert

Instructors should visit this web site in class for some humorous perspectives on the modern work place. Management is filled with serious models and prescriptions for success. This comic strip pokes fun at that seriousness and reveals some painful truths about bosses, workers, and life in organizations.

Chapter 16

Out-of-Class Exercise: Another Perspective on Organizational Change

Organizational change and its effects on productivity, people, and processes is one of the most intensely studied issues in management theory. Models and strategies abound, leaving the typical manager confused about which models work and what strategies are appropriate for a given situation.

This exercise is designed to take students to a web site that offers another perspective on organizational change. The purpose is not simply to expose students to another perspective, but rather to give them insight into the kinds of messages practicing managers are receiving from consultants and organizational change theorists.

Students should visit the following web site outside of class:

http://www.tiac.net/users/praxis/article.html

Students should read the brief article on organizational change featured at this web site. They should be prepared to discuss the following questions during the next class period:

1. After years of analyzing change and living in its midst, why should modern organizations, their managers, and employees still feel ill-prepared when change does occur?

2. To illustrate revolutionary change, Ralph Siu, Professor of Management Science at MIT, suggests that there is a new Organizational baseball game today. What does he mean by this analogy?

3. Do you think that organizational change occurs in the manner discussed in this article?

4. What role does the employee play in organizational change? How can the change process be managed to minimize employee stress and speed up the process of implementing change?

Chapter 17

Out-of-Class Exercise: A Look at Agile Manufacturing

Manufacturing organizations are constantly looking for more efficient and effective ways to produce products. The scientific management techniques of the turn of the century have long been replaced by other approaches. In the past few decades, manufacturing companies have adopted techniques that allow them to make optimal use of emerging information technologies. Among these techniques are lean manufacturing, flexible manufacturing, and now a new approach known as "agile manufacturing."

Agile manufacturing was first made famous in a book about the automobile industry titled *The Machine That Changed the World.* Agile manufacturing focuses on managing the "web" of relationships that manufacturing companies are involved in as part of the overall production process. The agile manufacturing approach in the automobile and aerospace industries is well articulated in a paper from the Massachusetts Institute of Technology at the following web site:

http://web.mit.edu/ctpid/www/agile/atlanta.html

Students should visit this web site outside of class and read the entire document, including the appendices. They should be prepared to discuss the following questions during the next class period.

1. What is agile manufacturing? How does it differ from other manufacturing techniques discussed in the text?

2. What new developments have made it possible for manufacturing companies to use the agile manufacturing approach?

3. What advantages will agile manufacturing offer companies compared to traditional approaches to manufacturing?

4. Can the techniques of agile manufacturing be transferred to a service environment? Draw a diagram showing the web of relationships for an athletic shoe retailer.

In-Class Exercise: Linking to a Variety of Operations Management Web Sites

The Internet is a wonderful place where individuals with widely diverse interests have an opportunity to explore and express those interests. Often times, individuals provide a valuable service for others by pursuing their interests on the net.

The web site at the address listed below was compiled by an individual named Ross L. Fink. Mr. Fink's interest in operations management has led him to develop the web site which has number of links to operations management web sites. His driving interest has provided the casual user with a valuable service. If one wishes to explore some aspect of operations management, Mr. Fink's web site is a good place to begin.

http://bradley.bradley.edu/~rf/opman.html

The above web site should be visited in class. Instructors should demonstrate to students the wealth of operations management links available at this site. Instructors may want to explore a few of the links to assess their value. It should be demonstrated that one can always return Mr. Fink's web site to re-orient and further explore other topics.

Chapter 18

Out-of-Class Exercise: The Inventory Management Newsletter

The Internet has made available to people a wide range of publications that would not ordinarily be accessible. This wide range of publications covers an equally wide range of

topic areas. Paradoxically, the broader the range of topic areas covered, the more narrow is the scope of individual publications.

The *Inventory Management Newsletter* is the type of publication that wouldn't ordinarily be available to people.

However, because publishing on the web is such a low-cost proposition, the Center for Inventory Management is able to publish material that is of use to people all over the world.

The web site listed below is the address for the *Inventory Management Newsletter:*

http://www.inventorymanagement.com/imnl1997.htm

Students should visit this web site outside of class and read at least two of the articles presented. Students should be encouraged to read articles that cover new or interesting topics, or that extend the discussion in the text. They should be prepared to discuss the articles they've read during the next class period. Instructors should lead the discussion, focusing on the following issues:

1. What are emerging trends in inventory management?
2. What approaches or techniques that you read about in the newsletter seem to contradict or revise what was discussed in the text?
3. What traditional inventory management techniques, if any, seem to be fading in popularity? Why is that happening?

Chapter 19

Out-of-Class Exercise: Data Warehousing and the World Wide Web

The nature of decision support systems is changing as rapidly as the technology used to create the systems. Database systems of the recent past were often set up to the needs of a single user. This created problems in that often more than one user needs the information. The other problem created by this approach is that the user-specific database system often could not communicate with other databases, making it difficult to analyze related data.

Enter the Internet with its power of networking individuals with diverse systems and needs. The new networking technologies are beginning to make proprietary databases a thing of the past. The new movement is toward "relational" databases, linking data from diverse sources to create rich new insights into organizational processes. The new insights are often difficult to obtain amidst the wealth of information that has suddenly become available. Managers have turned to a new technique known as "data mining" to help retrieve valuable insights from the variety of networked databases.

The web site listed below will expose students to these new developments in decision support systems. The web site features a discussion of relational on-line analytical processing (ROLAP), including discussions of the power of the web and data mining. It is located at the following address:

http://www.strategy.com/dwf/v9n6.htm#H

Students should visit the above web site outside of class. They should read the entire document and be prepared to discuss the following questions during the next class period:

1. What is relational on-line analytical processing (ROLAP)? How does it add anything new to the decision support systems available to managers?
2. What is data mining? Why do you think managers need to use data mining techniques?
3. What is data warehousing? How do managers use data warehousing?
4. What are the arguments that a manager can make in favor of investing in development of a ROLAP system? What new efficiencies and capabilities can reasonably be justified by moving to such a system?

Chapter 20

Out-of-Class Exercise: Developing an Entrepreneurial Mind Set

One of the most difficult parts of being an entrepreneur, a part that most likely cannot be taught, is developing an entrepreneurial mind set. An entrepreneurial mind set is the beliefs and attitudes one develops that will help carry the entrepreneur through the difficulties of starting and running their own business. This mindset has to be based in enthusiasm, a propensity for favoring action over contemplation, and an unwavering desire to be their own boss.

One way to develop this mindset is to get excited about the stories of others who have become successful entrepreneurs. Listening to successful entrepreneurs often gives students the sense that, "if they can do it, so can I." The enthusiasm for entrepreneurship often begins by listening to or reading about others' success.

The following web address links to *Inc.* magazine, the magazine for and about entrepreneurs. Each monthly issue of this magazine contains stories about people who saw a need and created a business to serve that need. The stories are often invigorating in that they tell the tale of average individuals who have become very successful through entrepreneurship. *Inc.* magazine can be viewed at the following web address:

http://www.inc.com/

Students should visit the web site outside of class. They should select the current issue of the magazine and choose to read at least one article about an entrepreneur. They should be prepared to discuss the following questions during the next class period:

1. What is the entrepreneur story that you read? What special background did the entrepreneur have that led to their success?
2. Did the story indicate to you in any way that entrepreneurship is only for a few "elite" individuals in our society? Why or why not?
3. What new product or service ideas do you think you could pursue as an entrepreneur?
4. What are the barriers you face to becoming an entrepreneur? How could those barriers be overcome?

In-Class Exercise: 10 Great Ideas for Starting a Health, Beauty or Fitness Business

The following web site features ideas on starting new businesses in the health, beauty, or fitness industries. Undergraduate students are often interested in starting businesses in these industries because they appeal to their current lifestyles. This web site will get them thinking about opportunities, and expose them to the wide range of business opportunities that exist for people with persistence and commitment.

**http://www.entrepreneurmag.com/
page.hts?N=1191&Ad=S**

Instructors should link to the above web site in class. There is a list of business opportunities in the various industries at this site. Instructors may want to click on one or more of the options to explore more in-depth the opportunities that exist. Discussion should center on what students think about the potential for the various options. What obstacles exist to starting such a business? What skills and abilities are required of the entrepreneur in the various industries? What is the future potential of the business?

Chapter 21

Out-of-Class Exercise: Resume Writing

Students on the verge of seeking their first management position are often in the dark about how to write an effective resume and cover letter. There are often resume-writing workshops on campuses, but few students have the time or inclination to attend. Although resumes alone will not win the critical first position, a poor resume can be the kiss of death.

The web site below offers students a wealth of tips on writing effective resumes and cover letters. Students should visit the following web site outside of class time and be prepared to discuss their own resumes during the next class period. They should be prepared to critique their and their classmates' resumes in light of what they have learned.

**http://www.careermag.com/careermag/newsarts/
resume.html**

Students should select at least three of the clickable items on this page to learn about tips on resume and cover letter writing. They should critique their own resumes in light of

what they learned and be prepared to critique other resumes during the next class period. This is not meant to be a critical discussion, but rather a time for students to provide one another with constructive feedback on the content and look of their resumes.

In-Class Exercise: Careers in Management

The web site listed below provides real-time graphs for a variety of career-related statistics. Instructors should visit this web site in class and discuss the data with students:

http://jwtworks.com/hrlive/factsfig/index.html

Click on the topic heading of choice. The site will automatically draw graphs of current trends in hiring, compensation, and educational requirements. Discussion should center on the meaning of the various graphs for students in their current situations. Instructors should also lead a discussion about what these data mean for employers.

Acculturation   The transfer of culture from one ethnic group to another. It is a gradual process where one or more minority groups is merged with a majority group.

Actions   The means, or specific activities, planned to achieve objectives that have been determined.

Activity   The work necessary to complete a particular event in a PERT network. An activity consumes time, which is the paramount variable in a PERT system. In PERT networks, three time estimates are used for each activity: an optimistic time, a pessimistic time, and a most likely time.

Affirmative Action Program   A program in which an employer specifies how the company plans to increase the number of minority and female employees.

Allocation Model   This type of management science model is used in a situation where several candidates or activities all compete for limited resources. It enables the user to allocate scarce resources to maximize some predetermined objective.

Altruism   An ethical standard which places highest value on behavior that is pleasurable and rewarding to society.

Americans with Disabilities Act of 1990   An antidiscrimination law aimed at integrating the disabled into the workforce. There are now estimated to be approximately 43 million Americans with some type of disability.

Anthropology   The behavioral science that studies learned behaviors of individuals and groups. It seeks general laws that explain intercultural and extracultural behavior. This includes social, technical, and family behaviors. It is often defined as the study of humans and their work.

Arbitration   A method used in labor-management disputes in which a third party listens to both sides,

analyzes the arguments, and makes a decision that is binding on the union and management.

Assimilation   A situation in which every person is expected to conform to the values and norms of the dominant culture.

Attitude   A person's tendency to feel and behave toward some object in some way.

Authority   The legitimate right to use assigned resources to accomplish a delegated task or objective; the right to give orders and to exact obedience. The legal bases for formal authority are private property, the state, or a Supreme Being.

Behavior   Any observable response given by a person.

Behavior Modification   An approach to motivation that uses operant conditioning: Operant behavior is learned on the basis of consequences. In management, if a behavior causes a desired outcome (for managers), then it is reinforced (positively rewarded), and because of its consequences is likely to be repeated. Thus, behavior is conditioned by adjusting its consequences.

Behavioral Approach to Management   A body of literature characterized by its concern for human behavior in the work environment. The school's primary means for acquiring knowledge is the scientific method, with emphasis on research. Chronologically, the behavioral approach to management thought followed the classical approach. Its first phase was identified with human relations theory, popular in the 1940s and early 1950s. Its second phase was the behavioral science approach, which came into popular use in the early 1950s.

Behavioral Change   Planned change in the attitudes, skills, and knowledge of organizational personnel.

Behavioral Motivation Theory   The behavioral approach to management advocates the pluralistic view of motivation, which emphasizes that many different needs influence behavior and that man is motivated by the desire to satisfy many needs.

Behavioral Science Approach   This approach to the study of management can be thought of as the study of observable and verifiable human behavior in organizations, using scientific procedures. It draws especially from psychology, sociology, and anthropology.

Behaviorally Anchored Rating Scales (BARS)   A set of rating scales developed by raters and/or rates that uses critical behavioral incidents as interval anchors on each scale. About 6 to 10 scales with behavioral incidents are used to derive the evaluation.

Benefits   Financial payments (e.g., insurance premiums) made by an employer over and above the base wages and salary.

Bill of Materials   A document that details the required components of each subassembly and finished good. The demand for components is derived from the demand for the subassemblies and finished goods.

Brainstorming   A technique for stimulating group creativity. The technique uses a series of rules to promote the generation of ideas while eliminating group members' feelings of inhibition.

Budgeting   Identifying the sources and levels of resources that can be committed to future courses of action an organization is planning to take.

Bureaucracy   An organizational design that relies on specialization of labor, a specific authority hierarchy, a formal set of rules and procedures, and rigid promotion and selection criteria.

Business Plan   A written report that provides an overview and analysis of a proposed business. The plan is the basis for presentations to prospective investors in the business.

Business Portfolio Matrix   A method commonly used in an organization's portfolio plan; the method was developed by the Boston Consulting Group. The basic purpose of the method is to assist management in deciding how much resource support should be budgeted to each strategic business unit.

Career   An individually perceived sequence of attitudes and behaviors associated with work-related experiences and activities over the span of a person's life.

Career Path   Beginning with a particular job, the sequence of jobs involved in promotion and advancement.

Career Planning   The process of systematically matching an individual's career aspirations with opportunities for achieving them.

Career Plateau   The point or stage of a career at which the individual has no opportunity for further promotion or advancement.

Career Stages   Distinct but interrelated steps or phases of a career, including the establishment stage, the advancement stage, the maintenance stage, and the withdrawal stage.

Carrying Costs   The costs incurred by carrying an inventory. They include such costs as the taxes and insurance on the goods in inventory, interest on money invested in inventory and storage space, and the costs incurred because of the obsolescence of the inventory.

Categorical Imperative   An ethical standard that judges behavior in its consistency with the principle: "Act as if the maxim of your action were to become a general law binding on everyone."

Central Data Bank   The core of a decision support system. The data bank contains all of the information vital to the organization and makes it readily available for decision making in other areas.

Centralization   A dimension of organization structure that refers to the extent to which authority is retained in the jobs of top management.

Certainty Decision   A decision in which the manager is certain about the state of nature or competitor action that will occur. Thus, the probability that a particular event will occur is 1.00.

Child Care   The care of employees' children—a benefit that some firms provide. There are some organizations that provide child care in organizationally sponsored day care centers. The first day care center opened in New York City in 1827.

Civil Rights Act of 1991   A law passed prohibiting discrimination on the basis of race and prohibiting racial harassment; the law returns the burden of proof that discrimination did not occur back to the employer and reinforces the illegality of employers' making hiring, firing, or promoting decisions based on race, ethnicity, sex, or religion.

Classical Approach to Management   A body of literature that represents the earliest attempts to define and describe the field of management. The approach's main focus is on formally prescribed relationships. Its primary means for acquiring knowledge are personal observation and case studies.

Classical Organizational Design   An approach to organizational design that relies on such management principles as unity of command, a balance between authority and responsibility, division of labor, and delegation to establish relationships between managers and subordinates.

Code of Ethics (or Code of Conduct)   Statement of a company's values, beliefs, and norms of ethical behavior, usually established by top management. The code should ideally provide employees with guidelines for handling ethical dilemmas as well as clarify the firm's position regarding areas of ethical uncertainty and concerning its relationships and responsibilities toward its different constituents.

Coercive Power   The power of a leader that is derived from fear. The follower perceives the leader as a person who can punish deviant behavior and actions.

Cognitive Dissonance   A state in which there is a discrepancy between a person's attitude and behavior.

Collective Bargaining   The process used by unions and management to reach a negotiated contract settlement.

Command Group   The group of employees who report to a single manager, as shown on an organizational chart.

Communication   The transmission of information and understanding through the use of common symbols.

Comparable Worth   The issue that relates to the fact that when women dominate an occupational field (such as nursing), the rate of pay for jobs within those occupations appears to be depressed unfairly when compared with the pay that men receive when working in jobs where they are the dominant incumbents within one occupation (e.g., ironworkers and construction).

Complexity   A dimension of organization structure that refers to the extent to which jobs in an organization are relatively specialized.

Concessionary Bargaining   The act of givebacks or concessions being made by the union to management as a result of economic problems; the firm's existence or long-term survival is the theme that management has used to secure concessions.

Concurrent Control   The techniques and methods that focus on the actual, ongoing activity of the organization.

Consideration   One of the two dimensions in the leadership model developed as a result of the 1945 Ohio State studies of leadership. This dimension reflects the degree to which a leader creates a work atmosphere of mutual trust, respect for subordinates' ideas, and consideration of subordinates' feelings.

Content Theories   Theories about human motivation that are concerned with identifying what it is within an individual or the work environment that energizes and sustains behavior.

Contingency Approach to Organization Design   A set of ideas contending that there is more than one "best way" to design an organization. Depending on the nature of such factors as strategy, environment, and technology, either the classical or neoclassical design might work.

Continuous Bargaining   A situation in which a joint labor-management committee meets on a regular basis to explore and solve problems.

Continuous Reinforcement   A reinforcement schedule that involves administering a reward each time a desired behavior occurs.

Controlling Function   All managerial activity undertaken to assure that actual operations go according to plan.

Cost Leadership Strategy   An overall corporate strategy that involves being the lowest-cost producer in the industry.

Critical Path   The longest path (in terms of time) in a PERT network, from the network beginning event to the network ending event.

Culture   A very complex environmental influence that includes knowledge, beliefs, law, morals, art, customs, and any other habits and capabilities an individual acquires as a member of society. It is important to be aware that cultures are learned, cultures vary, and culture influences behavior.

Decentralization   The delegation of the appropriate amount of decision-making authority. All organizations practice a certain degree of decentralization.

Decision Making   The process of thought and deliberation that results in a decision. Decisions, the output of the decision-making process, are means through which a manager seeks to achieve some desired state.

Decoding   The mental procedure that the receiver of a message uses to decipher the message.

Delegation   The process by which authority is distributed downward in an organization.

Delphi Technique   A technique used for group decision making. This technique involves the solicitation and comparison of anonymous judgments on the issue at hand through a series of sequential questionnaires.

Departmentalization   The process of grouping jobs together on the basis of some common characteristic such as product, process, client, location, or function.

Differentiation Strategy   An overall corporate strategy that involves creating real and perceived differences between the firm's products/services and those of competitors.

Direct Investment Entry Strategy   The strongest commitment to becoming an MNC, when management decides to begin producing the firm's products abroad. This strategy enables the firm to maintain partial to full control over production, marketing, and other key functions.

Direction   A method of concurrent control that refers to the manager's acts of communicating orders to subordinates and overseeing their work.

Discounted Rate of Return   The rate of return that equates future cash proceeds with the initial cost of an investment taking into account the time value of money.

Distinctive Competence   A factor that gives the organization an advantage over similar organizations.

Distinctive competencies are what the organization does best.

Distributive Bargaining A situation in which there is a fixed resource or issue and labor and management negotiate in this win-lose circumstance.

Diversification A strategy used by an organization when it seeks new products for new customers.

Downsizing A decision that involves laying people off in order to improve the efficiency and cost position of the company.

Downward Communication Communication that flows from individuals at higher levels of an organization structure to individuals at lower levels. The most common type of downward communication is job instructions transmitted from the superior to the subordinate.

Drug Testing An increasingly used procedure to identify drug abusers among job applicants and in some firms, employees. Controversy surrounds drug testing because of claims that it is an invasion of privacy and that the results are inaccurate in too many instances.

Dual Career Path A sequence of career moves designed to provide nonmanagerial professionals with the opportunity to advance upward, receiving the same rewards and prestige as their managerial counterparts while still working in their professional fields.

Econometric Model A sophisticated technique used to forecast both sales and availability of resources.

Economic Order Quality (EOQ) Model The economic order quantity model, which is used to resolve problems regarding the size of orders. A manager concerned with minimizing inventory costs could utilize the model to study the relationships between carrying costs, ordering costs, and usage.

Egoism An ethical standard which places higher value on behavior that is pleasurable and rewarding to the individual.

Elder Care As the US population ages, more attention is being paid to caring for parents and elder citizens. The care of elders is likely to be an important issue as the human resource management planners for benefits analyze the costs and the benefits.

Emergent Leader A person from within the group who naturally comes to lead or influence its members.

Employee Polygraph Protection Act of 1988 A law prohibiting private sector employers from using polygraph tests on applicants or employees—with a few exceptions.

Employee Stock Owner Plans (ESOPs) Plans that permit employees to secure ownership of the organization for which they work by purchasing stock.

Empowerment The act of providing employees at all levels the authority and responsibility to make decisions on their own.

Encoding The converting of a communication into an understandable message by a communicator.

Entrepreneur An individual who establishes and manages a business.

Equal Employment Opportunity Act of 1972 A law that has specific provisions about equal opportunities for employment.

Equal Employment Opportunity Commission (EEOC) A commission created with the authority to prohibit all forms of employment discrimination.

Equal Pay Act of 1963 A law forbidding employers to pay employees differently on the basis of sex.

Equity Theory A motivation explanation proposed by J. Stacy Adams. He proposed that when a person believes that her input/output ratio compared with that of another person is not in balance or fair, a state of inequity exists; the person would be motivated to bring her comparisons back to a state of equity.

Esteem Needs The needs for both the awareness of importance to others and for the regard accorded by others.

Ethics Principles that distinguish right from wrong behavior.

European Community (EC) An economic alliance of 12 European countries who have agreed to support mutual growth and to remove tariff and other trade barriers between the member nations.

European Currency Unit (ECU) The common currency that the 12 EC countries will use to replace individual nation currencies.

Event An accomplishment at a particular point in time on a PERT network. An event consumes no time.

Exception Principle A principle of management that deals with the regulation of information flow and states that (for purposes of reducing the likelihood of information overload) only significant deviations from policies and procedures should be brought to the attention of managers.

Expectancy Motivation Model A model that views motivation as a process governing choices. In this model, a person who has a goal weighs the likelihood that various behaviors will achieve that goal and is likely to select the behavior he expects to be most successful.

Expected Time (t_e) A time estimate for each activity that is calculated by using the following formula:

$$t_e = \frac{a + 4m + b}{6}$$

where a = optimistic time, m = most likely time, and b = pessimistic time.

Expected Value The average return of a particular decision in the long run if the decision maker makes the same decision in the same situation over and over again. The expected value is found by taking the value of an outcome if it should occur and multiplying that value by the probability that the outcome will occur.

Expert Power The power that individuals possess because followers perceive them to have special skills, special knowledge, or special expertise.

Export Entry Strategy The simplest way for a firm to enter a foreign market is by exporting. This strategy involves little or no change in the basic mission, objectives, and strategies, since the organization continues to produce all of its products at home. The firm usually secures an agent in the particular foreign market to facilitate the transactions with foreign buyers.

External Beneficiary A group or member of a group that has no apparent stake in an organization but benefits from the organization's successful activities nonetheless. External beneficiaries can be specific—a well-defined group, for example, whose needs can be affected by a corporation's actions—or general—society as a whole when a corporation's activities address environmental issues, for example.

External Change Forces Forces for change outside the organization, such as the pricing strategies of competitors, the available supply of resources, and government regulations.

Extinction A behavior modification practice that involves withholding positive rewards to change behavior.

Extrinsic Rewards Rewards such as pay, promotion, and time off that are given by a manager to motivate employees.

Fair Credit and Reporting Act of 1971 A law requiring a prospective employer to secure an applicant's permission before checking her references.

Fair Labor Standard Act of 1938 A law forbidding the employment of minors between 16 and 18 years of age in such hazardous occupations as coal mining, logging, and woodworking.

Family and Medical Leave Act of 1993 Federal legislation that provides employees up to 12 weeks of unpaid leave each year to care for family members or to tend to their own medical problems.

Feedback Control Techniques and methods that analyze historical data to correct future events.

First-Level Management The lowest level of the hierarchy. A manager at this level coordinates the work of nonmanagers but reports to a manager.

Flexible Manufacturing Technology A modern manufacturing method that, through use of the computer, integrates various operations within an organization.

Flextime A work schedule that gives a person some choice on the hours she will be present at work.

Focus Strategy An overall corporate strategy that involves developing either a cost leadership or differentiation strategy in a specific market segment of an industry.

Forecasting The process of using past and current information to predict future events. It is an important element of the planning function when it is used to make two basic determinations: (1) what level of activity can be expected during the planning period and (2) what level of resources will be available to support the projected activity. In a business organization, the critical forecast is the sales forecast.

Foreign Activities Entry Strategy As exports increase in importance to the firm, the company may decide that it can justify its own foreign activities. This decision usually involves joining with nationals in the foreign country to establish product and/or marketing facilities. The strategy differs from direct investment in that some type of association is formed with a local firm or individual, usually in the form of licensing or joint venture arrangements. Licensing is granting the right to produce and/or market the firm's product in another country to an outside firm. Joint venture arrangements involve foreign investors forming a group with local investors to begin a local business, with each group sharing ownership.

Formal Group A group formed due to its members' positions within the organization.

Formalization A dimension of organization structure that refers to the extent to which policies, rules, and procedures exist in written form.

Friendship Group An informal group that evolves because of some common characteristic such as age, political sentiment, or background.

Functional Job Analysis (FJA) A type of job analysis that focuses on four dimensions of an individual job—what the worker does in relation to data, people, and jobs; methods and techniques; equipment used; and products and services produced.

Geographic Expansion The stage of an organization's growth through which it continues to do what it has been, but in a larger geographic area by means of field units.

Good Movable personal property—one type of output produced by a system.

Grapevine An informal communication network in organizations that short-circuits the formal channels.

Graphic Rating Scales   A printed form with various job dimensions used by an appraiser to provide a rating for each appraisee.

Griggs v. *Duke Power*   A landmark Supreme Court decision stating that an employment test must fairly measure the knowledge or skills required for a job.

Group Assets   The advantages derived from the increase in knowledge that is brought to bear on a problem when a group examines it.

Group Cohesiveness   The attraction of individual members to a group in terms of the strength of the forces that impel them to remain active in the group and to resist leaving it.

Group Development   The phases or sequences through which a group passes: mutual acceptance, decision making, motivation, and control.

Group Liabilities   The negative features of groups, such as the group pressure that is expected to bring dissident members into line, the takeover by a dominant member, and the reduced creativity that results from the embarrassment of members about expressing themselves.

Group Negotiations   Negotiations that take place whenever the work of one group is dependent on the cooperation and actions of another group over which the first group's manager has no control.

Group Norm   Agreement among a group's members about how they should behave.

Groupthink   A phenomenon that occurs when a group believes that it is invincible, turns off criticism, attempts to bring noncomplying members into line, and feels that everyone is in agreement.

Hierarchy of Needs   A widely adopted pluralistic framework of motivation developed by psychologist A. H. Maslow. The theory stresses two ideas: (1) Only needs not yet satisfied can influence behavior; and (2) human needs are arranged in a hierarchy of importance—when one level has been satisfied, a higher-level need emerges and demands satisfaction. Maslow distinguishes five general classes of needs: physiological, safety, social, esteem, and self-actualization.

Honesty Tests   A specialized paper and pencil test designed to assess a person's honesty.

Horizontal Communication   A type of communication that occurs when the communicator and the receiver are at the same level in the organization.

Human Relations Approach   An approach to management that emphasizes the important role individuals play in determining the success or failure of an organization. It embarked on the critical task of compensating for some of the deficiencies in classical theory. Basically, it took the premises of the classical approach as given, but showed how these premises were modified as a result of individual behavior and the influence of the work group.

Human Resource Management   The process of accomplishing organizational objectives by acquiring, retaining, terminating, developing, and properly using the human resources in an organization.

Human Resource Planning   The process of estimating the size and makeup of the future workforce.

Implementation   The assignment and direction of personnel to carry out a plan.

Incremental Influence   This concept refers to the influence of a leader over and above the influence base best owed by position in the organization.

Individualism   The tendency of people to look after themselves and their immediate family.

Informal Groups   Natural groupings of people in response to some need.

Information Center   A central entity within an organization that gathers and processes information; it oversees the operation of the central data bank.

Initiating Structure   Leadership acts that develop job tasks and responsibilities for followers.

Instrumentality   A person's belief that various work-related outcomes will occur because of task performance.

Integrative Bargaining   A situation in which the union and management work at resolving a number of issues. There is a give-and-take atmosphere in the negotiation.

Interest Group   A group formed to achieve some job-related but personal objective.

Intergroup Conflict   The disagreements, hostile emotions, and problems that exist among groups. These conflicts emerge because of limited resources, communication problems, differences in perceptions and attitudes, and a lack of clarity.

Intermittent Reinforcement   A reinforcement schedule that involves rewarding desired behavior only periodically.

Internal Beneficiary   A group or member of a group that has an immediate and often conflicting stake in an organization. Customers, employees, and shareholders are all internal beneficiaries of organizations.

Internal Change Forces   Forces for change that occur within the organization, such as communication problems, morale problems, and decision-making breakdowns.

Interpersonal Communications   Communication flows from individual to individual in face-to-face and group settings, varying in form from direct orders to casual expressions.

Intragroup Conflict The disagreements and problems that exist among members within the same group. These conflicts can emerge due to incompatible goals, perceptions, or emotions.

Intrinsic Rewards Rewards such as self-regulation, pride, and increased self-worth that occur by performing a job.

Job Analysis The procedures for determining the tasks that make up a job, and the skills, abilities, and responsibilities an employee needs to do the job.

Job Depth The relative freedom that a jobholder has in the performance of assigned duties:

Job Description A statement derived from the job analysis that provides information about the job's title, duties, working conditions, materials and equipment used, potential hazards, and the kind of supervision involved.

Job Enlargement A form of despecialization in that the number of tasks performed by the employees is increased. The increase in tasks theoretically makes the job more interesting and challenging. Consequently, work becomes more psychologically rewarding.

Job Enrichment Suggested formally by Herzberg, this involves building into individual jobs greater scope for personal achievement, recognition, and responsibility. It is concerned primarily with strengthening the motivational factors and only incidentally with maintenance.

Job Evaluation Attaching a dollar value to a job so that comparisons of jobs on the basis of value can be made.

Job Range A reference to the number of activities performed on the job.

Job Specification A statement, derived from the job analysis, about the human qualifications needed to perform the job.

Joint Venture An alliance formed between a domestic firm or partner and a foreign firm or partner. The foreign firm or partner (the local) shares mutual ownership with a domestic firm or partner (e.g., United States, Canada).

Just-in-Time (JIT) Inventory Control A refined application of MRP that results in components becoming available at the precise moment in time when they are required. The effect of JIT is to reduce to a minimum the carrying cost of component parts.

Labor Management Relations Act of 1947 Also known as the Taft-Hartley Act, a law specifying that wages, hours, conditions of employment, and safety are *mandatory* issues for bargaining.

Lead Time The length of time between ordering and receiving an item of inventory. Inventory on hand must be sufficient to meet demand during the lead-time period.

Leader–Member Relations In the Fiedler situational model of leadership, a factor that refers to the degree of confidence, trust, and respect that followers have in the leader.

Leadership In the context of management theory, the ability of a person to influence the activities of followers in an organizational setting.

Legitimate Power The power that rank gives to a leader in the managerial hierarchy. For example, the department manager possesses more legitimate power than the supervisor because the department manager is ranked higher than the supervisor.

Less Developed Country (LDC) A country with a very low gross national product, very little industry, or a vastly unequal distribution of income, and with a very large number of poor.

Linear Programming A production planning technique with widespread applicability in organizations that produce repetitive and routine products and services. The technique enables management to make the optimal allocation of resources to alternative products and services.

Lockout A management action to keep employees from working by closing the firm with the intention of bringing pressure on union members to settle a labor dispute.

Maintenance Factors Distinguished by Herzberg in his two-factor theory of motivation, those conditions of the job that operate primarily to dissatisfy employees when they are not present. However, the presence of these factors does not build strong motivation among employees. Herzberg distinguished 16 of these factors (e.g., salary, job security, work conditions).

Management Development The process of educating and developing selected personnel so that they have the knowledge, skills, attitudes, and understanding needed to manage in the future.

Management Science Approach A body of literature characterized by its use of mathematical and statistical techniques to build models for the solution of production and operations problems. The approach's primary means for acquiring knowledge is mathematical deduction.

Managerial Grid Theory Also (now) known as the Leadership Grid, a personal–behavioral leadership theory that makes use of a two-dimensional grid on which a leader's style is plotted. The grid is used as a framework to help managers learn about their own style and keep track of their progression toward the ideal leadership style: (9,9) on the grid.

Managerial Roles   The organized sets of behavior that belong to the manager's job. The three main types of managerial roles discovered by such researchers as Mintzberg are interpersonal, informational, and decisional roles.

Manufacturing Resource Planning (MRP II)   An advanced version of material requirements planning, which integrates production planning, inventory control, and strategic planning.

Maquiladoras   A Spanish term that describes foreign plants that operate in Mexico as assembly units with special tariff privileges.

Market Development Strategies   Strategies that an organization uses when seeking new customers for its present products.

Market Penetration Strategies   Strategies that focus on improving the position of the organization's present products with its present customers.

Marketing Objectives   Goals established by an organization that relate to products, markets, distribution, and customer service. They focus on the prospects for longrun profitability.

Masculinity   The degree of achievement preference, assertiveness, and materialism that exists in a society.

Master Production Schedule   A document that details the planned production of all finished goods for a particular time period. The master production schedule is based on the strategic plan and the production plan.

Material Requirements Planning (MRP)   An inventory planning and controlling technique that involves identifying each component and subassembly of a complete product and then coordinating the ordering and delivering of those components and subassemblies. The technique usually requires a computer to deal with the mass of required information.

Maturity   As used in leadership theory, the term refers to the willingness of individuals and groups to take responsibility for directing their own behavior. The two dimensions of maturity are job maturity (ability to do the job) and psychological maturity (willingness to do the job).

Mechanistic System   An organizational design in which there is differentiation of job tasks, rigid rules, and a reliance on top-management objectives.

Mediation   The union–management use of a neutral third party to help resolve conflicts.

Mentor   An older or more experienced employee who helps a younger or less experienced person learn the job, the systems procedures, and the rituals of the organization. A mentor can offer counseling, guidance, support, and protection to the less experienced protégé.

Middle Management   The middle level of an administrative hierarchy. Managers at this level coordinate the work of managers and report to a manager.

Mission   A long-term vision of what an organization is trying to become. The mission is the unique aim that differentiates an organization from similar organizations. The basic questions that must be answered to determine an organization's mission are, "What is our business? What should it be?"

Mommy Track Career Path   A controversial strategy for helping women balance career and family demands, this career path enables a woman with young children to take time off or work part-time during critical child-rearing years.

Motivation   The inner strivings that initiate a person's actions.

Motivational Factors   Distinguished by Herzberg in his two-factor theory of motivation, those job conditions that, if present, operate to build high levels of motivation and job satisfaction. However, the absence of these factors does not prove highly dissatisfying. Herzberg distinguished six of these factors (e.g., achievement, recognition, advancement).

Moving Budget   A form of budgeting that involves periodic updating; for example, a 12-month budget will be updated each month and projected for the following 12 months.

Multinational Company (MNC)   A business firm doing business in two or more countries.

Neoclassical Organizational Design   An organizational design resting at the opposite end of the spectrum from classical design. The characteristics of this organization structure include low complexity, low formalization, and low centralization.

Noise   Any interference with the flow of a message from a sender to a receiver.

Nominal Group Technique (NGT)   A technique used to achieve a group decision through a combination of both verbal and nonverbal (written) stages. NGT typically takes the form of a structured group meeting that follows specific procedures and culminates in a group decision based on the mathematical calculation of independent prioritized voting.

Nonprogrammed Decisions   Decisions for novel and unstructured problems or for complex or extremely important problems. Nonprogrammed decisions deserve the special attention of top management.

Nonverbal Communication   A form of communication that takes place without the use of words. Typical nonverbal communications include body language and gestures.

North American Free Trade Agreement (NAFTA)   An economic alliance formed by the United States, Mexico, and Canada that pursues a free trade area and the removal of tariffs and trade barriers. Unlike the EC, the alliance does not cede significant national sovereignty over economic matters to any regional body.

Objective Probability   The odds of an outcome occurring based on historical evidence.

Objectives   Specified future conditions that an organization—or member of an organization—hopes to achieve.

Operant Conditioning   An approach to behavior modification that involves manipulating the consequences of behavior to change behavior.

Operations   A broad term used to describe the activities and flow of work, resources, and materials in goods- or service-producing organizations.

Ordering Cost   An element in inventory control models that comprises clerical, administrative, and labor costs; a major cost component that is considered in inventory control decisions. Each time a firm orders items for inventory, some clerical and administrative work is usually required to place the order, and some labor is required to put the items in inventory.

Organic System   An organizational system having the same characteristics as exist in a neoclassical design framework.

Organization "Fit"   The idea that, in order for an organization to achieve optimal performance, an organization design must be compatible with the technology it uses.

Organizational Change   The intentional attempt by management to improve the overall performance of individuals, groups, and the organization as a whole by altering the organization's structure, behavior, and technology.

Organizational Development (OD)   A method for facilitating change and development in structures and processes, people, and technology.

Organizational Objectives   The broad continuing aims that serve as guides for action and as the starting point for more specific and detailed operating objectives at lower levels in the organization. This book classifies organizational objectives into four categories: profitability, competitiveness, efficiency, and flexibility.

Organizational Portfolio Plan   A strategy a larger organization needs in order to set objectives for, make decisions about, and prioritize its various strategic business units (SBUs). Currently, the best known method is the Business Portfolio Matrix.

Organizational Psychology   The study of behavior and attitudes within an organization, including the effect of the organization upon the individual and the individual's effect on the organization.

Organizational Strategies   The general approaches that are utilized by the organization to achieve its organizational objectives. These approaches include market penetration, market development, product development, and diversification strategies.

Organizational Structure   The formally defined framework of task and authority relationships. The organizational structure is analogous to the biological concept of the skeleton.

Organizing Function   All managerial activity that results in the design of a formal structure of tasks and authority.

Payback Period   The length of time that it takes for an investment to pay for itself out of future funds.

Peer Relationship   A relationship between peers that provides support, feedback, information, and/or friendship.

Performance Appraisal   The formal evaluation of an individual's job performance.

Personal–Behavioral Leadership Theories   A group of theories based primarily on the personal and behavioral characteristics of leaders. These theories focus on *what* leaders do and/or *how* leaders behave in carrying out the leadership function.

Personality   The sum of an individual's traits or characteristics. These traits interact to create personality patterns.

Persuasion   The process of selling a plan to those who must implement it. The emphasis of persuasion lies in motivating through communicating a plan's merits rather than through use of an authoritative position.

Physiological (Basic) Needs   Needs of the human body, such as food, water, and sex.

Planning Function   All managerial activities that lead to the definition of objectives and to the determination of appropriate means to achieve those objectives.

Pluralism   A set of guidelines or principles, arranged in a hierarchy of importance, by which a person can make an ethical decision.

Policies   Guidelines for managerial action that must be adhered to at all times. Policymaking is an important management planning element for assuring that action is oriented toward objectives. The purpose of policies is to achieve consistency and direction and to protect the reputation of the organization.

Political Risk   The risk of losing any investment or management control over an asset in a foreign country because of instability or problems in the host country.

Political Risk Analysis   The use of forecasting techniques to assess the probability of various events or situations that can jeopardize the security of a foreign investment.

Position Analysis Questionnaire (PAQ)   A job analysis technique focusing on the actual behavior of the individual in the performance of the job.

Position Power   A factor in the Fiedler theory of leadership that refers to the power inherent in the leadership position.

Positive Reinforcement   A reward (e.g., praise, recognition, bonus) that results in an increase in the frequency of the rewarded response.

Power   The ability to influence another person's behavior.

Power Distance   The degree to which people in a society accept inequality in power among people and organizations.

Preliminary Control   Techniques and methods that attempt to maintain the quality and quantity of resources.

Process Approach to Organization Design   An approach to organization design that emphasizes how and why an organization moves from one design to another.

Process Theories   Theories about human motivation that try to explain and describe the process of how behavior is energized, directed, sustained, and finally stopped.

Product   The output (goods or services) of a productive system.

Product Development Strategies   Strategies in which an organization seeks to develop new products directed to its present customers.

Productivity   Any ratio of output to input. Other factors being equal, the higher the ratio, the more efficient is the use of inputs.

Profitability Objectives   The profit goals of an organization that include the ratios of profits to sales, profits to total assets, and profits to capital.

Program Evaluation and Review Technique (PERT)   A production planning technique with widespread applicability in organizations that produce large-scale, nonroutine products. The technique enables management to make the optimal allocation of resources to the activities that lead to completion of the product.

Programmed Decisions   Responses to repetitive and routine problems which are handled by a standard procedure that has been developed by management.

Psychology   The science of human behavior. It seeks general laws that explain individual and interpersonal behavior.

Punishment   The introduction of something disliked or the removal of something liked following a particular response to decrease the frequency of that response.

Quality   The totality of features and characteristics of a product or service that bear on its ability to satisfy stated or implied needs.

Quality Circles   A small group from the work unit, ranging in size from 4 to 15 members, who voluntarily meet on a regular basis to study quality control and productivity improvement techniques to identify and solve work problems.

Quality Funnel Principle   A principle in quality control which states that the cost of poor quality increases as the output passes progressively farther through the transformation process. The implication is that the cost of poor quality is minimized if detected and corrected in the input stage.

Rate of Return   The ratio of additional net income to the original cost.

Recruitment   Steps taken to staff an organization with the best-qualified people.

Referent Power   The power of a leader that is based on the leader's attractiveness. The leader is admired because of certain personal qualities, and the follower identifies closely with those qualities.

Reinforcement Theory   A motivation theory that focuses on the environment and its consequences and that considers the use of positive or negative reinforcers to motivate or create an environment of motivation.

Relationship Behavior   The extent to which leaders maintain personal relationships with members of their group through supportive, sensitive, and facilitative behavior.

Resources   Constraints on the course of action taken toward achieving an objective.

Reward Power   The power generated by followers' perception that compliance with the wishes of leaders can lead to positive rewards (e.g., promotion).

Risk Decisions   Decision situations in which managers do not know for certain the probability of occurrence of the state of nature or competitive actions. However, they have some past experience and/or data on which they can rely to develop probabilities. These probabilities are used with conditional values to determine expected values.

Robot   A reprogrammable, multifunctional manipulator designed to move material, parts, tools, or specialized devices through programmed motions.

Role Differentiation   The process of taking on different roles in a group.

Roles   The behaviors that people exhibit in a social context.

Safety Need   The need to be protected from physical harm, ill health, economic disaster, and the unexpected.

Safety Stock   The quantity of materials that management decides is necessary to have on hand at all times to guard against stock-outs due to unforeseen circumstances.

Salaries   Compensation based on time. The unit of time is a week, a month, or longer.

Sample Survey   Collection of data from a limited number of units that are assumed to be representative of the entire group.

Scientific Management   The practices introduced by Frederick W. Taylor to accomplish the management job. Taylor advocated the use of scientific procedures to find the one best way to do a job.

Self-Actualization Need   The need to fully realize one's potential.

Self-Fulfilling Prophecy   The notion that what a leader expects of someone else and the way the leader treats the other person will result in the expectation coming true. For example, if a manager treats a subordinate as though she is lazy, the subordinate will behave in a manner to support the treatment.

Sensitivity Training   An organizational change approach that focuses on the emotions and processes of interacting with people.

Separation   A situation in which the minority group is unable or unwilling to adapt to the dominant culture.

Service   An activity required by a customer or a client or work done for another person.

Services   Nonmonetary programs (e.g., gymnasium facilities) provided by companies to employees.

Sexual Harassment   Any unwelcome sexual advances, requests for sexual favors, or other verbal or physical contact of a sexual nature.

Situational Favorableness   The degree to which a (work) situation enables a leader to exert influence over a group. This concept is associated with Fiedler's theory of leadership.

Situational Theory of Leadership   An approach which advocates that leaders understand their own behavior, the behavior of their subordinates, and the situation before they utilize a particular leadership style. The application of this approach requires the leader to have diagnostic skills in human behavior.

Social Loafing   The tendency of a member in a group to not work hard or carry a fair share of the work by hiding within the group structure.

Social Need   The need for social interaction and companionship.

Social Obligation   The viewpoint that business social responsibility is satisfied when profit is pursued within the constraints of appropriate law.

Social Psychology   The branch of psychology dealing with the behavior of individuals as they relate to other individuals.

Social Reaction   The viewpoint that business social responsibility is satisfied when business pursues profit

legally and reacts to demands for correction of past wrongs.

Social Responsiveness   The viewpoint that business social responsibility is satisfied when business pursues profit legally, reacts to demands, and acts to prevent future wrongs and problems.

Sociology   The behavioral science that studies group behavior. It seeks general laws that explain intergroup and intragroup behavior.

Span of Control   The number of subordinates who report to a superior or the number of jobs to be included in a specific group. The span of control is a factor that affects the shape and height of an organization.

Staffing   A process that includes the forecasting of personnel needs and the recruitment, selection, placement, and training and development of employees.

Statistical Quality Control   The use of tools and techniques in a disciplined way to solve performance problems.

Stereotyping   The attribution of a whole set of traits to persons on the basis of their membership in particular groups.

Strategic Business Unit (SBU)   A division or product line of an organization that can be considered a business; an important part of the organization's portfolio plan in the strategic planning process. Management must decide which business to build, maintain, or eliminate.

Strategic Human Resource Management   The practice of placing human resources in an important position in developing the strategy of the firm. Human resources are becoming a major part of the strategic planning process in most firms concerned about competition and survival.

Strategic Planning   A planning process that involves taking information from the environment, deciding on long-range goals, selecting activities to achieve those goals, and allocating resources to those activities.

Strike   An employee action to stop work until a labor–management conflict is settled or a contract is signed.

Structural Change   A planned change of the formally prescribed task and authority relationships in an organization's design.

Subjective Probability   The estimated odds of an outcome occurring based on experience, intelligence, or intuition.

System   An entity consisting of several interrelated parts acting interdependently. The basic parts of any system are input, transformation, and output.

Task Behavior   The extent to which leaders are likely to organize and define the roles of followers, offer explanations, and direct work flow.

Task Group   A formal group of individuals working as a unit to complete a task.

Task Structure   In the Fiedler situational model of leadership, a factor that refers to the degree to which a job is laid out in detail or structured.

Team Building   A change technique that focuses on the interaction within a group to identify and solve problems and implement changes.

Technological Change   A planned change in the machinery, equipment, or techniques that are used to accomplish organizational goals.

Technology   The types and patterns of activity, equipment, and material and the knowledge or experience used to perform tasks. Technology is an important contingency variable in organization design theory.

Theory X and Theory Y   Douglas McGregor's theory that behind every management decision is a set of assumptions that a manager makes about human behavior. The Theory X manager assumes that people are lazy, dislike work, want no responsibility, and prefer to be closely directed. The Theory Y manager assumes that people seek responsibility, like to work, and are committed to doing good work if rewards are received for achievement.

Thorndike's Law of Effect   The theory that behavior resulting in a pleasant outcome will likely be repeated; behavior that results in an unpleasant outcome is not likely to be repeated.

Time-Series Analysis   A statistical technique for analyzing the relationship between a specified variable and time.

Top Management   The top level of an administrative hierarchy. Managers at this level coordinate the work of other managers but do not report to a manager.

Training   A continual process of helping employees to perform at a high level. Training may occur on the job or at a special training facility.

Trait Theory   Attempts to specify which personal characteristics (physical, personality, mental) are associated with leadership effectiveness. Trait theory relies on research that relates various traits to effectiveness criteria.

Uncertainty Avoidance   The extent to which people in a society feel threatened by ambiguous situations.

Uncertainty Decisions   Decision situations in which no past experiences or historical data are available. Any one of a number of criteria is employed, depending on the personality of the manager.

Unions   An employee organization that is certified (voted in by members) to represent workers in labor–management collective bargaining about job-related issues.

Universalistic Approach to Organization Design   A set of ideas that concludes that there exists only one effective design for all organizations regardless of setting.

Unsatisfied Need   The starting point in the process of motivation. It is a deficiency of something within the individual which provides the spark that leads to behavior.

Upward Communication   Communication that flows from individuals at lower levels of an organization structure to those at higher levels. Some of the most common upward communication flows are suggestion boxes, group meetings, and appeal or grievance procedures.

Valence   The value that a person (manager or nonmanager) assigns, because of her preference, to work-related outcomes.

Values   A lasting set of convictions held by a person and acquired early in life. Values often affect an individual's mode of conduct.

Variable Budgeting   A form of budgeting that targets expected costs at various potential output levels.

Variable Costs   Costs that vary with changes in production. For example, as the number of units produced increases, the amount of material used also increases. Thus, the cost of material used to produce a product would be an example of variable costs.

Vertical Integration   The stage of an organization's growth in which it either buys or creates other functions.

Volume Expansion   The stage of an organization's growth in which firms manufacture, sell, or distribute more of their product or service to existing customers.

Vroom-Yetton-Jago Theory   A situational theory of leadership that attempts to identify the appropriate leadership style for a given set of circumstances or situations. The leadership styles are defined by the extent to which the subordinates participate in decision making.

Wages   Compensations based on the time an employee works or the number of units produced.

Work Group   Also called a team, this is a collection of employees (managerial or nonmanagerial) who share certain norms and who strive to satisfy their needs through the attainment of the group goal(s).

Name/Company Name Index

Subject Index